Tuttle
Pocket
Indonesian
Dictionary

Indonesian-English
English-Indonesian

Katherine Davidsen

TUTTLE Publishing

Tokyo | Rutland, Vermont | Singapore

Published by Tuttle Publishing, an imprint of Periplus Editions (HK) Ltd.

www.tuttlepublishing.com

Copyright © 2007 Periplus Editions (HK) Ltd.
This Paperback edition Copyright © 2014 Periplus Editions (HK) Ltd.

Library of Congress Control No: 2007924328

ISBN 978-0-8048-4508-3

Distributed by:

North America, Latin America & Europe
Tuttle Publishing
364 Innovation Drive, North Clarendon, VT 05759-9436 U.S.A.
Tel: 1 (802) 773-8930 | Fax: 1 (802) 773-6993
info@tuttlepublishing.com
www.tuttlepublishing.com

Asia Pacific
Berkeley Books Pte. Ltd.
61 Tai Seng Avenue #02-12, Singapore 534167
Tel: (65) 6280-1330 | Fax: (65) 6280-6290
inquiries@periplus.com.sg
www.periplus.com

Indonesia
PT Java Books Indonesia
Kawasan Industri Pulogadung
Jl. Rawa Gelam IV No. 9, Jakarta 13930
Tel: (62) 21 4682-1088 | Fax: (62) 21 461-0206
crm@periplus.co.id
www.periplus.com

17 16 15 14   1410EP
8 7 6 5 4 3 2 1
Printed in Hong Kong

TUTTLE PUBLISHING® is a registered trademark of Tuttle Publishing,
a division of Periplus Editions (HK) Ltd.

Contents

iii

The Tuttle Story: "Books to Span the East and West"

Many people are surprised to learn that the world's largest publisher of books on Asia had its humble beginnings in the tiny American state of Vermont. The company's founder, Charles E. Tuttle, belonged to a New England family steeped in publishing.

Immediately after WWII, Tuttle served in Tokyo under General Douglas MacArthur and was tasked with reviving the Japanese publishing industry. He later founded the Charles E. Tuttle Publishing Company, which thrives today as one of the world's leading independent publishers.

Though a westerner, Tuttle was hugely instrumental in bringing a knowledge of Japan and Asia to a world hungry for information about the East. By the time of his death in 1993, Tuttle had published over 6,000 books on Asian culture, history and art—a legacy honored by the Japanese emperor with the "Order of the Sacred Treasure," the highest tribute Japan can bestow upon a non-Japanese.

With a backlist of 1,500 titles, Tuttle Publishing is more active today than at any time in its past—inspired by Charles Tuttle's core mission to publish fine books to span the East and West and provide a greater understanding of each.

Introduction

A brief introduction to Indonesian

Indonesian is the national language of the world's fourth-largest nation, spoken by at least 70 percent of the nation's 220 million people. It is a mother tongue to over 27 percent, connecting speakers of 750 regional languages. As a variety of Malay, it is also understood in Singapore and Malaysia, making it a major language of Southeast Asia. An Austronesian language, modern Indonesian developed from Riau Malay to become the official language of postwar independent Indonesia. It has borrowed widely from other languages and absorbed myriad influences, making it dynamic and always in flux.

Indonesian is considered relatively easy to learn, having very regular grammar. Adjectives follow the noun, as in French, and there is a wide range of verbs. Word order generally follows a subject-verb-object pattern. Words may be left out if the context is clear. Pronunciation is similar to Spanish or Italian, although accents vary.

Vowels:	**a**	as in *father*
	e	mostly as in *loosen* (swallowed "shwa" sound); sometimes as in *egg*. In older texts this is written as **é**
	i	as in *marine*
	o	as in *open*
	u	as in *blue*
Diphthongs:	**ai**	as in *aisle*
	au	as in *sauerkraut*

INTRODUCTION

Consonants: as in English, except for:

c	like **ch** in *child*
g	always hard, as in *gum*, never soft as in *gem*
kh	throaty sound as in *loch*
ng	as in *thing*
ngg	as in *finger* (ng+g)
r	rolled, as in Spanish
sy	**sh** as in *show*

The **Tuttle Pocket Indonesian Dictionary** aims to represent the modern, standard usage of Indonesian, through common entries, new terminology and authentic terms, as well as identify parts of speech. A helpful, unusual feature is that this volume does not presume knowledge of word structure, which is vital when using most quality Indonesian dictionaries. For example, the word *mengalahkan* is listed under *mengalahkan* as well as its base, *kalah* in this dictionary. In most dictionaries, only the latter would appear.

Selection of entries

By definition, a pocket dictionary is a selection of useful words and phrases, rather than a complete compendium. This dictionary attempts to reflect general, everyday usage throughout Indonesia and the English-speaking world, including words that are important to students, language learners and tourists. American spelling is used. Entries cover survival language for tourists, common everyday words, national culture and language heard on the street.

Guide to using this dictionary

The dictionary is divided into two sections, Indonesian–English and English–Indonesian. Entries are listed alphabetically, in the following order:

menghadap	entry (in bold, blue type)
halang: halangan	first word is not found (or commonly used) alone. Sub-entries follow after semi-colon, in bold black type
v	word type (ie part of speech). Not always given if more than one word type exists. eg. **cas** charge (could be *n*, *v*)
child *n* **children**	irregular plurals follow the noun symbol *n*
put *v* **put put**	irregular past tense forms (simple past and past perfect) follow the verb symbol *v*
[nait]	irregularly-spelt words are given in Indonesian phonetic pronunciation (see spelling guides)
malam	meaning (in plain type)
session, meeting; hearing	Similar meanings are divided by commas; other meanings are divided by a semi-colon
~ *tiri* stepmother; *bahasa* ~ mother tongue	Entries or sub-entries are indicated by ~ (in italics). On the left, ~ represents *ibu*.

ouch! ow! (expressions of pain) to (be able to) speak or use a language	Round brackets contain additional information; or perhaps an extra meaning.
baik ... maupun ... both ... and ...	... represents any word, in a set phrase
bersih, membersihkan, pembersih **nutty ← nut**	Where possible, all entries and sub-entries are grouped alphabetically. A left-pointing arrow indicates the base word.
abis → habis **went → go**	A right-pointing arrow shows an entry for further information or reference; or the base of an irregular past tense verb form.

Acknowledgments

I would like to thank everyone involved in this dictionary project. In particular, thanks to Eric M. Oey, Associate Professor Stuart O. Robson of Monash University, Nancy Goh, Tony Mansanulu, Judo Suwidji, and of course Johansjah Sugianto. I must also thank countless patient and helpful friends, the Sumirat family, the family of Moch. Yunus, the household of Fauzi Bowo, my own family in Melbourne, the Zeed family, and my students over the years. *Terima kasih banyak.*

Indonesian–English

A

abad *n* century; age, era;
~ *keemasan* golden age

abadi eternal, everlasting;
cinta ~ endless love;
mengabadikan *v* to
immortalize

abai *adj* neglectful; **mengabaikan** *v* to neglect, disregard, ignore

abang *n, pron* elder brother;
~ *None* Mr and Miss Jakarta
→ **bang**

abang: abangan *adj*
Javanese Muslim who
follows local traditions
rather than Islam (*cf.*
santri)

abdi ~ *dalem* court servant
at a Javanese palace;
pengabdian *n* service,
servitude, devotion

abis *coll* → **habis**

abjad *n* alphabet; *menurut* ~
in alphabetical order

abon *n* shredded dry meat,
eaten as a side-dish

abonemén *n* subscription,
billing

aborsi, abortus *n* abortion;
mengaborsi *v* to abort (a
fetus)

ABRI *abbrev Angkatan
Bersenjata Republik
Indonesia* Indonesian
Armed Forces

absén *adj* not present

abu *n* ash; ~ *rokok* cigarette
ash

abu-abu *adj* gray

AC *abbrev* air-conditioner,
air-conditioning

acak random, mixed

acar *n* finely-cut pickled
cucumber, shallot, carrot
and chilli, eaten with fried
rice, satay etc

acara agenda, program, event;
~ *hari ini* today's program;
pengacara *n* lawyer, solicitor

acu: mengacu *v* to refer to,
to use as a point of reference; **mengacukan** *v* to
point, refer to

acuh *(tidak/tak ~)* indifferent,
not care; ~ *tak* ~ to ignore,
take no notice of

acung: acungan *n* ~ *jempol*
thumbs-up

AD *abbrev Angkatan Darat* Army

ada *v* to be (present); to have, exist; ~ *Firman?* Is Firman here?; ~ *apa?* What's up? What's wrong?; *tidak* ~ there isn't, there aren't; not here; **ketidak-adaan** *n* absence, lack of; **ada-ada** ~ *saja* well, I never! Words fail me!; **adalah** *v* is, are (followed by a noun); *Rina* ~ *sepupu Dian* Rina is Dian's cousin; **adanya** *n* the existence of; *apa* ~ as it is, without any pretensions; **berada** *v* to be somewhere; *adj* well-to-do, well-off; **keberadaan** *n* presence; **keadaan** *n* situation, condition; ~ *darurat* emergency situation; **mengadakan** *v* to create, organize, make available; ~ *kampanye* to run a campaign; **seadanya** *adj* what's there; *makan* ~ eat what's there

adab: peradaban *n* culture, civilization

adalah *v* is, are (followed by a noun); *Rina* ~ *sepupu Dian* Rina is Dian's cousin ← **ada**

adanya *n* the existence of; *apa* ~ as it is, without any pretensions ← **ada**

adat *n* tradition, custom, customary law, esp. of an ethnic group; ~ *istiadat* customs and traditions; ~ *Sunda* Sundanese traditions

adegan *n* scene; ~ *panas* steamy scene

adi- *pref* higher; **adipura** *n* tidy town, cleanest town

adik *n* younger brother or sister; ~ *ipar* (younger) brother- or sister-in-law; ~ *laki-laki* (younger) brother; *kakak-ber*~ siblings; ~ *kandung* (younger) blood brother or sister; ~ *sepupu* cousin (of lower status)

adil *adj* just, righteous; **keadilan** *n* justice; **mengadili** *v* to try someone, put someone on trial; **pengadilan** *n* court of justice or law, trial; ~ *negeri* district court

adjéktiva, adjéktif *n* adjective

administrasi *n* administration, management;

~ *negara* public administration

adon: adonan *n* batter, dough, mixture

adu: mengadu *v* to complain, report; ~ *domba* to play two parties against each other; **mengadukan** *v* to report someone/something, to make a complaint about; **pengaduan** *n* complaint; *surat* ~ letter of complaint

aduh *ejac* ouch! ow! (expression of pain); *excl* oh! (expression of sorrow); wow!; ~ *sakit!* Ow, that hurts!; ~ *berat sekali* Oh, how difficult!

aduhai *ejac, lit* oh! *adj* amazing, outstanding

aduk *campur* ~ mixed up; **mengaduk** *v* to stir, mix

adzan → azan

Afganistan, Afghanistan *n* Afghanistan

Afrika *n* Africa; *orang* ~ African; ~ *Selatan (Afsel)* South Africa

agak *adv* rather, somewhat; ~ *gemuk* rather fat

agama *n* religion; ~ *Budha*

Buddhism; **beragama** *v* to have a religion; *Siti* ~ *Islam* Siti is Muslim; *adj* religious; **keagamaan** *adj* religious affairs

agar *conj* in order that/to

agar, agar-agar *n* a kind of jelly made from seaweed

agén *n* agent, agency, distributor; ~ *koran* news agency; ~ *rahasia* secret agent

agénda *n* agenda; appointment diary

agrowisata *n* agricultural tourism

agung *adj* high, supreme

Agustus *bulan* ~ August

ah *excl* oh (showing mild annoyance)

Ahad → Minggu

ahli *n* expert, specialist; member; ~ *bahasa* linguist; ~ *bedah* surgeon; ~ *hukum* legal adviser; ~ *waris* heir; **keahlian** *n* expertise

aib *n* shame

air *n* water; juice; ~ *bah* flood; ~ *jeruk* orange juice; ~ *ledeng* reticulated water; ~ *liur* saliva; ~ *mata* tears; ~ *minum*, ~ *putih* drinking water; ~ *muka* facial expression; ~ *pasang* incoming tide; ~ *suci* holy water; ~ *tawar* fresh water; ~ *terjun* waterfall; *buang* ~ to go to the toilet; **pengairan** *n* irrigation; **perairan** *n* territorial waters, waterworks

ajaib *adj* miraculous, strange; **keajaiban** *n* wonder, miracle

ajak: ajakan *n, inf* invitation; **mengajak** *v* to invite, ask out; to urge; ~ *jalan-jalan* to ask out; ~ *kawin*, ~ *nikah* to ask someone to marry you

ajal *n* moment of death; *sampai* ~*nya* to die

ajar: ajaran *n* teaching; *tahun* ~ academic year; **belajar** *v* to learn, study; **mempelajari** *v* to study something in depth; **mengajar** *v* to teach; **mengajari** *v* to teach someone; **mengajarkan** *v* to teach something; **pelajar** *n* pupil, student; **pelajaran** *n* lesson; *mata* ~ school subject; **terpelajar** *adj* educated;

pengajar *n* teacher; **pengajaran** *n* teaching, tuition

aju: mengajukan *v* to forward, propose; to submit

akad *n* contract, agreement; ~ *nikah* Muslim marriage contract

akadémi *n* academy, higher education; ~ *Angkatan Bersenjata (Akabri)* Armed Forces Academy

akal *n* mind, intellect; ~ *sehat* intellect, common sense; *mencari* ~ to find a way; **mengakali** *v* to find a way; to deceive, play a trick on

akan *v* will, going to (marks future time); *minggu yang* ~ *datang* next week; *prep* about, concerning, regarding; ~ *tetapi* however; *sudah lupa* ~ has forgotten about; **seakan-akan** *adv* as if, as though

akar *n* root; ~ *kuadrat* square root; **mengakar** *v* to take root

akbar *adj* big, great

akhir *n* end; ~*nya* finally; ~-~ *ini* recently; **akhiran** *n* ending, suffix; **berakhir** *v* to end; **mengakhiri** v to end, finish something; **terakhir** adj last, final, latest

akhirat n the hereafter

aki n vehicle battery

akibat n result, consequence; conj due to, consequently; ~nya as a result; **mengakibatkan** v to result in

akrab adj close, intimate, friendly; **keakraban** n closeness, intimacy

aksara n letter, character, alphabet; ~ Cina Chinese characters

aksén n accent; **beraksén** v to have a touch of

aksi n action, demonstration; ~ sepihak unilateral action; **beraksi** v to take action, do something

akta, akte n official document, certificate; ~ lahir, ~ kelahiran birth certificate; ~ nikah, ~ pernikahan marriage certificate

aktif adj activated, active, on, working; ~ di kampus involved in many university activities; **aktivitas** n activity; **beraktivitas** v to be doing something

aktual adj latest, up-to-date; berita ~ current affairs

aku pron I, me; **mengaku** v to admit, confess, acknowledge; to claim; ~ salah to admit guilt; **mengakui** v to admit something; to acknowledge, recognize; **pengakuan** n confession, acknowledgment; ~ dosa confession (Catholic)

akuntan n accountant; **akuntansi** n accounting

AL abbrev Angkatan Laut Navy

a.l. antara lain among others

ala adj in the style of, à la

alam n nature, world; ~ (ter)buka open-air; ~ semesta the universe; sumber daya ~ natural resources

alam: mengalami v to experience; **pengalaman** n experience; **berpengalaman** adj experienced, skilled

alamat n address; sign, omen; **beralamat** v to have an address; **mengalamatkan** v to address to; to indicate

alang-alang n tall, coarse grass

alangkah *adv* how ...! what a ...!; ~ *bagusnya!* how beautiful!

alas *n* foundation, basis, base; ~ *kaki* footwear; **alasan** *n* cause, reason, motive; **beralasan** *v* to have reason

alat *n* tool, instrument, means; ~ *kelamin* genitals; ~ *kontrasepsi*, ~ *KB* form of contraception; ~ *pendengaran* sense of hearing; ~ *bantu dengar* hearing aid; ~ *tulis* stationery; **peralatan** *n* equipment

album *n* album; ~ *foto* photo album

alérgi *n* allergy, allergic; ~ *terhadap mangga* allergic to mangoes

algojo *n* hangman, executioner

alhamdulillah *ejac, Isl* thanks be to God; bless you! (when sneezing)

aliansi *n* alliance; **beraliansi** *v* to be allied with

alih *v* to shift, change position; ~ *bahasa* translation; ~ *profesi* change of career; ~ *teknologi* to upgrade technology; **beralih** *v* to move, change; **mengalih(kan)** *v* to shift something; ~ *perhatian* to shift attention, change the subject; **peralihan** *n* transition, change

alinéa *n* paragraph

alir flow **aliran** *n* stream, current; ideology, school, sect; ~ *listrik* electric current; ~ *kepercayaan* unofficial religious movement; **beraliran** *v* to have an ideology; ~ *kiri* leftist; **mengalir** *v* to flow

alis *n* eyebrow; *mengangkat* ~ to raise your eyebrows

aljabar *n* algebra

Aljazair *n* Algeria

Alkitab *n* the Bible

alkohol *n* alcohol; **beralkohol** *v* containing alcohol; *minuman* ~ alcoholic drink

Allah *n* God, Allah; ~*u Akbar* God is great

almarhum *adj, m, Isl* the late; **almarhumah** *adj, f, Isl* the late

Almasih *n* the Messiah; *Kenaikan Isa* ~ Assumption

alpukat, apokat, avokat *n*
avocado; *jus* ~ avocado drink

**Alqur'an, Al-quran,
Alquran** *n* the Koran

AL(RI) *abbrev Angkatan
Laut (Republik Indonesia)*
(Indonesian) Navy

alu *n* pestle; ~ *lumpang*
mortar and pestle

aluminium *n* aluminium

alun-alun *n* town square

amal *n* charity; ~ *ibadah*
service to God; *konser* ~
charity concert; **beramal**
v to give to charity; *adj* charitable; **mengamalkan** *v* to
do something for charity; to
carry out

aman *adj* safe, in peace;
keamanan *n* safety,
security; **mengamankan** *v*
to make safe, restore order;
place in custody; **peng-
aman** *n* safety device

amanah, amanat, *n* message,
instruction, mandate

amarah → marah

amat *adv* very, extremely;
kasihan ~! poor thing!

amat: mengamati *v* to
watch closely, keep an
eye on; **pengamat** *n*

observer; **pengamatan** *n*
observation, monitoring

ambang *n* threshold,
doorstep, verge; ~ *pintu*
doorstep, verge

ambang: mengambang *v*
to float

ambar *n* ambergris; *batu*
~ amber

ambeien *n* hemorrhoids,
piles

ambil *v* to take; to subtract;
to bring; ~ *saja* help yourself; *Tiga* ~ *dua sama
dengan satu* Three minus
two is one; *Tolong* ~ *air*
Please bring some water;
mengambil *v* to take, get,
fetch; ~ *alih* to take over;
~ *keputusan* to make a
decision; **mengambilkan** *v*
to get something for someone; **pengambilan** *n* act of
taking, removal; ~ *gambar*
photo shoot; ~ *sumpah*
taking an oath

ambisi *n* ambition; **berambisi** *v* to have an ambition, have ambitions

ambruk *v* to collapse, break,
crash

ambulans *n* ambulance

amén: (me)ngamén v to sing in the street for money, busk; **pengamén** n street singer, busker

Amérika n America; ~ **Serikat** United States of America

amin *ejac* amen

amis *adj* putrid, smelling fishy

amnésti n amnesty

amplop n envelope; *coll* bribe; **kasih ~** hand over a bribe

ampuh *adj* powerful, potent

ampun n mercy, forgiveness, pardon; *ejac* Mercy! (expression of astonishment or disapproval); **minta ~** beg for mercy; **pengampunan** n pardon, reprieve, amnesty

amuk: mengamuk v to run amok, go berserk

amunisi, munisi n ammunition, munitions

anak n child; young (of an animal); member of a group; small part of a whole; ~ **angkat** adopted child; ~ **anjing** puppy; ~ **ayam** chick; ~ **buah** assistants, staff; ~ **bungsu** youngest child; ~ **cucu** descendants; ~ **emas** favorite; ~ **haram** illegitimate child; ~ **jalanan** street kid; ~ **kalimat** clause; ~ **kapal** crew, sailor; ~ **kembar** twins; ~ **kos** boarder; ~ **kucing** kitten; ~ **kunci** key; ~ **panah** arrow; ~ **perempuan** daughter; ~ **perusahaan** subsidiary company; ~ **sulung** eldest child; ~ **sungai** tributary, creek; ~ **tangga** rung of a ladder; ~ **tunggal** only child; ~ **yatim** orphan; ~ **tiri** stepchild; **menganaktirikan** v to treat as a second-class citizen; **anak-anak** n, pl children; **beranak** v (of animals) to give birth to, have offspring; **peranakan** n uterus; *adj* of mixed Chinese and Indonesian blood, Straits Chinese

analisa, analisis n analysis

ancam v to threaten; **ancaman** n threat; **mengancam** v to threaten, intimidate; **terancam** *adj* threatened

anda, Anda *pron* you (neutral, without status)

andai, andaikan, andaikata, andainya, seandainya *conj* if, supposing that; **mengandaikan** *v* to suppose, assume

andal *adj* reliable; **mengandalkan** *v* to rely on, trust

Andalas *n* Sumatra

andil *n* share, contribution

andong *n* four-wheeled horse-drawn carriage in Jogja and Solo

anéh *adj* strange, peculiar; **~nya** the strange thing is...; **keanéhan** *n* peculiarity, oddity

anéka *adj* all kinds of, various; ~ *jenis* all sorts; ~ *macam*, ~ *ragam* varied; ~ *warna* various colors, multicolored; **beranéka ~ ragam** various

anggap *v* to consider; **anggapan** *n* point of view, opinion; **menganggap** *v* to consider, regard; ~ *enteng* take lightly; *sudah dianggap saudara* to be considered part of the family

anggar *n* fencing (sport)

anggar: anggaran *n* budget, estimate

anggota *n* member; ~ *badan* limb; ~ *DPR* Member of Parliament; ~ *kehormatan* honorary member; ~ *keluarga* family member; **beranggotakan** *v* to have a membership, have as members; **keanggotaan** *n* membership; *kartu ~* membership card

anggrék *n* orchid

angguk, mengangguk *v* to nod

anggun *adj* elegant, stylish, graceful

anggur *n* wine, grapes; ~ *putih* white wine; *buah ~* grapes

anggur: menganggur *v* to be unemployed, idle; **pengangguran** *n* unemployment, unemployed person

angin *n* wind, breeze; ~ *ribut*, ~ *topan* cyclone, typhoon; *tambah ~* to pump up a tire

angka *n* figure, numeral, digit; score, mark; ~ *kelahiran* birth rate; ~ *Romawi* Roman numeral

angkasa *n* space, sky; ~ *luar* outer space

angkat *v* to lift; ~ *besi* weightlifting; ~ *tangan* give up; raise your hand; ~ *telepon* to pick up, answer the phone; *orang tua* ~ adoptive parents; **angkatan** *n* generation, year level (at school or university); force; ~ *darat (AD)* army; **berangkat** *v* to depart, leave; **keberangkatan** *n* departure; *pintu* ~ departure gate; **mengangkat** *v* to lift or pick up, raise; appoint; to remove, amputate; **perangkat** *n* equipment, tool; **seperangkat** *n* set, suite

angkét *n* survey (form)

angklung *n* bamboo instrument, played in an orchestra

angkot *n, coll* public minibus ← **angkutan kota**

angkuh *adj* arrogant, proud, conceited

angkut *v* to carry, lift, transport; **angkutan** *n* transport, transportation; ~ *darat* land transportation; ~ *kota (angkot)* city transportation; ~ *umum* public transport; **mengangkut** *n* to transport

angpao, angpau *n* a red envelope containing money, given at Chinese New Year

angsa *n* goose

angsur, mengangsur *v* to pay in instalments; **angsuran** *n* instalment

angus → **hangus**

aniaya: menganiaya *v* to mistreat, oppress; **penganiayaan** *n* oppression, mistreatment

anjak: beranjak *v* to move, shift

anjing *n* dog (also insult); ~ *herder* German shepherd; ~ *ras* pure-breed

anjlok *v* to derail; *kereta api* ~ derailed train

anjung: anjungan *n* gallery, upper level, ship's bridge; ~ *tunai mandiri (ATM)* automated teller machine (ATM)

anjur: menganjurkan *v* to suggest, propose

anoa *n* dwarf buffalo of Sulawesi

antak: berantakan *adj* messy, in a mess

antar take, escort; ~ *jemput* pick up and take home,

door-to-door; **mengantar** v to take, escort, accompany; **mengantarkan** v to take someone or something

antara conj between; ~ lain among others; di ~nya among them; **perantara** n broker, intermediary, go-between

antarbudaya adj cross-cultural

antarpropinsi adj interprovincial

antem: berantem v, coll to fight, scuffle ← **hantam**

anténa n antenna, aerial

anti- pref, adj against, resistant to; ~ peluru, bullet-proof; ~ perang, anti-war

anting n earring

antré, antri queue; **antréan** n queue; **mengantri** v to queue

anu um, er; n so-and-so, what's-its-name

anugerah n gift, grace, blessing

anut, menganut v to follow; **penganut** n follower, believer

anyam, menganyam v to weave, plait, braid;

anyaman n plait, braid; kursi ~ wicker chair

apa interrog, n what; ~ lagi what else; ~ saja anything; ~ kabar? how are you?; ~ boleh buat it can't be helped; **apa-apa** n something; bukan ~ nothing; tidak ~ it doesn't matter; **apabila** conj if, when; **berapa** interrog how many? what number?; ~ banyak? how much? how many?; ~ harganya? how much is it?; umur ~ how old; **beberapa** adj several, a number of; **mengapa** interrog why; tak ~ it doesn't matter; **ngapain** sl why, do what; **siapa** interrog, n who; ~ saja whoever; **siapa-siapa** n anybody

apakah, apa (question marker) ← **apa**

apal → **hafal**

apalagi adv, conj especially, moreover

aparat n government official

apartemén n apartment, flat

apek adj smelling musty, moldy

11

apel *n* apple; ~ *Malang* Malang apples

apél call; *v, coll* to visit your girlfriend's house

api *n* fire, flame; **berapi** *v* to produce fire; **berapi-api** *adj* fiery, fervent; **perapian** *n* fireplace, oven

apik *adj* neat, tidy

apit, mengapit *v* to pinch, press, squeeze; to flank

apokat → **alpukat**

apoték *n* pharmacy, chemist (shop), dispensary; **apotéker** *n* pharmacist

April *bulan* ~ April

apung float; **mengapung** *v* to float, be suspended; **terapung** *adj* drifting, floating

Arab *bahasa* ~ Arabic; *Laut* ~ the Arabian Sea; *orang* ~ an Arab

arah *n* direction; ~ *kiri* to the left; *berbelok* ~ to change direction; *satu* ~ one way; same direction; **mengarah** *v* to aim something towards; **mengarahkan** *v* to direct; **pengarahan** *n* direction, guidance, briefing; **searah** *adj* the same direction; **terarah** *adj* directed

arak *n* alcoholic drink

arak: arak-arakan *n* procession

arang *n* charcoal

arca *n* statue

arén *n* areca palm; *gula* ~ palm sugar

argo, argométer *n* taxi meter

arguméntasi *n* reasoning, argument

ari *kulit* ~ epidermis

ari-ari *n* placenta

arif *adj* wise, learned

arit *n* sickle

arogan *adj* arrogant

arsip *n* archive, file; **kearsipan** archives, archival

arti *n* meaning; ~*nya* it means, that is to say; *dalam* ~ in the context of; **berarti** *v* to mean; *adj* meaningful; **mengartikan** *v* to define, interpret → **erti**

artikel *n* article (in print media)

artis *n* celebrity; actor, actress or singer

arung ~ *jeram* white water rafting

arus *n* stream, current, flow; ~ *listrik* electric current

arwah *n* soul (of a dead person)

AS *abbrev Amerika Serikat* the United States

asa *n* hope

asal *n* origin; *~-usul* origins; **asal-asalan** *adv* carelessly, in any old way; **berasal** *v* to come from

asal, asalkan *conj* as long as, providing that

asam, asem sour, tamarind; acid; *~ manis* sweet and sour; *muka ~* sour look

asap *n* smoke, exhaust, pollution; vapor; *~ rokok* cigarette smoke; **berasap** *adj* smoky

asar *n, Isl* the afternoon prayer

asas, azas: berasas(kan) *adj* based on; **asasi, asazi** *adj* basic; *hak ~ manusia (HAM)* human rights

asbak *n* ashtray

asbés *n* asbestos

ASI *abbrev air susu ibu* breast milk

Asia *n* Asia; *bahasa ~* Asian languages; *orang ~* Asian; *~ Tenggara* Southeast Asia

asin *adj* salty, salted; **asinan** *n* sour vegetable and fruit dish

asing *adj* strange, alien, foreign; *orang ~* stranger; foreigner; *bahasa ~* foreign language; **mengasingkan** *v* to exile; **pengasingan** *n* exile

asli *adj* original, indigenous; *orang ~, penduduk ~* indigenous person, native

asma *n* asthma

asmara *n* romantic love, passion

aso, mengaso *v* to take a rest, break

asong: asongan *n* street vendor; goods sold on the street (cigarettes, magazines, drinking water etc)

aspal *n* asphalt

aspék *n* aspect, point of view

asrama *n* boarding house, dormitory, *mil* barracks

asri *adj* beautiful, scenic (of a view)

assalamualaikum, assalamu alaikum salam alaikum *gr, Isl* peace be upon you

astaga *ejac* gosh, golly

astagfirullah *ejac, Isl* God forbid

asuh care; *orang tua ~* foster parents; **pengasuh** *n* carer; *~ anak* nursemaid, babysitter

asyik *adj* fun; *adv* absorbed, engrossed; eager

atap *n* roof; **beratap** *v* to have a roof

atas *prep* up; *n* upper part; *~ nama* on behalf of; *di ~* on (top of), upon, above, over; upstairs; **atasan** *n* superior, boss; **mengatasi** *v* to overcome

atau *conj* or

atéis *adj* atheist

ati ampela *n* liver and gizzards

atlét, atlit *n* athlete; **atlétik** *cabang ~* athletics

atmosfér *n* atmosphere (around Earth)

atom *n* atom

atur arrange; **aturan** *n* rule, regulation; *~ main* rules of the game; **mengatur** *v* to arrange, organize, regulate; **peraturan** *n* rule, regulation; **teratur** *adj* organized, regular

aula *n* hall (at school), auditorium

aum roar; **mengaum** *v* to roar, growl (of tigers)

AU(RI) *abbrev Angkatan Udara (Republik Indonesia)* (Indonesian) Air Force

aus *adj* eroded, worn

Australia *n* Australia; *orang ~* Australian

autis *adj* autistic

avokad → alpukat

awak *n* person; *~ pesawat* cabin crew

awal beginning, early; **awalan** *n* prefix; **berawal** *v* to begin with; **meng-awali** *v* to start; to precede

awam *adj* common, lay; *orang ~* layman

awan *n* cloud; **berawan** *adj* cloudy, overcast

awas *ejac* be careful, beware; *~ ada anjing* beware of the dog; **mengawasi** *v* to supervise; **pengawasan** *n* supervision, control

awét *adj* durable, long-lasting; *~ muda* youthful; **mengawétkan** *v* to preserve (food)

ayah, Ayah *n, pron* father; ~ *bunda* parents

ayam *n* chicken, hen; ~ *betina* hen; ~ *jago*, ~ *jantan* rooster, cock; ~ *kampung* free-range chicken; ~ *negeri* battery hen

ayat *n* verse (of a religious text)

ayo come on, let's go

ayu *adj* beautiful; *pagar* ~ girl attendant at a wedding reception

ayun, mengayun *v* to rock, swing, sway; **ayunan** *n* swings; *main* ~ play on the swings

azan, adzan *n* call to prayer

B

bab *n* chapter

babak *n* round (in sport); half (in football)

babat *n* a kind of meat (from the stomach)

babat *wingko* ~ small coconut slice, a specialty of Semarang

babat: membabat *v* to cut or chop down, clear away; **pembabatan** *n* felling, chopping; ~ *hutan* (unregulated) deforestation

babi *n* pig, boar (also as an insult); ~ *hutan* wild boar; *daging* ~ pork

baca *v* to read; **bacaan** *n* reading material; **membaca** *v* to read; **pembaca** *n* reader

badai *n* hurricane, storm; ~ *topan* typhoon

badak *n* rhino, rhinoceros; ~ *air* hippo, hippopotamus; ~ *bercula satu* one-horned rhino

badan *n* body; board, committee

Badui, Baduy *orang* ~ a Sundanese sub-ethnic group

badut *n* clown

bagai *conj* like, as; **berbagai** *adj* various, several; **sebagai** *conj* like, as

bagaimana *interrog, conj* how, in what way

bagasi *n* baggage; boot (of vehicle); hold (of ship or aircraft)

bagi *v* divide; **bagian** *n* part, share, section; **berbagi** *v* to share; **membagi** *v* to divide, distribute; **pembagian** *n* distribution, division; **sebagian** *n* some, a section of

bagi *prep* for; ~ *saya* as for me

bagus *adj* good, fine, excellent (external qualities of concrete objects)

bah *n* flood; *air* ~ flood

bahagia *adj* happy, joyous; **berbahagia** *v* to be happy; **kebahagiaan** *n* happiness; **membahagiakan** *v* to make happy

bahan *n* materials, ingredients; cloth, fabric; ~ *bakar* fuel

bahari *Musium* ~ Maritime Museum

bahas *v* to discuss; **membahas** *v* to discuss, debate

bahasa *n* language; ~ *Indonesia* Indonesian; *ilmu* ~ linguistics; **berbahasa** *v* to (be able to) speak or use a language; *Nenek hanya* ~ *Jawa* Grandma only speaks Javanese; **peribahasa** *n* proverb, idiom

bahaya *n* danger; **berbahaya** *v* to be dangerous

bahkan *conj* moreover; on the contrary; indeed, even

bahu *n* shoulder; ~ *jalan* hard shoulder; ~~*mem*~ shoulder to shoulder, to help each other

bahwa *conj* that

baik *adj* good, fine, well, OK (ie. internal qualities of abstract objects); **baik-baik** *adj* fine; respectable; *Apa kabar?/*~ *saja* How are you?/Fine; ~ ... *maupun* ..., both ... and ...; ~ *hati* kind; **kebaikan** *n* goodness, kindness; **membaik** *v* to improve; **memperbaiki** *v* to repair, fix; **perbaikan** *n* repair, improvement; **sebaiknya** *adv* preferably, it's best if; **terbaik** *adj* the best

baja *n* steel

bajaj *n* three-wheeled motorized form of transport in Jakarta

bajak *n* plow; **membajak** *v* to plow

bajak, membajak *v* to hijack; to copy illegally;

bajakan *adj* pirated; *CD* ~ pirated CD; **pembajakan** *n* hijacking; piracy

baju *n, inf* clothes; clothing for the upper body; ~ *dalam* singlet; underwear; **berbaju** *v* to put on, wear clothes

bak *n* tub; ~ *mandi* large tank in the bathroom from which water is taken

bakal *adj* future, potential

bakar *v* to burn; **kebakaran** *n* fire; ~ *hutan* forest fire, bushfire; *Ada* ~! Fire!; **membakar** *v* to burn; **terbakar** *adj* burnt

bakat *n* talent, gift; **berbakat** *adj* talented, gifted

bakau, *n* mangrove

bakmi, **bami** *n* Chinese noodles

bakpao *n* steamed white bread with filling of nuts or chicken

bakpia *n* sweet cake from Jogja with nutty filling

bakso, **baso** *n* meatball; meatball soup; ~ *tahu* meatballs and tofu (specialty of Bandung)

baktéri *n* bacteria

bakti *n* service, devotion; **kebaktian** *n* (Protestant) service

baku *adj* standard

bakul *n* basket hung on a pole for selling goods

bakwan *n* dish of various sweetmeats, a specialty of Malang

bala ~ *Keselamatan* Salvation Army; ~ *tentara* army

balai *n* house, building, office; ~ *kota* town hall

balap race; **balapan** *n* race; ~ *mobil* car race; **membalap** *v* to race

balas reply; ~ *dendam* take revenge; **balasan** reply, answer; **membalas** *v* to reply, respond

balét *n* ballet

Bali *n pulau* ~ Bali; *bahasa* ~, *orang* ~ Balinese

balik *v* to return, reverse, retreat; ~ *nama* transfer of ownership; *n* back, flipside; return; **membalik** *v* to return, reverse, turn over; **membalikkan** *v* to turn something over; **sebaliknya** *conj* on the contrary;

terbalik *adj* overturned, upside-down, opposite

balon *n* balloon

balur: membalur *v* to smear or massage with oil

balut *v* to bandage; **pembalut** *n* sanitary pad

bambu *n* bamboo

ban *n* tire; ~ *serep* spare tire

banci *n* transvestite, cross-dressing male, often a prostitute; male homosexual (*derog*)

bandar *n* (sea) port

bandar *n* dealer (often in drugs), croupier

bandara *n* airport ← **bandar udara**

bandel *adj* naughty, disobedient

bandeng *ikan* ~ milkfish

banding *tiada* ~, *tidak ada* ~ incomparable, the best there is; *naik* ~ to appeal against a court decision; **membandingkan** *v* to compare something; **perbandingan** *n* comparison, ratio

bandrék *n* ginger drink

bang *pron* older brother (in Jakarta or Malay areas) → **abang**

bangau *n* heron

banget *adj, sl* fast, quick

bangga *adj* proud; **kebanggaan** *n* pride; something of which you are proud; **membanggakan** *v* to make proud, please

bangkai *n* corpse (usually of animals); *bunga* ~ the Rafflesia flower

bangkit, berbangkit *v* to rise, get up; **kebangkitan** *n* rise, awakening; **membangkit** *v* to rise, get up; **pembangkit** ~ *listrik* power station

bangkrut *adj* bankrupt; **kebangkrutan** *n* bankruptcy

bangku *n* bench (for sitting); stool; desk

bangsa *n* people, nation, race; ~ *Indonesia* the Indonesian people; **kebangsaan** *adj* national; **bangsawan** *n* aristocrat, member of royalty

bangsal *n* ward (in hospital), dormitory

bangsawan *n* aristocrat, member of royalty

bangun v get up, wake up

bangun: bangunan n building; **membangun** v to build or create; **pembangunan** n development

banjir n flood

bank n bank; ~ *negara* state-owned bank; **perbankan** adj banking; **bankir** n banker

bantah, membantah v to deny, dispute

bantai, membantai v to slaughter, kill viciously; **pembantaian** n slaughter, mass killings

bantal cushion; pillow; ~ *guling* bolster, Dutch wife

banteng n (Javan) ox

banting throw down, slam; ~ *harga* cut prices; **membanting** v to throw down (with a bang); ~ *pintu* to slam the door; ~ *tulang* to toil, work yourself to the bone

bantu v to help; **bantuan** n assistance, help, aid; **membantu** v to help (someone); **pembantu** n servant, maid; assistant; *kantor* ~ (larger) branch office

banyak adj many, much; **kebanyakan** n, adj too much; most

Bapa pron Father (title for own father or respected older man), also **Bapak**; *Chr* God, Father, Lord

bapa n father; ~ *permandian* godfather

Bapak pron Father (title for own father or respected older man)

bapak n father; ~ *angkat* adopted father; ~ *tiri* stepfather

Bappenas *Badan Perencanaan Pembangunan Nasional* National Development Planning Agency

baptis adj baptist; **membaptis** v to baptize, christen

bara n embers; **membara** v to glow with heat

barang n goods, things

barang adj some (indicating uncertainty); **barangkali** conj perhaps, maybe; **barangsiapa** pron whoever, whosoever

Barat n the West

barat *adj* west; ~ *daya* southwest; ~ *laut* northwest

Barelang *Batam, Rempang, Galang* group of islands in Riau Archipelago province

bareng *conj, sl* with; *v* to go together

baring: berbaring *v* to lie down

baris *n* line, row, rank; **barisan** *n* line; forces; *Bukit* ~ mountain range in Sumatra; **berbaris** *v* to line up

barongsai *n* Chinese dragon for dance performances

baru *adj* new, recent; just; ~~ *ini* just the other day; ~ *saja* just now; **pembaruan** *n* renewal; **terbaru** *adj* latest, newest; **barusan** *adv, sl* just now

basa: basa-basi *n* good manners, politeness; platitudes

basah *adj* wet, moist, soaked; ~ *kuyup* soaking wet

basi *adj* off, rotten, inedible (of food)

basmi destroy; **membasmi** *v* to exterminate, destroy, wipe out

batagor *n* fried tofu and meatballs, a specialty of Bandung ← **bakso tahu goréng**

Batak *adj* ethnic group of North Sumatra; *bahasa* ~, *orang* ~ Batak

batal *adj* cancelled; broken (a fast); **membatalkan** *v* to cancel, repeal

batang *n* trunk, stem, stick (of a tree); shaft; handle; penis; counter for long cylindrical objects; *rokok tiga* ~ three cigarettes; ~ *pohon* tree trunk; ~ *sungai* tributary

batas *n* limit, border; **berbatasan** *v* to be adjacent to; **membatasi** *v* to limit, restrict, curb something; **pembatas** *n* divider; ~ *buku* bookmark; **pembatasan** *n* restriction; **perbatasan** *n* border, frontier; **terbatas** *adj* limited; **keterbatasan** *n* limitation

baterai *n* battery

batik *n* application of wax onto fabric to create a pattern after dyeing; fabric or clothes with designs produced in this manner;

fabric or clothes resembling batik but with printed designs; ~ *cap* stamped batik; ~ *modern* batik produced with chemicals instead of wax; ~ *tulis* handmade batik; **membatik** *v* to apply wax onto fabric

batin, bathin *adj, n* inner, spiritual; soul, spirit

batok *n* shell, skull

batu *n* stone; ~ *apung* pumice; ~ *arang* charcoal; ~ *bara* coal; ~ *bata* brick; ~ *empedu* gallstones; ~ *pualam* marble; ~ *tulis* slate; inscription; **berbatu** *adj* rocky, stony

batuk *v* cough

bau *n, v, adj* smell, smelly; ~ *amis* fishy smell; **berbau** *v* to smell, have connotations of

baur: berbaur, membaur *v* to integrate, mix with others (of people); **pembauran** *n* integration, mixing of different ethnic groups

baut *n* bolt

bawa *v* to take, bring, carry; to conduct; ~ *diri* to conduct yourself; **membawa** *v* to take, bring, carry; to conduct; **membawakan** *v* to bring or carry for someone; to sing; **pembawa** *n* bearer, carrier; ~ *acara* host, MC; **terbawa** *adj* (accidentally) taken away; ~ *arus* swept away in the current

bawah *prep* below; *di* ~ below, under; *di* ~ *umur* underage

bawang *n* onion; ~ *bombai* (brown) onion; ~ *merah* red onion, shallot; ~ *putih* garlic

baya *n* age; *setengah* ~ middle-aged; **sebaya** *adj* the same age

bayam, bayem *n* spinach

bayang *n* shadow, image; **bayangan** *n* shadow; **terbayang** *adj* imagined, conceivable

bayar *v* to pay; **bayaran** *adj* paid, hired; **membayar** *v* to pay; ~ *di muka* to pay in advance; **pembayaran** *n* payment

bayi *n* baby

béa *n* tax, duty, excise; ~ *cukai* customs

béasiswa *n* scholarship, bursary

beban *n* burden, load; responsibility; **membebani** *v* to burden someone with something

bébas *adj* free; ~ *banjir* safe from floods; **kebébasan** *n* freedom; **membébaskan** *v* to exempt, liberate, free someone; **pembébasan** *n* liberation, release, exemption

bébék *n* duck

beberapa *adj* several, a number of ← **apa, berapa**

bebuyutan *adj* ancestral; arch enemy ← **buyut**

becak *n* pedicab, rickshaw tricycle; *tukang* ~ *bécak* driver

bécék *adj* muddy, wet

béda *adj* different; ~*nya* ... the difference is, ...; **ber-béda** *adj* different; **mem-bédakan** *v* to discriminate, differentiate between, consider different; **per-bédaan** *n* difference

bedah *n* surgery; ~ *plastik* plastic or cosmetic surgery; *ahli* ~ surgeon

bedak *n* powder

bedug, beduk *n* big drum, especially in a mosque

begadang *v* to stay up all night; to sleep late

begini *adv* like this, in this manner ← **ini**

begitu *adv* like that, in that manner ← **itu**

bégo *excl, adj, sl* idiot; stupid

béha *n* bra

bekal *n* provisions

bekas *adj* used, old, former (for objects); ~ *pakai* used; *barang* ~ second-hand goods

bekerja *v* to work; ~ *sama* to co-operate, work together ← **kerja**

beku *adj* frozen; **membeku** *v* to freeze; **membekukan** *v* to freeze something

bél *n* bell

béla *v* defend; ~ *diri* self-defense; **membéla** *v* to defend; **pembéla** *n* defender; **pembélaan** *n* defense

belah *n* crack, fissure, divide, splinter; ~ *pecah* crockery, breakable household goods; **belahan** *n* half, side; ~ *jiwa* other half (of a couple); **membelah** *v* to split in two; **sebelah** ~ *kiri* on the left (side); ~ *mana* which side, where; *rumah* ~ next door; **bersebelahan** *v* to be next to

belai, **membelai** *v* to stroke, caress

belajar *v* to learn, study ← **ajar**

belaka *adj, neg* only, mere, pure

belakang *prep, n* behind; back, rear; **belakangan** *adv* recently; after others; ~ *ini* recently; **terbelakang, terkebelakang** *adj* backward, neglected

belalang *n* grasshopper, locust

Belanda *n* the Netherlands, Holland; *bahasa* ~ Dutch (language); *orang* ~ Dutch (people)

belanja *v* to go shopping; **belanjaan** *n* shopping; **berbelanja** *v* to go shopping; **membelanjakan** *v* to spend money; **perbelanjaan** *pusat* ~ shopping center, mall

belantara *hutan* ~ forest, wilderness

belas ~ *kasih* pity, compassion

belas *n* number between 10–20; *lima* ~ fifteen; **belasan** *n* dozens; **sebelas** *n, adj* eleven; **kesebelasan** *n* team of eleven, soccer team

bélasungkawa *n* condolences

belatung *n* maggot

bélérang *n* sulfur

Bélgia *n* Belgium; *orang* ~ Belgian

beli *v* to buy; **membeli** *v* to buy, purchase; **membelikan** *v* to buy something for someone; **pembelian** *n* purchase

beliau *pron* he, she; him, her (respectful form of **dia**)

belimbing *n* starfruit

belit: **berbelit-belit** *v* to wind around; to ramble, try to wriggle out of something; **membelit** *v* to twist; **terbelit** *adj* twisted, involved

bélok *ber~~* windy, lots of bends and turns; **bélokan** *n*

bend, turn in the road;
berbélok, membélok v
to bend, turn; **mem-
bélokkan** v to turn, divert
something

belum adv not yet; ~
pernah until now, never
(but possibly in the future);
sebelum adj before; **sebelumnya** adv previously,
before

belut n eel

bémo n motorized three-
wheeled vehicle still
operating in a few parts
of Jakarta ← **bécak
bermotor**

benak n brains, mind

benam: terbenam adj set,
sunken

benang n thread; ~ *gigi*
dental floss; ~ *merah*
connecting thread (of a story
or series of happenings)

benar, bener adj true,
correct, right; **benar-benar**
adv truly, really; **ke-
benaran** n truth; **mem-
benarkan** v to confirm,
verify; to justify; **sebenarnya** adv in fact, actually →
betul

bencana n disaster,
catastrophe; ~ *alam* natural
disaster, act of God

benci v to hate; **kebencian** n
hatred; **membenci** v to hate

béncong n, sl transvestite;
m homosexual

benda n thing, object;
goods, valuables

bendahara n treasurer;
bishop (in chess); **per-
bendaharaan** n treasury

bendéra n flag

béndi n two-wheeled horse-
carriage

bendung: bendungan n
dam

bener → **benar**

bengkak adj swollen

béngkél n garage;
workshop; ~ *las* welding
workshop

béngkok adj bent, crooked;
membéngkokkan v to
bend something

bengkuang, bengkoang n
kind of small fruit with
brown skin and white flesh,
used in salads and cosmetics

benih n seed, germ, sperm

bening adj clear, transparent,
clean (of glass, water etc)

bénjol, bénjolan n mole, lump, tumor

bénsin n petrol, gasoline

bentak shout; **membentak** v to shout, scold, snap

bentar → **sebentar**

bénténg n fort, fortress

bentrok v to clash head-on; **bentrokan** n clash, conflict

bentuk n shape, form; **ber-bentuk** adj shaped, with the shape of; **membentuk** v to form, set up something (eg. committee); **terbentuk** adj formed, shaped, created

bentur: terbentur adj accidentally bumped

benua n continent

bepergian v to travel, be away ← **pergi**

beracun adj poisonous, containing poison; gas ~ poison gas ← **racun**

berada v to be somewhere; adj well-to-do, well-off ← **ada**

beragam adj various ← **ragam**

beragama adj religious; v to have a religion; Siti ~ Islam Siti is Muslim ← **agama**

berahi n lust, desire; heat (of animals); ~ tinggi (BT or bété) sexually excited, horny; bad-tempered

bérak v poo, defecate; n poo, feces

berakhir v to end ← **akhir**

beraksén v to have a touch of ← **aksén**

beralamat v to have an address ← **alamat**

beralasan adj with reason, reasonable ← **alas**

beraliansi v to be allied with ← **aliansi**

beralih v to move, change ← **alih**

beraliran v to have an ideology; ~ kiri leftist ← **alir**

beralkohol v containing alcohol; minuman ~ alcoholic drink ← **alkohol**

beramal v to give to charity; adj charitable ← **amal**

berambisi v to have an ambition, have ambitions ← **ambisi**

berambut adj hairy; v to have hair

beranak v (of animals) to give birth to, have offspring ← **anak**

25

beranda *n* veranda, balcony

beranéka ~ *ragam* various ← **anéka**

berang *adj* furious, enraged

beranggotakan *v* to have a membership, have as members ← **anggota**

berangkat *v* to depart, leave; **keberangkatan** *n* departure ← **angkat**

berangus *n* muzzle; **memberangus** *v* to muzzle, bridle

berani *adj* brave, courageous; **keberanian** *n* bravery, courage; **pemberani** *n* brave or courageous person, hero

beranjak *v* to move, shift ← **anjak**

berantakan *adj* messy, in a mess ← **antak**

berantas, memberantas *v* to wipe out, fight against; **pemberantasan** *n* destruction, fight against

berantem *v, coll* to fight, scuffle ← **antem, hantam**

berapa *interrog* how many? what number?; ~ *banyak?* how much? how many?; ~ *harganya?* how much is

it?; *umur* ~ how old; **beberapa** *adj* several, a number of; **seberapa** *tidak* ~ not many; ~ *jauh* as far as ← **apa**

berapi *adj* burning, fire-producing (of volcanoes); **berapi-api** *adj* fiery, fervent ← **api**

berarti *v* to mean; *adj* meaningful ← **arti**

beras *n* rice (husked and uncooked, as sold in shops)

berasal *v* to come from ← **asal**

berasap *adj* smoky ← **asap**

berasas(kan) *adj* based on ← **asas**

berat heavy, severe, difficult; weight; ~ *badan* body weight; ~ *bersih* net weight; ~ *sebelah* unbalanced, tending to favor one side; **keberatan** *n* objection; *v* to object; **memberatkan** *v* to burden, make heavy; *adj* incriminating

beratap *v* to have a roof ← **atap**

berawal *v* to begin with ← **awal**

berawan *adj* cloudy, overcast ← **awan**

berbagai *adj* various, several ← **bagai**

berbagi *v* to share ← **bagi**

berbahagia *v* to be happy ← **bahagia**

berbahasa *v* to (be able to) speak or use a language; *Nenek hanya ~ Jawa* Grandma only speaks Javanese ← **bahasa**

berbahaya *v* to be dangerous ← **bahaya**

berbaju *v* to put on, wear clothes ← **baju**

berbakat *adj* talented, gifted ← **bakat**

berbaring *v* to lie down ← **baring**

berbaris *v* to line up ← **baris**

berbatasan *v* to be adjacent to ← **batas**

berbatu *adj* rocky, stony ← **batu**

berbau *v* to smell, have connotations of ← **bau**

berbaur *v* to integrate, mix with others (of people) ← **baur**

berbéda *adj* different ← **béda**

berbelanja *v* to go shopping ← **belanja**

berbelit-belit *v* to wind around; to ramble, try to wriggle out of something ← **belit**

berbentuk *adj* shaped, with the shape of ← **bentuk**

berbicara *v* to speak; *~ dalam bahasa Sunda* to speak in Sundanese ← **bicara**

berbincang, berbincang-bincang *v* to chat, discuss ← **bincang**

berbintang *v* to have a star ← **bintang**

berbisa *adj* poisonous; *ular ~* poisonous snake ← **bisa**

berbisik *adj* whispering; *v* to whisper ← **bisik**

berbisnis *v* to do business ← **bisnis**

berbobot *adj* heavy, weighty ← **bobot**

berbohong *v* to lie ← **bohong**

berbondong-bondong *adv* in droves ← **bondong**

berbuah *v* to bear fruit, produce ← **buah**

berbuat *v* to do; ~ *salah* to do wrong ← **buat**

berbudaya *n* to have a culture ← **budaya**

berbuka ~ *puasa* to break the fast ← **buka**

berbukit *adj* hilly ← **bukit**

berbulu *adj* hairy; to have fur or feathers ← **bulu**

berbunga *v* to flower, blossom ← **bunga**

berbunyi *v* to sound, make a noise ← **bunyi**

berburu *v* to go hunting ← **buru**

bercabang *v* to be split, branched ← **cabang**

bercak *n* spot, blemish, pock (on body)

bercakap *v* to speak; **bercakap-cakap** *v* to chat ← **cakap**

bercampur *adj* mixed with ← **campur**

bercanda *v* to joke; ~ *kok* just kidding ← **canda**

bercas-cis-cus *v* to speak a European language ← **cas-cis-cus**

bercécéran *adj* scattered, dispersed ← **cécér**

bercelana *v* to wear trousers, trousered ← **celana**

bercerai *v* to be divorced ← **cerai**

berceramah *v* to give a lecture or talk ← **ceramah**

bercerita *v* to tell (a story) ← **cerita**

bercinta *v* to make love; to be in love ← **cinta**

bercita-cita, **bercita-citakan** *v* to dream of ← **cita-cita**

berciuman *v* to kiss each other ← **cium**

bercocok ~ *tanam* to work or till the soil ← **cocok**

bercorak *v* to have a design ← **corak**

bercucuran *v* to trickle down, drip, flow ← **cucur**

bercumbu *v* to flirt, flatter ← **cumbu**

berdagang *v* to trade, do business ← **dagang**

berdahak *n* containing phlegm or mucus; *batuk* ~ chesty cough ← **dahak**

berdamai *v* to make peace ← **damai**

berdampak *v* to have a (negative) effect ← **dampak**

berdandan *v* to dress, put on make-up ← **dandan**

berdansa *v* to dance (Western-style) ← **dansa**

berdarah *v* to bleed ← **darah**

berdasarkan *adj* based on; in accordance with, pursuant to ← **dasar**

berdasi *v* to wear a tie; *kaum* ~ white-collar workers ← **dasi**

berdaya *v* to have power; *tak* ~ powerless ← **daya**

berdebar *v* to beat quickly ← **debar**

berdebat *v* to have a debate ← **debat**

berdebu *adj* dusty ← **debu**

berdekap-dekapan, berdekapan *v* to embrace each other ← **dekap**

berdekatan *adj* close (of two or more things) ← **dekat**

berdémo *v* to hold a protest ← **démo**

berdémpét *adj* stuck together ← **démpét**

berdéndang *v* to sing, chant ← **déndang**

berdengung *v* to drone, hum, shake with sound ← **dengung**

berdenyut *v* to throb, to beat ← **denyut**

berdering *v* to ring, tinkle ← **dering**

berdesakan *v* to push each other ← **desak**

berdesir *v* to hiss, rustle ← **desir**

berdiam *v* to reside ← **diam**

berdikir *v, Isl* to say additional prayers ← **dikir, zikir**

berdoa *v* to pray, say a prayer ← **doa**

berdomisili *v* to be domiciled, reside ← **domisili**

berdosa *v* to sin, commit a sin ← **dosa**

berdua *adj* together, in pairs ← **dua**

berduka ~ *(cita)* to grieve, be in mourning ← **duka**

berduri *adj* thorny ← **duri**

berdusta *v* to lie ← **dusta**

beréaksi *v* to react ← **réaksi**

berebut *v* to fight for; **berebutan** *v* to fight each other for ← **rebut**

berédar *v* to circulate ← **édar**

berékor *v* to have a tail ← **ékor**

berembuk *v* to confer, discuss ← **rembuk**

berembus *v* to blow ← **embus**

berémosi *adj* emotional ← **émosi**

berempat *adj* in a group of four ← **empat**

berenang *v* to swim ← **renang**

berencana *v* to plan ← **rencana**

berendam *v* to soak ← **rendam**

berénérgi *adj* energetic, containing energy ← **énérgi**

bérés finished, ready; **membéréskan** *v* to clear up, make ready

berétika *adj* ethical; to behave ← **étika**

berfilsafat *v* to have a philosophy ← **filsafat**

berfirman *v* to utter, say; *Allah* ~ God said ← **firman**

berfokus *adj* focused ← **fokus**

berfoya-foya *v* to waste money, live frivolously ← **foya-foya**

berfungsi *v* to work, go; to act as ← **fungsi**

bergabung *v* to join together ← **gabung**

bergadang → **begadang**

bergairah *adj* lusty, passionate; enthusiastic ← **gairah**

bergambar *adj* illustrated ← **gambar**

bergandéngan ~ *tangan* to link arms or hands ← **gandéng**

berganti *v* to change; ~*ganti*, ~*an* in turns ← **ganti**

bergantung ~ *pada* to depend on ← **gantung**

bergaransi *adj* guaranteed ← **garansi**

bergaris *adj* lined ← **garis**

bergaul *v* to mix or associate with ← **gaul**

bergaung *v* to echo ← **gaung**

bergaya *adj* stylish, with style ← **gaya**

bergegas-gegas *v* to hurry ← **gegas**

bergelantungan *v* to hang from (of several things) ← **gelantung**

bergelar *v* titled ← **gelar**

bergelimang *adj* smeared ← **gelimang**

bergelimpangan *adj* sprawled all around

bergelombang *adj* wavy ← **gelombang**

bergema *v* to echo, reverberate ← **gema**

bergembira *v* to be happy, joyous ← **gembira**

bergéngsi *adj* prestigious ← **géngsi**

bergerak *v* to move ← **gerak**

bergerigi *adj* serrated, jagged ← **gerigi**

bergetar *v* to vibrate, tremble ← **getar**

bergilir, bergiliran *adj* in turns ← **gilir**

bergizi *adj* nutritious ← **gizi**

bergosip *v* to gossip ← **gosip**

bergoyang *v* to shake, sway; to dance ← **goyang**

bergulat *v* to wrestle, fight ← **gulat**

bergumam *v* to mumble ← **gumam**

berguna *adj* useful, worthwhile; *tidak* ~ useless ← **guna**

berhadapan *v* (~ *muka*) face to face ← **hadap**

berhadiah *adj* with prizes ← **hadiah**

berhak *v* to have a right to, be entitled to ← **hak**

berhalangan *v* to be prevented from, unable ← **halang**

berhamburan *adj* scattered about ← **hambur**

berharap *v* to hope ← **harap**

berharga *adj* precious, valuable ← **harga**

berhari-hari *adv* for days ← **hari**

berhasil *v* to succeed ← **hasil**

berhati-hati *v* to be careful ← **hati**

berhawa ~ *sejuk* cool climate ← **hawa**

berhenti *v* to stop, cease ← **henti**

berhias *v* to dress up, put on make-up ← **hias**

berhubung *conj* in connection to, related with; ~ *dengan* in connection with; **berhubungan** *v, pl* to have a link or connection ← **hubung**

beri v give; ~ *semangat* give a cheer; ~ *tahu* inform, let know → **beritahu; memberi** v to give; **memberikan** v to give someone (as an act of kindness); to give something (for someone); **pemberian** n present, gift, something given to someone

beribadah v to worship, serve ← **ibadah**

beribu, beribu-ribu adj thousands of ← **ribu**

berijazah adj certified, qualified ← **ijazah**

beriklim v to have a climate; ~ *dingin* to have a cool climate ← **iklim**

berikut adj following; ~ *itu* after that; *yang* ~, ~*nya* the next ← **ikut**

beriman adj religious ← **iman**

berimbang adj balanced, proportional ← **imbang**

beringin n banyan (tree)

berinisiatif v to take the initiative ← **inisiatif**

berirama adj rhythmical ← **irama**

berisi v to contain; adj full, filled out ← **isi**

berisik adj noisy, loud; to rustle ← **risik**

berisiko v to be risky ← **risiko**

beristeri, beristri adj, m married; *pria* ~ married man ← **isteri, istri**

beristirahat v to rest, take a break ← **istirahat**

berita n news, information; ~ *malam* evening news; **memberitakan** v to report

beritahu, beri tahu v to inform, let know; **memberitahu** v to advise, inform, tell; **pemberitahuan** n announcement, notice

berjabat, berjabatan ~ *tangan* to shake hands ← **jabat**

berjalan v to walk, move; ~ *dengan baik* to go well ← **jalan**

berjam-jam adj for hours and hours ← **jam**

berjamaah v, Isl to pray together, as a congregation ← **jamaah**

berjamur adj moldy; **berjamuran** v to pop up

everywhere ← **jamur**

berjangka *adj* for a term ← **jangka**

berjanji *v* to promise ← **janji**

berjasa *adj* meritorious, deserving of reward; *v* to perform a service ← **jasa**

berjéjér, berjéjéran *adj* in a row, in a line ← **jéjér**

berjemur *v* to sunbathe, sun yourself ← **jemur**

berjénggot *adj* bearded ← **jénggot**

berjilbab *v* to wear the veil ← **jilbab**

berjilid *adj* in volumes ← **jilid**

berjinjit-jinjit *v* to walk on tiptoe ← **jinjit**

berjogét *v* to dance ← **jogét**

berjongkok *v* to squat ← **jongkok**

berjuang *v* to fight, struggle ← **juang**

berjudi *v* to gamble ← **judi**

berjudul *v* to have a title; *adj* titled ← **judul**

berjumlah *v* to number ← **jumlah**

berjumpa *v* to meet ← **jumpa**

berjuta *v* to have millions of ← **juta**

berkabung *v* to mourn ← **kabung**

berkaitan *adj* related to ← **kait**

berkala *adj* regular; *secara* ~ periodically ← **kala**

berkali-kali *adv* repeatedly, again and again ← **kali**

berkalung *adj* wearing a necklace ← **kalung**

berkampanye *v* to (hold a) campaign; to join a parade for a candidate ← **kampanye**

berkantong *v* to have a pocket ← **kantong**

berkapasitas *v* with a capacity of ← **kapasitas**

berkarat *adj* rusty ← **karat**

berkas *n* bundle; file, dossier, brief

berkat *n* blessing; *conj* thanks to; **memberkati** *v* to bless; *Tuhan* ~ God bless; **pemberkatan** *n* consecration, blessing

berkata *v* to say, speak ← **kata**

berkawan *v* to have or be friends with ← **kawan**

berkecil ~ *hati* to be
  disappointed ← **kecil**
berkedip *v* to blink (two
  eyes) or wink (one eye);
  berkedip-kedip *adj*
  blinking ← **kedip**
berkedok *v* to hide behind
  a mask, pretend ← **kedok**
berkelahi *v* to quarrel,
  fight, fall out ← **kelahi**
berkelas *adj* classy ← **kelas**
berkeliaran *v* to swarm or
  wander about ← **keliar**
berkeliling *v* to go around
  ← **keliling**
berkelip *v* to twinkle, flicker
  ← **kelip**
berkeluarga *v* to have a
  family, be married ←
  keluarga
berkémah *v* to camp, go
  camping ← **kémah**
berkemas-kemas *v* to tidy
  up, pack ← **kemas**
berkembang *v* to develop,
  expand; ~ *biak* to breed,
  grow; *negara* ~ developing
  country ← **kembang**
berkencan *v* to go on a
  date ← **kencan**
berkepala *v* to have a head
  ← **kepala**

berkeramas *v* to wash your
  hair ← **keramas**
berkeringat *v* to sweat ←
  keringat
berkerja → **bekerja**
berkerudung *adj* veiled ←
  kerudung
berkerumun *v* to swarm,
  crowd ← **kerumun**
berkesan *adj* impressive ←
  kesan
berketombé *rambut* ~ dry
  scalp, dandruff ← **ketombé**
berkhayal *v* to dream,
  imagine ← **khayal**
berkibar *v* to wave, flutter
  ← **kibar**
berkiblat *v* to be oriented
  toward ← **kiblat**
berkilau *adj* glittering,
  sparkling ← **kilau**
berkisah *v* to tell a story ←
  kisah
berkisar *v* to revolve, rotate,
  turn ← **kisar**
berkoalisi *v* to be in a
  coalition ← **koalisi**
berkolaborasi *v* to
  collaborate, work together
  ← **kolaborasi**
berkoméntar *v* to (make a)
  comment ← **koméntar**

berkompromi *v* to (reach a) compromise ← **kompromi**

berkorban *v* to make sacrifices, do without ← **korban**

berkuah *adj* with a soup or sauce ← **kuah**

berkualitas *adj* quality ← **kualitas**

berkuasa *adj* powerful, mighty ← **kuasa**

berkubah *adj* domed ← **kubah**

berkuda *v* to ride a horse, go (horse-)riding ← **kuda**

berkuku *adj* having nails or claws; clawed ← **kuku**

berkulit to have skin, skinned; ~ *badak* thick-skinned ← **kulit**

berkuman *adj* full of germs, bacteria ← **kuman**

berkumandang *v* to echo ← **kumandang**

berkumpul *v* to assemble, meet ← **kumpul**

berkumur(-kumur) *v* to gargle ← **kumur**

berkunjung *v* to visit, pay a visit to ← **kunjung**

berkurang *v* to decrease, diminish, subside ← **kurang**

berlabuh *v* to anchor ← **labuh**

berlagak *v* to act, pretend ← **lagak**

berlainan *adj* differing, different ← **lain**

berlaku *adj* effective, valid; *v* to behave ← **laku**

berlalu *v* to pass ← **lalu**

berlambang *v* to have a symbol ← **lambang**

berlandaskan *adj* based on ← **landas**

berlangganan *v* to subscribe to ← **langgan**

berlangsung *v* to take place ← **langsung**

berlanjut *v* to continue ← **lanjut**

berlantai *v* to have floors, stories ← **lantai**

berlari *v* to run ← **lari**

berlatarkan *v* to have as a background, be based on ← **latar**

berlawanan *v* to be opposed ← **lawan**

berlayar *v* to sail ← **layar**

berlebihan *adj* excessive ← **lebih**

berlépotan → **belépotan**

berlian *n* diamond

berlibur *v* to go or be on holiday ← **libur**

berlindung *v* to (take) shelter ← **lindung**

berlipat ~ *ganda* many times over ← **lipat**

berlogat ~ *Jawa* to have a Javanese accent ← **logat**

berlokasi *adj* located ← **lokasi**

berlomba *v* to compete, race ← **lomba**

berlumuran *adj* smeared, stained ← **lumur**

berlutut to kneel (down) ← **lutut**

bermacam-macam *adj* various ← **macam**

bermain *v* to play; ~ *api* to play with fire ← **main**

bermaksud *v* to intend ← **maksud**

bermalam *v* to spend or stay the night ← **malam**

bermalas-malas(an) *v* to lie or laze around, be lazy ← **malas**

bermanfaat *adj* useful, of benefit ← **manfaat**

bermasalah *adj* problematic, troublesome ← **masalah**

bermérek *adj* branded ← **mérek**

bermimpi *v* to dream ← **mimpi**

berminat *v* to have an interest, be interested ← **minat**

berminggu-minggu *adv* for weeks ← **minggu**

berminyak *adj* oily, greasy ← **minyak**

bermotif *v* to have a design ← **motif**

bermuatan *v* to be laden with ← **muat**

bermuka *v* to have a face; ~ *dua* two-faced ← **muka**

bermukim *v* to reside, stay ← **mukim**

bermula *v* to start, begin ← **mula**

bermusuhan *v* to be enemies ← **musuh**

bermutu *adj* quality ← **mutu**

bernafaskan, bernapaskan *v* with a breath of ← **nafas**

bernafsu *adj* passionate, lusty ← **nafsu**

bernama *adj* named ← **nama**

berniat *v* to intend ← **niat**

bernostalgia *v* to reminisce, be nostalgic ← **nostalgia**

bernuansa *adj* with a touch of ← **nuansa**

bernyanyi *v* to sing ← **nyanyi**

bernyawa *adj* alive ← **nyawa**

berobat *v* to go to the doctor, seek medical advice ← **obat**

beroda *adj* wheeled ← **roda**

berolahraga *v* to do or play sport ← **olahraga**

berombak *adj* wavy ← **ombak**

berontak, memberontak *v* to rebel, revolt; **pemberontakan** *n* rebellion, revolt, mutiny

beroperasi *v* to operate, work, function ← **operasi**

berotot *adj* muscular ← **otot**

berpakaian *adj* dressed in ← **pakai**

berpandangan *v* to look at each other ← **pandang**

berpangkat *v* to have the rank of ← **pangkat**

berpantang *v* to not be allowed, abstain from;

makan ~ to be on a diet ← **pantang**

berpantulan *v* to reflect (of many things) ← **pantul**

berparas *v* to have a face or appearance ← **paras**

berpasang-pasangan *adv* in pairs ← **pasang**

berpegang *v* to hold onto ← **pegang**

berpendapat *v* to have an opinion, believe ← **dapat**

berpendidikan *adj* educated; *v* to have an education

berpengalaman *adj* experienced, skilled ← **alam**

berpengaruh *adj* influential ← **pengaruh**

berperan *v* to play the role or part ← **peran**

berperang *v* to wage war, go to war ← **perang**

berpésta *v* to (have a) party ← **pésta**

berpidato *v* to make a speech, give an address ← **pidato**

berpihak *v* to take sides ← **pihak**

berpikir *v* to think ← **pikir**

berpiknik *v* to have a picnic ← **piknik**

berpindah *v* to move ←
pindah

berpisah *v* to part, separate
← **pisah**

berpola *v* to have a pattern;
adj patterned ← **pola**

berpolitik *v* to play politics
← **politik**

berpori *adj* porous; *v* to
have pores ← **pori**

berpose *v* to pose for a
photograph ← **pose**

berposisi *v* to hold a
position, be positioned
← **posisi**

berpotongan *adj* of a certain
style or cut ← **potong**

berpréstasi *adj* prestigious;
successful ← **préstasi**

berprinsip *v* to have
principles; *adj* principled
← **prinsip**

berprofési *v* to have a
profession, work as ←
profési

berpuasa *v* to fast ← **puasa**

berpulang *v* to pass away,
die ← **pulang**

berpusar *n* to revolve,
whirl ← **pusar**

berpusat ~ *pada* to focus
or center on ← **pusat**

berputar *v* to rotate, turn ←
putar

bersabar *v* to be patient ←
sabar

bersahabat *adj* to be
friends ← **sahabat**

bersahaja *adj* simple,
natural ← **sahaja**

bersaing *v* to compete;
harga ~ competitive price
← **saing**

bersaksi *v* to testify ←
saksi

bersalah *adj* guilty ←
salah

bersalin *v* to give birth;
rumah sakit ~ maternity
hospital ← **salin**

bersalju *adj* snowy, snow-
covered ← **salju**

bersama *adv* together;
jointly ← **sama**

bersambung *adj* in parts; to
be continued ← **sambung**

bersampingan *adj* next to
each other ← **samping**

bersampul *adj* in an envelope or folder ← **sampul**

bersandar *v* to lean ←
sandar

bersandiwara *v* to pretend
← **sandiwara**

bertekuk v to bend your knees ~ *lutut* to surrender, go down on your knees ← **tekuk**

bertelanjang v to be bare; ~ *dada* bare-chested ← **telanjang**

bertelur v to lay an egg ← **telur**

bertéma v to have as a theme ← **téma**

berteman v to be friends ← **teman**

bertempat v to take place or happen; ~ *tinggal* to live or reside ← **tempat**

bertempur v to fight ← **tempur**

bertemu v to meet; *sampai* ~ *lagi* see you later, so long ← **temu**

bertengkar v to quarrel ← **tengkar**

bertentangan adj contradictory, contrary, opposing ← **tentang**

bertepatan adj coinciding with, at the same time as ← **tepat**

bertepuk tangan v to applaud, clap ← **tepuk tangan**

berteriak v to scream or shout ← **teriak**

berterima kasih v to be grateful or thankful ← **terima kasih**

bertetangga v to have neighbors ← **tetangga**

bertiga adj in a three ← **tiga**

bertindak v to act, take action ← **tindak**

bertingkat adj having different levels; *rumah* ~ two-storied house ← **tingkat**

bertinju v to box ← **tinju**

bertiup v to blow ← **tiup**

bertobat v to repent ← **tobat**

bertongkat adj with a stick ← **tongkat**

bertransaksi v to make a transaction ← **transaksi**

bertubuh v to have a body; ~ *gemuk* fat ← **tubuh**

bertukar v to change ← **tukar**

bertumpuk v to be in piles ← **tumpuk**

berturut-turut adj consecutive, successive ← **turut**

bertutur v to speak or talk ← **tutur**

bersanggama v to have sex ← **sanggama**

bersanggul v to wear a bun ← **sanggul**

bersangka v to suspect or think; ~ *buruk* to think the worst ← **sangka**

bersangkutan adj concerned, involved; *yang* ~ *(ybs)* person concerned or involved ← **sangkut**

bersantap v, pol to eat, partake of ← **santap**

bersatu v to unite ← **satu**

bersaudara v to be related; to have brothers and sisters; ~ *enam* to be one of six (children) ← **saudara**

bersayap adj winged ← **sayap**

bersebelahan conj next to ← **belah**

berseberangan adj opposing, in disagreement ← **seberang**

bersedia v to be prepared or willing ← **sedia**

bersedih v to be or feel sad ← **sedih**

bersejarah adj historic, historical ← **sejarah**

bersekolah v to go to school ← **sekolah**

bersekongkol v to plot, conspire against ← **kongkol**

bersekutu v to be allies ← **sekutu**

berselancar v to surf, go surfing ← **lancar**

berselang adj with an interval of; ~~*seling* alternating ← **selang**

berseléra v to have a taste or appetite for ← **seléra**

berselingkuh v to have an affair ← **selingkuh**

berselonjor adj with outstretched legs ← **selonjor**

berseloroh v to joke ← **seloroh**

bersemangat adj spirited, enthusiastic ← **semangat**

bersembahyang v to pray, perform a prayer ← **sembahyang**

bersembunyi v to hide (yourself) ← **sembunyi**

bersemi v to sprout buds ← **semi**

bersenandung v to hum, sing ← **senandung**

bersenang-senang *v* to enjoy yourself, have fun ← **senang**

bersenda ~ *gurau* to joke around ← **senda**

bersendawa *v* to burp, belch ← **sendawa**

bersénggolan *v* to bump into each other ← **sénggol**

bersenjata *adj* armed ← **senjata**

bersentuhan *v* to touch each other ← **sentuh**

bersenyawa *v* to become a chemical compound ← **senyawa**

bersepatu *adj* in shoes ← **sepatu**

bersepéda *v* to ride a bicycle ← **sepéda**

berserat *makanan* ~ high-fiber food ← **serat**

bersértifikat *adj* with papers (of a house) ← **sértifikat**

berseru *v* to call, cry; ~ *kepada* to call on, appeal ← **seru**

bersetubuh *v* to have sex ← **tubuh, setubuh**

bersiap *v* to get ready; **bersiap-siap** *v* to make preparations ← **siap**

bersifat *v* to have the quality of ← **sifat**

bersih *adj* clean, neat; **kebersihan** *n* cleanliness, hygiene; **membersihkan** *v* to clean; wipe out (eg. disease); **pembersih** *n* cleaning agent

bersikap *v* to display an attitude ← **sikap**

bersikeras *v* to maintain, stick to, be obstinate ← **keras**

bersila *duduk* ~ sit with crossed legs ← **sila**

bersilang *adj* crossed ← **silang**

bersilaturahmi *v* to maintain good relations, visit or meet friends ← **silaturahmi**

bersimpati *adj* sympathetic ← **simpati**

bersin *v* to sneeze

bersinambung *adj* continuous ← **sambung**

bersinar *v* to shine, gleam ← **sinar**

bersisik *adj* scaly, rough ← **sisik**

bersitegang *v* to stand fast, persevere ← **tegang**

bersiul *v* to whistle ← **siul**

berskala *v* to be on a scale; ~ *besar* large-scale ← **skala**

bersoda *adj* carbonated; *minuman* ~ carbonated drink ← **soda**

bersolék *v* to put on make-up, dress up ← **solék**

bersorak *v* to cheer, shout ← **sorak**

bersosok *v* to have a figure; ~ *tinggi* tall ← **sosok**

bersuami *adj, f* married; **bersuamikan** *v* to be married to ← **suami**

bersuara *v* to sound, have a voice ← **suara**

bersuit *v* to whistle using your fingers ← **suit**

bersulang *v* to toast, drink to ← **sulang**

bersumpah *v* to swear ← **sumpah**

bersusah ~ *payah* to work hard ← **susah**

bersyarat *adj* conditional ← **syarat**

bersyukur *adj* grateful ← **syukur**

bertaburan *adj* scattered over ← **tabur**

bertahap *adj* in stages ← **tahap**

bertahun-tahun *adv* for years and years ← **tahun**

bertakhta *v* to reign ← **takhta**

bertambah *v* to increase ← **tambah**

bertaméng *v* to hide behind, use as a shield or pretext ← **taméng**

bertanda *adj* marked ← **tanda**

bertanding *v* to compete, play ← **tanding**

bertanggal *tak* ~ undated ← **tanggal**

bertanggung jawab *adj* responsible ← **tanggung jawab**

bertanya *v* to ask; **bertanya-tanya** *v* to wonder, ask yourself ← **tanya**

bertaraf *adj* of a certain standard ← **taraf**

bertaruh *v* to bet ← **taruh**

bertato *adj* tattooed ← **t**

berteduh *v* to take shel ← **teduh**

bertékad *v* to be dete ← **tékad**

beruang *n* bear; ~ *putih* polar bear

berubah *v* to change ← **ubah**

beruban *v* to have gray hairs ← **uban**

berulang *v* to happen again, recur; **berulang-ulang** *adv* again and again, repeatedly ← **ulang**

berumah tangga *adj* married ← **rumah tangga**

berumur *adj* aged ← **umur**

berunding *v* to discuss ← **runding**

beruntun *adj* in a chain ← **runtun**

beruntung *adj* lucky, fortunate ← **untung**

berupa *adj* in the shape or form of ← **rupa**

berupaya *v* to make an effort, try ← **upaya**

berurusan *v* to have dealings with, deal with ← **urus**

berurut(-urut)an *adj* successive, consecutive, sequential ← **urut**

berusaha *v* to try, make an effort ← **usaha**

berusia *v* to be (aged) ← **usia**

berutang *v* to owe; ~ *budi* to have a debt of gratitude ← **utang**

berwajah *v* to have a face; ~ *muram* sour-faced ← **wajah**

berwarna *adj* colored ← **warna**

berwawasan *v* to have an outlook; ~ *luas* broad- or open-minded ← **wawas**

berwenang *adj* competent, in charge ← **wenang**

berwibawa *adj* esteemed, respected, of good standing ← **wibawa**

berwisata *v* to travel or holiday ← **wisata**

berwujud *v* in the form or shape of ← **wujud**

berziarah *v* to make a pilgrimage, visit a holy place ← **ziarah**

berzina *v* to commit adultery ← **zina**

bésan *n* relationship between two couples whose children have married

besar *adj* big, large, great; ~ *kepala* big-headed, arrogant; **besar-besaran** *adj* large-scale; **kebesaran** *n*

greatness; *adj* too big;
membesar *v* to get bigger,
grow; **membesarkan** *v* to
bring up, raise (children);
memperbesar *v* to enlarge
something; **terbesar** *adj*
largest, biggest

beserta *conj* along with,
and ← **serta**

besi *n* iron; ~ *tua* scrap
metal; *tukang* ~ blacksmith

bésok *adv* tomorrow; *coll*
in the future ← **ésok**

besuk *v* to visit someone in
hospital

betah *v* settle in, feel at home

betapa *adv* how (very);
~ *cantiknya!* How pretty
she is!; *conj* ~*pun* however
→ **alangkah**

Betawi original inhabitants
of Jakarta (since 1527);
orang ~ the Betawi people

beterbangan *v, pl* to fly
about ← **terbang**

betina *adj* female (of
animals); *anjing* ~ bitch

betis *n* calf, lower part of leg

beton *n* concrete

betul *adj* true, correct, right;
betul-betul *adv* truly,
completely; **kebetulan** *adv*

by chance, accidentally; *n*
coincidence; **membetul-
kan** *v* to correct, repair;
sebetulnya *adv* in fact,
actually

BI *abbrev* Bank Indonesia
Bank Indonesia, the central
reserve bank

bi *pron* Aunt; term of address
for older housemaid ← **bibi**

biadab *adj* uncivilized,
savage

biak, membiakkan *v* to
breed, cultivate

bianglala *n* rainbow

biar let, no matter if; ~*lah!*
Never mind!; ~*pun* even if,
although; **membiarkan** *v*
to let, allow, permit

biara *n* abbey, monastery,
convent; **biarawan** *n*
monk; **biarawati** *n* nun

biasa *adj* normal, usual,
common, ordinary; ~*nya*
usually; **kebiasaan** *n* habit,
custom; **terbiasa** *adj* used
to, accustomed

biaya *n* cost, expense (for
a service); ~ *hidup* cost of
living; **membiayai** *v* to
finance someone or
something

bibi *n, pron* aunt, sister of parent; mother's female cousin ← **bi**

bibir *n* lips

bibit *n* seedling

bicara *v* speak; **berbicara** *v* to speak; ~ *dalam bahasa Sunda* to speak in Sundanese; **membicarakan** *v* to discuss; **pembicaraan** *n* discussion

bidadari *n* fairy

bidan *n* midwife; **kebidanan** *n* midwifery

bidang *adj* spacious, wide; *n* area, field; *se~ tanah* piece of land

bihun *n* vermicelli noodles

bijak *adj* wise; **kebijakan** *n* policy

bijaksana *adj* wise, prudent; **kebijaksanaan** *n* caution, prudence; policy

biji *n* seed, grain; counter for very small objects; *sl* counter

bikin *v, coll* to make; ~ *marah* make angry; **bikinan** *n* product; ~ *Australia* made in Australia; **dibikin** *v* to be made → **buat**

biksu *n* Buddhist monk

bila, bilamana *conj* if (usually in written form)

bilang *v, sl* say; **dibilang** *v* to be said

bilas, membilas *v* rinse

biliar, bilyar *n* billiards

biliun, bilyun *n* billion (1,000,000,000); **biliunér** *n* billionaire

bimbang *adj* nervous, doubtful

bimbing *v* to lead, guide; **bimbingan** ~ *belajar (bimbel)* extra-curricular course to prepare for exams; **membimbing** *v* to lead, guide, coach

BIN *abbrev Badan Intelijen Negara* State Intelligence Agency

bin *n, Isl* son of (father's name); **binti** *n, Isl* daughter of (father's name)

bina *v* build up; ~ *raga* body-building; **membina** *v* to build up, found

binasa: membinasakan *v* to destroy, ruin

binatang *n* animal

binatu *n* (commercial) laundry

bincang: **berbincang**
(**-bincang**) v to chat,
discuss; **perbincangan** n
discussion

bingkai n frame; ~ *kaca-*
mata glasses frames; **mem-**
bingkai v to frame

bingkis: **bingkisan** n
wrapped or free gift

bingung adj confused;
kebingungan n confusion;
membingungkan adj
confusing

binokular n binoculars

bintang n star; ~ *berekor*
comet; ~ *tamu* guest star;
berbintang v to have a
star; *jenderal* ~ *tiga*
three-star general; **mem-**
bintangi v to star (in)

binti n, Isl daughter of
(father's name) ← **bin**

bintik n spot, stain, freckle

biodata n personal profile
(name, address, date of
birth, hobbies etc)

biola n violin, fiddle;
pemain ~ violinist

biologi *ilmu* ~ biology;
biologis adj biological

bioskop n cinema, movie
theater

bir n beer

biro n office, center;
~ *perjalanan* travel agent

birokrasi n bureaucracy;
red tape

biru adj blue; ~ *lebam* black
and blue; ~ *tua* dark blue;
membiru v to turn blue

bis ~ *surat* letter box,
mailbox (for posting)

bis, bus n bus; ~ *kota*
city bus

bisa v, aux can, be able;
bisa-bisa conj it could
happen that; **sebisanya,**
sebisa-bisanya adv as
well as you can, to the best
of your ability

bisa n poison (of animals),
venom; **berbisa** adj
poisonous; *ular* ~ poisonous
snake

bisbol n baseball

bisik whisper; **bisikan** n
whisper; ~ *hati* conscience;
berbisik adj whispering; v
to whisper; **membisik** v to
whisper something

bisnis n business, trade;
berbisnis v to do business

bistik n steak; ~ *ayam* cut
of barbecued chicken

bisu *adj* mute, dumb; ~ *tuli* deaf-mute; **membisu** *v* to be silent, say nothing

bius *n* drug; *obat* ~ anesthetic; **membius** *v* to drug, anesthetize

blak-blakan *adv* outspoken

blangko *n* form

blasteran *adj* mixed, hybrid; *Sari ~ Sunda-Jerman* Sari is half-Sundanese, half-German

bléwah *n* kind of melon

blits *n* flash (of camera)

blok *n* block (in addresses)

blokir, memblokir *v* to block; ~ *jalan* to block the road

bloknot *n* writing pad

blong *adj* loose, not taut; *remnya* ~ the brakes failed

bloon *adj* silly, naive, impressionable

bludak → **beludak**

blus *n* blouse

BNI *Bank Negara Indonesia* State Bank of Indonesia

bobo, bobok *v, sl* to sleep (children's language)

bobol: membobol *v* to break into

bobot *n* weight; **berbobot** *adj* heavy, weighty

bocor *v* to leak; **kebocoran** *n* leak; **membocorkan** *v* to leak something; **pembocoran** *n* leakage, divulging (of secrets)

bodoh *adj* stupid; **kebodohan** *n* stupidity, ignorance

boga *n* food, catering

bohlam *n* light bulb

bohong lie; **berbohong** to lie; **membohong** *v* to lie; **membohongi** *v* to lie to; **pembohong** *n* liar

boikot *n* boycott; **memboikot** *v* to boycott something

bokong *n* buttocks, bottom

boks *n* playpen, bassinet; *mobil* ~ (closed) truck

bola *n* ball; football, soccer; ~ *basket* basketball; ~ *mata* eyeball; *main* ~ play football

bolak-balik *adv* back and forth, to and fro, there and back

boléh may, can; allowed, permitted; okay; ~~ *saja* sure you can; **memperboléhkan** *v* to allow, permit

boling *n* ten-pin bowling; *main* ~ go bowling

bolong *adj* holey, perforated;
 membolongi *v* to pierce
bolos, membolos *v* to
 skip, be absent, play truant,
 wag, skive; ~ *sekolah* to
 skip school
bolpoin *n* ballpoint pen, biro
bom *n* bomb; **mengebom**
 v to bomb something;
 pengeboman *n* bombing
bon *n* bill, check, receipt;
 minta ~ may I have the
 bill?; *pakai* ~ make out a
 receipt before paying (at
 another counter)
boncéng, memboncéng *v*
 to ride with someone else
 on a two-wheeled vehicle,
 dink; to sponge or cadge a
 lift; **boncéngan** *n* passenger
**bondong: berbondong-
 bondong** *adv* in droves
bonéka *n* doll (like a person);
 soft toy (animal); puppet
bongkar, membongkar *v*
 to pull apart, dismantle;
 unpack; to unearth
bontot *n* youngest child in
 a family ← **buntut**
boorwater, borwater *n*
 boric acid (as an eye salve)
bor *n* drill; *mata* ~ drill bit

bordil *n* brothel, bordello;
 rumah ~ brothel
bordir, bordiran *n*
 embroidery, lace edging;
 membordir *v* to embroider
borgol *n* handcuffs; **memborgol** *v* to handcuff
boro-boro *conj* what's the
 point of ...? It's not even
 worth ...
borong, memborong *v* to
 buy up, buy in bulk;
 borongan *n* goods bought
 in bulk; *taksi* ~ un-metered
 taxi; **pemborong** *n* developer, contractor
boros *adj* wasteful;
 pemborosan *n* wastage
bos *pron, sl* boss, sir; *n* boss
bosan *adj* bored, fed up
 with, tired of; **mem-
 bosankan** *adj* boring,
 tiresome
botak *adj* bald; **kebotakan**
 n baldness, hair loss;
 membotaki *v* to shave,
 make bald
botok, bothok *n* Javanese
 side-dish of shredded
 coconut and fresh vegetables
botol *n* bottle; *teh* ~ bottled
 tea

boyong, memboyong *v* to take (someone) away

BPKB *abbrev Bukti Pemilik Kendaraan Bermotor* vehicle registration papers

BPS *abbrev Biro Pusat Statistik* Central Statistics Bureau

brahmana, brahmin, brahma *n* highest Hindu caste in Bali

BRAj *Bendoro Raden Ajeng* Javanese title for unmarried female aristocracy

brankas, brangkas *n* safe

Brasil *n* Brazil; *orang ~* Brazilian

BRAy *Bendoro Raden Ayu* Javanese title for married female aristocracy

brédel, membrédel *v* to muzzle, bridle, ban; **pembrédelan** *n* muzzling, being closed down

bréndi *n* brandy

bréngsék *excl* blast! damn!; *n* bastard!; *adj* damn, bloody; *~ lu!* You bastard!

brem *n* a soft white biscuit made from fermented rice

bréwok, beréwok *n* beard, whiskers, sideburns;

bréwokan *adj* whiskered, bearded

BRI *abbrev Bank Rakyat Indonesia* Indonesian People's Bank

brokat *n* brocade

brokoli *n* broccoli

bros *n* brooch

brosur *n* brochure; *~ wisata* travel brochure

bruder *n* Christian brother (Catholic)

bruto *adj* gross

bu *pron* Mother (to respected older women); Mum(my), Mom(my); *~ Haji* title for a woman who has completed the pilgrimage to Mecca

buah *n* fruit; piece, general counter for objects; *~ hati* darling (child); *~ nangka* jackfruit; *~ tangan* souvenir, gift brought home; **buah-buahan** *n* fruit(s); **sebuah** *adj* a, one (generic counter); *~ kursi* a chair

bual, membual *v* to foam; to froth at the mouth, talk rubbish

buang *v* to throw (away); *~ air* to urinate; *~ muka* look the other way; *~ sampah* throw rubbish away; **membuang** *v* to throw out; waste; exile; ~ *ingus* blow your nose; ~ *kesempatan* to waste an opportunity; **terbuang** *adj* thrown out, wasted

buas *adj* fierce, wild; *binatang* ~ wild animal

buat *prep* for; *v* to do, make; **buatan** *n* made in, product of; ~ *lokal* made locally; **berbuat** *v* to do; ~ *salah* to do wrong; **membuat** *v* to make; ~ *marah* to make angry; **pembuat** *n* producer; **pembuatan** *n* production, manufacture; **perbuatan** *n* act, deed

buaya *n* crocodile, alligator; ~ *darat* conman

bubar *v* to disperse, break up, spread out; **membubarkan** *v* to break something up

bubuk *n* powder, dust

bubur *n* porridge; ~ *ayam* chicken porridge; ~ *sumsum* porridge made from rice flour

budak *n* slave; **perbudakan** *n* slavery

budaya *n* culture; **berbudaya** *n* to have a culture; **kebudayaan** *n* culture, civilization; **membudaya** *v* to spread, become entrenched

Budha *agama* ~ Buddhism; *orang* ~ Buddhist

budi *n* goodness; intellect; ~ *pekerti* ethics, good behavior

budidaya *n* cultivation; **membudidayakan** *v* to cultivate, grow

bufét *n* buffet meal

bugar *adj* fit; **kebugaran** *pusat* ~ gym, fitness center

bugil *adj* naked, nude

Bugis ethnic group from South Sulawesi; *orang* ~, *bahasa* ~ Buginese

buih *n* foam, froth

bujang *adj* single, unmarried (man); **bujangan** *n* bachelor

bujuk, membujuk *v* to coax; ~ *rayu* to flatter; **bujukan** *n* enticement

bujur *n* longitude; vertical line down a sphere; ~ *timur* east longitude

buka open; ~ *baju* take off clothes; **berbuka** ~ *puasa* to break the fast; **membuka** v to open; ~ *rahasia* to reveal a secret; **membukakan** v to open (for someone); **pembuka** adj opening; **terbuka** adj open; *sidang* ~ public session

bukan no, not (of things, nouns); *Ini* ~ ? This one, isn't it?; ~ *main* extraordinary, no kidding!; ~*nya* isn't it ...?

buking, booking n booking; **membuking** v to book

bukit n hill; **berbukit** adj hilly

bukti n proof, evidence; **membuktikan** v to prove; **terbukti** adj proven

buku n book; ~ *harian* journal, diary; ~ *pelajaran* textbook; ~ *panduan* guide(book); ~ *petunjuk* directory; **pembukuan** n book-keeping

bulak-balik → **bolak-balik**

bulan n moon, month; ~ *Februari* February; ~ *madu* honeymoon; *ber~ madu* to go on a honeymoon; ~ *puasa* fasting month, Ramadan; ~ *purnama* full moon; *datang* ~ menstruate, have your period

bulat adj round; fat; **bulatan** n circle

bulé n, *derog* white person, whitey, paleface; albino

bulu n feather; fur; body hair; ~ *ayam* feather; ~ *domba* wool; ~ *mata* eyelashes; ~ *tangkis* badminton; **berbulu** adj hairy; to have fur or feathers

bumbu n spice, **membumbui** v to season

bumerang n boomerang; *Itu sudah menjadi ~ bagi Hari* It's come back to haunt Hari

bumi n earth, ground; ~ *hangus* scorched earth; **bumiputera, pribumi** n native inhabitant, son of the soil

BUMN abbrev Badan Usaha Milik Negara state-owned corporation

buncis n string bean

buncit adj pot-bellied, fat

bundar, bunder adj round; *meja bundar* round table; **bundaran** n roundabout

Bung *pron* brother; ~ *Karno* President Soekarno; *ayo* ~*!* Come on, mate!

bunga *n* flower, blossom; interest; ~ *mawar*, ~ *ros* rose; **berbunga** *v* to flower, blossom

bungalo *n* bungalow, cottage, one-story house

bungkam *adj* quiet, silent; **membungkam** *v* to keep silent

bungker, bunker *n* (underground) bunker, hiding place

bungkuk, bongkok *adj* crooked, bent; **membungkuk** *v* to bow, be hunched; **membungkukkan** ~ *badan* to bow

bungkus *n* takeaway, pack; *nasi* ~ a takeaway rice meal; **membungkus** *v* to wrap; ~ *kado* to wrap a gift

bungsu *n* youngest child in a family; *anak* ~, *si* ~ youngest child

bunting *adj* pregnant (of animals)

buntu *adj* one-way, useless; *jalan* ~ dead-end; cul-de-sac, court

buntut *n* tail; *sop* ~ oxtail soup; **membuntuti** *v* to follow someone

bunuh, membunuh *v* to kill; ~ *diri* kill yourself, commit suicide; **pembunuh** *n* murderer, killer; **pembunuhan** *n* murder, killing; **terbunuh** *adj* killed

bunyi *n* sound, noise; **berbunyi** *v* to sound, make a noise; **membunyikan** *v* to sound, ring something

bupati *n* regent; **kabupatén** *n* regency

buram *adj* cloudy, frosted, dull

buron *n* fugitive

bursa *n* exchange; ~ *efek* stock exchange

buru, memburu *v* to hunt, chase; **buruan, buron** *n* the hunted; **berburu** *v* to go hunting; **keburu** *sl* in time; too early; ~ *habis* already run out; **pemburu** *n* hunter; **pemburuan** *n* hunt, chase; **terburu-buru** *adj* in a hurry

buruh *n* laborer; ~ *bangunan* construction worker; *Hari* ~ Labor Day

buruk *adj* bad (of a situation, weather); ugly; *kabar* ~ bad news; **memburuk** *v* to worsen

burung *n* bird; ~ *béo* parrot; ~ *dara* pigeon, dove; ~ *gereja* sparrow; ~ *hantu* owl

busa *n* foam, lather; **berbusa** *adj* foamy; with a layer of foam

busana *n* clothing, wear; ~ *kantor* office wear

busuk *adj* rotten; *bau* ~ bad smell; **membusuk** *v* to rot

busung *adj* swollen, distended; ~ *lapar* disease caused by starvation

busur *n* bow

buta *adj* blind; ~ *huruf* illiterate

butik *n* boutique

butir *n* grain, counter for small oval objects; *tiga* ~ *telur* three eggs

butuh *v* need; **kebutuhan** *n* need, necessity; **membutuhkan** *v* to need something

buyung *n* boy, lad

buyut *n* ancestor from your great-grandparents' generation

C

C Celsius

ca → **cah**

cabai → **cabé**

cabang *n* branch; ~ *pohon* tree branch; **bercabang** *v* to be split, branched

cabé, cabai *n* chilli; ~ *rawit* small, hot red chilli

cabik shred; **tercabik-cabik** *adj* torn, to shreds

cabul *adj* obscene, indecent, rude; *film* ~ oh jpornographic film; **mencabuli** *v* to rape, assault someone

cabut *v* to pull out, remove; *sl* to leave; **mencabut** *v* to pull out, remove; ~ *gigi* to extract a tooth

cacar *n* pock, pox; ~ *air* chicken pox; **cacaran** *v* to have chicken pox

cacat *n* fault, defect, flaw; *adj* disabled, handicapped; ~ *lahir* birth defect; *orang* ~, *penyandang* ~ disabled or handicapped person

caci ~ *maki* insults; **mencaci** ~ *maki* to insult, abuse

cacing *n* worm; ~ *tanah* earthworm; **cacingan** *adj* to have (intestinal) worms

cadang *suku* ~ spare part; **cadangan** *adj* spare, reserve; stocks

cadel, cedal *adj* to have a speech impediment

cagar *n* preserve; ~ *alam* nature reserve

cagub *n* candidate for governor; gubernatorial candidate ← **calon gubernur**

cahar: pencahar *n* laxative

cahaya *n* light, shine, glow; ~ *bulan* moonlight; **pencahayaan** *n* lighting

cair flow; **cairan** *n* liquid; **mencair** *v* to melt, turn into liquid; **mencairkan** *v* to melt something; to make (funds) available

cakap *adj* **cakep** *sl* handsome; *sl* pretty

cakap: bercakap *v* to speak; **bercakap-cakap** *v* to chat; **percakapan** *n* conversation

cakar *n* claw; **mencakar** *v* to scratch; *dicakar kucing* scratched by a cat; **pencakar** ~ *langit* skyscraper

cakram *n* disc; discus; *lempar* ~ discus (throw); *rem* ~ disc brakes

cakrawala *n* horizon; sky

cakup: mencakupi *v* to include, cover; **pencakupan** *n* coverage

calo *n* ticket scalper, profiteer; **percaloan** *praktek* ~ profiteering

calon *n* candidate; ~ *suami* husband-to-be; **mencalonkan** *v* to nominate someone; **pencalonan** *n* nomination, candidacy

camar *burung* ~ seagull

camat *n* sub-district head; **kecamatan** *n* sub-district

cambuk *n* whip; **mencambuk** *v* to whip

camil, camilan → **cemil**

campak *n* measles; *penyakit* ~ measles

campur mix; ~ *baur* mix with society; ~*sari* a blend of traditional and modern Javanese music; ~ *tangan* get involved, interfere; ~ *aduk* all mixed up; **mencampuradukkan** *v* to mix up, confuse; **campuran** *n* mix, mixture; *anak* ~

child of mixed descent;
bercampur *adj* mixed
with; **mencampurkan** *v* to
mix something to

canda *n* joke; ~ *gurau*
joking, jokes; **bercanda** *v*
to joke; ~ *kok* just kidding

candi *n* temple, ancient
Hindu or Buddhist temple
or monument

candu *n* opium, drug;
kecanduan *n* addiction,
addicted to; ~ *obat* drug
addiction; **pecandu** *n*
addict

canggih *adj* sophisticated;
kecanggihan *n* sophistication

canggung *adj* awkward,
clumsy

cangkir *n* cup, mug; ~ *teh*
teacup; *se~ kopi* a cup of
coffee

cangkok graft, transplant;
~ *ginjal* liver transplant

cangkul *n* hoe; **cangkulan**
n card game; **mencangkul**
v to hoe

cantik *adj* beautiful, pretty;
kecantikan *n* beauty

cantum: mencantumkan *v*
to attach; **tercantum** *adj*

attached, included, inserted

cap *n* seal; brand, mark; ~
jempol thumbprint; ~ *pos*
postmark; **mengecap** *v* to
brand

cap go méh *n* 15th day
after Chinese New Year

capai, mencapai *v* to
reach, attain; **tercapai** *adj*
achieved

capcay, cap cai *n* chop suey,
Chinese vegetables in sauce

capék, capai *adj* tired;
kecapékan *adj* tired out; *n*
exhaustion

capem *n* branch office
← **cabang pembantu**

caprés *n* presidential
candidate ← **calon pré-
sidén**

capung *n* dragonfly

cara *n* way, style, means;
secara *adv* in a way; (used
to form adverbs)

cari *v* to look for, search for,
seek; **mencari** *v* to look or
search for, seek; ~ *makan*,
~ *nafkah* to earn a living; ~
tahu to try to find out;
mencari-cari *v* to search
repeatedly, everywhere;
pencarian *n* search, hunt

carter charter; **carteran** *adj*
chartered; **mencarter** *v* to
hire, charter

cas charge; **mengecas** *v*
to charge (electrical
equipment)

cas-cis-cus: **bercas-cis-
cus** *v* to speak a European
language (esp English)

cat *n* **cét** *coll* paint; ~ *air*
watercolors; ~ *basah* wet
paint; **mengecat** *v* to paint,
dye; ~ *rambut* to dye, color
your hair

catat, **mencatat** *v* to note;
catatan *n* notes; ~ *kaki*
footnotes; *buku* ~ notebook;
dengan ~ on the condition
or proviso; *kantor* ~ *sipil*
civil registry office; **tercatat** *adj* nored, registered;
surat ~ registered mail

catur *n* chess; **pecatur** *n*
chess player

cawat *n* loincloth

cc cubic centiliters, milliliters

CD compact disk

cébok to wash your bottom
after using the toilet;
cébokan *n* pail of water to
wash your bottom

cébol *n* dwarf, midget

cebur *v* to fall into water;
tercebur *adj* fallen into
water

cecak → **cicak**

cécér: **bercécéran** *adj*
scattered, dispersed

cedera, cidera injured,
injury; ~ *lutut* knee injury

cegah, **mencegah** *v* to
prevent, fight against;
pencegahan *n* prevention

cegat, **mencegat** *v* to hold
up, bar

ceguk, cekuk: **cegukan** *n*
hiccups; *v* to have the
hiccups

cék *n* cheque, check; ~
kosong blank cheque

cék, **mengecék** *v* to check,
confirm

cekal: **mencekal** *v* to prevent
from leaving the country ←
cegah dan tangkal

cekam, cengkam:
mencekam *adj* frightening,
ominous

cekat: **cekatan** *adj* clever,
good, adept

cékcok: **percékcokan** *n*
quarrel, dispute

cékér *n, sl* claw; ~ *ayam*
chicken feet (dim sum)

cekik, mencekik v to strangle; **tercekik** adj strangled

cekikik: cekikikan v to giggle

ceking adj thin, gaunt, skin and bones; si ~ skinny

Céko n the Czech Republic; bahasa ~, orang ~ Czech

cekung adj concave, sunken

cela n fault; **tercela** adj wrong

celah n gap, crack, crevice

celaka n accident, bad luck, misfortune; **kecelakaan** n accident, disaster

celana n trousers; ~ pendek shorts

celemék n apron

céléng, célengan n piggy bank, savings box

celetuk v **nyeletuk** sl to interrupt, call out, say suddenly

celup, mencelup v to dye, dip; **pencelupan** n dyeing process

celurit, clurit n crescent-shaped knife, sickle (traditionally carried by Madurese men)

cemar: mencemari v to dirty, pollute; **pencemaran**

n pollution; ~ udara air pollution; **tercemar** adj polluted

cemara n casuarina (tree)

cemas adj worried, anxious; **kecemasan** n anxiety, concern; **mencemaskan** adj worrying, sobering

cemberut adj bad-tempered, in a bad mood

cemburu adj jealous; ~ buta blind jealousy; **kecemburuan** n jealousy

cemerlang adj glittering, sparkling, brilliant

cemil, camil v to snack; **cemilan** n snack food

cempaka n a white kind of gardenia or magnolia

cempedak n fruit which is cut into slices and fried

cemplung: tercemplung adj fallen into water

cendana kayu ~ sandalwood; Pulau ~ Timor

cendawan n fungi, toadstool, mushroom

cendekia: cendekiawan n intellectual

cenderung v to tend; **kecenderungan** n tendency, trend

céndol *n* sweet drink of
  green rice flour, molasses
  and coconut milk
cendramata, cinderamata
  n souvenir, keepsake
cengéng *adj* whiny,
  complaining
cengkam → cekam
cengkéh *n* cloves
cengkeram *v* to grip;
  cengkeraman *n* grip,
  squeeze; **mencengkeram**
  v to grip, squeeze
centil *adj* attention-seeking,
  coquettish
centong ~ *nasi* spoon for
  serving rice
cepak *adj* shaven-headed;
  rambut ~ crew cut
cepat *adj* **cepet** *coll* fast,
  quick; *yang* ~, *dapat*
  first come, first served; ~
  marah quick-tempered;
  kecepatan *n* speed; **mempercepat** *v* to speed up,
  accelerate; **secepat** *conj*
  as fast as; ~ *mungkin*,
  secepat(-cepat)nya *adv* as
  fast as possible; **tercepat**
  adj fastest
ceplas-ceplos *adv* forth-
  right, blunt, straight from

  the heart (of speech or
  behavior)
ceplok *telur* ~ fried egg
ceprét → jeprét
cerah *adj* clear, sunny
cerai divorce; ~ *mati*
  widowed; **bercerai** *v* to be
  divorced; **menceerai(kan)** *v*
  to divorce someone;
  perceraian *n* divorce
ceramah *n* lecture, talk;
  ~ *agama* sermon;
  berceramah *v* to give a
  lecture or talk
cerber *n* short story ←
  cerita bersambung
cerdas *adj* intelligent,
  bright; **kecerdasan** *n*
  intelligence
cerdik *adj* clever, smart;
  cunning
cerét, crét: mencrét *v* to
  have diarrhea
ceréwét *adj* fussy, finicky,
  hard to please; talkative
céri *buah* ~ cherry
ceria *adj* happy, in a good
  mood
cerita, ceritera story, tale;
  ~ *bersambung* serial;
  ~ *pendek* (**cerpen**) short
  story; ~ *rakyat* folk tale;

~*nya panjang* it's a long story; **bercerita** *v* to tell (a story); **menceritakan** *v* to describe, relate

cermai, cermé *n* small, sour plum

cermat *adj* thorough, careful, accurate; **kecermatan** *n* precision, accuracy; **mencermati** *v* to observe closely

cermin mirror; **mencerminkan** *v* to reflect; **tercermin** *adj* reflected

cerna, mencerna *v* to digest; **pencernaan** *n* digestion

ceroboh *adj* careless

cerobong *n* chimney; ~ *asap* smokestack

cerocos → **nerocos**

cerpén *n* short story; **cerpénis** *n* short story writer ← **cerita péndék**

cerucut → **kerucut**

cerutu *n* cigar

cét → **cat**

cétak print; ~ *biru* blueprint; *barang* ~ printed material; *media* ~ print media; **cétakan** *n* mold; impression, printing;

mencétak *v* to print; **pencétak** *n* printer

cetus: mencetus *v* to say something unexpected

céwék *n, coll* girl, young woman; *adj* female

CGI Consultative Group on Indonesia

cicak, cecak *n* gecko, house lizard

cicil pay in instalments; **mencicil** *v* to pay by instalments

cicip taste; **mencicipi** *v* to try, taste something

cicit *n* great-grandchild

cidera → **cedera**

cidomo *n* horse-drawn cart in Lombok ← **cikar dokar mobil**

ciduk, cédok *n* dipper

Cik *pron* you, Sister (for Chinese women)

cikal ~ *bakal* origins

Cilé *n* Chile; *orang* ~ Chilean

cilik *adj* small, little

Cina *n* China; *derog* Chinese person; *bahasa* ~ Chinese (language); *orang* ~ Chinese (people); **Pecinan** *n* Chinatown

cincang minced; *daging* ~ mincemeat; **mencincang** *v* to mince, chop up

cincau *n* jelly made from cinchona leaves, used in drinks

cincin *n* ring; ~ *kawin* wedding ring

cinderamata, cendramata *n* souvenir, keepsake

cinta love, like; ~ *monyet* puppy love; **bercinta** *v* to make love; to be in love; **mencintai** *v* to love someone; **pencinta, pecinta** *n* lover; **tercinta** *adj* dear, beloved

ciprat: kecipratan *adj* be splashed, sprayed accidentally

cipta idea, creativity; **ciptaan** *n* creation; **mencipta, menciptakan** *v* to create, make; **pencipta** *n* creator; ~ *lagu* song-writer; **tercipta** *adj* created

ciri *n* characteristic, identifying mark; ~ *khas* special feature

cita ~ *rasa* taste; **cita-cita** *n* ideal, dream, ambition; **bercita-cita(kan)** *v* to dream of

citra *n* image

cium kiss; smell; ~ *pipi* peck, kiss on the cheek; ~ *tangan* kiss someone's hand (as a sign of respect); **ciuman** *n* kiss; **berciuman** *v* to kiss each other; **mencium** *v* to smell, to kiss; **tercium** *adj* smelt; found out

clurit → **celurit**

cm centimeter

coba *v, aux* try; please; *uji* ~ experiment; **mengujicobakan** *v* to test something; **cobaan** *n* trial, ordeal; **mencoba** *v* to try, attempt; **percobaan** *n* experiment, test

cobék, coék *n* pestle for grinding chillies

coblos, mencoblos *v* to vote, pierce

cocok fit, match, suitable; **bercocok** ~ *tanam* to work or till the soil; **kecocokan** *n* suitability, compatibility; **mencocokkan** *v* to match

cokelat, coklat chocolate; *rasa* ~ chocolate-flavored; *warna* ~ brown

colék pinch

colok *v* to put in a plug; **colokan** *n* power point; **mencolok, menyolok** *adj* glaring, standing out

colong: kecolongan *adj* robbed; lost unjustly

condong *v* lean, incline

congkél, mencongkél *n* to prise open

conték, mencontèk, menyontèk *v* to copy, cheat

contoh *n* example, model, sample; ~ *baik* a good example; ~*nya* for example

copét *n* pickpocket; **kecopétan** *adj* to be pickpocketed, robbed; *n* pickpocketing; **mencopét** *v* to pick someone's pocket

copot *v* to come off (accidentally)

corak *n* design, pattern, motif, style; **bercorak** *v* to have a design

corét scratch; **corét-corét** doodle, graffiti; **corétan** *n* scratch; **mencorét** *v* to scratch, cross out

corong *n* funnel, spout

coto *n* clear meat soup, specialty of Makassar

cs *cum suis* and associates

CSIS Centre for Strategic and International Studies

cuaca *n* weather

cubit pinch; **mencubit** *v* to pinch; **secubit** *n* pinch

cuci *v* to wash; ~ *darah* kidney dialysis; ~ *gudang* stocktake sale; ~ *mata* window-shopping; ~ *otak* brainwash; ~ *tangan* wash your hands; **cuclan** *n* laundry; **mencuci** *v* to wash, clean; ~ *cetak* to develop photos (negatives and prints)

cucu *n* grandchild

cucur flow, trickle; **bercucuran** *v* to trickle down, drip, flow

cuék *adj* uncaring, unfeeling, ignoring; independent; ~ *aja* who cares?

cuka *n* vinegar

cukong *n* wealthy businessman

cukup *adj* enough, sufficient; *adv* quite; **berkecukupan** *v* to have enough, get by; **secukupnya** *adv* sufficient, adequate

cukur shave; *pisau* ~ razor; **mencukur** *v* to shave

cula *n* horn

culik, menculik *v* to
kidnap; **penculikan** *n*
kidnapping

cuma, cuman *coll* but,
only; **cuma-cuma** free, at
no cost

cumbu flattery; **bercumbu**
v to flirt, flatter

cumi, cumi-cumi *n* squid

curah fall, pour; **mencurahkan** *v* to pour out; ~
tenaga to spend energy

curam *adj* steep, sloping,
precipitous

curang *adj* dishonest,
cheating; **kecurangan** *n*
cheating, dishonesty

curhat *v, coll* to pour out
your heart ← **curah hati**

curi steal; **curi-curi**
surreptitious, secret; **mencuri** *v* to steal; **pencuri** *n*
thief, burglar

curiga *adj* suspicious;
kecurigaan *n* suspicion;
mencurigai *v* to suspect
someone; **mencurigakan**
adj suspicious, suspect

cuti leave; ~ *hamil*
maternity leave

CV curriculum vitae

D

D2 *Diploma Dua* 2-year
diploma course

D3 *Diploma Tiga* 3-year
diploma course

da, dag, dah *gr* bye; **da-da**
gr (children) bye-bye

d/a *dengan alamat* care
of, c/-

dada *n* breast, chest,
bosom; *buah* ~ *f* breast;
telanjang ~ bare-chested

dadak: dadakan *adj* sudden;
mendadak *adj* sudden

dadar *telur* ~ omelet

daérah *n* region, territory,
area; provinces,
country(side); *bahasa* ~
regional language

daftar list, register, roll; ~
barang inventory, catalog;
~ *harga* price list; **mendaftar** *v* to register; **mendaftarkan** *v* to register
something; **pendaftaran** *n*
enrolment, registration;
terdaftar *adj* registered,
enrolled

dag → **da**

dagang trade; **dagangan** *v*
to sell goods informally; *n*

merchandise; **berdagang** v
to trade, do business; **pedagang** n merchant; **perdagangan** n commerce, trade

dag dig dug thump, thump,
thump (of heartbeat)

daging n meat, flesh; ~ *babi*
pork; ~ *sapi* beef

dagu n chin

dah → **da**

dahak n phlegm, mucus;
berdahak n containing
phlegm or mucus; *batuk* ~
chesty cough

dahi n forehead

dahsyat adj terrible, dreadful, awesome

dahulu adj before,
former(ly); first (more
formal than **dulu**); ~ *kala*
ancient times, the old days;
lebih ~ first(ly); **mendahului** v to precede,
overtake; **pendahuluan** n
introduction

daki: **mendaki** v to climb,
ascend; ~ *gunung* (to go)
mountaineering, bush-
walking

dakwa, dakwaan n charge,
accusation; **terdakwa** n the
accused

dakwah n mission, religious
proselytizing

dalam *pron* in, inside, into;
adj deep, profound; *celana*
~ underpants; *di* ~ in,
inside; *ke* ~ into; **kedalaman** n depth; **mendalam** adj
deep; **pedalaman** n inland,
hinterland

dalang, dhalang n puppeteer
(in shadow puppet plays);
mastermind; **mendalangi** v
to orchestrate (events)

dalih n excuse, pretext; reason

dalil n thesis, proposition,
theorem

**daluwarsa, kedaluwarsa,
kadaluwarsa** n expired,
overdue; *tanggal* ~ expiry
date, use-by date (food)

damai peace; **berdamai** v
to make peace; **men-
damaikan** v to reconcile,
pacify; **perdamaian** n
peace, reconciliation

damba v to long, yearn,
wish for; **dambaan** n idol,
dream; **mendambakan** v
to long or wish for

dampak n ill-effect;
berdampak v to have a
(negative) effect

dampar: terdampar *adj* beached, grounded, washed ashore

damping next to, close; **berdampingan** *adj* side by side; **mendampingi** *v* to accompany, flank; **pendamping** *n* companion; ~ *hidup* spouse; **pendampingan** *n* assistance

dan *conj* and

dana *n* funds, money, grant; **mendanai** *v* to fund something

danau *n* lake

dandan *v* to dress up, put on make-up; **dandanan** *n* dress, make-up; **berdandan** *v* to dress, put on make-up; **mendandani** *v* to decorate, dress, adorn

dangdut *n* popular Indian-inspired music; **dangdutan** *v* to go to a *dangdut* show; to dance to *dangdut* music

dangkal *adj* shallow, superficial

dansa *n* Western-style dance; **berdansa** *v* to dance

dapat find, get, obtain; be able to, can; ~ *kesulitan* to have difficulties;

mendapat *v* to obtain, receive; ~ *kabar* to receive news; **mendapatkan** *v* to obtain; discover; **pendapat** *n* opinion, point of view; **berpendapat** *v* to have an opinion, believe; **pendapatan** *n* income, revenue; **sedapatnya** *adv* what you can get

dapur *n* kitchen; ~ *rekaman* recording studio

dara *n* (young) girl; *anak* ~ young girl

darah *n* blood; ~ *tinggi* high blood pressure; *golongan* ~ blood group, type; **berdarah** *v* to bleed; **pendarahan** *n* bleeding

darat *n* land, shore; *ke* ~ ashore; **daratan** *n* mainland; **mendarat** *v* to land; **pendaratan** *n* landing (of vessel)

dari *prep* from, of; *conj* from the time; *selain* ~ except for; **daripada** *conj* than

darurat *adj* emergency, pressing

dasa *adj* ten; ~*lomba* decathlon; ~*sila* the Ten Commandments

dasar *n* base, basis, ~ foundation; *sl* all because; ~ *maling!* that's thieves for you!; *pada* ~*nya* in principle; **berdasarkan** *adj* based on; in accordance with, pursuant to; **mendasarkan** *v* to base on something

dasi *n* necktie; **berdasi** *v* to wear a tie

daster *n* house-coat, nightgown, nighty

data *n* data, information; **mendatakan** *v* to record, document, collect data on; **pendataan** *n* documentation

datang *v* to come, arrive; *minggu yang akan* ~ next week; **kedatangan** *n* arrival; **mendatang** *adj* coming, next; **mendatangkan** *v* to bring, import; **pendatang** *n* immigrant, migrant, newcomer

datar *adj* level, flat; **dataran** *n* plain; ~ *tinggi* plateau; **mendatarkan** *v* to make flat, level

datuk *pron* (male) head of family; title in Malay areas

daulat *adj* sovereign,

majesty; **kedaulatan** *n* sovereignty

daun *n* leaf; ~ *bawang* spring onion; ~ *bunga* petal; ~ *salam* bay leaf; ~ *telinga* ear; *hijau* ~ leaf green; **dedaunan** *n* leaves, foliage

daur *n* cycle; ~ *ulang* recycling; **mendaur-ulang** *v* to recycle

dawal *n* string (of musical instrument)

dawet *n* sweet Javanese drink of green rice flour, pink syrup and coconut milk

daya *n* power, energy; ~ *beli* purchasing power; ~ *kuda (DK)* horsepower; **berdaya** *v* to have power; *tak* ~ powerless; **memberdayakan** *v* to empower; **pemberdayaan** *n* empowerment

daya: memperdaya *v* to deceive, use, trick

Dayak generic name for indigenous (non-Malay) inhabitants of Kalimantan and Borneo; *orang* ~ Dayak

dayung *n* oar; **mendayung** *v* to stroke (an oar), row; to pedal

debar pulse, beat; ~ *jantung*

heart beat; **berdebar** *v* to beat quickly

debat *n* debate; **berdebat** *v* to have a debate; **perdebatan** *n* debate, discussion

débet, débit *n* debit; **mendébet** *v* to debit

debu *n* dust; **berdebu** *adj* dusty

dedaunan *n* leaves, foliage ← **daun**

deg: deg-degan *adj* anxious, worried

déh OK then, well; *Ayo, ~ !* Come on, then!; *Saya nasi goreng ~* I'll have fried rice then ← **sudah**

deham, dehem, mendeham *v* to clear the throat, cough

dékan *n* (university) dean

dekap: dekapan *n* embrace; **berdekap-dekapan, berdekapan** *v* to embrace each other

dékar: pendékar *n* (in martial arts) master, champion, leader

dekat *prep* close, near; *dalam waktu ~* soon; **berdekatan** *adj* close (of two or more things); **mendekati** *v* to approach;

pendekatan *n* approach; getting to know; **terdekat** *adj* closest, nearest

déklarasi *n* declaration; **mendéklarasikan** *v* to declare

delapan *adj* eight; *~ belas* eighteen; *~ puluh* eighty; *segi ~* octagon; **kedelapan** *adj* eighth

délman *n* two-wheeled horse-drawn carriage

demam *n* fever; *~ panggung* stage fright

demi *conj* for (the sake of); by; *~ Allah* I swear to God; *seorang ~ seorang* one by one

demikian *adv* such, so, in this way, thus; *se~ rupa sehingga* in such a way that

démo, démonstrasi *n* demo, demonstration, protest; **mendémo** *v* to protest against

démokrasi *n* democracy; **démokrat** *n* democrat; **démokratis** *adj* democratic

démonstrasi *n* demo, demonstration, protest

démpét: berdémpét *adj* stuck together

dénah *n* plan, map, diagram;

~ *rumah* house plan

denda fine; *kena* ~ be fined;
mendenda *v* to fine

dendam revenge; grudge

déndang *n* song, chant;
berdéndang *v* to sing, chant

dendéng *n* dried meat, jerky;
~ *rusa* dried venison meat

dengan *conj* with; ~
hormat Dear Sir or Madam
(in letter); ~ *sendirinya*
by itself; *sesuai* ~ in
accordance with

dengar *v* to hear; **kedengaran, terdengar** *adj*
audible; **mendengar** *v* to
hear; **mendengarkan** *v* to
listen; **memperdengarkan**
v to play, broadcast; **pendengar** *n* listener; **pendengaran** *n* hearing;
indera ~ sense of hearing

dengkul *n* knee

dengkur, mendengkur *v*
to snore; to purr (of a cat)

dengung *n* hum, buzz;
**berdengung, men-
dengung** *v* to drone, hum,
shake with sound

denyut pulse; throb; ~
jantung heartbeat; ~ *nadi*
pulse; **berdenyut** *v* to

throb, to beat

déodoran *n* deodorant

Dep. *Departemen*
(government) department,
ministry

Depag *Departemen Agama*
Department of Religion

depak, mendepak *v* to
kick something, kick out

depan *prep* front; *di* ~
front, in front of; *ke* ~ forward, to the front; *tahun* ~
next year

departemén *n* department,
ministry

Depdagri *Departemen
Dalam Negeri* Department
of Home Affairs, State
Department, Ministry of
the Interior

Depdikbud *Departemen
Pendidikan dan Kebu-
dayaan* Department of
Education and Culture

Dephankam *Departemen
Pertahanan dan Kea-
manan* Department of
Defense and Security

Depkeh *Departemen
Kehakiman* Department of
Justice

Depkes *Departemen*

Kesehatan Department of Health

Deplu *Departemen Luar Negeri* Department of Foreign Affairs

Depnaker *Departemen Tenaga Kerja* Department of Manpower

déposito *n* (bank) deposit

derajat *n* degree, rank

derap *n* stamp, clap, hitting sound

deras *adj* swift; heavy; *hujan* ~ heavy rain

dérék tow (a vehicle); *mobil* ~ tow truck; **mendérék** *v* to tow

dérét *n* row, line; **dérétan** *n* row

dering ring, chime; **berdering, mendering** *v* to ring, tinkle

derita *n* suffering; **menderita** *v* to suffer, endure; **penderitaan** *n* suffering

dermaga *n* pier, jetty

dermawan *n* donor, philanthropist; *adj* charitable

deru roar; **menderu** *v* to roar

désa *n* village; hometown; **pedésaan** *n* country(side), rural areas

desah *n* sigh, hiss, swish; **mendesah** *v* to sigh, make a swishing noise

désain, disain *n* design; *jurusan* ~ design major; **mendésain** *v* to design; **désainer** *n* designer

desak push; **mendesak** *adj* pressing, urgent; *v* to press, urge, push

Désémber *bulan* ~ December

desir hiss, rustle; **berdesir, mendesir** *v* to hiss, rustle

déterjén *n* detergent

detik *n* second

dévisa *n* foreign currency, foreign exchange; *cadangan* ~ exchange reserves

déwa *n, m* god; **mendéwakan** *v* to worship, idolize, put on a pedestal; **déwa-déwi, déwata** *n, pl, m & f* gods

déwan *n* council, board; ~ *Keamanan (PBB)* (UN) Security Council

déwasa adult; *orang* ~ adult, grown-up

déwata *n, pl, m & f* gods →
déwa

déwi *n, f* goddess → **déwa**

dh *dahulu* formerly

DI *abbrev* Darul Islam

di *prep* at; on; in; ~ *atas*
above, on top of; ~ *dalam*
inside; ~ *samping* beside

dia *pron* he, she, it; him, her
(often replaced by **–nya** for
possessive)

diabét, diabétés *(penyakit)*
~ diabetes

diagnosa *n* diagnosis;
mendiagnosa *v* to diagnose

dialék *n* dialect

diam silent, not moving;
diam-diam *adv* secretly;
pendiam *n* quiet, shy
person; **terdiam** *v* to fall
silent

diam: berdiam *v* to reside;
kediaman *n* residence

dian *n* lamp

diaré *n* diarrhea

dibikin *v, coll* to be made
← **bikin**

dibilang *v* to be said ←
bilang

didih: mendidih *adj* boiling

didik educate; *anak* ~ pupil
(of a teacher); **mendidik** *v*

to educate, bring up, teach;
pendidikan *n* education;
ilmu ~ pedagogy; **ber-
pendidikan** *adj* educated;
v to have an education

diét *n* diet; **berdiét** *v* to
diet, go on a diet

difaks *v* to be faxed ← **faks**

digips *v* to be in or have a
plaster cast ← **gips**

dilnfus *v* to be put on a drip
← **infus**

diklakson *v* to be tooted at
← **klakson**

dikontrakkan *adj* for rent,
lease ← **kontrak**

diktator *n* dictator

dikté *n* dictation; **mendikté**
v to dictate (terms)

dilarang *v* to be prohibited;
~ *masuk* no entry, no
admittance; ~ *merokok* no
smoking ← **larang**

dilélang for auction, tender
← **lélang**

dilém *v* to be glued ← **lém**

dimengerti *v* to be
understood ← **erti, arti**

dinamit *n* dynamite

dinas (to work at a)
government office

dinding *n* (inner) wall

ding *coll* no, I mean (as correction)

dingin *n* cold, cool, chilly; **kedinginan** *n* cold; feeling cold; **mendingin- kan** *v* to chill, cool; **pendingin** ~ *ruangan* air conditioning, cooling

dini *adj* very early, premature; ~ *hari* dawn, daybreak

dinosaurus *n* dinosaur

diopname *v* to be admitted to hospital, be hospitalized ← **opname**

dipéhakakan *v* to lose your job, be fired ← **pé ha ka, PHK**

dipél *v* to be mopped, cleaned ← **pél**

diperban *v* to be bandaged ← **perban**

dipermak *v* to be altered, shortened ← **permak**

dipingpong *v* to be sent here and there, messed about ← **pingpong**

diplomasi *n* diplomacy; **diplomat** *n* diplomat

diportal *v* to be blocked by a barrier, have a barrier lowered ← **portal**

diréksi *n* management, managing board; **diréktorat** *n* directorate; **diréktur** *n* director, manager

dirgahayu *ejac* long live!

dirgantara *n* sky, air; aerospace

diri *n* self; ~ *saya* me, myself; ~*nya* he, she; himself, herself

diri: berdiri *v* to stand, get up; **mendirikan** *v* to build, establish, erect; **terdiri** ~ *atas,* ~ *dari* to consist of, be based or founded on

dirjén *n* director-general ← **diréktor jéndéral**

dironsen *v* to be x-rayed ← **ronsen**

dirundung ~ *malang* to be cursed with or suffer bad luck ← **rundung**

dirut *n* (chief) director, director ← **diréktur utama**

disain → **désain**

disegani *v* to be respected ← **segan**

diselot *v* to be bolted ← **selot**

diserut *v* to be sharpened ← **serut**

disérvis *v* to be serviced ← **sérvis**

disetrap *v* to be punished (at school) ← **setrap**

disinar *v* to have radiotherapy or chemotherapy ← **sinar**

disinféktan, désinféktan *n* disinfectant

disiplin discipline, disciplined

diskét *n* diskette, disket

diskon *n* discount

diskors *v* to be suspended (from school, work etc) ← **skors**

diskoték *n* disco, nightclub

diskriminasi *n* discrimination; **mendiskriminasi(-kan)** *v* to discriminate against

distribusi *n* distribution; **mendistribusikan** *v* to distribute

distrik *n* district

disunat *v* to be circumcised ← **sunat**

ditilang *v* to be fined ← **tilang**

ditipéks *v* to be whited-out, corrected ← **tipéks**

Ditjén *n* Directorate-General ← **Diréktorat Jénderal**

divisi *n* division (of a company)

divonis *v* to be sentenced ← **vonis**

DIY *abbrev* Daerah Istimewa Yogyakarta Special Region of Yogyakarta

DKI *abbrev* Daerah Khusus Ibukota Special Capital City Region

dkk *dan kawan-kawan* and friends

dll *dan lain-lain* et cetera

doa *n* prayer; ~ *restu* blessing; *membaca* ~ to pray, say a prayer; **berdoa** *v* to pray, say a prayer; **mendoakan** *v* to pray for

dobel *adj* double, twice as much

dobrak, mendobrak *v* to break open, smash

dodol *n* soft, chewy sweet made from brown sugar or fruit

dok *pron* Doc, Doctor (used when addressing a doctor) ← **dokter**

dokar *n* (two-wheeled horse-drawn) buggy

dokter, dr *n* doctor, surgeon; ~ *gigi (drg)* dentist; ~ *hewan (drh)* vet; ~ *mata* oculist, optometrist;

kedokteran *adj* medical; *fakultas* ~ School of Medicine

Doktor, Dr *pron* title for holder of a Ph.D.

dokumén *n* document; **dokuméntasi** *n* documentation; **mendokuméntasi** *v* to document, file

dolar *n* dollar; ~ *Amerika* US dollar

DOM *abbrev Daerah Operasi Militer* region of military operations

domba *n* sheep

doméstik *adj* domestic, internal, national

domisili: berdomisili *v* to be domiciled, reside

dompét *n* purse, wallet; ~ *saya hilang!* I've lost my wallet!

donat *n* donut, doughnut

dong, donk *sl* you should know that; *Jangan begitu* ~ Please don't do that

dongéng *n* tale, story, fable

dongkrak *n* (car) jack, lever; **mendongkrak** *v* to jack, lever, raise

dor bang! (sound of gun, burst balloon, etc)

dorong *v* to push; **dorongan** *n* push, urge; **mendorong** *v* to push, encourage; **terdorong** *adj* pushed, shoved

dosa *n* sin; **berdosa** *v* to sin, commit a sin

dosén *n* (university) lecturer

dot *n* dummy; **mengedot** *v* to suck

doyan *v* to like, enjoy

DPA *abbrev Dewan Pertimbangan Agung* Supreme Advisory Council

DPR *abbrev Dewan Perwakilan Rakyat* People's Representative Council

DPRD *abbrev Dewan Perwakilan Rakyat Daerah* Regional People's Representative Council

Dr *Doktor pron* holder of a Ph.D.

dr *dokter* doctor

dra *doktoranda f* holder of a Bachelor's degree

drainase *n* drainage

drastis *adj* drastic; *turun* ~ fall drastically

drg *dokter gigi* dentist

drh *dokter hewan* vet(erinary surgeon)

drs *doktorandus m* holder of a Bachelor's degree

dsb *dan sebagainya* and so on

dua *adj* two; ~ *belas* twelve; ~ *kali* twice; ~ *puluh* twenty; **dua-duanya** *adj* both, the two of them; **berdua** *adj* together, in pairs; **kedua** *adj* second; **kedua(-dua)nya** *adj* both

dubes *n* ambassador; ← **duta besar**

dubur *n* anus

duda *n* widower; divorced man; ~ *cerai* divorced man

duduk *v* to sit, be placed; **kedudukan** *n* position; **menduduki** *v* to sit on something; to occupy; **penduduk** *n* inhabitant, citizen, resident; **pendudukan** *n* occupation

duga, menduga *v* to suppose, suspect; **dugaan** *n* suspicion

dugem *n, sl* jetset, nightlife, underworld ← **dunia gemerlap**

duh → **aduh**

duit *n, sl* money, cash, dirt, dosh; *cari* ~ earn a living

duka *n* sorrow; ~ *cita* grief, sorrow; **berduka** ~ *(cita)* to grieve, be in mourning

duku *n* small sweet fruit with light brown skin, clear flesh and large dark seed

dukun *n* traditional or spiritual healer, shaman

dukung support; **dukungan** *n* support; **mendukung** *v* to support; **pendukung** *n* supporter

dulang: mendulang *v* to pan (for gold); **pendulang** *n* prospector

dulu *adv* first, former, before; **duluan** *adv, coll* first, before others ← **dahulu**

dungu *adj* stupid, slow

dunia *n* world; ~ *akhirat* the hereafter; *juara* ~ world champion

dupa *n* incense

durasi *n* duration

durén → **durian**

durhaka *adj* treacherous, rebellious

duri *n* thorn; **berduri** *adj* thorny; **durian** *n* durian, spiky yellow-skinned fruit with a strong smell

dus *conj, coll* so, then
dus, dos *n* cardboard box
    ← **kardus**
dusta *n* lie, fib; **berdusta** *v*
to lie; **pendusta** *n* liar
dusun *n* hamlet, village
duta *n* envoy, messenger,
representative, ~ *besar*
ambassador; **kedutaan**
~ *(besar)* embassy
duyung *n* seacow
dwi- *pref* two; ~*bahasa*
bilingual; ~*fungsi* dual
function (of army);
~*mingguan* *adj* fortnightly;
~*warna* the Red-and-White
(Indonesian flag)

E

é *ejac* hey (showing
recognition, disagreement)
ébi *n* (dried) shrimp
écér: éceran *adj* retail;
harga ~ retail price
édar: édaran *n* circular;
berédar *v* to circulate;
mengédarkan *v* to
circulate something;

pengédar *n* dealer;
peregédaran *n* circulation
édisi *n* edition; **édit, mengédit** *v* to edit; **éditor** *n*
editor
éfisién *adj* efficient; *secara*
~ efficiently
égois *adj* egoist, egotistical
éh, é *ejac* I mean; *Datang
besok,* ~*, maksudnya lusa*
Come tomorrow, no, I
mean the day after
éja: éjaan *n* spelling;
~ *Yang Disempurnakan
(EYD)* reformed spelling of
1972; **mengéja** *v* to spell
éjék, mengéjék *v* to tease,
mock, ridicule
ékonom *n* economist;
ékonomi *n* economy; *ilmu*
~ economics; *kereta* ~
economy-class train
ékor *n* tail; counter for
animals; ~ *kuda* pony tail;
tiga ~ *kucing* three cats;
berékor *v* to have a tail
éks- *pref* ex-, former →
mantan
ékséksusi *n* execution;
mengéksékusi *v* to
execute (carry out the death
penalty)

éksékutif executive

ékskul *n* extra-curricular activities, classes outside school ← **ékstra kurikulér**

ékspatriat *orang* ~expatriate (esp. Caucasian)

éksplorasi *n* exploration (for mineral resources)

ékspor export; **meng-ékspor** *v* to export; **pengékspor** *n* exporter

éksprés *adj* express

ékstradisi *n* extradition; **mengékstradisi** *v* to extradite (someone)

élak, mengélakkan *v* to avoid, dodge, evade

éléktronik *adj* electronic; *media* ~ electronic media; **éléktronika** *n* electronics

éliminasi *n* elimination; **teréliminasi** *adj* eliminated → **singkir**

élit, élite [élit] *n* elite; ~ *politik* political elite; *daerah* ~ elite residential area

élok *adj* beautiful

élpiji *n* liquid petroleum gas, LPG

elu → **lu**

elus stroke, caress;

mengelus *v* to caress, stroke or pat (an animal)

émail *n* (tooth) enamel

email → **imél**

emak, mak *n* mother

émang → **mémang**

emas, mas *n* gold; ~ *kawin* dowry; *kesempatan* ~ golden opportunity; *tukang* ~ goldsmith

embék bleat *coll* sheep or goat

émbél-émbél *n* details; extra decorations

émbér *n* bucket, pail

embun *n* dew; **berembun** *adj* moist, dewy; **pengembunan** *n* condensation

embus, hembus blow; **embusan** *n* blow; bellows; **berembus, mengembus** *v* to blow

emis: mengemis *v* to beg; **pengemis** *n* beggar

émisi *n* emission; ~ *kendaraan* vehicle emissions

émosi, berémosi, émosional *adj* emotional

empal *n* slice of beef

empang *n* dam, fish pond

empas, mengempaskan ~ *diri* to throw yourself down

empat *adj* four; ~ *belas* fourteen; ~ *puluh* forty; **berempat** *adj* in a group of four; **keempat** *adj* fourth; **perempat** *n* quarter; *tiga* ~ three-quarters; **perempat- an, prapatan** *n* crossroads, intersection; **seperempat** *n* one quarter

empedu *n* gall, bile

empék-empék → **pémpék**

émpér, émpéran *n* awning; stall, booth

emping *n* chips made from the *melinjo* bean

empu *n* creese-maker

empuk *adj* soft, tender

emut, kemut, mengemut *v* to suck on (sweets etc)

én *conj, sl* and

énak *adj* nice, tasty, delicious; pleasant; *~nya* the good thing is, ...; ~ *saja*, ~ *aja* (sarcastically) that's nice! how dare they!; *tidak* ~ *badan* not feeling well; **énakan** *adj, sl* better, nicer, tastier; **keénakan** *adj* too enjoyable or good; **se- énaknya** *adv, neg* just how you like, at will

enam *adj* six; ~ *belas* sixteen;

~ *puluh* sixty; *segi* ~ hexagon; **keenam** *adj* sixth

éncér *adj* liquid, runny, watery

éncik, cik *pron* form of address to Chinese woman

encok *n* rheumatism, arthritis

endap: mengendap *v* to sink, silt up; **pengendapan** *n* siltation

énergi *n* energy; **berénérgi** *adj* energetic, containing energy; **énérgik** *adj* energetic → **tenaga**

enggak *coll* no, not ← **tidak**

enggan *adj* reluctant, unwilling; **keengganan** *n* reluctance

enggang *n* hornbill

engkau, kau, dikau *pron* you

engku *pron* title used for men in Malay areas

éngsél *n* hinge; joint

énsiklopédi, énsiklopédia *n* encyclopedia

entah who knows

entar soon ← **sebentar**

énténg *adj* light; flippant; *menjawab* ~ to give a light, flippant answer

épiséntrum *n* epicenter

eram: mengeram v to sit on eggs, brood, hatch

erang groan; **erangan** n groan, moan; **mengerang** v to groan, moan

erat adj close, solid, strong; **mempererat** v to strengthen, make closer

Éropa, Éropah n Europe; orang ~ European

érosi n erosion

erotis adj erotic

erti → **arti, mengerti**

és n ice; ~ krim, ~ puter ice cream; ~ teler sweet dessert with ice; lemari ~ refrigerator

esa, ésa n, lit one, only; Yang Maha ~ (YME) the one and only (God)

ésai, éséi n essay

ésok adv ~ hari tomorrow; **keésokan** ~ harinya the next day → **bésok**

éstafét n relay

étalase n shop window

étika n ethics, good manners; **berétika** adj ethical; v to behave

étnik, étnis n ethnic group; ~ Madura the Madurese (ethnic group); adj ethnic,

non-Western

étsa n sketch

évakuasi n evacuation → **ungsi**

EYD abbrev Ejaan Yang Disempurnakan reformed spelling, implemented in 1972

F

faham → **paham**

fajar n dawn, daybreak; ~ menyingsing crack of dawn

fakir ~ miskin poor person

faks n fax, facsimile; lewat ~ by fax; mesin ~ fax machine; **difaks** v to be faxed

fakultas n faculty; ~ Sastra Arts faculty

fakultatif adj not fixed; optional

fals adj off-key, false (of music)

falsafah → **filsafat**

famili adj related, distant family

fanatik n fan; fanatic

fans: ngefans *v, sl* to be a fan of

fantasi *n* fantasy, imagination

fase *n* phase

fasih *adj* fluent, eloquent; ~ *berbahasa Indonesia* to speak Indonesian fluently

fasis *adj* fascist; **fasisme** *n* fascism

fatal *adj* very bad; fatal

fatwa *n* fatwa, religious ruling

favorit *adj* favorite; *sekolah* ~ top school

FE *abbrev Fakultas Ekonomi* Faculty of Economics

Fébruari *bulan* ~ February

féderal *adj* federal; **féderasi** *n* federation

féng sui, hong sui *n* feng shui

fénoména *n* phenomenon

féodal, féodalis *adj* feudal, feudalistic; **féodalisme** *n* feudalism

féri *n* ferry

Fesbuk *n* Facebook

FH *abbrev Fakultas Hukum* Faculty of Law

fikir → **pikir**

fiksi *n* fiction; **fiktif** *adj* fictitious, fictional

Filipina *n* the Philippines; *orang* ~ Filipino, *f* Filipina

film *n* film; ~ *biru* blue film, pornographic film

filsafat, falsafah *n* philosophy; **berfilsafat** *v* to have a philosophy

final *adj* final; *babak* ~ final (match)

Finlandia *n* Finland; *bahasa* ~ Finnish; *orang* ~ Finn

firasat *n* presentiment, foreboding, bad feeling

firman *n* word of God; **berfirman** *v* to utter, say; *Allah* ~ God said

fisik *adj* physical

fisika *n* physics

fisiotérapi *n* physiotherapy

FISIP *abbrev Fakultas Ilmu Sosial dan Politik* Faculty of Social Science and Politics

fiskal *n* departure payment (for residents)

fitnah *n* slander, libel; **memfitnah** *v* to slander

FK *abbrev Fakultas Kedokteran* Faculty of Medicine

flék *n* blemish, spot (on face)

flu *n* flu, influenza; ~ *burung* bird flu

fokus *n* focus; ~ *pada* focus on; **berfokus** *adj* focused; **memfokuskan** *v* to focus something; ~ *diri* to focus yourself

fondasi *n* foundation (of a building)

formal, formil *adj* formal

formulir *n* (blank) form

fosil *n* fossil

foto *n* photo, photograph; ~*model* (professional) model; ~ *udara* aerial photo; **berfoto** *v* to take, pose for a photo; **fotokopi** *n* photocopy; *difotokopi* to be photocopied

foya: foya-foya, berfoya-foya *v* to waste money, live frivolously

frustrasi *adj* frustrated

FS *abbrev Fakultas Sastra* Faculty of Letters, Arts Faculty

fungsi *n* function; **ber-fungsi** *v* to work, go; to act as; **fungsionaris** *n* party functionary, official

fuyung hai, puyung hai *n* sweet-and-sour omelet

G

G. *Gunung* Mt (Mount, name of mountain)

G30S *Gerakan Tiga Puluh September* (alleged) 30th September Movement

GA Garuda (Indonesia Airways)

gabung connect, join; **gabungan** *adj* joint; *tim* ~ team (comprising various elements); **ber-gabung** *v* to join together; **menggabungkan** *v* to connect, combine, fuse

gadai *surat* ~ pawn ticket; **menggadaikan** *v* to pawn something; **pegadaian** *n* pawnshop

gadang *rumah* ~ traditional Minangkabau house

gadang → begadang

gading tusk, ivory

gadis *n* girl, maiden, virgin, unmarried woman; **kegadisan** *n* virginity

gado-gado *n* cooked salad with peanut sauce; *adj* mixed; *bahasa* ~ mixture of Indonesian and another language

gaduh: kegaduhan *n* noise, uproar

gadungan *adj* fake, false

gaét, gait, kait: menggaét *v* to get (on board), snatch, hook → **gait, kait**

gagah *adj* strong; ~ *perkasa* heroic; handsome

gagak *burung* ~ crow, raven

gagal *v* to fail; **kegagalan** *n* failure

gagang *n* handle; ~ *telepon* handset, telephone cradle

gagap stammer, stutter; ~ *teknologi (gaptek)* technophobe

gagas: gagasan *n* idea, concept

gagu *adj* mute

gaharu *kayu* ~ aloe wood, eaglewood

gaib *adj* mysterious, invisible

gairah *n* passion, lust; enthusiasm; **menggairahkan** *v* to excite, stimulate

gait: menggait *v* to pull, hook → **gaét, kait**

gajah *n* elephant

gaji *n* (monthly) salary, pay; ~ *bersih* net salary, take-home pay; **menggaji** *v* to pay, remunerate, employ

gak *sl* no, not → **enggak, tidak**

galah *n* long pole, spear; *lompat* ~ pole vault

galak *adj* fierce, wild, vicious; *anjing* ~ vicious dog; *guru yang* ~ strict teacher

galéri *n* gallery → **paméran**

gali *v* to dig; **galian** *n* excavations, diggings; **menggali** *v* to dig; **penggalian** *n* digging

gambar picture, drawing, illustration; **gambaran** *n* sketch, idea; **bergambar** *adj* illustrated; **menggambar** *v* to draw, depict; **menggambarkan** *v* to describe, illustrate

gamblang *adj* clear, obvious, plain

gamelan *n* traditional orchestra

gampang *adj, coll* easy; ~~ *susah* not as easy as it looks → **mudah**

ganas *adj* fierce, wild, ferocious; uncontrolled; *tumor* ~ malignant growth or lump

ganda double; -fold; ~ *putra* men's doubles

gandéng link, join; *truk ~* semi-trailer; **bergandéngan** *~ tangan* to link arms or hands

gandul *n* pendulum, clapper

gandum *n* wheat

gang *n* alley, lane

ganggu, mengganggu *v* to bother, disturb; **gangguan** *n* disturbance, interference; problem; **terganggu** *adj* bothered, disrupted, disturbed

ganja *n* marijuana

ganjal *v* to wedge; to fill a gap

ganjil *adj* uneven, odd; *angka ~* odd number

ganteng *adj, coll* handsome

ganti change, substitute; *~ baju, ~ pakaian* change your clothes; *~ rugi* compensation; **gantian** *v, sl* change over; **berganti** *v* to change; *~~ganti, ~an* in turns; **mengganti** *v* to change, substitute, replace; **menggantikan** *v* to substitute or replace someone/something; **pengganti** *n* replacement, substitute, successor

gantolé *n* hang-glider, hang-gliding

gantung hang; *~ diri* hang yourself; **bergantung** *~ pada* to depend on; **menggantung** *v* to hang, suspend; **tergantung** *adj* depending (on), it depends; **ketergantungan** *n* dependency

ganyang *v* to crush, wipe out

gapai: menggapai *v* to strive for, reach

gapték *n* technophobe ← **gagap téknologi**

gapura *n* (ornamental) gateway, entrance

gara-gara *adv, sl* all because of → **goro-goro**

garam *n* salt; *sudah makan ~* experienced, an old salt

garansi *n* guarantee (on a product); **bergaransi** *adj* guaranteed

garap: garapan *adj* produced by, product; **menggarap** *v* to work on, produce; *~ tanah* to till the land

garasi *n* carport, garage

gardu *n* post, station; *~ listrik* transmission station

garing *adj* dry, crisp

garis line, scratch; ~ *peperangan* front, front line; ~ *tengah* diameter; ~ *tegak lurus* perpendicular (line); **bergaris** *adj* lined; **menggarisbawahi** to underline, emphasize; **penggaris** *n* ruler

garmén *pabrik* ~ garment factory

garong *n* robber

garpu *n* fork

garuda *n* eagle, national symbol of Indonesia

garuk, menggaruk *v* to scratch, scrape; ~ *kepala* to scratch your head

gas *n* gas; ~ *bumi* natural gas; *menancap* ~ to step on the gas

gasing *n* (spinning) top; *main* ~ to spin a top

gatal *adj* itchy; *sl* lustful; **gatal-gatal** *v* to have a rash

gaul *v* to mix, associate; *adj, sl* trendy; **bergaul** *v* to mix or associate; **pergaulan** *n* mixing, social intercourse; association; ~ *bebas* promiscuity, permissiveness

gaun *n* (evening) gown

gaung *n* echo; **bergaung** *v* to echo

gawang *n* goal (in field sports); hurdle; *penjaga* ~ goalkeeper

gawat *adj* serious, very bad; *Unit* ~ *Darurat (UGD)* emergency ward

gaya energy, strength; style; ~ *berat*, ~ *bobot* gravity; **bergaya** *adj* stylish, with style

gayung *n* water dipper; stick

Gd. *gedung* building

gebrak blow, bang, hit; **menggebrak** *v* to hit or slam

gebuk hit, bash; **menggebuk** *v* to batter, bash

gebyar sparkle, glitter

gedé *adj, coll* big, large; ~ *rasa (GR)* stuck-up, full of yourself

gedor: menggedor *v* to bang on repeatedly

gedung *n* building, public hall; ~ *Arsip* State Archives

géér, gé ér, GR *adj, coll* stuck-up, full of yourself ← **gedé rasa**

gegar shake, quiver; ~ *budaya* culture shock; ~ *otak* concussion

gegas: bergegas-gegas v to hurry

gejala n symptom, sign

gejolak: bergejolak v to flare up, burst out

geladak n deck of a ship

geladi → **gladi**

gelagap: gelagapan confused; stammer, stutter

gelak laugh; ~ *tawa* burst or galc of laughter

gelandang: gelandangan n tramp, homeless person

gelang n bracelet; **pergelangan** ~ *kaki* ankle; ~ *tangan* wrist

gelanggang n arena, stadium; ~ *olah raga (GOR, gelora)* sports complex

gelantung hang, suspend; **bergelantungan** v to hang from (of several things)

gelap adj dark; *barang* ~ contraband, illegal goods; **kegelapan** n darkness; **menggelapkan** v to embezzle, misappropriate

gelar n title; **bergelar** v titled; **menggelar, menggelarkan** v to hold (an event)

gelatik *burung* ~ kind of bird, finch

gelédah, geladah, menggelédah v to search; to ransack

gelédék n lightning

gelembung n bubble

géléng: menggéléng, menggél-éngkan ~ *kepala* to shake your head

gelétak: tergelétak adj sprawled

geli ticklish; uncomfortable; **menggelikan** adj funny, comic; off-putting

geliat: menggeliat v to stretch, twist

gelimpang: tergelimpang adj sprawled; **bergelim-pangan** adj sprawled all around

gelincir: tergelincir adj skidded, slipped

gelisah adj nervous, restless; **kegelisahan** n anxiety, nerves

gelitik, menggelitik v to tickle

gelombang n wave; (radio) frequency; **bergelombang** adj wavy

gelora n storm, surge, passion; **gelanggang olah raga** sports complex

gelut: bergelut v to wrestle; to romp

gema n echo, reverberation; **bergema** v to echo, reverberate

gemar like, enjoy; **kegemaran** n hobby; **menggemari** v to like, enjoy; **penggemar** n fan, enthusiast

gemas, gemes coll cute, sweet (often said to children); annoyed; **menggemaskan** adj annoying

gembira adj cheerful, happy, joyous; **bergembira** v to be happy, joyous; **kegembiraan** n joy, happiness; **menggembirakan** adj exciting, happy

gembok n padlock; **menggembok** v to padlock

gembung, kembung adj filled with air, inflated; bloated; perut ~ bloated belly → **kembung**

gemerlap shine, sparkle

gemetar shiver, tremble; **gemetaran** adj shivering, trembling

gemilang glitter, shine; brilliant

gempa n quake, shudder;

~ bumi earthquake

gempar clamor, noise, uproar; **menggemparkan** v to cause a stir

gempur: menggempur v to attack, destroy

gemuk adj fat, plump, obese; n grease; jalur ~ busy route

gemuruh n thunder → **guruh**

gén n gene; **génétik** adj genetic; **génétika** n genetics; rekayasa ~ genetic engineering

genang: genangan n puddle, flood; **tergenang** adj flooded

genap adj even, complete, exact; angka ~ even number; **segenap** adj each, all

gencat: gencatan ~ senjata ceasefire, truce, armistice

gendang n (kettle) drum

géndong, menggéndong v to carry on the hip

gendut adj fat, pot-bellied

générasi n generation

génétik adj genetic; **génétika** n genetics; rekayasa ~ genetic engineering ← **gén**

géng, génk *n* gang

genggam fist; **genggam-an** *n* grip, grasp; **meng-genggam** *v* to grip, grasp

géngsi *n* prestige, face; **bergéngsi** *adj* prestigious

genit *adj* flirtatious

génsét *n* generator

gentar shiver, tremble

genténg *n* roof tile

góografi *n* geography (school subject) → **ilmu bumi**

gépéng *adj* flat, concave, sunken

gerabah *n* earthenware pot

gerah *adj* sultry, muggy

geraham *gigi* ~ molar

gerak move; ~ *badan* (physical) exercises; ~ *gerik* movements, body language; ~ *jalan* long march; demonstration; **gerakan** *n* movement; ~ *Aceh Merdeka (GAM)* Free Aceh Movement; **bergerak** *v* to move; **menggerakkan** *v* to move, shift something

gerangan can it be?

gerayang: menggerayangi *v* to grope

gerbang *n* gate, gateway, door; ~ *tol* toll gate; *pintu* ~ main gate

gerbong *n* carriage; ~ *restorasi* restaurant car

gerebek, gerebeg: meng-gerebek *v* to raid, search

geréja *n* church

gergaji *n* saw; **meng-gergaji** *v* to saw

gerhana *n* eclipse; ~ *bulan* lunar eclipse; ~ *matahari* solar eclipse

gerigi *n, pl* teeth, points; **bergerigi** *adj* serrated, jagged

gerilya *n* guerrilla

gerimis *(hujan)* ~ drizzle

gerobak *n* cart; ~ *kaki lima* itinerant food vendor; ~ *sampah* rubbish cart

gerogot: menggerogoti *v* to eat into, erode, gnaw on

gersang *adj* arid

gerutu: menggerutu *v* to grumble, complain, gripe

gesa: tergesa-gesa *adj* in a hurry or rush

gését rub; **gésékan** *n* stroke, scrape; **menggését** *v* to rub, scrape; ~ *biola* to play the violin; ~ *kartu* to swipe a card; **pergésékan** *n* friction

gésér: menggésér *v* to move aside or over; **pergéséran** *n* movement, shift

gesit *adj* nimble, adept, adroit

Gestapu *n* (alleged) 30th September Movement (in 1965) ← **Gerakan Séptémber Tiga Puluh**

getah *n* sap, latex, gum; ~ *bening* lymph gland

getar shake, tremor; **getaran** *n* vibration, shake, tremor; **bergetar** *v* to vibrate, tremble

Gg *gang* lane, alley

GIA Garuda Indonesia Airlines

giat *adj* active, busy; **kegiatan** *n* activity

gigi *n* tooth; ~ *palsu* false teeth; *gosok* ~ brush your teeth; *tusuk* ~ toothpick

gigil: menggigil *v* to shiver

gigit: menggigit *v* to bite

gila *adj* crazy, mad, insane

gilas, menggilas *v* to crush, pulverize, roll

giling *daging* ~ mincemeat; **menggiling** *v* to grind, mill

gilir: giliran *n* turn; **bergilir, bergiliran** *adj* in turns

gimana *coll* how; ~ *sih?* what about that? → **bagaimana**

gini *adv, coll* like this, in this way → **begini**

ginjal *n* kidney; *sakit* ~ kidney disease

giok *n batu* ~ jade

gips *n* plaster, plaster cast; **digips** *v* to be in or have a plaster cast

girang *adj* pleased, glad, happy

giring, menggiring *v* to herd, drive (cattle)

gitar *n* guitar

gitu *adv, coll* like that, in that way → **begitu**

giur: menggiurkan *adj* tempting, mouth-watering; **tergiur** *adj* tempted

gizi *n* nutrient; *ahli* ~ nutritionist; **bergizi** *adj* nutritious

gladi, geladi ~ *resik,* ~ *bersih* dress-rehearsal

goa, gua *n* cave, tunnel; ~ *Jepang* Japanese-built tunnel from World War II

goblok *derog* stupid, moron

goda tempt; **godaan** *n* temptation; **menggoda** *v* to tempt; **tergoda** *adj* tempted

godok boil; **menggodok** *v* to boil

golak: pergolakan *n* disturbance, upheaval

golf *n* golf; *lapangan ~, padang ~* golf course

Golkar *n, arch* Functional Group (Soehartoist party); *Partai ~* Golkar Party ← **Golongan Karya**

golok *n* machete, chopping knife

golong: golongan *n* group, category; rank; *~ Karya (Golkar) arch* Functional Group; *~ putih (golput)* 'white' group (abstainers in elections); **menggolong-kan** *v* to group, classify; **tergolong** *adj* to include, be part of or considered

gombal *adj* worthless

goncang, guncang rock, sway; **goncangan** *n* shock wave, quake; **menggon-cangkan** *v* to rock or make something move

gondok *n* goitre

gondrong (excessively) long hair

gong *n* gong

gonggong woof, sound of dog barking; **meng-gonggong** *v* to bark

gono-gini *n* shared goods and chattels during a marriage, split up during divorce

gonta-ganti *v* to change constantly; *~ pacar* to have had lots of boyfriends/girl-friends → **ganti**

GOR *abbrev Gelanggang Olah Raga* stadium, sports complex

gordén, hordén *n* curtain(s)

goréng fry; **goréngan** *n* fried snacks; **menggoréng** *v* to fry; **penggoréngan** *n* wok, frying pan; process of frying

gorés line, scratch; **gorésan** *n* scratch, stroke; **menggorés** *v* to scratch, make a stroke; **tergorés** *adj* scratched

gosip gossip; **menggosip-kan** *v* to gossip about something or someone

gosok rub; *minyak ~*
massage oil; **menggosok** *v*
to rub, polish; *~ sepatu* to
polish, shine shoes

gosong *adj* burnt, singed,
scorched; *bau ~* burnt smell

got *n* roadside drain or ditch

gotong carry; *~ royong*
mutual assistance; **menggotong** *v* to carry together

goyah *adj* unstable, wobbly

goyang shake, wobble,
unsteady; **bergoyang** *v* to
shake, sway; to dance;
menggoyangkan *v* to
shake or rock something

GR, gé ér *adj, coll* stuck-
up, full of yourself ← **gedé
rasa**

grafik *n* graph; diagram;
grafis *adj* graphic; *seni ~*
graphic design

graha, grha *n* building,
house; *Bina Graha*
presidential office

granat *n* grenade

grasi *n* pardon (from the
President); *memberi ~* to
pardon someone (for a
crime)

grogi *adj* nervous, groggy

grosir *n* wholesaler

grup *n* group (esp business)

gua → **goa**

gubernur *n* governor

gubris: menggubris *v* to
pay heed or attention to

gubuk *n* hut

guci *n* (earthenware) jar
or pot

gudang *n* warehouse, shed,
store

gugat sue; **gugatan** *n*
lawsuit, accusation; **menggugat** *v* to sue, accuse

gugup *adj* nervous

gugur *v* to fall, be killed
(in action) or eliminated;
keguguran *n* miscarriage;
menggugurkan *v* to abort

gugus cluster; *~ bintang*
constellation; **gugusan** *n*
bunch, group, cluster; *~
pulau* chain of islands

gula *n* sugar; *~ batu* sugar
lump; *~ Jawa* palm sugar

gulai, gulé *n* curry; *~
kambing* goat curry

gulat wrestling; **bergulat** *v*
to wrestle, fight

guling *(bantal) ~* bolster,
Dutch wife; *babi ~*
suckling pig; **mengguling**
v to roll

gulung: menggulung *v* to roll up

gumam, bergumam *v* to mumble; **menggumamkan** *v* to mumble or mutter something

gumpal *n* clot, lump; **gumpalan** *n* clot, lump

guna *n* use, benefit; for; *tidak ada ~nya* there's no use; **berguna** *adj* useful, worthwhile; *tidak ~* useless; **menggunakan** *v* to use; **pengguna** *n* user; **penggunaan** *n* usage, use

guna-guna *n* black magic

guncang, goncang rock, sway; **guncangan** *n* shock wave, quake; **menggun-cangkan** *v* to rock or make something move

gundul *adj* bald; **meng-gunduli** *v* to shave, denude, make bald

gunting scissors, cut; *~ kuku* nail clippers; **gun-tingan** *n* cutout; **meng-gunting** *v* to cut (out)

guntur *n* thunder

gunung *n* mountain, mount; remote area; *~ (ber)api* volcano; *~ Bromo* Mount Bromo; **gunungan** *n* symbolic mountain used in shadow-puppet plays; **pegunungan** *n* mountain range

gurah *n* rinsing, as an alternative medical treatment

guramé, guraméh, gurami *ikan ~* large freshwater fish

gurat: guratan *n* scratch

gurau *n* joke, jest

gurem *adj* tiny, insignificant

gurih *adj* tasty, delicious, mouth-watering

gurita *ikan ~* octopus

guru *n* teacher; *~ besar* professor; *~ kepala* headmaster; **perguruan** *~ tinggi* university

guruh *n* thunder

Gus, Bagus *title, m, Isl* East Javanese title

gusar *adj* angry, vexed

gusi *n* gums

gusti *n, pron, arch* lord; *~ Allah* the Lord God

gusur: menggusur *v* to evict, sweep aside, forcibly remove; **penggusuran** *n* eviction, forcible removal

H

H *hijriah* Islamic calendar

H. *Haji* title for man who has performed the major pilgrimage to Mecca

habis *adj* finished; empty; *adv* entirely; *coll* after, ~ *perkara* end of story; that was it; ~ *mandi, dia pergi* After washing, he went out; **kehabisan** *v* to run out of (water; food; stock); **menghabiskan** *v* to finish, use up, spend; **sehabis** *conj* after

hablur *n* crystal

hadap face; ~ *kiri* face left; **hadapan** *n* front; facing; *di* ~ in front of; **berhadapan** *(~ muka) v* face to face; **menghadap** *v* to face, appear before; **menghadapi** *v* to face someone or something; **terhadap** *conj* regarding; against; with respect to

hadiah *n* present, gift; prize; ~ *pertama* first prize; **berhadiah** *adj* with prizes

hadir present; available; *tidak* ~ absent; **hadirin** *n* audience; **kehadiran** *n* presence; attendance; **menghadiri** *v* to attend; **menghadirkan** *v* to present; to bring forward

hafal, hapal know by heart; **menghafalkan** *v* to learn by heart

hal *sl* hi!

haid *n* menstruation; *siklus* ~ menstrual cycle

Haj, hajj → **haji**

hajat *n* want, need, wish; *buang* ~ defecate; *punya* ~ hold a feast

haji *n, Isl* person who has made the pilgrimage to Mecca; *Lebaran* ~ Idul Adha, Feast of the Sacrifice (performed during the annual pilgrimage)

hajjah *Isl, f* title for a woman who has made the pilgrimage to Mecca

hak *n* right; ~ *azasi manusia (HAM)* human rights; ~ *milik* ownership; **berhak** *v* to have a right to, be entitled to

hak *n* heel

hakikat, hakékat *n* nature, essence; *pada ~nya* basically, essentially

hakim *n* judge; **kehakiman** Departemen ~ Department of Justice

hal *n* matter, case; ~ *ini* this; *dalam* ~ *itu* in that case

halal *adj*, *Isl* permitted (to eat); killed according to Islamic practice

halal bihalal *n* social gathering, usually after fasting month

halaman *n* yard, open area, page; ~ *rumah* yard

halang: halangan *n* obstacle; hindrance; **berhalangan** *v* to be prevented; unable; **menghalangi** *v* to hinder, prevent; **terhalang** *adj* blocked; prevented

hal-ihwal *n* related matters; circumstances ← **hal**

halilintar *n* lightning bolt, thunderclap

halte *n* stop; ~ *bis* bus stop

halus *adj* fine; soft; refined; *bahasa* ~ refined language; *makhluk* ~ spirit; **kehalusan** *n* delicacy; grace; **menghaluskan** *v* to refine; grind

HAM *abbrev* Hak Asasi Manusia Human Rights

hama *n* pest; plague

hamba *n, pron, arch* slave; me; your servant

hambar *adj* flavorless; bland

hambat, menghambat *v* to obstruct, impede, hamper; **hambatan** *n* obstacle

hambur: berhamburan *adj* scattered about; **menghamburkan** *v* to scatter; throw about

hamil *adj* pregnant; ~ *muda* first trimester; ~ *tua* heavily pregnant; **kehamilan** *n* pregnancy

hampa *adj* empty

hampar: hamparan ~ *sungai* flood plain

hampir *adv* nearly, almost; **hampir-hampir** *adv* very nearly

hanacaraka *n* Sundanese and Javanese alphabet → **honocoroko**

hancur smashed, crushed; **kehancuran** *n* destruction, ruin; **menghancurkan** *v* to smash, crush, destroy

handai ~ *tolan,* ~ *taulan* friends

handphone [hénpon; hénfon] *n* mobile phone, cell phone

handuk *n* towel

hangat *adj* warm, hot;
  kehangatan *n* warmth,
  friendliness
hangus *adj* burnt, scorched;
  expired; *bumi* ~ scorched
  earth; **membumihangus-
  kan** to conduct a scorched-
  earth policy
hansip *n* local security
  guard; paramilitary ←
  pertahanan sipil
hantam strike, blow;
  menghantam *v* to strike
hantar: menghantarkan *v*
  to conduct (electricity or
  heat); **penghantar** ~ *listrik*
  electrical conductor
hantu *n* ghost; **menghantui**
  v to haunt
hanya *adv* only
hanyut drift, float
hapé, HP *n* mobile phone,
  cell phone ← **handphone**
hapermot → **havermut**
haram *adj, Isl* forbidden,
  not permitted
harap hope; please; ~
  maklum please understand;
  harapan *n* hope, expectation; ~ *tipis* little hope;
  berharap *v* to hope;
  mengharapkan *v* to expect

hardik: menghardik *v* to
  shout at; scold
harga *n* price; value; ~ *beli*
  buying price; ~ *diri* dignity;
  self-worth; ~ *mati* fixed
  price; last offer; **berharga**
  adj precious; valuable;
  menghargai *v* to appreciate; **penghargaan** *n*
  appreciation; award;
  seharga *adj* of equal value;
  the same price
hari *n* day; ~ *besar* holiday;
  ~ *ini* today; ~ *kerja* weekday, working day; ~ *libur*
  holiday, day off; ~ *ulang
  tahun (HUT)* birthday,
  anniversary; *sepanjang* ~ all
  day long; *siang* ~ daytime;
  harian *adj* daily; **berhari-
  hari** *adv* for days; **sehari-
  hari** *adv* every day, daily;
  seharian *adv, coll* all day
harimau *n* tiger
harpa *n* harp
hart *n* hearts (in cards)
harta *n* wealth, belongings;
  ~ *benda* property; goods
  and chattels; ~ *karun*
  hidden treasure
haru emotion; touched;
  mengharukan *adj* moved,

touched (emotionally); **terharu** *adj* moved, touched

harum *adj* fragrant; perfumed; **keharuman** *n* fragrance

harus *v* must, ought to, have to; **keharusan** *n* obligation, necessity, requirement; **mengharuskan** *v* to require; **seharusnya** should

hasil *n* product; result; **berhasil** *v* to succeed; **keberhasilan** *n* success; **menghasilkan** *v* to produce; **penghasilan** *n* production; income

hasrat *n* desire; lust

hati *n* liver; heart; ~ *kecil* conscience; **hati-hati** take care; **berhati-hati** *v* to be careful; **memperhatikan** *v* to notice, pay attention to; **perhatian** *n* attention

haus *adj* thirsty; ~ *perhatian* longing for attention; **kehausan** *adj* to be thirsty; *n* thirst

havermut, hapermot *n* oatmeal porridge

hawa *n* air, atmosphere, climate; ~ *nafsu* passion; lust; **berhawa** ~ *sejuk* cool climate

hayat *n* life; *sampai akhir* ~ until the end of your life; **hayati** *adj* biological

hébat *adj* great; violent; terrific

héboh sensational; **meng-hébohkan** *v* to cause an uproar; *adj* sensational

héktar *n* hectare

héla, menghéla *v* to draw; drag; ~ *nafas* to sigh, draw a breath

helai *n* (counter) sheet; counter for thin flat objects; *se*~ *kertas* a piece of paper

hélat: perhélatan *n* celebration, feast

héli, hélikopter *n* helicopter

hélm *n* helmet

hémat *adj* economical, thrifty; ~ *air* save water; **menghémat** *v* to save on or economize

hémat *n* judgment; opinion

hembus, embus blow, puff; **menghembus** *v* to blow

hendak *v* to will, wish, intend; ~*nya* should; **kehendak** *n* will; **meng-hendaki** *v* to want

héngkang *v* to flee, leave

hening clear; quiet; ~ *cipta a* moment's silence

henti stop; **berhenti** *v* to stop, cease; **menghentikan** *v* to stop something; **memberhentikan** *v* to stop (a vehicle), to dismiss

hér resit a test or exam; *ujian* ~ make-up test or exam

héran *adj* astonished, amazed; **kehéranan** *n* astonishment; amazement; wonder; **menghérankan** *adj* astonishing, astounding

héwan *n* animal, beast; ~ *piaraan* pet

hias decorative; *ikan* ~ ornamental fish; **hiasan** *n* decoration; **menghiasi** *v* to adorn; to decorate something; **perhiasan** *n* jewellery

hibah *n* donation, bequest, gift; **menghibahkan** *v* to donate, bequeath

hibur: hiburan *n* entertainment; **menghibur** *v* to entertain; to comfort, console; **penghibur** *wanita* ~ escort, prostitute

hidang: hidangan *n* dish,

food served; **menghidangkan** *v* to serve up, offer

hidung *n* nose; ~ *mancung* straight nose; ~ *pesek* flat nose

hidup live; alive; lively; ~ *Indonesia!* Long live Indonesia!, *bunga* ~ cut flowers; *sepanjang* ~ lifelong; **kehidupan** *n* life, existence; **menghidupkan** *v* to bring to life; to start or turn on (a device); ~ *mesin* to turn on the engine

hijau, hijo, héjo *adj* green; ~ *toska* turquoise green; ~ *tua* dark green; *jalur* ~ nature strip, median strip

hijriah, H *tahun* ~ the Islamic calendar

hikmah *n* wisdom, insight, moral; *ada ~nya* there's some good of it

hilang disappear; lost, missing; *orang* ~ missing person; **kehilangan** *n* (feeling of) loss; *v* to lose something; **menghilang** *v* to disappear, vanish; **menghilangkan** *v* to remove

hilir, ilir downstream; ~ *mudik* back and forth, up and down

himpun: himpunan *n* association, gathering; **perhimpunan** *n* union, association, club

hina low, insulting; humble; **hinaan** *n* insult; **menghinakan** *v* to humiliate, insult; **penghinaan** *n* insult, libel (written), slander (spoken)

hindar: menghindar *v* to steer clear of, avoid; **menghindari** *v* to avoid something

Hindia *n* the Indies; ~ *Barat* the West Indies; ~ *Belanda* the Dutch East Indies

Hindu *agama* ~ Hinduism; *orang* ~ Hindu

hingga until; ~ *sekarang* up to now; **sehingga** *conj* to the point that, as far as, until, so that

hinggap *v* to land, perch (of a bird)

hirau: menghiraukan *v* to take heed, to listen to advice

hirup inhale; suck; *obat* ~ lozenge; **menghirup** *v* to breathe in

hitam *adj* black; ~ *manis* dark and pretty; ~ *putih* black and white; *daftar* ~ blacklist; *orang* ~ black person, Negro

hitung count; *ilmu* ~ arithmetic; **menghitung** *v* to count, calculate, reckon; **menghitungkan** *v* to count or calculate something; **perhitungan** *n* calculation; **terhitung** *adj* counted, included

Hj. *Hajjah* title for woman who has performed the major pilgrimage to Mecca

hobi *n* hobby

hoki *n* good luck or fortune

homo *m, sl (orang)* ~ homosexual, gay

honai *n* round hut in Papua (Irian Jaya)

Hongaria *n* Hungary; *bahasa* ~, *orang* ~ Hungarian

hong sui, féng sui *n* feng shui

honor, honorarium *n* fee (for a guest or part-time employee); **honorér** *adj* honorary

hordén, gordén *n* curtain(s)

horé *ejac* hooray!

horisontal *adj* horizontal; at one level; *konflik* ~

95

conflict within a group or level of society

hormat respect, honor; ~ *saya* yours faithfully; *memberi* ~ to salute, pay respect; **kehormatan** *n* respect; **menghormat, menghormati** *v* to honor or respect; **terhormat** *adj* respected; *yang* ~ to; dear

horoskop *n* horoscope

hotél *n* hotel; ~ *melati* cheap hotel; ~ *(ber)bintang lima* five-star hotel; **perhotélan** *n* hotel studies; hospitality

hubung: hubungan *n* link, connection, relationship; ~ *masyarakat (humas)* public relations (PR); **berhubung** *conj* in connection with, relating to; ~ *dengan* in connection with; **berhubungan** *v, pl* to have a link or connection; **menghubungi** *v* to contact someone; **menghubungkan** *v* to connect, join, link different parts; **penghubung** *n* switch, connector; *kata* ~ conjunction, connector; **perhubungan** *n*

communications, connection; ~ *udara* air route

hujan rain; ~ *batu*, ~ *es* hail; ~ *lebat* heavy rain, downpour; ~ *rintik-rintik* drizzle; *musim* ~ rainy season, monsoon; **kehujanan** *adj* caught in the rain

hujat: hujatan *n* insult, blasphemy; **menghujat** *v* to swear, blaspheme

hukum law; punish; ~ *fisika* laws of physics; ~ *perdata* civil code; ~ *pidana* criminal code; **hukuman** *n* punishment; ~ *mati* capital punishment, death penalty; ~ *penjara* imprisonment; **menghukum** *v* to punish, sentence, condemn

hulu *n* source, beginning; **penghulu** *n, Isl* local chief who performs marriage ceremonies

humas *n* PR, public relations ← **hubungan masyarakat**

huni: penghuni *n* occupant, resident

hunus: menghunus *v* to unsheathe, take out

huru ~*-hara* riot, uproar

huruf *n* letter, character;
~ *besar* capital letters,
upper case; ~ *bersambung*
cursive; ~ *cetak* block
letters, printing; ~ *hidup*
vowel; ~ *kecil* small letters,
lower case; ~ *mati* consonant; ~ *miring* italics
HUT *abbrev hari ulang
tahun* birthday, anniversary
hutan *n* forest, jungle,
wood; ~ *kota* urban forest;
~ *rimba* jungle; **kehutanan**
n forestry

I

ia *lit* he, she, it → **dia**
iba pity, compassion;
merasa ~ to feel sorry for
ibadah *n* worship, religious
devotion; **beribadah** *v* to
worship, serve
ibarat *conj* like, as, example
iblis *n* devil, Satan
Ibrani *bahasa* ~ Hebrew
ibu *n, pron, f* mother; ~
angkat adopted mother;
~ *bapak* parents; ~ *jari*

thumb; ~ *kos* concierge,
house-mother; ~ *kota*
capital (city); ~ *rumah
tangga* housewife, home-
maker; ~ *tiri* stepmother;
bahasa ~ mother tongue;
ibu-ibu *n, pl* ladies; *adj* of
an age to be a mother;
keibuan *adj* motherly
ICMI *abbrev Ikatan
Cendekiawan Muslim
se-Indonesia* Indonesian
Islamic Intellectuals
Association
idam: idaman *adj* dream,
ideal; *rumah* ~ dream
home; **mengidam** *v*
ngidam *coll* to crave (esp
of pregnant woman)
idap: mengidap *v* to
suffer from; **pengidap** *n*
sufferer
idé, ide *n* idea; ~ *gemilang*
great idea
idéntik *adj* identical, same;
~ *dengan* just like, the
same as
idéntitas *n* (proof of)
identity; *kartu* ~ ID card
IDI *abbrev Ikatan Dokter
Indonesia* Indonesian
Doctors' Association

idih *excl* yuck! (expressing disgust or revulsion)

idola *n* idol, star

Idul, Ied ul *Isl* ~ *Adha* Feast of the Sacrifice; ~ *Fitri* end of fasting celebrations

igau: mengigau *v* to talk in one's sleep, be delirious

ijab ~ *kabul Isl* marriage contract

ijazah *n* certificate, qualification; **berijazah** *adj* certified, qualified

ijin, izin permission; *minta* ~ ask permission; **mengijinkan** *v* to permit, allow

ikal *adj* curly

ikan *n* fish; ~ *air tawar* freshwater fish; ~ *asin* salty fish; ~ *emas* goldfish; ~ *hiu* shark; ~ *laut* saltwater fish; ~ *paus* whale; ~ *teri* anchovies, small fry; **perikanan** *n* fisheries

ikat tie, knot; weaving, ikat; ~ *pinggang* belt; **ikatan** *n* alliance, union; **mengikat** *v* to tie, fasten; **terikat** *adj* bound

iklan *n* advertisement

iklim *n* climate; **beriklim** *v* to have a climate; ~ *dingin* to have a cool climate

ikrar *n* promise, pledge, oath

ikut *v* join in, go along with; ~ *prihatin* feel concerned; ~ *serta* take part, participate; **keikutsertaan** *n* participation; **berikut** *adj* following; *yang* ~, ~*nya* the next; **mengikut** *v* to follow, accompany; **mengikuti** *v* to follow, join, participate in; ~ *kursus* to do a course; **pengikut** *n* participant; follower

ilir → **hilir**

ilmu *n* science, study; ~ *bumi* geography; ~ *filsafat* philosophy; ~ *fisika* physics; ~ *kimia* chemistry; ~ *pasti* the physical sciences, mathematics; ~ *sejarah* history

ilusi *n* illusion

imam *n, Isl, m* prayer leader in the mosque

iman *n* faith, belief; **beriman** *adj* religious

imbal: imbalan *n* compensation, reward, repayment

imbang balanced; **ber-imbang** *adj* balanced, proportional; **seimbang** *adj* balanced, well-proportioned; **keseimbangan** *n* balance

imél *n* email

imigrasi *n* immigration

imitasi *n* fake

Imlék *n (Tahun Baru)* ~ Chinese New Year

impi: impian *n* dream; **mengimpikan** *v* to dream of → **mimpi**

impor import; ~ *ekspor* import-export; **mengimpor** *v* to import; **pengimpor** *n* importer

inai *n* henna

inap stay the night; *rawat* ~ stay in hospital, be hospitalized; **menginap** *v* to stay the night, stay over; **penginapan** *n* accommodation, hotel

incar: mengincar *v* to set your sights on, target

inci *n* inch

indah *adj* beautiful; **keindahan** *n* beauty; **mengindahkan** *v* to take heed, pay attention to;

memperindah *v* to beautify

indekos → **kos**

indera, indra *n* sense; ~ *keenam* sixth sense; ~ *penglihatan* sense of sight

India *n* India; *orang* ~ Indian

Indian *orang* ~ Native American, (South) American Indian

Indo *orang* ~ person of mixed Western and Indonesian descent

Indonesia Indonesia; *Bahasa* ~, *orang* ~ Indonesian

induk mother (animal); ~ *ayam* mother hen; ~ *semang* house-mother, landlady; *kalimat* ~ main clause

indung mother, home; ~ *telur* ovary; *anak kucing dan* ~*nya* a kitten and its mother

industri *n* industry

inféksi *n* infection; **terinféksi** *adj* infected

inflasi *n* inflation

info, informasi *n* information, info

informatika *n* information technology (IT)

infus *n* (saline) drip; **diinfus** *v* to be put on a drip

ingat remember; *daya ~* memory; **ingatan** *n* memory; **mengingat** *v* to remember, bear in mind; **mengingatkan** *v* to remind someone about something; **memperingati** *v* to commemorate; **peringatan** *n* warning; commemoration, remembrance

Inggris Britain; England, English; *~ Raya* Great Britain; *bahasa ~* English; *orang ~* English; British

ingin *v* to wish, desire; **keinginan** *n* desire, wish; **menginginkan** *v* to wish for, desire

ingkar *v* to break (a vow etc); *~ janji* to break a promise

ingus *n* nasal mucus; **ingusan** *anak ~* toddler; still a child

ini *pron* this, these; **begini** *adv* like this

inisiatif, inisiatip *n* initiative, enterprise; **berinisiatif** *v* to take the initiative

injak *v* to tread, pedal; **menginjak** *v* to step, tread, or stamp on; *~ gas* to accelerate, step on the gas

injil *n* gospel, Bible; **penginjil** *n* preacher, evangelist

Inprés *n* Presidential Decree ← **Instruksi Présidén**

insaf, insyaf aware, conscious; realize

insan *n* human, person; **insani** *adj* human

insang *n* gill

insidén *n* incident

insinyur, Ir *n* engineer

inspéksi *n* inspection; **inspéktur** *n* inspector

instansi *n* agency, authority (esp state); *~ terkait* related agencies

instruksi *n* instruction; *~ Presiden (Inpres)* presidential decree

insya Allah *Isl* God willing

intai: mengintai *v* to spy on or watch, conduct surveillance

intan *n* diamond

intél *n* secret agent, spy; **intélijén** *n* secret intelligence

intélék n brains, intellect; **intéléktual** n intellectual → **cendekiawan**

interlokal adj long-distance (dialing); telepon ~ long-distance call

intérn adj internal

internasional adj international

intérnis n specialist (doctor)

interviu, interpiu n interview; **menginterviu** v to interview

inti n core, kernel, nucleus; ~nya basically; ~sari essence

intim adj intimate, close; hubungan ~ sexual relations

intip, mengintip v to peep at, spy on

intisari n essence, extract

IP abbrev indeks prestasi grade point average

IPA abbrev ilmu pengetahuan alam natural sciences

ipar in-law

IPB abbrev Institut Pertanian Bogor Bogor Agricultural University

IPS abbrev ilmu pengetahuan sosial social sciences

Ir insinyur title for holder of a degree in engineering or architecture

Irak n Iraq; orang ~ Iraqi

irama n rhythm; **berirama** adj rhythmical; with a rhythm

Iran n Iran; orang ~ Iranian

iri envy; ~ (hati) envious

Irian n (West) Papua, Irian; ~ Jaya Indonesian province between 1963 & 2000; orang ~ Papuan

irigasi n irrigation

iring: iring-iringan n parade, convoy; **mengiringi** v to accompany, escort; **pengiring** n escort, companion

iris slice thinly; **irisan** n slice; **mengiris** v to slice

irit economical; save money; **mengirit** v to economize

Irja n Irian Jaya, Papua ← **Irian Jaya**

Irlandia n Ireland; bahasa ~ Irish (Gaelic); orang ~ Irish

Isa n Jesus → **Yesus**

isak sob; **terisak(-isak)** adj sobbing

isap v to suck on; **isapan** ~ jempol lie, untruth;

mengisap v to suck;
~ *cerutu* to smoke a cigar
iseng for fun, not serious;
waste or kill time; ~ *aja*
just for fun
isi contents, volume, full;
berisi v to contain; *adj* full,
filled out, **mengisi** v to fill,
load; ~ *bensin* to fill up
with petrol; ~ *waktu* to fill
in time
Islam Islam; *agama* ~
Islam; *masuk* ~ to become
Muslim, convert to Islam;
orang ~ Muslim
isolasi n isolation, insulation;
adhesive tape; **terisolasi**
adj isolated
Isra Miraj n, *Isl* holiday
commemorating
Muhammad's ascent to
Heaven
Israél Israel; *orang* ~
Israeli
istana n palace; ~ *presiden*
presidential palace
isteri, istri n wife; ~ *kedua*
second wife; ~ *muda* new
or second wife; **beristeri,
beristri** *adj, m* married;
pria ~ married man
istilah n term, word; ~*nya* in

other words, you could say
istiméwa *adj* special;
keistiméwaan n special
quality; **mengistiméwa-
kan** v to treat as special
istirahat rest, recreation,
break; **beristirahat** v to
rest, take a break
istri, isteri n wife; ~ *kedua*
second wife; ~ *muda* new
or second wife; **beristeri,
beristri** *adj, m* married;
pria ~ married man
isu n issue, controversy
isya night prayer (during
the hours of darkness)
isyarat n signal, sign,
gesture; *bahasa* ~ sign
language; *memberi* ~ to
give a signal
Itali, Italia n Italy; *bahasa* ~,
orang ~ Italian
ITB *abbrev Institut Teknologi Bandung* Bandung
Institute of Technology
itik n duck
itu *pron* that, those; ~ *dia!*
that's the problem!; **begitu**
adv like that
iuran n contribution, regular
payment; ~ *keanggotaan*
membership fee

iya *coll* yes; ~ *ya* it is, isn't it?

izin, ijin permission; *minta* ~ to ask permission; **mengizinkan** *v* to permit, allow

J

Jabar *n* West Java ← **Jawa Barat**

jabat: jabatan *n* position, work; **berjabat(an)** ~ *tangan* to shake hands; **menjabat** *v* to hold; to work as; **pejabat** *n* (government) official

Jabotabék *n* Greater Jakarta ← **Jakarta Bogor Tangerang Bekasi**

jadi *v* to become, happen; *conj* so; ~ *orang* to succeed, make something of yourself; ~ *tidak?* Is it going ahead or not?; *tidak* ~ it didn't happen, it fell through; **kejadian** *n* event, happening; creation; **menjadi** *v* to be or become; **menjadikan** *v* to create, make; **terjadi** *v* to happen, become

jadwal *n* timetable, schedule; **menjadwalkan** *v* to timetable

jaga guard, nightwatchman; **menjaga** *v* to guard, keep watch; ~ *anak* to look after children, babysit

jagad, jagat *n* world; ~ *raya* universe, cosmos

jagal *tukang* ~ butcher; **pejagalan** *n* abattoir

jago *n* champion; cock, rooster; *si* ~ *merah* fire; **menjagokan** *v* to support

jagung *n* corn, maize; ~ *bakar* roasted sweet corn

jahat *adj* bad, wicked, evil; **kejahatan** *n* crime; **penjahat** *n* criminal

jahé *n* ginger

jahil, jail *adj* mischievous, naughty

jahit *v* to sew; *tukang* ~ tailor; **jahitan** *n* stitches; sewing; **menjahit** *v* to sew

jail → **jahil**

jaipong *tari* ~ modern Sundanese dance

jaja: menjajakan *v* to hawk, peddle; **penjaja** *n* hawker, pedlar

jajah: jajahan *n* colony, territory; **menjajah** *v* to colonize, rule another country; **penjajah** *n* colonizer, ruler, colonial power; **penjajahan** *n* colonization

jajan buy cheap goods, *uang* ~ pocket money; **jajanan** *n* cheap snacks

jajar: sejajar *adj* parallel

jaksa *n* judge; ~ *Agung* Attorney-General; **kejaksaan** *n* district attorney's office

jakun *n* Adam's apple

jala *n* fishing net; *roti* ~ kind of Malay pancake

jalak *n* starling, mynah

jalan street, road, way; walk; operate, go; ~ *besar* main road; ~ *keluar* exit, way out; ~ *masuk* entrance; ~ *raya* highway; ~ *tikus* back street; *rawat* ~ outpatient; **jalan-jalan** *v* to go for a walk; to go out (for fun); **jalanan** *n* streets, on the road; **berjalan** *v* to walk, move; ~ *dengan baik* to go well; **menjalani** *v* to undergo, do; **menjalankan**

v to operate, run, set in motion; **perjalanan** *n* journey, trip; *agen* ~ travel agency

jalang *adj* wild, untamed

jalar *adj* creeping; *ubi* ~ sweet potato

jalin, jalinan *n* net, network; **menjalin** *v* to forge links, network

jalur lane, track; ~ *khusus* fast track; ~ *lambat* slow lane; ~ *sepeda* bicycle lane

jam *n* hour; clock; ~ *berapa?* what time is it?; ~ *besuk* visiting hours; ~ *buka* opening hours; ~ *dinding* (wall) clock; ~ *karet* rubber time, lack of punctuality; ~ *lima* five o'clock; ~ *malam* curfew; ~ *praktek* consulting hours; ~ *tangan* (wrist)watch; **berjam-jam** *adj* for hours and hours

jamak *adj* plural, more than one; *bentuk* ~ plural form

jaman, zaman *n* age, era, time, period; ~ *dahulu,* ~ *dulu* in the old days, times past; ~ *Belanda* the Dutch era; ~ *purbakala* prehistoric times; ~ *saya* in my day; *ketinggalan* ~ outdated

jamblang *nasi* ~ rice dish, specialty of the Cirebon area

jambrét snatch; **menjambrét** *v* to snatch

jambu *n (buah)* ~ guava, rose-apple; kind of fruit; ~ *air* rose apple; ·· *batu*, ~ *biji* guava

jamin, menjamin *v* to guarantee, promise; **jaminan** *n* guarantee; *surat* ~ letter of guarantee; **terjamin** *adj* guaranteed

jamrud, zamrud *n* emerald

Jamsosték *n* state social security system ←
Jaminan Sosial Tenaga Kerja

jamu *n* traditional herbal medicine; ~ *kuat* aphrodisiac; tonic

jamu: perjamuan *n* feast, party; entertainment

jamur *n* mushroom, mold, fungus; ~ *kaki* athlete's foot; **berjamur** *adj* moldy; **berjamuran** *v* to pop up everywhere

janda *n* widow; ~ *cerai* divorced woman, divorcée; **menjanda** *v* to be widowed, live as a widow

jangan *neg* don't, do not; ~ *begitu* don't do (or say) that; **jangan-jangan** *adv*, *neg* or else, otherwise, maybe even

janggal *adj* odd, strange; **kejanggalan** *n* oddity, anomaly

janggut, jénggot *n* beard, goatee; **berjénggot** *adj* bearded

jangka *n* distance, term; ~ *pendek* short term; **berjangka** *adj* for a term

jangkar *n* anchor

jangkit: menjangkiti *v* to infect; **terjangkit** *adj* infected

jangkrik, jéngkerik *n* cicada, cricket

janin *n* fetus, embryo

janji promise; **janjian** *v, sl* to make a date, promise; **berjanji** *v* to promise; **menjanjikan** *v* to promise something; **perjanjian** *n* agreement, contract

jantan male (animal), manly

jantung *n* heart, core; ~ *kota* city center, heart of the city; *serangan* ~ heart attack

Januari *bulan* ~ January

janur *n* decoration woven from coconut leaves, used at weddings; ~ *kuning* wedding decoration

jarah: menjarah *v* to loot; **penjarah** *n* looter; **penjarahan** *n* looting

jarak *n* distance, space

jarang *adj, adv* seldom, rare, rarely, hardly ever

jari *n* finger; ~ *kaki* toe; ~ *kelingking* little or baby finger; ~ *manis* ring finger; ~ *telunjuk* forefinger, index finger; ~ *tengah* middle finger; **jari-jari** *n, pl* spokes

jaring net, shoal; **jaringan** *n* network; **menjaring** *v* to fish with a net; to filter or sift

jarum *n* needle; hand; ~ *jam* hand (of a clock or watch); *arah* ~ *jam* clockwise; ~ *suntik* (injection) needle

jas *n* coat; ~ *hujan* raincoat

jasa *n* service, merit; ~ *boga* catering service; **berjasa** *adj* meritorious, deserving of reward; *v* to perform a service

jatah *n* ration, serve

Jateng *n* Central Java ← **Jawa Tengah**

jati ~ *diri* identity; **sejati** *adj* genuine, original, real

Jatim *n* East Java ← **Jawa Timur**

jatuh fall; ~ *cinta,* ~ *hati* fall in love; ~ *sakit* fall ill; *bintang* ~ shooting star; **kejatuhan** *n* fall; *adj* be struck by something falling; **menjatuhkan** *v* to fell, let drop; **terjatuh** *adj* (accidentally) fallen

jauh *adj* far; *jarak* ~ long-distance; ~~ *hari* well in advance; **kejauhan** *adj* too far; **menjauhi** *v* to avoid; **sejauh** *conj* how far; ~ *mana* to what point

Jawa *n*; ~ *Barat (Jabar)* West Java; *bahasa* ~, *orang* ~ Javanese; *pulau* ~ Java

jawab answer, reply; **jawaban** *n* answer, reply, response; **menjawab** *v* to answer, reply; **terjawab** *adj* answered

jawi *tulisan* ~ Malay writing in Arabic script

jebak: jebakan *n* trap; **menjebak** *v* to trap; **terjebak** *adj* trapped, caught; ~ *macet* caught in traffic

jeblos to push or stick through

jebol to collapse, fall apart, break through; **jebolan** *n* graduate

jeda *n* pause, break, ceasefire

jejak *n* footprint, track; ~ *langkah* footprint; **menjejaki** *v* to step on, trail, trace

jejaka *n* bachelor, young single man

jéjér row, line; **berjéjér, berjéjéran** (stand) in a row, in a line; **menjéjérkan** *v* to place in rows

jelajah: menjelajahi *v* to travel through or explore a place

jelang: menjelang *v* to approach (usu time)

jelas *adj* clear, obvious; **menjelaskan** *v* to explain, clarify; **penjelasan** *n* explanation

jelék *adj* bad, ugly; ~*nya* the bad side is; **menjelékkan** *v*

to criticize, say bad things about

jelita *adj, f* beautiful, charming

jelma: menjelma *v* to be incarnated, turn into, materialize

jemaah, jemaat *n* congregation, followers of a religion; **berjamaah** *v, Isl* to pray together, as a congregation

jemari *n* finger; *jari* ~ fingers → **jari**

jembatan *n* bridge; ~ *besi* iron bridge; ~ *gantung* suspension bridge

jempol *n* thumb

jemput pick up; **jemputan** *n* vehicle which picks you up; **menjemput** *v* to pick up

jemu *adj* sick or tired of, bored

jemur dry (in the sun); **jemuran** *n* clothes or food drying in the sun; **berjemur** *v* to sunbathe, sun yourself; **menjemur** *v* to air, dry in the sun; ~ *baju cucian* to hang out the washing

jenak: sejenak *adv* briefly, a moment

jenaka *adj* funny, amusing, cute

jenazah *n* dead body, corpse

jendéla *n* window

jénder *n* gender; *soal ~* gender issue

jénderal *n* general; *~ bintang empat* four-star general; *Brigadir-~ (Brigjen)* Brigadier-General; *~ (Polisi)* Police General

jénggot, janggut *n* beard; *kebakaran ~* lose your head, unable to cope; **berjénggot** *adj* bearded

jéngkél *adj* annoyed; **menjéngkélkan** *adj* annoying

jéngkol *n* pungent vegetable

jenis *n* kind, sort, type; species; *~ kelamin* sex, gender; *lawan ~* opposite sex; **sejenis** *adj* same type or species

jentik *~ nyamuk* mosquito larvae

jenuh *adj* fed up, bored; saturated; *lemak ~* saturated fats

Jepang *n* Japan; *bahasa ~, orang ~* Japanese

jepit *n* tweezers; **jepitan** *n* clip; tweezers; *~ rambut*

hair clip; **menjepit** *v* to pinch, squeeze; **terjepit** *adj* pinched, caught in an uncomfortable situation

jeprét: *jeprétan,* **penjeprét** *n* stapler; **menjeprét** *v* to snap, staple; *~ foto* to take a photo

jerami *n* straw

jerapah *n* giraffe

jerat snare, trap, noose; **menjerat** *v* to snare, trap; **terjerat** *adj* snared, trapped, caught

jerawat *n* pimple; **jerawatan** *adj* pimply

jerit scream, shriek; **jeritan** *n* scream, shriek; **menjerit** *v* to scream, shriek

Jerman *n* Germany; *bahasa ~, orang ~* German

jernih *adj* clear, transparent, pure; *air ~* clear water

jero: jeroan *n* innards

jeruji *n* trellis, iron bars

jeruk *buah ~* orange, mandarin; *~ limau* lime; *~ nipis* lemon; *rasa ~* orange(-flavored)

jerumus: terjerumus *adj* plunged into

jéwér: menjéwér *v* to pinch someone's ear, scold

jihad *n, Isl* crusade, holy war

jijik *adj* disgusting, revolting, filthy; *rasa* ~ disgust; **menjijikkan** *adj* disgusting, revolting, foul

jika, jikalau *conj* if, should

jilat lick; **menjilat** *v* to lick; *sl* to suck up, flatter

jilbab *n, Isl* (full) veil; **berjilbab** *v* to wear the veil

jilid *n* volume; **berjilid** *adj* in volumes; **menjilid** *v* to bind; **penjilidan** *n* binding (process)

jimat *n* lucky charm, talisman

jin *n* spirit; *dunia* ~ spirit world

jinak *adj* tame, domesticated, friendly

jingga *adj* orange (color)

jinjing *tas* ~ carrybag; **menjinjing** *v* to carry by hand

jinjit: berjinjit-jinjit *v* walk on tiptoe

jintan *n* cumin

jip *mobil* ~ jeep

jiplak: menjiplak *v* to copy, plagiarize

jitu *adj* exact, accurate; *penembak* ~ sniper

jiwa *n* life, soul; ~ *raga* body and soul; *ilmu* ~ psychology; **kejiwaan** *adj* mental

Jl(n) *Jalan* street, road

jodoh *n* life partner, match; *m* Mr Right; **menjodohkan** *v* to set up, match

jogét, jogéd (spontaneous) dance; **berjogét** *v* to dance

jok *n* seat (in vehicle); ~ *belakang* back seat

joki *n* jockey; paid passenger (to avoid traffic restrictions)

joli *sejoli dua* ~ a couple

jompo *adj* elderly; *rumah* ~ old persons' home, senior citizens' home

jongkok, berjongkok *v* to squat

joran *n* fishing rod

jorok *adj* obscene, disgusting; sloppy; *cerita* ~ dirty story

jorok: menjorok *v* to stick out, protrude

jotos fist; *adu* ~ fistfight

jua only; also, too

jual *v* to sell; ~ *beli* business, buying and selling; **jualan** *v* to sell informally; **menjual** *v* to sell; **penjual** *n* seller, dealer; **penjualan** *n* sale, sales; **terjual** adj sold; habis ~ sold out

juang: berjuang v to fight, struggle; **memperjuangkan** v to fight for; **perjuangan** n battle, fight, struggle

juara n champion; ~ satu firat plaoe; **kojuaraan** n championship; **menjuarai** v to win (a competition)

jubah n gown, robe

judes adj mean, cruel, bitchy

judi v to gamble; main ~ to gamble; **berjudi** v to gamble; **penjudi** n gambler; **perjudian** n gambling

judul n title; **berjudul** adj titled

juga too, also

jujur adj honest; **kejujuran** n honesty

Juli bulan ~ July

juling adj cross-eyed; mata ~ squint

Jumat, Jum'at hari ~ Friday; ~ Agung Good Friday; sholat ~ Friday prayers

jumlah n amount, total, sum, number; ~ korban total casualties; **berjumlah** v to number; **menjumlahkan** v to add (up)

jumpa meet; ~ pers press conference; **berjumpa** v to meet

Juni bulan ~ June

junior, yunior n junior; student in a younger year level; co-worker of a lower rank

juntai: menjuntai v to dangle

juragan n boss, master

jurang n ravine, gorge

jurnal n journal; **jurnalis** n journalist, reporter → **wartawan**

juru expert, skilled; ~ bahasa interpreter; ~ bicara spokesperson; ~ masak cook; ~ mudi helmsman; ~ rawat nurse; ~ tulis clerk; **kejuruan** adj technical

juru: penjuru n corner

jurus: jurusan n direction; major (at university)

jus n juice; ~ alpukat avocado juice

justru adv precisely, exactly

juta n million; sepuluh ~ ten million; **jutaan** adj millions; **berjuta** v to have millions of; **jutawan** n millionaire

K

K. *kali* creek, stream, river

KA *abbrev kereta api* train

Ka *Kepala* head of section

Kab. *Kabupaten* regency

kabar *n* news; ~ *angin*, ~ *burung* rumor; ~ *baik* good news; I'm well; ~*nya* people say; **mengabari** *v* to tell or inform someone; **mengabarkan** *v* to announce, report

kabel *n* cable

kabin *n* cabin (of a ship or aeroplane); *bagasi* ~ cabin luggage

kabinét *n* cabinet

kabul: mengabulkan *v* to grant, approve, consent to; **terkabul** *adj* granted

kabung: berkabung *v* to mourn; **perkabungan** *n* mourning

kabupatén *n* regency

kabur *adj* blurry, hazy

kabur *v* to disappear, vanish

kabut *n* fog, mist

kaca *n* glass; ~ *mata* glasses, spectacles; ~ *mata hitam* sunglasses, dark glasses; ~ *pembesar*

magnifying glass; ~ *spion* rear-view mirror; *tukang* ~ glazier

kacang *n* bean, legume; ~ *kapri* snow pea; ~ *kedelai* soybean, soya bean; ~ *mede* cashew (nut); ~ *merah* kidney bean; ~ *panjang* kind of long bean; ~ *polong* (green) pea; ~ *tanah* peanut

kacau *adj* disordered, confused, chaotic; **mengacaukan** *v* to mix or mess up

kadal *n* lizard

kadaluwarsa, kedaluwarsa *adj* expired; *tanggal* ~ expiry date, use-by date (food) ← **daluwarsa**

kadang, kadang-kadang, terkadang *adv* sometimes, occasionally

kadar *n* level, degree; **sekadar** *adj* just; ~*nya* as necessary

kafé *n* café, bar, pub, nightspot

kaféin *n* caffeine

kafir *n, Isl* infidel, pagan

kagét *n* startled, surprised; *pasar* ~ temporary street

111

market; *rasa* ~ surprise;
mengagétkan *v* to surprise,
startle

kagum *adj* admiring;
mengagumi *v* to admire;
pengagum *n* admirer

-kah (suffix to make a question) *bisa*~? Can?, *tidak* ~
Isn't?

kaidah *n* law, rule; ~ *fisika*
laws of physics

kail *n* fishing rod

kailan *n* Chinese broccoli,
kailan

kain *n* cloth; ~ *kafan*
shroud; ~ *kebaya* national
dress for women

kais, mengais *v* to scratch;
~ *rejeki* to scratch a living

kaisar *n, pron* emperor;
kekaisaran *n* empire

kait hook; **kaitan** *n* relationship, link; *tidak ada* ~*nya*
unrelated; **berkaitan** *adj*
related to; **mengaitkan** *v* to
link, connect, join; **pengait**
n catch ← **gaét, gait**

kaji: kajian *n* studies; **mengkaji** *v* to study, investigate

kaji: mengaji, ngaji *v* to recite
or read the Koran; **pengaji-
an** *n* Koranic recitation

kak *pron* term for older
sibling or slightly older
person; **kakak** *n pron* elder
brother or sister; ~ *laki-laki*
elder brother

kakap *ikan* ~ large fish

kakas: perkakas *n* tool,
implement

kakatua *n burung* ~
cockatoo

kakék *n, pron* grandfather;
old man

kaki *n* foot, leg; ~ *langit*
horizon; ~ *tangan*
henchman, stooge

kaku *adj* stiff, frozen

kakus *n* toilet, outhouse

kala *n* time; *conj* when; *ada*
~*nya* sometimes; **berkala**
adj regular; *secara* ~
periodically

kalah lose, be defeated;
~ *cepat* miss out, too slow;
kekalahan *n* defeat, loss;
mengalahkan *v* to
conquer, defeat

kalajengking *n* scorpion

kalang: kalangan *n* circle,
group

kalau *conj* if; **kalau-kalau**
conj in case; **kalaupun**
conj even if

Kalbar *n* West Kalimantan
← **Kalimantan Barat**

kalbu *n* heart

kaldu *n* broth; ~ *sapi* beef stew

kalem *adj* calm, steady

kaléndar, kalénder *n* calendar ~ *Masehi* Christian calendar

kaléng *n* tin, can; *ikan* ~ tinned fish; *surat* ~ anonymous letter

kali time, times; *satu* ~, *se*~ once; *dua* ~ twice; *enam* ~ six times; **berkali-kali** *adv* repeatedly, again and again; **sekali** *adv* once; very; *besar* ~ very large; **sekali-sekali, sesekali** *adv* every now and then, occasionally; **sekali-kali** *jangan* ~ never (do this); **sekalian** *adv* all together, all at once; *adv,* *coll* at the same time; **sekaligus** *adv* all at once; **seka-lipun** *conj* even though

kali *n* creek, stream, river; ~ *Brantas* the River Brantas

kali *coll* maybe, perhaps ← **barangkali**

kalian *pron, pl* you; *anda* *se*~ all of you

Kalimantan *n* Kalimantan, Borneo; ~ *Timur (Kaltim)* East Kalimantan; ~ *Utara* Malaysian Borneo, North Borneo

kalimat *n* sentence

kalkun *n* turkey

Kalsél *n* South Kalimantan
← **Kalimantan Selatan**

Kalteng *n* Central Kalimantan ← **Kalimantan Tengah**

Kaltim *n* East Kalimantan
← **Kalimantan Timur**

kalung *n* necklace

kamar *n* room; *sl* bedroom; ~ *belajar* study; ~ *dagang* chamber of commerce; ~ *kecil* toilet, lavatory; ~ *makan* dining room; ~ *mandi* bathroom; ~ *pas* fitting room; ~ *tamu* room for receiving guests, front room; ~ *tidur* bedroom

kambing *n* goat, sheep; *daging* ~ goat; mutton, lamb

kamboja *bunga* ~ frangi-pani

Kamboja *n* Cambodia; *bahasa* ~ Khmer; *orang* ~ Cambodian

113

kaméra *n* camera

kami *pron excl* we, us, our; (very polite) I

Kamis *hari ~* Thursday

kampanye *n* campaign; **berkampanye** *v* to (hold a) campaign; to join a parade for a candidate

kampung, kampong *n* village, hometown; *~ halaman* hometown; *~ Melayu* Malay quarter; *pulang ~* to go home to the village; **kampungan** *adj* uneducated, backward, provincial

kampus *n* university, campus

kamu *pron sing* you (to children and familiars); *~ punya* yours

kamus *n* dictionary; *~ dwibahasa* bilingual dictionary; *~ saku* pocket dictionary

kan, 'kan you know; isn't it? ← **bukan**

Kanada *n* Canada; *orang ~* Canadian

kanan *adj* right; *~ kapal* starboard; *ke ~* to the right; *tangan ~* right hand

kancil *n* mouse-deer; smart car used as a taxi ← **kendaraan angkutan niaga cilik irit dan lincah**

kancing *n* button, stud; *~ pencet* press-stud; *lubang ~* buttonhole; **mengancing** *v* to button

kandang *n* stable, pen; *~ anjing* kennel, doghouse; *~ ayam* chicken coop; *~ kuda* stable

kandas *adj* stranded, aground; *v* to fail

kandung *n* uterus; bladder; *~ empedu* gall bladder; *~ kemih* bladder; **kandung-an** *n* fetus, unborn child; contents; **mengandung** *v* to contain, carry; to be pregnant

kangen *adj* long for, miss; *rasa ~* longing

kangguru, kanguru *n* kangaroo

kangkung *n* water spinach

kanibal *n* cannibal

kanker *n* cancer; *~ darah* leukaemia; *~ payudara* breast cancer

kano *n* canoe

kantin *n* canteen

kantong, kantung *n* pocket, pouch; **berkantong** *v* to have a pocket

kantor *n* office; ~ *cabang*, ~ *perwakilan* branch office; ~ *pos* post office; ~ *pusat* head office; *pergi ke* ~ go to work; **perkantoran** *n* office block

kantuk: mengantuk, ngantuk *adj* sleepy

kantung → kantong

kanwil *n* regional office ← kantor wilayah

kaos → kaus

kapak *n* ax

kapal *n* ship, vessel; ~ *api*, ~ *uap* steamer; ~ *induk* aircraft carrier; ~ *penumpang* passenger ship; ~ *perang* warship; ~ *selam* submarine; ~ *tempur* fighter; ~ *terbang* aeroplane, airplane; *awak* ~ crew; **perkapalan** *n* shipping

kapan *interrog* when; ~ *saja* whenever, any time; **kapan-kapan** *adv* one day, some time in the future

kapas *n* cotton, cotton wool

kapasitas *n* capacity;

berkapasitas *v* with a capacity of

kapitalis capitalist; **kapitalisme** *n* capitalism

kapling, kavling, kaveling, kav *n* block (in addresses)

Kapolda *n* Regional Chief of Police ← Kepala Polisi Daérah

Kapolrés *n* Local Chief of Police ← Kepala Polisi Résort

Kapolri *n* National Chief of Police ← Kepala Polisi Republik Indonésia

Kapolsék *n* Section Chief of Police ← Kepala Polisi Séktor

kapsul *n* capsule

kapuk, kapok *n* kapok

kapulaga *n* cardamom

kapur *n* lime(stone), chalk

karam *adj* shipwrecked; *v* to sink

karamba *n* large basket for catching fish

karambola, karambol *n* children's game

karamél *n* caramel pudding; *rasa* ~ caramel-flavored

karang *n* coral reef; *batu* ~ coral reef

karang: karangan *n* essay;
~ *bunga* bouquet; **mengarang** *v* to write, compose;
lomba ~ essay competition; **pengarang** *n* author,
writer, composer

karantina *n* quarantine

karapan ~ *sapi* Madurese
bull races

karat *n* rust; **karatan,
berkarat** *adj* rusty

karat *n* carat; *emas delapan
belas* ~ eighteen-carat gold

karbol *n* carbolic acid, floor
cleaner

karburétor, karburator *n*
carburettor

karcis *n* ticket (of small
value); ~ *bis* bus ticket;
~ *masuk* entrance ticket;
~ *kereta api* local train
ticket; *loket* ~ ticket office

kardus *n* cardboard (box)

karé → **kari**

karédok *n* Sundanese fresh
salad with peanut sauce

karena *conj* because, since

karét *n* rubber; rubber
band; ~ *gelang* rubber
band; *kebun* ~ rubber
plantation; *permen* ~
chewing gum

kari, karé *n* curry; ~ *ayam*
chicken curry

karikatur *n* caricature

karpét *n* carpet

karton *n* cardboard

kartu *n* card; ~ *merah* red
card (in soccer); (in game)
nama name card; ~ *pos* postcard;
~ *pelajar* student card; ~
remi playing cards; ~ *truf*
trump card, trumps; *main* ~
play cards

kartun *n* cartoon, anime;
kartunis *n* cartoonist

karuan, keruan *tidak* ~
very badly, in chaos

karung *n* sack

karunia: mengaruniai *v* to
bless

karya *n* works; **karyawan** *n*
(salaried) employee;
karyawati *n, f* (salaried)
employee

kasa *kain* ~ gauze, muslin

Kasad *n* Army Chief of
Staff ← **Kepala Staf
Angkatan Darat**

kasar *adj* rough, rude,
vulgar; **kekasaran** *n*
coarseness, roughness

kasatmata *adj* clear, with
the naked eye

kasét *n* cassette

kasih, kasi *v, coll* give;
~ *lihat* show; ~ *pinjam*
lend; ~ *tahu* inform, tell;
mengasih *v* to give

kasih *n* affection, love;
~ *ibu* mother's love;
sayang love; **kasihan** pity,
feel sorry for; ~ *dia* poor
thing!; **kekasih** *n* darling,
sweetheart, beloved

kasir, kassa *n* cashier

kasmaran *adj* in love,
smitten ← **asmara**

kasta *n* caste

kasuari *burung* ~ cassowary

kasur *n* mattress

kasus *n* case

kata *n* word; ~ *benda* noun;
~ *kerja* verb; ~*nya*, ~ *orang*
people say; ~ *pengantar*
preface; ~ *sifat* adjective;
lawan ~ antonym; *dengan*
~ *lain* in other words;
berkata *v* to say, speak;
mengatakan *v* to say

katak *n* frog, toad

katalog *n* catalog

katédral *n* cathedral

Katolik Catholic; *agama* ~
Catholicism; *orang* ~
Catholic

katrol *n* pulley

katulistiwa, khatulistiwa *n*
the Equator

katun *n* cotton

katup *n* valve

kau *pron, s* you (to equals
or inferiors) ← **engkau**

kaum *n* people, community;
~ *intelektual* intellectuals;
~ *kolot* conservatives; ~
wanita women

kaus, kaos *n* stocking,
sock; garment; ~ *kaki*
sock; stocking; ~ *oblong*
T-shirt; ~ *tangan* glove,
mitten

kav, kavling, kaveling →
kapling

kawah *n* crater

kawal guard; **kawalan** *n*
escort, guard; **mengawal** *v*
to guard, escort; **pengawal**
n (body)guard, sentry

kawan *n* friend; ~ *baik*
good friend; **kesetia-
kawanan** *n* loyalty;
kawanan *n* flock, swarm;
berkawan *v* to have or be
friends with; **sekawan** *tiga*
~ a trio (of friends)

kawas: kawasan *n* area,
region

kawat *n* wire; ~ *berduri* barbed wire; ~ *listrik* electrical wire

kawi *bahasa* ~ Old Javanese

kawin *v* marry, mate; ~ *lari* elope; ~ *muda* marry young, ~ *silang* cross-breed; ~ *siri* marry in secret; *musim* ~ on heat; **kawinan** *n, coll* wedding ceremony or reception; **mengawinkan** ~ *anak* to marry off a son or daughter; **perkawinan** *n* marriage, wedding; ~ *campuran* mixed marriage

kawula ~ *muda* youth, young people

kaya *adj* rich; ~ *raya* very rich; *orang* ~ *baru* new money, nouveau riche; **kekayaan** *n* wealth, riches

kayak, kaya *conj, coll* like, as; **kayaknya** it seems, apparently

kayu *n* wood; ~ *bakar* firewood; ~ *cendana* sandalwood; ~ *jati* teak; ~ *manis* cinnamon; ~ *meranti* kind of reddish wood, morantee

kayuh: mengayuh *v* to paddle or pedal something; ~ *sepeda* to ride a bicycle

KB *abbrev kelompok bermain* playgroup

KB *abbrev Keluarga Berencana* Family Planning

KBRI *abbrev Kedutaan Besar Republik Indonesia* Embassy of the Republic of Indonesia

ke *prep* to, towards; ~ *atas* up, upwards; ~ *dalam* into; ~ *luar* out; ~ *muka* to the front; ~ *samping* to the side; ~ *tengah* to the middle

keadaan *n* situation, condition; ~ *darurat* emergency situation ← **ada**

keadilan *n* justice ← **adil**

keagamaan *adj* religious affairs ← **agama**

keahlian *n* expertise ← **ahli**

keajaiban *n* wonder, miracle ← **ajaib**

keakraban *n* closeness, intimacy ← **akrab**

keamanan *n* safety, security ← **aman**

keanéhan *n* peculiarity, oddity ← **anéh**

keanggotaan *n* membership; *kartu* ~ membership card ← **anggota**

kearsipan archives, archival ← **arsip**

kebahagiaan *n* happiness ← **bahagia**

kebaikan *n* goodness, kindness ← **baik**

kebakaran *n* fire; ~ *hutan* forest fire, bushfire; *ada* ~! fire! ← **bakar**

kebaktian *n* (Protestant) service ← **bakti**

kebal *adj* resistant, immune; **kekebalan** *n* immunity

kebanggaan *n* pride; something of which you are proud ← **bangga**

kebangkitan *n* rise, awakening ← **bangkit**

kebangkrutan *n* bankruptcy ← **bangkrut**

kebangsaan *adj* national ← **bangsa**

kebanyakan *n, adj* too much; most ← **banyak**

kebatinan *n* mysticism ← **batin**

kebaya *n, f* women's blouse worn as national costume

kebébasan *n* freedom ← **bébas**

kebenaran *n* truth ← **benar**

kebencian *n* hatred ← **benci**

keberadaan *n* presence ← **ada**

keberangkatan *n* departure; *pintu* ~ departure gate ← **angkat, berangkat**

keberanian *n* bravery, courage ← **berani**

keberatan *n* objection; *v* to object ← **berat**

keberhasilan *n* success ← **hasil**

kebersihan *n* cleanliness, hygiene ← **bersih**

kebesaran *n* greatness; *adj* too big ← **besar**

kebetulan *adv* by chance, accidentally; *n* coincidence ← **betul**

kebiasaan *n* habit, custom ← **biasa**

kebidanan *n* midwifery ← **bidan**

kebijakan *n* policy ← **bijak**

kebijaksanaan *n* caution, prudence; policy ← **bijaksana**

kebingungan *n* confusion ← **bingung**

kebiri: mengebiri *v* to castrate, neuter

kebisingan *n* noise, buzz ← **bising**

kebocoran *n* leak ← **bocor**

kebodohan *n* stupidity, ignorance ← **bodoh**

kebotakan *n* baldness, hair loss ← **botak**

kebudayaan *n* culture, civilization ← **budaya**

kebugaran *n* health; *pusat* ~ gym, fitness center ← **bugar**

kebuli *nasi* ~ lamb and rice dish of Middle Eastern origin

kebun, kebon *n* garden, plantation; ~ *binatang* zoo; ~ *kopi* coffee plantation; ~ *raya* botanical garden; *tukang* ~ gardener; **berkebun** *v* to garden, do gardening; **perkebunan** *n* plantation, estate; ~ *teh* tea plantation

keburu *adj, adv, coll* in time; too early; ~ *habis* already run out ← **buru**

kebut: mengebut *v* to speed

kebutuhan *n* need, necessity ← **butuh**

kecam; mengecam *v* to criticize; **kecaman** *n* criticism

kecamatan *n* sub-district ← **camat**

kecanduan *n* addiction, addicted to; ~ *obat* drug addiction ← **candu**

kecanggihan *n* sophistication ← **canggih**

kecantikan *n* beauty ← **cantik**

kécap *n* soy sauce; ~ *asin* soy sauce; ~ *manis* sweet soy sauce

kecapékan *adj* tired out; *n* exhaustion ← **capék**

kecapi *n* Sundanese zither

kecelakaan *n* accident, disaster ← **celaka**

kecemasan *n* anxiety, concern ← **cemas**

kecemburuan *n* jealousy ← **cemburu**

kecenderungan *n* tendency, trend ← **cenderung**

kecepatan *n* speed ← **cepat**

kecerdasan *n* intelligence ← **cerdas**

kecermatan *n* precision, accuracy ← **cermat**

kecéwa *adj* disappointed; **kekecéwaan** *n* disappointment; **mengecéwakan** *v* to disappoint; *adj* disappointing

kecil *adj* small, little; young; ~ *hati* disappointed, offended; *orang* ~ the little people, the poor; *dari* ~, *sejak* ~ since youth; **berkecil** ~ *hati* to be disappointed; **kekecilan** *adj* too small; **mengecilkan** *v* to make smaller, decrease

kecipratan *adj* be splashed, sprayed accidentally ← **ciprat**

kecocokan *n* suitability, compatibility ← **cocok**

kecolongan *adj* to be robbed; to lose unjustly ← **colong**

kecopétan *adj* to be pickpocketed, robbed; *n* pickpocketing ← **copét**

kecuali *conj* except; **kekecualian, pengecualian** *n* exception; **terkecuali** *tidak* ~, *tanpa* ~ without exception

kecubung *batu* ~ ruby

kecurangan *n* cheating, dishonesty ← **curang**

kecurigaan *n* suspicion ← **curiga**

kecut *adj* sour, acidic

kecut *adj* shrivelled; **pengecut** *n* coward

kedai *n* stall, kiosk

kedalaman *n* depth ← **dalam**

kedaluwarsa, kadaluwarsa *adj* expired; *tanggal* ~ expiry date, use-by date (food) ← **daluwarsa**

kedamaian *n* peace ← **damai**

kedap *adj* free from; ~ *air* waterproof; ~ *suara* soundproof; ~ *udara* air-tight

kedatangan *n* arrival ← **datang**

kedaulatan *n* sovereignty

kedekatan *n* close relationship ← **dekat**

kedelai, kedelé soy; *susu kacang* ~ soya milk, soymilk

kedelapan *adj* eighth ← **delapan**

kedengaran *adj* audible ← **dengar**

121

kediaman *n* residence ←
diam

kedinginan cold; feeling
cold ← **dingin**

kedip blink; wink; **berkedip** *v* to blink (two
eyes) or wink (one eye);
berkedip-kedip *adj* blink-
ing; **mengedipkan** ~ *mata*
to blink

kedok: berkedok *v* to hide
behind a mask, to pretend

kedokteran *adj* medical
← **dokter**

kedondong *buah* ~ kind
of fruit

kedua *adj* second;
kedua(-dua)-nya *adj* both
← **dua**

kedudukan *n* position ←
duduk

kedutaan ~ *(besar)* embassy
← **duta**

keempat *adj* fourth ←
empat

keénakan *adj* too enjoyable
or good ← **énak**

keenam *adj* sixth ← **enam**

keengganan *n* reluctance
← **enggan**

keésokan ~ *harinya* the
next day ← **ésok, bésok**

kegadisan *n* virginity ←
gadis

kegaduhan *n* noise, uproar
← **gaduh**

kegagalan *n* failure ←
gagal

kegelapan *n* darkness ←
gelap

kegelisahan *n* anxiety,
nerves ← **gelisah**

kegemaran *n* hobby ←
gemar

kegembiraan *n* joy,
happiness ← **gembira**

kegiatan *n* activity ← **giat**

kegigihan *n* perseverance,
tenacity ← **gigih**

keguguran miscarry,
miscarriage ← **gugur**

kehabisan *v* to run out of
(water, food, stock) ← **habis**

kehadiran *n* presence,
attendance ← **hadir**

kehakiman *Departemen* ~
Department of Justice ←
hakim

kehalusan *n* delicacy, grace
← **halus**

kehamilan *n* pregnancy ←
hamil

kehancuran *n* destruction,
ruin ← **hancur**

kehangatan *n* warmth, friendliness ← **hangat**

keharusan *n* obligation, necessity, requirement ← **harus**

kehausan to be thirsty; thirst ← **haus**

kehendak *n* will, wish; **mengehendaki** *v* to wish, want ← **hendak**

kehéranan *n* astonishment, amazement, wonder ← **héran**

kehidupan *n* life, existence ← **hidup**

kehilangan (feeling of) loss ← **hilang**

kehormatan *n* respect ← **hormat**

kehujanan *adj* caught in the rain ← **hujan**

kehutanan *n* forestry ← **hutan**

keibuan *adj* motherly ← **ibu**

keikutsertaan *n* participation ← **ikut serta**

keilmuan *adj* scientific ← **ilmu**

keindahan *n* beauty ← **indah**

keinginan *n* desire, wish ← **ingin**

keistiméwaan *n* special quality ← **istiméwa**

kejadian *n* event, happening; creation ← **jadi**

kejahatan *n* crime ← **jahat**

kejaksaan *n* district attorney's office ← **jaksa**

kejam *adj* cruel, merciless; **kekejaman** *n* cruelty

kejam: mengejamkan ~ mata to close your eyes

kejang *adj* stiff; **berkejang** *v* to have convulsions

kejanggalan *n* oddity, anomaly ← **janggal**

kejap: sekejap *n* moment, flash, blink; *dalam ~ mata* in a moment, in the twinkling of an eye

kejar *v* chase; **kejar-kejaran** *v* chase each other; **mengejar** *v* to chase; *~ waktu* to race against the clock

kejatuhan *n* fall; *adj* be struck by something falling ← **jatuh**

kejauhan *adj* too far ← **jauh**

kejawén *n* Javanese traditional mysticism

kejiwaan *adj* mental ← **jiwa**

kejora *bintang ~* morning star

kéju *n* cheese

kejuaraan *n* championship ← **juara**

kejujuran *n* honesty ← **jujur**

kejurnas *n* national championship → **kejuaraan nasional**

kejuruan *adj* technical ← **juru**

kejut *adj* surprised, startled; **mengejutkan** *adj* surprising, startling; *v* to surprise or startle; **terkejut** *adj* surprised

kék whether it's this, or that; *sate ~, soto ~, saya mau* whether it's satay or soup, I'll have some

kekacauan *n* chaos ← **kacau**

kekaisaran *n* empire ← **kaisar**

kekal *adj* everlasting, eternal

kekalahan *n* defeat, loss ← **kalah**

kekang *n* bridle; *tali ~* rein

kekar *adj* solid, strong

kekasaran *n* coarseness, roughness ← **kasar**

kekasih *n* sweetheart, beloved, darling; *~ gelap* secret love ← **kasih**

kekayaan *n* wealth, riches ← **kaya**

kekecéwaan *n* disappointment ← **kecéwa**

kekecilan *adj* too small ← **kecil**

kekecualian *n* exception ← **kecuali**

kékéh: terkékéh-kékéh *v* to laugh

kekejaman *n* cruelty ← **kejam**

kekeliruan *n* mistake, error ← **keliru**

kéker *n* binoculars, field glasses

kekerasan *n* violence; *~ di dalam rumah, ~ domestik* domestic violence; *~ terhadap perempuan* violence against women ← **keras**

kekeringan *n* dryness, aridity ← **kering**

kekosongan *n* emptiness ← **kosong**

kekuasaan *n* power; authority ← **kuasa**

kekuatan *n* strength, power ← **kuat**

kekuatiran *n* worry, fear ← **kuatir**

kekurangan *n* shortcoming (of a person), lack; flaw, mistake, defect ← **kurang**

kel. *keluarga* family

kelab, klab *n* club; ~ *malam* nightclub

kelabu *adj* gray, cloudy; **mengelabui** *v* to trick, pull the wool over someone's eyes ← **abu**

keladi *tua tua* — the older, the more

kelahi: berkelahi *v* to quarrel, fight, fall out; **perkelahian** *n* fight, scuffle

kelahiran *n* birth; *adj* born; ~ *Semarang* born in Semarang ← **lahir**

kelainan *n* abnormality ← **lain**

kelak later, in the future

kelakuan *n* act, behavior ← **laku**

kelalaian *n* forgetfulness, negligence ← **lalai**

kelam *adj* dark, dull

kelamaan *adj* too long (a time) ← **lama**

kelambu *n* mosquito net

kelamin *penyakit* ~ venereal disease, sexually transmitted disease (STD)

kelancaran *n* smoothness, good progress, fluency ← **lancar**

kelapa *n* coconut; ~ *muda* young coconut; ~ *sawit* oil-palm; *air* ~ coconut milk; coconut juice; *pohon* ~ coconut palm

kelaparan *n* hunger, famine, starvation; *adj* very hungry ← **lapar**

kelas *n* class; ~ *kakap* big-time

kelautan *adj* maritime; *Departemen Perikanan dan* ~ Department of Fisheries and Marine Affairs ← **laut**

kelayakan *n* suitability ← **layak**

keledai *n* donkey

kelelap *adj* submerged, sunken into water

kelelawar, kelalawar *n* bat

keleluasaan *n* freedom (of choice) ← **leluasa**

kelemahan *n* weakness ← **lemah**

kelembaban *n* humidity ← **lembab**

kelembutan *n* softness ← **lembut**

keléngkéng *buah* ~ small lychee ← **léngkéng**

kelenjar *n* gland; ~ *getah bening* lymph gland; ~ *prostat* prostate

kelénténg, klénténg *n* Chinese temple, pagoda

keléréng *n* marble, *main* ~ to play marbles

keliar: berkeliaran *v* to swarm or wander about

kelicikan *n* trickery, cunning ← **licik**

kelihatan *adj* visible; ~*nya* apparently, it seems ← **lihat**

keliling around; edge, perimeter; ~ *dunia* go around the world; **ber-keliling** *v* to go around; **mengelilingi** *v* to circle, go around

kelim *n* seam

kelincahan *n* agility ← **lincah**

kelinci *n* rabbit; ~ *percobaan* guinea-pig

kelingking *n* little or baby finger

kelip: berkelip *v* to twinkle, flicker

kelipatan *n* multiple ← **lipat**

keliru *adj* wrong, mistaken; **kekeliruan** *n* mistake, error

kélok *n* bend, curve

kelola: mengelola *v* to manage, run; **pengelolaan** *n* management

kelom, klompen *n* clogs

kelompok *n* group; ~ *bermain (KB)* playgroup; ~ *kerja* working group

kelonggaran *n* facility, dispensation ← **longgar**

kelontong *pedagang* ~ pedlar, hawker; *toko* ~ shop selling cheap goods

kelopak ~ *mata* eyelid

keluar go out; be issued; *prep* out, outside; **keluaran** *n* issue, edition, version; **mengeluarkan** *v* to issue, send out, release, publish ← **ke luar**

keluarga *n* family; ~ *Berencana (KB)* state family planning program; ~ *besar* extended family; *kartu* ~ family ID card; *kepala* ~ head of the family; *tunjangan* ~ family allowance; **berkeluarga** *v* to have a family, be married

keluh sigh; ~ *kesah* complain; **keluhan** *n* complaint; **mengeluh** *v* to complain

kelupaan *n* something forgotten ← **lupa**

kelupas, mengelupas *v* to peel, come off (of a skin)

kelurahan *n* administrative unit, village ← **lurah**

kemacetan *n* jam; ~ *lalu lintas* traffic jam ← **macet**

kémah *n* tent; **berkémah** *v* to camp, go camping; **perkémahan** *n* camping, camp

kemahiran *n* skill ← **mahir**

kemajuan *n* progress, advance ← **maju**

kemaksiatan *n* immorality, vice ← **maksiat**

kemalaman *adv* too late (at night); after dark ← **malam**

kemalingan *v* to be robbed ← **maling**

kemaluan *n* genital, sex organ ← **malu**

kemampuan *n* ability, capability ← **mampu**

kemangi *n* Indonesian mint

kemanisan *adj* too sweet ← **manis**

kemarahan *n* anger ← **marah**

kemarau *musim* ~ dry season

kemari here, in this direction; *ke sana* ~ here and there

kemarin *adv* yesterday; the other day; last; ~ *dulu* the day before yesterday

kemas: kemasan *n* packaging; **berkemas-kemas** *v* to tidy up, pack

kematian *n* death, passing ← **mati**

kemauan *n* want, will, desire ← **mau**

kembali back, return; again; *(terima kasih)* ~ you're welcome; **kembalian** *n* small change; **kembalinya** *n* the return; **mengembalikan** *v* to give or send back, return

kembang *n* flower; ~ *api* fireworks, sparkler; ~ *kol* cauliflower; ~ *sepatu* hibiscus; **berkembang** *v* to develop, expand; ~ *biak* to breed, grow; *negara* ~ developing country; **mengembangkan** *v* to develop something;

perkembangan *n* development

kembar *n* twin; ~ *tiga* triplets; *saudara* ~ twin

kembung, gembung *adj* filled with air, inflated; bloated; *perut* ~ bloated belly

keméja *n* Western-style shirt (with collar)

kemelaratan *n* poverty ← **melarat**

kemelék-hurufan *n* literacy ← **melék**

kemenakan → **keponakan**

kemenangan *n* victory ← **menang**

kementerian *n* ministry, department, office ← **menteri**

kemérah-mérahan *adj* reddish ← **mérah**

kemerdékaan *n* freedom, independence, liberty ← **merdéka**

kemerosotan *n* descent, deterioration ← **merosot**

kemesraan *n* intimacy ← **mesra**

keméwahan *n* luxury ← **méwah**

kemih *saluran* ~ urinary tract

kemilau shiny, sheen

kemiri *n* candle nut

Kemis → **Kamis**

kemis, emis: mengemis *v* to beg; **pengemis** *n* beggar

kemiskinan *n* poverty ← **miskin**

kemocéng, kemucing *n* feather duster

kempés, kempis *adj* deflated, flat; hollow; *ban* ~ flat tire

kemudahan *n* ease, facility ← **mudah**

kemudi *n* rudder, steering wheel; **mengemudikan** *v* to drive, steer; **pengemudi** *n* driver

kemudian *conj* then; *di* ~ *hari* in the future, later on

kemuka: mengemukakan *v* to put forward, advance, nominate; **terkemuka** *adj* prominent ← **ke muka**

kemuliaan *n* honor, glory; ~ *Tuhan* the glory of God ← **mulia**

kemunduran *n* deterioration, decline ← **mundur**

kemungkinan *n* possibility ← **mungkin**

kemurnian *n* purity ← **murni**

kemut, emut, mengemut *v* to suck on, chew

kena touch; **kenapa** *coll* why, how come; what did you say?; **mengenai** *conj* about, concerning

kenaikan *n* rise, raise; ~ *gaji* pay rise ← **naik**

kenakalan *n* naughtiness ← **nakal**

kenal *v* to know, be acquainted with; **kenalan** *n* acquaintance; **mengenal** *v* to know, be acquainted with, recognize; **memperkenalkan** *v* to introduce; **perkenalan** *n* introduction; **terkenal** *adj* well-known

kenang recall; **kenangan** *n* memories; **kenang-kenangan** *n* souvenir, keepsake; **mengenang** *v* to commemorate, remember

kenang-kenangan *n* souvenir, keepsake ← **kenang**

kenapa *interrog, coll* why, how come; what did you say? ← **kena apa**

kenari *burung* ~ canary

kencan *n* date; ~ *buta* blind date; **berkencan** *v* to go on a date

kencang tight, taut; **mengencangkan** *v* to tighten

kencing urine; urinate; ~ *manis* diabetes; *saluran* ~ urinary tract

kencur *beras* ~ traditional Javanese drink

kendali *n* reins; **mengendalikan** *v* to control; **pengendalian** *n* control; ~ *mutu* quality control; **terkendali** *adj* controlled

kendang *n* small drum → **gendang**

kendara: kendaraan *n* vehicle; ~ *bermotor* motor vehicle; ~ *umum* public transport

kendi *n* earthen water flask

kendor, kendur *adj* slack, loose

kenduri *n* feast, celebration

kenegaraan *adj* state (affairs) ← **negara**

kenék, kernét *n* bus assistant acting as conductor

kenikmatan *n* pleasure, enjoyment ← **nikmat**

kening *n* forehead, brow

kental *adj* thick, sticky, congealed; *logat* ~ thick accent; *susu* ~ condensed milk

kentang *n* potato; *coll* french fries; ~ *goreng* hot potato chips, french fries

kentut fart, break wind

kenyal *adj* elastic, rubbery

kenyamanan *n* comfort ← **nyaman**

kenyang *adj* full, not hungry

kenyataan *n* fact ← **nyata**

kéong *n* snail

Kep. *kepulauan* archipelago, chain of islands

kepada *prep* to (someone); ~ *yang terhormat (kpd yth)* to (on letters)

kepagian *adj* too early ← **pagi**

kepahitan *n* bitterness ← **pahit**

kepailitan *n* bankruptcy ← **pailit**

kepal fist; **kepalan** *n* fist; **mengepal** *v* to form a fist

kepala *n* head, chief; ~ *batu* obstinate; ~ *kantor* boss; ~ *susu* cream; ~ *pusing* headache

kepandaian *n* ability, intelligence ← **pandai**

kepanduan *n* scouting, Scouts; *n, f* guiding, Guides ← **pandu**

kepanjangan *adj* too long ← **panjang**

kepasrahan *n* submission ← **pasrah**

kepastian *n* certainty ← **pasti**

kepedasan *adj* too hot or spicy ← **pedas**

kepedulian *n* concern ← **peduli**

kepegawaian *adj* staff, personnel ← **pegawai**

kepekatan *n* thickness, viscosity ← **pekat**

kepemimpinan *n* leadership (qualities) ← **pimpin**

kepéndékan *n* abbreviation ← **péndék**

kepéngén, kepingin *v, coll* really want to ← **péngén**

kepentingan *n* importance, interest ← **penting**

keperawanan *n* virginity ← **perawan**

kepercayaan *n* belief, faith ← **percaya**

kepergian *n* departure ← **pergi**

keperluan *n* needs, requirements ← **perlu**

kepikiran *adj* considered, thought of, sprang to mind ← **pikir**

keping *n* piece (counter for flat objects); splinter; ~ *kayu* woodchip

kepingin → **kepéngén**

kepiting *n* crab

kepodang, kepudang *burung* ~ oriole

kepolosan *n* simplicity, straight-forwardness, lack of pretension ← **polos**

kepompong *n* cocoon

keponakan, kemenakan *n* niece or nephew; cousin; ~ *laki-laki* nephew; ~ *perempuan* niece; ~ *satu buyut* second cousin

Kepprés *n* Presidential Decree ← **keputusan Présidén**

kepraktisan *n* practicality ← **praktis**

keprésidénan *adj* presidential ← **présidén**

Kepri *Kepulauan Riau* Riau Archipelago, a province in Sumatra

kepribadian *n* personality ← **pribadi**

keprihatinan *n* concern ← **prihatin**

kepul: berkepul, mengepul *v* to smoke, billow

kepulauan *n* archipelago, chain

kepung, mengepung *v* to surround, encircle, besiege; **kepungan** *n* encirclement, surrounded area

kepunyaan *n* possession, belonging ← **punya**

kepustakaan *n* bibliography, list of references; literature ← **pustaka**

keputihan *n* thrush, vaginal itching (white discharge) ← **putih**

keputusan *n* decision, decree ← **putus**

kera *n* ape

kerabat *n* relative, family

keracunan *adj* poisoned; ~ *makanan* food poisoning ← **racun**

keraguan, keragu-raguan *n* doubt, uncertainty ← **ragu**

kerah *n* collar

kerajaan *n* kingdom; ~ *Inggris* the United Kingdom ← **raja**

kerajinan *n* crafts; ~ *tangan* handicrafts ← **rajin**

kerak *n* crust; ~ *bumi* the Earth's crust

keram cramp

keramahan *n* friendliness ← **ramah**

keramaian *n* noise, din; lively atmosphere ← **ramai**

keramas, berkeramas to wash your hair

keramat *adj* holy, sacred; *tempat* ~ place sacred to locals

keramik ceramic, earthenware

keran *n* tap, faucet; *buka* ~ turn on the tap

kerang *n* shell; mollusc; *kulit* ~ seashell

kerangka *n* skeleton, framework

keranjang *n* basket; ~ *sampah* rubbish or garbage bin, trash can

kerap *adv* often; ~ *kali* often, frequently

keras *adj* hard, strong; severe, strict, violent; loud; ~ *kepala* stubborn; **bersi-keras** *v* to maintain, stick to, be obstinate; **kekerasan**

n violence; ~ *di dalam rumah*, ~ *domestik* domestic violence; ~ *terhadap perempuan* violence against women; **mengeras-kan** *v* to make something harder, louder; **pengeras** ~ *suara* loudspeaker

kerasan *coll* settled, comfortable, feel at home ← **rasa**

keraton, kraton *n* Javanese palace

kerawang, karawang *n* filigree embroidery

kerbau, kebo *n* buffalo

kerdil *n* dwarf

kérék *n* pulley; **mengérék** *v* to hoist, pull; ~ *bendera* to raise the flag

kerén *adj, coll* great, cool; trendy

kerendahan *n* lowness; ~ *hati* humility ← **rendah**

keresahan *n* restlessness, nervous energy ← **resah**

keresak, keresek rustle, sound of rustling leaves

keréta *n* train; carriage; ~ *api* train; ~ *ekspres* express train; *gerbong* ~ carriage

keributan n disturbance; loud noise ← **ribut**

kericuhan n chaos ← **ricuh**

kerikil n gravel, pebble; small but annoying problem

kerinduan n longing, craving ← **rindu**

kering adj dry; **kekeringan** n dryness, aridity; **mengeringkan** v to dry something; **pengering** ~ rambut hair dryer

keringat n sweat, perspiration; ~ dingin cold sweat; mandi ~ soaked in sweat; **keringatan** adj sweaty, sweating; **berkeringat** v to sweat

keripik, kripik n small chip or crisp; ~ singkong cassava chips

keriput n wrinkle, line

keris, kris n traditional dagger, creese

keriting curl, curly; clubs (in cards); **mengeriting** ~ rambut to perm your hair

kerja work; job, occupation; ~ bakti community work; ~ sama co-operation; mencari ~ to look for work; **kerjaan** n work, job, things

to do; **kinerja** n performance; **bekerja** v to work; ~ sama to co-operate, work together; **mengerjakan** v to do, carry out; **pekerja** n worker, laborer; **pekerjaan** n work, profession

kernét, kenék n assistant on a bus or truck

kernyit. mengernyit ·- dahi, ~ kening to frown

kerobohan n collapse ← **roboh**

kerok traditional treatment for minor illnesses by rubbing the back with a coin; biang ~ agitator; **kerokan** v to be massaged in this way; **mengerok** v to rub someone's back with a coin

keroncong, kroncong n traditional songs and music of Portuguese origin

kerongkongan n throat

keropos adj eroded, eaten away; tulang ~ osteoporosis; **mengeropos** v to be eaten away, eroded

keroyok, mengeroyok v to beat savagely in a mob

kertas *n* paper; ~ *kado*
wrapping paper; ~ *pasir*
sandpaper; ~ *tebal* cardboard; *uang* ~ banknotes
keruan, karuan *tidak* ~
very badly, unthinkably
kerucut, cerucut *n* cone
kerudung, kudungan *n, Isl*
veil; **berkerudung** *adj* veiled
kerugian *n* loss; damage
← **rugi**
keruh *adj* turbid, cloudy
keruk dredge; *kapal* ~
dredger; **mengeruk** *v* to
dredge, scrape out
kerupuk, krupuk *n* large
cracker, crisp, chip; ~
udang prawn cracker
kerusakan *n* damage ←
rusak
kerusuhan *n* riot, disturbance
← **rusuh**
kerut *n* wrinkle; **mengerut**
v to shrink, shrivel,
contract; **mengerutkan**
~ *kening* to frown
kesabaran *n* patience ←
sabar
kesadaran *n* consciousness,
awareness ← **sadar**
kesakitan *adj* in pain ←
sakit

kesaksian *n* evidence,
testimony; *memberi* ~ to
give evidence, bear witness
← **saksi**
kesaktian *n* magic power
← **sakti**
kesal *adj* **kesel** *coll*
annoyed, in a bad mood
kesalahan *n* mistake ←
salah
kesampaian *adj* achieved,
reached, realized ← **sampai**
**kesamping: mengesam-
pingkan** *v* to put to one
side ← **ke samping**
kesan *n* impression; **berkesan, mengesankan** *adj*
impressive; **terkesan** *adj*
impressed; seemed
kesasar *coll* to lose your
way, (get) lost ← **sasar**
kesatu *adj, sl* first; **kesatuan** *n* unity ← **satu**
kesayangan favorite, pet
← **sayang**
kesebelasan *n* team of
eleven, soccer team ←
belas
kesediaan *n* readiness,
willingness ← **sedia**
kesedihan *n* sadness,
sorrow ← **sedih**

kesuburan

keséhatan *n* health ← **séhat**

keseimbangan *n* balance ← **imbang**

kesejahteraan *n* welfare ← **sejahtera**

kesejukan *n* coolness ← **sejuk**

keselamatan *n* safety; salvation ← **selamat**

keselarasan *n* harmony ← **laras**

keselek, keselak *adj* choking (due to food or drink) ← **selak**

keseléo sprain; sprained; *kaki* ~ sprained foot

keseluruhan *secara* ~ totally, completely ← **seluruh**

kesemak, kesemek *buah* ~ sweet, soft fruit with orange flesh, persimmon

kesempatan *n* opportunity ← **sempat**

kesempitan *n* narrowness ← **sempit**

kesemutan *v* to have pins and needles ← **semut**

kesenangan *n* amusement, hobby ← **senang**

kesengsaraan *n* torture, misery, suffering ← **sengsara**

kesenian *n* art (form) ← **seni**

kesepakatan *n* agreement ← **pakat**

kesepian *n* loneliness, solitude ← **sepi**

kését *n* door mat

kesetiaan *n* allegiance, faithfulness ← **setia**

kesetiakawanan *n* solidarily ← **setia kawan**

kesetrum *v, coll* to receive an electric shock ← **setrum**

kesiangan *adj* late, too late in the day ← **siang**

kesiapan *n* readiness, willingness ← **siap**

kesibukan *n* activity, fuss, bustle, business ← **sibuk**

kesimpulan *n* conclusion ← **simpul**

kesinambungan *n* continuity ← **sambung**

kesopanan *n* manners, politeness ← **sopan**

kesopan-santunan *n* manners, etiquette ← **sopan santun**

kesoréan *adv* too late ← **soré**

kesuburan *n* fertility ← **subur**

135

kesucian *n* purity; virginity ← **suci**

kesukaan *n* hobby; enjoyment ← **suka**

kesukaran *n* difficulty ← **sukar**

kesukuan *adj* ethnic, tribal ← **suku**

kesulitan *n* difficulty, trouble ← **sulit**

kesungguhan *n* earnestness, sincerity, truth ← **sungguh**

kesunyian *n* quiet, still ← **sunyi**

kesurupan *v* to be possessed by a spirit or ghost ← **surup**

kesusahan *n* trouble, difficulty ← **susah**

kesusasteraan, kesusastraan *n* literature ← **sastra**

ketagihan *adj* addicted to ← **tagih**

ketahuan to be found out ← **tahu**

ketakutan *adj* frightened, terrified, scared ← **takut**

ketan *n* sticky rice; ~ *bakar* grilled slices of sticky rice; *bubur ~ hitam* black sticky rice porridge

ketangkasan *n* agility, dexterity ← **tangkas**

ketapél *n* catapult

ketat *adj* tight, strict; *baju ~* tight clothes; *keamanan ~* high security

ketawa *v, coll* to laugh → **tawa**

ketegangan *n* tension ← **tegang**

kéték → **kétiak**

ketekunan *n* diligence, dedication ← **tekun**

kétél *n* boiler, kettle

ketéla *n* yam

ketelaténan *n* patience, perseverance ← **telatén**

ketelédoran *n* carelessness ← **telédor**

ketelitian *n* accuracy, care ← **teliti**

ketemu *v, coll* to meet ← **temu**

ketenangan *n* calm, peace ← **tenang**

ketenaran *n* popularity ← **tenar**

ketenteraman *n* peace ← **tenteram**

ketentuan *n* condition, stipulation ← **tentu**

keterangan *n* explanation ← **terang**

keterbatasan *n* limitation ← **batas**

keterlaluan *n* excess, too much ← **lalu**

keterlambatan *n* delay ← **lambat**

keterlibatan *n* involvement, association ← **libat**

ketertiban *n* discipline, order ← **tertib**

ketetapan *n* regulation; stipulation ← **tetap**

ketiadaan *n* absence, lack ← **tiada, tidak ada**

kétiak, kéték *n* armpit

ketiduran *v* to fall asleep ← **tidur**

ketiga *adj* the third ← **tiga**

ketik *v* type; *juru* ~ typist; **mengetik** *v* to type

ketika *conj* when (in past); ~ *itu* at that time

ketimbang *conj, coll* than; instead of ← **timbang**

ketimpangan *n* inequality, imbalance; ~ *sosial* social inequality ← **timpang**

ketimun → **mentimun**

ketimuran *adj* Eastern, Oriental ← **timur**

ketinggalan *adj* left behind; ~ *kereta api* to miss a train ← **tinggal**

ketinggian *n* altitude, height ← **tinggi**

ketinting *n* water taxi used on the rivers of Kalimantan

ketok *v* to knock; panel-beat; ~ *magic* 'magic' panel-beating

ketombé *n* dandruff; **ketombéan** *v, coll* to have dandruff; **berketombé** *rambut* ~ dry scalp, dandruff

ketoprak *n* Betawi dish of vegetables in peanut sauce; folk play

ketrampilan *n* skill ← **trampil**

ketua *n* chief, chair, president, elder; ~ *RT* neighborhood leader; *wakil* ~ deputy chair

ketuban *air* ~ amniotic fluid

ketuhanan *n* divinity, deity; belief in God ← **tuhan**

ketuk, ketok knock; **mengetuk** *v* to knock

ketularan *adj* infected, caught something ← **tular**

ketulusan ~ *hati* sincerity ← **tulus**

ketumbar n (ground) coriander

ketupat n coconut fronds woven into a diamond-shape for cooking rice

keturunan n descendant; *WNI* ~ Indonesian of Chinese descent ← **turun**

ketus adj sharp (of words)

keuangan n finance ← **uang**

keunggulan n superiority ← **unggul**

keunikan n unique thing, uniqueness ← **unik**

keuntungan n advantage, profit ← **untung**

kewajiban n obligation, duty ← **wajib**

kewarganegaraan n citizenship ← **warga negara**

kewaspadaan n caution ← **waspada**

kewenangan n authority ← **wenang**

keyakinan n belief, conviction, faith ← **yakin**

kg kilogram

khas adj special, specific

khasiat n benefit, special effect

khatulistiwa, katulistiwa n the Equator

khawatir, kuatir v to worry, fear; *jangan* ~ don't worry; **kekuatiran** n worry, fear; **menguatirkan** v to worry about something

khayal: khayalan n dream, hallucination; **berkhayal** v to dream, imagine

khianat: mengkhianati v to betray someone; **pengkhianat** n traitor

khidmat n respect

khitan n circumcision; **khitanan** n feast held in honor of a circumcision; **mengkhitan(kan)** v to circumcise

khotbah v sermon; **peng-khotbah** n preacher

khusus adj special, particular; *~nya* in particular, especially

ki, kiai, kyai n, pron, Isl religious leader; ~ *Haji* title for leader who has completed the pilgrimage to Mecca

kiamat *hari* ~ day of judgment

kian adv such; increasingly, more and more; **sekian** adv so much, this much; ~ *banyak* so many, so much; ~ *dulu* that's all for now (used in speeches and letters)

kias: kiasan *n* figure of speech, metaphor

kiat *n* means, way, method

kibar: berkibar(-kibar) *v* to wave, flutter; **mengibarkan** *v* to wave, unfurl

kiblat, qiblat *n* direction of Mecca; **berkiblat** *v* to be oriented toward

kibor *n* keyboard

kidal *adj* left-handed

kijang *n* barking deer, kind of antelope

kikir *adj* stingy, tight, miserly

kikis *adj* scraped; **mengikis** *v* to erode, eat away; **terkikis** *adj* eaten away, eroded

kilang *n* refinery, mill; ~ *minyak* oil refinery; **perkilangan** *n* refinery

kilap shine; **mengkilap** *v* to shine, gleam

kilas ~ *balik* flashback; **sekilas** *n* flash, glance

kilat *n* lightning

kilau: berkilau *adj* glittering, sparkling

kilir twist; **terkilir** *adj* twisted, sprained

kilo *n* kilo, kilogram; kilometer; *se~ pisang* a kilo of bananas; **kiloan** *adv* by the kilogram, in kilograms

kimia *n* chemistry

kimono *n* kimono; dressing gown

KIM(S) *abbrev Kartu Izin Menetap [Sementara]* (temporary) residence permit for foreigners

kina *n* quinine; *pohon ~* cinchona tree

kincir *n* wheel; ~ *air* waterwheel; ~ *angin* windmill

kinerja *n* performance ← **kerja**

kini *adv* now, nowadays (often when comparing with past); **terkini** *adj* the latest

kios *n* stall, kiosk; **kiostél, kiospon** *n* small phone agency, phone kiosk ← **kios télépon**

kipas *n* fan; ~ *angin*, ~ *listrik* (electric) fan

kiper *n* (goal)keeper

kiprah: berkiprah *v* to move, dance, be active in

kira v to think, guess, estimate; **kira-kira** adv approximately, around, about; **kiranya** adv hopefully; **mengira** v to assume, think; **memper-kirakan** v to estimate, calculate; **perkiraan** n estimate, guess; **terkira** tak ~ unsuspected, not thought of

kiri adj left; ~ kanan left and right; ~ kapal port, portside; belok ~ turn left

kirim n send; ~ salam to send your best wishes; **kiriman** n parcel; **mengi-rim** v to send; **pengirim** n sender; **pengiriman** n dispatch, forwarding; **terkirim** adj sent

kisah n tale, story; ~ sejati true story; **berkisah** v to tell a story; **mengisahkan** v to tell the story of

kisar: berkisar v to revolve, rotate, turn

kismis n sultana, currant

kita pron we, us, our (inclusive); ~ punya our

kitab n holy book; ~ suci holy book

kitar: sekitar adv around; near; prep around; **sekitar-nya** di ~ around (a place); dan ~ and environs

KITAS abbrev Kartu Izin Tinggal Sementara temporary residence permit for foreigners

KK abbrev kepala keluarga head of family, household

KKN abbrev korupsi, kolusi, nepotisme corruption (collusion and nepotism)

klakson n horn; **diklakson** v to be tooted at

klarinét n clarinet

klasik adj classic, classical

klénténg, kelénténg n Chinese temple, pagoda

klép, kelép n valve, catch

klién n client

klinik n clinic

kliping n news clipping

klisé n cliché

klop → **kelop** adj suitable, comfortable

klosét n cistern (of toilet)

klub n (sports) club; ~ tenis tennis club

KM abbrev Kapal Motor ship

km kamar room (in a hotel); kilometer

knalpot *n* exhaust pipe, muffler

koalisi *n* coalition; **berkoalisi** *v* to be in a coalition

kobar: kobaran ~ *api* flame

koboi *n* cowboy

kocék *n, sl* pocket

kocok *mie* ~ kind of noodles; **mengocok** *v* to shake, shuffle

Kodam *n* Regional Military Komando ← **Komando Daérah Militér**

kode *n* code; ~ *pos* postcode

kodok *n* frog; *gaya* ~ frogkick; *mobil* ~ Volkswagen VW, Beetle

kodrat *n* nature

Kodya *n* municipality, city ← **kotamadya**

koi *ikan* ~ Japanese carp

koin *n* coin

kok you know (emphasizing contrary argument); *tidak apa-apa* ~ really, it's OK; *interrog* how come, why

koki *n* cook

kokoh, kukuh *adj* strong, robust

kokok *n* crowing

kokpit *n* cockpit

Kol. *kolonel* colonel

kol *n* cabbage

kolaborasi *n* collaboration; **berkolaborasi** *v* to collaborate, work together

kolak *n* sweet fruit stew; ~ *pisang* banana *kolak*

kolam *n* pond; ~ *ikan* fish pond; ~ *renang* swimming pool

koléga *n* colleague

koléksi *n* collection

koléra *n* cholera

kolintang *n* large wooden xylophone from Minahasa

Kolombia *n* Colombia

kolonél *n, pron* colonel

kolong *n* space under a large object; ~ *meja* under the table; ~ *tempat tidur* under the bed

kolonial *adj* colonial; **kolonisasi** *n* colonization → **jajah**

kolor *n* drawstring shorts; *celana* ~ (boxer) shorts

kolot *n* old-fashioned, out of date; conservative

kolusi *n* collusion

koma *n* comma

komandan *n* commander

komando *n* command

kombinasi *n* combination

Komdak *abbrev Komando Daerah Kepolisian* Regional Military Command, large police complex in south Jakarta

koméntar *n* comment; **berkoméntar** *v* to (make a) comment; **mengoméntari** *v* to comment on; **koméntator** *n* (sports) commentator

komik *(buku)* ~ comic (book); **komikus** *n* comic book author or artist

komisaris *n* commissioner; ~ *polisi* superintendent of police; *dewan* ~ commission

komisi *n* committee, commission; ~ *Pemilihan Umum (KPU)* Electoral Commission

komité *n* committee → **panitia**

kompas *n* compass

kompeténsi *n* competence

komplék, kompléks, kompléx *n* housing complex, compound

komplét, komplit *adj* complete

komplot: komplotan *n* plot

komponis *n* composer

kompor *n* stove, cooker; ~ *gas* gas cooker

komprés *n* compress, pack; ~ *dingin* ice pack

kompromi *n* compromise; **berkompromi** *v* to (reach a) compromise

komputer *n* computer; **komputerisasi** *n* computerization

komunis *adj n* communist; **komunisme** *n* communism

konci → **kunci**

kondang *adj* famous, well-known

kondé *n, f* small bun worn with national costume; *tusuk* ~ hair pin

kondéktur *n* conductor, guard (on a train or city bus)

kondisi *n* condition

kondom *n* condom

kondusif *adj* conducive, allowing

konéksi *n* connections, contacts (at an institution)

konferénsi, konperénsi *n* conference; ~ *Asia-Afrika* the Asian-African conference

konfrontasi *n* confrontation; Indonesian aggression towards Malaysia in the 1960s

Kong Hu Cu Confucius, Confucian, Confucianism

kongkol: sekongkol, bersekongkol *v* to plot, work against; **persekongkolan** *n* plot, intrigue

konglomerat *n* wealthy financier

kongrés *n* congress, convention

KONI *abbrev* **Komite Olahraga Nasional Indonesia** Indonesian National Sports Commission

konsékuén *adj* consistent, logical

konséling *n* counselling; **konsélor** *n* counsellor

konsén, konséntrasi *adj* focused, concentrating

konsép *n* concept, draft

konsér *n* concert; *nonton ~* to go to a concert

konstruksi *n* construction, building

konsul *n* consul; **konsulat** *n* consulate; *~ jenderal (konjen)* consulate-general

konsultan *n* adviser, consultant

konsumén *n* consumer

kontak contact

kontés *n* contest

kontra *adj* against, opposing, anti

kontrak *n* contract; **kontrakan** *n* rented (house); **dikontrakkan** *adj* for rent, lease

kontrol *n* control

konyol *adj* silly, foolish

kop *n* head; *~ surat* letterhead

koper, kopor *n* suitcase, baggage

koperasi *n* co-operative, co-op

kopi *n* coffee; *~ pahit* black coffee without sugar; *~ susu* white or milk coffee; *~ tubruk* ground coffee

kopi *n* copy; *~ darat* meet face-to-face → **fotokopi**

kopiah *n, Isl* flat-topped cap; national headwear for men → **péci**

kopyor *n* very soft coconut flesh; *es ~* sweet drink made from this coconut

koran *n* newspaper

korban *n* victim; ~ *jiwa*
fatality; ~ *luka* injured;
berkorban *v* to make
sacrifices, do without;
mengorbankan *v* to sacrifice; **pengorbanan** *n* (act
of) sacrifice

Korea *n* Korea; ~ *Selatan
(Korsel)* South Korea; ~
Utara North Korea; *bahasa*
~, *orang* ~ Korean

korék ~ *api* matches; **mengorék** *v* to scrape, scratch

koréksi *n* correction;
mengoréksi *v* to correct

korma, kurma *n* date;
pohon ~ date palm

kornét, kornéd *n* (tinned)
corned beef

Korsél *n* South Korea ←
Koréa Selatan

kortsléting, korsléting *n*
short-circuit

korup *adj* corrupt; **korupsi**
n corruption; *adj* corrupt;
~ *kolusi dan nepotisme
(KKN)* corruption; **koruptor**
n corrupt person

Korut *n* North Korea ←
Koréa Utara

kos board, lodging; ~ *putri*
female boarding-house;

terima ~ boarder wanted;
uang ~ boarding fee; **kos-
kosan** *n* boarding-houses,
rooms for board

kosa ~ *kata* vocabulary

kos-kosan *n* boarding-
houses, rooms for board ←
kos

kosong *adj* empty, blank;
hollow; zero; ~ *melom-
pong* completely empty;
kekosongan *n* emptiness;
mengosongkan *v* to
empty

Kostrad *n* Army Regional
Strategic Command ← **Ko-
mando Stratégis Ang-
katan Darat**

kota *n* town, city; **perkotaan** *n* metropolitan area;
kotamadya *n* municipality

kotak *n* box; square; ~
surat letter box; *nasi* ~ box
meal of rice and side-dishes;
kotak-kotak *adj* check

kotamadya *n* municipality
← **kota**

kotéka *n* penis sheath, worn
in Papua

Kotip, Kotif *n* administrative city, municipality ←
kota administratif

144

kotor *adj* dirty, filthy; gross; *gaji* ~ gross salary; **kotoran** *n* excrement; dirt

Kp. *kampung* village; densely-inhabited area in city

kran → **keran**

kraton, keraton *n* Javanese palace

krédit *n* credit; ~ *rumah* home loan; *kartu* ~ credit card

kribo *rambut* ~ Afro

kriminal *adj* criminal; **kriminolog** *n* criminologist

kring sound of telephone ringing

kripik, keripik *n* small chip or crisp; ~ *kentang* potato chips, ~ *singkong* cassava chips

krisis *n* crisis; ~ *moneter (krismon)* financial crisis of 1997-8

kristal crystal

Kristen *adj* Christian, Protestant; *agama* ~ Christianity, Protestantism; *gereja* ~ Protestant church

Kristus *Yesus* ~ Jesus Christ

krupuk → **kerupuk**

ksatria, kesatria *n* knight, warrior; *adj* chivalrous

KTP *abbrev Kartu Tanda Penduduk* national identity card

KTT *abbrev Konperensi Tingkat Tinggi* (international) high-level conference

ku, -ku *pron* I, my, mine; *rumah*~ my home

KUA *abbrev, Isl Kantor Urusan Agama* Religious Affairs Office

kuah *n* soup, sauce, gravy (accompanying a food); **berkuah** *adj* with a soup or sauce

kuala *n* mouth, confluence

kualat *adj* cursed; disastrous

kuali *n* wok, cooking pot

kualitas, kwalitas *n* quality; **berkualitas** *adj* quality → **mutu**

kuas *n* brush (for art or cosmetics); paintbrush

kuasa *n* power; ~ *hukum* legal counsel; **berkuasa** *adj* powerful, mighty; **kekuasaan** *n* power; authority; **menguasai** *v* to control, have power over

kuat *adj* strong; *tidak* ~ *berdiri* unable to stand up;

kekuatan *n* strength, power; **memperkuat** *v* to reinforce, make stronger; **terkuat** *adj* the strongest

kuatir, khawatir *v* to worry, fear; *jangan* ~ don't worry; **kekuatiran** *n* worry, fear; **mengualirkan** *v* to worry about something

Kuba *n* Cuba

kubik *adj* cubic; *liter* ~ cubic liter

kubis *n* cabbage

kubu *n* block, faction

kubur *n* grave, tomb; **kubur-an** *n* cemetery, graveyard; ~ *Cina* Chinese cemetery; **menguburkan** *v* to bury; **terkubur** *adj* buried in an accident

kucing *n* cat; ~ *angora* Persian cat; ~ *kampung* alley cat; ~ *Siam* Siamese cat

KUD *abbrev Koperasi Unit Desa* village co-operative

kuda *n* horse; ~ *hitam* dark horse; ~ *laut* seahorse; ~ *nil* hippo, hippopotamus; **ber-kuda** *v* to ride a horse, go (horse-)riding

kudéta *n* coup, *coup d'etat*; ~ *militer* military coup

kuduk *bulu* ~ hairs on the back of your neck

kudung, kerudung *n* loose veil; **berkudung** *v* to wear a loose veil

kudus *adj, Chr* holy

kué *n* cake, pastry; ~ *kering* biscuit; ~ *pasar* traditional cakes

kuil *n, Ch, Hind* temple

kuis *n* quiz

kuitansi → **kwitansi**

kuku *n* nail (of people), claw (of animals); *cat* ~ nail polish; *penyakit* ~ *mulut* foot and mouth disease

kukuh, kokoh *adj* strong, robust; **mengukuhkan** *v* to strengthen, to ratify; **pen-gukuhan** *n* strengthening, reinforcement; ratification

kukus steam; **mengukus** *v* to steam (food)

kulai: terkulai *adj* sprawled, splayed, fallen

kuliah *n* lecture; *v, coll* to study at university or college

kulit *n* skin, hide (of animals); leather; peel, rind (of fruit); ~ *imitasi* imitation leather; ~ *jeruk* orange rind; ~ *telur* eggshell; **ber-kulit** to have skin, -skinned

kulkas *n* refrigerator, fridge

kumal *adj* dishevelled, dingy, grubby

kuman *n* germ, bacteria; **berkuman** *adj* full of germs, bacteria

kumandang echo; **ber-kumandang** *v* to echo

kumat, komat relapse

kumbang *n* beetle; bumblebee

kumis *n* mustache

kumpul *v* to get together, gather; ~ *kebo* to live together without marrying; **kumpulan** *n* collection; group; ~ *puisi*, ~ *cerita pendek* anthology; **berkumpul** *v* to assemble, meet; **mengumpulkan** *v* to collect, gather; **ngumpul** *v, sl* to get or come together; **perkumpulan** *n* associa-tion, club; assembly

kumuh *adj* dirty, slummy; *daerah* ~ slum

kumur *obat* ~ mouthwash; **berkumur(-kumur)** *v* to gargle

kunang-kunang *n* firefly

kunci key; lock; fastener; ~ *kombinasi* combination lock; ~ *mobil* car lock; ~ *slot* bolt; *juru* ~ gatekeeper; *saksi* ~ key witness; **men-gunci** *v* to lock (up)

kuncup *n* bud

kuning *adj* yellow; *coll* light brown; *n* saffron, turmeric; ~ *telur* yolk; *sakit* ~ jaundice; **kunIngan** *n* brass

kunjung: kunjungan *n* visit, excursion; **ber-kunjung** *v* to visit, pay a visit to; **mengunjungi** *v* to visit a place

kuno *adj* ancient, historic; old-fashioned, out-of-date, conservative

kuntum *n* ripening bud

kunyah: mengunyah *v* to chew

kunyit, kunir, kuning *n* saffron; turmeric

kupang *n* edible shellfish

kupas peel; **mengupas** *v* to peel; to analyze

kuping *n* ear; **menguping** *v* to eavesdrop, listen in

kupon *n* coupon

kupu: kupu-kupu *n* butterfly

kura: kura-kura *n* tortoise

kurang *adj, adv* less, lacking; ~ *ajar* rude; ~ *lebih* more or less, about; ~ *tahu* don't really know; **berkurang** *v* to decrease, diminish, subside; **kekurangan** *n* shortcoming (of a person), lack; flaw, mistake, defect; **mengurangi** *v* to take from, subtract, minus; **sekurang(-kurang)nya** *adv* at least

kuras, menguras *v* to clean out, drain

kurban, qurban *n, Isl* sacrifice, usu goats or cattle

kurcaci *n* gnome, dwarf

kurét *n* curette

kurikulum *n* curriculum

kurir *n* courier

kurma, korma *n* date

kurs *n* exchange rate

kursi *n* chair, seat; ~ *empuk* armchair; ~ *goyang* rocking chair; ~ *malas* easy chair; ~ *panjang* sofa; ~ *roda* wheelchair

kursus course; ~ *kilat* crash course

kurun time; ~ *waktu* period, length of time

kurung cage; **mengurung** *v* to cage, put in a cage, lock up

kurus *adj* thin, skinny; ~ *kering,* ~ *kerempeng* as thin as a rake

kusén, kosén *n* frame (of door or window)

kusir *n* coachman, driver

kuskus *n* cuscus

kusta *penyakit* ~ leprosy

kusut *adj* tangled, tousled, unkempt; complicated

kutak, utak: mengutak-ngatikkan *v* to work on or tinker with

kutik: berkutik *v* to move slightly, budge; **mengutik** *v* to tinker with; to touch on

kutil *n* wart

kutip, mengutip *v* to quote, cite an extract; **kutipan** *n* extract, quotation

kutu *n* louse, flea; ~ *buku* bookworm; ~ *busuk* bedbug

kutub *n* pole; ~ *selatan* the South Pole; ~ *utara* the North Pole; *beruang* ~ polar bear

kutuk curse; **kutukan** *n* curse; **mengutuk** *v* to

curse; **terkutuk** *adj* cursed, accursed

kwalitas → **kualitas**

kwantitas → **kuantitas**

kwétiau, kwétiauw *n* large Chinese egg noodles

kwitansi, kuitansi *n* bill, receipt

kyai → **ki, kiai**

L

la → **lha**

laba *n* profit, gain; ~ *bersih* net profit; ~ *kotor* gross profit

laba: laba-laba *n* spider; *rumah* ~, *sarang* ~ cobweb

labil *adj* unstable, unreliable; *tanah* ~ shaky ground

laboratorium, lab *n* laboratory

labu *n* gourd, pumpkin, squash

labuh: pelabuhan port, harbor; **berlabuh** *v* to anchor

lacak: melacak *v* to trace; **pelacak** *anjing* ~ sniffer dog

laci *n* drawer; chest of drawers, dresser

lacur: pelacur *n* prostitute; **pelacuran** *n* prostitution

lada *n* pepper

ladang *n* field; area of opportunity; ~ *minyak* oilfield; ~ *padi* dry ricefield; **berladang** *v* to cultivate the land

lafal *n* pronunciation; **melafalkan** *v* to pronounce

laga *n* fight; *film* ~ action film

lagak: berlagak *v* to act, pretend

lagi *adv* again; more; **lagipula** *n* furthermore, moreover

lagi *sl* in the act of; ~ *makan* eating → **sedang**

lagipula *n* furthermore, moreover ← **lagi pula**

lagu *n* song, music; ~ *anak-anak* children's song; ~ *daerah* song or music from a certain region; ~ *kebangsaan* national anthem; ~ *lama* old song; ~ *Natal* Christmas carol

-lah added after a word to soften the message; *baik*~ OK then; *mari*~ let us go

lahan *n* ground, land, terrain; ~ *kosong* waste land

149

lahar *n* lava

lahir born; external; ~*nya* the birth of; **kelahiran** *n* birth; *adj* born; ~ Semarang born in Semarang; **melahirkan** *v* to give birth to; to create; **terlahir** *adj* born

lain *adj* other, different; ~ *lagi* different again; **kelainan** *n* abnormality; **melainkan** *conj* rather, instead; **selain** except, apart from

lajang *adj* single, unmarried; **melajang** *v* to live as a single

laju fast, rapid, quick; rate; **melaju** *v* to proceed quickly

lajur *n* lane (one of many); ~ *kiri* left lane → **jalur**

lakban *n* adhesive tape

laki *adj, sl* male; *n, sl* husband; ~ *bini* man and wife; **lelaki** *adj, n* male; **laki-laki** *adj, n* male; *saudara* ~ brother; *anak* ~ son

lakon *n* play; act

laksa *n* Malay dish of vermicelli noodles with chicken in coconut sauce

laksamana *n* admiral

laksana *conj* like, as; **melaksanakan** *v* to realize,

execute, carry out; **pelaksanaan** *n* realization, execution

laku *adj* popular, in vogue; salable; ~ *keras* selling like hot cakes; **berlaku** *adj* effective, valid; *v* to behave; **kelakuan** *n* act, behavior; **melakukan** *v* to do, perform, carry out; **selaku** *adj* (acting) as, in the capacity of

lalai *adj* careless, negligent; **kelalaian** *n* forgetfulness, negligence

lalap, lalapan *n* raw vegetables, eaten as a side-dish

lalat, laler *n* fly

lalu *conj* then; *adj* last; ~ *lintas* traffic; *bulan (yang)* ~ last month; **berlalu** *v* to pass; **melalui** *v* to pass through; *conj* through, via; **selalu** *adv* always; **terlalu** *adv* too; **keterlaluan** *adj* too much, overly, unacceptable

lama *adj* long; old, former; **lama-lama** *adj* too long; *jangan* ~ don't be too long; **kelamaan** *adj* too long (a time); **selama** *conj* for, during, as long as; **selama-**

nya *adv* always, forever

laman *n* webpage, website

lamar, melamar *v* to apply; **lamaran** *n* application; proposal; *surat ~* application letter

lambai: melambaikan *v* to wave something; *~ tangan* to wave (goodbye)

lamban *adj* slow

lambang *n* symbol, **berlambang** *v* to have a symbol; **melambangkan** *v* to symbolize, represent

lambat *adj* slow, late; *~ laun* gradually; **melambatkan** *v* to slow down; **selambat-lambatnya** *adv* at the latest; **terlambat** *adj* (too) late, delayed; **keterlambatan** *n* delay

lambung *n* stomach

lambung: melambung *v* to bounce; **melambungkan** *v* to bounce something

lamin: pelaminan *n* bridal sofa where the couple greet guests

laminasi *n* laminating; **melaminasi** *v* to laminate

lampau past; **terlampau** *adj* too, extremely

lampias: melampiaskan *v* to release, indulge in

lampion *n* paper lantern

lampir: lampiran *n* attachment, appendix; **melampirkan** *v* to attach, enclose; **terlampir** *adj* attached, enclosed

lampu *n* light, lamp; *~ lalu lintas, ~ merah* traffic light; *~ sen* indicator, *~ senter* flashlight; *~ sorot* searchlight

lampung: pelampung *n* floater; flotation device; *baju ~* lifejacket

lamun: melamun *v* to daydream, fantasize

lancang *adj* impudent, impolite, shameless

lancar *adj* smooth, fluent; **kelancaran** *n* smoothness, good progress, fluency; **selancar** *papan ~* surfboard; **berselancar** *v* to surf, go surfing

lancip *adj* pointed, pointy

lancong: pelancong *n* tourist

landa: melanda *v* to engulf, attack, hit

landak *n* porcupine, echidna

landas *n* base, ground;
  lepas ~ take-off
langgan: langganan *n*
  subscription; regular customer; **berlangganan** *v* to
  subscribe to; **pelanggan** *n*
  subscriber, customer
langgar *n, Isl* small prayer
  house
langgar: melanggar *v* to
  disobey, offend; ~ *hukum*
  to break the law; **pelang-**
  garan *n* violation
langgeng *adj* everlasting,
  eternal
langit *n* sky; **langit-langit** *n*
  palate, roof of your mouth;
  ceiling
langka *adj* rare
langkah *n* step; ~ *demi* ~
  step by step; **melangkah** *v*
  to step
langlang: melanglang ~
  buana to see the world,
  travel great distances
langsam slow
langsing *adj* slim, slender
langsung *adj* direct,
  straight; **berlangsung** *v* to
  take place
lanjur: terlanjur *adv* too
  late, already

lanjut *adj* advanced, further;
  lanjutan *n* continuation;
  berlanjut *v* to continue;
  melanjutkan *v* to continue
  something; **selanjutnya**
  adv then, after that
lansia *adj* elderly → **lanjut**
  usia
lantai *n* floor (of building),
  story (of house); ~ *bawah*
  ground floor
lantar: lantaran *conj*
  because, the reason
  being
lantar: terlantar, telantar
  adj neglected, abandoned
lantas *adv* then, next
lantik, melantik *v* to install,
  inaugurate; **pelantikan** *n*
  inauguration
lantun: melantunkan ~
  lagu to sing (a song)
lanud *n* airfield ← **lapang-**
  an udara
lap *n* rag, cloth; **mengelap**
  v to wipe, mop
lapang *adj* wide, spacious;
  lapangan *n* field; ~ *kerja*
  job vacancy; ~ *tenis* tennis
  court; ~ *terbang*, ~ *udara*
  (lanud) airfield, airport
lapar *adj* hungry; **kela-**

paran n hunger, famine, starvation; adj very hungry

lapis layer, fold, lining; kue ~ layer cake; ~ legit kind of layer cake; **lapisan** n coat, layer

lapor, melapor v to report; **laporan** n report; **melaporkan** v to report, inform

laptop n laptop computer, notebook

lapuk rotten, decayed

larang: melarang v to ban, prohibit, forbid; **dilarang** v prohibited; ~ masuk no entry, no admittance; ~ merokok no smoking; **larangan** n ban, prohibition; **terlarang** adj forbidden, banned

laras n pitch, key, scale; **selaras** adj harmonious; **keselarasan** n harmony

larat: melarat adj miserable, poor; poverty-stricken; hidup ~ live in poverty; **kemelaratan** n poverty

lari run; ~ estafet relay (race); ~ gawang hurdles; lomba ~ race; **berlari** v to run; **melarikan** v to run off with, abduct, kidnap; ~ diri

to run away, flee, escape; **pelari** n runner

laris adj popular, in great demand

laron n flying white ant

larut dissolve; ~ malam late at night; **larutan** n solution; **melarutkan** v to dissolve

las weld; tukang ~ welder; **mengelas** v to weld

laskar n army, troops

lata: melata v to crawl, creep; binatang ~ reptile

latar n base; ~ belakang background; **berlatarkan** v to have as a background, be based on

latih, melatih v to train; **latihan** n training, practice, exercise; **pelatih** n coach, trainer; **pelatihan** n training

Latin Amerika ~ Latin America; bahasa ~ Latin; lagu ~ Spanish-language song

lauk n side-dish; ~ pauk side-dish

laut n sea; ~ Tengah the Mediterranean; bajak ~ pirate; kapal ~ ship; **lautan** n ocean; ~ Hindia the Indian Ocean; ~ Teduh,

153

~ *Pasifik* the Pacific Ocean;
kelautan *adj* maritime;
melaut *v* to go to sea;
pelaut *n* sailor, seaman
lawak: melawak *v* to joke,
jest; **pelawak** *n* comedian,
comic, clown
lawan *n* opponent, adver-
sary; opposite; ~ *kata*
opposite, antonym; **berla-**
wanan *v* to be opposed;
melawan *v* to oppose,
resist; **perlawanan** *n* opposition, resistance
lawat: melawat *v* to visit,
make a trip
layak, laik *adj* proper, suitable; **kelayakan** *n* suitability; **selayaknya** *adv*
properly, should
layan: layanan *n* service;
melayani *v* to serve;
pelayan *n* waiter, *m* waitress *f* attendant; **pelayanan**
n service
layang: layang-layang
kite; **melayang** *v* to float
(in the air)
layar sail; ~ *perak* television; **berlayar** *v* to sail;
pelayaran *n* voyage
layat: melayat *v* to visit a

house in mourning, pay
your respects
layu wither, wilt
lazim *adj* usual
LBH *abbrev Lembaga*
Bantuan Hukum Legal Aid
Agency
lebah *n* bee
lébar *adj* wide, broad;
lébarnya *n* width;
melébarkan *v* to widen
Lebaran *n* Idul Fitri, first two
days after the Ramadan fast
lébarnya *n* width ← **lébar**
lebat *adj* thick, dense
lebih *adv* more; ~ *baik,* ~
bagus better; ~ *buruk,* ~
jelek worse; **berlebihan**
adj excessive; **kelebihan** *n*
extra, excess; **melebihi** *v* to
exceed, surpass
lécéh: melécéhkan *v* to
insult; **pelécéhan** ~
seksual sexual harassment
lécét sore, blister; *luka* ~
blister
léci *n* lychee
ledak: ledakan *n* explosion;
meledak *v* to explode;
meledakkan *v* to explode
or detonate something;
peledak *bahan* ~ explosive

lédék, melédék *v* to tease, provoke

lédéng, léding *tukang* ~ plumber

lédré, lédri *pisang* ~ thinly sliced banana chips, a specialty of Malang

lega *adj* relieved; **melegakan** *adj* reassuring, consoling

lógal *adj* legal; **melégalisasi, melégalisir** *v* to legalize

légénda *n* legend, myth; **légéndaris** *adj* legendary

légong *tari* ~ Balinese trance dance performed by young girls

léhér *n* neck

lejit: melejit *namanya* ~ she suddenly became famous

lekas *adj* fast, quick, speedy; *(semoga)* ~ *sembuh* get well soon

lekat *adj* close; sticky, adhesive; **melekat** *v* to stick; **pelekat** *bahan* ~ adhesive

lekuk *n* hollow, cavity; concave

lelah *adj* tired, weary; **melelahkan** *adj* tiring

lelaki, laki-laki *adj* male; *n* man, male

lélang *n* auction; *juru* ~ auctioneer; **dilélang** for auction, tender

lelap *adj* sound, fast, completely; *tidur* ~ sound asleep

lélé *ikan* ~ catfish

léléh melt, run; **meléléh** *v* to drip, run

leluasa *adj* free, unrestricted; **keleluasaan** *n* freedom (of choice)

lelucon → **lucu**

leluhur *n* ancestor → **luhur**

lém *n* glue; ~ *tikus* sticky paper to catch rats; **dilém** *v* to be glued

lemah *adj* weak; **kelemahan** *n* weakness

lemak *n* fat; grease

lemari, almari *n* cupboard, closet, shelf; ~ *baju* wardrobe

lemas, lemes *adj* weak, drained; *mati* ~ suffocated, drowned

lembab, lembap *adj* humid, damp, moist; **kelembaban** *n* humidity; **pelembab, pelembap** *n* moisturizer

lembaga *n* institute, foundation, board; ~ *swadaya masyarakat (LSM)* non-government organization (NGO)

lembah *n* valley

lembam, lebam *adj* slow, inert; *gas ~* inert or noble gas

lembap → **lembab**

lembar *n* sheet (of paper), page

lembék *adj* soft, weak, flimsy

lembing *n* javelin, spear; *lempar ~* javelin (throw)

lembur *v* to work overtime, stay late

lembut *adj* soft, gentle; **kelembutan** *n* softness; **pelembut** *n* softener

lémpar, melémpar *v* to throw; **lémparan** *n* throw; **melémpari** *v* to pelt, throw something at; **melémpar-kan** *v* to throw something; **terlémpar** *adj* thrown, flung

lémpéng *n* large slightly curved shell; **lémpéngan** ~ *bumi* tectonic plate

lemper *n* sweet cake of sticky rice with a meat filling

léna: terléna *adj* confused, bewildered

léncéng: meléncéng *v* to deviate, go out of your way

lendir *n* mucus

lengan *n* arm, sleeve; *baju ~ panjang* long-sleeved shirt

lénggang *adj* swaying

lengkap *adj* complete; **melengkapi** *v* to furnish, supply; **perlengkapan** *n* outfit, equipment

léngkéng, keléngkéng *n (buah)* ~ small lychee

léngkét *adj* sticky, close

lengkuas *n* a kind of spice, galingale → **laos**

lengkung *adj* bent, convex; **melengkung** *v* to arch

léngsér *v* to abdicate, descend from power

lénong *n* Betawi folk play

lénsa *n* lens; ~ *kontak* contact lenses

lentéra *n* lantern

lentur *adj* elastic, pliable

lenyap *adj* disappeared, gone, vanished

lepas loose, free; escape; ~ *kendali* out of control; **melepaskan** *v* to release, let free; **pelepasan** *n* departure, farewell; **selepas** *prep, conj* after

léréng *n* slope

lés (to attend) a private class or course; ~ *piano* piano lesson; *guru* ~ private teacher

lésbi lesbian

lését: melését *v* to slip, skid, to miss the target; **pelésétan** *n* parody; **terpelését** *adj* slipped

lestari: melestarikan *n* to preserve, maintain; **pelestarian** *n* protection, preservation

lesu *adj* tired, weary

lesung *n* dimple, hollow; ~ *pipi* dimple

letak place, location; **letaknya** *n* the location, position; **meletakkan** *v* to put in place, set down; **terletak** *adj* situated, located

letih *adj* tired

létnan *n* lieutenant; ~ *kolonel (letkol)* lieutenant-colonel

letus: letusan *n* eruption; **meletus** *v* to erupt

léver *n* liver → **hati**

léwat *prep* past; via; *jam empat* ~ *lima* five past four; **meléwati** *v* to pass or go through; **meléwatkan** *v* to miss something

lezat *adj* delicious, tasty

lho you know (used to emphasize a statement, often denying something); *ejac* well!; *gitu* ~ like that, you know

liang *n* hole, passage; ~ *kubur* grave

liar *adj* wild, untamed; unregulated

liat *adj* tough

Libanon *n* Lebanon

libat: melibatkan *v* to involve, include; **terlibat** *adj* involved, implicated; **keterlibatan** *n* involvement, association

libur be free, on holiday (from school or work); **liburan** *n* holiday; ~ *sekolah* school holidays; **berlibur** *v* to go or be on holiday; **meliburkan** *v* to give a holiday to

licik *adj* cunning, tricky; **kelicikan** *n* trickery, cunning

licin *adj* smooth; slippery

lidah *n* tongue

lidi *n* palm-leaf rib; *sapu ~* small broom

liga *n* (football) league

lihat *v* to see; *~ halaman sebelah (lhs)* please turn over (PTO); **kelihatan** *adj* visible; *~nya* apparently, it seems; **melihat** *v* to see, look; **melihat-lihat** *v* to look around, have a look; **memperlihatkan** *v* to show, display

liku: berliku-liku *adj* twisted, complicated

lilin *n* candle; wax; *es ~* icypole, iced lolly

lilit turn, twist; **lilitan** *n* turn, twist; **terlilit** *adj* caught up, twisted

lima *adj* five; *~ belas* fifteen; *~ puluh* fifty; *ke~* fifth; *kembar ~* quin-tuplets; *simpang ~* five-way intersection

limbah *n* waste; *~ nuklir* nuclear waste

limpa *n* spleen

limpah: melimpah *adj* overflowing, abundant; **melimpahkan** *v* to shower upon

lincah *adj* nimble, deft, agile; **kelincahan** *n* agility

lindas: melindas *v* to run over, squash; **terlindas** *adj* run over

lindung: berlindung *v* to (take) shelter; **melindungi** *v* to protect, shelter; **pelindung** *n* protective device; **perlindungan** *n* protection

lingkar *n* ring, circle, cir-cumference; *jalan ~* ring road; **lingkaran** *n* circle; **melingkari** *v* to circle or surround

lingkung: lingkungan *n* environment, surroundings, circle

lingkup *n* scope, reach

linglung *adj* dazed, confused

lintah *n* leech

lintang across, latitude; **melintang** *adj* horizontal, across

lintas: lintasan *n* path, route; **melintas** *v* to pass by

lipat fold; *dua kali ~* double, twice; **lipatan** *n* fold; **berlipat** *~ ganda* many times over; **kelipatan** *n* multiple; **melipat** *v* to fold

LIPI *abbrev Lembaga Ilmu Pengetahuan Indonesia* Indonesian Institute of Sciences

lipstik *n* lipstick

liput: liputan *n* coverage, reporting; **meliputi** *v* to include, cover

lirik: melirik *v* to steal a glance

lisan *adj* oral, verbal

listrik electric, electricity

litbang *n* research and development (R & D) ← **penelitian dan pengembangan**

liter *n* liter, litre

liwet *nasi* ~ rice cooked in coconut milk, a specialty of Solo

LN *abbrev luar negeri* overseas, foreign

lo → **lho**

lobak *n* radish

lobang → **lubang**

logam *n* metal; *uang* ~ coins, small change

logat *n* accent; **berlogat** ~ *Jawa* to have a Javanese accent

logika *n* logic

logistik *n* logistics

loh → **lho**

lohor *Isl* the midday prayer

lok, lokomotif *n* locomotive

lokakarya *n* seminar, workshop

lokal *adj* local; *hujan* ~ local showers

lokasi *n* location; **berlokasi** *adj* located

lokét *n* counter, desk, ticket window or office; ~ *retour* counter for return tickets

lokomotif, lok *n* locomotive

lolong howl; **melolong** *v* to howl (of dogs)

lolos *v* to escape; succeed, progress

lomba race, competition, contest; **berlomba** *v* to compete, race

lombok *n* chilli

lompat jump, leap; ~ *jauh* long jump; ~ *tinggi* high jump; **melompat** *v* to jump, leapfrog

loncat jump (over something); ~ *indah* diving; *papan* ~ springboard; **meloncat** *v* to spring, jump

loncéng *n* bell

longgar *adj* loose, wide; **kelonggaran** *n* facility, dispensation; **melonggar-kan** v to loosen (restrictions)

longsor slip; *tanah* ~ landslide

lonjak: melonjak v to increase sharply, peak

lonjong *adj* oval

lontar *daun* ~ palm leaves once used as writing material

lontar throw; ~ *martil* hammer throw; **melontarkan** v to throw

lontong n cooked, solid slab of rice

loper n delivery boy

loréng *adj* striped; *baju* ~ camouflage gear, cammo

lorong n path; lane, alley

Lorosae *Timor* ~ East Timor

lorot: melorot v to fall, drop, plummet

losmén n guest house, accommodation, cheap hotel

loték n a dish of fresh vegetables with peanut sauce

loténg n attic, loft

loteré, lotré n lottery

lotot: melotot v to stare or gape at, with bulging eyes

lotré → loteré

lowong *adj* vacant; **lowongan** *adj* wanted, vacancy

loyang n cake tin, tray, mould

LSM *abbrev lembaga swadaya masyarakat* non-government organization (NGO)

Lt. *lantai* floor, level

lu *sl* you; *derog* you (bastard); *pergi* ~ get lost

luang *adj* free, empty; *waktu* ~ spare time; **peluang** n chance, opportunity

luap: meluap v to overflow, swell, wash

luar out, external; ~ *biasa* outstanding, extraordinary; ~ *negeri* overseas, abroad; *orang* ~ outsider, stranger; **keluar** go out; be issued; *prep* out, outside; **keluaran** n edition, version, issue; **mengeluarkan** v to issue, publish, send out, release

luas wide, broad; space; **luasnya** n width; area; **memperluas** v to widen, expand, enlarge

lubang, lobang n hole, passage; ~ *hidung* nostril; ~ *di jalan* pothole; **melubangi** v to pierce, put a hole in

lubuk *n* deep pool; ~ *hati* depth of your heart

lucu *adj* cute, sweet; funny; odd; **melucu** *v* to make jokes, be funny

lucut: melucuti *v* to strip or pull off

ludah *n* saliva, spit; **meludah** *v* to spit

lugu *adj* naive, gullible

luhur *adj* lofty, noble, esteemed; **leluhur** *n* ancestor

luka wound; injured; ~ *bakar* burn; ~ *parah* badly wounded or injured; ~ *ringan* mild injury; **melukai, melukakan** *v* to hurt or wound

lukis *v* to paint, draw; **lukisan** *n* painting, picture, portrait (of a person); **melukis** *v* to paint, draw; **pelukis** *n* painter, artist

lulus *v to* pass; ~ *ujian* pass an exam; *tidak* ~ fail; **lulusan** *n* graduate

lumas: pelumas *n* lubricant

lumayan *adv, adj* quite, not bad, fairly

lumba-lumba *n* dolphin, porpoise

lumbung ~ *padi* rice silo or barn

lumpang *n* pestle, rice pounder

lumpia *n* spring rolls

lumpuh *adj* paralysed, lame; ~ *layuh* polio; **melumpuhkan** *v* to knock out, paralyse

lumpur *n* mud

lumrah *adj* usual, accepted, common

lumur smear; **berlumuran** *adj* smeared, stained; **melumuri** *v* to smear, cover with

lumut *n* moss; *hijau* ~ moss green, bright green

lunak *adj* soft

lunas *adj* paid off, in full; **melunasi** *v* to pay off

luncur: meluncurkan *v* to launch, set in motion

luntur fade, lose color, run

lupa *v* to forget; **kelupaan** *n* something forgotten; **melupakan** *v* to forget something; **terlupakan** *tak* ~ unforgettable

lurah *n* head of a *kelurahan*, village chief; **kelurahan** *n* administrative unit, village

lurik *kain* ~ striped cloth

lurus *adj* straight; **meluruskan** *v* to straighten

lusa *adv* the day after tomorrow; **besok** ~ tomorrow or the day after

lusin *n* dozen, twelve; **selusin** *n* a dozen

lutung *n* black monkey

lutut *n* knee; **berlutut** to kneel (down)

luwes *adj* attractive, well-presented

M

M *Masehi* Christian calendar

m meter

maaf sorry; *minta* ~ apologize, say you're sorry; *(mohon)* ~ *lahir (dan) batin* ask forgiveness for all sins (at Idul Fitri); **bermaaf-maafan** *v, Isl* to beg forgiveness of each other (at Idul Fitri); **memaafkan** *v* to forgive, pardon

maag, mag *n, coll* stomach (disorder); *obat* ~ antacid; *sakit* ~ weak stomach, gastric pain

mabes *n* headquarters; ~ *Polri* National Police Headquarters ← **markas besar**

mabuk *adj* drunk; ill; motion sickness; ~ *jalan* carsick; ~ *laut* seasick; *orang* ~ drunk

macam *n* kind, sort, model; **macam-macam** *adj, neg* all sorts; **bermacam-macam** *adj* various; **semacam** *adj* a kind or type of

macan *n* large spotted cat; *n, coll* tiger; ~ *kumbang* leopard, panther; ~ *tutul* cheetah

macet, macét *adj* jammed, blocked; traffic jam; ~ *total* gridlock; **kemacetan** *n* jam; ~ *lalu lintas* traffic jam

madani *adj* civil

madrasah *n, Isl* school, college

madu *n* honey; co-spouse; **memadu** *v* to cheat on

madya *adj* medium, middle

magang (do) work experience, apprentice

magnét → **maknit**

magrib, maghrib *n* sunset; sunset (prayer)

maha- *adj* great; *Tuhan Yang ~ kuasa* Almighty God

mahal *adj* expensive, dear; *jual ~* have a high asking price

mahar *n, Isl* dowry, bride price

mahasiswa *n* (university or college) student; **mahasiswi** *n, f* (female) student

mahir *adj* expert, skilled; **kemahiran** *n* skill

mahkamah *n* court of law; *~ Agung* High Court

mahkota *n* crown, crest

main *v* to play, do (a sport); *~ golf* play golf; *~ piano* play the piano; **main-main** *v* to joke around, not be serious; **mainan** *n* toy; **bermain** *v* to play; *~ api* to play with fire; **memainkan** *v* to play something; *~ biola* to play the violin; **permainan** *n* game, match

maizéna *n* corn

majalah *n* magazine; *~ bulanan* monthly (magazine)

majelis *n* assembly, council

majemuk *adj* compound, complex

majikan *n* employer

maju go forward, advance, progress, improve; *~ mundur* back and forth; **kemajuan** *n* progress, advance

mak *pron* mother; *~ comblang* matchmaker

maka *conj* therefore, so, then; **makanya** *conj* that's why, so

makalah *n* paper, essay

makam *n* grave; *Taman ~ Pahlawan* Heroes' Cemetery; **memakamkan** *v* to bury; **pemakaman** *n* funeral, burial

makan *v* to eat; *~ dulu* said when eating first before others; *~ hati* be upset; *~ malam* (eat or have) dinner; *~ waktu* take (time); *kereta ~* restaurant car; **makanan** *n* food; **memakan** *v* to eat, consume, take; *~ obat* to take a pill or capsule

makanya *conj* that's why, so ← **maka**

makaroni *n* macaroni

Makasar, Makassar *n* Macassar (formerly Ujung Pandang); *bahasa ~, orang ~* Macassarese

makhluk, mahluk *n* creature

maki, mencaci-maki *v* to insult, abuse; **memaki, memaki-maki** *v* to insult, heap abuse on

makin *adv* increasingly; ~ *lama*, ~ *besar* the longer, the bigger; **semakin** *adv* even more

maklum *v* to know, be aware of; *agar* ~ let it be known; **memaklumi** *v* to be aware of, accept

makmur *adj* prosperous

makna *n* meaning

maknit, magnét *n* magnet

maksiat *adj* immoral

maksimal maximal(ly); **maksimum** *n* maximum

maksud *n* purpose, intention, meaning; ~ *saya* I mean; **bermaksud** *v* to intend; **dimaksud(kan)** *v* to be meant or intended

mal, mol *n* shopping center, mall

Maladéwa the Maldives

malah, malahan instead, rather, on the other hand

Malaka, Melaka *n* Malacca

malam *n* night, evening;

~ *Jumat* Thursday night; *Jumat* ~ Friday night; ~ *hari* at night; ~ *Natal* Christmas Eve; **malam-malam** *adv* late at night; **bermalam** *v* to spend or stay the night; **kemalaman** *adv* too late (at night); after dark; **semalam** *adv* last night; **semalaman** *adv* all night long

malang *adj* unlucky

malas *adj* lazy, can't be bothered; **bermalas-malas(an)** *v* to lie or laze around, be lazy

Malaysia *n* Malaysia; *bahasa* ~, *orang* ~ Malaysian

maling *n* thief; **kemalingan** *v* to be robbed

malu *adj* shy, ashamed, embarrassed; *jangan* ~ don't be shy; **malu-malu** *adj* shy; **kemaluan** *n* genital, sex organ; **memalukan** *adj* embarrassing; **pemalu** shy (person)

mam, mam-mam *v, ch* eat

Mami, Mi *pron, coll* Mom, Mommy (in Westernized circles)

mampet *adj* stuck, blocked, jammed; *hidung* ~ blocked nose

mampir *v* to drop in, call on

mampu *adj* able, capable; *adj* well-off; *kurang* ~ poor, not well-off; **kemampuan** *n* ability, capability

mana *pron* where, which; ~ *mungkin* how could it be?; ~ *saja* whichever; *dari* ~ from where; *di* ~ where; *di* ~ *saja* wherever; *ke* ~ where; **mana-mana** *di* ~, *ke* ~ everywhere

mana-mana *di* ~, *ke* ~ everywhere ← **mana**

manca- *adj* many; ~*negara* international, overseas

mancing → **pancing**

mancung *adj* straight (of noses)

mancur *air* ~ fountain ← **pancur**

Mandar ethnic group in South Sulawesi; *bahasa* ~, *orang* ~ Mandarese

mandau *n* knife used in Kalimantan

mandek, mandeg stop, cease, get stuck, stagnate

mandi bathe, take a bath, wash (the body); ~ *lulur* traditional body scrub; **bermandi** *v* to bathe; ~ *keringat* to be soaked in sweat; **memandikan** *v* to wash someone; **permandian** *n* christening, baptism; *bapak* ~ godfather

mandor *n* supervisor, overseer

mandul *adj* infertile, sterile, childless

manfaat *n* benefit, use; **bermanfaat** *adj* useful, of benefit; **memanfaatkan** *v* to take advantage of, (draw) benefit from

mangga *n* mango

manggis *n* mangosteen

manggung *v, coll* to perform ← **panggung**

mangkal *v, coll* to use as a base, wait for work ← **pangkal**

mangkok, mangkuk *n* bowl

mangsa *n* prey

mani *air* ~ sperm

manik: manik-manik *n* beads

manis *adj* sweet; pretty; nice; **manisan** *n* sweets, candy; sugared snacks;

kemanisan *adj* too sweet;
pemanis ~ *buatan* artificial
sweetener

manja spoilt; *anak* ~ spoilt
child; **memanjakan** *v* to
spoil someone

mantan *adj* former (of
people); ~ *Presiden* former
President; ~ *suami* ex-
husband

mantap *adj* stable, steady

mantel *n* (long) coat, raincoat

mantu *n* son- or daughter-
in-law; *v* to marry off a son
or daughter → **menantu**

manula *n* old person, senior
citizen → **manusia lanjut
usia**

manusia *n* human (being);
humanity; **perikemanusiaan** *adj* humanitarian

manyar *burung* ~ weaverbird

map *n* folder

mapan *adj* settled, comfortable

marah *adj* angry; *cepat* ~,
gampang ~ short-tempered,
hot-headed; **marah-marah**
frequently angry; in a bad
mood; **kemarahan** *n* anger;
memarahi *v* to scold, be

angry with; **pemarah** *adj*
bad-tempered

Maret *bulan* ~ March

marga *n, lit* road; *Jasa*
~ Indonesian Highway
Corporation

marga *n* (Batak) family name

margarin *n* margarine

margasatwa *n* wild animals,
fauna

mari let's go, come on;
please (said when someone
begs leave); ~*lah* let us

marinir *n* Marines

markas *n* office, headquarters; ~ *besar (mabes)*
headquarters

markisa *n* kind of passion-
fruit

marmer *n* marble

marmot, marmut *n* guinea
pig, marmot

Maroko, Marokko *n*
Morocco

martabak *n* large fried
snack with filling; ~ *telur*
kind of omelet

martabat *n* dignity, rank

mas, emas *n* gold; ~ *kawin*
dowry; ~ *putih* platinum,
white gold; *tukang* ~
goldsmith

Mas *pron, m* address for elder brother, male person slightly older than yourself, or worker in service industry

masa *n* time, period; ~ *depan* future; ~ *lalu* past; *sepanjang* ~ forever

masa, masak no! I can't believe it! it's not possible (expression of disbelief)

masak cook; cooked; **masakan** *n* food, cooking, dish; ~ *Cina* Chinese food, Chinese cuisine; **memasak** *v* to cook

masalah *n* problem; ~*nya* the problem is; *tidak* ~ no problem; **bermasalah** *adj* problem, troublesome

masam, masem *adj* sour; acid

Maséhi *adj* Christian

masih *adv* still, yet

masing: **masing-masing** *pron* each, respectively

masinis *n* train driver, engineer

masjid, mesjid *n* mosque

maskapai ~ *penerbangan* airline

maskara *n* mascara, eye-shadow

masker *n* surgical mask

massa *n* the masses, the public; **massal** *adj* mass

masuk *v* to come in, enter; ~ *akal* make sense, logical; ~ *angin* have or catch a cold; **memasuki** *v* to enter (illicitly); **memasukkan** *v* to put in, insert, import, enter; **termasuk** *adj* including

masya Allah it is God's will, heavens above!

masyarakat *n* society; ~ *madani* civil society; **kemasyarakatan** *adj* social

mata *n* eye; ~ *air* spring, well; ~ *angin* direction, compass point; ~ *kaki* ankle; ~ *keranjang* wandering eye; ~ *uang* currency; **mata-mata** *n* spy

matahari *n* sun; *bunga* ~ sunflower; ~ *terbenam* sunset; ~ *terbit* sunrise

mata-mata *n* spy ← **mata**

matang *adj* ripe, cooked, mature; *setengah* ~ medium, half-cooked

matématika *n* mathematics, maths

matéri *n* material; **matérial** *adj* material; **matérialis** *adj* materialist

mati die; go out, be extinguished; ~ *lampu* blackout; ~ *suri* coma; **kematian** *n* death, passing; **mematikan** *v* to kill, extinguish, put out

matras *n* mat (in gymnastics or martial arts)

mau *v* to want, will; ~ *tidak* ~ whether you want to or not, there's no avoiding it; **kemauan** *n* want, will, desire

maut *n* death; *malaikat* ~, *malaikatul* ~ angel of death

maya *dunia* ~ cyberspace

mayat *n* corpse

mayor *pron* major; ~ *Jenderal (Mayjen)* Major-General

Mbak *pron, f* address for elder sister, female person slightly older than yourself, or worker in service industry

mbok *coll* perhaps (softens message)

Mbok *pron, f* mother; address for female servants

MCK *abbrev mandi cuci kakus* toilet and bathing facilities

mébel, meubel *n* furniture

medali, médali *n* medal

médan *n* field, plain, square; ~ *perang* battlefield

medok *adj* very thick (of an accent, esp Javanese)

méga *n* cloud

megah *adj* glorious, luxurious, grand

Méi *bulan* ~ May

méja *n* table; ~ *hijau* court (of law); ~ *makan* dining table; ~ *tulis* desk

Mekah, Mekkah *n* Mecca

mekar *v* to blossom; **pemekaran** *n* expansion, development

Méksiko *n* Mexico

melacak *v* to trace ← **lacak**

meladéni *v* to serve someone ← **ladén**

melafalkan *v* to pronounce ← **lafal**

melahirkan *v* to give birth to; to create ← **lahir**

melainkan *conj* rather, instead

melajang *v* to be single ← **lajang**

melaju *v* to proceed quickly ← **laju**

Melaka, Malaka *n* Malacca

melaksanakan *v* to realize, execute, carry out ← **laksana**

melakukan *v* to do, perform, carry out ← **laku**

melalui *v* to pass through; *conj* through, via ← **lalu**

melamar *v* to apply ← **lamar**

melambaikan *v* to wave something; ~ *tangan* to wave goodbye ← **lambai**

melambangkan *v* to symbolize, represent ← **lambang**

melambatkan *v* to slow down ← **lambat**

melambung *v* to bounce; **melambungkan** *v* to bounce something ← **lambung**

melaminasi *v* to laminate ← **laminasi**

melampiaskan *v* to release, indulge in

melampirkan *v* to attach, enclose

melamun *v* to day-dream, fantasize ← **lamun**

melanda *v* to engulf, attack, hit ← **landa**

melanggar *v* to disobey, offend; ~ *hukum* to break the law ← **langgar**

melangkah *v* to step ← **langkah**

melanglang ~ *buana* to see the world, travel great distances ← **langlang**

melanjutkan *v* to continue something ← **lanjut**

mélankolis *adj* melancholic

melantik *v* to install, inaugurate ← **lantik**

melantunkan ~ *lagu* to sing (a song) ← **lantun**

melapor *v* to report; **melaporkan** *v* to report, inform ← **lapor**

melar stretch, expand

melarang *v* to ban, prohibit, forbid ← **larang**

melarat *adj* miserable, poor, poverty-stricken; *hidup* ~ live in poverty; **kemelaratan** *n* poverty

melarikan *v* to run off with, abduct, kidnap; ~ *diri* to run away, flee, escape ← **lari**

melarutkan *v* to dissolve ← **larut**

melas: memelas *adj* pathetic, pitiful

melata v to crawl, creep; *binatang* ~ reptile ← **lata**

melati n jasmine

melatih v to train ← **latih**

melaut v to go to sea ← **laut**

melawak v to joke, jest ← **lawak**

melawan v to oppose, resist ← **lawan**

melawat v to visit, make a trip ← **lawat**

melayang v to float (in the air) ← **layang**

melayani v to serve ← **layan**

melayat v to visit a house in mourning, to pay your respects ← **layat**

Melayu Malay; Indonesian; *bahasa* ~, *orang* ~ Malay

melébarkan v to widen ← **lébar**

melebihi v to exceed, surpass ← **lebih**

melécéhkan v to insult ← **lécéh**

meledak v to explode; **meledakkan** v to explode or detonate something ← **ledak**

melédék n to tease, provoke ← **lédék**

melegakan adj reassuring, consoling ← **lega**

melégalisasi, melégalisir v to legalize ← **légalisasi**

melejit *namanya* ~ she suddenly became famous ← **lejit**

melék awake, eyes open; ~ *huruf* literate; **kemelék-hurufan** n literacy

melekat v to stick ← **lekat**

melelahkan adj tiring ← **lelah**

meléléh v to drip, run ← **léléh**

melémpar v to throw; **melémpari** v to pelt, throw something at; **melémparkan** v to throw something ← **lémpar**

meléncéng v to deviate, go out of your way ← **léncéng**

melengkapi v to furnish, supply ← **lengkap**

melengkung v to arch ← **lengkung**

melepaskan v to release, let free ← **lepas**

melését v to slip, skid; to miss the target; **pelésétan, plésétan** n parody ← **lését**

170

melestarikan *n* to preserve, maintain ← **lestari**

meletakkan *v* to put in place, set down ← **letak**

meletus *v* to erupt ← **letus**

meléwati *v* to pass or go through; **meléwatkan** *v* to miss something ← **léwat**

melibatkan *v* to involve, include ← **libat**

meliburkan *v* to give a holiday to ← **libur**

melihat *v* to see, look; **melihat-lihat** *v* to look around, have a look; **memperlihatkan** *v* to show, display ← **lihat**

melimpah *adj* overflowing, abundant; **melimpahkan** *v* to shower upon ← **limpah**

melindas *v* to run over, squash ← **lindas**

melindungi *v* to protect, shelter ← **lindung**

melingkari *v* to circle or surround ← **lingkar**

melintang *adj* horizontal, across ← **lintang**

melintas *v* to pass by ← **lintas**

melipat *v* to fold ← **lipat**

meliputi *v* to include, cover ← **liput**

melirik *v* to steal a glance ← **lirik**

melolong *v* to howl (of dogs) ← **lolong**

melompat *v* to jump, leap-frog ← **lompat**

mélon *n* rockmelon, cantaloupe

meloncat *v* to spring, jump (over something) ← **loncat**

melonggarkan *v* to loosen (restrictions) ← **longgar**

melonjak *v* to increase sharply, peak ← **lonjak**

melontar, melontarkan *v* to throw ← **lontar**

melorot *v* to fall, drop, plummet ← **lorot**

melotot *v* to stare or gape at, with bulging eyes ← **lotot**

meluap *v* to overflow, swell, wash ← **luap**

melubangi *v* to pierce, put a hole in ← **lubang**

melucu *v* to make jokes, be funny ← **lucu**

melucuti *v* to strip or pull off ← **lucut**

meludah *v* to spit ← **ludah**

melukai, melukakan *v* to
hurt or wound ← **luka**

melukis *v* to paint, draw
← **lukis**

melumpuhkan *v* to knock
out, paralyze ← **lumpuh**

melumuri *v* to smear, cover
with ← **lumur**

melunasi *v* to pay off ←
lunas

meluncurkan *v* to launch,
set in motion ← **luncur**

melupakan *v* to forget
something ← **lupa**

meluruskan *v* to straighten
← **lurus**

memaafkan *v* to forgive,
pardon ← **maaf**

memadai *adj* enough,
sufficient ← **pada**

memadamkan *v* to put out,
extinguish ← **padam**

memadu *v* to cheat on ←
madu

memadukan *v* to combine,
unite ← **padu**

memahami *v* to understand,
comprehend ← **paham**

memahat *v* to sculpt, chisel
← **pahat**

memainkan *v* to play
something; ~ *biola* to play

the violin ← **main**

memakai *v* to wear; to use
~ *kacamata* to wear glasses
← **pakai**

memakamkan *v* to bury ←
makam

memakan *v* to eat, consume,
take; ~ *obat* to take a pill or
capsule ← **makan**

memaki, memaki-maki *v*
to insult, heap abuse on ←
maki

memaklumi *v* to be aware
of, accept ← **maklum**

memaksa *v* to force ←
paksa

memaku *v* to nail ← **paku**

memalsukan *v* to falsify,
forge ← **palsu**

memalukan *adj* embarrassing ← **malu**

memamérkan *v* to display,
exhibit ← **pamér**

memanaskan *v* to heat (up)
← **panas**

memancarkan *v* to broadcast ← **pancar**

memancing *v* to fish (with
hook and line) ← **pancing**

memancung *v* to cut off;
~ *kepala* to behead or
decapitate ← **pancung**

memandang *v* to view, consider ← **pandang**

memandikan *v* to wash someone ← **mandi**

memandu *v* to guide ← **pandu**

memanfaatkan *v* to take advantage of, (draw) benefit from ← **manfaat**

mémang *conj* **émang** *coll* indeed

memanggang *v* to roast, bake, toast ← **panggang**

memanggil *v* to call ← **panggil**

memangkas *v* to cut, shear, trim ← **pangkas**

memangku *v* to take on (your lap) ← **pangku**

memanjakan *v* to spoil someone ← **manja**

memanjat *v* to climb

memantau *v* to observe, watch ← **pantau**

memaparkan *v* to explain ← **papar**

memar *adj* bruised

memarahi *v* to scold, be angry with ← **marah**

memarut *v* to grate ← **parut**

memasak *v* to cook ← **masak**

memasang *v* to put up, attach, fix; ~ *iklan* to advertise; ~ *lampu* to switch on a light ← **pasang**

memasarkan *v* to market ← **pasar**

memasok *v* to supply ← **pasok**

memastikan *v* to confirm, make sure, ascertain ← **pasti**

memasuki *v* to enter (illicitly); **memasukkan** *v* to put in, insert, import, enter ← **masuk**

mematahkan *v* to break ← **patah**

mematikan *v* to kill, extinguish, put out ← **mati**

mematok *v* to fix, set ← **patok**

mematuhi *v* to obey ← **patuh**

membaca *v* to read ← **baca**

membagi *v* to divide, distribute ← **bagi**

membahagiakan *v* to make happy ← **bahagia**

membahas *v* to discuss, debate ← **bahas**

membaik *v* to improve ← **baik**

membajak v to hijack; to copy illegally ← **bajak**

membajak v to plough ← **bajak**

membakar v to burn ← **bakar**

membalap v to race ← **balap**

membalas v to reply, respond ← **balas**

membalik v to return, reverse, turn over; **membalikkan** v to turn something over ← **balik**

membalut v to bandage ← **balut**

membandingkan v to compare something ← **banding**

membanggakan v to make proud, please ← **bangga**

membangkit v to rise, get up ← **bangkit**

membangun v to build or create

membangunkan v to wake someone up ← **bangun**

membantah v to deny, dispute ← **bantah**

membantai v to slaughter, kill viciously ← **bantai**

membanting v to throw down (with a bang); ~ *pintu*

to slam the door; ~ *tulang* to toil, work yourself to the bone ← **banting**

membantu v to help (someone) ← **bantu**

membaptis v to baptize, christen ← **baptis**

membasahi v to moisten, wet ← **basah**

membasmi v to exterminate, destroy, wipe out ← **basmi**

membatalkan v to cancel, repeal ← **batal**

membatasi v to limit, restrict, curb something ← **batas**

membatik n to apply wax onto fabric ← **batik**

membaur v to integrate, mix with others (of people) ← **baur**

membawa v to take, bring, carry; conduct; **membawakan** v to bring or carry for someone; to sing ← **bawa**

membawahi v to head a section (with staff under you) ← **bawah**

membayar v to pay; ~ *di muka* to pay in advance ← **bayar**

membebani v to burden someone with something; **membebankan** v to charge something to someone ← **beban**

membébaskan v to exempt, liberate, free someone ← **bébas**

membédakan v to discriminate, diffcrentiate between, consider as different ← **béda**

membeku v to freeze; **membekukan** v to freeze something ← **beku**

membéla v to defend ← **béla**

membelah v to split in two ← **belah**

membelanjakan v to spend money ← **belanja**

membeli v to buy, purchase; **membelikan** v to buy something for someone ← **beli**

membélok v to bend, turn; **membélokkan** v to turn, divert something ← **bélok**

membenarkan v to confirm, verify; justify ← **benar**

membenci v to hate ← **benci**

membéngkokkan v to bend something ← **béngkok**

membentak v to shout, scold, snap ← **bentak**

membentuk v to form, set up something (eg. committee) ← **bentuk**

memberangus v to muzzle, bridle ← **berangus**

memberantas v to wipe out, fight against ← **berantas**

memberatkan v to burden, make heavy; *adj* incriminating ← **berat**

memberéskan v to clear up, make ready ← **bérés**

memberhentikan v to stop (a vehicle); dismiss

memberi v to give ← **beri**

memberitahu v to advise, inform, tell ← **beritahu**

memberitakan v to report ← **berita**

memberkati v to bless; *Tuhan* ~ God bless ← **berkat**

memberontak v to rebel, revolt ← **berontak**

membersihkan v to clean; wipe out (eg disease) ← **bersih**

membesar *v* to get bigger, grow; **membesarkan** *v* to bring up, raise (children) ← **besar**

membetulkan *v* to correct, repair ← **betul**

membiakkan *v* to breed, cultivate ← **biak**

membiarkan *v* to let, allow, permit ← **biar**

membiayai *v* to finance someone or something ← **biaya**

membicarakan *v* to discuss ← **bicara**

membilas *v* to rinse ← **bilas**

membimbing *v* to lead, guide, coach ← **bimbing**

membina *v* to build up, found ← **bina**

membinasakan *v* to destroy, ruin ← **binasa**

membingkai *v* to frame ← **bingkai**

membingungkan *adj* confusing ← **bingung**

membintangi *v* to star in ← **bintang**

membiru *v* to turn blue ← **biru**

membisik *v* to whisper ← **bisik**

membisu *v* to be silent, say nothing ← **bisu**

membius *v* to drug, anesthetize ← **bius**

memblokir *v* to block; *jalan* to block the road ← **blokir**

membobol *v* to break into ← **bobol**

membocorkan *v* to leak something ← **bocor**

membohong *v* to lie; **membohongi** *v* to lie to someone ← **bohong**

memboikot *v* to boycott something ← **boikot**

membolongi *v* to pierce ← **bolong**

membolos *v* skip, be absent, play truant, wag, skive; ~ *sekolah* to skip school ← **bolos**

memboncéng *v* to ride with someone else on a two-wheeled vehicle, dink; to sponge or cadge a lift ← **boncéng**

membongkar *v* to pull apart, dismantle; to unpack; to unearth ← **bongkar**

membordir *v* to embroider ← **bordir**

memborgol *v* to handcuff ← **borgol**

memborong *v* to buy up, buy in bulk ← **borong**

membosankan *adj* boring, tiresome ← **bosan**

membotaki *v* to shave, make bald ← **botak**

memboyong *v* to take (someone) away ← **boyong**

membrédel *v* to muzzle, bridle, ban ← **brédel**

membual *v* to foam; to froth at the mouth, talk rubbish ← **bual**

membuang *v* to throw out; to waste; to exile; ~ *ingus* blow your nose; ~ *kesempatan* waste an opportunity ← **buang**

membuat *v* to make; ~ *marah* to make angry ← **buat**

membubarkan *v* to break something up ← **bubar**

membudaya *v* to spread, become entrenched ← **budaya**

membudidayakan *v* to cultivate, grow ← **budidaya**

membujuk *v* to coax ← **bujuk**

membuka *v* to open; ~ *rahasia* to reveal a secret; **membukakan** *v* to open (for someone) ← **buka**

membuktikan *v* to prove ← **bukti**

membumbui *v* to season ← **bumbu**

membungkam *v* to keep silent ← **bungkam**

membungkuk *v* to bow, be hunched; **membungkuk-kan** ~ *badan* to bow ← **bungkuk**

membungkus *v* to wrap; ~ *kado* wrap a gift ← **bungkus**

membuntuti *v* to follow someone ← **buntut**

membunuh *v* to kill; ~ *diri* to kill yourself, commit suicide ← **bunuh**

membunyikan *v* to sound, ring something ← **bunyi**

memburu *v* to hunt, chase ← **buru**

memburuk *v* to worsen ← **buruk**

membusuk *v* to rot ← **busuk**

membutuhkan *v* to need something ← **butuh**

memecahkan v to break; to solve; ~ *soal* to solve a problem ← **pecah**

memecat v to fire, dismiss ← **pecat**

memedulikan v to care or be bothered about ← **peduli**

memegang v to hold, grasp ← **pegang**

memejamkan ~ *mata* to close your eyes ← **pejam**

memelas *adj* pitiful, pathetic ← **belas**

memelésétkan v to up-end, send off-course; change ← **pelését**

memelihara v to take care of, look after, cultivate ← **pelihara**

memelintir, memelintirkan v to twist ← **pelintir**

memelopori v to pioneer, lead ← **pelopor**

memelotot v to stare, have bulging eyes; **memelotot-kan** ~ *mata* to stare ← **lotot**

memeluk v to hug or embrace ← **peluk**

memencét v to press (a button, key) ← **pencét**

meméndékkan v to shorten ← **péndék**

memengaruhi v to influence, affect ← **pengaruh**

memenggal v to cut off, amputate ← **penggal**

memenjara, memenjara-kan v to put in prison, imprison ← **penjara**

meménsiunkan v to pension off ← **pénsiun**

mementaskan v to stage, present ← **pentas**

mementingkan v to make important, emphasize ← **penting**

memenuhi v to fulfill, meet requirements ← **penuh**

memeragakan v to display, show ← **peraga**

memérah v to blush ← **mérah**

memerankan v to portray, play the role of ← **peran**

memeras v to squeeze, press; to blackmail, extort ← **peras**

memercayai v to trust someone; **mempercaya-kan** v to entrust with ← **percaya**

memeriahkan v to liven up, enliven ← **meriah**

memeriksa v to examine or

178

investigate; ~ *ulang* to review ← **periksa**

memerintah *v* to rule, govern, reign; **memerintahkan** *v* to order or command something ← **perintah**

memerkosa *v* to rape ← **perkosa**

memerlukan *v* to need, require ← **perlu**

memesan *v* to order ← **pesan**

memesona, memesonakan *adj* enthralling, enchanting ← **pesona**

memetik *v* to pick; to strum ← **petik**

memfitnah *v* to slander ← **fitnah**

memfokuskan *v* to focus something; ~ *diri* to focus yourself ← **fokus**

memicu *v* to trigger, set off ← **picu**

memijat *v* to massage ← **pijat**

memikirkan *v* to think about ← **pikir**

memilih *v* to choose or select; to elect or vote (for) ← **pilih**

memiliki *v* to own, possess ← **milik**

memimpikan *v* to dream of ← **mimpi**

memimpin *v* to lead ← **pimpin**

memindahkan *v* to move, transfer ← **pindah**

meminggir *v, coll* to move to the side, pull over ← **pinggir**

meminjam *v* to borrow; **meminjami** *v* to lend someone; **meminjamkan** *v* to lend something ← **pinjam**

meminta *v* to ask for, request; **meminta-minta** *v* to beg, ask for money ← **minta, pinta**

memisah *v* to separate; **memisahkan** *v* to separate something ← **pisah**

memojokkan *v* to force into a corner ← **pojok**

memompa *v* to pump ← **pompa**

mémori *n* (electronic) memory

memotivasi *v* to motivate ← **motivasi**

memotong *v* to cut, deduct; to slaughter, amputate; to interrupt ← **potong**

memotrét *v* to photograph ← **potrét**

mempelai *kedua* ~ bridal couple; ~ *pria* groom; ~ *wanita* bride

mempelajari *v* to study something in depth ← **ajar**

memperbaiki *v* to repair, fix ← **baik**

memperbesar *v* to enlarge something ← **besar**

memperboléhkan *v* to allow, permit ← **boléh**

mempercepat *v* to speed up, accelerate ← **cepat**

memperdaya *v* to deceive, use, trick ← **daya**

memperdengarkan *v* to play, broadcast ← **dengar**

memperebutkan *v* to seize, take by force ← **rebut**

mempererat *v* to strengthen, make closer ← **erat**

memperhatikan *v* to notice, pay attention to ← **hati**

memperingati *v* to commemorate ← **ingat**

memperjuangkan *v* to fight for ← **juang**

memperkenalkan *v* to introduce ← **kenal**

memperkirakan *v* to estimate, calculate ← **kira**

memperkuat *v* to reinforce, make stronger ← **kuat**

memperluas *v* to widen, expand, enlarge ← **luas**

mempermasalahkan *v* to make a problem out of ← **masalah**

mempermudah *v* to make easier ← **mudah**

memperoléh *v* to obtain, get ← **oléh**

memperolok *v* to tease, taunt ← **olok**

memperpanjang *v* to extend, make longer ← **panjang**

memperparah *v* to make worse, aggravate ← **parah**

memperpéndék *v* to shorten, make even shorter ← **péndék**

mempersatukan *v* to unite various things ← **satu**

mempersembahkan *v* to offer (up), present ← **sembah**

mempersiapkan *v* to prepare something, get something ready ← **siap**

mempersilakan *v* to invite

someone to do something
← **sila**

mempersoalkan v to
question, discuss ← **soal**

mempertahankan v to
defend or maintain ← **tahan**

**mempertanggung-
jawabkan** v to account for
← **tanggung jawab**

mempertanyakan v to
query ← **tanya**

mempertimbangkan v to
consider ← **timbang**

mempraktékkan v to put
into practice ← **praktek**

memprihatinkan adj
worrying ← **prihatin**

memprioritaskan v to
prioritize ← **prioritas**

memproduksi v to produce
← **produksi**

mempromosikan v to
promote ← **promosi**

memprotés v to (make a)
protest ← **protés**

mempunyai v to have,
own, possess ← **punya**

memuakkan adj revolting,
disgusting ← **muak**

memuaskan adj satisfactory
← **puas**

memuat v to contain ← **muat**

memudar v to fade ← **pudar**

memugar v to restore,
renovate ← **pugar**

memuja v to worship ← **puja**

memuji v to praise

memukul v to hit, beat,
strike ← **pukul**

memulai v to start or begin
something ← **mula, mulai**

memulangkan v to give
back; to send back, repatriate ← **pulang**

memuliakan v to honor,
glorify ← **mulia**

memungkinkan adj
conducive; v to enable,
make possible ← **mungkin**

memungut v to pick up,
collect ← **pungut**

memusatkan v to focus;
~ perhatian to concentrate
← **pusat**

memusingkan ~ kepala
puzzling ← **pusing**

memusnahkan v to destroy;
pemusnahan n act of
destruction ← **musnah**

memusuhi v to fight
against, antagonize, make
an enemy of ← **musuh**

memutar v to wind; to
rotate; ~ balik to turn

around, do a U-turn;
memutar-balikkan *v* to
reverse, distort; **perputaran** *n* rotation ← **putar**

memutuskan *v* to terminate
or break; to decide ← **putus**

menaati *v* to obey or follow
something ← **taat**

menabrak *v* to collide with;
menabrakkan *v* to ram
something into ← **tabrak**

menabuh *v* to beat (a drum)
← **tabuh**

menabung *v* to save or
deposit money ← **tabung**

menabur *v* to scatter or
sprinkle ← **tabur**

menafsirkan *v* to interpret
something ← **tafsir**

menagih *v* to ask for
payment, bill ← **tagih**

menahan *v* to bear, endure;
to detain; ~ *diri* to hold
yourself back, restrain
yourself ← **tahan**

menaiki *v* to ride, mount,
get on; **menaikkan** *v* to
raise, hoist ← **naik**

menakdirkan *v* to determine,
to predestine ← **takdir**

menakjubkan *adj* astonishing, amazing ← **takjub**

menaklukkan *v* to defeat,
conquer, subdue ← **takluk**

menaksir *v* to estimate,
appraise, value; to like, find
someone or something
attractive ← **taksir**

menakutkan *v, adv*
frightening; to frighten or
scare ← **takut**

menamatkan *v* to end,
finish, conclude ← **tamat**

menambah *v* to add to or
in-crease; **menambahi** *v* to
increase something;
menambahkan *v* to add
something to ← **tambah**

menambal *v* to mend,
patch, darn; ~ *gigi* to fill a
tooth, have a filling ←
tambal

menampakkan *v* to show,
make appear ← **tampak**

menampar *v* to slap ←
tampar

menampilkan *v* to present
← **tampil**

menampung *v* to collect,
hold ← **tampung**

menanak ~ *nasi* to cook
rice ← **tanak**

menanam *v* to plant or
grow; to invest ← **tanam**

menandai *v* to mark ←
tanda

menandatangani *v* to sign
something ← **tanda
tangan**

menang *v* to win; **kemenangan** *n* victory;
pemenang *n* winner,
victor

menangani *v* to handle ←
tangan

menanggapi *v* to respond,
reply ← **tanggap**

menanggulangi *v* to deal
or cope with ← **tanggu-
lang**

menanggung *v* to
guarantee, be responsible
← **tanggung**

menangis *v* to cry ←
tangis

menangkap *v* to catch,
capture ← **tangkap**

menanjak *adj* rising,
climbing, steep ← **tanjak**

menantang *v* to challenge;
adj challenging ← **tantang**

menanti-nanti *v* to wait for
a long time; **menantikan** *v*
to wait for ← **nanti**

menantu *n* son- or daugh-
ter-in-law → **mantu**

menanyai *v* to question
someone; **menanyakan** *v*
to ask about ← **tanya**

menara *n* tower; minaret
(of a mosque)

menari *v* to dance, perform
a traditional dance; **menari-
nari** *v* to dance about ← **tari**

menarik *v* to pull or draw;
adj interesting, attractive
← **tarik**

menaruh *v* to put (away)
← **taruh**

menasihati *v* to advise ←
nasihat

menawan *v* to detain, take
someone prisoner, intern
← **tawan**

menawar *v* to bargain;
menawarkan *v* to offer or
bid ← **tawar**

menayangkan *v* to telecast,
show on TV ← **tayang**

mencabuli *v* to rape,
assault someone ← **cabul**

mencabut *v* to pull out,
remove; ~ *gigi* extract a
tooth ← **cabut**

mencaci ~ *maki* to insult,
abuse ← **caci**

mencair *v* to melt, turn into
liquid; **mencairkan** *v* to

183

melt something; to make
(funds) available ← **cair**

mencakar v to scratch ←
cakar

mencakupi v to include,
cover ← **cakup**

mencalonkan v to nominate
someone ← **calon**

mencambuk v to whip ←
cambuk

mencampuradukkan v to
mix up, confuse; **mencampurkan** v to mix something
to ← **campur**

mencantumkan v to attach
← **cantum**

mencapai v to reach, attain
← **capai**

mencari v look or search
for, seek; **mencari-cari** v to
search repeatedly, every-
where ← **cari**

mencarter v to hire, charter
← **carter**

mencatat v to note (down)
← **catat**

mencatut ~ *nama* to use
someone else's name illegally

mencegah v to prevent,
fight against ← **cegah**

mencegat v to hold up, bar
← **cegat**

mencekal v to prevent
from leaving the country
← **cekal**

mencekam *adj* frightening,
ominous ← **cekam**

mencekik v to strangle ←
cekik

mencelup v to dye, dip ←
celup

mencemari v to dirty,
pollute ← **cemar**

mencemaskan *adj* worrying, sobering ← **cemas**

mencengkeram v to grip,
squeeze ← **cengkeram**

mencerai, menceraikan v
to divorce someone ←
cerai

menceritakan v to
describe, relate ← **cerita**

mencermati v to observe
closely ← **cermat**

mencerminkan v to reflect
← **cermin**

mencerna v to digest ←
cerna

mencétak v to print ←
cétak

mencetus v to say something unexpected ← **cetus**

mencicil v to pay by
instalments ← **cicil**

mencicipi v to try, taste something ← **cicip**

mencincang v to mince, chop up ← **cincang**

mencintai v to love someone ← **cinta**

mencipta, menciptakan v to create, make ← **cipta**

mencium v to smell; to kiss ← **cium**

mencoba v to try, attempt ← **coba**

mencoblos v to vote, pierce ← **coblos**

mencocokkan v to match ← **cocok**

mencolok adj glaring, standing out ← **colok**

méncong adj bent, skewed, not straight

mencongkél n to prise open ← **congkél**

menconték v to copy, cheat ← **conték, sonték**

mencopét v to pick someone's pocket ← **copét**

mencorét v to scratch, cross out ← **corét**

méncrét v to have diarrhea

mencubit v to pinch ← **cubit**

mencuci v to wash, clean ← **cuci**

mencukur v to shave ← **cukur**

menculik v to kidnap ← **culik**

mencurahkan v to pour out ← **curah**

mencuri n to steal ← **curi**

mencurigai v to suspect someone; **mencurigakan** adj suspicious, suspect ← **curiga**

mendadak adj sudden ← **dadak**

mendaftar v to register; **mendaftarkan** v to register something ← **daftar**

mendahului v to precede, overtake ← **dahulu**

mendaki v to climb, ascend; ~ *gunung* (to go) mountaineering, bushwalking ← **daki**

mendalam adj deep ← **dalam**

mendalangi v to orchestrate (events) ← **dalang**

mendamaikan v to reconcile, pacify ← **damai**

mendambakan v to long or wish for ← **damba**

mendampingi v to accompany, flank ← **damping**

mendanai *v* to fund something ← **dana**

mendandani *v* to decorate, dress, adorn ← **dandan**

mendapat *v* to obtain, receive; ~ *kabar* to receive news; **mendapatkan** *v* to obtain; discover ← **dapat**

mendarat *v* to land ← **darat**

mendasarkan *v* to base on something ← **dasar**

mendatakan *v* to record, document, collect data on ← **data**

mendatang *adj* coming, next; **mendatangkan** *v* to bring, import ← **datang**

mendatarkan *v* to make flat, level ← **datar**

mendaur-ulang *v* to recycle ← **daur ulang**

mendayung *v* to stroke (an oar), row; to pedal ← **dayung**

mendébet *v* to debit ← **débet**

mendeham *v* to clear the throat, cough ← **deham**

mendekati *v* to approach ← **dekat**

mendémo *v* to protest against ← **démo**

mendenda *v* to fine ← **denda**

mendengar *v* to hear; **mendengarkan** *v* to listen; ~ *lagu* listen to music ← **dengar**

mendengkur *v* to snore; to purr (of a cat) ← **dengkur**

mendengung *v* to drone, hum, shake with sound ← **dengung**

mendepak *v* to kick something, kick out ← **depak**

mendérék *v* to tow ← **dérék**

mendering *v* to ring, tinkle ← **dering**

menderita *v* to suffer, endure ← **derita**

mendesah *v* to sigh, make a swishing noise ← **desah**

mendésain *v* to design ← **désain**

mendesak *adj* pressing, urgent; *v* to press, urge, push ← **desak**

mendesir *v* to hiss, rustle ← **desir**

mendéwakan *v* to worship, idolize, put on a pedestal ← **déwa**

mendiagnosa *v* to diagnose ← **diagnosa**

mendiang *adj* the late

mendidih *adj* boiling ←
 didih

mendidik *v* to educate,
 bring up, teach ← **didik**

mendikté *v* to dictate
 (terms) ← **dikté**

mending, mendingan *adj,
 coll* better, better off

mendirikan *v* to build,
 establish, erect ← **diri**

mendiskriminasi, men-
 diskriminasikan *v* to
 discriminate against ←
 diskriminasi

mendistribusikan *v* to
 distribute ← **distribusi**

mendoakan *v* to pray for
 ← **doa**

mendobrak *v* to break
 open, smash ← **dobrak**

mendokuméntasi *v* to
 document, file ← **doku-
 méntasi**

mendongkrak *v* to jack,
 lever, raise ← **dongkrak**

mendorong *v* to push,
 encourage ← **dorong**

menduduki *v* to sit on something; to occupy ← **duduk**

mendukung *v* to support
 ← **dukung**

mendulang *v* to pan (for
 gold) ← **dulang**

mendung *adj* cloudy,
 overcast

menebak *v* to guess ←
 tebak

menebang *v* to fell, cut
 down ← **tebang**

menebus *v* to pay a ransom
 ← **tebus**

menegakkan *v* to erect; to
 uphold or maintain ←
 tegak

menegangkan *adj* tense,
 stressful ← **tegang**

menegaskan *v* to clarify,
 point out, affirm ← **tegas**

meneguk *v* to gulp or
 guzzle ← **teguk**

menegur *v* to speak to,
 address; to warn, rebuke,
 tell off ← **tegur**

menekan *v* to press;
 menekankan *v* to stress,
 emphasize ← **tekan**

menelan *v* to swallow
 something ← **telan**

menélépon *v* to ring (up),
 call, (tele)phone ←
 télépon

meneliti *v* to investigate or
 research ← **teliti**

menelusuri *v* to follow, go along, trace ← **telusur**

menemani *v* to accompany ← **teman**

menémbak *v* to shoot ← **témbak**

menémbok *v* to wall something up ← **témbok**

menembus *v* to pierce, stab ← **tembus**

menempati *v* to occupy, take a place; **menempatkan** *v* to place ← **tempat**

menémpél *v* to stick or adhere to; **menémpélkan** *v* to stick, paste or glue something ← **témpél**

menempuh ~ *ujian v* to do an exam ← **tempuh**

menemui *v* to meet up with, arrange to meet; ~ *ajal* to die; **menemukan** *v* to discover ← **temu**

menenangkan *v* to calm someone (down) ← **tenang**

menendang *v* to kick ← **tendang**

menengah *adj* intermediate ← **tengah**

menéngok *v* to look or see; to look in on someone ← **téngok**

menentang *v* to oppose, resist ← **tentang**

menénténg *v* to carry dangling from the hand ← **ténténg**

menentukan *v* to decide, determine, stipulate ← **tentu**

menenun *v* to weave ← **tenun**

menepati *v* to fulfill; ~ *janji* to keep a promise ← **tepat**

menepuk *v* to pat, slap ← **tepuk**

menerangkan *v* to explain ← **terang**

menerapkan *v* to apply something ← **terap**

menerbangkan *v* to fly something ← **terbang**

menerbitkan *v* to publish, issue ← **terbit**

meneriakkan *v* to shout something ← **teriak**

menerima *v* to receive, accept ← **terima**

menerjemahkan *v* to translate (writing); to interpret (speaking) ← **terjemah**

menerobos *v* to break through ← **terobos**

menertawakan *v* to laugh at ← **tawa**

menertibkan *v* to keep order, discipline ← **tertib**

meneruskan *v* to continue, keep doing something ← **terus**

menetap *v* to stay; **menetapkan** *v* to appoint, fix, stipulate ← **tetap**

menetas *v* to hatch ← **tetas**

menéték *v* to suck, feed from the breast ← **téték**

menétralkan *v* to neutralize ← **nétral**

menéwaskan *v* to kill someone ← **téwas**

mengabadikan *v* to immortalize ← **abadi**

mengabaikan *v* to neglect, disregard, ignore ← **abai**

mengabari *v* to tell or inform someone; **mengabarkan** *v* to announce, report ← **kabar**

mengaborsi *v* to abort (a fetus) ← **aborsi**

mengabulkan *v* to grant, approve, consent to ← **kabul**

mengacaukan *v* to mix or mess up ← **kacau**

mengacu *v* to refer to, to use as a point of reference; **mengacukan** *v* to point, refer to ← **acu**

mengadakan *v* to create, organize, make available; ~ *kampanye* to run a campaign ← **ada**

mengadili *v* to try someone, put someone on trial; to punish ← **adil**

mengadu *v* to complain, report; **mengadukan** *v* to report someone/something, to make a complaint about ← **adu**

mengaduk *v* to stir, mix ← **aduk**

mengagétkan *v* to surprise, startle ← **kagét**

mengagumi *v* to admire ← **kagum**

mengais *v* to scratch; ~ *rejeki* to scratch a living ← **kais**

mengaitkan *v* to link, connect, join ← **kait**

mengajak *v* to invite, ask out; to urge; ~ *jalan-jalan* to ask out; ~ *kawin*, ~ *nikah* to ask someone to marry you ← **ajak**

189

mengajar *v* to teach; **mengajari** *v* to teach someone; **mengajarkan** *v* to teach something ← **ajar**

mengaji *v* to recite or read the Koran ← **kaji**

mengajukan *v* to forward, propose; to submit ← **aju**

mengakali *v* to find a way; to deceive, play a trick on ← **akal**

mengakar *v* to take root ← **akar**

mengakhiri *v* to end, finish something ← **akhir**

mengakibatkan *v* to result in ← **akibat**

mengaku *v* to admit, confess, acknowledge; to claim; ~ *salah* to admit guilt; **mengakui** *v* to admit something; to acknowledge, recognize ← **aku**

mengalahkan *v* to conquer, defeat ← **kalah**

mengalamatkan *v* to address to; to indicate ← **alamat**

mengalami *v* to experience ← **alam**

mengalih(kan) *v* to shift something; ~ *perhatian* to

shift attention, change the subject ← **alih**

mengalir *v* to flow ← **alir**

mengamalkan *v* to do something for charity; to carry out ← **amal**

mengamankan *v* to make safe, restore order; to place in custody ← **aman**

mengamati *v* to watch closely, keep an eye on ← **amat**

mengambang *v* to float ← **ambang**

mengambil *v* to take, get, fetch; ~ *alih* to take over; ~ *keputusan* to make a decision; **mengambilkan** *v* to get something for someone ← **ambil**

mengamén *v* ngamén *coll* to sing in the street for money, busk ← **amén**

mengamuk *v* to run amok, go berserk ← **amuk**

mengancam *v* to threaten, intimidate ← **ancam**

mengancing *v* to button ← **kancing**

mengandaikan *v* to suppose, assume ← **andai**

mengandalkan *v* to rely on, trust ← **andal**

mengandung v to contain, carry; to be pregnant ← **kandung**

menganggap v to consider, regard; ~ *enteng* to take lightly; *sudah dianggap saudara* considered part of the family ← **anggap**

mengangguk v to nod ← **angguk**

menganggur v to be unemployed, idle ← **anggur**

mengangkat v to lift or pick up, raise; to appoint; to remove, amputate ← **angkat**

mengangkut v to transport ← **angkut**

mengangsur v to pay in instalments ← **angsur**

menganiaya v to mistreat, oppress ← **aniaya**

menganjurkan v to suggest, propose ← **anjur**

mengantar v to take, escort, accompany; **mengantarkan** v to take someone or something ← **antar**

mengantri v to queue ← **antré, antri**

mengantuk *adj* sleepy → **kantuk**

menganut v to follow ← **anut**

menganyam v to weave, plait, braid ← **anyam**

mengapa why; *tak* ~ it doesn't matter ← **apa**

mengapung v to float, be suspended ← **apung**

mengarah v to aim something towards; **mengarahkan** v to direct ← **arah**

mengarang v to write, compose ← **karang**

mengartikan v to define, interpret as ← **arti**

mengaruniai v to bless ← **karunia**

mengasih v to give ← **kasih**

mengasingkan v to exile ← **asing**

mengasuransikan v to insure ← **asuransi**

mengatakan v to say ← **kata**

mengatasi v to overcome ← **atas**

mengatur v to arrange, organize, regulate ← **atur**

mengaum v to roar, growl (of tigers) ← **aum**

mengawal *v* to guard, escort ← **kawal**

mengawali *v* to start; to precede ← **awal**

mengawasi *v* to supervise ← **awas**

mengawétkan *v* to preserve (food) ← **awét**

mengawinkan ~ *anak* to marry off a son or daughter ← **kawin**

mengayuh *v* to paddle or pedal something; ~ *sepeda* to ride a bicycle ← **kayuh**

mengayun *v* to rock, swing, sway ← **ayun**

mengebom *v* to bomb something ← **bom**

mengecap *v* to brand ← **cap**

mengecas *v* to charge (electrical equipment) ← **cas, charge**

mengecat *v* to paint, dye; ~ *rambut* to dye, color your hair ← **cat**

mengecék *v* to check, confirm ← **cék**

mengecéwakan *v* to disappoint; *adj* disappointing ← **kecéwa**

mengecilkan *v* to make smaller, decrease ← **kecil**

mengédarkan *v* to circulate something ← **édar**

mengedipkan ~ *mata* to blink ← **kedip**

mengédit *v* to edit ← **édit**

mengedot *v* to suck ← **dot**

mengéja *v* to spell ← **éja**

mengejar *v* to chase; ~ *waktu* to race against the clock ← **kejar**

mengéjék *v* to tease, mock, ridicule ← **éjék**

mengejutkan *adj* surprising, startling; *v* to surprise or startle ← **kejut**

mengéksékusi *v* to execute (carry out the death penalty) ← **éksékusi**

mengékspor *v* to export ← **ékspor**

mengékstradisi *v* to extradite (someone) ← **ékstradisi**

mengelabui *v* to trick, pull the wool over someone's eyes ← **kelabu, abu**

mengélakkan *v* to avoid, dodge, evade ← **élak**

mengelap *v* to wipe, mop ← **lap**

mengelas *v* to weld ← **las**

mengelilingi *v* to circle, go around ← **keliling**

mengelola *v* to manage, run ← **kelola**

mengeluarkan *v* to issue, send out, release ← **keluar**

mengeluh *v* to complain ← **keluh**

mengelupas *v* to peel, come off (of a skin) ← **kelupas**

mengelus *v* to caress, stroke or pat (an animal) ← **elus**

mengemaskan *v* to package ← **kemas**

mengembalikan *v* to give or send back, return ← **kembali**

mengembangkan *v* to develop something ← **kembang**

mengembus *v* to blow ← **embus**

mengemis *v* to beg ← **emis, kemis**

mengempaskan ~ *diri* to throw yourself down ← **empas**

mengemudikan *v* to drive, steer ← **kemudi**

mengemukakan *v* to put forward, advance, nominate ← **ke muka**

mengemut *v* to suck on (sweets etc) ← **emut, kemut**

mengenai *conj* about, over, on, concerning ← **kena**

mengenal *v* to know, be acquainted with, recognize; **memperkenalkan** *v* to introduce ← **kenal**

mengenang *v* to commemorate, remember ← **kenang**

mengencangkan *v* to tighten ← **kencang**

mengendalikan *v* to control ← **kendali**

mengendap *v* to sink, silt up ← **endap**

mengepak *v* to pack ← **pak**

mengepakkan ~ *sayap* to flutter wings ← **kepak**

mengepal *v* to form a fist ← **kepal**

mengepél *v* to mop (up) ← **pél**

mengepul *v* to smoke, billow ← **kepul**

mengepung *v* to surround, encircle, besiege ← **kepung**

mengerang *v* to groan, moan ← **erang**

mengeraskan *v* to make something harder, louder ← **keras**

mengérék *v* to hoist, pull; *~ bendera* to raise the flag ← **kérék**

mengerém *v* to brake ← **rém**

mengerikan *adj* terrifying, horrifying ← **ngeri**

mengeringkan *v* to dry something ← **kering**

mengeriting *~ rambut* to perm your hair ← **keriting**

mengerjakan *v* to do, carry out ← **kerja**

mengernyit *~ dahi, ~ kening* to frown ← **kernyit**

mengerok *v* to rub someone's back with a coin ← **kerok**

mengeropos *v* to be eaten away, eroded ← **keropos**

mengeroyok *v* to beat savagely in a mob ← **keroyok**

mengerti *v* to understand; **dimengerti** *v* to be understood; **pengertian** *n* understanding ← **erti, arti**

mengerut *v* to shrink, shrivel, contract; **mengerutkan** *~ kening* to frown ← **kerut**

mengesahkan *v* to validate, ratify, legitimize, legalize ← **sah**

mengesampingkan *v* to put to one side ← **ke samping**

mengesankan *adj* impressive ← **kesan**

mengetahui *v* to know something, have knowledge of ← **tahu**

mengetik *v* to type ← **ketik**

mengetuk *v* to knock ← **ketuk**

menggabungkan *v* to connect, combine, fuse ← **gabung**

menggadaikan *v* to pawn something ← **gadai**

menggaét *v* to get (on board), snatch, hook ← **gaét, gait, kait**

menggairahkan *v* to excite, stimulate, enthuse ← **gairah**

menggait *v* to pull, hook ← **gait, gaét, kait**

menggaji *v* to pay, remunerate, employ ← **gaji**

menggali *v* to dig ← **gali**

menggambar *v* to draw, depict; **menggambarkan** *v*

to describe, illustrate ←
gambar
mengganggu v to bother,
disturb ← **ganggu**
mengganti v to change,
substitute, replace; **menggantikan** v to substitute or
replace someone/something
← **ganti**
menggantung v to hang,
suspend ← **gantung**
menggarap v to work on,
produce; ~ *tanah* to till the
land ← **garap**
menggarisbawahi v to
underline, emphasize ←
garis
menggaruk v to scratch,
scrape; ~ *kepala* to scratch
your head ← **garuk**
menggebrak v to hit or
slam ← **gebrak**
menggebuk v to batter,
bash ← **gebuk**
menggedor v to bang on
repeatedly ← **gedor**
menggelapkan v to
embezzle, misappropriate
← **gelap**
**menggelar, menggelar-
kan** v to hold (an event)
← **gelar**

menggelédah v to search;
to ransack ← **gelédah**
**menggéléng, menggé-
léngkan** ~ *kepala* to shake
your head ← **géléng**
menggelikan *adj* funny,
comic off-putting ← **geli**
menggelitik v to tickle ←
gelitik
menggemari v to like,
enjoy ← **gemar**
menggemaskan *adj*
annoying ← **gemas**
menggembirakan *adj*
exciting, happy; *berita yang*
~ good news ← **gembira**
menggembok v to
padlock ← **gembok**
menggemparkan v to
cause a stir ← **gempar**
menggempur v to attack,
destroy ← **gempur**
menggéndong v to carry
on the hip ← **géndong**
menggenggam v to grip,
grasp ← **genggam**
menggerakkan v to move,
shift something ← **gerak**
menggerayangi v to grope
← **gerayang**
menggerebek v to raid,
search ← **gerebek**

menggergaji *v* to saw ←
gergaji

menggerogoti *v* to eat into,
erode, gnaw on ← **gerogot**

menggerutu *v* to grumble,
complain, gripe ← **gerutu**

menggésék *v* to rub,
scrape; ~ *biola* to play the
violin; ~ *kartu* to swipe a
card ← **gésék**

menggésér *v* to move aside
or over ← **gésér**

menggigil *v* to shiver ←
gigil

menggigit *v* to bite ← **gigit**

menggilas *v* to crush,
pulverize ← **gilas**

menggiling *v* to grind, mill
← **giling**

menggiring *v* to herd, drive
(cattle) ← **giring**

menggiurkan *adj* tempting,
mouth-watering ← **giur**

menggoda *v* to tempt ←
goda

menggodok *v* to boil ←
godok

menggolongkan *v* to
group, classify ← **golong**

menggoncangkan *v* to
rock or make something
move ← **goncang**

menggoréng *v* to fry ←
goréng

menggorés *v* to scratch,
make a stroke ← **gorés**

menggosipkan *v* to
gossip about something
or someone ← **gosip**

menggosok *v* to rub,
polish; ~ *sepatu* to
polish, shine (shoes) ←
gosok

menggotong *v* to carry
together ← **gotong**

menggoyangkan *v* to
shake or rock something ←
goyang

menggugat *v* to sue,
accuse ← **gugat**

menggugurkan *v* to abort
← **gugur**

mengguling *v* to roll ←
guling

menggulung *v* to roll up
← **gulung**

menggumamkan *v* to
mumble or mutter some-
thing ← **gumam**

menggunakan *v* to use ←
guna

mengguncangkan *v* to
rock or make something
move ← **guncang**

mengGunduli v to shave, denude, make bald ← **gundul**

mengGunting v to cut (out) ← **gunting**

mengGusur v to evict, sweep aside, forcibly remove ← **gusur**

menGhabiskan v to finish, use up, spend ← **habis**

menGhadap v to face, appear before; **menghadapi** v to face someone or something ← **hadap**

menGhadiri v to attend; **menghadirkan** v to present, bring forward ← **hadir**

menGhafalkan v to learn by heart ← **hafal**

menGhaluskan v to refine, grind ← **halus**

menGhambat v to obstruct, impede, hamper ← **hambat**

menGhamburkan v to scatter, throw about ← **hambur**

menGhancurkan v to smash, crush, destroy ← **hancur**

menGhantam v to strike ← **hantam**

menGhantarkan v to conduct (electricity or heat) ← **hantar**

menGhantui v to haunt ← **hantu**

menGharapkan v to expect ← **harap**

menGhardik v to shout at, scold ← **hardik**

menGhargai v to appreciate ← **harga**

menGharukan adj moved, touched (emotionally) ← **haru**

menGharuskan v to require ← **harus**

menGhasilkan v to produce ← **hasil**

menGhébohkan v to cause an uproar; adj sensational ← **héboh**

menGhéla v to draw, drag; ~ nafas to sigh, draw a breath ← **héla**

menGhémat v to save on or economize ← **hémat**

menGhembus v to blow ← **hembus**

menGhendaki v to want ← **hendak**

menGhentikan v to stop something ← **henti**

menGhérankan adj astonishing, astounding ← **héran**

menghiasi *v* to adorn, decorate something ← **hias**

menghibahkan *v* to donate, bequeath ← **hibah**

menghibur *v* to entertain; to comfort, console ← **hibur**

menghidangkan *v* to serve up, offer ← **hidang**

menghidupkan *v* to bring to life, start or turn on (a device); ~ *mesin* to turn on the engine ← **hidup**

menghilang *v* to disappear, vanish; **menghilangkan** *v* to remove ← **hilang**

menghinakan *v* to humiliate, insult ← **hina**

menghindar *v* to steer clear, avoid; **menghindari** *v* to avoid something ← **hindar**

menghiraukan *v* to take heed, listen to advice ← **hirau**

menghirup *v* to breathe in ← **hirup**

menghitung *v* to count, calculate, reckon; **menghitungkan** *v* to count or calculate something ← **hitung**

menghormat, menghormati *v* to honor or respect

menghubungi *v* to contact someone; **menghubungkan** *v* to connect, join, link different parts ← **hubung**

menghujat *v* to swear, blaspheme ← **hujat**

menghukum *v* to punish, sentence, condemn ← **hukum**

menghunus *v* to unsheathe, take out ← **hunus**

mengibarkan *v* to wave, unfurl ← **kibar**

mengidam *v* to crave (esp of pregnant woman) ← **idam**

mengidap *v* to suffer from ← **idap**

mengigau *v* to talk in one's sleep, be delirious ← **igau**

mengijinkan *v* to permit, allow ← **ijin, izin**

mengikat *v* to tie, fasten ← **ikat**

mengikis *v* to erode, eat away ← **kikis**

mengikut *v* to follow, accompany; **mengikuti** *v* to follow, join, participate in; ~ *kursus* to do a course ← **ikut**

mengimpikan v to dream of ← **impi**

mengimpor v to import ← **impor**

menginap v to stay the night, stay over ← **inap**

mengincar v to set your sights on, target ← **incar**

mengindahkan v to take heed, pay attention to; **memperindah** v to beautify ← **indah**

mengingat v to remember, bear in mind; **mengingat-kan** v to remind someone about something ← **ingat**

menginginkan v to wish for, desire ← **ingin**

menginjak v to step, tread, or stamp on; ~ *gas* to accelerate, step on the gas ← **injak**

mengintai v to spy on or watch, conduct surveillance ← **intai**

menginterviu v to interview ← **interviu**

mengintip v to peep at, spy on ← **intip**

mengira v to assume, think ← **kira**

mengirim v to send ← **kirim**

mengiringi v to accompany, escort ← **iring**

mengiris v to slice ← **iris**

mengirit v to economize ← **irit**

mengisahkan v to tell the story of ← **kisah**

mengisap v to suck; to smoke; ~ *cerutu* to smoke a cigar ← **isap**

mengisi v to fill, load; ~ *bensin* fill up with petrol; ~ *waktu* to fill in time ← **isi**

mengistiméwakan v to treat as special ← **istiméwa**

mengizinkan v to permit, allow ← **izin, ijin**

mengkaji v to study, investigate ← **kaji**

mengkhianati v to betray someone ← **khianat**

mengkhitan(kan) v to circumcise ← **khitan**

mengkilap v to shine, gleam ← **kilap**

mengkudu n kind of root, used as a spice

mengobati v to treat, cure ← **obat**

mengobral *v* to put on sale
← **obral**

mengobrol *v* to chat ← **obrol**

mengobyék *v* to have a job
on the side, moonlight ←
obyék

mengocok *v* to shake,
shuffle; ~ *kartu* to shuffle
cards ← **kocok**

mengolah *v* to process,
treat ← **olah**

mengolés *v* to grease,
spread, lubricate; **mengolési** *v* to grease something; **mengoléskan** *v* to
smear with something ←
olés

mengomél *v* to complain,
grumble, whinge, whine ←
omél

mengoméntari *v* to com-
ment on ← **koméntar**

mengompol *v* to wet your
pants, the bed ← **ompol**

mengoper *v* to transfer,
hand over; ~ *bola* to pass
the ball ← **oper**

mengoplos *v* to mix in
another liquid illegally ←
oplos

mengorbankan *v* to
sacrifice ← **korban**

mengorék *v* to scrape,
scratch

mengoréksi *v* to correct ←
koréksi

mengosongkan *v* to empty
← **kosong**

menguap *v* to yawn ← **kuap**

menguap *v* to evaporate or
steam ← **uap**

menguasai *v* to control,
have power over ← **kuasa**

menguatirkan *v* to worry
about something ← **kuatir**

memguatkan *v* to strengthen;
memperkuat *v* to reinforce,
make stronger ← **kuat**

mengubah *v* to change or
alter ← **ubah**

menguber *v, coll* to chase,
go after ← **uber**

menguburkan *v* to bury ←
kubur

mengucap, mengucapkan
v to say or express something; ~ *terima kasih* to say
thank you; to thank ← **ucap**

mengudarakan *v* to broadcast or air ← **udara**

menguji *v* to examine or
test ← **uji**

mengukir *v* to carve or
engrave ← **ukir**

mengukuhkan v to strengthen; to ratify ← **kukuh**

mengukur v to measure ← **ukur**

mengukus v to steam (food) ← **kukus**

mengulang v to repeat, do again; **mengulangi** v to repeat something ← **ulang**

mengulur-ulur v to spin out, take a long time; **mengulurkan** v to extend something ← **ulur**

mengumpat v to curse, swear ← **umpat**

mengumpet v to hide or conceal yourself ← **umpet**

mengumpulkan v to collect, gather ← **kumpul**

mengumumkan v to announce or declare ← **umum**

mengunci v to lock (up) ← **kunci**

mengundang v to invite (formally) ← **undang**

mengundi v to conduct a draw or lottery ← **undi**

mengundurkan v to postpone ← **undur**

mengungkap v to uncover; **mengungkapkan** v to express ← **ungkap**

mengungsi v to evacuate or flee; **mengungsikan** v to evacuate someone ← **ungsi**

mengunjungi v to visit a place ← **kunjung**

menguntungkan v to profit; *adj* profitable ← **untung**

mengunyah v to chew ← **kunyah**

mengupas v to peel; to analyze ← **kupas**

mengupil v to pick your nose ← **upil**

menguping v to eavesdrop, listen in ← **kuping**

menguraikan v to explain; to untangle ← **urai**

mengurangi v to take from, subtract, minus ← **kurang**

menguras v to clean out, drain ← **kuras**

mengurung v to cage, put in a cage, lock up ← **kurung**

mengurus v to arrange, organize, manage ← **urus**

mengurut v to massage ← **urut**

mengusahakan *v* to try, endeavor to ← **usaha**

mengusik *v* to tease, make fun of ← **usik**

mengusir *v* to drive away or out, chase away, expel ← **usir**

mengusulkan *v* to propose or suggest ← **usul**

mengusut *v* to investigate, sort out ← **usut**

mengutak-atik, mengutak-ngatikkan *v* to work on or tinker with ← **kutak, utak-atik**

mengutamakan *v* to give preference or priority to ← **utama**

mengutarakan *v* to put forward ← **utara**

mengutik *v* to tinker with; to touch on ← **kutik, utik**

mengutip *v* to quote, cite an extract ← **kutip**

mengutuk *v* to curse ← **kutuk**

mengutus *v* to send or delegate ← **utus**

meniadakan *v* to undo or cancel ← **tiada, tidak ada**

meniduri *v* to sleep with someone, have sex with

someone; **menidurkan** *v* to put to sleep ← **tidur**

menikah *v* to marry, get married; **menikahi** *v* to marry someone ← **nikah**

menikam *v* to stab ← **tikam**

menikmati *v* to enjoy ← **nikmat**

menilai *v* to evaluate, appraise

menimbang *v* to weigh (up) ← **timbang**

menimbulkan *v* to give rise, bring to the surface ← **timbul**

menimbun *v* to pile up, accumulate; to hoard

menimpa *v* to fall upon, befall ← **timpa**

menindaklanjuti *v* to take a step or measure ← **tindak lanjut**

menindik *v* to pierce (ears) ← **tindik**

meninggal ~ *(dunia)* to die; **meninggalkan** *v* to leave (behind), abandon ← **tinggal**

meningkat *v* to rise, increase, improve; **meningkatkan** *v* to increase or raise the level of something ← **tingkat**

202

meninjau v to observe, view; ~ *kembali* to review ← **tinjau**

menipis v to become thin ← **tipis**

menipu v to trick, deceive ← **tipu**

meniru v to copy or imitate ← **tiru**

menit n minute

menitip v to leave in someone's care, entrust ← **titip**

meniup v to blow ← **tiup**

menjabat v to hold; to work as ← **jabat**

menjadi v to be or become; **menjadikan** v to create, make ← **jadi**

menjadwalkan v to timetable ← **jadwal**

menjaga v to guard, keep watch ← **jaga**

menjagokan v to support ← **jago**

menjahit v to sew ← **jahit**

menjajah v to colonize, rule another country ← **jajah**

menjajakan v to hawk, peddle ← **jaja**

menjalani v to undergo, do; **menjalankan** v to operate, run, set in motion ← **jalan**

menjalin v to forge links, network ← **jalin**

menjambrét v to snatch ← **jambrét**

menjamin v to guarantee, promise ← **jamin**

menjanda v to be widowed, live as a widow ← **janda**

menjangan n deer

menjangkiti v to infect ← **jangkit**

menjanjikan v to promise something ← **janji**

menjarah v to loot ← **jarah**

menjaring v to fish with a net; to filter or sift ← **jaring**

menjatuhkan v to fell, let drop ← **jatuh**

menjauhi v to avoid ← **jauh**

menjawab v to answer, reply ← **jawab**

menjebak v to trap ← **jebak**

menjejaki v to step on, trail, trace ← **jejak**

menjéjérkan v to place in rows ← **jéjér**

menjelajahi v to travel through or explore a place ← **jelajah**

menjelang v to approach (usu time) ← **jelang**

menjelaskan *adj* to explain, clarify ← **jelas**

menjelékkan *v* to criticize, say bad things about ← **jelék**

menjelma *v* to be incarnated, turn into, materialize ← **jelma**

menjemput *v* to pick up; ~ *bola* to be proactive ← **jemput**

menjemur *v* to air, dry in the sun; ~ *baju cucian* to hang out the washing ← **jemur**

menjéngkélkan *adj* annoying ← **jéngkél**

menjepit *v* to pinch, squeeze ← **jepit**

menjeprét *v* to snap, staple; ~ *foto* to take a photo ← **jeprét**

menjerat *v* to snare, trap ← **jerat**

menjerit *v* to scream, shriek ← **jerit**

menjéwér *v* to pinch someone's ear, scold ← **jéwér**

menjijikkan *adj* disgusting, revolting, foul ← **jijik**

menjilat *v* to lick; *sl* to suck up, flatter ← **jilat**

menjilid *v* to bind ← **jilid**

menjinjing *v* to carry by hand ← **jinjing**

menjiplak *v* to copy, plagiarize ← **jiplak**

menjodohkan *v* to set up, match ← **jodoh**

menjorok *v* to stick out, protrude ← **jorok**

menjual *v* to sell ← **jual**

menjuarai *v* to win (a competition) ← **juara**

menjumlahkan *v* to add (up) ← **jumlah**

menjuntai *v* to dangle ← **juntai**

menobatkan *v* to install, crown ← **nobat**

menodong *v* to threaten or hold up at knifepoint ← **todong**

menolak *v* to refuse, reject ← **tolak**

menoléh *v* to look in a different direction, turn your head ← **toléh**

menolong *v* to help or assist ← **tolong**

menomersatukan *v* to put first, give priority ← **nomer satu**

menonaktifkan *v* to release

from active service, non-
activate ← **nonaktif**

menonjok v to punch, hit
← **tonjok**

menonjol v to stick out,
protrude; *adj* prominent ←
tonjol

menonton v to watch, look
on ← **tonton**

menopang v to prop up,
support ← **topang**

méns *coll* period; *lagi* ~
have your period; *sakit* ~
menstrual pain

mensosialisasikan v to
introduce to the public,
disseminate ← **sosial-
isasi**

mensponsori v to sponsor
← **sponsor**

mensubsidi v to subsidize
← **subsidi**

mensukséskan v to make
something succeed ←
suksés

menswastakan v to
privatize ← **swasta**

mensyukuri v to appreciate,
be thankful ← **syukur**

mentah *adj* raw, uncooked,
not ripe; *bahan* ~ raw
materials

méntal, méntalitas *n* way
of thinking, mentality

mentéga *n* butter

mentéréng *adj* dressed up,
fancy

menteri *n* minister; ~
Dalam Negeri (Mendagri)
Minister of Home Affairs;
~ *Luar Negeri (Menlu)*
Foreign Minister;
kementerian *n* ministry,
department, office

mentimun, timun *n*
cucumber

mentraktir v to invite out,
shout, treat, pay for another
← **traktir**

menuang, menuangkan v
to pour something ←
tuang

menuding v to accuse,
point the finger ← **tuding**

menuduh v to accuse ←
tuduh

menugaskan v to assign
someone, give a task to ←
tugas

menuju v to approach, go
towards ← **tuju**

menukar v to change;
menukarkan v to change
something ← **tukar**

menular v to infect; *adj* contagious, infectious; *penyakit* ~ contagious disease ← **tular**

menulis v to write ← **tulis**

menumbuk v to pound (rice), crush, grind ← **tumbuk**

menumpahkan v to spill something ← **tumpah**

menumpang v to make use of someone else's facilities; to get a lift or ride ← **tumpang**

menumpuk v to pile up ← **tumpuk**

menunaikan v to pay cash; to fulfill ← **tunai**

menunda v to delay, put off, postpone; **menundakan** v to delay or postpone something ← **tunda**

menunduk v to bow your head; **menundukkan** v to bow or lower something; to defeat ← **tunduk**

menung: termenung *adj* lost in thought

menunggang v to ride; ~ *kuda* to ride a horse ← **tunggang**

menunggu v to wait for something; **menunggu-nunggu** v to wait a long time for ← **tunggu**

menunjuk v to indicate, point out, refer to; **menunjukkan** v to show, point out; ~ *jalan* to give directions ← **tunjuk**

menuntut v to claim or demand ← **tuntut**

menurun v to fall, drop, decline; **menurunkan** v to lower or reduce ← **turun**

menurut *conj* according to; ~ *pendapat saya* in my opinion ← **turut**

menusuk v to stab, prick, pierce ← **tusuk**

menutup v to close or shut; **menutupi** v to cover (up) ← **tutup**

menyabotase v to sabotage ← **sabotase**

menyadap v to tap (rubber, telephones) ← **sadap**

menyadari v to realize, be aware of ← **sadar**

menyadur v to rewrite, adapt ← **sadur**

menyahut v to answer, reply, respond ← **sahut**

menyaingi *v* to compete with ← **saing**

menyajikan *v* to serve, present, offer ← **saji**

menyakiti *v* to hurt, treat badly; **menyakitkan** *adj* painful ← **sakit**

menyaksikan *v* to witness ← **saksi**

menyala *v* to burn, blaze; **menyalakan** *v* to light, set fire to ← **nyala**

menyalami *v* to greet ← **salam**

menyalin *v* to copy ← **salin**

menyalip *v* overtake, slip past ← **salip**

menyalurkan *v* to channel ← **salur**

menyamakan *v* to equate, consider the same ← **sama**

menyamar *v* to be in disguise ← **samar**

menyambar *v* to pounce on, strike ← **sambar**

menyambung *v* to join, continue; **menyambung-kan** *v* to connect to (something else) ← **sambung**

menyambut *v* to welcome or receive ← **sambut**

menyampaikan *v* to deliver, hand over, pass on ← **sampai**

menyampingi *v* to escort, accompany, flank ← **samping**

menyandar *v* to lean ← **sandar**

menyandera *v* to take hostage ← **sandera**

menyangka *v* to suspect, suppose, presume; *tidak ~* never thought ← **sangka**

menyangkal *v* to deny ← **sangkal**

menyangkut *v* to involve, concern; *conj* about ← **sangkut**

menyanjung *v* to flatter ← **sanjung**

menyanyi *v* to sing; **menyanyikan** *v* to sing something ← **nyanyi**

menyapa *v* to greet ← **sapa**

menyapu *v* to sweep or wipe ← **sapu**

menyarankan *v* to suggest ← **saran**

menyaring *v* to filter (through), screen, select ← **saring**

menyasar *v* to lose your way, get lost ← **sasar**

menyatakan *v* to declare, state, certify ← **nyata**

menyatu *v* to become one; **menyatukan** *v* to unite various things ← **satu**

menyayangi *v* to love ← **sayang**

menyebabkan *v* to cause ← **sebab**

menyebalkan *adj* annoying, tiresome ← **sebal**

menyebarkan *v* to spread something ← **sebar**

menyebarluaskan *v* to disseminate, spread something ← **sebar luas**

menyeberang *v* to cross ← **seberang**

menyebut *v* to mention, name, say ← **sebut**

menyederhanakan *v* to simplify ← **sederhana**

menyediakan *v* to prepare, get ready ← **sedia**

menyedihkan *adj* depressing, sad ← **sedih**

menyedot *v* to suck (up) ← **sedot**

menyegarkan *adj* refreshing ← **segar**

menyégel *v* to seal (off), close up (a building) ← **ségel**

menyejukkan *adj* cooling, refreshing ← **sejuk**

menyekolahkan *v* to send to school ← **sekolah**

menyelam *v* to dive ← **selam**

menyelamatkan *v* to save, rescue ← **selamat**

menyelenggarakan *v* to run, hold, organize ← **selenggara**

menyelesaikan *v* to finish, end, settle; ~ *masalah* to overcome a problem ← **selesai**

menyeléwéng *v* to deviate; to have an affair ← **seléwéng**

menyelidiki *v* to investigate ← **selidik**

menyelimuti *v* to (cover with a) blanket ← **selimut**

menyelinap *v* to sneak, move quietly ← **selinap**

menyelip *v* to slip; **menyelipkan** *v* to slip an object (into something) ← **selip**

menyelubungi *v* to veil or cover ← **selubung**

menyelundup *v* to sneak in illegally, infiltrate;

208

menyelundupkan *v* to smuggle (in) ← **selundup**

menyematkan *v* to pin, fasten with pins ← **semat**

menyembah *v* to pay homage to, worship ← **sembah**

menyembelih *v* to slaughter, butcher ← **sembelih**

menyembuhkan *v* to curc, heal ← **sembuh**

menyembunyikan *v* to hide or conceal something ← **sembunyi**

menyemburkan *v* to spit or spray something out ← **sembur**

menyemir *v* to polish ← **semir**

menyempatkan ~ *diri* to make time to ← **sempat**

menyempit *v* to (become) narrow ← **sempit**

menyemprot *v* to spray; **menyemprotkan** *v* to spray with something ← **semprot**

menyempurnakan *v* to perfect, complete ← **sempurna**

menyenangkan *adj* pleasing, agreeable ← **senang**

menyendiri *v* to go off by yourself ← **diri**

menyengat *v* to sting ← **sengat**

menyénggol *v* to bump, brush, tweak ← **sénggol**

menyentuh *v* to touch ← **sentuh**

menyépak *v* to kick (out) ← **sepak**

menyepakati *v* to agree to ← **sepakat, pakat**

menyepélékan *v* to make light of, treat lightly ← **sepélé**

menyerah *v* to surrender, give in, give up; **menyerahkan** *v* to hand over ← **serah**

menyerang *v* to attack ← **serang**

menyerap *v* to absorb, soak up ← **serap**

menyerbu *v* to attack (as a group), charge on, invade ← **serbu**

menyérét *v* to drag ← **sérét**

menyerobot *v* to push in front ← **serobot**

menyertai *v* to accompany ← **serta**

menyerukan *v* to call or appeal for ← **seru**

menyerupai *v* to resemble, be similar to ← **rupa**

menyesal *v* to regret; **menyesalkan** *v* to feel bad about, regret (another's action) ← **sesal**

menyesatkan *adj* misleading, confusing ← **sesat**

menyesuaikan *v* to adapt, bring into line ← **sesuai**

menyetél *v* to tune, set, adjust; ~ *mesin mobil* to tune the engine ← **setél**

menyetir *v* to drive ← **setir**

menyetor *v* to pay in, deposit ← **setor**

menyetrika *v* to iron ← **setrika**

menyetujui *v* to agree to, approve, ratify ← **tubuh, setubuh**

menyéwa *v* to rent; hire; **menyéwakan** *v* to let (a house), hire out, lease ← **séwa**

menyiapkan *v* to prepare something, get something ready ← **siap**

menyiarkan *v* to telecast, broadcast, disseminate ← **siar**

menyibukkan ~ *diri* to keep yourself busy, spend your time ← **sibuk**

menyidik *v* to investigate ← **sidik, selidik**

menyikat *v* to brush ← **sikat**

menyiksa *v* to torture ← **siksa**

menyimak *v* to hear, monitor ← **simak**

menyimpan *v* to keep, save up, store ← **simpan**

menyimpang *v* to deviate ← **simpang**

menyimpulkan *v* to conclude or summarize ← **simpul**

menyindir *v* to insinuate, allude ← **sindir**

menyinggung *v* to touch on; ~ *perasaan* to offend someone, hurt someone's feelings ← **singgung**

menyingkapkan *v* to open something slightly; ~ *rahasia* to reveal a secret ← **singkap**

menyingkatkan *v* to abbreviate, shorten ← **singkat**

menyingkir *v* to step or
move aside; **menyingkir-
kan** *v* to remove, brush
aside ← **singkir**

menyiram *v* to pour, water
(plants); **menyirami** *v* to
pour onto ← **siram**

menyisakan *v* to leave
behind ← **sisa**

menyisihkan *v* to set aside
← **sisih**

menyisipkan *v* to insert ←
sisip

menyisir *v* to comb, check
thoroughly ← **sisir**

menyita *v* to confiscate
← **sita**

menyobék *v* to tear off ←
sobék

menyodok *v* to poke ←
sodok

menyodomi *v* to sodomize
← **sodomi**

menyodori *v* to hand to, offer;
menyodorkan *v* to offer up,
put forward ← **sodor**

menyogok *v* to bribe ←
sogok

menyongsong *v* to welcome,
greet ← **songsong**

menyonték *v* to copy, cheat
← **conték, sonték**

menyoroti *v* to light up,
illuminate, focus on ←
sorot

menyortir *v* to sort, organize
← **sortir**

menyuap *v* to feed by
hand; to bribe ← **suap**

menyuarakan *v* to voice ←
suara

menyucikan *v* to purify,
cleanse ← **suci**

menyudutkan *v* to push into
a corner, deflect ← **sudut**

menyuguhi *v* to offer
(food), present (a performance) ← **suguh**

menyukai *v* to like ← **suka**

menyulam *v* to embroider
← **sulam**

menyulap *v* to conjure up;
to make something vanish
or change ← **sulap**

menyulih-suarakan *v* to
dub ← **sulih**

menyulitkan *v* to make
difficult, complicate, cause
problems ← **sulit**

menyuluh *v* to illuminate;
to inform ← **suluh**

menyumbang *v* to contribute, make a donation ←
sumbang

211

menyumbat v to plug, stop ← **sumbat**

menyunatkan v to have someone circumcised ← **sunat**

menyundul ~ *bola* to head the ball (in soccer) ← **sundul**

menyuntik v to inject or vaccinate ← **suntik**

menyunting v to edit ← **sunting**

menyupir v to drive ← **supir**

menyurati v to write a letter to ← **surat**

menyuruh v to command, order ← **suruh**

menyusahkan v to bother, make difficult ← **susah**

menyusu v to feed, suckle; **menyusui** v to feed ← **susu**

menyusul v to follow, go after ← **susul**

menyusun v to heap or pile; to arrange, organize, compile ← **susun**

menyusut v to shrink, become smaller ← **susut**

méong meow; *coll* puss, cat

mépét *adj* tight, squeezed

meraba v to feel or grope something; **meraba-raba** v

to feel around or grope (in the dark) ← **raba**

meracik ~ *obat* to mix up medicine ← **racik**

meracuni v to poison ← **racun**

meradang v to become inflamed; to become angry ← **radang**

meragukan v to doubt something ← **ragu**

mérah *adj* red; ~ *jambu* pink; ~ *tua* dark red, maroon; **kemérah-mérahan** *adj* reddish; **memérah** v to blush; **pemérah** ~ *pipi* rouge

merahasiakan v to keep secret ← **rahasia**

meraih v to reach for; to achieve ← **raih**

merajaléla v to be out of control, act violently ← **rajaléla**

merajut v to knit; to crochet ← **rajut**

merak n peacock

merakit v to assemble ← **rakit**

meralat v to correct a mistake ← **ralat**

meramaikan v to liven up, enliven ← **ramai**

meramal v to tell fortunes;
meramalkan v to predict,
foretell ← **ramal**

merampas v to take by
force, rob, plunder ←
rampas

merampok v to rob, hold
up ← **rampok**

merana v to suffer, waste
away; to live miserably, in
poverty

merancang v to plan,
design ← **rancang**

merang n rice-straw

merangkak v to crawl ←
rangkak

merangkap v to hold
another position (tempo-
rarily) ← **rangkap**

merangkul v to hug,
embrace; to get someone
involved ← **rangkul**

merangsang v to stimulate,
excite ← **rangsang**

merantai v to chain up ←
rantai

merantau v to sail away,
seek your fortune, settle
overseas ← **rantau**

merasa v to think, feel;
merasakan v to feel something ← **rasa**

meratakan v to level, flatten
← **rata**

meratap v to lament, wail
← **ratap**

meraung v to roar ←
raung

merawat v to nurse, care
for; to maintain, look after
← **rawat**

merayakan v to celebrate
← **raya**

merayap v to crawl, creep
← **rayap**

merayu v to tempt, flatter,
seduce ← **rayu**

mercon n fireworks

mercu n top, summit; ~
suar lighthouse

merdéka *adj* free, independent; **kemerdékaan** n
freedom, independence,
liberty

merdu *adj* sweet, melodious,
honeyed

meréboisasi v to reforest,
replant trees ← **réboisasi**

merebus v to boil (in)
water ← **rebus**

merebut v to snatch,
capture; **merebutkan** v
to snatch something ←
rebut

213

meredakan *v* to soothe; to calm something down ← **reda**

mérek *n* brand, make (vehicle), label (clothes); **bermérek** *v* to have a label, branded

meréka *pron, pl* they, them, their; ~ *punya* theirs

merekam *v* to record ← **rekam**

merekayasa *v* to engineer ← **rékayasa**

merékonstruksi *v* to reconstruct ← **rékonstruksi**

merekrut *v* to recruit ← **rekrut**

merélakan *v* to approve, agree to ← **réla**

merem be asleep, eyes shut

meremajakan *v* to revitalize, refurbish, update ← **remaja**

meremas *v* to press, squeeze, knead ← **remas**

merembes *v* to seep in, leak, ooze ← **rembes**

meréméhkan *v* to belittle, treat as unimportant ← **réméh**

merencanakan *v* to plan ← **rencana**

merendahkan *v* to lower; to humiliate ← **rendah**

merendam *v* to soak something ← **rendam**

merengék *v* to whimper, whine ← **réngék**

merenggut *v* to snatch, tug ← **renggut**

merénovasi *v* to renovate ← **rénovasi**

merenung *v* to daydream ← **renung**

meréparasi *v* to repair ← **réparasi**

merépotkan *v* to make someone busy or go to some trouble ← **répot**

meresahkan *adj* disturbing, worrying ← **resah**

meresap *v* to be absorbed, penetrate, seep into ← **resap**

merésépkan *v* to write a prescription for a drug ← **resép**

meresmikan *v* to formalize, make official ← **resmi**

merestui *v* to agree to, give your blessing to ← **restu**

meriah *adj* merry, lively; **memeriahkan** *v* to liven up, enliven

214

meriam *n* cannon

meriang feel unwell, sick

meributkan *v* to make a fuss about ← **ribut**

merica *n* pepper

merilis *v* to release, put out ← **rilis**

merinding *v* to have goose-bumps or an eerie feeling, be spooked ← **rInding**

merindukan *v* to miss, long for ← **rindu**

meringankan *v* to ease, relieve, make easier ← **ringan**

merintih *v* to moan or groan ← **rintih**

merintis *v* to trace; to pioneer ← **rintis**

merisaukan *v* to worry about ← **risau**

mérk → **mérek**

merobék *v* to tear up, shred ← **robék**

merobohkan *v* to knock down, demolish ← **roboh**

merogoh *v* to grope around, search for (inside something else) ← **rogoh**

merokok *v* to smoke ← **rokok**

merombak *v* to pull down, demolish; to reorganize ← **rombak**

merompak *v* to commit piracy ← **rompak**

meronta, meronta-ronta *v* to struggle, squirm to get loose ← **ronta**

merosot *v* fall down, descend, plummet; **kemerosotan** *n* descent, deterioration ← **rosot**

merpati *n* pigeon, dove

mertua *n* parents-in-law; *ibu* ~ mother-in-law

merubah → **mengubah**

merugikan *v* to hurt, harm, injure ← **rugi**

merujuk *v* to refer to, use as a source ← **rujuk**

meruncing *v* to become critical or sharp ← **runcing**

merundingkan *v* to discuss something, deliberate ← **runding**

meruntuhkan *v* to destroy overthrow ← **runtuh**

merupakan *v* to be, form, constitute ← **rupa**

merusak *v* to spoil, damage; **merusakkan** *v* to destroy, break ← **rusak**

més *n* company accommodation or housing, boarding house

mésem smile

méses *n* chocolate sprinkles

mesin *n* machine, engine; ~ *jahit* sewing machine

mesjid, masjid *n* mosque; ~ *agung,* ~ *raya* great mosque

meski, meskipun *conj* although, even though

mesra *adj* intimate, close; **kemesraan** *n* intimacy

mesti, musti *v, aux* should; ~*nya* should; **semestinya** should have (been)

méter *n* meter; metre; **méteran** *n* tape measure

meterai, méterai *n* seal

méteran *n* tape measure ← **méter**

métode *n* method

méwah *n* luxurious; **keméwahan** *n* luxury

mewajibkan *v* to enforce or make obligatory ← **wajib**

mewakili *v* to represent ← **wakil**

mewarisi *v* to inherit ← **waris**

mewarnai *v* to color (in) ← **warna**

mewaspadai *v* to watch out for, guard against ← **waspada**

mewawancarai *v* to interview ← **wawancara**

mewujudkan *v* to make something real, realize something ← **wujud**

meyakini *v* to convince someone; **meyakinkan** *adj* convincing, believable ← **yakin**

mi, mie *n* noodles; ~ *ayam* chicken noodles; ~ *goreng* fried noodles; ~ *rebus* boiled noodles (in soup)

migrasi *n* migration; **bermigrasi** *v* to migrate; **migran** *n* migrant → **imigrasi, pendatang**

migrén *n* migraine

mik, mikrofon *n* microphone, mike

mikroskop *n* microscope

mili, miliméter *n* millimeter

miliar, milyar *n* billion → **milyar**

milik *n* property, possession; ~ *negara* state-owned; **memiliki** *v* to own, possess; **pemilik** *n* owner

milis *n* mail list

milisi *n* militia

militan *adj* militant; **militér** *n* military

milyar, miliar *n* billion; **milyarder** *n* billionaire

mimbar *n* pulpit, platform, forum

mimisan nose bleed, blood nose

mimpi dream; ~ *buruk* night mare, bad dream; ~ *indah* sweet dreams; **bermimpi** *v* to dream; **memimpikan** *v* to dream of → **impi**

min → **minus**

minal aidin (wal faidzin) greeting at Idul Fitri

Minang, Minangkabau ethnic group of West Sumatra; *bahasa* ~, *orang* ~ Minang

minat *n* interest, attention; **berminat** *v* to have an interest, be interested

minder to lack confidence, low self-esteem; to feel inferior

minggir *v, coll* move to one side, pull over (on the road) → **pinggir**

minggu *n* week; Sunday; ~ *depan* next week; ~ *ini* this

week; ~ *yang lalu*, ~ *kemarin* last week; *hari* ~ Sunday; *malam* ~ Saturday night; **berminggu-minggu** *adv* for weeks; **mingguan** *n* weekly (publication); **seminggu** *adj* a week

miniatur *adj* miniature

minim, minimal, minimum minimum, minimal(ly)

minoritas *n* minority

minta *v* to ask, beg, request; to apply for; ~ *uang* to ask or beg for money; **minta-minta** *v* to beg (alms); **meminta** *v* to ask for, request; **permintaan** *n* request

minum drink; ~ *obat* to take (liquid) medicine; **minuman** *n* drink; ~ *hangat* hot drink, beverage; ~ *keras* alcoholic drink, liquor

minus, min *adj* minus

minyak *n* oil; ~ *kelapa* coconut palm oil; ~ *mentah* crude oil; ~ *rambut* hair tonic or oil; ~ *tanah* kerosene; ~ *wangi* perfume; ~ *zaitun* olive oil; **berminyak** *adj* oily, greasy; **perminyakan** *n* oil and gas

miring *adj* sloping, slanting; not straight; *berita* ~ negative story; *tulisan* ~ italic

misa *n, Cath* mass; ~ *agung* high mass

misal *n* example; **misalnya, misalkan** for example, for instance

misi *n* mission; **misionaris** *n* missionary

miskin *adj* poor, lacking in; *orang* ~ the poor; **kemiskinan** *n* poverty

mistéri *n* mystery; **mistérius** *adj* mysterious

mistik, mistis *adj* mystical

mitos *n* myth

mitra *n* partner, friend

mobil *n* car; ~ *baja* armored car, tank; ~ *jenazah* hearse; ~ *kuno* vintage car; ~ *mewah* luxury car

modal *n* capital, fund; *menanam* ~ to invest (capital)

mode *n* fashion, trend

modél *n* model

modérn *adj* modern

moga: moga-moga, semoga may, hopefully

mogok strike; break down; ~ *kerja* strike; ~ *makan* hunger strike

mohon *v* to request, ask, beg; please; ~ *diri* to take leave; ~ *perhatian* attention please; **permohonan** *n* request, application → **pohon**

mol → **mal**

molék *adj* pretty, charming; *kecil* ~ delicate

molor stretch, become longer

momong take care of a baby; **momongan** *n* baby, child

Monas *n* National Monument in Central Jakarta ← **Monumén Nasional**

moncong *n* muzzle, nose

mondar-mandir *v* to go back and forth, to and fro

mondok *v, coll* to board, stay ← **pondok**

monopoli *n* monopoly

monorél *n* monorail

monoton *adj* monotonous

montir *n* mechanic

montok *adj* plump, rounded, well filled-out

monumén *n* monument; ~ *Nasional (Monas)* National Monument

monyét *n* monkey; *derog* term of abuse

monyong *adj* sticking out, protruding (of teeth), like a dog's muzzle

moral, moril moral; *dukungan* ~ moral support

motif *n* design, pattern, motif; **bermotif** *v* to have a design

molif *n* motive; **motivasi** *n* motivation; **bermotivasikan** *v* to be motivated by; **memotivasi** *v* to motivate

moto *n* MSG, monosodium glutamate; motto, chant ← **Ajinomoto**

motor *n* motorcycle, (motor)bike

MPR *abbrev Majelis Permusyarawatan Rakyat* People's Consultative Council

-mu *pron, poss, s* your; *buku*~ your book → **kamu**

mua *n* eel

muak loathe; disgusted, fed up; **memuakkan** *adj* revolting, disgusting

mual *adj* nauseous, queasy, sick

mualaf *n, Isl* recent convert

muara *n* mouth (of a river); **bermuara** *v* to have a mouth, empty into

muat contain; *tidak* ~ it won't fit; **muatan** *n* load, cargo; **bermuatan** *v* to be laden with; **memuat** *v* to contain

muda *adj* young; *hijau* ~ light green; **pemuda** *n* youth; young man

mudah *adj* easy; ~ *marah* easily angry, quick-tempered; **mudah-mudahan** *adv* hopefully; **kemudahan** *n* ease, facility; **mempermudah** *v* to make easier

mudik *v* to go upstream, back to the village

mujur straight on; lucky

muka *n* face, front, surface; *di* ~ in front of; *ke* ~ to the front, forward; **mengemukakan** *v* to put forward, advance, nominate; **terkemuka** *adj* prominent; **bermuka** *v* to have a face; ~ *dua* two-faced; **permukaan** *n* surface; ~ *air* water level; *di atas* ~ *laut* above sea level

mukim: bermukim v to reside, stay; **permukiman** n housing, residential area

mula beginning, start; **mula-mula** adv in the beginning, at first; **bermula** v to start, begin; **memulai** v to start or begin something; **pemula** n beginner; **permulaan** n beginning; **semula** adv originally

mulai v to begin, start; ~ tanggal 23 Desember from December 23; **memulai** v to start or begin something ← **mula**

mula-mula adv in the beginning, at first ← **mula**

mulas stomach upset, loose stomach

mulia adj honorable, noble; logam ~ precious metal; **kemuliaan** n honor, glory; **memuliakan** v to honor, glorify

mulus adj smooth, flawless

mulut n mouth; ~ kotor filthy mouth

mumpung v to make the most of, capitalize on

muncrat v to spurt, spray

muncul v to appear, turn up

mundur v to go backwards, reverse, retreat; to resign; **kemunduran** n deterioration, decline → **undur**

mungil adj small, tiny, delicate; rumah ~ small house

mungkin conj maybe, possibly; tidak ~ impossible; **kemungkinan** n possibility; **memungkinkan** adj conducive; v to enable, make possible

munisi → **amunisi**

muntabér n diarrhea and vomiting ← **muntah bérak**

muntah v to vomit, throw up

mur n nut

murah adj cheap; ~ hati generous; ~ senyum always smiling; **termurah** adj the cheapest

murai burung ~ magpie

muram adj gloomy, sombre, mournful

murid n pupil, student

murni adj pure; only; **kemurnian** n purity

murung adj gloomy, despondent

musang n civet cat

muséum → **musium**

mushola, musholla, mushalla n, Isl small prayer-house

musibah n disaster, calamity; kena ~ suffer a disaster

musik n music; **pemusik, musikus, musisi** n musician

musim n season; ~ bunga, ~ semi spring; ~ dingin winter; ~ gugur autumn, fall; ~ panas summer; **musiman** adj seasonal

musium, muséum n museum

Muslim adj, Isl Muslim; baju ~ Islamic dress ← **Islam**

musnah adj destroyed; **memusnahkan** v to destroy; **pemusnahan** v act of destruction

mustahil adj impossible

musti → **mesti**

musuh n enemy; ~ bebuyutan arch-enemy; **memusuhi** v to fight against, antagonize, make an enemy of; **permusuhan** n enmity, animosity, hostility

musyawarah: bermusyawarah v to deliberate, discuss

mutakhir adj modern, latest

mutasi n change (in status), mutation

mutiara n pearl; ibu ~ mother-of-pearl

mutlak adj absolute, unconditional

mutu n quality; **bermutu** adj quality

Myanmar n Myanmar, Burma; bahasa ~, orang ~ Burmese

N

naas adj unfortunate

nabati adj vegetable, plant; lemak ~ vegetable fats

nabi n, Isl, Chr prophet

nada n note, tone, sound; ~ dering ringtone; ~sela call waiting

nadi n pulse

nafas, napas breath, breathe; **bernafas** v to breathe; **bernafaskan** v with a breath of; **pernafasan** *n* breathing, respiration; ~ *buatan* artificial respiration; *sistem* ~ respiratory system

nafkah *n* means of livelihood

nafsu *n* desire, ~ *makan* appetite; **bernafsu** *adj* passionate, lusty

naga *n* dragon; *Tahun* ~ Year of the Dragon

nah, na well, well then; look! ~ *lu* well then, how about that?

Nahdlatul Ulama (NU) *n* Islamic social organization

naif *adj* naive → **lugu**

naik go up, climb, rise, ascend; ~ *gunung* to climb a mountain; ~ *haji* to go on the pilgrimage to Mecca; ~ *pesawat* to board, boarding; ~ *pangkat* to be promoted; ~ *pitam* get angry; **kenaikan** *n* rise, raise; ~ *gaji* pay rise; **menaiki** *v* to ride, mount, get on; **menaikkan** *v* to raise, hoist

nak *pron* child, son, lass → **anak**

nakal *adj* naughty; **kenakalan** *n* naughtiness

nakhoda *n* captain (of a ship)

naluri *n* instinct

nama *n* name; ~ *depan* first name; ~ *kecil* everyday name, nickname; ~ *keluarga* family name, surname; **bernama** *adj* named; **menamakan** *v* to call, name; **ternama** *adj* famous, well-known

nampak → **tampak**

namun *conj* however, yet

nanah *n* pus; **bernanah** *v* to fester

nanas, nenas *n* pineapple

nangka *n* jackfruit

nanti *adv* later; ~ *dulu* not now, later on; ~ *malam* tonight; ~ *sore* this afternoon; **menanti** *v* to wait; **menanti-nanti** *v* to wait for a long time; **menantikan** *v* to wait for

napas, nafas breath, breathe; **bernapas** *v* to breathe; **bernapaskan** *v* with a breath of; **pernapasan** *n* breathing, respiration; ~ *buatan* artificial respiration; *sistem* ~ respiratory system

napi *n* prisoner, inmate, criminal → **narapidana**

napsu → **nafsu**

nara: narapidana *n* prisoner, inmate, criminal; **narasumber** *n* source (person)

narik *v, coll* to work as a driver of public transport ← **tarik**

narkoba *n* (illegal) drugs, narcotics and other banned substances ← **narkotik, psikotropika dan obat terlarang**

narkotika *n* narcotics

nasabah *n* (bank) customer

naséhat → **nasihat**

nasi *n* (cooked) rice; ~ *goreng* fried rice; ~ *rames* rice with side-dishes

nasib *n* fate, lot, destiny

nasihat, naséhat *n* advice; **menasihati** *v* to advise; **penasihat** *n* adviser

nasional *n* national; **nasionalis** *n* nationalist; **nasionalisme** *n* nationalism

naskah *n* manuscript, original (text); *penulis* ~ script writer

Nasrani *adj* Christian

Natal *Hari* ~ Christmas Day; *Malam* ~ Christmas Eve; **natalan** *v, coll* to celebrate Christmas

naung: naungan *n* shade, shelter; protection; *di bawah* ~ under the auspices of

nb *abbrev nota bene* note (well)

ndak, nggak, enggak *coll* no, not ← **tidak**

nébéng *v, sl* to sponge, get a lift, use something without paying ← **tébéng**

nécis *adj* well-dressed

negara *n* state, country; ~ *tetangga* neighbor; *antar* ~ international; *Ibu* ~ First Lady; *lambang* ~ national symbol; **kenegaraan** *adj* state (affairs); **negarawan** *n* statesman

negeri *n* country, land; ~ *jiran* neighbor, Malaysia; *dalam* ~ national, domestic, internal

nékad, nékat reckless; stubborn; **kenékatan** *n* determination, resolve, recklessness

nelayan *n* fisherman

nenas → **nanas**

nénék *n, pron* grandmother; great-aunt; female relative of grandmother's generation; ~ *buyut* great-grandmother; ~ *moyang* ancestors → **Nék**

Néng *pron* term of address for girl or young woman in western Java

néon *n* neon

népotisme *n* nepotism

neraca *n* scales, balance

neraka *n* hell

nerocos, nyerocos *v, coll* to talk too much, blather, chatter or rattle on ← **cerocos**

nétral *adj* neutral; **ménétralkan** *v* to neutralize

ngabén Balinese funeral ceremony

ngaji *v, coll* to recite or read the Koran; *guru* ~ Arabic teacher ← **kaji**

nganga: ternganga *adj* gaping, flabbergasted, wide open

ngantor *v, coll* to go to work ← **kantor**

ngantuk *adj, coll* sleepy ← **antuk**

ngarang *v, coll* to make something up (off the top of your head) ← **karang**

ngefans *v, sl* to be a fan of; ~ *berat* to be a great fan of ← **fans**

ngeri *adj* terrified, **mengerikan** *adj* terrifying, horrifying

ngetém *v, coll* to wait for passengers (of public transport) ← **tém**

ngetrén, ngetréand *adj, coll* trendy, fashionable ← **tréand**

nggak, enggak, ndak *coll* no, not → **tidak**

ngilu *adj* painful (of teeth), smarting; *rasa* ~ pain

ngobrol *v, coll* to chat ← **obrol**

ngomong *v, coll* to speak, talk; **ngomong-ngomong** *adv* by the way

ngompol *v, coll* to wet your pants, the bed ← **ompol**

ngorok *v, coll* to snore; to sleep

ngotot *v, coll* to be stubborn, refuse to back down → **otot**

nguping *v, coll* to eavesdrop, listen in ← **kuping**

niaga *n* commerce; **per-niagaan** *n* commerce, trade, business

niat *n* intention; **berniat** *v* to intend

nih *pron, sl* this, these; here; *ini* ~ this one → **ini**

nihil *adj* nothing, nil

nikah *pol* marry; **menikah** *v* to marry, get married; **menikahi** *v* to marry someone; **pernikahan** *n* wedding

nikmat *adj* enjoyable, delicious; **kenikmatan** *n* pleasure, enjoyment; **menikmati** *v* to enjoy

nila *n* indigo; *ikan* ~ a kind of freshwater fish

nilai *n* value, worth; mark, grade (at school); ~ *tambah* added value; **menilai** *v* to evaluate, appraise; **penilaian** *n* evaluation; **ternilai** *tidak* ~ priceless, invaluable

NIM *abbrev Nomor Induk Mahasiswa* (university) student number

ninabobo lullaby; sing to sleep

NIP *abbrev Nomor Induk Pegawai* civil servant number

nir- *pref* without; **nirlaba** *adj* non-profit, not for profit

nisan *n* headstone, gravestone

NKRI *abbrev Negara Kesatuan Republik Indonesia* the unitary state of the Republic of Indonesia

Nn. *abbrev Nona* Miss, title for unmarried woman, especially a non-Indonesian

nobat: menobatkan *v* to install, crown

noda *n* stain

nol *adj* zero, nil

nomor, nomer *n* number; event, match; ~ *urut* queue number; ~ *cantik* lucky mobile phone number; ~ *satu* number one, first; **menomersatukan** *v* to put first, give priority

non- *pref* not; non-; **nonaktif** *adj* not in active service; **menonaktifkan** *v* to release from active service, non-activate; **nonformal** *adj* irregular, informal; **nonpri(bumi)**

adj ethnic Chinese, non-indigenous

Non, Nona *pron* Miss

nonaktif *adj* not in active service

nonformal *adj* irregular, informal

nongkrong → **tongkrong**

nonpri, nonpribumi *adj* ethnic Chinese, non-indigenous ← **pribumi**

nonton *v, coll* to watch, look on ← **tonton**

Nopémber → **November**

norak *adj, coll* tasteless, vulgar, tacky

norit *n* diarrhea tablets, made from black carbon

Norwégia *n* Norway

nostalgia, nostalgi *n* nostalgia; **bernostalgia** *v* to reminisce, be nostalgic

not *n* note (music)

nota *n* note, memo; bill, account

notaris *n* notary

Novémber, Nopémber *bulan* ~ November

nr *abbrev nomor* number

ntar, entar *sl* just a minute, wait → **sebentar**

NTB *abbrev Nusa*

Tenggara Barat West Nusa Tenggara (the lesser Sunda islands)

NTT *abbrev Nusa Tenggara Timur* East Nusa Tenggara (the lesser Sunda islands)

NU *abbrev* Nahdlatul Ulama, Islamic organization based in East Java

nuansa *n* touch, nuance; **bernuansa** *adj* with a touch of

nuklir *adj* nuclear; *bom* ~ nuclear bomb

numpang → **tumpang**

nurani *adj* inner; *hati* ~ inner self, conscience

nuri *burung* ~ parrot

nusa *n* island; ~ *Tenggara* the Lesser Sunda Islands; **Nusantara** *n* Indonesia

Ny. *abbrev Nyonya* Madam, title for married woman, especially a non-Indonesian

-nya *suf, poss* added to words to indicate possession; the; *itu ibu*~ that's her mother

nyala flame, blaze, burn; **menyala** *v* to burn, blaze; **menyalakan** *v* to light, set fire to

nyali *n* guts, bravery

nyaman *adj* comfortable, pleasant; **kenyamanan** *n* comfort

nyamuk *n* mosquito

nyanyi sing; **nyanyian** *n* song; **bernyanyi, menyanyi** *v* to sing; **menyanyikan** *v* to sing something; **penyanyi** *n* singer, vocalist; ~ *latar* backing vocalist

nyaring *adj* clear, loud, shrill

nyaris *adv, neg* nearly, almost

nyata *adj* clear, obvious, plain; **kenyataan** *n* fact; **menyatakan** *v* to declare, state, certify; **pernyataan** *n* statement, declaration

nyawa *n* soul, life; *tiga puluh* ~ thirty lives; **bernyawa** *adj* alive

nyekar *v, coll* to strew flower petals on a grave; to visit a grave → **sekar**

nyenyak *adj* sound asleep

Nyepi *n* Balinese Day of Seclusion

nyeri *n* pain; ~ *haid* menstrual pain or cramp

nyerocos *v, coll* to talk too

much, blather, chatter or rattle on ← **cerocos**

nyiur *n* coconut palm

nyonya *pron, f* term of address for a married woman, Madam; Mrs; ~ *rumah* the lady (mistress) of the house; *untuk* ~ for Madam; ~ *Iskandar* Mrs Iskandar

O

o *excl* oh; ~ *ya* oh yes, by the way

oase *n* oasis

obah → **ubah**

obat *n* medicine; ~ *batuk* cough medicine; ~ *merah* mercurochrome; ~ *nyamuk* mosquito repellent; **berobat** *v* to go to the doctor, seek medical advice; **mengobati** *v* to treat, cure; **pengobatan** *n* treatment

obor *n* torch

obrak-abrik: mengobrak-abrik *v* to upset, turn upside-down

obral *n* sale; **mengobral** *v* to put on sale

obrol: **mengobrol** *v* **ngobrol** *coll* to chat; **obrolan** *n* chat

obyék *n* object; ~ *wisata* tourist destination, sight; **obyéktif** *adj* objective

obyék: **ngobyék** *v, coll* to have a job on the side, moonlight

OD *abbrev* overdose

odol *n, arch* toothpaste

ogah *adj, sl* unwilling, reluctant

ojék, ojég *n* motorcycle taxi; *pangkalan* ~ place where motorcycle taxis wait; *tukang* ~ motorcycle taxi driver

oké *sl* okay, OK

oknum *n, neg* individual (causing trouble in a group or company)

oksigén *n* oxygen

Oktober *bulan* ~ October

olah manner, process; ~*raga* sport; **olahan** *adj* processed; **mengolah** *v* to process, treat; **pengolahan** *v* processing

olahraga *v* sport; ~ *bela diri* self-defense; **berolahraga**

v to do or play sport; **olahragawan** *n, m* sportsman

oléh *conj* by, through; ~ *karena* because of, due to; **oléh-oléh** *n* souvenir; **memperoléh** *v* to obtain, get; **peroléhan** *n* acquisition

oléng *adj* on a lean, leaning to one side

olés: **olésan** *n* smear; **mengolés** *v* to grease, spread, lubricate; **mengolési** *v* to grease something; **mengoléskan** *v* to smear with something

oli, olie *n* (engine) oil; *ganti* ~ drain sump oil

Olimpiade *n* the Olympics, the Olympic Games

olok: **memperolok** *v* to tease, taunt

Om, Oom *pron* Uncle; term of address to extended family, parents' friends, friends' parents etc

ombak *n* wave; **berombak** *adj* wavy

ombang-ambing: **ter-ombang-ambing** *v* to bob (up and down), float; to fluctuate

omél: mengomél v to
complain, grumble, whinge,
whine ← omél

omong chat, talk, speak;
~ kosong nonsense; omo-
ngan n chat; gossip; ngo-
mong v, coll to speak, talk;
ngomong-ngomong by
the way

ompol: mengompol v to
wet the bed, wet your pants

ompong adj toothless

ompréng: ompréngan n
truck converted into a
passenger vehicle, unofficial taxi

onani n masturbation;
melakukan ~ to masturbate

onar n stir, commotion

oncom n fermented soy-
bean cake

ondé: ondé-ondé n small
round cakes made of green
peanuts, covered in sesame
seeds

ondél: ondél-ondél n giant
figures used in Betawi
celebrations

onderdil n (automotive)
spare part

ongkos n cost (for a
service), expense, charge;

~ hidup cost of living,
living expenses; ~ pen-
giriman cost of freight or
postage

ONH abbrev ongkos naik
haji cost of the package
covering the major
pilgrimage to Mecca

ons ounce

onta → unta

oper, mengoper v to
transfer, hand over; ~ bola
to pass the ball

operasi n operation;
beroperasi v to operate,
work, function

opini n opinion

oplos: mengoplos v to
mix in another liquid
illegally

OPM abbrev Organisasi
Papua Merdeka Free
Papua Organisation,
secessionist movement

opname go into hospital,
hospitalization; diopname
v to be admitted to hospital,
be hospitalized

opor ~ ayam chicken in
coconut sauce, traditionally
eaten at Idul Fitri

oposisi n opposition

optik optician; optical

orak: orak-arik n scrambled egg with beans

orang n person, human; ~ *asing* foreigner, stranger; ~ *awam* layman, public; ~ *banyak* public, people; ~ *Barat* Westerner; ~ *baru* newcomer; ~ *besar* person in power or authority; ~ *Cina,* ~ *Tionghoa* (ethnic) Chinese; ~ *gila* tramp; mentally-ill person; ~ *Indonesia* Indonesian; ~ *Islam* Muslim; ~ *kulit putih* white person; ~ *Kristen* Christian Protestant; ~ *tua* parents; **orang-orangan** n doll, dummy; **perorangan** adj personal, individual; **seorang** a (person); counter for people; ~ *Arab* an Arab; ~ *diri* alone, single-handedly; **perseorangan** adj individual; **seseorang** n a certain person, somebody

orang conj, coll because; expression of surprise or defensiveness; ~ *saya baru pulang jam 12 malam* I only got home at midnight (so how would I know?)

oranye adj orange

Orba n New Order, Suharto's rule ← **Orde Baru**

orde n order; ~ *Lama (Orla)* Old Order

organisasi n organization; *aktif dalam* ~ active in a movement or group

orgel, organ n organ

orisinal, orisinil adj original

orkés n orchestra; ~ *Melayu* Malay orchestra, traditional music group

ormas n social or people's organization ← **organisasi masyarakat**

orok n (newborn) baby

oséng: oséng-oséng n stir-fried vegetables

OSIS abbrev *Organisasi Siswa Intrasekolah* high school students' organization, Student Council

ospék n O-week, (school) orientation → **oriéntasi studi dan pengenalan kampus**

otak n brain

otak: otak-otak n steamed fish cakes, baked in banana leaves

otda *n* regional autonomy ← **otonomi daérah**

otomatis *adj* automatic; *secara* ~ automatically

otomotif *adj* automotive

otonomi *n* autonomy; ~ *daerah (otda)* regional autonomy

otopét *n* scooter

otorita, otoritas *n* authority

otot *n* muscle; *nyeri* ~ cramp; **berotot** *adj* muscular; **ngotot** *v, coll* to be stubborn, refuse to back down

oven *n* oven, kiln; *cat* ~ vehicle paint applied through heat

overdosis, OD overdose

oya, o ya oh yes, by the way

P

P. *abbrev Pulau* Island

pabrik factory

pacar *n* boyfriend, girlfriend; **pacaran** *v, coll* to be going out, to go out, date

paceklik *n* famine; *masa* ~ hard times before the harvest

pacu *n* spur; **pacuan** ~ *kuda* racecourse

pacul *n* hoe

pada *prep* in, at, on (expressing time); to; ~ *hari itu* on that day

pada *coll, pl* pluralizing word; *sudah* ~ *pulang* everybody's going home

pada: memadai *v* enough, sufficient

padahal *conj* whereas, however

padam put out, extinguish; **memadamkan** *v* to put out, extinguish; **pemadam** *pasukan* ~ *kebakaran* fire brigade

padan: padanan *n* synonym; something that matches or fits

padang *n* field, plain; ~ *pasir* desert, sand dune

padat *adj* dense, full, crammed

padi *n* (unhusked) rice

padu fused; **memadukan** *v* to combine, unite; **per- paduan** *n* blend, synthesis; **terpadu** *adj* integrated

pagar *n* fence; hedge; ~ *hidup* hedge

231

pagi *n* morning; ~ *buta* in the early hours of the morning; *makan* ~ breakfast; **pagi-pagi** *adv* (very) early; **kepagian** *adj* too early

paguyuban *n* group, association

paha *n* thigh; ~ *ayam* chicken leg; *lipat* ~ groin

pahala *n* reward, merit

paham, faham *v* to understand, know; **memahami** *v* to understand, comprehend

pahat chisel; **memahat** *v* to sculpt, chisel; **pemahat** *n* sculptor

pahit *adj* bitter

pahlawan *n* hero

pai *n* pie

pailit *adj* bankrupt; **kepailitan** *n* bankruptcy

pajak tax; ~ *Bumi Bangunan (PBB)* land tax, household rates; ~ *pendapatan*, ~ *penghasilan* income tax

pajang: pajangan *n* display

pak: mengepak *v* to pack

Pak, Bapak *pron* Father; term of address to older, respected men

pakai, paké wear; use;

pakaian *n* clothes, dress; ~ *dalam* underwear; **berpakaian** *adj* dressed in; **memakai** *v* to wear; to use; ~ *kacamata* to wear glasses; **pemakai** *n* user; **pemakaian** *n* use, usage; **terpakai** *adj* used, in use

pakar *n* expert, authority

pakat: sepakat *v* to agree; **kesepakatan** *n* agreement; **menyepakati** *v* to agree to

pakét *n* packet, package, promotion; ~ *hemat (pahe)* cheap package

pakis *n* fern

Pakistan *n* Pakistan; *orang* ~ Pakistani

paksa force; *kerja* ~ forced labor; **memaksa** *v* to force; **pemaksaan** *n* force, pressure; **terpaksa** *adj* forced

paku *n* nail; **memaku** *v* to nail

paku *n* fern

pala *buah* ~ nutmeg; *bunga* ~ mace

palak: pemalak *n* extortionist, someone who demands payment

palang *n* barrier, bar, cross; ~ *Merah* Red Cross

palawija *n* secondary crop, planted in dry season

palem *n* palm

Palestina *n* Palestine; *orang* ~ Palestinian

paling *adv* most; at the most; ~ *baik* the best; ~ *jelek* the worst

palsu *adj* false, forged; *identitas* ~ fake ID; *rambut* ~ wig; *sumpah* ~ perjury; *uang* ~ counterfeit money; **memalsukan** *v* to falsify, forge

palu *n* hammer, gavel (in court); ~ *arit* hammer and sickle

palung *n* trough, riverbed

PAM *abbrev Perusahaan Air Minum* company providing reticulated water, water board

pamali *n* taboo

paman *n* uncle, male relative of parents' generation; ~ *Sam* Uncle Sam (America)

pamér show off; **paméran** *n* exhibition; **memamérkan** *v* to display, exhibit

pamit, pamitan, berpamit *v* to take leave

pamor *n* prestige, lustre, glow

pamrih *n* reward; *tanpa* ~ altruistic, without expecting anything in return

PAN *abbrev Partai Amanat Nasional* People's Mandate Party

panah *n* bow; **panahan** *n* archery; **pemanah** *n* archer

panas *adj* hot, warm; ~ *badan* body temperature; *coll* high temperature; ~ *dingin* hot and cold; ~ *hati* angry; ~ *terik* dry heat; hot and dry; **kepanasan** *n* heat; *adj* too hot; **memanaskan** *v* to heat (up)

panca *adj* five; **Pancasila** *n* Indonesian state philosophy of five principles

pancar: pancaran *n* emission; **memancarkan** *v* to broadcast; **pemancar** *n* transmitter

pancaroba *n* change of season; *musim* ~ transition between seasons

Pancasila *n* Indonesian state philosophy of five principles

panci *n* saucepan, pan

pancing: memancing *v* to fish (with hook and line);

terpancing *adj* hooked, caught up; involved

pancung: memancung *v* to cut off; ~ *kepala* to behead or decapitate

pancur: pancuran, pancoran *n* fountain; shower

pandai *adj* clever; ~ *besi* smith; **kepandaian** *n* ability, intelligence

pandan *daun* ~ pandanus leaf, used for green coloring in food

pandang see, gaze; **pandangan** *n* view, sight; **berpandangan** *v* to look at each other; **memandang** *v* to view, consider; **pemandangan** *n* view

pandu guide, scout, pilot; **kepanduan** *n* scouting, Scouts; *n, f* guiding, Guides; **memandu** *v* to guide

panén *n* harvest, windfall

Pangab *n* Commander-in-Chief of the Armed Forces ← **Panglima Angkatan Bersenjata**

pangan *n* food

Pangdam *n* Regional Commander ← **Panglima Daérah Militér**

pangéran *n* prince

panggang *n* roast, bake, toast; *ayam* ~ roast chicken; **memanggang** *v* to roast, bake, toast; **pemanggangan** *n* spit

panggil call; **panggilan** *n* call, summons; *wanita* ~ callgirl; **memanggil** *v* to call

panggul *n* hip

panggung *n* stage; **manggung** *v, coll* to perform

pangkal *n* base; **pangkalan** *n* terminal, base; ~ *udara (lanud)* air base; **mangkal** *v, coll* to use as a base, wait for work

pangkas cut; ~ *rambut* barber; **memangkas** *v* to cut, shear, trim

pangkat *n* rank, class; to the power of; **berpangkat** *v* to have the rank of

pangku lap; **pangkuan** *n* lap; **memangku** *v* to take on (your lap)

panglima *n* commander; ~ *besar* general for life; ~ *tertinggi* commander-in-chief

pangsa *n* segment

pangsit *n* wonton, dumpling

234

panik panic

panitera n clerk, secretary

panitia n committee, board

panjang adj long; ~nya
length; bulat ~ cylindrical;
~ lebar detailed; (empat)
persegi ~ rectangle; ~
tangan light-fingered, a
thief; ~ umur long life;
kepanjangan adj too long;
memperpanjang v to
extend, make longer;
sepanjang conj, adj as long
as; ~ jalan the whole way

panjat climb; ~ pinang
climbing a greased areca-
nut palm, an Independence
Day competition; ~ tebing
abseiling; **memanjat** v to
climb; **memanjatkan** v to
send up; ~ doa to offer
prayers

pantai n beach, coast; ~
batu pebble beach; ~
Gading Ivory Coast

pantang forbidden, prohibited; ~ menyerah never
give up, never say die; ~
mundur never look back;
berpantang v to not be
allowed, abstain from;
~ makan to be on a diet

pantas adj proper, decent,
right; **sepantasnya** adv
proper, rightly

pantat n bottom, backside

pantau: pantauan n
observation; **memantau** v
to observe, watch; **pemantau** n observer, monitor;
pemantauan n monitor-
ing

panti n building; ~ asuhan
orphanage; ~ jompo old
people's home

pantul: pantulan n reflection; **memantulkan** v to
reflect something

pantun n traditional poem
(of four lines)

panu n white spots caused
by skin fungus

panut: panutan n leader,
good example ← **anut**

papa adj destitute, poor;
kaum ~ the destitute, the
poor

papan n plank, board,
bench; ~ catur chessboard;
~ tulis blackboard, whiteboard; ~ tuts keyboard

papar: memaparkan v to
explain

papaya → **pepaya**

Papi, Pi *pron* Papa, Daddy (in Westernized circles)

paprika *n* red or green pepper, paprika

Papua Nugini *n* Papua New Guinea, PNG; *orang* ~ Papuan

para pluralizes the following word; ~ *pemirsa* viewers; ~ *pendengar* listeners

parabola *n* satellite dish; parabola; *TV* ~ satellite TV

paraf *n* initials

paragraf *n* paragraph → **alinéa**

parah *adj* grave, serious, bad; *sakit* ~ gravely ill; **memperparah** *v* to make worse, aggravate

parang *n* chopper, machete

paras *n* face; **berparas** *v* to have a face or appearance

parasut *n* parachute → **payung**

parau *adj* hoarse

paré, paria, peria *n* kind of bitter gourd or squash

parfum *n* perfume

pari *bintang* ~ Southern Cross; *ikan* ~ ray

paria → **paré**

paripurna *sidang* ~ plenary session

parit *n* (roadside) ditch

pariwara *n* advertisement

pariwisata *n* tourism; *bis* ~ tourist bus; **kepariwisataan** *n* tourist industry

parkir park (a vehicle); *tempat* ~ car park, parking lot; *tukang* ~ parking attendant

parkit *burung* ~ parakeet

parlemén *n* parliament

parodi *n* parody

parpol *n* (political) party ← **partai politik**

partai *n* party; ~ *Amanat Nasional (PAN)* National Mandate Party; ~ *Demokrasi Indonesia Perjuangan (PDIP)* Indonesian Democratic Party of Struggle; ~ *Demokrat* Democratic Party, Democrats; ~ *Kebangkitan Bangsa (PKB)* Party of National Awakening; ~ *Persatuan Pembangunan (PPP, P3)* United Development Party; ~ *politik (parpol)* political party

paru, paru-paru *n* lung

paruh, paro *n* half, part;
kerja ~ waktu work part-
time; **separuh** *n* half

paruh *n* bill, beak

parut grater; **memarut** *v* to
grate

pas exact, just (as); fit

pasak *n* peg, wooden nail

pasal *n, leg* paragraph,
section; *conj* regarding,
concerning

pasang *n* pair, couple;
pasangan *n* pair; **berpasangan** *adv* in pairs;
sepasang *n* a pair of

pasang, memasang *v* to
put up, attach, fix; *~ iklan*
to advertise; *~ lampu* to
switch on a light, light a
lamp; **pemasangan** *n*
installation

pasang *~ surut* rise and
fall, ebb and flow

pasar *n* market, bazaar;
~ dunia global market; *~
gelap* black market; *~ raya,
pasaraya* supermarket;
memasarkan *v* to market;
pemasaran *n* marketing

pasca [pasca, paska] *pref*
after, post-; *~ krismon* after
the financial crisis; **pasca-**

sarjana *adj* post-graduate

pasfoto *n* passport (-sized)
photo

pasién *n* patient

pasif *adj* passive

pasir *n* sand; *gula ~* (white)
sugar

Paskah *n* Easter; *Hari ~*
Easter Sunday

pasok: pasokan *n* supply;
memasok *v* to supply;
pemasok *n* supplier

paspor *n* passport

pasrah *adj* accepting,
fatalistic

pasta *n* paste; pasta,
spaghetti; *~ gigi* toothpaste

pastél *n* samosa, small
pasty containing vegetables,
egg and vermicelli noodles

pasti sure, certain, definite;
kepastian *n* certainty;
memastikan to confirm,
make sure, ascertain

pastor *n, Cath* priest

pasuk: pasukan *n* troops;
~ khusus elite troops,
special troops

patah break, fracture (of
bones); *~ hati* broken-heart-
ed; *~ semangat* lose heart;
~ tulang break or fracture a

bone; **mematahkan** *v* to break

patok: patokan *n* standard, peg; **mematok** *v* to fix, set

patri solder; kaca ~ stained glass

patroli *n* patrol

patuh *adj* loyal, obedient; **mematuhi** *v* to obey

patung *n* statue, figurine; **pematung** *n* sculptor

patung: patungan *v* to pay together; to work together; perusahaan ~ joint venture

patut *adj* decent, proper, deserving; **sepatutnya** *adv* rightly, properly

paus ikan ~ whale

Paus ~ Benedictus XVI Pope Benedict XVI

pause, pauze *n* break, half-time (in sport); adem ~ break

paut: terpaut *adj* fastened, bound; separated

pavilyun, paviliun *n* smaller house attached to a larger one

pawai *n* procession, parade

payah *adj* difficult, serious; tired

payudara *n, f* breast

payung *n* umbrella; parachute

PBB *abbrev* Persatuan Bangsa-Bangsa United Nations, UN

PBB *abbrev* Pajak Bumi dan Bangunan Land and Building Tax

PD II *abbrev* Perang Dunia Kedua Second World War

PDAM *abbrev* Perusahaan Daerah Air Minum regional water board

PDIP *abbrev* Partai Demokrasi Indonesia Perjuangan Indonesian Democratic Party of Struggle

Pdt. *abbrev* Pendeta (Protestant) minister, clergyman

Pébruari → Fébruari

pecah break, smash; curdled (of milk); (barang) ~ belah earthenware; **pecahan** *n* piece, fragment; fraction; **memecah** ~ belah to break into fragments, cause divisions; **memecahkan** *v* to break; to solve; ~ soal to solve a problem

pecandu *n* addict ← candu

pecat fired, sacked, dismissed; **memecat** *v* to fire, dismiss; **pemecatan** *n* sacking, dismissal

pecatur *n* chess player ← **catur**

pecel ~ *lele* catfish with rice and side-dishes; *nasi* ~ rice and salad with peanut sauce

péci *n* black, flat-topped cap worn by men, also with national dress

Pecinan *n* Chinatown ← **Cina**

pecinta *n* lover ← **cinta**

pecundang lose, be beaten

pedagang *n* merchant ← **dagang**

pedanda *n* Balinese priest

pedang *n* sword

pedas *adj* spicy, hot; **kepedasan** *adj* too hot or spicy

pédé, PD *sl* self-confidence; *kurang* ~ lacking self-confidence ← **percaya diri**

pedes → **pedas**

pedésaan *n* country(side), rural areas ← **désa**

pedih, perih smart, sting

pédikur *n* pedicure

pedoman *n* compass; guide; manual

peduli *v* **perduli** *coll* to care, bother; *tidak* ~ not care; **kepedulian** *n* concern; **memedulikan** *v* to care or be bothered about

Peg. *abbrev* Pegunungan (mountain) range

pegadaian *n* pawnshop ← **gadai**

pegal *adj* sore, cramped, stiff; ~ *linu* aches and pains

pégang, pegang hold, grip, grasp; **berpegang** *v* to hold onto; **memegang** *v* to hold, grasp

pegas *n* spring; *kasur* ~ spring bed

pegawai *n* official, employee; ~ *negeri* public or civil servant; **kepegawaian** *adj* staff, personnel

pegunungan *n* mountain range ← **gunung**

péhaka, PHK to lose your job, be unemployed; **dipéhakakan** *v* to lose your job, be fired ← **putus hubungan kerja**

pejabat *n* (government) official ← **jabat**

pejagalan *n* abattoir ← **jagal**

pejam: memejamkan ~
mata to close your eyes

pekan *n* week; market;
~ *Olahraga Nasional
(PON)* National Sports
Week, national champion-
ships; *akhir* ~ weekend

pekat *adj* thick, strong,
concentrated; *hitam* ~ pitch
black

pekerja *n* worker, laborer;
pekerjaan *n* work, profession ← **kerja**

pekerti *n* character, nature

pekik scream, yell

pél *kain* ~ rag for mopping
the floor; *obat* ~ floor
disinfectant; **mengepél** *v*
to mop (up); **dipél** *v* to be
mopped, cleaned

pelabuhan port, harbor ←
labuh

pelacak *anjing* ~ sniffer
dog ← **lacak**

pelacur *n* prostitute; **pelacuran** *n* prostitution ← **lacur**

pelajar *n* pupil, student;
pelajaran *n* lesson; *mata* ~
school subject ← **ajar**

pelaju *n* commuter ← **laju**

pelaksanaan *n* realization,
execution ← **laksana**

pelaminan *n* bridal sofa
where the couple greet
guests ← **lamin**

pelampung *n* floater,
flotation device; *baju* ~
lifejacket ← **lampung**

pelan, perlahan: pelan-
pelan, perlahan-lahan
adv slowly, softly

pelana *n* saddle

pelancong *n* tourist ←
lancong

pelanggan *n* subscriber,
customer ← **langgan**

pelanggaran *n* violation ←
langgar

pelangi *n* rainbow

pelan-pelan *adv* slowly,
softly ← **pelan**

pelantikan *n* inauguration
← **lantik**

pelanting: terpelanting *v*
to fall heavily

pelari *n* runner ← **lari**

pelat *n* plate; ~ *merah*
government number plate;
~ *polisi* (vehicle) number
plate, license plate

pelatih *n* coach, trainer;
pelatihan *n* training ← **latih**

pelaut *n* sailor, seaman ←
laut

pelawak n comedian, comic, clown ← **lawak**

pelayan n waiter m, waitress f, attendant; **pelayanan** n service ← **layan**

pelayaran n voyage ← **layar**

pelbagai, berbagai adj all kinds or sorts of, various ← **bagai**

pelécéhan n contempt; ~ seksual sexual harassment ← **lécéh**

peledak bahan ~ explosive ← **ledak**

pélek n rim of wheel ← **vélg**

pelekat bahan ~ adhesive ← **lekat**

pelembab, pelembap n moisturizer ← **lembab**

pelembut n softener ← **lembut**

pelengkap n accessory; **perlengkapan** n outfit, equipment ← **lengkap**

pelepasan n departure, farewell; acara ~ goodbye (party) ← **lepas**

pelését: terpelését adj slipped, skidded; tripped; **memelésétkan** v to up-end; to send off-course;

pelésétan, plésétan n parody ← **lését**

pelestarian n protection, preservation ← **lestari**

pelihara take care of; **peliharaan** hewan ~ pet; **memelihara** v to take care of, look after; to cultivate; **pemeliharaan** n care, maintenance, cultivation; **terpelihara** adj well cared-for, well-maintained → **piara**

pélikan burung ~ pelican

pelindung n protective device ← **lindung**

pelintir: memelintir(kan) v to twist; **terpelintir** adj twisted

pelipis n temple (on head)

pelir buah ~ testicles

pelita n, lit (oil) lamp; light

pelitur polish

Pélni n National Shipping Line, state passenger shipping service ← **Pelayaran Nasional Indonésia**

pelopor n pioneer, leader, forerunner; **memelopori** v to pioneer, lead

pelor → **peluru**

pelosok n remote place

pelotot: melotot, memelotot *v* to stare, have bulging eyes; **memelototkan** ~ *mata* to stare ← **lotot**

peluang *n* opportunity; ~ *kerja* job opportunity; **berpeluang** *v* to have an opportunity, a chance ← **luang**

peluh *n* sweat, perspiration

peluit, pluit *n* whistle

peluk hug; ~ *cium* hugs and kisses; **pelukan** *n* embrace; **memeluk** *v* to hug or embrace; ~ *agama* to follow a religion; **pemeluk** *n* follower, adherent

pelukis *n* painter, artist ← **lukis**

pelumas *n* lubricant ← **lumas**

peluntur *n* laxative ← **luntur**

pelupa *n* forgetful person ← **lupa**

peluru *n* bullet; ~ *kosong* blank (cartridge)

pelurusan *n* straightening ← **lurus**

pemadam *pasukan* ~ *kebakaran* fire brigade ← **padam**

pemahat *n* sculptor ← **pahat**

pemain *n* player, actor; ~ *film* actor; ~ *bola basket* basketballer ← **main**

pemakai *n* user; **pemakaian** *n* use, usage ← **pakai**

pemakaman *n* funeral, burial ← **makam**

pemaksaan *n* force, pressure ← **paksa**

pemalak *n* extortionist, someone who demands payment ← **palak**

pemalu shy (person) ← **malu**

pemancar *n* transmitter ← **pancar**

pemandangan *n* view ← **pandang**

pemanggangan *n* spit ← **panggang**

pemanis ~ *buatan* artificial sweetener ← **manis**

pemantau *n* observer, monitor; **pemantauan** *n* monitoring ← **pantau**

pemarah *adj* bad-tempered ← **marah**

pemasangan *n* installation ← **pasang**

pemasaran *n* marketing ← **pasar**

pemasok *n* supplier ← **pasok**

pematang *n* small dike (in a rice field)

pematung *n* sculptor ← **patung**

pembabatan *n* felling, chopping; ~ *hutan* (unregulated) deforestation ← **babat**

pembaca *n* reader ← **baca**

pembagian *n* distribution, division ← **bagi**

pembalut *n* sanitary pad ← **balut**

pembangkit ~ *listrik* power station ← **bangkit**

pembangunan *n* development ← **bangun**

pembantaian *n* slaughter, mass killings ← **bantai**

pembantu *n* servant, maid; assistant; *kantor* ~ (larger) branch office ← **bantu**

pembaruan *n* renewal ← **baru**

pembatas *n* divider; ~ *buku* bookmark; **pembatasan** *n* restriction ← **batas**

pembauran *n* integration, mixing of different ethnic groups ← **baur**

pembawa *n* bearer, carrier; ~ *acara* host, MC ← **bawa**

pembayaran *n* payment ← **bayar**

pembébasan *n* liberation, release, exemption ← **bébas**

pembéla *n* defender; **pembélaan** *n* defense ← **béla**

pembelian *n* purchase ← **beli**

pembenihan ~ *buatan* artificial insemination ← **benih**

pembentukan *n* formation, act of forming ← **bentuk**

pemberani *n* brave or courageous person, hero ← **berani**

pemberantasan *n* destruction, fight against ← **berantas**

pemberdayaan *n* empowerment; *Kementerian ~ Perempuan* Ministry for the Empowerment of Women ← **daya**

pemberian *n* present, gift, something given to someone ← **beri**

pemberitahuan *n* announcement, notice ← **beritahu**

pemberkatan *n* consecra-
tion, blessing ← **berkat**

pemberontakan *n* rebellion,
revolt, mutiny ← **berontak**

pembersih *n* cleaning agent
← **bersih**

pembicaraan *n* discussion
← **bicara**

pembocoran *n* leakage,
divulging (of secrets) ←
bocor

pembohong *n* liar ←
bohong

pemborong *n* developer,
contractor ← **borong**

pemborosan *n* wastage ←
boros

pembrédelan *n* muzzling,
being closed down ← **brédel**

pembuat *n* producer; maker;
pembuatan *n* production,
manufacture ← **buat**

pembuka *adj* opening; *kata*
~ preface ← **buka**

pembukuan *n* book-keeping
← **buku**

pembunuh *n* murderer,
killer; ~ *bayaran* hitman,
hired killer; **pembunuhan**
n murder, killing ← **bunuh**

pemburu *n* hunter; **pemburuan** *n* hunt, chase ← **buru**

Pémda *n* Regional
Government → **Pemerintah
Daérah**

pemecatan *n* sacking,
dismissal ← **pecat**

pemekaran *n* expansion,
development ← **mekar**

pemeliharaan *n* care,
maintenance, cultivation ←
pelihara

pemeluk *n* follower, adherent
← **peluk**

pemenang *n* winner, victor
← **menang**

pementasan *n* staging,
production ← **pentas**

pemérah ~ *pipi* rouge ←
mérah

pemeran *n* actor, actress ←
peran

pemerasan *n* blackmail,
extortion ← **peras**

pemeriksa *n* examiner;
pemeriksaan *n* examination,
investigation ← **periksa**

pemerintah *n* government;
pemerintahan *n* administration, government ←
perintah

pemerkosaan *n* act of
raping, rape ← **perkosa,
kosa**

pemersatu *n* unifying
agent, unifier ← **satu**

pemesanan *n* order,
request ← **pesan**

pemetik *n* picker; ~ *daun
teh* tea-picker ← **petik**

pemicu *n* trigger ← **picu**

pemikir *n* thinker;
pemikiran *n* thinking,
consideration ← **pikir**

pemilihan *n* election; ~
umum (pemilu) general
election ← **pilih**

pemilik *n* owner ← **milik**

pemilu *n* general election
← **pemilihan umum**

pemimpin *n* leader ←
pimpin

pemindahan *n* transfer,
shifting, removal ←
pindah

peminjam *n* borrower;
kartu ~ borrowing card

pemirsa *n* television
audience, viewer ← **pirsa**

pemisahan *n* separation ←
pisah

permohonan *n* request,
application ← **mohon**

pémpék, mpék mpék *n*
fried fish-cakes, a specialty
of Palembang

pémprop, pemprov *n*
provincial government ←
pemerintah propinsi

pemuda *n* youth; young
man ← **muda**

pemugaran *n* restoration,
renovation ← **pugar**

pemula *n* beginner ←
mula

pemulangan *n* return,
repatriation ← **pulang**

pemulihan *n* recovery,
restoration ← **pulih**

pemungutan *n* collection;
~ *suara* vote ← **pungut**

pemusik *n* musician ←
musik

pemusnahan *n* act of
destruction ← **musnah**

pemutaran *n* screening;
~ *perdana* opening
screening, opening night
(of a film) ← **putar**

pemutih *n* bleach ← **putih**

pemutusan *n* termination,
breaking-off; ~ *hubungan
kerja (PHK)* to lose your
job ← **putus**

péna *n* (fountain) pen, quill

penaksiran *n* evaluation
← **taksir**

penakut *n* coward ← **takut**

penambang *n* miner ← **tambang**

penampakan *n* appearance ← **tampak**

penampilan *n* performance ← **tampil**

penampung *n* container; **penampungan** *n* reception, place that receives something ← **tampung**

penanaman ~ *modal* investment ← **tanam**

penanganan *n* handling ← **tangan**

penanggalan *n* calendar, dating ← **tanggal**

penanggulangan *n* tackling, fight against ← **tanggulang**

penangkal ~ *petir* lightning rod ← **tangkal**

penangkapan *n* capture, arrest ← **tangkap**

penari *n* dancer ← **tari**

penasaran *adj* curious, inquisitive, impatient

penasihat *n* adviser ← **nasihat**

penat *adj* tired

penawar *n* antidote ← **tawar**

penawaran *n* offer, bid ← **tawar**

pencahar *n* laxative ← **cahar**

pencahayaan *n* lighting ← **cahaya**

pencak ~ *silat* traditional self-defense

pencakar ~ *langit* skyscraper ← **cakar**

pencakupan *n* coverage ← **cakup**

pencalonan *n* nomination, candidacy ← **calon**

pencar: terpencar *adj* dispersed

pencarian *n* search, hunt ← **cari**

pencegahan *n* prevention ← **cegah**

pencelupan *n* dyeing process ← **celup**

pencemaran *n* pollution; ~ *udara* air pollution ← **cemar**

pencernaan *n* digestion ← **cerna**

pencét press; **memencét** *v* to press (a button, key); **terpencét** *adj* accidentally pressed

pencétak *n* printer ← **cétak**

pencil: terpencil *adj* isolated, remote

pencinta *n* lover ← **cinta**

pencipta *n* creator; ~ *lagu* song-writer ← **cipta**

penculikan *n* kidnapping ← **culik**

pencuri *n* thief, burglar ← **curi**

pendaftaran *n* enrollment, registration ← **daftar**

pendahuluan *n* introduction ← **dahulu**

pendam: terpendam *adj* hidden, concealed

pendamping *n* companion; ~ *hidup* spouse; **pendampingan** *n* assistance ← **damping**

pendapa → **pendopo**

pendapat *n* opinion, point of view; **pendapatan** *n* income, revenue ← **dapat**

pendarahan *n* bleeding ← **darah**

pendaratan *n* landing (of vessel) ← **darat**

pendataan *n* documentation ← **data**

pendatang *n* immigrant, migrant; newcomer ← **datang**

péndék *adj* short; ~ *kata* in short; ~*nya* in a word; **kependékan** *n* abbreviation;

meméndékkan *v* to shorten; **memperpéndék** *v* to shorten, make even shorter

pendékar *n* (in martial arts) master, champion, leader ← **dékar**

pendekatan *n* approach; getting to know ← **dekat**

pendengar *n* listener; **pendengaran** *n* hearing; *indera* ~ sense of hearing ← **dengar**

penderitaan *n* suffering ← **derita**

pendéta *n, Chr* minister, clergyman, vicar; *Hind* priest

pendiam *n* quiet, shy person ← **diam**

pendidikan *n* education; *ilmu* ~ pedagogy ← **didik**

pendingin ~ *ruangan* air conditioning, cooling ← **dingin**

pendopo, pendapa *n* traditional large roofed verandah in front of an official residence

penduduk *n* inhabitant, citizen, resident; **pendudukan** *n* occupation ← **duduk**

pendukung *n* supporter ←
dukung

pendulang *n* prospector ←
dulang

pendusta *n* liar ← **dusta**

penebangan *n* logging;
~ *liar* illegal logging ←
tebang

peneliti *n* researcher;
penelitian *n* research ←
teliti

penémbak *n* marksman,
gunman ← **témbak**

penemu *n* inventor, dis-
coverer; **penemuan** *n*
invention, discovery ←
temu

penerangan *n* information;
lighting, enlightenment ←
terang

penerapan *n* application
← **terap**

penerbang *n* pilot, aviator;
penerbangan *n* flight;
aviation ← **terbang**

penerbit *n* publisher ← **terbit**

penerimaan *n* receipt ←
terima

penerjemah *n* translator;
~ *tersumpah* sworn translator; **penerjemahan** *n*
translation ← **terjemah**

penerjun ~ *(payung)*
parachutist, sky diver ←
terjun

penerus *n* successor;
someone who continues
another's work ← **terus**

penetapan *n* appointment
← **tetap**

pengabdian *n* service,
servitude, devotion ← **abdi**

pengacara *n* lawyer,
solicitor ← **acara**

pengadilan *n* court of justice or law; trial; ~ *negeri*
district court ← **adil**

pengaduan *n* complaint;
surat ~ letter of complaint
← **adu**

pengagum *n* admirer ←
kagum

pengairan *n* irrigation ← **air**

pengajar *n* teacher; **pengajaran** *n* teaching, tuition
← **ajar**

pengakuan *n* confession,
acknowledgment; ~ *dosa*
confession (Catholic) ←
aku

pengalaman *n* experience
← **alam**

pengaman *n* safety device
← **aman**

248

pengamat *n* observer; **pengamatan** *n* observation, monitoring ← **amat**

pengambilan *n* act of taking, removal; ~ *gambar* photo shoot; ~ *sumpah* taking an oath ← **ambil**

pengamón *n* street singer, busker ← **amén**

pengampunan *n* pardon, reprieve, amnesty ← **ampun**

penganan *n* snack, food

pengangguran *n* unemployment, unemployed person ← **anggur**

penganiayaan *n* oppression, mistreatment ← **aniaya**

pengantin, pengantén *n, f* bride; *n, m* (bride)groom; marrying couple; ~ *baru* newlyweds; *busana* ~ wedding dress or costume; *mobil* ~ bridal car; ~ *pria* (bride)groom; ~ *wanita* (bride) bride

penganut *n* follower, believer ← **anut**

pengap *adj* stuffy; stale, musty

pengarahan *n* direction, guidance, briefing ← **arah**

pengarang *n* author, writer, composer ← **karang**

pengaruh *n* influence; ~ *obat* effect of medicine or drugs; **berpengaruh** *adj* influential; **memengaruhi** *v* to influence, affect; **terpengaruh** *adj* affected or influenced

pengasingan *n* exile ← **asing**

pengasuh *n* carer; ~ *anak* nursemaid, babysitter ← **asuh**

pengawal *n* (body)guard, sentry ← **kawal**

pengawasan *n* supervision, control ← **awas**

pengeboman *n* bombing ← **bom**

pengecualian *n* exception ← **kecuali**

pengecut *n* coward ← **kecut**

pengédar *n* dealer; **pengédaran** *n* circulation; ~ *udara* air circulation ← **édar**

pengékspor *n* exporter ← **pengékspor**

pengelolaan *n* management ← **kelola**

249

pengembunan *n* condensation ← **embun**

pengemis *n* beggar ← **emis, kemis**

pengemudi *n* driver ← **kemudi**

péngén, pingin, kepéngén, kepingin *v, coll* to really want to

pengendalian *n* control; ~ *mutu* quality control ← **kendali**

pengendapan *n* siltation ← **endap**

pengeras ~ *suara* loudspeaker ← **keras**

pengering ~ *rambut* hair dryer ← **kering**

pengertian *n* understanding ← **erti, arti**

pengetahuan *n* knowledge ← **tahu**

penggal: memenggal *v* to cut off, amputate

penggalian *n* digging ← **gali**

pengganti *n* replacement, substitute, successor ← **ganti**

penggaris *n* ruler ← **garis**

penggemar *n* fan, enthusiast ← **gemar**

penggoréngan *n* wok, frying pan; process of frying ← **goréng**

pengguna *n* user; **penggunaan** *n* usage, use ← **guna**

penggusuran *n* eviction, forcible removal ← **gusur**

penghantar ~ *listrik* electrical conductor ← **hantar**

penghargaan *n* appreciation, award ← **harga**

penghasilan *n* production; income ← **hasil**

penghibur *wanita* ~ escort, prostitute ← **hibur**

penghinaan *n* insult, libel (written), slander (spoken) ← **hina**

penghubung *n* switch, connector; *kata* ~ conjunction, connector ← **hubung**

penghulu *n, Isl* local chief who performs marriage ceremonies ← **hulu**

penghuni *n* occupant, resident ← **huni**

pengidap *n* sufferer ← **idap**

pengikut *n* participant; follower ← **ikut**

pengimpor *n* importer ← **impor**

penginapan *n* accommodation, hotel ← **inap**

penginjil *n* preacher, evangelist ← **injil**

pengirim *n* sender; **pengiriman** *n* dispatch, forwarding ← **kirim**

pengiring *n* escort, companion ← **iring**

pengkhianat *n* traitor ← **khianat**

pengkhotbah *v* preacher ← **khotbah**

pengobatan *n* treatment ← **obat**

pengolahan *v* processing ← **olah**

pengorbanan *n* (act of) sacrifice ← **korban**

penguapan *n* evaporation ← **uap**

penguji *n* examiner ← **uji**

pengukuhan *n* strengthening, reinforcement; ratification ← **kukuh**

pengukuran *n* measuring, measurement ← **ukur**

pengumuman *n* notice, announcement ← **umur**

pengunduran *n* postponement, delay ← **undur**

pengungsi *n* refugee, evacuee; **pengungsian** *n* evacuation ← **ungsi**

pengurus *n* manager, organizer; ~ *besar* board of directors, executive ← **urus**

pengusaha *n, m* businessman, *f* businesswoman ← **usaha**

penindasan *n* oppression ← **tindas**

pening *adj* dizzy; ~ *kepala* dizzy, light-headed

peningkatan *n* rise, increase ← **tingkat**

peninjau *n* observer; **peninjauan** *n* observation, review ← **tinjau**

penipu *n* con man, trickster; **penipuan** *n* deception ← **tipu**

peniti *n* safety-pin; brooch

penitipan *n* care; *tempat* ~ *anak* child-minding center, creche ← **titip**

penjahat *n* criminal

penjaja *n* hawker, pedlar ← **jaja**

penjajah *n* colonizer, ruler, colonial power; **penjajahan** *n* colonization ← **jajah**

penjara n prison, jail; **memenjara(kan)** v to put in prison, imprison

penjarah n looter; **penjarahan** n looting ← **jarah**

penjelasan n explanation ← **jelas**

penjeprét n stapler ← **jeprét**

penjilidan n binding (process) ← **jilid**

penjual n seller, dealer; **penjualan** n sale, sales ← **jual**

penjudi n gambler ← **judi**

penjuru n corner

penolakan n refusal, rejection ← **tolak**

penonton n spectator, audience; *para* ~ audience; ladies and gentlemen ← **tonton**

penopang n prop, support ← **topang**

pénsil n pencil

pénsiun pension, retired; ~ *dini* early pension; **pénsiunan** n pensioner **meménsiunkan** v to pension off

pentahbisan n consecration, ordination ← **tahbis**

pentas stage; **mementaskan** v to stage, present; **pementasan** n staging, production

péntil n valve

penting adj important; ~*nya* the importance; *urusan* ~ urgent business; **kepentingan** n importance, interest; **berkepentingan** v to have an interest in; *yang* ~ concerned party; **mementingkan** v to make important, emphasize

pentol: pentolan n boss, big shot

penugasan n assignment ← **tugas**

penuh adj full; ~ *sesak* crowded, chock-full; *sehari* ~ a full or whole day; **memenuhi** v to fulfill, meet requirements; **sepenuhnya** adv fully, completely; **terpenuhi** adj satisfied, fulfilled

penulis n author, writer; ~ *novel* novelist ← **tulis**

penumpang n passenger ← **tumpang**

penuntut n claimant, plaintiff, prosecuting party ← **tuntut**

penurut *adj* obedient, meek ← **turut**

penutup *n* stopper, lid; end ← **tutup**

penutur *n* speaker; ~ *asli* native speaker ← **tutur**

penyadap *n* tapper; **penyadapan** *n* tapping ← **sadap**

penyair *n* poet ← **syair**

penyajian *n* presentation ← **saji**

penyakit *n* disease, illness, complaint; ~ *anjing gila* rabies; ~ *jiwa* mental problem; ~ *gula* diabetes; ~ *menular seksual (PMS)* sexually transmitted disease (STD), venereal disease ← **sakit**

penyaluran *n* channelling ← **salur**

penyambutan *n* welcoming, welcome ceremony ← **sambut**

penyanderaan *n* taking of hostages ← **sandera**

penyanyi *n* singer, vocalist; ~ *latar* backing vocalist ← **nyanyi**

penyaringan *n* filtration, screening ← **saring**

penyebab *n* cause ← **sebab**

penyebar *n* carrier, infectious person ← **sebar**

penyeberangan *n* crossing ← **seberang**

penyegar *minuman* ~ tonic, energy drink ← **segar**

penyelam *n* diver ← **selam**

penyelamatan *n* rescue (operation) ← **selamat**

penyelenggara *n* organizer; *panitia* ~ organizing committee ← **selenggara**

penyelesaian *n* solution, settlement ← **selesai**

penyelidik *n* investigator, detective; **penyelidikan** *n* investigation ← **selidik**

penyelundup *n* smuggler ← **selundup**

penyembelih *n* butcher, slaughterer; **penyembelihan** *n* slaughter ← **sembelih**

penyembuhan *n* cure, healing ← **sembuh**

penyerahan *n* handing over, handover ← **serah**

penyerang *n* attacker; **penyerangan** *n* attack, aggression ← **serang**

penyerapan *n* absorption ← **serap**

penyerbuan n attack, charge, invasion ← **serbu**

penyetélan n tuning ← **setél**

penyiar n announcer ← **siar**

penylidikan n investigation ← **selidik, sidik**

penyihir n wizard, witch, sorcerer ← **sihir**

penyiksaan n torture, torment ← **siksa**

penyimpangan n aberration, deviation ← **simpang**

penyisiran n combing, checking ← **sisir**

penyitaan n confiscation, seizure ← **sita**

pényok, péyot, péot adj dented

penyu n turtle; *rumah ~* (tortoise) shell

penyulap n magician, conjurer ← **sulap**

penyulingan n distillation ← **suling**

penyuluh n scout; education worker ← **suluh**

penyumbatan n blockage ← **sumbat**

penyunting n editor; **penyuntingan** n editing ← **sunting**

penyusun n compiler, author ← **susun**

pepatah n proverb, saying

pepaya, papaya n pawpaw, papaya

peperangan n battle ← **perang**

pépés method of cooking by steaming or roasting in banana leaves; *~ tahu* steamed tofu; *~ ikan* steamed fish; **pépésan** n food cooked in this way; *~ kosong* lies

pepet n shwa, unemphasized e in Indonesian

pépét: mépét sl tight; **kepépét** adj, sl in a fix, trapped; no time, rushed

Per. abbrev Perusahaan company

pér n spring

perabot n tools; *~ dapur* kitchen utensils; *~ rumah* furniture; **perabotan** n furnishings

peradaban n culture, civilization ← **adab**

peraga n visual aid; **memeragakan** v to display, show; **peragawati** n, f model

perahu *n* (sail)boat; ~ *layar* sailing boat; *naik* ~ go on board, travel by boat

perairan *n* territorial waters; waterworks ← **air**

perajin *n* craftsman, artisan ← **rajin**

pérak *n* silver; silver coin; *medali* ~ silver medal; *perajin* ~ silversmith; *seratus* ~ one hundred rupiah

perakitan *n* assembly ← **rakit**

peralatan *n* equipment ← **alat**

peralihan *n* transition, change ← **alih**

perampok *n* robber; **perampokan** *n* robbery ← **rampok**

peran *n* part, role; **berperan** *v* to play the role or part; **memerankan** *v* to portray, play the role of; **pemeran** *n* actor, actress

peranakan *n* uterus; *adj* of mixed Chinese and Indonesian blood, Straits Chinese ← **anak**

perancang *n* designer, planner; ~ *busana* fashion designer ← **rancang**

Perancis, Prancis *n* France; *bahasa* ~, *orang* ~ French

perang *n* war; ~ *Dunia Kedua* World War II; ~ *gerilya* guerrilla war; **perang-perangan** *n* war games; paintball; **berperang** *v* to wage war, go to war; **memerangi** *v* to fight against; **peperangan** *n* battle

pérang → **pirang**

perangkap *n* trap; **memerangkap** *v* to trap, catch; **terperangkap** *adj* trapped, caught

perangkat *n* equipment, tool ← **angkat**

perangko, prangko *n* (postage) stamp; *mengumpulkan* ~ to collect stamps

perang-perangan *n* war games; paintball ← **perang**

perangsang *adj, n* stimulant ← **rangsang**

perantara *n* broker, intermediary, go-between ← **antara**

perantauan *n* abroad, in another place ← **rantau**

255

peranti, piranti *n* apparatus, equipment; ~ *lunak* software

perapatan → **prapatan**

perapian *n* fireplace, oven ← **api**

peras, memeras *v* to squeeze, press; to blackmail, extort; **pemerasan** *n* blackmail, extortion

perasaan *n* feeling ← **rasa**

peraturan *n* rule, regulation ← **atur**

perawan *n* virgin; **keperawanan** *n* virginity

perawat *n* nurse, sister; **perawatan** treatment; maintenance, upkeep ← **rawat**

perayaan *n* celebration ← **raya**

perbaikan *n* repair, improvement ← **baik**

perban *n* bandage, dressing; **diperban** *v* to be bandaged

perbandingan *n* comparison, ratio ← **banding**

perbankan *adj* banking

perbatasan *n* border, frontier ← **batas**

perbédaan *n* difference ← **béda**

perbelanjaan *pusat* ~ shopping center, mall ← **belanja**

perbendaharaan *n* treasury ← **bendahara**

perbincangan *n* discussion ← **bincang**

perboden, perboten → **verboten**

perbuatan *n* act, deed ← **buat**

perbudakan *n* slavery ← **budak**

percakapan *n* conversation ← **cakap**

percaya trust, believe; ~ *akan* believe in; ~ *diri (PD)* self-confidence; **kepercayaan** *n* belief, faith; **mempercayai** *v* to trust someone; **mempercayakan** *v* to entrust with; **terpercaya** *adj* trusted, reliable

percékcokan *n* quarrel, dispute ← **cékcok**

perceraian *n* divorce ← **cerai**

percobaan *n* experiment, test ← **coba**

percuma in vain

perdagangan *n* commerce, trade ← **dagang**

perdamaian *n* peace, reconciliation ← **damai**

perdana *adj* first, starter; ~ Menteri Prime Minister; *paket* ~ starter kit

perdata *hukum* ~ civil law

perdebatan *n* debate, discussion ← **debat**

perduli → **peduli**

peredam *n* device to muffle or reduce noise ← **redam**

perekat *n* glue, adhesive → **rekat**

peréli *n* rally driver ← **réli**

peremajaan *n* renewal, revitalization ← **remaja**

perempat *n* quarter; *tiga* ~ three-quarters; **perempatan** *n* crossroads, intersection ← **empat**

perempuan *n* woman, female; ~ *jalanan* streetwalker; *hak* ~ women's rights

perenang *n* swimmer ← **renang**

perencanaan *n* planning ← **rencana**

peresmian *n* formal ceremony, inauguration ← **resmi**

perétél → **prétél**

pergaulan *n* mixing, social intercourse; association; ~ *bebas* promiscuity, permissiveness ← **gaul**

pergelangan ~ *kaki* ankle; ~ *tangan* wrist ← **gelang**

pergésékan *n* friction ← **gésék**

pergéséran *n* movement, shift ← **gésér**

pergi go, leave; ~ *jauh* travel far; *sedang* ~, *lagi* ~ out, not here; **bepergian** *v* to travel, be away; **kepergian** *n* departure

pergok: tepergok *adj* caught in the act, caught red-handed

pergolakan *n* disturbance, upheaval ← **golak**

perguruan ~ *tinggi* university ← **guru**

perhatian *n* attention ← **hati**

perhélatan *n* celebration, feast ← **hélat**

perhiasan *n* jewelery ← **hias**

perhimpunan *n* union, association, club ← **himpun**

perhitungan *n* calculation ← **hitung**

perhotélan *n* hotel studies, hospitality ← **hotél**

perhubungan *n* communications, connection; ~ *udara* air route ← **hubung**

peri- *pref* concerning; **perihal** *n* subject; *conj* about, concerning; **perikemanusiaan** *n* humanitarianism; **ber-perikemanusiaan** *adj* humane

peri *n* fairy; *ibu* ~ fairy godmother

periang *n* cheerful person ← **riang**

peribahasa *n* proverb, idiom

perih, pedih smart, sting

perihal *n* subject; *conj* about, concerning

perikanan *n* fisheries ← **ikan**

perikemanusiaan *adj* humanitarianism ← **manusia**

periksa investigate, check; **memeriksa** *v* to examine or investigate; ~ *ulang* to review; **pemeriksa** *n* examiner; **pemeriksaan** *n* examination, investigation

perincian *n* details, detailed explanation ← **rinci**

perintah order, command; **menjalankan** ~ to carry out orders; **memerintah** *v* to rule, govern, reign; **memerintahkan** *v* to order or command something; **pemerintah** *n* government; **pemerintahan** *n* administration, government

perintis *n* pioneer ← **rintis**

période *n* period, time

perisai *n* shield

périskop *n* periscope

peristiwa *n* incident, occurrence, happening

periuk *n* cooking pot

perjalanan *n* journey, trip; *agen* ~ travel agency ← **jalan**

perjanjian *n* agreement, contract ← **janji**

perjuangan *n* battle, fight, struggle ← **juang**

perjudian *n* gambling ← **judi**

perkakas *n* tool, instrument

perkantoran *n* office block ← **kantor**

perkapalan *n* shipping ← **kapal**

perkara *n* matter, case, affair

perkasa *adj* powerful; manly, virile

perkawinan *n* marriage, wedding; ~ *campuran* mixed marriage ← **kawin**

perkedél *n* (potato) patty, croquette; ~ *jagung* corn patty

perkelahian *n* fight, scuffle ← **kelahi**

perkémahan *n* camping, camp ← **kémah**

perkembangan *n* development ← **kembang**

perkenalan *n* introduction ← **kenal**

perkici *burung* ~ rainbow lorikeet

perkiraan *n* estimate, guess ← **kira**

perkosa: memerkosa *v* to rape, violate; **pemerkosaan** *n* rape, raping; **perkosaan** *n* rape

perkotaan *n* metropolitan area ← **kota**

perkumpulan *n* association, club; assembly ← **kumpul**

perkusi *n* percussion

perkutut *burung* ~ turtle-dove

perlahan, pelan, perlahan-lahan, pelan-pelan *adv* slowly, softly

perlawanan *n* opposition, resistance ← **lawan**

perlengkapan *n* outfit, equipment ← **lengkap**

perlindungan *n* protection ← **lindung**

perlu need, necessary; **keperluan** *n* needs, requirements; **memerlukan** *v* to need, require

permadani *n* carpet

permainan *n* game, match ← **main**

permaisyuri, permaisuri *n* queen

permak, vermak alteration to clothes; **dipermak** *adj* altered, shortened

permandian *n* christening, baptism; *bapak* ~ godfather ← **mandi**

permén *n* sweet, lolly, candy

permintaan *n* request; *atas* ~ by request ← **minta**

perminyakan *n* oil and gas ← **minyak**

permisi excuse me; ~ *dulu* excuse me, excuse yourself

permohonan *n* request, application ← **mohon**

permukaan *n* surface; ~ *air* water level; *di atas* ~ *laut* above sea level ← **muka**

permukiman *n* housing, residential area ← **mukim**

permusuhan *n* enmity, animosity, hostility ← **musuh**

pernafasan, pernapasan *n* breathing, respiration; ~ *buatan* artificial respiration; *sistem* ~ respiratory system ← **nafas**

pernah *adv* ever; once; have + past perfect form of verb; *saya* ~ *ke Bali* I've been to Bali; ~ *makan bebek?* Have you ever eaten duck?; *Tidak* ~ Never

perniagaan *n* commerce, trade, business ← **niaga**

pernikahan *n* wedding ← **nikah**

penilaian *n* evaluation ← **nilai**

pernis *n* varnish

pernyataan *n* statement, declaration ← **nyata**

peroléhan *n* acquisition ← **oléh**

perombakan *n* reorganization ← **rombak**

perompak *n* pirate ← **rompak**

péron *n* platform; *karcis* ~ platform ticket

perona ~ *mata* eyeshadow; ~ *pipi* rouge ← **rona**

perosok: terperosok *adj* fallen, sunk, plunged

perosotan *n* (children's) slide ← **rosot**

perpaduan *n* blend, synthesis ← **padu**

perpisahan *n* parting, farewell; *acara* ~, *pesta* ~ farewell (party) ← **pisah**

perpustakaan *n* library ← **pustaka**

pérs *n* press, media

persahabatan *n* friendship; *pertandingan* ~ friendly (match) ← **sahabat**

persaingan *n* competition; ~ *ketat* intense competition ← **saing**

persalinan *n* childbirth ← **salin**

persamaan *n* similarity, likeness, resemblance; equation ← **sama**

persatuan *n* union, association ← **satu**

persaudaraan *n* brotherhood, fraternity; sisterhood; family ties ← **saudara**

persediaan *n* stock, supply ← **sedia**

persegi *adj* square; sided → **segi**

persekongkolan *n* plot, intrigue, conspiracy ← **kongkol**

persekutuan *n* alliance, partnership ← **sekutu**

perselingkuhan *n* affair ← **selingkuh**

perselisihan *n* dispute, difference of opinion ← **selisih**

persembahan *n* offering; product or service ← **sembah**

persembunyian *n* hiding place, hideout ← **sembunyi**

persén *n* percent; *seratus* ~ one hundred percent; **persénan** *n* tip; **perséntase, proséntase** *n* percentage

persendian *n* joints ← **sendi**

perserikatan *n* federation; ~ *Bangsa-Bangsa (PBB)* the United Nations (UN) ← **serikat**

perséro *adj* proprietary limited (Pty Ltd); **perséroan** *n* company; ~ *terbatas* proprietary limited ← **séro**

persétan *ejac* go to hell! ← **sétan**

persetubuhan *n* sexual intercourse ← **tubuh, setubuh**

persetujuan *n* agreement, approval ← **tuju, setuju**

persiapan *n* preparations ← **siap**

persidangan *n* meeting, assembly; (extended) court session ← **sidang**

persimpangan *n* intersection ← **simpang**

persis *adv* exactly; ~ *ibunya* just like his mother

persoalan *n* problem, issue, matter ← **soal**

personalia, personél *adj* personnel, staff

pertahanan *n* defense

pertama *adj* first; **pertama-tama** *adv* first of all

pertamanan *adj* parks and gardens ← **taman**

pertambahan *n* increase ← **tambah**

pertambangan *n* mining ← **tambang**

Pertamina *n* state-run national oil and gas company ← **Perusahaan Pertambangan Minyak dan Gas Bumi Negara**

261

pertanda *n* sign, omen, indication ← **tanda**

pertandingan *n* contest, competition, match ← **tanding**

pertanian *n* agriculture; *sekolah* ~ agricultural college ← **tani**

pertanyaan *n* question; *mengajukan* ~ to ask questions ← **tanya**

pertempuran *n* battle ← **tempur**

pertemuan *n* meeting ← **temu**

pertengahan *n* middle; *Abad* ~ the Middle Ages ← **tengah**

pertengkaran *n* quarrel ← **tengkar**

pertiga *dua* ~ two-thirds; **pertigaan** *n* T-junction ← **tiga**

pertikaian *n* quarrel, disagreement ← **tikai**

pertimbangan *n* consideration ← **timbang**

pertiwi *ibu* ~ motherland, native country

pertokoan *n* shopping center or complex, mall ← **toko**

pertolongan *n* help, assistance, aid; ~ *pertama* first aid ← **tolong**

pertukaran *n* exchange ← **tukar**

pertumbuhan *n* growth, development ← **tumbuh**

pertunangan *n* engagement ← **tunang**

pertunjukan *n* show, performance ← **tunjuk**

perubahan *n* change, alteration ← **ubah**

perumahan *n* housing (complex) ← **rumah**

Perumnas National Housing → **Perumahan Nasional**

perundingan *n* discussion; *meja* ~ discussion table ← **runding**

perunggu *n* bronze

peruntungan *n* (good) fortune or luck ← **untung**

perupa *n* sculptor ← **rupa**

perusahaan *n* company ← **usaha**

perut *n* stomach, belly; ~ *buncit* pot belly; pregnant; ~ *kapal* hold

perwakilan *n* representation, delegation ← **wakil**

perwalian *n* guardianship, representation ← **wali**

perwira *n* officer; ~ *tinggi* general

pesan message, instruction, order; **pesanan** *n* order; *antar* ~ delivery; **memesan** *v* to order; **pemesanan** *n* order, request

pesantrén *n* Islamic boarding school → **santri**

pesat *adj* fast, rapid

pesawat *n* machine; ~ *telepon* telephone; ~ *terbang* aeroplane, airplane

pésék *adj* flat-nosed

pésér → **sepésér**

peserta *n* participant ← **serta**

pesiar *n* trip, cruise; *kapal* ~ cruise ship, pleasure craft

pésimis *adj* pessimistic

pesindén *n, f* singer accompanying a gamelan orchestra

pesing *bau* ~ stink of urine

pesisir *n* coast; *batik* ~ batik from the north coast of Java

pesona *n* magic; **memesona(kan)** *adj* enthralling, enchanting; **terpesona** *adj* enthralled, enchanted

pésta *n* party, celebration;

~ *perkawinan*, ~ *pernikahan* wedding reception; **berpésta** *v* to (have a) party; **dipéstakan** *v* to be celebrated with a party

péstisida *n* pesticide

pesuruh *n* messenger, errand boy; ~ *kantor* office boy ← **suruh**

pét *topi* ~ cap

peta *n* map, chart; ~ *dunia* world map; *buku* ~ atlas; *buku* ~ *jalan* road atlas, street directory

petai → **peté**

petak *n* compartment, division; *rumah* ~ tenement, communal house

petang *adj, form* late afternoon to evening (from around 2.30 to sunset); *berita* ~ evening news

petani *n* farmer ← **tani**

petas: petasan *n* firecracker, fireworks

peté, petai *n* stinkbean

peténis *n* tennis player ← **ténis**

peternak *n* (cattle) farmer; **peternakan** *n* cattle farm, ranch ← **ternak**

péterséli *n* parsley

peti *n* chest, case, box; ~ *es* ice-box; ~ *kemas* packing case, freight box; ~ *mati* coffin

petik pluck; **petikan** *n* extract, quotation; **memetik** *v* to pick; to strum; **pemetik** *n* picker; ~ *daun teh* tea-picker

petinju *n* boxer ← **tinju**

petir *n* thunder, lightning; *disambar* ~ to be struck by lightning

petis *tahu* ~ fried tofu with a spicy sauce

petisi *n* petition

pétrokimia *adj* petrochemical

pétromaks *lampu* ~ kerosene lantern

Pétruk *n* clown figure in shadow-puppet plays

petunjuk *n* instruction, direction ← **tunjuk**

pewarna *n* dye, stain ← **warna**

pewawancara *n* interviewer ← **wawancara**

péyot, péot, pényok *adj* dented

PHK *abbrev, euph* pemutusan hubungan kerja unemployment

piagam *n* charter

piala *n* trophy, cup; ~ *Sudirman* Sudirman Cup (badminton)

piano *n* piano; **pianis** *n* pianist

piatu *n* motherless child; *yatim* ~ orphan

piawai *adj* expert, skilled

picik *adj* narrow; *berpikiran* ~ to be narrow-minded

picu *n* trigger; **memicu** *v* to trigger, set off; **pemicu** *n* trigger

pidana *hukum* ~ criminal law; **terpidana** *n* the condemned

pidato *n* speech, address; ~ *pembukaan* opening speech; **berpidato** *v* to make a speech, give an address

pigura *n* picture frame

pihak *n* party; side; ~ *ayah* paternal line, father's side; *di satu* ~ on the one side; **berpihak, sepihak** *adj* unilateral

pijak: pijakan *n* foothold, something to stand on; ~ *kaki* pedal

pijar *lampu* ~ light bulb

pijat, pijit massage; *panti* ~ massage parlor; *tukang* ~

masseur; **memijat** *v* to massage

pikat: terpikat *adj* attracted, enchanted

pikir, fikir *v* to think; **pikiran** *n* thought, idea; **berpikir** *v* to think; **kepikiran** *v* considered, thought of, sprang to mind; **memikirkan** *v* to think about; **pemikir** *n* thinker; **pemikiran** *n* thinking, consideration

piknik *n* picnic; **berpiknik** *v* to have a picnic

pikul: memikul *v* to bear, carry on the shoulder

pikun *adj* senile, dotty

pil *n* (contraceptive) pill, tablet

PIL *n, abbrev* lover, another man ← **pria idaman lain**

pilar *n* pillar

pilek sniffle, have a cold or runny nose

pilem → **film**

pilih choose; ~ *kasih* take sides; **pilihan** *n* choice, selection; *adj* select; **memilih** *v* to choose or select; to elect or vote (for); **pemilihan** *n* election; ~

umum (pemilu) general election

pilkada *n* local or regional election ← **pemilihan kepala daérah**

pilu moved

pimpin: pimpinan *n* leadership, guidance; administration; **memimpin** *v* to lead; **pemimpin** *n* leader; **kepemimpinan** *n* leadership (qualities); **terpimpin** *adj* led, guided

pinak: beranak-pinak *v* to have (many) descendants

pinang *n* areca nut; *seperti ~ dibelah dua* like two peas in a pod; **meminang** *v* to propose, ask for a girl's hand in marriage

pincang *adj* crippled, lame; *kaki ~* bad or gammy leg

pindah move; change; ~ *agama* change religions; ~ *rumah* (house); **berpindah** *v* to move; **memindahkan** *v* to move, transfer; **pemindahan** *n* transfer, shifting, removal

pinggan *n* bowl, plate

pinggang *n* waist

pinggir *n* edge, border;

pinggiran n edges, outskirts; ~ *kota* city outskirts or limits; **meminggir** v **minggir** v, coll to move to the side, pull over; **terpinggirkan** adj cast aside, marginalized

pingit: pingitan n seclusion

pingpong n table tennis, pingpong; **dipingpong** v to be sent here and there, messed about

pingsan faint, collapse; unconscious; *jatuh* ~ to faint (away)

pinguin n penguin

pinisi, phinisi *kapal* ~ Buginese cargo boat

pinjam borrow; **pinjaman** n loan; **meminjam** v to borrow; **meminjami** v to lend someone; **meminjamkan** v to lend something; **peminjam** n borrower; *kartu* ~ borrowing card

pinsét n tweezers

pinta: (me)minta v to request, ask for; **(me)minta-minta** v to beg, ask for money; **permintaan** n request; *atas* ~ by request

pintar adj **pinter** coll clever

pintas: sepintas ~ *lalu* at first glance

pintu n door, gate; ~ *air* sluice, floodgates; ~ *darurat* emergency exit; ~ *geser* sliding door; ~ *keluar* exit; ~ *masuk* entrance

pipa n pipe, tube; ~ *karet* rubber tube

pipi n cheek

pipih adj flat

pipis n, ch wee, pee, go to the toilet

piramida n pyramid

pirang, pérang adj, m blond, f blonde, fair-haired

piranti, peranti n apparatus, equipment; ~ *lunak* software

piring n plate, dish; *mencuci* ~ to wash the dishes; *tari* ~ dance from West Sumatra performed with plates; ~ *terbang* flying saucer; **piringan** n plate-shaped object

pirsa: pemirsa n television audience, viewer

pisah separate, split; ~ *ranjang* separate (of a couple); **berpisah** v to part, separate; **memisah** v to separate; **memisahkan** v to separate something; **pemisahan** *n* separation; **perpisahan** *n* parting, farewell; *acara ~, pesta ~* farewell (party); **terpisah** *adj* separated

pisang *n* banana; *~ goreng (pisgor)* fried banana

pisau *n* knife; *~ bedah* scalpel

pispot *n* chamber pot, potty

pita *n* ribbon; *~ suara* vocal cords; *cacing ~* tapeworm

piton *n (ular) ~* python

piutang *n* credit → **utang**

piyama *n* pyjamas, pajamas

PKB *abbrev Partai Kebangkitan Bangsa* Party of National Awakening

PKI *abbrev Partai Komunis Indonesia* Indonesian Communist Party

PKS *abbrev Partai Keadilan Sejahtera* Justice and Prosperity Party

plafon *n* ceiling

plagiat *n* plagiarism; **plagiator** *n* someone who copies or commits plagiarism

plakat *n* placard, poster

planolog *n* town planner; **planologi** *n* town planning

plastik *adj* plastic; *n* plastic bag, carrier bag

plat → **pelat**

platina *n* platinum

pléno *adj* plenary; *sidang ~* plenary session, full session

pléster *n* sticking plaster, bandaid

PLN *abbrev Perusahaan Listrik Negara* State Electricity Corporation

plong *adj* relieved

PLTA *abbrev Pembangkit Listrik Tenaga Air* hydroelectric power station

PLTPB *abbrev Pembangkit Listrik Tenaga Panas Bumi* geothermal power station

PLTU *abbrev Pembangkit Listrik Tenaga Uap* steam power station

pluit → **peluit**

plus *adj* plus, added; *kacamata ~* long-sighted glasses; *nilai ~* added bonus

PM *abbrev Perdana Menteri* Prime Minister

PMI *abbrev Palang Merah Indonesia* Indonesian Red Cross

PNG *abbrev Papua Nugini* Papua New Guinea

PNI *abbrev Partai Nasional Indonesia* Indonesian National Party

PNS *abbrev Pegawai Negeri Sipil* civil servant

poci *n* teapot

poco: poco-poco *n* line dance from North Sulawesi

pocong *n* ghost (wrapped in a shroud); *sumpah ~* oath taken while wrapped in a shroud

poco-poco *n* line dance from North Sulawesi

pohon *n* tree; *~ beringin* banyan (tree); *~ cendana* sandalwood tree; *~ cemara* casuarina (tree); *~ jati* teak

pohon → **mohon**

poin *n* point, mark

pojok *n* corner; **pojokan** *n, sl* corner; **memojokkan** *v* to force into a corner; **ter-pojok(kan)** *adj* forced into a corner

pokok main; *~ kalimat* subject of a sentence; *~nya* basically, the main thing is; *~ pembicaraan* discussion topic; *gaji ~* base salary

pola *n* pattern; *~ baju* sewing pattern; **berpola** *v* to have a pattern; *adj* patterned

Polandia *n* Poland

Polda *n* Regional Police; *~ Metro Jaya* Jakarta Metropolitan Police station ← **Polisi Daérah**

polés polish

poligami *n* polygamy

poliklinik, poli *n* polyclinic, doctor's surgery; *~ gigi* dentist's surgery; *~ umum* GP's surgery, doctor's surgery

polisi *n* police; *~ militer* military police; *~ wanita (polwan)* policewoman; *kantor ~* police station

politik *n* politics; **berpolitik** *v* to play politics; **politikus** *n politisi* politician; **politis** *adj* political

polos *adj* plain, unpretentious; smooth; *baju ~* plain shirt; **kepolosan** *n* simplicity, straight-forwardness, lack of pretension

Polri *n* Indonesian police force

polsék *n* local police station ← **polisi séktor**

polusi *n* pollution; *~ udara*

air pollution; **polutan** *n*
pollutant

Polwan *n* policewoman ←
polisi wanita

pompa pump; ~ *angin* air
pump; ~ *bensin* petrol
station, gasoline pump, service station; **memompa** *v*
to pump

PON *n* National Sports
Week, national champion-
ships ← **Pekan Olahraga
Nasional**

pon *n* pound

ponco *n* poncho, cloak

pondok *n* hut, cottage; ~
pesantren (ponpes) Islamic
boarding school; **mondok**
v, coll to board, lodge, stay

pong *tahu* ~ tofu eaten with
spicy sauce

pongah *adj* arrogant

poni *n* fringe, bangs

ponpés *n* Islamic boarding
school ← **pondok
pesantrén**

pontang: pontang-panting
adv helter-skelter

pop *n* pop (music)

popok *n* napkin, diaper

populér *adj* popular;
popularitas *n* popularity

pori *n* pore; **berpori** *adj*
porous, having pores

porno *adj* pornographic;
film ~ porn(ographic) film;
pornoaksi *n* pornographic
actions; **pornografi** *n*
pornography

poros *n* axis

porselén *n* porcelain

porsi *n* serve, portion

portal *n* iron gateway into a
building complex; barrier
blocking access into a
complex; **diportal** *v* to be
blocked by a barrier, have a
barrier lowered

Portugal, Portugis *n*
Portugal; *bahasa* ~, *orang*
~ Portuguese

pos *n* post; ~ *kilat* express
mail; ~ *penjagaan*, ~
satpam security post; ~
udara airmail

pose *n* pose (for a photograph); **berpose** *v* to pose
for a photograph

posisi *n* position; **berposisi** *v* to hold a position,
be positioned

positif *adj* positive; **berpikir**
~ to think positive

poskamling *n* neighborhood security post ← **pos keamanan lingkungan**

posko *n* post (for a political party or fund-raising effort) ← **pos koordinasi**

posyandu *n* all-in-one government administrative office ← **pos pelayanan terpadu**

pot *n* pot, vase; ~ *bunga* vase (indoors), flowerpot (outdoors)

potong piece, cut; ~ *kambing* slaughter a goat; ~ *rambut* cut your hair, get your hair cut; hairdresser, barber (for men); **potongan** *n* discount, reduction; cut (of clothes); **berpotongan** *adj* of a certain style or cut; **memotong** *v* to cut, deduct; to slaughter, amputate; to interrupt; **terpotong** *adj* cut (off)

potrét *n* portrait; photograph of a person; *tukang* ~ photographer; **memotrét** *v* to photograph

PP *abbrev pulang pergi* there and back, shown on public transport

PPN *abbrev Pajak Penda-* *patan Nasional* National Income Tax, a goods and services tax at restaurants and hotels

PPP (P3) *abbrev Partai Persatuan Pembangunan* United Development Party, a Muslim party

PR *abbrev pekerjaan rumah* homework

pra- *pref* pre-, before; ~*karsa* initiative; ~*nikah* pre-marital; ~*sangka* prejudice

prada *n* coating, leaf

prajurit *n* soldier

prakarsa *n* initiative; *mengambil* ~ to take the initiative

prakték, praktik *n* practice; practical; ~ *umum* general practitioner's; **mempraktékkan** *v* to put into practice; **praktis** *adj* practical; **kepraktisan** *n* practicality

pramugari *n, f* stewardess, air hostess; cabin crew; **pramugara** *n, m* steward; cabin crew

Pramuka *n* Scouts → **Praja Muda Karana**

Prancis → **Perancis**

prangko → **perangko**

prapatan, perapatan *n, coll* crossroads, intersection

prasangka *n* prejudice

prasmanan *adj* buffet-style

prédikat *dengan* ~ with the title or designation

préman *n* thug

prémi *n* (insurance) premium

présdir *n* president-director ← **présidén diréktur**

préséntasi *n* (oral) presentation

présiden *n* president; **keprésidénan** *adj* presidential

préstasi *n* performance, achievement; **berpréstasi** *adj* prestigious; successful

pria *n* male, man

pribadi *n* self, individual, personality; *saya* ~ personally; *secara* ~ privately; **kepribadian** *n* personality

pribumi *n* **pri** *coll* native inhabitant, indigenous Indonesian; **non-pri** *coll* ethnic Chinese

prihatin concerned, worried; **keprihatinan** *n* concern; **memprihatinkan** *adj* worrying

primadona *n* primadonna

primitif *adj* primitive

prinsip *n* principle; **berprinsip** *v* to have principles; *adj* principled

prioritas *n* priority; ~ *tinggi* high priority; **memprioritaskan** *v* to prioritize

priyayi *n* upper class, esp in colonial era

problém, problim *n* problem

prodéo *n* leg without paying court costs, free

produk *n* product → **buatan; produksi** *n* production; **memproduksi** *v* to produce

profési *n* profession; **berprofési** *v* to have a profession, work as; **profésional** *adj* professional

profésor *n* professor → **guru besar**

profil *n* profile, outline

prokém *bahasa* ~ Jakarta teen slang

proklamasi *n* proclamation (of independence); **proklamator** *n* proclaimer (of independence)

promosi *n* promotion; **mempromosikan** *v* to promote

propinsi *n* province

271

proporsi *n* proportion;
proporsional *adj* proportional, reasonable
prosa *n* prose
prosédur *n* procedure;
prosédural *adj* procedural
prosés *n* process; court case;
memproséskan *v* to process
protés protest; **memprotés**
v to (make a) protest
Protéstan *n* Protestant →
Kristen
protokol *jalan ~* main street
(passed through by official
visitors)
provokasi *n* provocation;
provokator *n* trouble-maker,
provocateur
proyék *n* project, scheme
PRT *pembantu rumah
tangga* household servant
Ps. *pasar* market
psikiater [sikiater] *n* psychiatrist → **jiwa**
psikolog [sikolog] *n* psychologist; **psikologi** *n*
psychology → **jiwa**
PT *abbrev Perseroan
Terbatas* Pty Ltd
PU *abbrev Pekerjaan
Umum* Public Works
pualam *n* marble

puas *adj* satisfied, content;
memuaskan *adj* satisfactory
puasa fast; *~ nasi* give up
eating rice; *~ Senin Kamis*
fast on Mondays and
Thursdays; *membatalkan ~*
to break your fast (inten-
tionally); **berpuasa** *v* to fast
puber *n* puberty; *masa ~*
puberty
pucat *adj* pale; *adj, coll*
scared
pucuk *n* shoot, sprout
pudar faded, washed-out;
memudar *v* to fade
pudel *anjing ~* poodle
puding *n* pudding, dessert
pugar: **memugar** *v* to restore, renovate; **pemugaran**
n restoration, renovation
puing *n* ruins; rubble
puisi *n* poetry (esp Western); **puitis** *adj* poetic
puja worship; **pujaan** *n*
something worshipped or
idolized; **memuja** *v* to
worship
pujaséra *n* food court,
collection of food stalls
← **pusat jajan serba rasa**
puji praise; *~ Tuhan Chr*

thank God, Praise the Lord;
pujian *n* praise; **memuji** *v*
to praise; **terpuji** *adj*
highly-praised

pukul strike; *form* hour; ~
tiga belas 1 pm; ~ *rata* in
general; **pukulan** *n* strike,
beat, hit; **memukul** *v* to hit,
beat, strike; **terpukul** *adj*
hard-hit

pula *adv* also, too; again

pulang *v* to go home,
return; ~ *hari* to return on
the same day, not stay
overnight; ~ *pergi (PP)*
there and back, both ways;
berpulang *v* to pass away,
die; **memulangkan** *v* to
give back; to send back,
repatriate; **pemulangan** *n*
return, repatriation

pulau *n* island; ~ *Dewata*
Bali, Island of the Gods; ~
karang coral island, atoll; ~
Seribu the Thousand Islands;
antar ~ between islands,
inter-island; **kepulauan** *n*
archipelago, chain

pulen *nasi* ~ delicious,
well-cooked rice

pulih recovered; **pemulihan**
n recovery, restoration

pulpén *n* fountain pen

pulsa *n* unit of credit (for a
telephone)

puluh *dua* ~ twenty; *tiga* ~
thirty; *empat* ~ forty; *lima*
~ fifty; **puluhan** *n* dozens;
tahun delapan ~ the eight-
ies; **sepuluh** *n* ten

pun emphasizing particle;
too, also; even; then

punah *adj* extinct

punai *burung* ~ kind of
green pigeon

puncak *n* peak, summit,
top; ~ *gunung* mountain-top,
summit; ~ *popularitas* peak
of popularity; *pimpinan* ~
top-level management

pundak *n* shoulder

pundi *n* piggybank, purse;
~ *amal* charitable fund

punggung *n* back; *tulang* ~
spine; **memunggungi** *v* to
turn your back on

pungli *n* unofficial charge
← **pungutan liar**

pungut pick up; *anak* ~
adopted child; **memungut**
v to pick up, collect

puntung ~ *rokok* cigarette
butt

punya have, own; *orang*

273

tidak ~ the poor, the have-nots; *yang* ~ the owner; **kepunyaan** *n* possession, belonging; **mempunyai** *v* to have, own, possess

pupuk *n* fertilizer; ~ *kandang* manure, dung

pura *n* Balinese or Hindu temple

pura-pura pretend, fake

purba *adj* ancient; **purbakala** *n* ancient times

puri *n* palace, castle

purna- *pref* post-, after; **purnabakti** *adj* retirement; **purnawirawan** *n* retired soldier

purnawirawan *n* retired soldier

puruk: terpuruk *adj* hidden, buried, sunk

pus *n, coll* pussycat

pusaka *n* heirloom, inheritance

pusar *n* navel, belly button; ~ *kepala* crown; **pusaran** *n* vortex; ~ *air* eddy, whirlpool; ~ *angin* whirlwind; **berpusar** *v* to revolve, whirl

pusat *n* center; ~ *berat* center of gravity; **berpusat** ~ *pada* to focus or center

on; **memusatkan** *v* to focus; ~ *perhatian* to concentrate

pusing *adj* dizzy; ~ *tujuh keliling* completely confused; ~ *kepala* headache; **memusingkan** ~ *kepala* puzzling

puskésmas *n* clinic, public health center ← **pusat keséhatan masyarakat**

pustaka *n, lit* book; *daftar* ~ list of references; **kepustakaan** *n* bibliography, list of references; literature; **perpustakaan** *n* library; **pustakawan** *n* librarian

putar turn around, rotate; **putaran** *n* round, revolution; **berputar** *v* to rotate, turn; ~ *balik* to turn around, do a U-turn; **memutar** *v* to wind; to rotate; **memutarbalikkan** *v* to reverse, distort; **perputaran** rotation; **pemutaran** *n* screening; ~ *perdana* premiere, opening night (of a film); **seputar** *adj* around, about

putera → **putra**

puteri → **putri**

putih *adj* white; ~ *telur* albumen, egg white; *merah*

~ red and white; **keputihan** n thrush, vaginal itching (white discharge); **memutihkan** v to whiten, bleach; **pemutih** n bleach

puting n nipple

putra, putera n, pol son; ~ *mahkota* crown prince; ~-*putri* children, sons and daughters

putri, puteri n, pol daughter; ~ *duyung* mermaid; ~ *malu* a kind of shrub

putus broken off; ~ *asa* give up hope; ~ *sekolah* leave or drop out of school (prematurely); **keputusan** n decision, decree; **memutus** v to break; ~ *hubungan* to break or sever contact; **memutuskan** v to terminate or break; to decide; **pemutusan** n termination, breaking-off; ~ *hubungan kerja (PHK)* to lose your job; **terputus** adj cut off; **terputus-putus** v to keep cutting out

puyeng adj dizzy, confused; with a headache

puyuh *burung* ~ quail

puyung hai → **fuyung hai**

Q

Quran *al*-~ the Koran

R

raba: rabaan n caress, stroke; **meraba** v to feel or grope something; **meraba-raba** v to feel around or grope (in the dark)

rabat n rebate, (bulk) discount

Rabu, Rebo *hari* ~ Wednesday

rabun adj blurry; ~ *dekat* long-sighted; ~ *jauh* short-sighted

racik: racikan n blend, concoction; prescription; **meracik** ~ *obat* to mix up medicine

racun n poison (not from animals); ~ *tikus* rat poison; **beracun** adj poisonous, containing poison; **keracunan** adj poisoned; ~ *makanan* food poisoning; **meracuni** v to poison

rada *adv, coll* quite, rather

radang *adj* inflamed; ~ *paru-paru* pneumonia; **meradang** *v* to become inflamed; to become angry

radio *n* radio; ~ *Republik Indonesia (RRI)* Indonesian state radio

rafia *tali* ~ plastic twine

raga *n* body; **peraga** *n* visual aid; **memeragakan** *v* to model, show; **peragawati** *n, f* model

ragam *n* manner, way; kind; **beragam** *adj* various; **seragam** *n* uniform

ragi *n* yeast

ragos *n, sl* gossip (queen) ← **raja gosip**

ragu doubt, doubtful; **ragu-ragu** *adj* doubtful, unsure; **keragu(-ragu)an** *n* doubt, uncertainty; **meragukan** *v* to doubt something

rahang *n* jaw; *tulang* ~ jawbone

rahasia *n* secret, mystery; ~ *umum* open secret; **merahasiakan** *v* to keep secret

rahim *n* uterus, womb

raib vanished, disappeared

raih: meraih *v* to reach for; to achieve

raja *n* king; ~ *singa* syphilis; **kerajaan** *n* kingdom; ~ *Inggris* the United Kingdom

rajaléla: merajaléla *v* to be out of control; to act violently

rajin *adj* diligent, hardworking, industrious; ~ *belajar* study hard; **kerajinan** *n* crafts; ~ *tangan* handicrafts; **perajin** *n* craftsman, artisan

rajungan *n* kind of small edible crab

rajut: rajutan *n* knitting, crochet work; **merajut** *v* to knit; to crochet

rak *n* shelf; ~ *buku* bookshelf; ~ *piring* dish rack

rakét *n* racquet, racket

rakit *n* raft; **merakit** *v* to assemble; **perakitan** *n* assembly

raksasa giant

rakus *adj* greedy

rakyat *n* people; ~ *jelata* common people, proletariat

ralat *n* correction, errata; **meralat** *v* to correct a mistake

rama → romo

Ramadan Muslim fasting month

ramah *adj* friendly; ~ *tamah* informal get-together; **keramahan** *n* friendliness

ramai, ramé *adj* busy, lively; crowded; **ramai-ramai** *adv* in a group, together; **keramaian** *n* noise, din; lively atmosphere; **meramaikan** *v* to liven up, enliven

ramal: ramalan *n* prediction, prophecy, forecast; ~ *cuaca* weather forecast; **meramal** *v* to tell fortunes; **meramalkan** *v* to predict, foretell

Ramayana *n* Hindu epic, performed in shadow-puppet plays and other traditional arts

rambah: merambah ~ *hutan* to clear away the forest, clear the land

rambut *n* hair; ~ *lurus* straight hair; ~ *ikal*, ~ *keriting* curly hair; **rambutan** *n* rambutan, fruit with hairy red skin; **berambut** *adj* hairy; *v* to have hair

ramé → ramai

rami *n* hemp, jute

rampas, merampas *v* to take by force, rob, plunder; **rampasan** *n* booty, plunder, loot

ramping *adj* slender

rampok, merampok *v* to rob, hold up; **perampok** *n* robber; **perampokan** *n* robbery

ramu: ramuan *n* mixture

rana: merana *v* to suffer, waste away; to live miserably, in poverty

rancang: rancangan *n* plan, design; **merancang** *v* to plan, design; **perancang** *n* designer, planner; ~ *busana* fashion designer

rangka *n* skeleton, framework; *dalam* ~ in connection with, in the context of ← **kerangka**

rangkai: rangkaian *n* combination, series

rangkak: merangkak *v* to crawl

rangkap multiple; *tiga* ~ three copies, in triplicate; **merangkap** *v* to hold another position (temporarily)

rangkap → perangkap

277

rangkul, merangkul *v* to hug, embrace

rangsang: rangsangan *n* stimulation; **merangsang** *v* to stimulate, excite; **perangsang** *n* stimulant

ranjang *n* bed

ranjau *n* mine; ~ *darat* land mine; *kapal penyapu* ~ minesweeper

ranking, rangking [réng-king] *n* process of ranking marks in class

ransel *n* backpack; *turis* ~ backpacker

rantai *n* chain; **merantai** *v* to chain up

rantau *n* abroad, across the sea; **merantau** *v* to sail away, seek your fortune, settle overseas; **perantauan** *n* abroad, in another place

ranting *n* twig; small branch (of parties, banks)

rapat *adj* close to; tight; **merapat** *v* to move closer

rapat meeting, meet

rapi *n* neat, tidy, organized

rapot, rapor *n* (school) report

rapuh *adj* brittle, weak

ras *n* breed; pure-bred

rasa feel, feeling; sense; taste; ~*nya* it appears, it seems; ~ *malu* shame; ~ *pahit* bitterness, bitter taste; *saya* ~ I think, I feel; **kerasan** *coll* feel at home; **merasa** *v* to think, feel; **merasakan** *v* to feel something; **perasaan** *n* feeling; **terasa** *v* to be felt

rasi *n* constellation; **serasi** *adj* suited, compatible

rasul *n* prophet, messenger of God, apostle

rata *adj* flat, even, level; **rata-rata** *adv* equally; on average; **meratakan** *v* to level, flatten

rata-rata *adv* equally; on average ← **rata**

ratu *n* queen

ratus *dua* ~ two hundred; **beratus-ratus** *adj* hundreds of; **seratus** *adj* one hundred, a hundred

raung: meraung *v* to roar

raut ~ *muka* (facial) expression, look on your face

raut: rautan ~ *pensil* pencil sharpener

rawa *n* swamp, marsh

rawan *adj* vulnerable, troubled, unsafe

rawat: merawat *v* to nurse, care for; to maintain, look after; perawat *n* nurse, sister; perawatan treatment; maintenance, upkeep

rawon *n* black meat soup from East Java

raya *adj* great, greater; hari ~ holiday, feast day; Idul Fitri; *Indonesia* ~ the national anthem; merayakan *v* to celebrate; perayaan *n* celebration

rayap *n* termite, white ant; kena ~, dimakan ~ eaten by termites; merayap *v* to crawl, creep

rayu: rayuan *n* flattery; ~ *gombal* sweet talk; merayu *v* to tempt, flatter, seduce

razia *n* raid, spot-check

réaksi *n* reaction; beréaksi *v* to react

réalitas *n* reality

rebab *n* two-stringed musical instrument

rebana *n* tambourine

Rebo → Rabu

réboisasi *n* reforestation; meréboisasi *v* to reforest, replant trees

rebus *v* boil, boiled; merebus *v* to boil in water

rebut, merebut *v* to snatch, capture; rebutan *v* fighting for something; berebut *v* to fight for; berebutan *v* to fight each other for; merebutkan *v* to snatch something; memperebutkan *v* to seize, take by force

red. *abbrev redaksi* editor, (ed)

reda: meredakan *v* to soothe; to calm something down

redaksi *n* editors, editorial staff; redaktur *n* editor

redam *adj* faint, muffled; peredam *n* device to muffle or reduce noise

redup dim, go out

référénsi *n* reference; *surat* ~ reference (for a job)

réformasi *n* reform (esp after 1998); réformis *adj* reformist, pro-reform

regu *n* group, team

rejeki, rezeki, rizki *n* fortune, luck; livelihood, living

rekam: rekaman *n* recording; ~ *video* video recording; merekam *v* to record

rekan *n* colleague, partner,

279

associate; **rekanan** *n*
regular service provider
rekat: perekat *n* glue,
adhesive
rékayasa *n* engineering;
merekayasa *v* to engineer
rékening *n* (bank) account;
~ *tabungan* savings
account
réklamasi *n* reclamation;
tanah ~ reclaimed land
rékoméndasi *n* recommendation
rékonstruksi *n* reconstruc-
tion (of an incident);
merékonstruksi *v* to
reconstruct
rékor *n* record; ~ *dunia*
world record
rékréasi *n* recreation, relaxing, fun
rekrut recruit; **merekrut** *v*
to recruit
réktor *n* vice-chancellor,
rector; **réktorat** *n* vice-
chancellor's office
rél *n* rail; ~ *kereta api*
railway line, railroad, train
tracks
réla, réd(h)a, ridha, ridho
willing; **relawan** *n* volunteer; **merélakan** *v* to

approve, agree to
rélaks → rilék, riléks
rélasi *n* customer, client
rélatif *adj* relative
réli *n* (vehicle) rally; **peréli**
n rally driver
rém *n* brake; ~ *tangan* hand
brake; **mengerém** *v* to brake
remaja *n* teen, adolescent,
young single person, youth;
meremajakan *v* to revitalize, refurbish, update;
peremajaan *n* renewal,
revitalization
remas, meremas *v* to
press, squeeze, knead
rématik *n* rheumatism
rembes: merembes *v* to
seep in, leak, ooze
rembuk, rembug: berembuk
v to confer, discuss
réméh *adj* small, unimportant, trifling; **meréméhkan** *v* to belittle, treat
as unimportant
rempah *n* spice; **rempah-
rempah** *n* spices
rempéyék, péyék *n* peanut
crisps
renang swimming; *baju*
~ swimming costume,
swimsuit; **berenang** *v*

to swim; **perenang** *n* swimmer

rencana *n* plan, program, draft; ~ *Undang-Undang (RUU)* draft act; **berencana** *v* to plan; **merencanakan** *v* to plan; **perencanaan** *n* planning

rénda *n* lace; **berénda** *adj* lacy, lace

rendah *adj* low, humble; ~ *hati* humble; **kerendahan** *n* lowness; ~ *hati* humility; **merendahkan** *v* to lower; to humiliate; **terendah** *adj* lowest

rendam soak; **berendam** *v* to soak; **merendam** *v* to soak something; **terendam** *adj* inundated, flooded, soaked

rendang *n* meat cooked in coconut milk

réngék: meréngék *v* to whimper, whine

renggang *adj* distant, apart

renggut: merenggut *v* to snatch, tug

rénovasi renovation; **merénovasi** *v* to renovate

renta *adj* worn

rentak: serentak *adj* all at once, simultaneous, at the same time

rentan *adj* susceptible

rentang: rentangan *n* stretch, span

renung: renungan *n* reflection, musing, contemplation; **merenung** *v* to daydream

renyah *adj* crisp, crispy

réog *n* trance dance, most famously in Ponorogo, East Java

Rep. *Republik* Republic

réparasi *n* repair(s); **meréparasi** *v* to repair ← **baik**

répatriasi *n* repatriation

répot very busy; bothered; **répot-répot** *v* to go to great trouble; **merépotkan** *v* to make someone busy or go to some trouble

républik *n* republic; ~ *Indonesia* the Republic of Indonesia

reruntuhan, runtuhan *n* ruins → **runtuh**

resah *adj* restless; **keresahan** *n* restlessness, nervous energy; **meresahkan** *adj* disturbing, worrying

resap: meresap v to be absorbed; to penetrate, seep into

résé → **risi**

résénsi, risénsi n review; ~ *buku* book review

resép n recipe; prescription; **meresépkan** v to write a prescription for a drug

resépsi n reception; ~ *perkawinan*, ~ *pernikahan* wedding reception; **resépsionis** n receptionist

resérse n detective, forensic

résidivis n repeat offender

resik adj clean

resmi adj official, formal; *kunjungan* ~ state visit; *pakaian* ~ formal dress; *secara* ~ officially; **meresmikan** v to formalize, make official; **peresmian** n formal opening, inauguration

résolusi n resolution

réspon, réspons respond, response; **réspondan** n respondent

résto n up-market restaurant

réstoran n restaurant

réstorasi n restoration

restu n blessing; **merestui** v to agree to, give your blessing to

retak adj cracked; **retakan** n crack, fissure

retrét n, Chr retreat, period of religious contemplation

réuni n (school) reunion

révolusi n revolution; *zaman* ~ the Indonesian Revolution, 1945-9; **révolusionér** adj revolutionary

réwél adj fussy, troublesome, difficult

rezeki, rizki → **rejeki**

RI abbrev Republik Indonesia Republic of Indonesia

riak n ripples of water

riak n phlegm

riam n (river) rapids

riang adj cheerful; **periang** n cheerful person

riang → **meriang**

rias *kamar* ~ dressing room; *meja* ~ dressing table; *tukang* ~ make-up artist; **riasan** n make-up

riba n high interest on a loan, usury

ribu n thousand; *sepuluh* ~

ten thousand; **beribu(-ribu)** *adj* thousands of; **seribu** *adj* one thousand, a thousand

ribut noise; noisy; **keributan** *n* disturbance; loud noise

ricuh *adj* chaotic, out of control; **kericuhan** *n* chaos

rijstafel [réstafel] *n* colonial-style dinner of rice with small trays of side-dishes

rilék, riléks, rélaks relax, relaxed

rilis release (of an album or film); **merilis** *v* to release, put out

rimba *n* jungle, forest

rinci detail; **rincian** *n* details; **perincian** *n* details, detailed explanation

rindang *adj* leafy, shady

rinding: merinding *v* to have goose-bumps or an eerie feeling, be spooked

rindu longing; ~ *akan*, ~ *pada* long for, miss; *benci tapi* ~ love-hate relationship; **kerinduan** *n* longing, craving; **merindukan** *v* to miss, long for

ring *n* (boxing) ring

ringan *adj* light, easy; ~

tangan light-fingered; prone to violence; *kredit* ~ easy credit; **meringankan** *v* to ease, relieve, make easier

ringgit *n* ringgit, Malaysian currency (100 cents)

ringkas: ringkasan *n* summary, synopsis

rintang: rintangan *n* obstacle; barricade

rintih moan; **merintih** *v* to moan or groan

rintis: merintis *v* to pioneer; **perintis** *n* pioneer

risalah, risalat *n* pamphlet, brochure, circular

risau *adj* uneasy, anxious; **merisaukan** *v* to worry about

risénsi → **résénsi**

risét *n* research; ~ *dan teknologi (ristek)* research and technology; *meng-adakan* ~ to do research

risih, risi, résé feel uncomfortable

risik: berisik *adj* noisy, loud; *v* to rustle

risiko *n* risk; **berisiko** *adj* risky

riskan *adj* risky

risték *n* research and
technology ← **risét dan
téknologi**

riwayat *n* story, tale; ~ *hidup*
biography; curriculum
vitae, CV

RM *abbrev Rumah Makan*
restaurant, roadhouse

robah, rubah → **ubah**

robék *adj* torn (of cloth),
holey; *tangan* ~ grazed or
cut arm; **merobék** *v* to tear
up, shred

roboh, rubuh collapse;
pohon ~ tree that has been
blown down; **kerobohan** *n*
collapse; **merobohkan** *v* to
knock down, demolish

roda *n* wheel; ~ *gigi* cog;
~ *stir* steering wheel; *kendaraan* ~ *dua* two-wheeled
vehicles; **beroda** *adj*
wheeled

rodi *kerja* ~ forced labor

roh *n* spirit, ghost; **rohani**
adj spiritual, religious; *lagu*
~ *Chr* gospel or religious
song

rok *n* skirt; dress; ~ *mini*
miniskirt; ~ *pensil* straight
skirt

rokok *n* cigarette; ~ *kretek*

clove cigarette; *uang* ~ tip;
merokok *v* to smoke

roma *bulu* ~ body hair, hair
on the back of your neck

romansa *n* romance,
romantik *adj* romantic

Romawi, Rumawi *adj*
Roman; *huruf* ~ Roman
letters or numerals

rombak: merombak *v* to
pull down, demolish; to
reorganize; **perombakan** *n*
reorganization

rombong: rombongan *n*
group, party

romo, Romo *n, pron, Cath*
(Catholic) priest, Father

rompak: merompak *v* to
commit piracy; **perompak**
n pirate

rompi *n* waistcoat, vest

romusa, romusya *n* forced
laborer under the Japanese
occupation

rona *n* color, shade; **perona**
~ *mata* eyeshadow; ~ *pipi*
rouge

ronda patrol; ~ *malam*
night watch, night patrol

ronde *n* round (in sport)

rondé *wedang* ~ Javanese
warm drink

rongga *n* cavity, hollow, hole

rongkong → **kerong-kongan**

ronsen → **rontgen**

ronta: meronta(-ronta) *v* to struggle, squirm to get loose

rontak → **berontak**

rontgen [ronsen], **ronsen** *n* x-ray; *hasil* ~ x-ray (photograph); **dironsen** *v* to be x-rayed

rontok fall out, shed; *musim* ~ autumn, fall

rosario *n, Cath* rosary

rosot: merosot *v* to fall down, descend, plummet; **kemerosotan** *n* descent, deterioration; **perosotan** *n* (children's) slide

rotan *n* rattan; *kursi* ~ wicker chair

roti *n* bread, bun; ~ *gandum* (brown or wholemeal) bread; ~ *kismis* currant bun; ~ *panggang* toast; *tempat* ~ bread basket, bread bin

royal *adj* extravagant, wasteful (with money)

Rp. rupiah

RRC *abbrev Republik Rak-yat Cina* People's Republic of China

RRI *abbrev Radio Republik Indonesia* Indonesian state radio

RS *abbrev rumah sakit* hospital

RSJ *abbrev Rumah Sakit Jiwa* mental hospital

RSU *abbrev Rumah Sakit Umum* public hospital

RT/RW *abbrev Rukun Tetangga/Rukun Warga* neighborhood association/citizens' association

ruang *n* space, room; ~ *angkasa* outer space; ~ *kelas* classroom; ~ *makan* dining room; ~ *periksa* consultation room; ~ *tunggu* waiting room; **ruangan** *n* room; hall

ruas *n* space between joints; ~ *jari* knucklebone, phalanx

rubah *n* fox

rubuh collapse, fall down ← **roboh**

rudal *n* guided missile ← **peluru kendali**

rugi loss, lose out; *untung* ~ gains and losses, pros and

285

cons; **kerugian** n loss;
damage; **merugikan** v to
hurt, harm, injure

rujak n fruit salad with
spicy sauce; ~ *cingur* fruit
salad with beef snout

rujuk reconciliation (after
separation)

rujuk: rujukan n reference;
merujuk v to refer to, use
as a source

rukan n office with a dwelling upstairs, shophouse ←
rumah kantor

ruko n shophouse ←
rumah toko

rukun *adj* harmonious;
~ *warga (RW)* citizens'
association; ~ *tetangga
(RT)* neighborhood
association; *hidup* ~ live
in harmony

rukun n pillar, principle; *lima*
~ *Islam* five pillars of Islam

rumah n house; ~ *gadai*
pawnshop; ~ *hantu* haunted
house; ~ *jabatan* official
residence; ~ *keong* snail's
shell; ~ *lelang* auction
house; ~ *makan* restaurant;
~ *panjang* (Dayak) long-
house; ~ *sakit* hospital; ~

sakit jiwa mental hospital,
asylum; ~ *sewa* rented
house; *di* ~ at home; *isi* ~
household, people in a
house; ~ *tangga* household,
family; **berumah tangga**
adj married; **perumahan** n
housing (complex)

rumbai n tassel

rumbia n sago palm; sago
palm thatch

rumpun: serumpun *adj*
related, of one family;
bahasa ~ languages related
to Indonesian

rumput n grass, lawn;
~ *kering* hay

rumus n formula

runcing *adj* sharp, pointed;
bambu ~ bamboo spear;
meruncing v to become
critical or sharp

runding: berunding v to
discuss; **merundingkan** v
to discuss something,
deliberate over; **perun-
dingan** n discussion; *meja*
~ discussion table

runtuh fall down, collapse;
runtuhan, reruntuhan n
ruins; **meruntuhkan** v to
overthrow

runtun: beruntun *adj* in a chain; *tabrakan* ~ pile-up

rupa shape, appearance, look; ~*nya* it seems, appears; **rupa-rupa** *adj* all kinds of; **berupa** *adj* in the shape or form of; **merupakan** *v* to be, to form, constitute; **rupawan** good-looking (person); **serupa** *adj* similar

rupiah *n* rupiah, Indonesian currency

rusa *n* deer

rusak *adj* broken, damaged, destroyed, spoilt; ~ *parah* badly damaged; **kerusakan** *n* damage; **merusak** *v* to spoil, damage; **merusakkan** *v* to destroy, break

Rusia *n* Russia; *bahasa* ~, *orang* ~ Russian

rusuh restless, disturbed; **kerusuhan** *n* riot, disturbance

rusuk *n* flank, side; *tulang* ~ rib

rute *n* route

rutin *adj* routine; **rutinitas** *n* routineness, boredom

ruwet *adj* complicated

S

saat *n* moment, time; ~ *ini* at this moment

sabar *adj* patient; *tidak* ~ impatient; **bersabar** *v* to be patient; **kesabaran** *n* patience

sabda *n, pol* word; ~ *Tuhan* the word of God

sabit *n* sickle; *bulan* ~ crescent moon

sablon *n* screen-printed cloth banner; screen-printing

sabot: menyabot, menyabotase *v* to sabotage; **sabotase** *n* sabotage

Sabtu *hari* ~ Saturday

sabuk *n* belt, sash; ~ *hitam* black belt (in martial arts); ~ *pengaman* safety belt, seat belt

sabun *n* soap; ~ *colek* liquid soap for scrubbing clothes; ~ *cuci piring* dish-washing liquid; *opera* ~ soap opera

sabung ~ *ayam* cock fighting

sabut ~ *kelapa* coconut fiber

sadap: sadapan *n* something tapped; **menyadap** *v*

to tap (rubber, telephones);
penyadap *n* tapper;
penyadapan *n* tapping

sadar conscious, aware;
tidak ~ unconscious; **kesadaran** *n* consciousness,
awareness; **menyadari** *v* to
realize, be aware of

sadis *adj* sadistic, cruel

sado *n* two-wheeled horse
carriage

sadur, saduran *n* plating,
coating; ~ *emas* gold-
plated, gilt

sadur: saduran *n* adaptation, rewrite; **menyadur** *v*
to rewrite, adapt

safari *n* safari, tour

safir *batu* ~ sapphire

sagu *n* sago

sah *adj* legal, legitimate,
valid; *tidak* ~ illegal,
illegitimate; **mengesah-
kan** *v* to validate, ratify,
legitimize, legalize

sahabat *n* friend; ~ *pena*
pen friend, penpal; **bersahabat** *adj* to be friends;
persahabatan *n* friendship

sahaja, bersahaja *adj*
simple, natural; **kesahaja-
an** *n* simplicity ← **saja**

saham *n* share; *main* ~ play
the share market

sahur, saur *n, Isl* meal
before dawn during fasting
month

sahut, menyahut *v* to
answer, reply, respond

saing compete; **saingan** *n*
competitor, the competi-
tion; **bersaing** *v* to compete; **menyaingi** *v* to compete with; **persaingan** *n*
competition; ~ *ketat* intense
competition

saja, aja *adv* only, just;
-ever; *itu* ~ just that ←
sahaja

sajadah, sejadah *n, Isl*
prayer mat or rug

sajak *n* rhyme; poem

saji serve; *siap* ~ ready to
serve, ready to eat; **sajian** *n*
dish; offering; **sesajén** *n*
ritual offering; **menyajikan**
v to serve, present, offer

Saka *Tahun* ~ Balinese
calendar

sakelar *n* (electric) switch

saking *conj, coll* all
because of, due to, as a
result of

sakit sick, ill; pain, ache; ~

gigi toothache; ~ *hati* offended, hurt; ~ *kepala* headache; ~ *keras* gravely ill; ~ *perut* stomach ache, upset stomach; ~*sakitan* often ill, frequently unwell; **kesakitan** *adj* in pain; **menyakiti** *v* to hurt, treat badly; **menyakitkan** *adj* painful; **penyakit** *n* disease, illness, complaint; ~ *jiwa* mental problem; ~ *gula* diabetes; ~ *menular seksual (PMS)* sexually transmitted disease (STD), venereal disease

sakral *adj* holy, sacred

saksi witness; ~ *mata* eyewitness; **bersaksi** *v* to testify; **kesaksian** *n* evidence, testimony; **menyaksikan** *v* to witness

saksofon *n* saxophone

sakti *adj* magically or supernaturally powerful; **kesaktian** *n* magic power

saku *n* pocket

salah *adj* wrong, mistaken, faulty; ~ *alamat* wrong address, wrong person; ~ *cetak* misprint; ~ *faham* misunderstanding; ~ *satu*

one of; ~ *sambung* wrong number; ~ *urat* strained muscle; *kalau tidak* ~ if I'm not mistaken; **bersalah** *adj* guilty; **kesalahan** *n* mistake; **menyalahkan, mempersalahkan** *v* to blame

salak *buah* ~ fruit with a hard brown skin like a snake, snakefruit

salam peace; ~ *alaikum Isl* peace be upon you; ~ *hormat* respectfully yours, yours sincerely; ~ *saya* best wishes, regards; **menyalami** *v* to greet

saldo *n* balance; ~ *terakhir* current balance

saléh → **soléh**

salep *n* ointment, cream

salib *n* cross

salin copy, duplicate; *baju* ~ change of clothes, spare clothes; **salinan** *n* copy; **bersalin** *v* to give birth; *rumah sakit* ~ maternity hospital; **menyalin** *v* to copy; **persalinan** *n* childbirth

saling *pron* each other, mutual; ~ *mencintai* to love each other

salip, menyalip v overtake, slip past

salju n snow; *main ~* play in the snow; *manusia ~* snowman; **bersalju** adj snowy, snow-covered

salon n beauty salon, hairdresser's

salto n somersault

salur: saluran n channel; *~ pernafasan* windpipe, esophagus; **menyalurkan** v to channel; **penyaluran** n channelling

salut v, coll to admire, salute

sama adj, adv same, both; *~ sekali* neg completely; *~ rata* equal, level; **sama-sama** you're welcome; adv both, equally; **bersama** adv together; jointly; **menyamakan** v to equate, consider the same; **persamaan** n similarity, likeness, resemblance; equation; **sesama** adj fellow, another; *~ manusia* fellow human being

samar: samaran n disguise, alias; *nama ~* pseudonym, alias; **menyamar** v to be in disguise

sama-sama you're welcome; adv both, equally ← **sama**

sambal, sambel n chilli sauce; *~ ulek* fresh(ly ground) chilli sauce

sambar: menyambar v to pounce on, strike

sambil v, aux while, at the same time; *~ lalu* in passing

sambung connect; **sambung-menyambung** adj continuously; **sambungan** n connection; **bersinambung** adj continuous; **bersambung** adj in parts; to be continued; **menyambung** v to join, continue; **menyambungkan** v to connect to (something else); **tersambung** adj connected

sambut welcome; **sambutan** n reception, welcome; **bersambut, menyambut** v to welcome or receive; **penyambutan** n welcoming, welcome ceremony

samenléven v to live together (outside marriage) → **kumpul kebo**

sampah n rubbish, garbage,

trash, waste; *tempat* ~ rubbish bin, garbage can, trashcan; *tukang* ~ garbage man

sampai, sampé arrive, reach; until; ~ *dengan* to, until, up to the point of, as far as; ~ *jumpa,* ~ *nanti* see you later; **kesampaian** *adj* achieved, reached, realized; **menyampaikan** *v* to deliver, hand over, pass on

sampanye *n* champagne

samping *n* side; *dari* ~ *ke* ~ from side to side; *di* ~ next to, beside(s); **sampingan** *n* side-job, extra work; **bersampingan** *adj* next to each other; **menyampingi** *v* to escort, accompany, flank

sampo *n* shampoo; ~ *anti-ketombe* anti-dandruff shampoo

sampul *n* cover, folder, envelope; **bersampul** *adj* in an envelope or folder

samudera, samudra *n* ocean; ~ *Atlantik* Atlantic Ocean; ~ *Hindia,* ~ *Indonesia* Indian Ocean

sana *adv* yonder, over there (far from speaker and

listener); *di* ~ over there (far from both speaker and listener); ~*-sini* here and there

sanak ~ *saudara* relatives, family

sanatorium *n* sanatorium (esp for respiratory illnesses)

sanca *ular* ~ python

sandal *n* sandals (open-toed shoes); ~ *jepit* thongs, flip flops

sandar: sandaran *n* support, prop; ~ *kursi* chair back; **bersandar, menyandar** *v* to lean

sandera *n* hostage; **menyandera** *v* to take hostage; **penyanderaan** *n* taking of hostages

sandi *n* code, cipher; ~ *rahasia, nomor* ~ secret code

sandiwara *n* drama, play; **bersandiwara** *v* to pretend

sandung: sandungan *batu* ~ stumbling block; **tersandung** *adj* to stumble on, trip (up) on

sang *pref, pol* used to denote respect; ~ *Merah Putih* the Red and White (Indonesian flag)

sangat *adv* very, extremely; *amat* ~ terribly

sanggama, senggama *n* sexual relations; **ber-sanggama** *v* to have sex

sanggar *n* workshop, studio

sanggul *n* bun (worn with women's national costume); **bersanggul** *v* to wear a bun; **disanggul** *v* to have your hair put into a bun

sanggup *v, aux* to be able to, to be capable of

sangka *v* to guess, suspect; **sangkaan** *n* suspicion; **bersangka** *v* to suspect or think; ~ *buruk* to think the worst; **menyangka** *v* to suspect, suppose, presume; *tidak* ~ never thought; **ter-sangka** *n (yang)* ~ suspect

sangkal, menyangkal *v* to deny

sangkar *n* cage

sangkut ~ *paut* connection, link; **bersangkutan** *adj* concerned, involved; *yang* ~ *(ybs)* person concerned or involved; **menyangkut** *v* to involve, concern; *conj* about; **tersangkut** *adj* involved; caught, snagged

sanjung: menyanjung *v* to flatter; **tersanjung** *adj* flattered

sanksi *n* disciplinary action, sanction

Sansekerta, Sanskerta *bahasa* ~ Sanskrit

santa *tit, f, Chr* Saint; **santo** *tit, m, Chr* Saint

santai *adj* relaxed, easy-going, informal

santan *n* coconut milk (used in cooking)

santap, bersantap *v, pol* to eat, partake of; **santapan** *n* meal, dish, food

santer *adj* strong, rife

santét *n* black magic; *dukun* ~ witchdoctor, sorcerer; **disantét** *v* to have spells cast on you, be a victim of black magic

santo *tit, m, Chr* Saint

santri *n* student at an Islamic school (esp a boarder); strict Muslim; **pesantrén** *n* Islamic boarding school

santun *adj* polite, well-mannered; **santunan** *n* benefit, compensation (from insurance)

saos → **saus**

sapa greet; **sapaan** n greeting; **menyapa** v to greet

sapi n cow; ~ *perah* dairy cow; endless source; *anak* ~ calf; *susu* ~ cow's milk

sapta *pref* seven

sapu broom; ~ *tangan* handkerchief, hanky; *tukang* ~ cleaner, sweeper; **menyapu** v to sweep or wipe

saput: tersaput ~ *awan* clouded over

SARA *adj* communal, sectarian; related to ethnicity, religion, race or socioeconomic group ← **suku agama ras antargolongan**

saraf n nerve; *penyakit* ~ nervous disorder

saran n suggestion; ~ *saya* I suggest, my suggestion; **menyarankan** v to suggest

sarana n facility, means; ~ *umum* public amenity; *pra*~ infrastructure

sarang n nest; ~ *lebah* beehive; ~ *burung* bird's nest

sarap: sarapan n breakfast

sarat → **syarat**

sardin, sardén *ikan* ~ sardine

sari n essence, extract; flower; ~ *bunga* pollen

sariawan, seriawan (mouth) ulcer, have an ulcer

saring filter; **saringan** n filter, sieve; **menyaring** v to filter (through), screen, select; **penyaringan** n filtration, screening

sarjana n university graduate; ~ *ekonomi* economics graduate; ~ *muda* undergraduate

sarung n sarong; cover, case; ~ *bantal* pillowcase, pillowslip

Sasak ethnic group of Lombok; *bahasa* ~, *orang* ~ Sasak

sasana n boxing stadium

sasando n harp-like musical instrument from Timor

sasar: sasaran n target; **menyasar** v, **kesasar** *coll* to lose your way, (get) lost

sastra n literature; ~ *Indonesia* Indonesian literature; **kesusasteraan, kesusastraan** n literature; **sastrawan** n literary figure

sate, satai n satay, kebab; ~ *ayam* chicken satay; ~ *ke-*

linci rabbit satay; ~ *kambing* goat satay

satpam *n* security guard ← **satuan pengamanan**

satu *adj* one; ~ *sama lain* each other; ~ *per* ~ one by one; **satu-satu** *adv* one by one, individually; ~*nya* the only; **satuan** *n* unit; **bersatu** *v* to be united; **kesatu** *adj, sl* first; **kesatuan** *n* unity; **menyatu** *v* to become one; **menyatukan, mempersatukan** *v* to unite various things; **pemersatu** *n* unifying agent, unifier; **persatuan** *n* union, association

satwa *n* animal, fauna

saudara *n* family (member); sibling, brother, sister; *pron* you; brother, sister; ~ *angkat* person considered family; ~ *perempuan* sister; ~ *sepupu* cousin; *hubungan* ~ family relationship; **bersaudara** *v* to be related; to have brothers and sisters; **persaudaraan** *n* brotherhood, fraternity; sisterhood; family ties; **saudari** *pron, f* you, sister;

~ *saudara*~ brothers and sisters

sauh *n* anchor; *membuang* ~ to cast anchor

oauna *n* sauna; small steaming box in a salon

saung *n* open-air restaurant by a fish-pond, esp in West Java

saus, saos *n* sauce, gravy; ~ *tomat* tomato sauce

sawah *n* (irrigated or wet) rice paddy, ricefield

sawi *n* bok choy, mustard greens; green leafy vegetable; ~ *putih* Chinese cabbage

sawo *n* brown, sweet fruit; sapodilla; ~ *matang* brown-skinned

saya *pron* I, me, my; ~ *sendiri* I (myself); *kepada* ~ to me; *komputer* ~ my computer

sayang pity, regret; love; *pron* darling; ~*ku* my darling; ~ *sekali* what a pity; **kesayangan** favorite, pet; **menyayangi** *v* to love; **tersayang** *adj* dear, dearest

sayap *n* wing; ~ *kiri* left-wing; ~ *roda* mudguard, fender; **bersayap** *adj* winged

sayat: sayatan *n* slice; ~ *daging* slice of meat

sayembara *n* contest, competition

sayup: sayup-sayup *adv* faintly; ~ *kedengaran* faintly audible

sayur *n* vegetable; ~ *asem* sour vegetable soup; ~ *hijau* greens, green vegetables; ~ *lodeh* vegetables in coconut milk; ~ *mayur* (all kinds of) vegetables; **sayur-sayuran** *n* vegetables

SD *abbrev Sekolah Dasar* primary/elementary school

SDM *abbrev sumber daya manusia* human resources

seadanya *adj* what's there; *makan* ~ eat what's there ← **ada**

seakan-akan *conj* as if, as though ← **akan**

seandainya *conj* supposing, if ← **andai**

searah *adj* the same direction ← **arah**

sebab *n* reason, cause; *conj* because; ~*nya* the reason is, the reason being; **menye-**

babkan *v* to cause; **penyebab** *n* cause

sebagai *conj* like, as

sebagian *n* some, a section of ← **bagi**

sebaiknya *adv* preferably, it's best if ← **baik**

sebal *adj* fed up, annoyed, cheesed off; **menyebalkan** *adj* annoying, tiresome

sebaliknya *adv* on the contrary, on the other hand ← **balik**

sebar: menyebarluaskan *v* to disseminate, spread something; **menyebarkan** *v* to spread, distribute; **penyebar** *n* carrier, infectious person

sebaya *adj* of the same age ← **baya**

sebelah *prep* next to; *n* half, side; ~ *mana* which side, where; *(di)* ~ *kanan* on the right (side); *rumah* ~ next door ← **belah**

sebelas *adj* eleven ← **belas**

sebelum *prep* before; ~ *Masehi (SM)* BC, before Christ; ~ *waktunya* prematurely; **sebelumnya** *adj*

previously, before(hand)
← **belum**

sebenarnya *adv* in fact,
actually ← **benar**

sebentar *n* a moment, minute, while; ~ *lagi* in a few
minutes, soon

seberang *prep* other side,
across; *negeri* ~ overseas,
foreign country; **menye-
berang** *v* to cross; **penyeberangan** *n* crossing

seberapa *tidak* ~ not much,
not many ← **apa**

sebetulnya *adv* in fact,
actually ← **betul**

sebisanya, sebisa-bisanya
adv as well as you can, to
the best of your ability ←
bisa

sebuah *adj* a, one (generic
counter); ~ *kursi* a chair
← **buah**

sebut mention; ~ *saja* take
(for instance); **sebutan** *n*
mention; **menyebut** *v* to
mention, name, say;
disebut-sebut *v* to be
frequently mentioned;
tersebut *adj* (afore)men-
tioned, said

secara *adv* in a way; used

to form adverbs; ~ *curang*
dishonestly → **cara**

secepat *conj* as fast as;
~ *mungkin*, **secepat-
(-cepat)nya** *adv* as fast as
possible ← **cepat**

secubit *n* pinch ← **cubit**

secukupnya *adj* sufficient,
adequate ← **cukup**

sedak: tersedak *adj*
choking

sedan: tersedan-sedan
adj sobbing

sedang *aux* while, -ing;
~ *tidur* sleeping; **sedangkan** *conj* whereas, while

sedang *adj* medium,
moderate

sedangkan *conj* whereas,
while ← **sedang**

sedap *adj* delicious, tasty

sedapatnya *adv* what you
can get ← **dapat**

sedekah *n* alms, charity,
handout; **bersedekah** *v* to
make a donation

sederhana *adj* simple,
plain; *rumah sangat* ~
(RSS) basic housing;
menyederhanakan *v* to
simplify

sedia ready, prepared;

willing; **bersedia** v to be prepared or willing; **kesediaan** n readiness, willingness; **menyediakan** v to prepare, get ready; **persediaan** n stock, supply; **tersedia** adj available, prepared

sedih adj sad; **bersedih** v to be or feel sad; **kesedihan** n sadness, sorrow; **menyedihkan** adj depressing, sad

sedikit adj a little, a few, a bit; ~ banyak at least, some; ~ demi ~ bit by bit, gradually; ~nya lack, paucity ← **dikit**

sedot suck; **sedotan** n straw; **menyedot** v to suck (up)

sedu sob; ~ sedan sobs; **tersedu-sedu** v to sob, sniffle

seénaknya adv, neg just how you like, at will ← **énak**

segala adj all, every; ~ sesuatu all (kinds of); **segala-galanya** n everything, the lot

segan adj reluctant, averse; **disegani** v to be respected

segar adj fresh; ~ bugar fit and healthy; **menyegarkan** adj refreshing; **penyegar** minuman ~ tonic, energy drink

ségel seal, stamp; **menyégel** v to seal (off), close (a building)

segenap adj each, all ← **genap**

segera adv immediately, directly; soon; ~ dibuka opening soon; dengan ~ express, immediately

segi n side, angle; point of view; ~ empat square, rectangle; ~ tiga triangle; dari ~ from the point of view of; **persegi** adj square, rectangular; ~ empat square, rectangle

segini → **ini**

segitu → **itu**

sehabis conj after ← **habis**

seharga adj of equal value, the same price ← **harga**

sehari-hari adv every day, daily; **seharian** adv, coll all day ← **hari**

seharusnya should ← **harus**

séhat *adj* healthy; **kesé-hatan** *n* health

sehingga *conj* until, to the point that, as far as; so that ← **hingga**

seimbang *adj* balanced, well-proportioned ← **imbang**

sejadah → **sajadah**

sejahtera *adj* prosperous; **kesejahteraan** *n* welfare

sejajar *adj* parallel ← **jajar**

sejak, semenjak *conj* since, from the time when

sejarah *n* history; **berseja-rah** *adj* historic, historical

sejati *adj* original, genuine, real ← **jati**

sejauh *conj* how far; ~ *mana* to what point ← **jauh**

sejenak *adv* briefly, a moment ← **jenak**

sejenis *adj* of the same type or species ← **jenis**

sejoli *dua* ~ a couple ← **joli**

sejuk *adj* cool; **kesejukan** *n* coolness; **menyejukkan** *adj* cooling, refreshing

sekadar *adj* just; ~*nya* as necessary ← **kadar**

sekali *adv* very; *indah* ~ very beautiful

sekali *adv* once; ~ *waktu* once upon a time; *jangan* ~~*kali* never (do this); **sekali-sekali, sesekali** *adv* every now and then, occasionally

sekalian *adv* all together, all at once; *adv, coll* at the same time ← **kali**

sekaligus *adv* all at once ← **kali**

sekalipun *conj* even though ← **kali**

sekali-sekali *adv* every now and then, occasionally ← **kali**

sekarang *adv* now, at present; ~ *ini* nowadays; ~ *juga* immediately

sekarat *adj* dying

sekat bar, block, partition

Sekatén *n* folk festival in Jogjakarta celebrating the Prophet Muhammad's birthday

sekawan *tiga* ~ a trio (of friends) ← **kawan**

sekejap *n* moment, flash, blink; *dalam* ~ *mata* in a moment, in the twinkling of an eye ← **kejap**

séken *adj, coll* second-hand

sekian *adv* so much, this much; ~ *banyak* so many, so much; ~ *dulu* that's all for now ← **kian**

sekilas *n* flash, glance ← **kilas**

sekitar *prep* around; *adv* around; near; **sekitarnya** *di* ~ around (a place); *dan* ~ and environs ← **kitar**

sékjén *n* secretary-general ← **sékretaris jénderal**

Séknég *n* State Secretary, Minister of the Interior ← **Sékretaris Negara**

sekolah *n* school; institute of learning; ~ *Dasar (SD)* primary school, elementary school; ~ *kejuruan* vocational school, technical college; ~ *luar biasa* special school; ~ *menengah* secondary school, high school; ~ *menengah atas (SMA)* senior high school; ~ *perawat* nursing school; ~ *tinggi* college; *alat-alat* ~ school supplies; *kepala* ~ principal; **bersekolah** *v* to go to school; **menyekolah-kan** *v* to send to school

sekongkol, bersekongkol

v to plot, conspire against; **persekongkolan** *n* plot, intrigue, conspiracy ← **kongkol**

sekop, skop *n* spade, shovel; spades (in cards)

sékretariat *n* secretariat; **sékretaris** *n* secretary; ~ *jenderal (sekjen)* secretary-general

sekrup *n* screw

séks *n* sex; *hubungan* ~ sexual relations, sexual intercourse; **séksual** *adj* sexual

seksama, saksama *adj* careful, thorough, detailed

séksi *n* section

séksi *adj* sexy ← **seks**

sékte *n* sect

séktor *n* sector

sekurangnya, sekurang-kurangnya *adv* at least ← **kurang**

sekuriti *n* security

sekutu *n* partner, ally; **bersekutu** *v* to be allies; **persekutuan** *n* alliance, partnership

sékwilda *n* provincial secretary ← **sékretaris wilayah daérah**

sél *n* cell

sela *n* gap, pause

selada, salada, salat *n* salad; lettuce

selai *n* jam; ~ *jeruk* marmalade; ~ *kacang* peanut butter

selain *conj* except, besides, apart from ← **lain**

selaku *conj* as, in the capacity of ← **laku**

selalu *adv* always ← **lalu**

selam diving; *baju* ~ diving suit; **menyelam** *v* to dive; **penyelam** *n* diver

selama *conj* during, as long as; **selamanya** *adv* always, forever ← **lama**

selamat safe; congratulations; ~ *berbahagia* congratulations (at a wedding); ~ *datang* welcome; ~ *jalan* goodbye; bon voyage, have a safe trip; ~ *malam* good evening; ~ *sore* good afternoon; ~ *tidur* good night; ~ *tinggal* goodbye; ~ *ulang tahun* happy birthday; happy anniversary; *dengan* ~ safe and sound; *memberi* ~ to congratulate; **selamatan** *n* (thanksgiving)

feast; **keselamatan** *n* safety; salvation; **menyelamatkan** *v* to save, rescue; **penyelamatan** *n* rescue (operation)

selambat-lambatnya *adv* at the latest ← **lambat**

selancar *papan* ~ surfboard; **berselancar** *v* to surf, go surfing ← **lancar**

Sélandia Baru *n* New Zealand

selang *n* interval; ~ *sehari* every other day, every second day; **berselang** *adj* with an interval of; ~~-*seling* alternating

selang *n* hose

selanjutnya *adv* then, after that ← **lanjut**

selaput *n* membrane; ~ *dara* hymen

selaras *adj* harmonious, in harmony; **keselarasan** *n* harmony ← **laras**

Selasa *hari* ~ Tuesday

selat *n* strait; ~ *Malaka* the Straits of Malacca

selatan *adj* south; *Sumatera* ~ South Sumatra; *daerah* ~ southern region, the south

selayaknya *adv* properly,

should ← **layak**

selebaran *n* leaflet, brochure, newsletter

sélébritis, séléb *n* celebrity

selédri *n* celery

séléksi *n* selection; *lolos* ~ be selected

seléndang, sléndang *n* shawl; sash worn over the shoulder with women's national costume

selenggara: menyeleng-garakan *v* to run, hold, organize; **penyelenggara** *n* organizer

selepas *prep, conj* after ← **lepas**

seléra *n* appetite, taste; ~ *tinggi* good taste; expensive tastes; **berseléra** *v* to have a taste or appetite for

selesai finished, over; **menyelesaikan** *v* to finish, end, settle; ~ *masalah* to overcome a problem; **penyelesaian** *n* solution, settlement

selesma, selésma having a cold; cold

seléwéng: menyeléwéng *v* to deviate; to have an affair; **penyeléwéngan** *n* affair, deviation

selidik: menyelidiki *v* to investigate; **penyelidik** *n* investigator, detective; **penyelidikan** *n* investigation

selimut *n* blanket; **menye-limuti** *v* to (cover with a) blanket

seling: selingan *n* change, break

selingkuh, berselingkuh *v* to have an affair; **per-selingkuhan** *n* affair

selip: menyelip *v* to slip; **menyelipkan** *v* to slip an object (into something); **terselip** *adj* fallen or slipped into

selisih *n* difference; **perselisihan** *n* dispute, difference of opinion

selok: selokan *n* ditch, trench

selonjor sit with legs sticking out in front; **berselonjor** *adj* with outstretched legs

selop *n* slipper

seloroh: berseloroh *v* to joke

selot: diselot *v* to be bolted

sélotip *n* sellotape, adhesive or sticky tape

selubung: menyelubungi
v to veil or cover

seluk ~ *beluk* ins and outs,
details

selundup: selundupan
barang ~ contraband,
smuggled goods; **menye-
lundup** *v* to sneak in illegally, infiltrate; **menyelundupkan** *v* to smuggle (in);
penyelundup *n* smuggler

seluruh *adj* entire, whole; ~
dunia all over the world;
seluruhnya *adv* completely;
adj all; **keseluruhan**
secara ~ totally, completely

selusin *n* a dozen ← **lusin**

semacam *adj* a kind or
type of ← **macam**

semak shrub, bush; ~
belukar scrub; **semak-
semak** *n* bush(land), scrub

semakin *adv* even more
← **makin**

semak-semak *n* bush(land),
scrub ← **semak**

semalam *adv* last night;
semalaman *adv* all night
long ← **malam**

semampai *tinggi* ~ tall and
slender

semangat *n* spirit, enthusi-

asm; *kurang* ~ lacking
enthusiasm; **bersemangat**
adj spirited, enthusiastic

semanggi *n* clover leaf

semangka *n* watermelon

semat, menyematkan *v* to
pin, fasten with pins

sembah *n* homage, tribute,
respect; **menyembah** *v* to
pay homage to, worship;
mempersembahkan *v* to
offer (up), present; **persembahan** *n* offering;
product or service

sembahyang pray, prayer;
bersembahyang *v* to pray,
perform a prayer

sembako *n* nine daily
necessities ← **sembilan
bahan pokok**

sembarang *adj* any, whichever; **sembarangan** *adj*
arbitrary, random

sembelih: menyembelih *v*
to slaughter, butcher; **penyembelih** *n* butcher,
slaughterer; **penyembelihan** *n* slaughter

sembelit constipation,
constipated

sembilan *adj* nine; ~ *belas*
nineteen; ~ *puluh* ninety

semboyan *n* motto, slogan

sembrono *adj* thoughtless, reckless

sembuh recovered, better; *cepat ~*, get well soon; **menyembuhkan** *v* to cure, heal; **penyembuhan** *n* cure, healing

sembunyi hide, conceal; **sembunyi-sembunyi** *adv* secretly, in secret; **bersembunyi** *v* to hide (yourself); **menyembunyikan** *v* to hide or conceal something; **persembunyian** *n* hiding place, hideout

sembur: semburan *n* spout, fountain; outpouring; *~ air panas* geyser; **menyemburkan** *v* to spit or spray something out

semén *n* (wet) cement

semenanjung *n* peninsula; *~ Melayu* Malaya, the Malay Peninsula

semenjak, sejak *conj* since

sementara *conj* during; *adj* temporary; *~ itu* in the meantime, meanwhile; *buat ~, untuk ~* for the time being

semestinya should have

(been) ← **mesti**

semi: bersemi *v* to sprout buds

seminggu *adj* a week ← **minggu**

semir polish; *~ sepatu* shoe polish; *tukang ~* shoeshine boy; **menyemir** *v* to polish

semoga may, hopefully ← **moga**

sempat chance, opportunity; *kalau ~* when possible; *tidak ~* not get the chance to; **kesempatan** *n* opportunity; **menyempatkan** *~ diri* to make time to

sempit *adj* narrow; **berpikiran** *~* narrow-minded; **kesempitan** *n* narrowness; **menyempit** *v* to (become) narrow

sempoa *n* abacus

semprot squirt; spurt; **semprotan** *n* spray-gun; **menyemprot** *v* to spray; **menyemprotkan** *v* to spray with something

sempurna *adj* perfect, complete; **menyempurnakan** *v* to perfect, complete

semrawut *adj* haphazard, uncontrolled

semu *adj* false, apparent

semua *adj* all; ~*nya* all, everyone

semula *adv* originally ← **mula**

semur *n* meat or tofu dish with soy sauce

semut *n* ant; **kesemutan** *v* to have pins and needles

sén cent

senam *n* gymnastics, aerobics; exercise; ~ *hamil* pre-natal exercises; ~ *pagi* morning exercise; *baju* ~ leotard

senandung hum; **bersenandung** *v* to hum, sing

senang *adj* happy, content; *v* to like; ~ *nonton TV* to like watching TV; **bersenang-senang** *v* to enjoy yourself, have fun; **kesenangan** *n* amusement, hobby; **menyenangkan** *adj* pleasing, agreeable

senantiasa *adv* always

senapan *n* rifle

sénat *n* senate; ~ *mahasiswa* student council

senda ~ *gurau* joke; **bersenda** ~ *gurau* to joke around

sendat: tersendat *adj* jammed, blocked

sendawa: bersendawa *v* to burp, belch

sendi *n* joint; **persendian** *n* joints

sendiri *adv* alone; *pron* self; *salah* ~ it's your own fault; *dengan* ~*nya* automatic, by itself; **sendiri-sendiri** *adv, pl* alone, individually; **sendirian** *adv* alone, single-handedly; **menyendiri** *v* to go off by yourself; **tersendiri** *adj* its own; apart, separate ← **diri**

séndok *n* spoon; ~ *makan* (dessert)spoon; ~ *teh* teaspoon; ~ *garpu* spoon and fork

Senén → Senin

séng *n* zinc

sengaja *adv* deliberately, on purpose; *tidak* ~ unintentionally

sengat sting; **sengatan** *n* sting, bite; **menyengat** *v* to sting

senggama → sanggama

senggang *adj* free, unoccupied

304

sénggol brush, bump; *pasar* ~ crowded market; **bersénggolan** *v* to bump into each other; **menyénggol** *v* to bump, brush, tweak; **tersénggol** *adj* bumped, brushed

sengkéta *n* dispute; *tanah* ~ disputed land

sengsara misery; **kesengsaraan** *n* torture, misery, suffering

sengsem: kesengsem *adj, coll* engrossed in, absorbed with

seni *n* art; ~ *lukis* painting; ~ *pahat* sculpture; ~ *peran* drama; *nilai* ~ artistic value; **kesenian** *n* art (form); **seniman** *n, m* **seniwati** *n, f* artist

seni *air* ~ urine

Senin, Senén *hari* ~ Monday

sénior *n* person in higher class or of higher position

senja *n* twilight, dusk

senjata *n* weapon; ~ *api* firearm, gun; **senjata** *adj* armed

sénsasi *n* sensation; **sénsasional** *adj* sensational

sénsor *n* censor; *kena* ~, **disensor** censored; **menyénsor** *v* to censor, cut out

sénsus *n* census

sentak: sentakan *n* jerk

sénter *n (lampu)* ~ flashlight, torch

sénti *n* centimeter, centimetre; *berapa* ~ how many centimeters, how long ← **séntiméter**

sentil: sentilan *n* flick, nudge

sentiméter, sénti *n* centimeter, centimetre

séntral central

sentuh touch; **sentuhan** *n* touch; **bersentuhan** *v* to touch each other; **menyentuh** *v* to touch; **tersentuh** *adj* touched

senyap *adj* quiet, still; *sunyi* ~ completely still or quiet

senyawa *n* compound; **bersenyawa** *v* to become a chemical compound

senyum smile

seorang a (person); counter for people; ~ *Arab* an Arab; ~ *diri* alone, single-handedly ← **orang**

sépak kick; ~ *bola* soccer,
football; ~ *bola Amerika*
gridiron; ~ *bola Australia*
Australian rules (football);
~ *takraw* game played with
a rattan ball; ~ *terjang* behavior, activity; **menyépak**
v to kick (out)

sepakat *v* to agree; **kesepakatan** *n* agreement;
menyepakati *v* to agree to
← **pakat**

sepanjang *conj, adj* as long
as; ~ *jalan* the whole way
← **panjang**

séparatis separatist; **sépa-
ratisme** *n* separatism

separo, separuh *n* half ←
paruh

sepasang *n* a pair of ←
pasang

sepatu *n* shoe; ~ *hak tinggi*
high heels; ~ *kets,* ~ *olahraga* running or sports
shoes, sneakers; ~ *lars,*
~ *bot* boots; ~ *roda* roller-
blades, rollerskates; ~
sandal sandals; **bersepatu**
adj in shoes

sepatutnya *adv* rightly,
properly ← **patut**

sepéda *n* bicycle, (push)-
bike; ~ *motor* motor bike;
naik ~ to ride a bike; **bersepéda** *v* to ride a bicycle

sepélé *adj* unimportant,
trifling; *hal* ~ trifle; **menyepélékan** *v* to make
light of, treat lightly

sepenuhnya *adv* fully,
completely ← **penuh**

seperempat *n* one quarter
← **empat**

seperti *conj* like; ~*nya* it
seems

sepertiga *adj* one-third
← **tiga**

sepésér *tidak ada* ~ *pun* to
have not even a cent ←
pésér

sepi *adj* quiet, still, lonely;
kesepian *n* loneliness,
solitude

sepihak *adj* unilateral ←
pihak

sepintas ~ *lalu* at first
glance ← **pintas**

sepoi: sepoi-sepoi *angin*
~ breeze, zephyr

seprei, seprai *n* (bed)sheet

Séptémber *bulan* ~
September

sepuh ~ *perak* silver plating; **sepuhan** *n* gilt

sepuh *adj, coll* elderly

sepuluh *n* ten ← **puluh**

sepupu *n* cousin ← **pupu**

sepur *n, coll* railway (line); rail; platform

seputar *adj* around, about ← **putar**

serabut *n* fiber, fibre

seragam *n* uniform ← **ragam**

serah hand over, transfer; ~ *terima* hand over to someone else; **menyerah** *v* to surrender, give in, give up; **menyerahkan** *v* to hand over; **penyerahan** *n* handing over, handover; **terserah** *adj* it depends; up to you

serai, séréh *n* lemon grass, citronella

serak *adj* hoarse

serakah *adj* greedy

seram *adj* weird, creepy

serambi *n* verandah

serang attack; **serangan** *n* attack, raid; ~ *fajar* dawn raid; **menyerang** *v* to attack; **penyerang** *n* attacker; **penyerangan** *n* attack, aggression

serangga *n* insect, bug

serap absorb; *daya* ~ absorbency; **menyerap** *v* to

absorb, soak up; **penyerapan** *n* absorption

serasi *adj* suited, compatible, harmonious ← **rasi**

serat *n* fiber, fibre; **berserat** *makanan* ~ high-fiber food

seratus *adj* one hundred, a hundred ← **ratus**

Serawak *n* Sarawak

serba *adj* all kinds of, various; ~*-serbi* all kinds of; ~ *salah* damned if you do, damned if you don't; wrong whatever you do

serban, sorban *n* turban

serbét *n* serviette, table napkin

serbu: **menyerbu** *v* to attack (as a group), charge, invade; **penyerbuan** *n* attack, charge, invasion

serbuk *n* powder; ~ *besi* iron filings; ~ *bunga* pollen; ~ *gergaji* sawdust

séréal *n* (breakfast) cereal

séréh, serai *n* lemon grass, citronella

serémpét: **menyerémpét** *v* to scrape, scratch against

serentak *adj* all at once, simultaneous, at the same time

307

sérep *adj* reserve, change

sérét, menyérét *v* to drag; **tersérét** *adj* dragged

seri *n* draw, tie

séri *n* series; *film ~* serial, series

seribu *adj* one thousand, a thousand ← **ribu**

serigala *n* wolf

serikat, sarékat, syarikat union, united; *~ buruh* labor union; **perserikatan** *n* federation; *~ Bangsa-Bangsa (PBB)* the United Nations (UN)

serikaya → **srikaya**

sering *adv* often, frequently; *~ sakit* sickly; **keseringan** *n* frequency; *adv* too often

sérius *adj* serious

séro *n* share; **perséro** *adj* proprietary limited (Pty Ltd); **perséroan** *n* company; *~ terbatas (PT)* proprietary limited (Pty Ltd)

serobot push in front; **menyerobot** *v* to push in front

seroja *(bunga) ~* kind of lotus

sérong *adj* on an angle, oblique

serpih, serpihan *n* shred, bit, piece; *~ kayu* wood chip

serta *conj* (together) with; *~-merta* automatically, immediately; **keikutsertaan** *n* participation; **beserta** *conj* along with, and; **menyertai** *v* to accompany; **peserta** *n* participant

sértifikat *n* certificate; **bersértifikat** *adj* with papers (of a house)

seru shout, call; *kata ~* exclamation; **seruan** *n* call, cry, exclamation; **berseru** *v* to call, cry; **menyerukan** *v* to call or appeal for

seru *adj* exciting, great

seruling, suling *n* flute

serumpun *adj* related, of one family; *bahasa ~* related languages ← **rumpun**

serupa *adj* similar; **menyerupai** *v* to resemble, be similar to ← **rupa**

sérvis *n* repairs, service, maintenance; **disérvis** *v* to be serviced

sesajén *n* ritual offering ← **saji**

sesak *adj* close, dense, crowded; ~ *dada*, ~ *napas* short of breath; asthmatic

sesal regret; **menyesal** *v* to regret; **menyesalkan** *v* to feel bad about, regret (another's action)

sesama *adj* fellow, another; ~ *manusia* fellow human being ← **sama**

sesat lost; **menyesatkan** *adj* misleading, confusing; **tersesat** *adj* lost

sesekali *adv* every now and then, occasionally ← **kali**

seseorang *n* somebody, a certain person ← **orang**

sesuai *adj* in accordance with, appropriate; **menyesuaikan** *v* to adapt, bring into line; **penyesuaian** *n* adaptation ← **suai**

sesuap *n* mouthful; ~ *nasi* a mouthful of rice; something to eat ← **suap**

sesuatu *n* something ← **suatu**

sesudah *prep* after; ~ *itu*, **sesudahnya** after that, then ← **sudah**

sesungguhnya *adv* actually, really ← **sungguh**

setahu *conj* as far as is known; ~ *saya* as far as I know ← **tahu**

sétan, syaitan *n* devil, demon; **persétan** *ejac* go to hell!

setasiun, stasiun, setasion *n* (railway) station; *kepala* ~ stationmaster

setél *n* set; **setélan** *n* set, suit

setél, menyétel *v* to tune, set, adjust; ~ *mesin mobil* to tune an engine; **penyetélan** *n* tuning

setelah *prep* after; ~ *itu* after that, then ← **telah**

setempat *adj* local ← **tempat**

setengah *adj* half; ~ *mati* half-dead; very hard; *jam* ~ *dua* half past one; **setengah-setengah** *adv* half-heartedly ← **tengah**

seterusnya *adv* after that, henceforth ← **terus**

setia *adj* faithful; ~ *kawan* solidarity; loyal; **kesetiakawanan** *n* solidarity; **kesetiaan** *n* allegiance, faithfulness

setiap *adj* each, every; ~ *saat* any time ← **tiap**

setidaknya, setidak-tidaknya *adv* at least ← **tidak**

setinggi *adj* as high as ← **tinggi**

setingkat *adj* of the same level ← **tingkat**

setir ~ *kanan* right-hand drive; **menyetir** *v* to drive

Sétnég *n* State Secretariat, Ministry of the Interior ← **Sékrétariat Negara**

setop: setopan *n, coll* traffic lights

setor: setoran (make a) deposit; *n* minimal amount taxi drivers must earn per day; **menyetor** *v* to pay in, deposit

setrap: disetrap *v* to be punished (at school)

setrika, seterika iron; **setrikaan** *n* (clothes for) ironing; **menyetrika** *v* to iron

setrip, strip *n* (diagonal) slash; strip; section of a mobile phone battery symbol

setrum *n* current; **kesetrum** *v, coll* to receive an electric shock

setubuh: bersetubuh *v* to have sex; **persetubuhan** *n* sexual intercourse

setuju agree, agreed; **bersetuju** *v* to agree; **menyetujui** *v* to agree to, approve, ratify; **persetujuan** *n* agreement, approval ← **tuju**

seumpamanya *conj* for instance ← **umpama**

seumur *adj* the same age; lifelong; ~ *hidup* for life, lifelong ← **umur**

séwa hire, rent; ~ *VCD* VCD rental; *uang* ~ rent; **menyéwa** *v* to rent, hire; **menyéwakan** *v* to let (a house), hire out, lease

sewaktu-waktu *adv* at any moment; every now and then ← **waktu**

sewenang-wenang *adv* tyrannically, arbitrarily ← **wenang**

SH *abbrev Sarjana Hukum* legal graduate, LL.B

shio *n* Chinese horoscope, based on year born

sholat, shalat, solat *Isl* (perform) one of the five daily prayers; ~ *magrib* sunset prayer; ~ *isya*

evening prayer; ~ *subuh*
dawn prayer; ~ *lohor* midday
prayer; ~ *asar* afternoon
prayer; ~ *id* mass prayer at
Idul Fitri or Idul Adha

si *pref* used before the name
of a familiar third party

sia: sia-sia *adj* pointless,
useless

siaga *adj* alert, on guard,
ready; ~ *satu* red alert

sial unlucky; **sialan** *ejac*
damn! hell!

siang *n* day; late morning,
early afternoon (usu between
10 am and 3 pm); ~ *ini* this
morning, this afternoon; ~
malam day and night; ~
bolong broad daylight;
makan ~ lunch; *masih* ~
it's still morning, it's only
early afternoon; **kesiangan**
adj late, too late in the day

siap ready; ~ *pakai* ready-
to-wear, ready to use;
kurang ~ under-prepared;
bersiap *v* to get ready;
bersiap-siap *v* to make
preparations; **kesiapan** *n*
readiness, willingness;
**menyiapkan, memper-
siapkan** *v* to prepare some-

thing, get something ready;
persiapan *n* preparations

siapa *interrog, pron* who; ~
namanya what's their name;
~ *lagi* who else; ~ *punya*
whose is this; ~ *saja* anybody; **siapa-siapa** *pron,
neg* nobody; *bukan* ~ nobody (important)

siar: siaran *n* telecast,
broadcast; **menyiarkan**
v to telecast, broadcast,
disseminate; **penyiar** *n*
announcer

siar: pesiar *n* trip, cruise;
kapal ~ cruise ship; pleasure craft

siasat *n, neg* tactics, strategy

sia-sia *adj* pointless, useless

sibuk *adj* busy; engaged (of
phones); *nada* ~ busy tone;
kesibukan *n* activity, fuss,
bustle, business

sidang *n* session, meeting;
hearing; ~ *istimewa* special
assembly (of parliament);
~ *pengadilan* court hearing,
court session; **persidangan**
n meeting, assembly;
(extended) court session

sidik ~ *jari* fingerprints;
menyidik *v* to investigate;

penyidikan *n* investigation ← **selidik**

sifat *n* quality, nature, character; **bersifat** *v* to have the quality of

sih used as a filler; *saya tidak keberatan* I myself have no objection

sihir *n* spells, witchcraft; *ilmu* ~ black magic; **penyihir** *n* wizard, witch, sorcerer

sikap *n* attitude; **bersikap** *v* to display an attitude

sikat brush; ~ *gigi* toothbrush; ~ *rambut* hairbrush; **menyikat** *v* to brush

siklus *n* cycle

siksa torture; **siksaan, penyiksaan** *n* torture, torment; **menyiksa** *v* to torture; **tersiksa** *adj* tortured

siku *n* elbow; bracket; ~ *segi tiga* right angle

sila *n* principle

sila: bersila *duduk* ~ sit with crossed legs

sila: silakan, silahkan please (when offering); ~ *duduk* please sit down, please be seated; ~ *masuk* please come in; **mempersi-**

lakan *v* to invite someone to do something

silam *adj* past, ago

silang cross, across; **bersilang** *adj* crossed

silat traditional self-defense

silaturahmi *n* good relations, friendship; **bersilaturahmi** *v* to maintain good relations, visit or meet friends

silau *adj* blinded, dazzled

silét *n* razor, scalpel

silih ~ *berganti* to take turns, replace

silsilah *n* family tree, pedigree (of an animal)

siluman *adj* invisible

SIM *n* driver's license, driving license; ~ *C* motorcycle license; *membuat* ~ to get your driver's license ← **Surat Izin Mengemudi**

simak: menyimak *v* to hear, monitor

simpan *v* to keep, put; **simpanan** *n* something kept; *uang* ~ savings, deposit; *wanita* ~ kept woman, lover; **menyimpan** *v* to keep, save up, store

simpang cross; ~ *empat*

312

crossroads, intersection;
~ *tiga* T-junction; **ber-
simpang** *v* to branch;
menyimpang *v* to deviate; **penyimpangan** *n*
aberration, deviation; **per-
simpangan** *n* intersection

simpati *n* sympathy; **bersimpati** *adj* sympathetic;
simpatik *adj* amiable,
likeable

simpul *n* knot; **kesimpulan**
n conclusion; **menyimpulkan** *v* to conclude or
summarize

**sinambung, bersinam-
bung** *adj* continuous ←
sambung

sinar *n* ray, beam; ~ *matahari* sunbeam; **bersinar** *v*
to shine, gleam

sindir, menyindir *v* to
insinuate, allude; **sindiran**
n allusion, insinuation

sinéas *n* cinematographer;
sinétron *n* local TV comedy or drama ← **sinéma
éléktronik**

singa *n* lion; ~ *betina*
lioness; *anak* ~ (lion) cub

Singapura *n* Singapore;
orang ~ Singaporean

singgah *v* to drop by, call
at, stop over

singgung, menyinggung *v*
to touch on; ~ *perasaan* to
offend someone, hurt someone's feelings; **tersinggung** *adj* offended, hurt

singkap: menyingkapkan *v*
to open something slightly;
~ *rahasia* to reveal a secret

singkat *adj* short, brief,
concise; ~*nya* in brief; ~
kata, secara ~ in brief,
briefly; **singkatan** *n* abbreviation; **menyingkatkan** *v*
to abbreviate, shorten

singkir: menyingkir *v* to
step or move aside;
menyingkirkan *v* to remove,
brush aside; **tersingkir** *adj*
eliminated, swept aside

singkong *n* cassava; *daun* ~
cassava leaves; *ubi* ~ cassava

sini *adv* here; *di* ~ here;
dari ~ from here; *ke* ~ here
← **ini**

sinsé, sin shé *n* Chinese
doctor, practitioner of
Chinese medicine or
acupuncture

sintal *adj* well-fed, rounded;
shapely

313

Sinterklas *n* Santa Claus

sinting *adj* silly, crazy

sinyal *n* signal

siomay, sio may *n* fishcakes eaten with peanut sauce

sipil *adj* civil

sipir *n* prison warden, jailer

sipit *adj* narrow, slanting (of eyes); *mata ~* slanted eyes (esp of East Asians)

siput *n* snail

siram *v* to pour; **siraman** *n* bathing ceremony before a wedding; **menyiram** *v* to pour, water (plants); **menyirami** *v* to pour onto

sirat: tersirat *adj* implied

siréne *n* siren

sirih *n* betel; *makan ~* chew betel

sirip *n* fin; *sup ~ ikan hiu* shark fin soup

sirkuit *n* (racing) circuit, race track

sirkus *n* circus

sirna *adj* vanished, disappeared

sirop *n* syrup, cordial

sirsak *n* soursop, green-skinned fruit with white fleshy interior; *air ~, jus ~* soursop juice

sisa *n* rest, remainder, remains; **menyisakan** *v* to leave behind; **tersisa** *adj* leftover

sisi *n* side; *~ buruk* bad side, shortcoming

sisik *n* scale (of fish)

sisip: menyisipkan *v* to insert

sisir *n* comb; hand (of bananas); *se~ pisang* a bunch of bananas; **menyisir** *v* to comb, check thoroughly; **penyisiran** *n* combing, checking

siskamling *n* neighborhood security system ← **sistém keamanan lingkungan**

sistém, sistim *n* system

siswa *n* pupil; *~ -siswi* pupils; **siswi** *n, f* pupil

sita confiscate, seize; **menyita** *v* to confiscate; **penyitaan** *n* confiscation, seizure

situ *di ~* there (close to listener); *dari ~* from there; *ke ~* there ← **itu**

situasi *n* situation

situs *n* site; *~ internet* website; *~ purbakala* archeological site

siul: bersiul *v* to whistle

siuman *v* to recover consciousness, come round

SK *abbrev Surat Keputusan* decree, binding decision

skala *n* scale; **berskala** *v* to be on a scale; ~ *besar* large-scale

skétsa *n* sketch

skor *n* score

skors: diskors *v* to be suspended (from school or work); **skorsing** *n* suspension

Skotlandia *n* Scotland

SLI *abbrev Sambungan Langsung Internasional* international direct dialling

SLJJ *abbrev Sambungan Langsung Jarak Jauh* long-distance direct dialling

SLTA *abbrev Sekolah Lanjutan Tingkat Atas* Senior High School

SLTP *abbrev Sekolah Lanjutan Tingkat Pertama* Junior High School

SM *abbrev sebelum Masehi* before Christ, BC

SMA *abbrev Sekolah Menengah Atas* Senior High School

SMP *abbrev Sekolah Menengah Pertama* Junior High School

SMU *abbrev Sekolah Menengah Umum* Senior High School

soal *n* question, issue, problem, matter; *conj* on the topic of; ~*nya* the problem is; ~ *kecil* small matter; ~ *ujian* exam question; **mempersoalkan** *v* to question, discuss; **persoalan** *n* problem, issue, matter

sobat *n* friend, comrade; ~ *karib* close friend

sobék torn (esp of paper); **menyobék** *v* to tear

soda *air* ~ soda water; **bersoda** *adj* carbonated; *minuman* ~ carbonated drink

sodok: sodokan *n* shot (in billiards); **menyodok** *v* to poke

sodomi *n* sodomy; **menyodomi** *v* to sodomize

sodor: menyodori *v* to hand to, offer; **menyodorkan** *v* to offer up, put forward

sofbol *n* softball; *pemain* ~ softballer

sogok *uang* ~ bribe; **sogok-an** *n* bribe; **menyogok** *v* to bribe

sohor: tersohor *adj* famous

sohun, so'un *n* vermicelli noodles

sok *coll* pretend; as if; ~ *tahu* be a know-all

sokong support; **sokongan** *n* support

sol ~ *sepatu* (shoe) sole

solar *n* diesel fuel

solat → **sholat**

soléh, saléh *adj* pious, religious

solék: bersolék *v* to put on make-up, dress up

solusi *n* solution

somasi *n* summons

sombong *adj* arrogant, stuck-up

songkét *n* (*kain*) ~ woven cloth, often with gold thread

songsong: menyongsong *v* to welcome, greet

sonték → **conték**

sop *n* (western-style) soup; ~ *ayam* chicken broth

sopan *adj* polite, well-mannered; ~ *santun* good manners; **kesopanan** *n*

manners, politeness; **kesopan-santunan** *n* manners, etiquette

sopir → **supir**

sorak cheer, shout; applause; **bersorak** *v* to cheer, shout

soré (late) afternoon, early evening; ~ *hari* late in the day; **soré-soré** *adv* late in the day; **kesoréan** *adv* too late

sorga → **surga**

sori *sl* sorry, pardon

sorot *n* beam of light; **sorotan** *n* focus; **menyoroti** *v* to light up, illuminate, focus on

sortir, menyortir *v* to sort, organize

sosial *adj* social; *visa* ~ *budaya (sosbud)* sociocultural visa; **sosialisasi** *n* socialization; **mensosial-isasikan** *v* to introduce to the public, disseminate

sosis *n* sausage

sosok *n* figure; **bersosok** *v* to have a figure; ~ *tinggi* tall

sospol sociopolitic, social studies and politics ← **sosial politik**

soto *n* clear soup; ~ *ayam* chicken soup

sotong *ikan* ~ cuttlefish, squid

so'un → **sohun**

spanduk *n* large banner

Spanyol *n* Spain; *bahasa* ~ Spanish

spasi *n* space, spacing

SPBU *abbrev setasiun pompa bensin umum* petrol/fuel/gasoline station

spérma *n* sperm

spésial *adj* special

spidol *n* felt-tip marker or pen, texta; whiteboard marker

spion *n* spy; ~ *Melayu derog* (inept) local agent

spiral *n* IUD (intra-uterine device)

spons, spon *n* sponge

sponsor *n* sponsor; **men-sponsori** *v* to sponsor

spontan *adj* spontaneous

sreg *adj, coll* comfortable, fitting

Sri *Dewi* ~ goddess of rice; ~ *Langka* Sri Lanka; ~ *Paus* the Pope, Holy Father

srikaya, serikaya *n* custard-apple

SS *abbrev Sarjana Sastra* Bachelor of Arts, BA

ST *abbrev Sarjana Teknik* Bachelor of Engineering, BEng

stabil *adj* stable

stabilo *n* highlighter, fluorescent marker

stadion *n* (sports) stadium

stadium *n* stage (of an illness); ~ *tiga* advanced

stasiun → **setasiun**

status *n* (marital) status

stémpel, setémpel *n* official stamp

STNK *abbrev Surat Tanda Nomor Kendaraan* motor vehicle license

stopkontak *n* power point, electricity socket

stoplés *n* glass jar for storing crackers & other loose food

strata *n* level; ~ *satu (S1)* bachelor degree

stréng *adj* strict, harsh, disciplinarian

strés, setrés stress(ed)

stupa *n* stupa, bell-shaped dome covering a Buddha statue

suai: sesuai *adj* in accordance or keeping

with; **menyesuaikan** v to adapt; ~ *diri dengan* to adapt yourself to; **penye-suaian** n adaptation

suaka n asylum; ~ *politik* political asylum; *mencari* ~ to seek asylum; *pencari* ~ asylum seeker

suami n husband; ~ *isteri* husband and wife, married couple; **bersuami** *adj, f* married; **bersuamikan** v to be married to

suap n mouthful; bribe; **suapan** n bribe; **menyuap** v to feed by hand; to bribe; **sesuap** n mouthful

suara n voice; vote; ~ *bulat* unanimous; ~ *terbanyak* majority vote; *memberi* ~ to (cast a) vote; **bersuara** v to sound, have a voice; **menyuarakan** v to voice

suasana n atmosphere

suatu *adj* a (certain); ~ *hari* one day; **sesuatu** n something

subsidi n subsidy; **men-subsidi** v to subsidize

subuh n dawn

subur *adj* fertile; **kesuburan** n fertility

subyék n subject

suci *adj* pure, holy; ~ *hama* sterile; **kesucian** n purity; **menyucikan** v to purify, cleanse

sudah *aux* **udah** *coll* already; indicates past time; **sesudah** *prep* after; **sesu-dahnya** after that, then

sudétan n diversion, canal → **sodét**

sudi *adj* willing; ~*kah* would you be willing to; please; *tidak* ~ unwilling

sudut n corner, angle, perspective, point of view; **menyudutkan** v to push into a corner, deflect

suguh: suguhan n something offered or presented; **menyuguhi** v to offer (food), present (a performance)

suhu n temperature; ~ *badan* body temperature; ~ *kamar* room temperature

suit whistling sound; **suit-an** n whistle; **bersuit** v to whistle using your fingers

suka v to like; *adv* often; ~ *damai* peace-loving; ~ *duka* good and bad times, happiness and sadness; ~ *menolong* helpful, likes helping out; **kesukaan** *n* hobby; enjoyment; **menyukai** *v* to like

sukar *adj* difficult, hard; **kesukaran** *n* difficulty

sukaréla *adj* voluntary; **sukarélawan** *n* volunteer ← *réla*

suksés *n* success; *semoga* ~ good luck, every success; **mensukséskan** *v* to make something succeed

suku *n* tribe; part; ~ *bangsa* ethnic group; ~ *kata* syllable; **kesukuan** *adj* ethnic, tribal

sulam: **sulaman** *n* embroidery; **menyulam** *v* to embroider

sulang: **bersulang** *v* to toast, drink to

sulap magic, conjure; *bermain* ~ to do magic; *tukang* ~ magician, conjurer; **sulapan** *n* conjuring, magic; **menyulap** *v* to conjure up; to make something vanish or change; **penyulap** *n* magician, conjurer

Sulawési, Sulawesi *(pulau)* ~ Sulawesi, Celebes

sulih substitute; ~ *suara* dubbing; **menyulihsuarakan** *v* to dub; **penyulih** ~ *suara* dubber; **penyulihan** ~ *suara* dubbing

suling, seruling *n* flute

suling: **penyulingan** *n* distillation

sulit *adj* difficult, complicated, hard; ~ *bicara* find it hard to speak; *masa* ~ hard times; **kesulitan** *n* difficulty, trouble; **menyulitkan** *v* to make difficult, complicate, cause problems

Sulsel *n* South Sulawesi ← **Sulawési Selatan**

Sulteng *n* Central Sulawesi ← **Sulawési Tengah**

Sultra *n* Southeast Sulawesi ← **Sulawési Tenggara**

suluh *n* torch; **menyuluh** *v* to illuminate; to inform; **penyuluh** *n* scout; education worker

Sulut *n* North Sulawesi ← **Sulawési Utara**

Sumatera, Sumatra *(pulau)* ~ Sumatra; ~ *Barat (Sumbar)* West Sumatra; ~

Selatan (Sumsel) South
Sumatra; ~ Utara (Sumut)
North Sumatra

sumbang adj false, out
of tune

sumbang: sumbangan n
contribution, donation;
menyumbang v to contribute, make a donation

Sumbar n West Sumatra ←
Sumatera Barat

sumbat plug; cork, stopper;
menyumbat v to plug,
stop; **penyumbatan** n
blockage

sumber n source; well; ~
minyak oilwell; ~ air source

sumbing bibir ~ harelip,
cleft palate

sumbu n fuse; wick (of a
candle)

sumpah curse; oath; ~
jabatan oath of office; di
bawah ~ under oath;
bersumpah v to swear

sumpek adj crowded,
stuffy

sumpit n chopsticks;
sumpitan n blowpipe

Sumsel n South Sumatra
← **Sumatera Selatan**

sumsum n bone marrow

sumur n well; ~ bor
artesian well

Sumut n North Sumatra ←
Sumatera Utara

sun peck on the cheek; kiss;
memberi ~ to kiss on the
cheek

sunat: sunatan n circumcision (celebration); **disunat** v to be circumcised;
menyunatkan v to have
someone circumcised

Sunda bahasa ~, orang ~
Sundanese

sundul, menyundul ~ bola
to head the ball (in soccer);
sundulan n header

sungai n river; ~ Mahakam
the Mahakam (River)

sungguh adj real, true;
sungguh-sungguh adj
serious; **kesungguhan** n
earnestness, sincerity, truth;
sesungguhnya adv actually,
really; **sungguhpun** conj
although, even though

suntik: suntikan n vaccination, injection; needle;
menyuntik v to inject or
vaccinate

sunting: menyunting v to
edit; **penyunting** n editor;

320

penyuntingan *n* editing

sunyi *adj* lonely, still, quiet;
kesunyian *n* quiet, still

supaya *conj* in order that,
so (used before nouns)

supir, sopir *n* driver, chauffeur; ~ *truk* truck driver;
menyupir *v* to drive

suram *adj* gloomy, dark

surat *n* letter; certificate,
card; ~ *cinta* love-letter; ~
edaran circular; ~ *ijazah*
diploma, certificate; ~
kabar newspaper; ~ *kawin*,
~ *nikah* marriage certificate;
~ *lahir* birth certificate; ~
keterangan written statement; ~ *kuasa* proxy letter;
~ *wasiat* (last) will and
testament; **menyurati** *v* to
write a letter to

surau *n*, *Isl* small prayer-
house

surga, syurga, sorga *n*
heaven, paradise

suri *ibu* ~ the Queen Mother

Suriah *n* Syria; *orang* ~ Syrian

Suriname *n* Surinam; *orang*
~ Surinamese, a Surinamer

suruh order, ask; tell;
suruhan *n* messenger,
errand-boy; **menyuruh** *v* to
command, order; **pesuruh**
n messenger, errand boy; ~
kantor office boy

surup: kesurupan *v* to be
possessed by a spirit or ghost

surut *v* to recede; *air* ~
low tide

surya *sang* ~ the Sun;
tenaga ~ solar energy

sus *kue* ~ small sweet buns
containing rum-flavored
cream

susah difficult; trouble,
sorrow; ~ *makan* won't eat;
berusaha ~ *payah* to work
hard; **kesusahan** *n* trouble,
difficulty; **menyusahkan** *v*
to bother, make difficult

susila *adj* modest, polite;
tuna~ immoral

suster *n* nurse(maid); *n*,
Cath nun

susu *n* milk; *n*, *sl* breast; ~
bubuk powdered milk; ~
formula milk formula; ~
kaleng condensed milk;
menyusu *v* to feed, suckle;
menyusui *v* to feed; *binatang* ~ mammals

susul: susulan *ujian* ~
make-up exams; **menyusul**
v to follow, go after

susun heap, pile; *rumah ~ (rusun)* block of flats, apartment block; **susunan** *n* arrangement, organization, system; *~ kalimat* sentence structure; **menyusun** *v* to heap or pile; to arrange, organize, compile; **penyusun** *n* compiler, author

susut to shrink; **menyusut** *v* to shrink, become smaller

sutera, sutra *n* silk

sutradara *n* director

swa- *pref* self-; *~daya* self-sufficient; *~layan* self-serve; supermarket; *~sembada* self-sufficient

swasta *adj* private; **menswastakan** *v* to privatize

Swédia *n* Sweden

Swis *n* Switzerland; *orang ~* Swiss

switer *n* jumper, pullover, sweater

syahid, sahid *Isl mati ~* martyr

syair *n* poem; **penyair** *n* poet

syal *n* shawl, scarf

syarat, sarat *n* condition, terms; *dengan ~* on condition; *tanpa ~* unconditional;

bersyarat *adj* conditional

syariah *hukum ~* Islamic law

syukur, sukur thanks, thanksgiving; thank goodness; *puji ~ Chr* thank God; **bersyukur** *adj* grateful; **mensyukuri** *v* to appreciate, be thankful

syuting *n* shooting (a film or TV program)

T

taat *adj* obedient; religious; **menaati** *v* to obey or follow something

tabah *adj* strong, resolute, brave

tabel *n* table, chart

tabiat *n* character, nature, temperament

tabir *n* curtain, screen; *~ surya* sunscreen, sunblock

tabrak collide; *~ lari* hit and run; **tabrakan** *n* collision, accident; **menabrak** *v* to collide with; **menabrakkan** *v* to ram something into;

tertabrak *adj* to be hit; ~ *mobil* hit by a car

tabu taboo

tabuh *n* drum; drumstick; **menabuh** *v* to beat (a drum)

tabung *n* container, tube; *bayi* ~ test-tube baby; **tabungan** *n* savings; ~ *pos* postal savings account; *uang* ~ savings; **menabung** *v* to save or deposit money

tabur scatter, sprinkle; ~ *bunga* to scatter flowers on a grave; **bertaburan** *adj* scattered over; **menabur** *v* to scatter or sprinkle

tadi *adv* just now; ~*nya* originally, at first; ~ *pagi* this morning; ~ *malam* last night

tafsir: menafsirkan *v* to interpret something

tagih, menagih *v* to ask for payment, bill; **tagihan** *n* amount due, bill; **ketagihan** *adj* addicted to

tahan bear, stop, last; ~ *air* waterproof; ~ *lama* durable, lasting; *tidak* ~ can't bear; **tahanan** *n* prisoner, detainee; custody, detention; **menahan** *v* to bear, endure; to detain; ~ *diri* to hold yourself back, restrain yourself; **mempertahankan** *v* to defend or maintain; **pertahanan** *n* defense; **tertahan** *adj* held back, prevented

tahap *n* stage, phase; **bertahap** *adj* in stages

tahbis: penahbisan *n* consecration, ordination

tahi *n* shit, feces; ~ *lalat* mole

tahta → **takhta**

tahu [tau] *v* to know; ~ *diri* humble; *tidak* ~ *malu* shameless, without shame; **tahu-tahu** *adv* suddenly, unexpectedly; **ketahuan** *v* to be found out; **mengetahui** *v* to know something, have knowledge of; **pengetahuan** *n* knowledge; **setahu** *conj* as far as is known; ~ *saya* as far as I know

tahu *n* tofu; ~ *tempe* tofu and unprocessed soybean cake

tahun *n* year; ~ *anggaran* financial year; ~ *Baru* New Year; ~ *Baru Cina*, ~ *Baru Imlek* Chinese New Year; ~ *kabisat* leap year; ~ *Masehi* Christian calendar; **tahunan**

323

adj annual, yearly; **bertahun-tahun** *adv* for years and years

tahu-tahu *adv* suddenly, unexpectedly ← **tahu**

taipan *n* magnate, wealthy financier

Taiwan *n* Taiwan; *orang* ~ Taiwanese

tajam *adj* sharp; *otaknya* ~ sharp(-witted); **ketajaman** *n* sharpness

taji *n* spur (of a cock)

tajuk *n* crown; editorial; ~ *rencana* editorial

tak no, not; ~ *terhingga* endless, infinite; ~ *kan*, ~*kan* will not, won't ← **tidak**

takar: takaran *n* measuring container or spoon

takbir: takbiran *v malam* ~ eve of Idul Fitri when this statement is chanted

takdir *n* fate, predestination; **menakdirkan** *v* to determine, to predestine

takhayul, tahayul, takhyul *n* superstition

takhta, tahta *n* throne; ~ *Suci* the Holy See; *naik* ~ ascend to the throne; **bertakhta** *v* to reign

takjub: menakjubkan *adj* astonishing, amazing

takkan will not, won't ← **tak kan**

takluk *v* to surrender, give in, **menaklukkan** *v* to defeat, conquer, subdue

takraw *n* small rattan ball

taksi *n* taxi; ~ *argo* metered taxi

taksir guess; **taksiran** *n* estimate, valuation, appraisal; **menaksir** *v* to estimate, appraise, value; to like, find someone or something attractive; **penaksiran** *n* evaluation

takut *adj* scared, afraid; ~ *mati* scared of dying; ~ *Tuhan* God-fearing; *jangan* ~ don't be afraid; *rasa* ~ fear; **ketakutan** *adj* frightened, terrified, scared; **menakutkan** *v, adv* frightening; to frighten or scare; **penakut** *n* coward

takwa *adj* piety; **bertakwa** *n* pious

tala *garpu* ~ tuning fork

talak *n, Isl* repudiation; step towards divorce

talang *n* (roof) gutter

talenan *n* chopping or cutting board

tali *n* rope, cord, tie; ~ *keluarga* family ties; ~ *pengikat* string; ~ *pusar* umbilical cord; ~ *sepatu* shoelace; **pertalian** *n* connection, relationship

talk *n* talc, talcum powder ← **bedak**

tamak *adj* greedy

taman *n* garden, park; ~ *bacaan*, ~ *pustaka* reading room, library; ~ *budaya* cultural center; ~ *kanak-kanak (TK)* kindergarten; **pertamanan** *adj* parks and gardens

tamasya view; spectacle; excursion

tamat end, finish; ~ *sekolah* graduate; ~ *usia* die; **tamatan** *n* graduate; **menamatkan** *v* to end, finish, conclude

tambah add; **tambahan** *n* addition, increase; **bertambah** *v* to increase; **menambah** *v* to add to or increase; **menambahi** *v* to increase something; **menambahkan** *v* to add

something to; **pertambahan** *n* increase

tambak *n* dam, pond; dike, levee, embankment; ~ *udang* shrimp pond, shrimp farm

tambal *n* patch; ~ *ban* tire repair; **tambalan** *n* patch, darn (on a sock); **menambal** *v* to mend, patch, darn

tambang *n* mine; ~ *batu bara* coal mine, colliery; ~ *emas* gold mine; **penambang** *n* miner; **pertambangan** *n* mining

tambang *n* thick rope, tow line

tambat tie up, tether; **tertambat** *adj* tied up, moored

tambun *adj* corpulent, fat

tambur *n* drum

taméng *n* shield; **bertaméng** *v* to hide behind, use as a shield or pretext

tampak visible, appear; ~*nya* it seems, apparently; **menampakkan** *v* to show, make appear; **penampakan** *n* appearance, visitation

tampan *adj, m* handsome

tampang *n* appearance; *coll* face; *jual* ~ succeed on looks alone; show off

tampar slap, smack; **menampar** v to slap

tampil v to appear; **menampilkan** v to present; **penampilan** n performance

tampung: menampung v to collect, hold; **penampung** n container; **penampungan** n reception, place that receives something; **tertampung** adj contained

tamu n guest, visitor; ~ negara state guest; ~ tak diundang uninvited guest; ruang ~ front room, living room; room for receiving guests

tanah n earth, ground, land, soil; country; ~ air Indonesia; ~ leluhur ancestral home; ~ liat clay; minyak ~ kerosene

tanak: menanak ~ nasi to cook rice

tanam: tanaman n plant; ~ merambat vine, climbing plant; **menanam** v to plant or grow; to invest

tancap layar ~ open-air makeshift cinema; ~ gas step on the gas, accelerate

tanda n sign, mark, symbol; ~ bayar receipt; ~ seru exclamation mark; ~ tanya question mark; ~ tangan signature; **menandatangani** v to sign something; **bertanda** adj marked; **menandai** v to mark; **pertanda** n sign, omen, indication

tandas adj finished, wiped out, desolated

tanding n match, equal; **bertanding** v to compete, play; **pertandingan** n contest, competition, match

tandu n litter

tanduk n horn

tandus adj infertile, barren

tangan n hand, arm; sleeve; kemeja ~ panjang long-sleeved shirt; **menangani** v to handle; **penanganan** n handling

tangga n ladder, stair(case); ~ nada musical scale

tanggal n date; ~ lahir date of birth; ~ muda early in the month; ~ tua late in the month; **bertanggal** tak ~ undated; **penanggalan** n calendar, dating; **tertanggal** adj dated

tanggap: tanggapan n

response, reaction; **menang-gapi** *v* to respond, reply

tangguh *adj* strong, powerful

tanggul *n* dike, levee, embankment

tanggulang: menanggulangi *v* to deal or cope with; **penanggulangan** *n* tackling, fight against

tanggung *adj* guaranteed; ~ *jawab* responsibility; **bertanggung jawab** *v* to be responsible; **mempertanggungjawabkan** *v* to account for; **tanggungan** *n* dependent; responsibility; **menanggung** *v* to guarantee, be responsible; **pertanggungan** *n* responsibility; insurance

tangis *isak* ~ crying; **tangisan** *n* weeping, crying; **menangis** *v* to cry

tangkai *n* stem, stalk; ~ *bunga* flower stem

tangkal: penangkal ~ *petir* lightning rod

tangkap, menangkap *v* to catch, capture; **penangkapan** *n* capture, arrest; **tertangkap** *adj*

caught; ~ *basah* caught in the act

tangkas *adj* agile, adroit, deft; **ketangkasan** *n* agility, dexterity

tangki *n* tank

tani *n* farmer; **petani** *n* farmer; **pertanian** *n* agriculture; *sekolah* ~ agricultural college

tanjak: tanjakan *n* rise, ascent, climb; **menanjak** *adj* rising, climbing, steep

tanjung *n* cape; ~ *Harapan* the Cape of Good Hope; **semenanjung** *n* peninsula; ~ *Melayu* the Malay Peninsula

tanpa *prep, conj* without

tantang challenge; **tantangan** *n* challenge; **menantang** *v* to challenge; *adj* challenging

tante *pron, pol* term of address to a familiar but unrelated woman, esp of mother's generation, in Westernized circles

tanya ask; ~ *jawab* question and answer session; **bertanya** *v* to ask; **bertanya-tanya** *v* to wonder, ask yourself; **menanyai** *v* to question someone; **menanyakan** *v* to ask about; **mempertanyakan** *v* to query; **pertanyaan** *n* question; *mengajukan* ~ to ask questions

tapa: **pertapa** *n* ascetic, hermit, recluse

tapak, telapak ~ *kaki* sole; footprint; ~ *tangan* palm

tapal ~ *batas* border, frontier

tapal ~ *kuda* horseshoe

tapé, tapai *n* fermented rice

tapi → **tetapi**

taplak ~ *meja* tablecloth

tapol *n* political prisoner ← **tahanan politik**

tar, tart *kue* ~ (birthday) cake

taraf *n* standard, level; ~ *hidup* standard of living; **bertaraf** *adj* of a certain standard

tarawih, tarawéh (to go to) evening prayers at the mosque during Ramadan

tari *n* (traditional) dance; ~ *lenso* dance with a handkerchief; ~*tarian* traditional dancing; **tarian** *n* (traditional) dance;

menari *v* to dance, perform a traditional dance; **menari-nari** *n* to dance about; **penari** *n* dancer

tarif, tarip *n* tariff, fare, rate

tarik pull; ~*menarik* push and pull; ~ *tambang* tug-of-war; **menarik** *v* to pull or draw; *adj* interesting, attractive; **narik** *v, coll* to work as a driver of public transport; **tertarik** *adj* attracted, interested

taring *n* tusk; fang; *gigi* ~ fang, incisor, canine tooth

taruh *v* to place, put; **taruhan** bet, wager; **bertaruh** *v* to bet; **menaruh** *v* to put (away); **mempertaruhkan** *v* to stake, risk, bet; ~ *nyawa* to risk your life

taruna, teruna *n* youth; cadet

tas *n* bag; ~ *pinggang* bum bag; ~ *tangan* handbag

tasbih, tasbéh *n, Isl* prayer beads

tata *n* system, layout; ~ *acara* agenda, program; ~ *bahasa* grammar; ~ *negara* civics, state administration; ~ *rambut* hairstyle; ~ *usaha* administration

tatanan n arrangement, system; ~ *sosial* social structure

tato n tattoo; **bertato** adj tattooed

tauco, taoco n brown sauce made from fermented soybeans

taugé, taogé, togé n bean sprouts

tawa laugh, laughter; **tawaan** n object of fun; **ketawa** *coll* **tertawa** v to laugh or smile; **menerta-wakan** v to laugh at

tawan: tawanan n prisoner of war (POW), detainee; **menawan** v to detain, take someone prisoner, intern

tawar bargain; **menawar** v to bargain; *tawar-~* bargaining; **menawarkan** v to offer or bid; **penawaran** n offer, bid

tawar adj bland, plain, tasteless; **penawar** n antidote

tawon n bee

tawur: tawuran n gang or street fight, often among schoolboys

tayang ~ *ulang* repeat, rerun; **tayangan** n program,

telecast; ~ *langsung* live telecast; ~ *tunda* delayed telecast; **menayangkan** v to telecast, show on TV

téater n theatre (building), theater; drama group

tebak guess; **tebakan** n guess; *tebak-~* *coll* guessing game; **menebak** v to guess

tebal adj thick; ~ *muka*, ~ *telinga* thick-skinned

tebang fall, be cut down (of trees); **menebang** v to fell, cut down; **penebangan** n logging; ~ *liar* illegal logging

tébar: menébarkan v to scatter; to cast (a net)

tebing n cliff, gorge, steep bank

tebu n sugarcane; *air* ~ sugar-cane juice; *ladang* ~ cane fields

tebus: tebusan n ransom; **menebus** v to pay a ransom

teduh adj shady; quiet, still; **berteduh** v to take shelter

téga v to have the heart to, dare to; ~*nya* how could you have the heart

tegak adj upright, erect; ~

lurus perpendicular, 90-degree angle; **menegakkan** *v* to erect; to uphold or maintain; ~ *hukum* to uphold the law

tegang *adj* tense, stressed, strained; **bersitegang** *v* to stand fast, persevere; **ketegangan** *n* tension; **menegangkan** *adj* tense, stressful

tegap *adj* strong, upright, sturdy

tegar *adj* stubborn, determined, resolute

tegas *adj* clear, distinct; **menegaskan** *v* to clarify, point out, affirm

tégel *n, arch* (floor) tile ← **ubin**

tegor → **tegur**

teguh *adj* firm, fast, strong, solid

teguk *n* gulp, swallow, draft; **tegukan** *n* swallow, gulp; **meneguk** *v* to gulp or guzzle

tegun: tertegun *adj* taken aback

tegur speak; rebuke; ~ *sapa* say hello; **teguran** *n* warning, rebuke; greeting;

menegur *v* to speak to, address; to warn, rebuke, tell off

téh *n* tea; ~ *melati* jasmine tea; ~ *poci* tea made in an earthenware pot, specialty of the Tegal area; ~ *tawar* black tea no sugar; *kantong, celur* ~ tea-bag

tékad, tékat will, determination; **bertékad** *v* to be determined

tekan press; **tekanan** *n* pressure, stress; **menekan** *v* to press; **menekankan** *v* to stress, emphasize; **tertekan** *adj* stressed, pushed, pressured

teka-teki *n* riddle, puzzle; ~ *silang (TTS)* crossword

téken *v* to sign, initial

téknik, téhnik *n* engineering; *adj* technical; ~ *mesin* civil engineering

téknis *adj* technical; **téknisi** *n* technician

téknologi *n* technology; ~ *tinggi* advanced technology

téko *n* kettle, teapot

téks *n* text; subtitle

tékstil *n* textile

ték-ték *mi* ~ wandering

noodle sellers who tap on their carts

tekuk ~ *lutut* bend your knee; **bertekuk** *v* to bend your knees; ~ *lutut* to surrender

tekukur *n* a kind of dove

tekun *adj* hard-working; **ketekunan** *n* diligence, dedication

telaah study, research

teladan *n* example, model

telaga *n* lake

telah *adv* already; **setelah** *conj* after

telan *v* to swallow; **menelan** *v* to swallow something; **tertelan** *v* accidentally swallowed

telanjang *adj* naked, nude, bare; ~ *bulat* stark-naked; ~ *kaki* barefoot; **bertelanjang** *v* to be bare; ~ *dada* bare-chested

telanjur, terlanjur *adj* neglected, abandoned

telapak, tapak ~ *kaki* sole; footprint; ~ *tangan* palm

telat *adv, coll* (too) late

telatén *adj* patient, persevering; **ketelaténan** *n* patience, perseverance

telédor *adj* careless; **keteledoran** *n* carelessness

téléfon → **télepon**

télékomunikasi *n* telecommunications

telekung *n* women's prayer shawl

telentang *adj* on your back, prone ← **lentang**

télepon, télépon, téléfon telephone; ~ *seluler (ponsel)* mobile phone; **menélépon** *v* to ring (up), call, (tele)phone

téler *adj* drunk, intoxicated; exhausted

télévisi, tévé, tivi *n* television, TV; *menonton* ~ to watch TV

telinga *n* ear

teliti *adj* accurate, careful, meticulous; **ketelitian** *n* accuracy, care; **meneliti** *v* to investigate or research; **peneliti** *n* researcher; **penelitian** *n* research

Télkom *n* state telephone company

telor → **telur**

teluk *n* bay, gulf; *~ Bone* the Gulf of Bone; *~ Jakarta* Jakarta Bay

telur, telor *n* egg; *~ ayam* egg; *~ ikan* roe (as food), spawn; *~ puyuh* quail egg; **bertelur** *v* to lay an egg

telusur: menelusuri *v* to follow, go along, trace

tém: ngetém *v, coll* to wait for passengers (of public transport)

téma *n* theme; **bertéma** *v* to have as a theme

teman *n* friend; **berteman** *v* to be friends; **menemani** *v* to accompany

tembaga *n* copper; *~ kuning* brass; *~ perunggu* bronze; *~ putih* pewter

témbak shoot, fire; *supir ~* unregistered taxi driver; **témbakan** *n* shot, shooting; **menémbak** *v* to shoot; **penémbak** *n* marksman, gunman; **tertémbak** *adj* shot (accidentally)

tembakau *n* tobacco

tembang *n* (esp Jav traditional) song

témbok *n* (concrete or outer) wall

tembus pierce, penetrate; **tembusan** *n* copy; **menembus** *v* to pierce, stab

tempa *besi ~* wrought iron

tempat *n* place; *~ istirahat* rest area; *~ kerja* workplace; *~ lahir* birthplace, place of birth; *~ sabun* soap dish; *~ tidur* bed; *~ tinggal* home, residence; *~ pemakaman umum (TPU)* public cemetery; *pada ~nya* proper; **bertempat** *v* to take place or happen; *~ tinggal* to live or reside; **menempati** *v* to occupy, take a place; **menempatkan** *v* to place; **setempat** *adj* local

témpé *n* unrefined soybean curd; *~ penyet* thin, fried slices of tempe

témpél stick to; **menémpél** *v* to stick or adhere to; **menémpélkan** *v* to stick, paste or glue something

tempéléng *v* to slap, box someone's ears

témpo *n* time, pace; *~ dulu, ~ doeloe* the olden days, colonial times; *~ hari* the other day, recently

tempuh: menempuh *v* to

endure, go through; to take on, take up; ~ *jalan* to go your way; ~ *ujian* to do an exam
tempur fight, combat; *pesawat* ~ fighter; **bertempur** *v* to fight; **pertempuran** *n* battle
tempurung *n* coconut shell; ~ *kepala* skull; ~ *lutut* kneecap, patella
temu find, locate; **temuan** *n* find, discovery; **bertemu** *v* to meet; *sampai* ~ *lagi* see you later, so long; **ketemu** *v, coll* to meet; **menemui** *v* to meet up with, arrange to meet; ~ *ajal* to die; **menemukan** *v* to discover; **penemu** *n* inventor, discoverer; **penemuan** *n* invention, discovery; **pertemuan** *n* meeting
tenaga *n* energy, power; ~ *kerja* manpower, workforce; ~ *listrik* electricity; ~ *nuklir* nuclear energy
tenang *adj* calm, still, quiet; **ketenangan** *n* calm, peace; **menenangkan** *v* to calm someone (down)
tenar *adj* well-known,

popular; **ketenaran** *n* popularity
ténda *n* tent
tendang kick; **tendangan** *n* kick; ~ *pertama* kick-off; **menendang** *v* to kick
tengah middle, in the middle of, half; ~ *hari* midday, noon; ~ *malam* midnight; **tengah-tengah** *prep* middle; **menengah** *adj* intermediate; *kaum* ~ middle class; **pertengahan** *n* middle; *Abad* ~ the Middle Ages; **setengah** *adj* half; ~ *mati* half-dead; very hard; *jam* ~ *dua* half past one; **setengah-setengah** *adv* half-heartedly
ténggang *n* period; ~ *waktu* time frame
tenggara *adj* southeast
tenggelam sink, sunken; drown
tenggiling *n* anteater
tenggiri *ikan* ~ mackerel
tenggorok, tenggorokan *n* throat; *sakit tenggorokan* sore throat
tengkar: bertengkar *v* to quarrel; **pertengkaran** *n* quarrel

tengkorak *n* skull

tengkurap, tengkurup *adv* on your front or face; *tidur ~* to sleep on your stomach

téngok, menéngok *v* to look or see; to look in on someone

tenis *n* tennis; **peténis** *n* tennis player

ténsi *n* blood pressure

tentang *conj* about, concerning; **bertentangan** *adj* contradictory, contrary, opposing; **menentang** *v* to oppose, resist

tentara *n* soldier

ténténg, menénténg *v* to carry dangling from the hand

tenteram, tentram *adj* peaceful, calm; **ketenteraman** *n* peace

tentu *adj* certain, sure, definite; *~nya, ~ saja* of course; **ketentuan** *n* condition, stipulation; **menentukan** *v* to decide, determine, stipulate; **tertentu** *adj* definite, fixed, certain

tenun *kain ~* woven cloth; **tenunan** *n* weaving, woven fabric; **menenun** *v* to weave

téori *n* theory

tepat *adj* precise, exact; *~ guna* appropriate; **bertepatan** *adj* coinciding with, at the same time as; **menepati** *v* to fulfill; *~ janji* to keep a promise

tepergok *adj* caught in the act, caught red-handed ← **pergok**

tepi edge, side; *~ jalan* side of the road; *~ laut* seaside

tepuk *~ tangan* clap, applause; **bertepuk tangan** *v* to applaud, clap; **menepuk** *v* to pat, slap

tepung *n* flour; *~ beras* rice flour; *~ maizena* wheat flour; *~ terigu* flour

ter- *pref* (before adjectives) the most; **terbaik** *adj* the best; **tercantik** *adj* the most beautiful; **tertinggi** *adj* the highest

tér *n* tar

tera: **tertera** *adj* printed, stamped

terakhir *adj* last, final, latest ← **akhir**

terali *n* trellis, lattice work

terang *adj* clear; **terang-terangan** *adj* frank, open; **keterangan** *n* explanation;

menerangkan *v* to explain;
penerangan *n* information,
enlightenment; lighting

terap: **terapan** *adj* applied;
menerapkan *v* to apply
something; **penerapan** *n*
application

térapi *n* therapy; *fisio~*
physiotherapy

terapung *adj* drifting, floating ← **apung**

terarah *adj* directed ← **arah**

téras *n* balcony, terrace

terasa *v* to be felt ← **rasa**

terasi *n* shrimp paste

teratai *(bunga)* ~ lotus

teratur *adj* organized,
regular ← **atur**

terawang: menerawang *v*
to look through something
translucent

terbaik *adj* the best ← **baik**

terbakar *adj* burnt ← **bakar**

terbalik *adj* overturned,
upside-down, opposite ←
balik

terbang *v* fly; **beterbangan** *v, pl* to fly about;
menerbangkan *v* to fly
something; **penerbang** *n*
pilot, aviator; **penerbangan** *n* flight; aviation;

perusahaan ~ airline

terbaru *adj* latest, newest
← **baru**

terbatas *adj* limited ← **batas**

terbawa *adj* (accidentally)
taken away; ~ *arus* swept
away in the current ← **bawa**

terbayang *adj* imagine,
conceivable ← **bayang**

terbelakang *adj* backward,
neglected; **keterbelakang-
an** *n* backwardness, neglect
← **belakang**

terbelit *adj* twisted, involved
← **belit**

terbenam *adj* set, sunken
← **benam**

terbentuk *adj* formed,
shaped, created ← **bentuk**

terbentur *adj* accidentally
bumped

terbesar *adj* largest, biggest
← **besar**

terbit *v* to rise, appear; **terbitan** *n* publication, edition; **menerbitkan** *v* to
publish, issue; **penerbit** *n*
publisher

terbuang *adj* thrown out,
wasted ← **buang**

terbuka *adj* open; *sidang* ~
public session ← **buka**

terbukti *adj* proven ← **bukti**

terbunuh *adj* killed ← **bunuh**

terburu-buru *adj* in a hurry ← **buru**

tercantum *adj* attached, included, inserted ← **cantum**

tercapai *adj* achieved ← **capai**

tercatat *adj* registered; *surat* ~ registered mail ← **catat**

tercebur *adj* fallen into water ← **cebur**

tercekik *adj* strangled ← **cekik**

tercela *adj* wrong ← **cela**

tercemar *adj* polluted ← **cemar**

tercemplung *adj* fallen into water ← **cemplung**

tercepat *adj* fastest ← **cepat**

tercermin *adj* reflected ← **cermin**

tercinta *adj* dear, beloved ← **cinta**

tercipta *adj* created ← **cipta**

tercium *adj* smelt; found out ← **cium**

terdaftar *adj* registered, enrolled ← **daftar**

terdakwa *n* the accused ← **dakwa**

terdampar *adj* beached, grounded, washed ashore ← **dampar**

terdekat *adj* closest, nearest ← **dekat**

terdengar *adj* audible ← **dengar**

terdiam *v* to fall silent ← **diam**

terdiri ~ *atas,* ~ *dari* to consist of, be based or founded on ← **diri**

terdorong *adj* pushed, shoved ← **dorong**

teréliminasi *adj* eliminated ← **éliminasi**

terendah *adj* lowest ← **rendah**

terendam *adj* inundated, flooded, soaked ← **rendam**

terganggu *adj* bothered, disrupted, disturbed ← **ganggu**

tergantung *adj* depending (on), it depends ← **gantung**

tergelétak *adj* sprawled ← **gelétak**

tergelimpang *adj* sprawled ← **gelimpang**

tergelincir *adj* skidded, slipped ← **gelincir**

336

tergenang *adj* flooded ←
genang

tergesa-gesa *adj* in a hurry
or rush ← **gesa**

tergiur *adj* tempted ← **giur**

tergoda *adj* tempted ← **goda**

tergolong *adj* to include,
be part of or considered ←
golong

tergorés *adj* scratched ←
gorés

terhadap *conj* regarding,
against, with respect to ←
hadap

terhalang *adj* blocked,
prevented ← **halang**

terharu *adj* moved, touched
← **haru**

terhormat *adj* respected;
yang ~ to, dear ← **hormat**

teriak scream, yell; **berteriak** *v* to scream or shout;
meneriakkan *v* to shout
something

terigu *n* wheat

terikat *adj* bound ← **ikat**

terima *tanda* ~ receipt; ~
kasih thank you; **menerima**
v to receive, accept; **penerimaan** *n* receipt

terima kasih thank you,
thanks; **berterima kasih** *v*

to be grateful or thankful

terinféksi *adj* infected ←
inféksi

teripang, tripang *n* sea
slug, sea cucumber, trepang

terisak, terisak(isak) *adj*
sobbing ← **isak**

terisolasi *adj* isolated ←
isolasl

terjadi *v* to happen, become
← **jadi**

terjal *adj* very steep, precipitous

terjamin *adj* guaranteed ←
jamin

terjang kick, thrust

terjangkit *adj* infected ←
jangkit

terjatuh *adj* (accidentally)
fallen ← **jatuh**

terjawab *adj* answered ←
jawab

terjebak *adj* trapped, caught;
~ *macet* caught in traffic
← **jebak**

terjemah: terjemahan *n*
translation; **menerjemahkan** *v* to translate (writing);
to interpret (speaking);
penerjemah *n* translator;
penerjemahan *n* translation

terjepit *adj* pinched, caught in an uncomfortable situation ← **jepit**

terjerat *adj* snared, trapped, caught ← **jerat**

terjerumus *adj* plunged into ← **jerumus**

terjual *adj* sold; *habis ~* sold out ← **jual**

terjun dive, fall; go down; **penerjun** *~ (payung)* parachutist, sky diver

terkabul *adj* granted ← **kabul**

terkadang *adv* sometimes, occasionally ← **kadang**

terkebelakang *adj* backward ← **belakang**

terkecuali *tidak ~, tanpa ~* without exception ← **kecuali**

terkejut *adj* surprised ← **kejut**

terkemuka *adj* prominent ← **ke muka**

terkenal *adj* well-known ← **kenal**

terkendali *adj* controlled ← **kendali**

terkesan *adj* impressed; seemed ← **kesan**

terkikis *adj* eaten away,

eroded ← **kikis**

terkilir *adj* twisted, sprained ← **kilir**

terkini *adj* the latest ← **kini**

terkira *tak ~* unsuspected, not thought of ← **kira**

terkirim *adj* sent ← **kirim**

terkuat *adj* the strongest ← **kuat**

terkubur *adj* buried in an accident ← **kubur**

terkuras *adj* drained ← **kuras**

terkutuk *adj* cursed, accursed ← **kutuk**

terlahir *adj* born ← **lahir**

terlalu *adv* too; **keterlaluan** *n* excess, too much ← **lalu**

terlambat *adj* (too) late, delayed ← **lambat**

terlampau *adj* too, extremely ← **lampau**

terlampir *adj* attached, enclosed ← **lampir**

terlanjur, telanjur *adj* too late, already ← **lanjur**

terlantar → **telantar**

terlarang *adj* forbidden, banned ← **larang**

terlémpar *adj* thrown, flung ← **lémpar**

terléna *adj* confused, bewildered ← **léna**

terletak *adj* situated, located ← **letak**

terlibat *adj* involved, implicated ← **libat**

terlilit *adj* caught up, twisted ← **lilit**

terlindas *adj* run over ← **lindas**

terlupakan *tak* ~ unforgettable ← **lupa**

termasuk *adj* including ← **masuk**

termenung *adj* lost in thought ← **menung**

terminal *n* (bus) terminal, bus station

termurah *adj* the cheapest ← **murah**

ternak *n* cattle, livestock; **peternak** *n* (cattle) farmer; **peternakan** *n* cattle farm, ranch

ternama *adj* famous, well-known ← **nama**

ternganga *adj* gaping, flabbergasted, wide open ← **nganga**

ternilai *tidak* ~ priceless, invaluable ← **nilai**

terobos break through, pierce; **terobosan** *n* break-through; **menerobos** *v* to

break through

terompét *n* trumpet; *pemain* ~ trumpet player, trumpeter

térong, térung, terung *n* eggplant, aubergine; small green eggplant eaten raw with salads

teropong *n* telescope, binoculars

terowong: terowongan *n* tunnel, shaft

terpadu *adj* integrated ← **padu**

terpakai *adj* used, in use ← **pakai**

terpaksa *adj* forced ← **paksa**

terpal *n* tarpaulin

terpancing *adj* hooked, caught up; involved ← **pancing**

terpaut *adj* fastened, bound; separated ← **paut**

terpelajar *adj* educated ← **ajar**

terpelanting *v* to fall heavily ← **pelanting**

terpelését *adj* slipped, skidded; tripped ← **pelését**

terpelihara *adj* well cared-for, well-maintained ← **pelihara**

terpelintir *adj* twisted ← **pelintir**

terpencar *adj* dispersed ←
pencar

terpencét *adj* accidentally
pressed ← **pencét**

terpencil *adj* isolated,
remote ← **pencil**

terpendam *adj* hidden,
concealed ← **pendam**

terpengaruh *adj* affected
or influenced ← **pengaruh**

térpentin, térpéntin *n*
turpentine, turps

terpenuhi *adj* satisfied,
fulfilled ← **penuh**

terperangkap *adj* trapped,
caught ← **perangkap**

terpercaya *adj* trusted,
reliable ← **percaya**

terperosok *adj* fallen, sunk,
plunged ← **perosok**

terpesona *adj* enthralled,
enchanted ← **pesona**

terpidana *n* the condemned
← **pidana**

terpikat *adj* attracted,
enchanted ← **pikat**

terpimpin *adj* led, guided
← **pimpin**

terpisah *adj* separated ←
pisah

terpojok, terpojokkan *adj*
forced into a corner ←
pojok

terpotong *adj* cut (off) ←
potong

terpuji *adj* highly-praised
← **puji**

terpukul *adj* hard-hit ←
pukul

terpuruk *adj* hidden, buried,
sunk ← **puruk**

terputus *adj* cut off;
terputus-putus *v* to keep
cutting out ← **putus**

tersambung *adj* connected
← **sambung**

tersandung *adj* to stumble
on, trip (up) on ← **sandung**

tersangka *n (yang)* ~suspect

tersangkut *adj* involved;
caught, snagged ←
sangkut

tersanjung *adj* flattered ←
sanjung

tersaput ~ *awan* clouded
over ← **saput**

tersayang *adj* dear, dearest
← **sayang**

tersebut *adj* (afore)men-
tioned, said ← **sebut**

tersedia *adj* available,
prepared ← **sedia**

terselip *adj* fallen or slipped
into ← **selip**

tersendat *adj* jammed, blocked ← **sendat**

tersendiri *adj* its own; apart, separate ← **diri, sendiri**

tersénggol *adj* bumped, brushed ← **sénggol**

tersentuh *adj* touched ← **sentuh**

tersenyum *v* to smile ← **senyum**

terserah *adj* it depends; up to you ← **serah**

tersérét *adj* dragged ← **sérét**

tersesat *adj* lost ← **sesat**

tersiksa *adj* tortured ← **siksa**

tersinggung *adj* offended, hurt ← **singgung**

tersingkir, tersingkirkan *adj* eliminated, swept aside ← **singkir**

tersirat *adj* implied ← **sirat**

tersisa *adj* leftover ← **sisa**

tersohor *adj* famous ← **sohor**

tertabrak *adj* hit; ~ *mobil* hit by a car ← **tabrak**

tertahan *adj* held back, prevented ← **tahan**

tertambat *adj* tied up, moored ← **tambat**

tertanggal *adj* dated ← **tanggal**

tertangkap *adj* caught; ~ *basah* caught in the act ← **tangkap**

tertarik *adj* attracted, interested ← **tarik**

tertawa *v* to laugh; **menertawakan** *v* to laugh at ← **tawa**

tertegun *adj* taken aback ← **tegun**

tertekan *adj* stressed, pushed, pressured ← **tekan**

tertelan *adj* accidentally swallowed ← **telan**

tertémbak *adj* shot (accidentally) ← **témbak**

tertentu *adj* definite, fixed, certain ← **tentu**

tertera *adj* printed, stamped ← **tera**

tertib *adj* orderly, organized, disciplined; **ketertiban** *n* discipline, order; **menertibkan** *v* to keep order, discipline

tertidur *adj* fallen asleep ← **tidur**

tertimpa *adj* hit or struck by; to suffer ← **timpa**

tertolong *adj* saved, rescued ← **tolong**

tertuduh *n* the accused ← **tuduh**

tertukar *adj* changed by
accident ← **tukar**

tertulis *adj* written ← **tulis**

tertunda *adj* delayed, post-
poned ← **tunda**

tertusuk *adj* pricked, jabbed
← **tusuk**

tertutup *adj* closed ← **tutup**

teruji *adj* tested ← **uji**

terulang *adj* repeated ←
ulang

terumbu *n* coral

terungkap *adj* expressed,
revealed ← **ungkap**

terurai *adj* hanging loose
← **urai**

terus *adv* straight on; continuous, constant; ~ *menerus*
constantly, continually; ~
terang direct, straightforward; **terusan** *n* extension;
canal; **terus-terusan** *adv*
constantly, continuously;
meneruskan *v* to continue,
keep doing something;
penerus *n* successor;
someone who continues
another's work; **seterusnya**
adv after that, henceforth

terutama *adv* especially,
particularly ← **utama**

tetangga *n* neighbor;

bertetangga *v* to have
neighbors

tetap *adj* fixed, definite,
constant; *adv* still; **ketetapan** *n* regulation; stipulation; **menetap** *v* to stay;
menetapkan *v* to appoint,
fix, stipulate; **penetapan** *n*
appointment

tetapi, tapi *conj* but

tetas: menetas *v* to hatch

téték *n, sl* breast; **menéték**
v to suck, feed from the
breast

tétés drip, drop; **tétésan** *n*
drip, drop, droplet

Tétum, Tétun *bahasa* ~
Tetum, language of East
Timor

tetumbuhan → **tumbuh**

tévé, tivi *n* TV ← **télévisi**

téwas *v* to be killed, die;
killed in action; **menéwaskan** *v* to kill someone

Thai *bahasa* ~, *orang* ~
Thai; **Thailand** *n* Thailand

THR *abbrev Tunjangan Hari
Raya* holiday bonus, paid at
Idul Fitri or Christmas

tiada no; there isn't any,
there aren't any; ~ *lagi*
there is no other; no more;

ketiadaan *n* absence, lack;
meniadakan *v* to undo or
cancel ← **tidak ada**

tiang *n* pillar, pole, mast;
~ *bendera* flagpole

tiap, setiap *adj* each, every;
~ *saat* any time

tiba *v* to arrive or come;
tiba-tiba *adv* suddenly

**tidak, tak, ndak, nggak,
enggak** no, not; ~ *pasti*
uncertain; **ketidakpastian**
n uncertainty; **setidak-
(tidak)nya** *adv* at least

tidur sleep; asleep; ~ *pulas,*
~ *nyenyak* sleep heavily,
sleep well; *kurang* ~ not
enough sleep; **tiduran** *v* to
lie down, rest; **ketiduran** *v*
to fall asleep; **meniduri** *v* to
sleep with someone, have
sex with someone; **me-
nidurkan** *v* to put to sleep;
tertidur *adj* fallen asleep

tifa *n* large drum from Papua

tifus, tipus *n* typhoid (fever)

tiga *adj* three; ~ *belas* thirteen; ~ *puluh* thirty; ~ *kali*
three times; **bertiga** *adj* in
threes; **ketiga** *adj* the third;
sepertiga *adj* one-third;
pertigaan *n* T-junction

tikai: bertikai *v* to quarrel
or disagree; **pertikaian** *n*
quarrel, disagreement

tikam stab; **tikaman** *n* stab;
menikam *v* to stab

tikar *n* mat; *gulung* ~ to
close shop; to go bankrupt

tikét *n* (relatively expensive)
ticket; ~ *kereta api* (long-
distance) train ticket; ~
pesawat plane ticket

tikung: tikungan *n* bend,
curve

tikus *n* (small) mouse, (large)
rat; ~ *besar* rat

tilang *n* traffic fine; **ditilang**
v to be fined ← **bukti
pelanggaran**

tilas *napak* ~ retrace your
steps, make a journey again

tim *n* team

tim *nasi* ~ steamed rice with
chicken

timah *n* tin; ~ *campuran*
pewter; ~ *hitam* lead; ~
putih tin

timbal ~ *balik* mutual,
reciprocal

timbang ~ *rasa* consider
another person's feelings;
timbangan *n* scales; **ketimbang** *conj, coll* compared

with; **menimbang** v to weigh (up); **mempertimbangkan** v to consider; **pertimbangan** n consideration

timbel, timbal n lead; *tanpa ~ (TT)* lead-free (fuel)

timbul emerge; **menimbulkan** v to give rise, bring to the surface

timbun n pile, heap; **menimbun** v to pile up, accumulate; to hoard

timpa: menimpa v to fall upon, befall; **tertimpa** *adj* hit or struck by; to suffer

timpang: ketimpangan n inequality, imbalance

Timteng n the Middle East ← **Timur Tengah**

Timtim n, *arch* East Timor, Timor Loro Sae ← **East Timor**

timun, mentimun n cucumber; *~ laut* sea cucumber, trepang; *~ suri* large cucumber, often eaten at fast-breaking ← **mentimun**

timur *adj* east; *~ laut* northeast; *~ Tengah (Timteng)* Middle East; *bintang ~* morning star; **ketimuran** *adj* Eastern, Oriental

tindak act, deed; *~ lanjut* follow-up; *~ pidana* criminal act; **menindaklanjuti** v to take a step or measure; **tindakan** n action, measure, step; *~ pencegahan* preventive measure; **bertindak** v to act, take action

tindas: penindasan n oppression

tindik *~ telinga* pierced ears; **menindik** v to pierce (ears)

tinggal v to live, stay, remain; *rumah ~* dwelling; **ketinggalan** *adj* left behind; **meninggal** *~ (dunia)* to die; **meninggalkan** v to leave (behind), abandon

tinggi *adj* high, tall; *~nya* height; **ketinggian** n altitude, height; **setinggi** *adj* as high as

tingkah action; *~ laku* behavior, actions

tingkat n level, floor, story, grade; *~ pemula* beginner; **tingkatan** n grade, degree, level; **bertingkat** *adj* having different levels; **meningkat** v to rise, increase, improve; **meningkatkan** v to increase or raise the level of something; **setingkat** *adj* of the same level

tinja *n* excrement, feces, sewage

tinjau: tinjauan *n* review; **meninjau** *v* to observe, view; ~ *kembali* to review; **peninjau** *n* observer; **peninjauan** *n* observation

tinju *n* boxing; fist; **bertinju** *v* to box; **petinju** *n* boxer

tinta *n* ink; *habis* ~ out of ink

Tionghoa *adj, pol* Chinese; *orang* ~ Chinese

tipe *n* type, sort

tipék, tipéks: ditipéks *v* to white-out, be corrected

tipis *adj* thin; *kemungkinan* ~ slim chance; **menipis** *v* to become thin

tipu trick, cheat; ~ *daya* scam, con; **menipu** *v* to trick, deceive; **penipu** *n* con man, trickster; **penipuan** *n* deception

tipus, tifus *n* typhoid (fever)

tirai *n* curtain

tiri *adj* step-; *adik* ~, *kakak* ~ stepbrother or stepsister

tiru, meniru *v* to copy or imitate; **tiruan** *n* imitation, fake

tisu *n* tissue; ~ *basah* wipe

titik *n* dot, point; full stop, period; ~ *dua* colon; ~ *koma* semicolon

titip, menitip *v* to leave in someone's care, entrust; **titipan** *n* parcel, something sent with another person; **penitipan** *n* care; *tempat* ~ *anak* child-minding center, creche

tiup blow; **bertiup** *v* to blow; **meniup** *v* to blow

tivi, tévé *n* TV ← **télévisi**

TK *abbrev Taman Kanak-kanak* kindergarten, pre-school

TKI *abbrev Tenaga Kerja Indonesia* Indonesian worker migrant

TKW *abbrev Tenaga Kerja Wanita* Indonesian female migrant worker

Tn. *Tuan* Mr, Sir, used for males, usually non-Indonesians

TNI *abbrev Tentara Nasional Indonesia* Indonesian National Army/Armed Forces

toalét, toilét n toilet, washroom

tobat, bertobat v to repent

todong, menodong v to threaten or hold up at knifepoint

togél n illegal small-scale gambling, lottery or bingo game ← **toto gelap**

toh adv, coll still, after all

tokék n large gray house gecko

toko n shop, store; ~ mas, ~ emas jewelery shop; ~ roti bakery; ~ swalayan supermarket; **pertokoan** n shopping center or complex, mall

tokoh n figure, character; ~ dunia world figure; ~ utama main character

tol n toll; jalan ~ toll road; pintu ~ tollbooth, tollgate

tolak v to refuse, reject; **menolak** v to refuse, reject; **penolakan** n refusal, rejection

toléh: menoléh v to look in a different direction, turn your head

tolol adj stupid

tolong help; please; minta ~ please help me; **menolong** v to help or assist; **pertolongan** n help, assistance, aid; ~ pertama first aid; **tertolong** adj saved, rescued; tidak ~ beyond help

tomat n tomato

tombak n spear

tombol n knob, button

tong n drum, barrel, bin

tongkang n barge

tongkat n stick, cane; **bertongkat** adj with a stick

tongkol ikan ~ tuna (fish)

tongséng n goat and cabbage curry

tonjok, menonjok v to punch, hit

tonjol: menonjol v to stick out, protrude; adj prominent

tonton: tontonan n show, performance; **menonton, nonton** v to watch, look on; **penonton** n spectator, audience; para ~ audience; ladies and gentlemen

topang: menopang v to prop up, support; **penopang** n prop, support

topéng n mask; tari ~ kind of traditional masked dance

topi *n* hat; ~ *pet* cap

Toraja Toraja, ethnic group of central Sulawesi; *bahasa* ~, *orang* ~ Toraja

tosérba *n* general store; department store ← **toko sérba ada**

totok *adj* full-blood; *Cina* ~ (overseas) Chinese

TPA *abbrev tempat pembuangan akhir* tip, rubbish dump

tradisi *adj* tradition (not *adat*); **tradisional** *adj* traditional

trah *n* lineage, descent

traktir, mentraktir *v* to invite out, shout, treat, pay for another

trampil *adj* skilled; **ketrampilan** *n* skill

transaksi *n* (bank) transaction; **bertransaksi** *v* to make a transaction

transisi *n* transition

transmigrasi *n* transmigration (from Java to other islands)

trayék *n* route (of public transport)

trén, tréndé *n* trend, fashion; **ngetrén** *adj, coll* trendy, fashionable

tribune *n* [tribun] stand, open area in a stadium or concert hall

triplék, tripléks *n* plywood, used for ceilings

triwulan *n* quarter (of a year); trimester; term (when four terms in a year)

trompét *n* trumpet

tropis *adj* tropical

trotoar *n* pavement, sidewalk

truk *n* truck

tsb. *tersebut* the aforementioned

tt(d) *tertanda* signed

TTS *abbrev teka-teki silang* crossword

tua *adj* old; dark (of colors); **ketua** *n* chair(person); chief

tuak *n* palm wine

tuan, Tn *pron* master, sir (esp for foreigners); **tuan-tuan** *pron* gentlemen

tuang *v* to pour; **menuang, menuangkan** *v* to pour something

tuan-tuan *pron* gentlemen ← **tuan**

tubuh *n* body; **bertubuh** *v* to have a body; ~ *gemuk* fat

tuding: tudingan *n* accusation; **menuding** *v* to accuse, point the finger

tuduh: tuduhan *n* charge, accusation; **menuduh** *v* to accuse; **tertuduh** *n* the accused

tugas *n* task, duty, function; **menugaskan** *v* to assign someone, give a task to; **penugasan** *n* assignment

tugu *n* monument, column

tuh *pron, coll* that; *itu ~* that one ← *itu*

Tuhan *n, pron* God, Allah; **tuhan** *n* god; **ketuhanan** *n* divinity, deity; belief in God

tuju: tujuan *n* direction, destination; aim, goal; **menuju** *v* to approach, go towards; **setuju** agree, agreed; **menyetujui** *v* to agree to, approve, ratify; **persetujuan** *n* agreement, approval

tujuh *adj* seven; *~ belas* seventeen; *~ puluh* seventy

tukang *n* (unskilled) worker; handyman; *~ cat* painter; *~ cukur* barber; *~ roti* baker;

bread-seller; *~ sepatu* cobbler, shoemaker

tukar *v* to exchange; *~ menukar* barter; *~ tambah* trade in; **bertukar** *v* to change; **menukar** *v* to change; **menukarkan** *v* to change something; **pertukaran** *n* exchange; **tertukar** *adj* changed by accident

tulang *n* bone; *~ belakang* spine

tular: ketularan *adj* infected, caught something; **menular** *v* to infect; *adj* contagious, infectious; **penyakit** *~* contagious disease

tulén *adj* real, pure, genuine

tuli *adj* deaf

tulip, tulpen *n* tulip

tulis *v* to write; **tulisan** *n* writing, script; *~ halus* calligraphy; **menulis** *v* to write; **penulis** *n* author, writer; *~ novel* novelist; **tertulis** *adj* written

tulus *adj* sincere

tumbang fall, fallen

tumbén *adj, coll* unusual, never before, rare

tumbuh *v* to grow; **tetum-buhan, tumbuh-tumbuh-an** *n* plants; **tumbuhan** *n* a growth; plant; **pertumbu-han** *n* growth, development

tumbuk, menumbuk *v* to pound (rice), crush, grind

tumis *v* to stir-fry, sautée; ~ *sayur* stir-fried veg-etables

tumit *n* heel (of foot)

tumpah spill, spilt; **menum-pahkan** *v* to spill some-thing

tumpang: menumpang *v* to make use of someone else's facilities; to get a lift or ride; **penumpang** *n* passenger

tumpeng *nasi* ~ rice shaped in a tall cone, made on special occasions

tumpuk *n* heap, pile; **ber-tumpuk** *v* to be in piles; **menumpuk** *v* to pile up

tumpul *adj* blunt

tuna- *pref* without

tunai *n* cash; **menunaikan** *v* to pay cash; to fulfill

tunang: tunangan *n, f* fiancée; *n, m* fiancé; *v, coll* to be engaged; **pertu-nangan** *n* engagement

tunas *n* shoot, sprout

tunda delay; **menunda** *v* to delay, put off, postpone; **menundakan** *v* to delay or postpone something; **ter-tunda** *adj* delayed, post-poned

tunduk *v* to bow to, submit, obey; **menunduk** *v* to bow your head; **menundukkan** *v* to bow or lower something; to defeat

tunggak: tunggakan *n* debt

tunggal *adj* single, sole; *orang tua* ~ single parent

tunggang: menunggang *v* to ride; ~ *kuda* to ride a horse

tunggu *v* to wait; ~ *dulu* wait a minute; **menunggu** *v* to wait for something; **menunggu-nunggu** *v* to wait a long time for

tungku *v* furnace, oven

tunjang: tunjangan *n* allowance, bonus; ~ *Hari Raya (THR)* one month's extra pay, awarded on a religious holiday

tunjuk, menunjuk *v* to indicate, point out, refer to;

349

menunjukkan *v* to show, point out; **pertunjukan** *n* show, performance; **petunjuk** *n* instruction, direction

tuntas *adj* complete, total

tuntut claim; **tuntutan** *n* claim, charge; **menuntut** *v* to claim or demand; **penuntut** *n* claimant, plaintiff, prosecuting party

tupai *n* squirrel

tur *n* tour; **turis** *n* tourist

Turki *n* Turkey

turun *v* to descend, fall, come down; **~temurun** from generation to generation, hereditary; **keturunan** *n* descendant; **WNI ~** Indonesian of Chinese descent; **menurun** *v* to fall, drop, decline; **menurunkan** *v* to lower or reduce

turut *v* to take part, join; **~ serta** participate, take part; **~ berduka cita** express your condolences; **berturut-turut** *adj* consecutive, successive; **menurut** *conj* according to; **penurut** *adj* obedient, meek

tuslah *n* surcharge; **~**

Lebaran surcharge on transport at Idul Fitri

tusuk skewer, needle; poke; **~ jarum** acupuncture; **~ sate** satay stick; **menusuk** *v* to stab, prick, pierce; **tertusuk** *adj* pricked, jabbed

tuts *n* key, button

tutul *adj* spotted

tutup lid, cover; closed, shut; **~ botol** bottle-cap; **~ mulut** keep your mouth shut; **menutup** *v* to close or shut; **menutupi** *v* to cover (up); **penutup** *n* stopper, lid; end; **tertutup** *adj* closed

tutur speak; **bertutur** *v* to speak or talk; **penutur** *n* speaker; **~ asli** native speaker

TV *abbrev* teve, tivi, televisi television; **menonton ~** to watch TV

TVRI *abbrev* Televisi Republik Indonesia Indonesian state-owned television

U

uang *n* money; ~ *kembali* change; ~ *muka* down payment; ~ *sekolah* school fees, tuition; ~ *tunai* cash; **keuangan** *n* finance; *Menteri* ~ Minister of Finance

uap *n* steam, vapor; **menguap** *v* to evaporate or steam; **penguapan** *n* evaporation

ubah change; **berubah** *v* to change; **mengubah** *v* to change or alter; **perubahan** *n* change, alteration

uban *n* (strand of) gray or white hair; **beruban** *v* to have gray hairs

ubi *n* edible tuber or root; sweet potato, yam; ~ *kayu* cassava

ubin *n* (floor) tile

ubur-ubur *n* jellyfish

ucap say; **ucapan** *n* greetings; ~ *selamat* congratulations; **mengucap, mengucapkan** *v* to say or express something; ~ *terima kasih* to say thank you; to thank

udah → **sudah**

udang *n* shrimp

udara *n* air, atmosphere; *angkatan* ~ *(AU)* air force; *tekanan* ~ air pressure, atmospheric pressure; **mengudarakan** *v* to broadcast or air

udik → **mudik**

UGM *abbrev Universitas Gadjah Mada* Gadjah Mada University, in Yogyakarta

UI *abbrev Universitas Indonesia* University of Indonesia, in Jakarta

ujar speak, say

uji test; ~ *coba* experiment, trial; **ujian** *n* test, exam(ination); ~ *lisan* oral test; ~ *masuk* entrance test; ~ *tertulis* written exam or test; **menguji** *v* to examine or test; **penguji** *n* examiner; **teruji** *adj* tested

ujung *n* point, end; ~ *jari* fingertip

ukir, **mengukir** *v* to carve or engrave; **ukiran** *v* carving

Ukraina *n* (the) Ukraine

ukur measure; **ukuran** *n* size, measurement; ~ *sedang* medium size; **mengukur** *v* to measure; **pengukuran** *v* measuring, measurement

351

ulah *n* behavior, manners

ulama *n, Isl* religious leader(s)

ulang repeat; ~ *alik* back and forth, both ways; *pesawat* ~ *alik* shuttle; ~ *tahun* birthday, anniversary; **ulangan** *n* test; **berulang** *v* to happen again, recur; **berulang-ulang** *adv* again and again, repeatedly; **mengulang** *v* to repeat, do again; **mengulangi** *v* to repeat something; **terulang** *adj* repeated

ular *n* snake

ulat *n* worm, caterpillar

ulet *adj* diligent, hard-working

ulos *n* woven cloth used in Batak ceremonies

ultah *n* birthday, anniversary ← **ulang tahun**

ulur: uluran *n* assistance, help; ~ *tangan* helping hand; **mengulur-ulur** *v* to spin out, take a long time; **mengulurkan** *v* to extend something

umat *n* people (of one faith); ~ *Islam* the Muslim community

umbi *n* tuber; **umbi-umbian** *n* tubers

umpama *n* example; ~*nya* for example; **seumpama-nya** *conj* for instance

umpan *n* bait

umpat, mengumpat *v* to curse swear; **umpatan** *n* oath, swear word

umpat, umpet: umpet-umpetan *n, coll* hide and seek; **mengumpet** *v* to hide or conceal yourself

umroh, umrah *n* minor pilgrimage to Mecca

umum *adj* general, public, common; *(pada)* ~*nya* generally, in general; **meng-umumkan** *v* to announce or declare; **pengumuman** *n* notice, announcement

umur *n* age; **berumur** *adj* aged; **seumur** *adj* the same age; lifelong; ~ *hidup* for life, lifelong

Unair *n* Airlangga University (in Surabaya) ← **Univérsitas Airlangga**

undang, mengundang *v* to invite (formally); **undangan** *n* invitation; formal event

undang: undang-undang *n* law, act; ~ *Dasar* constitution

undi *n* lot; **undian** *n* lottery;
mengundi *v* to conduct a
draw or lottery
undur, mundur *v* to reverse,
go back; **mengundurkan** *v*
to postpone; **pengunduran**
n postponement, delay
unggas *n* poultry, bird
unggul *adj* superior, **keunggulan** *n* superiority
unggun *api ~* (camp) fire
ungkap *v* to express, reveal;
ungkapan *n* expression;
mengungkap *v* to uncover;
mengungkapkan *v* to
express; **terungkap** *adj*
expressed, revealed
ungsi: **mengungsi** *v* to
evacuate or flee; **mengungsikan** *v* to evacuate someone; **pengungsi** *n* refugee,
evacuee; **pengungsian** *n*
evacuation
ungu *adj* purple; *~ muda*
violet
uni *n* union; *~ Arab Emirat*
United Arab Emirates;
~ Eropa (UE) European
Union (EU); *~ Soviet*
Soviet Union
unik *adj* unique; **keunikan**
n unique thing, uniqueness

univérsitas *n* university
unjuk *~ gigi* show your
teeth; *~ rasa* demonstration
Unpad *n* Padjadjaran
University (in Bandung) ←
Univérsitas Padjadjaran
unsur *n* element
unta, onta *n* camel; *burung
~* ostrich
untai string; counter for
string-like objects; **untaian**
n string, chain; **teruntai** *adj*
dangling, strung up
untuk *prep* for
untung advantage, gain,
profit; luck; **beruntung** *adj*
lucky, fortunate; **keun-
tungan** *n* advantage,
profit; **menguntungkan**
v to profit; *adj* profitable;
peruntungan *n* (good)
fortune or luck
upacara *n* ceremony; *~
pemakaman* funeral; *~
pernikahan, ~ perkawinan*
wedding ceremony
upah *n* wage, wages
upaya *n* effort; **berupaya** *v*
to make an effort, try
upik *n* nickname for a girl, esp
in Sumatra; *buyung ~* boy
and girl, son and daughter

upil *n* snot, bogey, nasal mucus; **mengupil** *v* to pick your nose

urai: uraian *n* explanation, analysis; **menguraikan** *v* to explain; to untangle; **terurai** *adj* hanging loose

urap *n* vegetable salad with grated coconut

urat *n* tendon, vein; muscle; ~ *saraf* nerve

uréa *pupuk* ~ kind of fertilizer

urus organize, arrange; **urusan** *n* arrangement, dealing, affair; *bukan* ~ *saya* none of my business; **berurusan** *v* to have dealings with, deal with; **mengurus** *v* to arrange, organize, manage; **pengurus** *n* manager, organizer; ~ *besar* board of directors, executive

urut order in a series; **urutan** *n* order, sequence; **berurut-(-urutan)** *adj* successive, consecutive, sequential

urut massage, rub; **mengurut** *v* to massage

urutan *n* order, sequence ← **urut**

usah *tidak* ~ not necessary

usaha *n* effort; *dunia* ~ business world; **berusaha** *v* to try, make an effort; **mengusahakan** *v* to try, endeavor to; **pengusaha** *n, m* businessman; *n, f* businesswoman; **perusahaan** *n* company

usai *adj* over, finished

USG ultrasonogram

usia *n, pol* age; ~ *lanjut* old age; **berusia** *v* to be (aged)

usik: mengusik *v* to tease, disturb

usil *adj* annoying, cheeky

usir, mengusir *v* to drive away or out, chase away, expel

uskup *n* bishop; ~ *agung* archbishop

usul *n* origin

usul propose, suggest; motion; *atas* ~ on the suggestion of; **mengusulkan** *v* to propose or suggest

usus *n* intestine; ~ *besar* large intestine; ~ *buntu* appendix

usut: mengusut *v* to investigate, sort out

utak ~*atik* fiddle or tinker with ← **kutak-katik**

utama *adj* main; **meng-utamakan** *v* to give preference or priority to; **terutama** *adv* especially, particularly

utang, hutang *n* debt; ~ piutang debits and credits; *surat* ~ IOU (I owe you); **berutang** *v* to owe

utara *adj* north; **meng-utarakan** *v* to put forward

utas *n* string (of beads)

utuh *adj* whole, complete, untouched

utus, mengutus *v* to send or delegate; **utusan** *n* delegate, deputy; mission

UU *abbrev Undang-Undang* legal statutes

UUD *abbrev Undang-Undang Dasar* constitution

V

vakansi, pakansi vacation, on holiday

vaksin *n* vaccine; **vaksinasi** *n* vaccination

vakum *n* vacuum

valas *n* foreign currency ← **valuta asing**

validasi *n* validation; **divalidasi** *v* to be validated

valuta *n* currency; ~ *asing (valas)* foreign currency

vampir *n* vampire

vanili *n* vanilla

variasi *n* accessories (esp vehicle), variation

varisés *n* varicose veins

vas *n* vase

végétarian *adj* vegetarian

vélg, véleg, pélek *n* wheel rim

véntilasi *n* ventilation

verboden, perboden no entry

vermak → **permak**

vérsi *n* version

versnéling → **persnéling**

véspa *n* moped, motor scooter

vétsin *n* MSG (monosodium glutamate)

vidéo video

Viétnam *n* Vietnam; *bahasa* ~, *orang* ~ Vietnamese

vihara, wihara *n* Buddhist temple or monastery

vila *n* villa, holiday house, summer cottage

visi ~ *dan misi* mission statement

vital *adj* vital; *alat* ~ vital organs; genitals

vocer, voucer *n* credit voucher (for mobile phones)

vokal *adj* vocal, outspoken; *huruf* ~ vowel; **vokalis** *n* vocalist

voli *bola* ~ volleyball

volume *n* volume, size, bulk

vonis *n* ruling; sentence; ~ *mati* death sentence; **divonis** *v* to be sentenced

W

wabah *n* epidemic, plague; ~ *belalang* locust plague; ~ *flu burung* bird flu epidemic

wadah *n* pot, container, place to put something

waduk *n* reservoir; dam

wafat *v, pol* to pass away or die; ~ *1970* died 1970

wagub *n* deputy governor ← **wakil gubernur**

wah *excl* wow! oh! *adj* amazing, outstanding; *adj* fantastic, wonderful

wahana *n* vehicle, means

wahyu *n* revelation, vision, inspiration

Waisak, Wésak *n* Buddhist New Year

wajah *n, pol* face; **berwajah** *v* to have a face; ~ *muram* sour-faced

wajan *n* wok

wajar *adj* natural

wajib compulsory; must, obliged; ~ *militér* military service; **berwajib** *adj* responsible, competent; **kewajiban** *n* obligation, duty; **mewajibkan** *v* to enforce or make obligatory

wajik *n* diamonds (card suit); diamond-shaped cake of sticky rice

wakaf *Isl tanah* ~ land donated to the local Muslim community

wakil *n* representative, substitute; *adj* vice; ~ *presiden* vice-president; **mewakili** *v* to represent; **perwakilan** *n* representation, delegation

waktu *n* time, hours; *conj* when; *pada* ~*nya* in due time, at the right time;

sewaktu-waktu *adv* at any moment; every now and then

walafiat *sehat* ~ healthy, hale and hearty, in good health

walaikum *Isl* ~ *salam* and upon you be peace (said in response to *salam alaikum*)

walau, walaupun *conj* although

walét *burung* ~ swift; *rumah* ~ building where swiftlet nests are cultivated

Walhi *n* Indonesian environmental group ← **Wahana Lingkungan Hidup Indonésia**

wali *n* guardian; saint; **perwalian** *n* guardianship, representation

wals, walsa *n* waltz

-wan *suf, m* -man, one who does something

wana- *pref* forest

wangi fragrant; perfume; **wangi-wangian, wewangian** *n* scents, perfumes

wanita *n* woman

waprés *n* vice-president ← **wakil présidén**

waralaba *n* franchise

waras *adj* sane, healthy

warga *n* citizen; **warganegara** *n* citizen, national; ~ *Indonesia (WNI)* Indonesian citizen; **kewarganegaraan** *n* citizenship

waris: warisan *n* inheritance; **mewarisi** *v* to inherit

warna *n* color; ~ *putih* white; ~*-warni* colorful, multicolored; **berwarna** *adj* colored; **mewarnai** *v* to color (in); **pewarna** *n* dye, stain

warnét *n* Internet café ← **warung internét**

warpostél *n* office where you can make calls, and send post and faxes ← **warung pos dan télékomunikasi**

warta *n* news; ~ *berita* news (items); **wartawan** *m* **wartawati** *f* journalist, reporter

warteg *n* small, cheap food stall ← **warung Tegal**

wartél *n* small office where you can make calls and send faxes ← **warung télékomunikasi**

waru *pohon* ~ kind of hibiscus tree

357

warung *n* stall, small local shop; ~ *kopi* coffee stall

waserai *n* (commercial) laundry

wasiat *n* will

wasir *n* hemorrhoids

wasit *n* umpire, referee

waslap *n* washcloth, flannel

waspada *adj* on guard, careful, cautious; **kewaspadaan** *n* caution; **mewaspadai** *v* to watch out for, guard against

wassalam *Isl* and upon you be peace (used in response to *assalamualaikum*); best regards (in closing letters)

wastafel *n* basin, sink (in bathroom)

watak *n* nature, character

-wati *suf, f* -woman, one who does something

wawancara *n* interview; **mewawancarai** *v* to interview; **pewawancara** *n* interviewer

wawas: wawasan *n* outlook, view, concept; **berwawasan** *v* to have an outlook; ~ *luas* broad or open mind

wayang *n* puppet; ~ *golek* wooden, three-dimensional puppet; ~ *kulit* shadow pup-

pet (performance); ~ *orang* traditional performance with actors

WC [wé sé] *n* toilet, bathroom, lavatory

wedang *n* warm Javanese beverage; ~ *jahe* warm ginger drink

wéker *n* alarm; *jam* ~ alarm clock; *memasang* ~ to set the alarm

wenang: berwenang *adj* competent, in charge; **kewenangan, wewenang** *n* authority; **sewenang-wenang** *adv* tyrannically, arbitrarily

wésel *n* money order; *pos* ~ postal money order

wewangian → **wangi**

wewenang *n* authority ← **wenang**

WIB *abbrev Waktu Indonesia Barat* Western Indonesian time

wibawa *n* authority, esteem; **berwibawa** *adj* esteemed, respected, of good standing

wihara, vihara *n* Buddhist temple or monastery

wijén *n* sesame seed

wilayah *n* area, territory;

kantor ~ regional office

windu *n* eight-year cycle; **sewindu** *adj* eight years

wira-: wirausaha *n* business; **wiraswasta** *n, m* businessman *f* businesswoman

wisata *n* tourism, travel; *biro* ~ travel agent; **berwisata** *v* to travel or holiday; **wisatawan** *n* tourist; ~ *mancanegara (wisman)* foreign tourist; ~ *Nusantara (wisnu)* domestic or local tourist

wiski *n* whisky, whiskey

wisma *n* house, building

wisuda graduate

WIT *abbrev Waktu Indonesia Timur* Eastern Indonesian time

WITA *abbrev Waktu Indonesia Tengah* Central Indonesian time

WNA *abbrev warga negara asing* foreign national

WNI *abbrev warga negara Indonesia* Indonesian national

wol *n* wool

wong *conj, coll* because; what do you mean?

wortel *n* carrot

WTS *abbrev wanita tuna susila* immoral woman, *euph* prostitute

wudu, wudhu, wudlu *n, Isl* ritual ablutions before praying; *tempat* ~ tap for washing before praying

wujud *n* existence; **berwujud** *v* in the form or shape of; **mewujudkan** *v* to make something real, realize something

wulan *catur* ~ trimester, term; ~ *(cawu) ketiga* third term

X

X *sinar* ~ X-ray

Y

ya, iya yes

ya *ejac* oh, O; ~ *Allah* oh God!

yad. *yang akan datang* future

Yahudi *adj* Jewish; *agama* ~

Judaism; *bahasa* ~ Yiddish; *orang* ~ Jewish, Jew

yaitu *conj* namely, that is

yakin *adj* sure, convinced; **keyakinan** *n* belief, conviction, faith; **meyakini** *v* to believe, be convinced; **meyakinkan** *adj* convincing, believable

yakni *conj* namely

Yaman *n* Yemen

yang *conj* that, which, who; ~ *biru* the blue one; ~ *lalu* in the past; ~ *akan datang* in the future

yatim *n* orphan, fatherless child; ~ *piatu* orphan

yayasan *n* foundation (not for profit)

yl. *yang lalu* in the past

YME *abbrev Yang Maha Esa* the One and Only, when referring to God

yoni *n* square hole, traditional female symbol

Yordania *n* Jordan

yth. *yang terhormat* the respected, used when addressing letters

yts. *yang tersayang* dear, used when addressing letters to family or friends

yuk → **ayo**

Yunani *n* Greece; *bahasa* ~, *orang* ~ Greek

yunior junior (at work or school)

Z

zaitun *n* olive

zakat, jakat *n* alms

zaman, jaman *n* age, era, time, period; ~ *dahulu,* ~ *dulu* in the old days, times past; *ketinggalan* ~ outdated

zamrud, jamrud *n* emerald; ~ *khatulistiwa* emeralds of the Equator (ie. Indonesia)

zat, jat *n* element, substance

zébra *n* zebra

ziarah *n* pilgrimage, visit to a holy place or cemetery; **berziarah** *v* to make a pilgrimage, visit a holy place

zikir, dikir, dzikir *Isl* (recite) additional prayers

zina, zinah *n* adultery; sex outside marriage; **berzina** *v* to commit adultery

zona *n* zone

English–Indonesian

A

& co *and Company* cs
(cum suis)

a *art* (sebelum huruf mati)
satu, suatu, se~; per, tiap; ~
cigarette sebatang rokok →
batang; ~ *dog* seekor
anjing → **ékor**; ~ *house*
sebuah rumah → **buah**; ~
man seorang lelaki →
orang; ~ *month* sebulan

abacus *n* sempoa

abandon *v* mengabaikan,
menelantarkan; **abandoned**
v, adj terabaikan, telantar

abattoir *n* [abatuar]
pejagalan

abbey *n* biara; **abbot** *n, m*
kepala biarawan

abbreviate *v* menyingkatkan, memendekkan;
abbreviation *n* singkatan,
kependekan

abdicate *v* lengser, turun
takhta

abdomen *n* perut

abduct *v* menculik; **abduc-
tion** *n* penculikan; **abduc-
tor** *n* penculik

ability *n* [abiliti] kemampuan, kesanggupan, kepan-
daian ← **able**

able *adj* [ébel] bisa, mampu,
sanggup

abnormal *adj* tidak normal,
tidak biasa; **abnormality**
n cacat

aboard *adj* di atas kendaraan; *to go* ~ naik kapal

abolish *v* menghapus,
meniadakan; **abolition** *n*
penghapusan, pencabutan

Aborigine *n* [Aborijini]
orang Aborijin, penduduk
asli Australia; **Aboriginal**
adj, n orang Aborijin

abort *v* menggugurkan;
abortion *n* pengguguran,
aborsi

about *prep* tentang, mengenai, seputar (sebuah
topik); sekitar, keliling
(sebuah tempat); *they know
their way* ~ *town* mereka
tahu jalan di kota; kurang
lebih, kira-kira (jumlah); ~
to segera akan

above *prep* [abav] (di)
atas; lebih daripada; ~ *all*

361

terutama, yang paling penting

abrasion *n* luka ringan, goresan pada kulit; **abrasive** *adj* (bersifat) kasar

abridged *adj* singkat; ~ *dictionary* kamus singkat

abroad *adv* luar negeri, negeri orang; *Liz has gone* ~ Liz sudah pergi ke luar negeri

abrupt *adj* tiba-tiba; kasar, kurang sopan

absence *n* ketidakhadiran; **absent** *adj* tidak hadir; ~*minded* sering lupa

absolute *adj* mutlak, total; **absolutely** *adv* secara mutlak, betul

absorb *v* menyerap; ~*ed in* asyik; **absorbent** *adj* menyerap; **absorption** *n* serapan, absorpsi; penyerapan

abstain *v* tidak ikut (memilih dalam pemilihan suara), menjadi netral; berpantang

abstract *adj* abstrak; tidak konkret; ~ *art* seni abstrak, aliran abstrak; *n* ringkasan

absurd *adj* gila, tidak masuk akal

abundance *n* kelimpahan; **abundant** *adj* berlimpah (ruah)

abuse *n* [abyus] penganiayaan, penyalahgunaan; kekerasan; *child* ~ kekerasan terhadap anak-anak; *v* [abyuz] menganiaya, menyalahgunakan, memperlakukan dengan kasar

academic *adj* akademis; ~ *record* hasil rapot atau nilai; *n* akademisi; **academy** *n* akademi, sekolah tinggi

accelerate *v* mempercepat; menginjak gas (di mobil); **accelerator** *n* (pedal) gas

accent [aksént] *n* logat, aksen, nuansa

accept *v* menerima; **acceptable** *adj* layak, dapat diterima; **acceptance** *n* penerimaan

access *n* akses; *v* mendapat, memakai; **accessible** *adj* terjangkau, dekat

accessory: accessories *n, pl* aksesoris, variasi (pada mobil), perlengkapan

accident *n* [aksident] kecelakaan; *it was an* ~

acquire

tidak sengaja; **accidental** *adj*
kebetulan, tidak disengaja
accommodation *n*
penginapan, akomodasi
accompaniment *n* [akam-
paniment] pengiringan;
accompany *v* menemani,
mengantarkan, mengiringi
accomplice *n* [akamplis]
kaki tangan, antek
accomplish *v* melaksanakan; **accomplishment** *n*
prestasi
accord *n* persepakatan, persetujuan; **accordance** *in*
~ *with* sesuai dengan;
according ~ *to* menurut;
accordingly *adv* oleh
karena itu, maka
account *n* rekening (bank);
pertanggung jawab; laporan,
cerita; ~ *for* mempertanggungjawabkan; **account-
ancy** *n* akuntansi; **accountant** *n* akuntan
accumulate *v* bertumpuk;
menghimpun
accuracy *n* [akurasi]
ketelitian, ketepatan; **accurate** *adj* teliti, cermat, tepat
accusation *n* tuduhan;
accuse *v* menuduh,

menuding; **accused** *the* ~
terdakwa, tergugat, tertuduh
accustomed *adj* terbiasa
ace *n* (kartu) as; *adj, coll*
mahir, hebat
ache *n* [ék] sakit, pegal;
head~ sakit kepala, pusing
kepala; *tooth*~ gigi ngilu; *v*
sakit; rindu
achieve *v* mencapai,
meraih; **achievement** *n*
prestasi
acid *n* asam; *adj* pahit
acknowledge *v* [aknolej]
mengakui; menyebut
(sebagai ucapan terima
kasih); **acknowledgment**
n pengakuan; ucapan terima
kasih
acne *n, pl* [akni] jerawat
(terutama yang besar dan
sulit sembuh)
acorn *n* biji pohon ek
acoustic *adj* [akustik] ~ *guitar*
gitar (klasik); **acoustics** *n*
keadaan suara atau musik
berbunyi di dalam ruangan,
akustik
acquaintance *n* kenalan
acquire *v* memperoleh;
acquisition *n* perolehan,
barang yang diperoleh

363

acquit *v* membebaskan dari tuduhan, menyatakan tidak bersalah; **acquittal** *n* pembebasan

acre *n, ark* [éker] ukuran tanah (0.46 hektar)

acrobat *n* akrobat, pesenam

across *prep* (di) seberang, melintang, lintas; mendatar

act *n* perbuatan; babak, lakon (dalam pertunjukan); undang-undang; **caught in the** ~ tertangkap basah; *v* berbuat, bertindak; ~*ing* pemangku jabatan; **action** *n* perbuatan, aksi; proses; ~ **film** film laga; **to take** ~ bertindak; **activate** *v* menghidupkan, menggerakkan; **active** *adj* giat, rajin, sibuk, aktif; hidup (telepon genggam); **activist** *n* aktivis; **activity** *n* kegiatan, kesibukan; **actor** *n, m* aktor, pemain (film); **actress** *n, f* aktris, pemain (film); **actual** *adj* **actually** *adv* sebenarnya

acupuncture *n* tusuk jarum

acute *adj* parah, akut; ~ **attack** serangan mendadak (penyakit)

AD *abbrev Anno Domini* M (Masehi)

adapt *v* menyesuaikan; menyadur; **adaptable** *adj* mudah menyesuaikan diri, supel

add *v* bertambah, menambah, menambahkan

addict *n* pecandu; **addiction** *n* ketagihan, ketergantungan

addition *n* tambahan, penambahan, jumlah; **in** ~ **to** ditambah lagi, lagipula; **additional** *adj* tambahan, ekstra ← **add**

address *n* alamat, adres; pidato; *v* mengalamatkan (surat); berpidato; menegur, menyapa

adequate *adj* cukup, memadai

adhesive *adj* lengket; *n* lem

adjacent *adj* berdekatan, berdampingan, bersebelahan

adjoining *adj* berdampingan

adjust *v* menyetel, mencocokkan, mengatur, menyesuaikan; **adjustment** *n* penyetelan, pengaturan, penyesuaian

administer *v* memerintah, mengelola, mengurus;

aeronautical

melaksanakan; memberikan;
administration n; **admini-**
strative adj pemerintahan;
pemerintah; pelaksanaan;
pemberian; **administrator**
n pemerintah, pelaksana,
pengurus

admirable adj mengagumkan,
patut dikagumi ← **admire**

admiral n laksamana

admiration n kekaguman;
admire v mengagumi;
admirer n pengagum

admission n penerimaan,
izin masuk; pengakuan;
admit v menerima, mengizinkan masuk; mengakui;
admittance no ~ dilarang
masuk

adolescent n remaja, anak
puber

adopt v mengangkat atau
memungut anak; mengambil;
adoptive adj ~ child anak
angkat, anak pungut

adorable adj lucu, meng-
gemaskan, manis, jelita;
adore v memuja; sangat
mencintai, gila akan

adult adj dewasa; n orang
dewasa

adultery n zinah

advance n kemajuan; uang
muka; in ~ di muka, ter-
lebih dahulu, sebelumnya; v
maju; memajukan, mem-
percepat

advantage n untung,
keuntungan

advent n kedatangan; before
the ~ of computers sebelum
munculnya zaman komputer

adventure n petualangan

adverb n kata keterangan
(pada kata kerja)

advertise v mengiklankan,
memasang iklan; **advertiser**
n pihak yang memasang
iklan; **advertisement** n
iklan, pariwara, reklame

advice n [advais] nasihat,
saran; **advise** v [advaiz]
menasihati; **advisor** n
penasihat

advocate n [advokat] orang
yang memperjuangkan,
pembela; v [advokét]
menyeru agar

aerial n [érial] antena; adj
angkasa, udara

aeronautical adj, n aero-
nautika, ilmu penerbangan;
~ engineering teknik
penerbangan; **aerospace** n

365

bidang angkasa dan
penerbangan

affair *n* perkara, hal, soal,
urusan; perselingkuhan,
cerita cinta

affect *v* mempengaruhi;
affection *n* rasa kasih
sayang; **affectionate** *adj*
memperlihatkan kasih
sayang

affiliate: affiliated *v, adj*
berafiliasi dengan

affirmative *n* ya

affix *n* kata imbuhan

afflict *v* melanda; *~ed by*
terkena, menderita;
affliction *n* penderitaan

afford *v* mampu (membayar
dll) *I can't ~ it* saya tidak
mampu (membayar atau
membeli); **affordable** *adj*
terjangkau (harganya)

afraid *adj* takut

Africa *n* Afrika; **African** *adj*
berasal dari Afrika; *n* orang
Africa

Afro-American *n* orang
Amerika berkulit hitam
(keturunan Afrika); orang
Negro

after *prep*, *conj*, *adv*
kemudian; *prep* setelah,

sesudah; *~ all* lagipula;
meskipun demikian; *to be*
~ mendesak, mengejar;

afternoon *n* sore, petang;
sesudah jam 12 siang
sampai dengan matahari
terbenam; *good ~* selamat
siang (jam 12–15); selamat
sore (jam 15–19); **after-
wards** *prep* sesudahnya,
kemudian

again *adv* (sekali) lagi; *~*
and ~ berulang kali,
berkali-kali; *then ~* tapi

against *prep* terhadap;
berlawanan, bertentangan

agate *n* [aget] batu akik

age *n* umur, usia; *under~*
di bawah umur; abad;
the Middle ~s Abad
Pertengahan

agency *n* agen, perwakilan;
news~ kantor berita ←
agent

agenda *n* agenda, acara;
rencana; *on the ~* direncana-
kan, masuk agenda

agent *n* agen, wakil

aggravate *v* memperparah,
mengganggu

aggression *n* penyerangan,
serangan, agresi; **aggressive**

adj galak, bersifat menyerang, agresif

agile *adj* gesit; **agility** *n*
ketangkasan, kecerdasan,
kegesitan

agitate *v* mengganggu, mengguncangkan, menghasut;
agitation *n* kekacauan,
penghasutan; **agitator** *n*
pengacau, penghasut;
pengaduk

AGM *abbrev Annual General
Meeting* rapat tahunan

ago *adv* lalu, lampau, silam;
three days ~ tiga hari yang
lalu

agony *n* kesakitan,
penderitaan; sakratulmaut

agrarian *adj* berkaitan
dengan tanah pertanian

agree *v* setuju, bersepakat;
menyetujui, mengiyakan; *~
to* menyetujui, mengabulkan;
agreement *n* persetujuan,
kesepakatan, perjanjian

agricultural *adj* berkaitan
dengan pertanian; *~ science*
ilmu pertanian; **agriculture**
n pertanian

agronomics *n* agronomi

AH *abbrev after hours* r, rmh
(rumah)

ahead *adv* [ahéd] di depan,
di muka, terlebih dahulu ←
head

aid *n* bantuan, pertolongan;
first ~ pertolongan pertama;
v membantu, menolong

**AIDS (Acquired Immune
Deficiency Syndrome)** *n*
AIDS; *~ patient* orang
dengan HIV/AIDS
(ODHA)

aim *n* sasaran, maksud,
tujuan; *v* membidik,
mengincar, menuju

ain't *sl* tak, tidak ← **is not**

air *n* udara; angin; *~ mail* pos
udara; *by ~* dengan pesawat
terbang; *on ~* mengudara; *v*
menjemur, menganginkan;
aircraft *n* pesawat terbang,
kapal terbang; **air crew** *n*
awak kabin; **air force** *n*
angkatan udara; **airer** *n*
jemuran; **airline** *n* perusahaan penerbangan, mas-
kapai penerbangan; **airliner**
pesawat (terbang) penump-
ang; **airplane, aeroplane**
n pesawat terbang; **airport**
n bandara, bandar udara;
air raid *n* serangan udara;
airship *n* kapal udara;

airsick *adj* mabuk (udara);
airtight *adj* kedap udara
aisle *n* [ail] lorong
alarm *n* weker; tanda bahaya;
rasa kaget; *v* membuat
kaget, mengagetkan
albatross *n* elang laut
alcohol *n* alkohol, minuman keras; **alcoholic** *n*
peminum berat, pemabuk;
adj beralkohol
alert *n* tanda (bahaya); *red ~*
siaga satu; *on the ~* berjaga-
jaga; *v* memperingatkan;
adj siaga, waspada
algebra *n* aljabar
Algeria *n* Aljazair; **Algerian**
adj berasal dari Aljazair
alien *n* [élien] makhluk
asing, orang asing; *adj* asing
alight *adj* menyala; bercahaya
align [alain] **alignment** *n*
kesejajaran
alike *adj* serupa, mirip ← **like**
alive *adj* (dalam keadaan)
hidup ← **live**
all *adj* [ol] semua, seantero;
sekalian, seluruh; *~ in ~*
sesudah dipertimbangkan
matang-matang; *~ but*
hampir-hampir; semua
kecuali; *~ day* sepanjang

hari, seharian; *~ over* habis;
di mana-mana; *~ right*
baiklah; *~ of us* kita semua;
not at ~ sama sekali tidak;
all-round *adj* umum
allegation *n* tuduhan,
tudingan; pengakuan, per-
nyataan
allergic *adj* mempunyai
alergi; *~ to cheese* ada
alergi keju; **allergy** *n* alergi
alley *n* [ali] lorong, gang; *~
cat* kucing kampung
alliance *n* [alaiens] perserikatan, persekutuan,
gabungan; **allied** *adj*
serikat, sekutu, gabungan
← **ally**
alligator *n* [aligétor] buaya
(bermoncong pendek)
allocate *v* mengalokasikan,
memperuntukkan; **alloca-
tion** *n* alokasi, peruntukan
allow *v* mengizinkan, mem-
perbolehkan, memperkenan-
kan; **allowance** *n* tunjangan,
uang harian, uang saku
alloy *n* logam campuran
allusion *n* sindiran
ally [alai] *n* sekutu; *v*
bersekutu
almanac *n, arch* almanak

almighty *adj* [olmaiti] maha kuasa

almond *n* kacang almond, buah badam

almost *adv* [olmost] hampir, nyaris

alone *adj, adv* sendiri, seorang diri; hanya, saja

along *prep* sepanjang; *adj* ~ *(with)* bersama (dengan); *all* ~ selama ini; **alongside** *adj* di sisi, di tepi

aloof *adj* sombong

aloud *adj* dengan suara keras, dengan suara nyaring

alphabet *n* abjad, aksara, alfabet; *the Latin* ~ huruf Rumawi

alpine *adj* gunung

already *adv* [olrédi] sudah, telah

also *adv* [olso] juga, pula, pun

alter *v* mengubah; memperbaiki; **alteration** *n* perubahan; perbaikan

alternate *v* berselang-seling, menyelang-nyeling; *adj* berselang-seling; **alternative** *n* pilihan lain, alternatif

although *conj* [oltho] meskipun, walaupun

altitude *n* ketinggian, tinggi

altogether *adj* [oltogéther] semuanya, secara keseluruhan; *neg* sama sekali

aluminium, aluminum *n* aluminium; ~ *foil* kertas perak

alumni [alamnai] *n, pl* lulusan universitas tertentu

always *adv* selalu, senantiasa

am *abbrev ante meridiem* pagi, siang (jam 0.00–12.00)

amateur *adj, n* [amater] amatir; tidak profesional

amaze *v* mengherankan, menakjubkan, mengagumkan; **amazement** *n* rasa heran, rasa kagum

ambassador *n* duta besar

amber *n* ambar

ambiguous *adj* ambigu, kurang jelas

ambition *n* ambisi, cita-cita; **ambitious** *adj* berambisi, mempunyai cita-cita tinggi

ambulance *n* ambulans

ambush *n* serangan mendadak, penyerapan; *v* menyerang secara mendadak, menyergap

amen *ejac* amin

amendment *n* pembetulan; amandemen

amenities *n, pl* fasilitas, sarana

America *n* Amerika (Serikat); *North* ~ Amerika Utara; **American** *n* orang America; *adj* berasal dari Amerika

amethyst *n* batu kecubung

amiable *adj* [émiabel] ramah, baik hati

amicably *adv* secara baik-baik

ammonia *n* amonia

ammunition *n* amunisi

amnesty *n* grasi, amnesti, pengampunan

among [amang], **amongst** *prep* di tengah, di antara

amount *n* jumlah, banyaknya; *v* berjumlah, menjadi

amphibian *n* binatang yang tinggal di dua dunia, seperti katak

amplifier *n* pengeras; **amplify** *v* memperbesar

amputate *v* memotong anggota badan, meng-amputasi; **amputation** *n* amputasi

amulet *n* jimat

amuse *v* menghibur; **amused** *adj* terhibur, tertawa; **amusement** *n*

hiburan, kesenangan; ~ *park* taman hiburan; **amusing** *adj* lucu, menyenangkan

an *art* (sebelum huruf vokal) satu, suatu, se~; per, tiap; ~ *apple* sebuah apel → **buah**; ~ *egg* sebutir telur → **butir**; ~ *envelope* sehelai amplop → **helai**; ~ *owl* seekor burung hantu → **ekor**

anaemia → **anemia**

anaesthesia → **anesthesia**

anal *adj* ~ *sex* sodomi ← **anus**

analysis *n* analisa, analisis, uraian; *in* ~ sedang men-jalankan terapi dengan psi-kiater; **analyze** *v* meng-analisa, meneliti

anatomy *n* anatomi, ilmu urai tubuh

ancestor *n* leluhur, nenek moyang; **ancestry** *n* silsilah, nenek moyang

anchor *n* [anker] sauh, jangkar; *v* membuang sauh, berlabuh

ancient *adj* [énsyent] kuno, zaman purbakala; ~ *Egypt* Mesir Kuno

& co *and company* cs (cum suis)

and *conj* dan, serta, bersama; ~ *so on* dan lain sebagainya

anecdote *n* lelucon, cerita, anekdot

anemia *n* [animia] kurang darah, anemia

anesthetic *n* obat bius; *general* ~ bius total; *local* ~ bius lokal

angel *n* [énjel] malaikat

anger *n* [angger] kemarahan, murka; *v* membuat marah

angle *n* [anggel] sudut; *right* ~ tegak lurus

angle: angling *n* memancing; ~ *rod* joran; **angler** *n* pemancing

Anglo- *adj* [angglo] Inggris; ~*Saxon* berdarah Inggris (bukan Wales, Skotlandia atau Irlandia)

angry *adj* marah, murka ← **anger**

animal *n* binatang, hewan, satwa

animation *n* semangat; kartun animasi, anime

ankle *n* [angkel] pergelangan kaki

annexe, annex *n* pavilyun; *v* mencaplok, menggabungkan; **annexation** *n* penggabungan

annihilate *v* [anaihilét] membinasakan, membasmi, memusnahkan; **annihilation** *n* pembinasaan, pembasmian, pemusnahan

anniversary *n* (hari) ulang tahun, hari jadi; hari peringatan (tidak digunakan untuk makhluk hidup); *wedding* ~ hari ulang tahun perkawinan

annotate *v* membubuhi catatan; **annotation** *n* catatan

announce *v* mengumumkan, memberitahukan; **announcer** *n* penyiar; **announcement** *n* pengumuman, maklumat

annoy *v* mengganggu, mengusik; **annoying** *adj* mengganggu, menjengkelkan

annual *adj* tahunan; ~ *general meeting* rapat tahunan; **annually** *adv* setiap tahun

annul *v* membatalkan, mencabut

anonymous *adj* tanpa nama, anonim; ~ *letter* surat kaleng

another *n, adj* satu lagi, yang lain

371

answer *n* [anser] jawaban, jalan keluar (dari masalah); *v* menjawab, membalas (surat)

ant *n* semut; *white ~s* rayap

Antarctic *adj* berasal dari Antartika; *the ~*, **Antarctica** *n* Antartika, Kutub Selatan

antenna *n* antena

anthem *n* lagu wajib; *national ~* lagu kebangsaan

anthology *n* kumpulan, antologi, bunga rampai

anthropological *adj* berkaitan dengan antropologi; **anthropologist** *n* antropolog; **anthropology** *n* ilmu antropologi

anti- *adj* anti-, anti, bersifat melawan; *~septic* obat anti-kuman

anticipate *v* mengantisipasi, mengharapkan, menanti-nanti; **anticipation** *n* harapan

anticlimax *n* kekecewaan, hasil yang berbeda dengan harapan ← **anti**

antics *n, pl* tingkah lucu, kelucuan

antidote *n* penawar ← **anti**

antipathy *n* antipati, perasaan tidak suka, perasaan benci ← **anti**

antique *n* barang kuno, barang antik; *adj* kuno, antik

antlers *n, pl* tanduk rusa

antonym *n* lawan kata

anus *n* [énus] dubur

anvil *n* landasan, paron

anxiety *n* [angzayeti] kecemasan, kegelisahan, kekuatiran; **anxious** *adj* [angsyes] gelisah, cemas

any *adj* [éni] sesuatu, beberapa, sembarang; *neg* sedikit pun; *~ one* mana saja; *do you have ~ food?* apakah ada makanan?; *~ color is fine* warna apa saja boleh; **anybody, anyone** *n* siapa pun, siapa saja; **anyhow** *adv* bagaimanapun; **anything** *n* apa saja, apa pun; **anywhere** *n* di mana saja; *adv* ke mana saja

apart *adv* terpisah; *~ from* selain, kecuali

apartment *n* apartemen, rumah susun

ape *n* kera, siamang

APEC *abbrev* Asia-Pacific Economic Cooperation APEC, Kerjasama Ekonomi Asia Pasifik

apologize *v* minta maaf;
apology *n* permintaan maaf
apostle *n* [aposel] rasul
appall *adj* ngeri, heran;
appalling *adj* mengerikan,
sangat buruk
apparatus *n* perkakas,
aparat, alat
apparent *adj* nyata, jelas,
kentara; **apparently** *adv*
tampaknya, ternyata ←
appear
appeal *n* permohonan,
permintaan, seruan; banding;
v naik banding; **appealing**
adj menarik, menawan
appear *v* tampak, muncul,
timbul, menghadap;
appearance *n* tampang,
penampilan
appendix *n* lampiran; usus
buntu
appetite *n* selera, nafsu
makan
applaud *v* bertepuk tangan,
memuji; **applause** *n* tepuk
tangan
apple *n* buah apel
appliance *n* peranti,
pesawat, alat
applicable *adj* berlaku,
dapat diterapkan ← **apply**

applicant *n* pelamar,
pemohon; **application** *n*
(surat) lamaran; penerapan,
pemakai; ~ *form* formulir
(pendaftaran); **apply** *v*
berlaku; menerapkan,
menggunakan; ~ *for a job*
melamar untuk pekerjaan
appoint *v* menunjuk,
menetapkan, mengangkat;
appointed *adj* yang
ditentukan
appraisal *n* taksiran
evaluasi
appreciate *v* [aprisyiét]
berterima kasih; meng-
hargai, menilai; mengerti;
appreciation *n* penghargaa-
an; pengertian; taksiran
apprehensive *adj* kuatir,
gelisah
apprentice *n* [apréntis]
murid
approach *n* pendekatan; *v*
mendekati, menuju (tem-
pat); menjelang (waktu)
appropriate *adj* patut,
layak, pantas, sesuai
approval *n* [apruval] izin,
persetujuan; **approve** *v*
memperkenankan, meng-
izinkan, menyetujui

approximate *adj* kira-kira, kurang lebih; **approximately** *adv* kira-kira, kurang lebih

apricot *n* [éprikot] aprikot

April *n* [Épril] bulan April

aqua *adj* biru toska

aquarium *n* akuarium, kolam ikan

aquatic *adj* [akuotik] berhubungan dengan air atau laut; ~ *center* kompleks kolam renang

aqueduct *n* jalan air (di atas tanah)

Arab *n* orang Arab; *adj* berasal dari daerah Arab; *Uni Emirat ~ (UEA)* United Arab Emirates (UAE); **Arabia** *n* [Arébia] (daerah) Arab; *Saudi ~ Arab Saudi*; **Arabian** *adj* berasal dari Arab; **Arabic** *n* [Arabik] bahasa Arab; ~ *script* huruf Arab

arbitrary *adj* tanpa aturan, secara acak

arcade *n* lorong atau gang beratap; ~ *game* mesin permainan di tempat umum

arch *n* garis lengkung; busur; **archer** *n* pemanah; **archery** *n* panahan

archeological *adj* purbakala; **archeologist** *n* ahli purbakala; **archeology** *n* ilmu purbakala

archipelago *n* [arkipélago] kepulauan, gugusan pulau; *the Malay ~* Nusantara

architect *n* [arkitekt] arsitek; ~ *lanskap* landscape architect; **architecture** *n* arsitektur

archive, archives *n* [arkaiv] arsip

Arctic *adj* Arktik, Artik, berasal dari kawasan Kutub Utara; *the ~ (Circle)* daerah (lingkaran) Arktik

are *v, pl* → **be**

area *n* [éria] daerah, wilayah, kawasan

Argentina *n* [Arjentina] Argentina; **Argentinian** *n* orang Argentina; *adj* berasal dari Argentina

argue *v* [argyu] berdebat, bertengkar; memperdebatkan, membantah; **argument** *n* pertengkaran; alasan, dalih

arid *adj* gersang, kering; *semi-~* kering

aristocracy *n* kaum ningrat; **aristocrat** *n* orang ningrat,

artist

bangsawan; **aristocratic**
adj bersifat ningrat atau
bangsawan

arithmetic *n* ilmu berhitung

ark *n* bahtera

arm *n* lengan, tangan (baju)

arm *n* senjata; *v* memper-
senjatai

armchair *n* kursi sofa, kursi
tamu

armor *n* baju baja; *~ed car*
mobil lapis baja

armpit *n* ketiak

army *n* tentara, bala tentara;
angkatan darat

aroma *n* bau harum, aroma;
aromatic *n* berbau harum;
aromatherapy *n* aroma-
terapi, pengobatan atau
relaksasi dengan wewan-
gian

around *prep* sekeliling,
sekitar, seputar; dekat; *adj*
kira-kira

arrange *v* mengurus, menata,
mengatur; mengaransemen
(lagu); *~d marriage* penjo-
dohan; **arrangement** *n*
penataan, pengaturan, perjanjian; aransemen

arrest *n* penahanan,
penangkapan; *cardiac ~*

serangan jantung; *under*
~ ditahan; *v* menahan,
menangkap

arrival *n* kedatangan; **arrive**
v datang, tiba

arrogance *n* kesombongan,
keangkuhan; **arrogant** *adj*
sombong, angkuh

arrow *n* (anak) panah

art *n* seni lukis; kesenian; **arts**
n kesenian; sastra (jurusan);
arty *adj* (sok) artistik

arterial *adj* [artirial] *~ road*
jalan arteri; **artery** *n* pembuluh nadi, arteri

arthritis *n* [arthraitis] encok,
radang sendi

article *n* barang, benda; pasal,
bab (hukum); kata sandang

articulate *adj* menguasai
bahasa, pandai menyuarakan
pikiran

artifact *n* benda atau barang
bersejarah

artificial *adj* buatan, palsu;
~ insemination pembuahan
buatan

artillery *n* artileri; *heavy ~*
senjata berat, meriam

artist *n* seniman, seniwati;
artis (seni peran); **artistic**
adj artistik, indah ← **art**

375

as *adv, conj* sama, se-; seperti; karena, sebab; ~ *big* ~ *a house* sebesar rumah; ~ *for me* kalau saya; ~ *if* seolah-olah

asbestos *n* asbes

ascend *v* naik, mendaki, memanjat; **ascent** *n* kenaikan; tanjakan

ash *n* abu; ~ *Wednesday* Rabu Abu

ashamed *adj* malu

ashore *adj* di darat; *to go* ~ naik ke darat ← **shore**

ashtray *n* asbak

Asia *n* [Ésya] Asia; *Southeast* ~ Asia Tenggara; **Asian** *n* orang Asia; *adj* berhubungan dengan Asia

aside *adv* di sebelah; ~ *from* selain dari ← **side**

ask *v* bertanya, minta, memohon; ~ *after* bertanya mengenai (orang); ~ *out* mengajak berkencan

asleep *adj* sedang tidur; *to fall* ~ tertidur

asparagus *n* asparagus

aspect *n* segi pandangan, sudut pandangan, aspek

asphalt *n* [asyfalt] aspal

aspiration *n* cita-cita,

harapan, aspirasi

ass *n* keledai; *sl* pantat

assassinate *v* membunuh tokoh terkenal; **assassination** *n* pembunuhan tokoh terkenal

assault *n* serangan, serbuan; *v* menyerang, menyerbu

assemble *v* berkumpul, berhimpun, bersidang; mengumpulkan; merakit; **assembly** *n* perkumpulan, perhimpunan, sidang; perakitan; apel (di sekolah)

assent *v* memperkenankan, mengizinkan, menyetujui

assert *v* menyatakan dengan tegas; **assertive** *adj* berani

assess *v* menaksir, menilai; **assessment** *n* taksiran, penilaian

asset *n* aset, modal

assignment *n* tugas

assimilate *v* membaur; **assimilation** *n* pembauran, asimilasi

assist *v* menolong, membantu; **assistance** *n* pertolongan, bantuan; *may I be of* ~? bisakah saya bantu?; **assistant** *n* pembantu, asisten

associate n kawan, mitra, rekan; v bergaul; mengaitkan, menghubungkan; **association** n gabungan, persatuan, asosiasi

assorted adj bermacam jenis

assume v menganggap; **assumption** n asumsi, prasangka

assurance n kepastian, jaminan, janji; **assure** v memastikan, menjamin

asterisk n tanda bintang

asthma n (penyakit) asma, sesak dada

astonish v mengherankan, menakjubkan; **astonished** adj heran; **astonishment** n keheranan

astound v **astounding** adj mengejutkan, mengherankan

astrologer n [astrolojer] peramal; **astrology** n nasib menurut bintang, astrologi

astronomer n astronom, ahli bintang; **astronomy** n (ilmu) astronomi, ilmu bintang

astute adj cerdik, berakal

asylum n [asailum] suaka,

tempat perlindungan; ~-*seeker* pencari suaka

at prep di; pada; ~ *all* sama sekali; ~ *home* di rumah; betah; ~ *last* akhirnya; ~ *least* paling tidak; ~ *once* sekarang juga; ~ *times* kadang-kadang; ~ *seven o'clock* pada jam tujuh

atheist n [éthiest] ateis

athlete n [athlit] atlet, olahragawan; pelari; **athletic** adj [athlétik] kuat, berotot, fit; **athletics** n cabang atletik, lari

Atlantic *the ~ (Ocean)* Laut Atlantik; *the South ~* Laut Atlantik Selatan

atlas n atlas, buku peta; *road ~* buku peta jalan

ATM abbrev *automated teller machine* ATM (anjungan tunai mandiri)

atmosphere n suasana; hawa, udara; angkasa, atmosfer

atoll n pulau karang, atol

atom n atom; ~ *bomb* bom nuklir, bom atom; **atomic** adj berkaitan dengan atom, nuklir; ~ *energy* tenaga nuklir

atrocity n kekejian, keke-

jaman, kebengisan
attach v menambat,
melekatkan, mengaitkan,
melampirkan; **attaché** n
[atasyé] atase; **attached**
adj terlampir; berpasangan;
sayang; **attachment** n
lampiran; rasa sayang
attack n serangan; v
menyerang
attempt n usaha, percobaan;
v mencoba, berusaha
attend v hadir; menghadiri;
~ to melayani; merawat;
attendance n kehadiran;
attendant n pelayan; flight
~ pramugari, pramugara
attention n perhatian; **atten-
tive** adj penuh perhatian
attic n loteng
attitude n sikap, pendirian;
sl keberanian
attorney n [atérni] pengacara;
~-general Jaksa Agung
attract v menarik atau
memikat (hati); **attraction**
n daya tarik, daya pikat;
atraksi; tourist ~ obyek
wisata; **attractive** adj
menawan
attribute v menghubungkan,
mengaitkan

auction n lelang; ~ house
rumah lelang; v melelangkan;
auctioneer n juru lelang
audible adj kedengaran,
terdengar
audience n para penonton,
tamu, hadirin
audit n pemeriksaan
keuangan; v memeriksa
keuangan, mengaudit;
auditor n akuntan
audition n audisi; v mengikuti audisi
August n bulan Agustus
aunt n [ant] **aunty, auntie**
sl bibi, tante; great-~
saudara perempuan dari
kakek atau nenek
Australia n [Ostrélia]
Australia; **Australian** n
orang Australia; adj berasal
dari Australia
authentic adj asli, otentik
author n pengarang, penulis
authority n otoritas,
kekuasaan; yang berwajib,
instansi; ahli, pakar;
authorization n kewenangan; **authorize** v mengizinkan
autism n [otizem] autisme;
autistic adj autis

autobiographical *adj* yang berkaitan dengan pengalaman sendiri; **autobiography** *n* otobiografi

automatic *adj* otomatis, dengan sendirinya

autonomous *n* otonom; **autonomy** *n* otonomi; *regional* ~ otonomi daerah (otda)

autopsy *n* otopsi, bedah mayat

autumn *n* [otum] musim gugur

auxiliary *adj* bantu, pembantu; ~ *verb* kata kerja bantu

Av, Ave *Avenue* Jl (Jalan)

available *adj* tersedia

avenge *v* membalas dendam (terutama atas kematian)

avenue *n* [avenyu] jalan

average *n adj* rata-rata; *on* ~ rata-rata

aviary *n* [éviari] kandang burung yang besar

avocado *n* alpukat

await *v* menantikan ← **wait**

awake *v* **awoke awoken** bangun; *adj* dalam keadaan bangun; **awaken** *v* bangun;

awakening *n* kesadaran; awal ← **wake**

award *n* penghargaan; *v* memberi penghargaan

aware *adj* sadar akan, menyadari; **awareness** *n* kesadaran

away *adj* tidak di sini, tidak ada; dari tempat itu; *go* ~! pergilah!; *he's* ~ *today* dia tidak masuk hari ini

awe *n* [o] perasaan kagum; **awful** *adj* dahsyat, mengerikan

awkward *adj* kikuk, canggung; **awkwardness** *n* kecanggungan

ax, axe *n* kapak

axis *n* [aksis] poros, sumbu

axle *n* [aksel] as roda

B

B & B *abbrev* **bed and breakfast** losmen, penginapan murah yang termasuk sarapan

BA *abbrev* **Bachelor of Arts** SS (Sarjana Sastra)

babble *v* berceloteh, mengoceh; bicara tanpa kendali

babe *n, sl* [béb] bayi; cewek; **baby** *n* bayi; *adj* anak; *a ~ elephant* anak gajah; *~sit v* menjaga anak; **babysitter** *n* penjaga anak

baboon *n* babon

bachelor *n* bujangan, jejaka; *~'s degree* S1 (Strata Satu); *~ of Arts (BA)* Sarjana Sastra (SS)

back *n* belakang, punggung, balik; *at the ~ of* di belakang; *adj* di belakang; *adv* ke belakang, mundur; *~ and forth* mondar-mandir, bolak-balik; *~ seat* jok belakang; *v* mendukung, mendanai; *~ down* akhirnya menyerah; *~ up* bertumpuk, menjadi antrean panjang; **backbone** *n* tulang belakang; **backdrop** *n* latar belakang (di panggung); **background** *n* latar belakang; **backing** *n* sokongan, dukungan; **backside** *n, sl* pantat; **backstreet** *adj, sl* tidak resmi, lewat pintu belakang; **backstroke** *n* gaya punggung; **backward,**

backwards *adj, adv* ke belakang, mundur

bacon *n* irisan daging babi asap; *beef ~* daging sapi yang diasap seperti *bacon*

bacteria *n, pl* bakteri, kuman

bad *adj* jelek, buruk, kurang baik; *~ dream* mimpi buruk; *~-mannered* tidak sopan

badge *n* lencana, pin

badger *n* sejenis binatang hutan di Eropa, luak

baffled *adj* bingung

bag *n* tas, karung; *bum ~* tas pinggang; *carry~* tas tenteng, keresek; *v, sl* memesan tempat

baggage *n* [bagej] bagasi, koper, tas; *left ~* penitipan tas

baggy *adj* kendor, kebesaran

bail *n* uang jaminan; *~ out* menyelamatkan

bait *n* umpan; *v* menggoda, mengumpani

bake *v* membakar; **baker** *n* tukang memasak roti; *~'s dozen* tiga belas; **bakery** *n* toko roti

balance *n* keseimbangan; neraca, timbangan; *fin* saldo; *v* menimbang; **balanced** *adj* berimbang balcony *n* balkon, teras, beranda

bald *adj* botak, gundul, plontos

ball *n* bola; ~*boy*, ~*girl* orang yang mengambilkan bola selama pertandingan tenis; *n* pesta berdansa; *on the* ~ cerdas, sadar

ballerina *n* p pebalet; **ballet** *n* [balé] balet

balloon *n* balon; *hot-air* ~ balon udara

ballot *n* [balet] pemilihan suara, pengambilan undi; ~ *box* kotak suara

bamboo *n* bambu

ban *n* larangan; *v* melarang; **banned** *adj* dilarang

banana *n* pisang

band *n* gerombolan, geng, kawanan; grup (band); gelang

bandage *n* [bandej] perban; *v* memerban, membalut

bandanna *n* ikat kepala

bandit *n* bandit, penyamun

bang *ejac* dor!, suara keras; *v* berdentang; membanting

banish *v* membuang; **banishment** *n* pembuangan

bank *n* bank; tepi, sisi (sungai); **banker** *n* bankir; **banknote** *n* uang kertas; **bankrupt** *adj* bangkrut, pailit; **bankruptcy** *n* kepailitan

banner *n* spanduk

banquet *n* [bankuet] perjamuan lengkap

baptism *n* permandian; **baptist** *n* pembaptis; *John the* ~ Yohanes Pembaptis; Yahya; **baptize** *v* memper-mandikan, membaptis

bar *n* palang pintu, batang, halangan, rintangan; tempat minum, kafe; *v* memalang, menghalangi, merintangi; melarang

barb *n* duri; ~*ed wire* kawat berduri

barbarian *n* barbar, orang biadab

barbecue, barbeque, BBQ *n* acara memanggang daging di luar rumah; *v* memanggang daging

barber *n* tukang cukur

bare *adj* telanjang, polos; hanya; *v* menelanjangi, memamerkan; **barefoot** *adj* dengan kaki telanjang; **barely** *adj* hampir tidak

bargain *n* [bargen] pembelian yang murah; *v* tawar-menawar, menawar

barge *n* tongkang

bark *n* kulit kayu; gonggongan anjing; *v* menggonggong

barn *n* gudang (tempat menyimpan jerami, rumput kering dsb)

baron *n* baron (gelar bangsawan)

barracks *n* barak, tangsi, asrama

barrel *n* tong; laras bedil

barren *adj* tandus, gersang; tidak subur, mandul

barricade *n* [barikéd] rintangan, barikade; *v* memblokir, merintangi

barrier *n* palang, penghalang, rintangan

barrister *n* advokat, pengacara (yang tampil di pengadilan)

barrow *n* gerobak

bartender *n* pelayan yang menyediakan minuman di bar atau kafe ← **bar**

barter *n* niaga tukar-menukar barang, barter; *v* tukar-menukar barang, barter, membarter

base *n* markas, dasar; *v* berdasar, mendasarkan

basic *adj* asasi, pokok; *the* ~s prinsip-prinsip dasar

basil *n* [bazil] sejenis kemangi

basin *n* baskom, wastafel; lembah, daerah aliran sungai (DAS)

basket *n* keranjang, bakul, basket; ~*ball* bola basket

bass *n* [bés] bas

bastard *n* anak haram, anak yang lahir di luar nikah; *sl* brengsek, bajingan

bat *n* alat pemukul (dalam olahraga); *v* memukul bola (dalam kriket, bisbol dsb)

bat *n* kelelawar, kampret, kalong

batch *n* sejumlah; seri (keluaran barang)

bath *n* (bak) mandi; *to take a ~, have a ~* mandi; ~*robe* kimono; ~*tub* bak untuk mandi rendam; **bathe** *v* [béth] mandi; **bathroom** *n* kamar mandi; *may I use your ~?* boleh saya ke WC?

baton *n* tongkat kecil

battalion *n* batalyon

battery *n* baterai

battle n pertempuran, peperangan; perjuangan; v bertempur, berjuang; **battler** n pejuang, orang kecil; **battleship** n kapal perang, kapal tempur

bay n teluk; ~ *leaf* daun salam

bazaar n [bezar] pasar kaget

BBC abbrev British Broadcasting Corporation penyiar nasional Inggris

BC abbrev before Christ SM (sebelum Masehi)

BE abbrev Bachelor of Economics SE (Sarjana Ekonomi)

be v **was been** menjadi, adalah

beach n pantai, pesisir; v mendamparkan diri

bead n manik-manik; tetesan

beam n balok; sinar (cahaya); v bersinar, tersenyum lebar

bean n buncis, kacang; *kidney* ~ kacang merah; *string* ~ kacang panjang

bear n beruang; *polar* ~ beruang putih

bear v **bore, born** memikul, menahan; bersalin; melahirkan

beard n [bird] jenggot

bearing n sikap; arah, tujuan, pengaruh

beast n binatang; orang yang bengis

beat n pukulan; irama, ritme; v **beat, beaten** memukul, mengalahkan

beautiful adj [byutifal] cantik (perempuan), asri (pemandangan), bagus, indah; **beauty** n kecantikan, keindahan; wanita cantik

beaver n sejenis berang-berang

became v, pf → **become**

because conj [bikoz] (oleh) karena, sebab; ~ *of* karena, lantaran

become v [bikam] **became become** menjadi; **becoming** adj cocok, menarik

bed n tempat tidur, ranjang; ~ *and breakfast (B & B)* hotel kecil; **bedroom** n kamar (tidur); **bedspread, bedcover** n selimut

bee n lebah, tawon, kumbang

beef n daging sapi

beehive n sarang lebah ← **bee**

been v, pf → **be**

383

beer *n* bir
beetle *n* kumbang
before *prep* di muka, depan; sebelum; *adv* sebelum; **beforehand** *adv* terlebih dahulu
beg *v* meminta-minta, mengemis; memohon; ~ *your pardon* maaf; **beggar** *n* pengemis
begin *v* **began begun** mulai, memulai; **beginning** *n* awal, permulaan
behalf *on* ~ *of* atas nama, demi
behave *v* berkelakuan (baik); ~ *yourself* berkelakuan baik, sopan; **behavior** *n* perilaku
behind *n* [behaind] belakang; *sl* pantat; *prep* di belakang, ke belakang; *adv* tertinggal, ketinggalan
being *n* makhluk; keadaan → **be**
Belgian *n* orang Belgia; **Belgium** *n* [Béljum] Belgia
belief *n* **beliefs** pendapat, kepercayaan, iman, agama; **believe** *v* percaya, berpendapat
bell *n* bel, lonceng, genta

bellow *v* berteriak; meneriakkan
belly *n* (bagian bawah) perut; ~ *button* pusar
belong *v* milik, termasuk kepunyaan; **belongings** *n, pl* barang milik
beloved *n* [belovéd] *adj* yang dicintai, yang dikasihi, yang disayangi
below *prep* di bawah, ke bawah
belt *n* ikat pinggang, sabuk; *seat* ~ sabuk pengaman; *v, sl* mencambuk
bench *n* bangku, tempat duduk
bend *n* belokan; *v* **bent bent** membelok, melengkung
beneath *prep* di bawah
beneficial *adj* menguntungkan, bermanfaat; **benefit** *n* manfaat, untung; ~ *concert* konser amal; *for the* ~ *of* demi; *v* menguntungkan
BEng *abbrev* Bachelor of Engineering ST (Sarjana Teknik), Ir (insinyur)
bent *v, pf* → **bend**; *adj* bengkok, tidak lurus; *sl* homoseksual
bequest *n* warisan

384

beret *n* [béré] baret, pici

Bermuda ~ *shorts* sejenis celana pendek

berth *n* kamar, bilik kapal; tempat

beside *prep* di sisi, di dekat; kecuali, di luar, selain dari; **besides** *adv, prep* lagipula, ditambah lagi

best *adj* paling bagus, paling baik, terbaik; ~ *man* pendamping pengantin pria; ~*seller* laris terjual; *the* ~ *part of* bagian terbesar; *it's (all) for the* ~ lebih baik begitu

bet *n* taruhan; *a safe* ~ kemungkinan besar; *v* **bet bet** bertaruh

betray *v* mengkhianati; **betrayal** *n* pengkhianatan

better *adj* lebih baik; sembuh; ~ *not* lebih baik jangan; *your* ~*s* orang di atas, orang tua; *v* memperbaiki, mengungguli

between *prep* (di) antara, di tengah

beverage *n* minuman (terutama yang panas)

beware *adj* awas, berhati-hati; ~ *of the dog* awas anjing

beyond *prep* (di) sebelah, lebih (jauh), melampaui, melebihi

BH *abbrev business hours* k, ktr (kantor)

bias *n* [bayas] kecenderungan; **biased** *adj* tidak berimbang

Bible *n* [baibel] Injil, Alkitab

bicycle *n* [baisikel] sepeda; ~ *path* jalur sepeda

bid *n* tawaran, usaha; *v* **bid bidden** menawar; **bidding** *n* penawaran

big *adj* besar, gemuk; raksasa; ~ *brother* abang, kakak (laki-laki); ~*-headed* sombong, egois; ~ *shot* tokoh penting, orang besar; ~ *toe* jempol kaki

bigamy *n* hal beristeri atau bersuami dua

bike *n* sepeda (motor); *v* naik sepeda; *trail* ~ sepeda motor gunung; **biker** *n* penggemar sepeda motor

bilingual *adj* [bailingguel] dwibahasa; **bilingualism** *n* kemampuan berbahasa lebih dari satu

bill *n* bon, rekening, nota; wesel, daftar; rancangan

undang-undang (RUU);
paruh (pada burung); *v*
menagih
billiards *n, pl* bilyar
billion *n* satu milyar
(1 000 000 000); **billionaire**
n milyarder
bin *n* tempat sampah, tong;
dust~, rubbish ~ tempat
sampah
bind *v* [baind] **bound**
bound menjilid; mengikat;
binder *n* map; **binding** *n*
penjilidan
binoculars *n, pl* teropong,
binokular
biographer *n* [bayografer]
penulis biografi; **biog-
raphy** *n* biografi, riwayat
hidup
biologist *n* [bayolojist] ahli
biologi; **biology** *n* ilmu
biologi
bird *n* burung; *~ cage*
sangkar burung; *~'s eye
view* pandangan dari atas
birth *n* kelahiran; *~day*
hari ulang tahun, hari jadi;
~mark tahi lalat; *~ mother*
ibu kandung
biscuit *n* [bisket] biskuit,
kue kering

bisexual *adj* [baiséksyual]
biseks
bishop *n* uskup
bit *n* sedikit, sepotong; *not
a ~* sedikit pun tidak, sama
sekali tidak; *v, pf →* **bite**
bitch *n* anjing betina;
perempuan jelek
bite *n* gigitan; *v* **bit bitten**
menggigit
bitter *adj* pahit
bizarre *adj* [bizar] luar
biasa aneh
black *adj* hitam, gelap;
~board papan tulis; *~
market* pasar gelap, tidak
resmi; *~out* mati lampu;
~smith pandai besi; *in ~
and white* di atas kertas,
hitam di atas putih; *v ~ out*
pingsan; **blackmail** *n* pemerasan; *v* memeras
bladder *n* kandung kemih;
~ infection infeksi saluran
kemih
blade *n* mata pisau
blame *n* kesalahan; *v* menyalahkan, menyalahi (orang)
blank *n* tempat kosong;
peluru kosong; *mental ~*
tiba-tiba lupa; *adj* kosong,
hampa

blanket *n* selimut; *v* menye-limuti

blasphemy *n* penghinaan terhadap Tuhan, cacian, makian

blast *n* angin kencang, letupan, tiupan; *ejac* keparat

blaze *n* kebakaran; *v* me-nyala; **blazing** *adj* menyala

blazer *n* jas (setengah resmi)

bleach *n* pemutih; *v* memu-tihkan (baju)

bleak *adj* suram, gelap

bleat *n* embekan; *v* mengembik

bleed *nose~* mimisan; *v* **bled bled** berdarah; **bleeding** *adj* berdarah

blend *n* campuran; *v* ber-baur; mencampur

bless *v* memberkati; *~ you Isl* alhamdulillah (sesudah bersin); *God ~ you Chr* Tuhan memberkati; **bless-ing** *n* pemberkatan; doa restu

blew *v, pf* → **blow**

blind *n* [blaind] horden, penutup jendela, kerai; *v* menyilaukan, membuta-kan; *~ed* silau; *adj* buta; **blindfold** *n* kain penutup

mata; *v* menutup mata dengan kain; **blindly** *adj* membabi buta, tanpa melihat atau berpikir

blink *n* kedipan mata, kejapan mata; *v* mengedip, mengejapkan mata; **blink-ing** *adj* berkedip-kedip

bliss *n* kebahagiaan; **blissful** *adj* bahagia, berbahagia

blister *n* lecet, lepuh; *v* menjadi lecet, melepuhkan

blitz *n* serangan kilat

bloat *~ed* bengkak, kem-bung

block *n* balok; blok; *v* merintangi, membatasi, menghambat; *~ed* ter-sumbat, mampet

blond *adj, m* **blonde** *f* (berambut) pirang

blood *n* darah; *~ relation* saudara kandung, hubungan darah; *~ vessel* pembuluh darah; **bloodstain** *n* bekas darah; **bloody** *adj* berdarah; *sl* gila, persetan; *~ hell* persetan

blossom *n* bunga; *cherry ~* sakura; *v* berbunga

blot *n* noda (tinta)

blouse *n* [blauz] blus

387

blow *n* pukulan, tamparan; tiupan; *v* **blew blown** bertiup; meniup; ~ *your nose* membuang ingus, bersin; **blowpipe** *n* sumpitan

blubber *v* menangis dengan keras

blue *adj* biru; ~ *blood* bangsawan, darah biru; ~*collar* pekerja berpenghasilan rendah; ~ *film* film porno; ~*print* cetakan biru; ~ *ribbon* mutu tertinggi; hadiah pertama; *to feel* ~ bersedih; *out of the* ~ tiba-tiba

bluff *n* pura-pura; *v* berpurapura, berlagak

blunder *n* [blander] kesalahan besar; *v* berbuat salah

blunt *adj* tumpul

blur *n* kabur; **blurred, blurry** *adj* kabur, kurang jelas

blurb *n* paragraf mengenai isi buku di sampul belakang

blush *v* memerah (muka); **blusher** *n* pemerah pipi, perona pipi

BMed *abbrev* Bachelor of Medicine SK (Sarjana Kedokteran)

BO *abbrev* body odor bau badan

boar *n* babi jantan

board *n* papan; karton, kertas tebal, kardus; dewan; *on* ~ di kapal, di pesawat, bersama; *v* naik pesawat; mondok, kos; ~ *and lodging* kos (termasuk makanan); **boarder** *n* anak kos; **boarding** ~ *house* rumah kos, asrama (sekolah); ~ *pass n* pas naik pesawat; ~ *school* sekolah dengan asrama

boast *n* bualan; *v* membual

boat *n* kapal, perahu

bob *v* membungkuk; turun naik

bobbin *n* bobin, gulungan

body *n* badan, tubuh; organisasi, himpunan; **bodyguard** *n* pengawal pribadi; **bodysurfing** *n* berselancar tanpa papan

bog *n* rawa, payau; *v* terhenti (kendaraan)

boil *n* bisul; *on the* ~ sedang memanas; *v* mendidih; merebus; **boiler** *n* ketel (kukus)

bold *adj* berani; ~ *type* huruf tebal

bother

bolt *n* baut, slot; *v* mengunci; kabur

bomb *n* [bom] bom; *v* mengebom; **bomber** *n* pesawat pengebom; **bombing** *n* pengeboman

bond *n* pengikat; ikatan; kewajiban; obligasi

bone *n* tulang; gading; *jaw~* tulang rahang; *adj* gading

bonfire *n* api unggun

bonnet *n* topi (untuk bayi atau perempuan)

book *n* buku, kitab, novel; *v* memesan; *~case*, *~ shelf* lemari buku; **booking** *n* pemesanan, buking; **book-keeper** *n* akuntan; bandar taruhan; **book-keeping** *n* pembukuan; **booklet** buku kecil, buklet; **bookseller** penjual buku, toko buku; **bookshop** *n* toko buku; **bookworm** *n* kutu buku

boom *n* ledakan; *v* meledak; *ejac* dor!

boost *n* dorongan, kemajuan; **booster** *n* tambahan

boot *n* sepatu (bot), sepatu lars; *v* menghidupkan (komputer); *re~* menghidupkan (komputer) kem-

bali; *~ polish* semir sepatu

booth *n* loket, gerai

bootlace *n* tali sepatu (bot) ← **boot**

booze *sl, n* minuman keras

border *n* tepi, sisi; perbatasan, tapal batas; *v* berbatasan dengan; membatasi

bore *n* orang atau kegiatan yang membosankan; mengebor; **boring** *adj* membosankan, menjemukan

bore *v, pf* → **bear**

born *v, pf* dilahirkan, lahir, terlahir → **bear**

borrow *v* pinjam, meminjam; *~er* orang yang meminjam

boss *n* pemimpin, bos; **bossy** *adj* suka menyuruh

botanist *n* ahli tumbuh-tumbuhan, ahli botani; **botany** *n* tumbuh-tumbuhan

both *adj* kedua, kedua(-kedua)nya; *both ... and ...* baik ... maupun ...

bother *n* repot, kesusahan; *v* merepotkan, menyusahkan; mengganggu

bottle *n* botol

bottom *n* bawah, pantat, alas; *adj* bawah; *at the ~ of* di bawahnya, di tempat bawah

bought *v, pf* [bot] → **buy**

bounce *n* lambungan; semangat; *v* melambung, memantul; **bouncy** *adj* bersifat melambung

bound *v* melompat, berlari-lari; *~ for* menuju; *v, pf* → **bind**

bounds *out of* ~ di luar daerah yang diizinkan; **boundary** *n* (tapal) batas

bounty *n* hadiah uang

bouquet [buké] karangan bunga, buket

bow [bau] *n* tundukan; haluan; *v* membungkukkan badan, menunduk; menyerah

bow [bo] *n* busur

bowels *n, pl* [bauls] usus

bowl *n* [bol] mangkuk, pinggan

bowling *n* boling

box *n* kotak, dus, peti; tinju; *v* bertinju; meninju; **boxer** *n* petinju; **boxing** *n* tinju; *~ Day* tanggal 26 Desember

boy *n* anak lelaki; *~ scout* pramuka, pandu

boycott *n* boikot; *v* memboikot

boyfriend *n, m* pacar

boyish *adj* seperti anak lelaki ← **boy**

brace *n* penahan; *~s* kawat gigi

bracelet *n* [bréslét] gelang (berantai)

bracket *n* tanda kurung

brag *v* membual, menyombong

braid *n* kepang

brain *n* otak, benak; *~s* akal sehat; otak (makanan); **brainwash** *v* mencuci otak

brake *n* rem; *hand~* rem tangan; *v* mengerem

bran *n* sejenis sereal

branch *n* cabang; bagian; *~ office* kantor cabang; *v* bercabang

brand *n* cap, merek; *~-new* sama sekali baru

brandy *n* brendi

brass *n* kuningan

brave *adj* berani; **bravery** *n* keberanian

brawl *n* tawuran, pertikaian; *v* tinju, bergumul

Brazil *n* Brasil; ~ *nut* kacang Brazil; **Brazilian** *n* orang Brasil; *adj* berasal dari Brasil

bread *n* [bréd] roti; *short~* semacam biskuit

breadth *n* [brédth] lebar

break *n* [brék] istirahat, rehat, jeda; patah, putus; *v* **broke broken** memecahkan, mematahkan; **breakdown** *n* perincian; kegagalan, kerusakan; **breakfast** [brékfast] *n, v* sarapan, makan pagi

breakwater *n* [brékwater] tembok laut

breast *n* [brést] dada, payudara; *sl* susu, tetek; ~ *cancer* kanker payudara; ~ *milk* ASI (air susu ibu)

breath *n* [bréth] nafas, napas; **breathe** *v* [brith] bernafas, menarik nafas

breed *n* ras; *v* **bred bred** mengembangbiakkan; mendidik; **breeder** *n* peternak; **breeding** *n* trah, nenek moyang; sopan santun

breeze *n* angin sepoi-sepoi

brew *n* minuman panas; *v* membuat minuman

(terutama bir); **brewery** *n* tempat pembuatan bir

bribe *n* uang sogok, uang suap; *v* menyogok, menyuap; **bribery** *n* suapan, sogokan; ~ *and corruption* KKN (korupsi, kolusi, nepotisme)

brick *n* batu bata; ~ *kiln* oven pembakaran keramik; **bricklayer** *n* tukang batu

bridal *adj* berkaitan dengan acara pernikahan; **bride** *n, f* pengantin wanita, mempelai wanita; **bridegroom** *n, m* pengantin pria

bridge *n* jembatan; *foot~* jembatan kaki; *suspension* ~ jembatan gantung; *v* menjembatani, mempertemukan

brief *adj* pendek, ringkas, singkat; **briefing** *n* rapat pendek, penyebaran informasi

brigade *n* [brigéd] regu, pasukan; *fire* ~ pasukan pemadam kebakaran

bright *n* [brait] terang, gemilang; cerdik, cemerlang, pandai

brilliant *adj* gemilang, berseri

brim *n* tepi, pinggir (topi)

bring *v* **brought brought**
[brot] membawa; ~ *about*
menghasilkan, meng-
akibatkan; ~ *on* menyebabkan, mendatangkan; ~ *up*
membesarkan

brink *n* sisi, tepi, pinggir

brisk *adj* cepat; segar, dingin

Britain *n* [Briten] Britania
coll Inggris; *Great* ~
Inggris Raya; **British** *adj*
berasal dari Inggris

brittle *adj* rapuh

broad *adj* lebar, luas;
~*minded* berwawasan luas

broadcast *n* siaran; *v*
broadcast broadcast
menyiarkan

broccoli *n* brokoli

broke, broken *v, pf* ←
break *adj* rusak

broker *n* makelar, calo,
perantara

bronze *n* perunggu

brooch *n* [broc] bros

brook *n* kali, anak sungai

broom *n* sapu

Bros *abbrev* **brothers**
bersaudara

broth *n* kaldu

brothel *n* tempat pelacuran,
bordil

brother *n* [brather] kakak
atau adik lelaki; saudara;
~*-in-law* (adik atau kakak)
ipar; **brotherhood** *n*
persaudaraan

brought *v, pf* → **bring**

brown *adj* (warna) coklat

brownies *n, pl* kue coklat

bruise *n* [bruz] memar;
bruised *adj* memar,
bengkak

brunette *n, f* [brunét]
wanita yang berambut
coklat

brush *n* sikat, kuas (alat
seni); *v* menyikat

brutal *adj* brutal, bengis,
kasar; **brutality** *n*
kebrutalan, kebengisan,
kekasaran

BSc *abbrev Bachelor of
Science* SSi (Sarjana
Sains)

bubble *n* gelembung; *v*
membual; menggelem-
bung; **bubbly** *adj* bersoda;
ceria

buck *n* rusa jantan; *sl* dolar

bucket *n* ember

buckle *n* [bakel] gesper

bud *n* kuntum; *v* berkuntum,
bersemi

Buddha *n* Budha;
Buddhism *n* agama
Budha; **Buddhist** *n* orang
Budha; *adj* berkaitan
dengan agama Budha

budge *v* bergerak sedikit

budgerigar, budgie *n*
sejenis burung bayan kecil

budget *n* [bajét] anggaran; *v*
menganggarkan

buffalo *n* kerbau

buffer *n* penyangga; ~ *zone*
daerah penyangga

buffet *n* [bafé] bufet,
prasmanan

bug *n* serangga, kumbang,
kutu; *v* mengganggu

buggy *n* kereta atau
kendaraan kecil

build *v* [bild] **built built**
mendirikan, membangun,
membina; **builder** *n*
pemborong; **building** *n*
gedung, bangunan

bulb *n* lampu pijar, bola
lampu, bohlam

bulge *v* membengkak,
menonjol

bulk *n* tumpukan, timbunan;
bulky *adj* besar, bertumpuk

bull *n* sapi jantan; ~*fighter*
matador; ~*fighting*

pertandingan antara
manusia dan banteng; ~*'s
eye* sasaran

bullet *n* peluru; ~*train*
shinkansen

bulletin *n* selebaran, berita
kilat

bully *n* orang yang men-
akut-nakuti atau mengejek
orang lain; *v* menakut-
nakuti orang lain

bump *n* pukulan, tonjokan;
v menabrak; **bumpy** *adj*
tidak rata, bergelombang

bun *n* sanggul, konde; roti
berbentuk bola, biasanya
manis

bunch *n* tandan, gugus,
segenggam; segerombolan

bundle *n* [bandel] berkas,
paket; *v* membungkus

bunk *n* ranjang yang
sempit; ~ *bed* ranjang yang
bertingkat

bunker *n* [bangker] ruang
bawah tanah, bungker

bunny *n, sl* kelinci

buoy *n* [boi] pelampung

burden *n* beban; muatan,
tanggungan; *v* membebani,
memberatkan

bureau *n* [byuro] kantor,

biro; meja tulis; **bureau-cracy** *n* [byurokrasi] birokrasi; **bureaucrat** *n* birokrat

burglar *n* maling; *cat* ~ maling yang masuk dari atas bangunan; **burglary** *n* kemalingan

burial *n* [bérial] pemakaman ← **bury**

burn *n* luka terkena panas, luka bakar; *v* **burned burnt** menyala; membakar; **burner** *n* sumbu

burp *n* sendawa; *v* bersendawa

burrow *n* liang (binatang); *v* menggali liang

burst *v* **burst burst** meletus; menyembur

bury *v* [béri] mengubur, menanam

bus *n* bis

bush *n* [busy] semak belukar

busily *adv* [bizili] dengan sibuk ← **busy**

business *n* pekerjaan; perkara, urusan; perdagangan, perniagaan; perusahaan; ~*-like* profesional; **businessman** *n, m*; **busi-nesswoman** *n, f* pengusaha, wiraswasta

busy *adj* [bizi] sibuk; **busybody** *n* orang yang suka ikut campur, raja gosip

but *conj* tetapi, tapi, namun; kecuali

butcher *n* [bucer] jagal, tukang potong, tukang daging, pembantai; toko daging

butt *n* puntung (rokok)

butter *n* mentega

butterfly *n* kupu-kupu; gaya kupu-kupu

button *n* kancing; *v* ~ *(up)* mengancing

buy *n* [bai] pembelian; *v* **bought bought** [bot] membeli; **buyer** *n* pembeli

buzz *n* dengung, deru; *v* mendengung, menderu

by *prep* oleh, dengan; ~ *yourself* sendiri; ~ *the* ~, ~ *the way* ngomong-ngomong; ~ *God* demi Allah

bye *ejac* selamat jalan, selamat tinggal; ~ ~ *child* selamat jalan, selamat tinggal

BYO *abbrev* bring your own bawa sendiri (minuman keras)

C

C *abbrev Celsius* Celsius

c *cent* sen

cab *n* bagian depan truk; ~ *driver* supir taksi

cabbage *n* [kabej] kol, engkol, kubis

cabin *n* bagian depan truk; ~ *crew* awak kabin; ~ *luggage* bagasi kabin; *log* ~ pondok (dibuat dari balok kayu)

cabinet *n* kabinet; lemari

cable *n* [kébel] kabel; ~ *TV* TV kabel

cactus *n* **cacti** kaktus

caddy *n* kedi

cadet *n* kadet; semacam pramuka

café, cafe *n* kafe, warung kopi

cage *n* sangkar, kurungan; *v* mengurung

cake *n* kue; ~ *mix* adonan kue

calcium *n* kalsium, zat kapur

calculate *v* menghitung-hitung, memperhitungkan, menaksir; **calculation** *n* perhitungan; **calculator** *n* kalkulator

calendar *n* kalender, alma-nak; penanggalan; *Islamic* ~ tahun hijriah

calf *n* [kaf] betis

calf *n* [kaf] anak sapi

call *n* [kol] panggilan, seruan; percakapan telepon; kunjungan; *v* memanggil; menelepon; ~ *at* mampir di; ~ *on* berkunjung ke, men-gunjungi; ~ *out* berteriak; ~ *box* telepon umum; ~*girl* wanita panggilan, pelacur; **caller** *n* penelepon; tamu

calligrapher *n* [kaligrafer] orang yang bisa membuat tulisan tangan indah; **callig-raphy** *n* tulisan tangan yang indah; *Arabic* ~ kaligrafi

calm *n* [kam] ketenangan, keteduhan; *v* menenangkan, menenteramkan; *adj* tenang, teduh

Cambodia *n* Kamboja; **Cambodian** *adj* berasal dari Kamboja

came *v, pf* → **come**

camel *n* [kamel] unta

camera *n* kamera

camouflage *n* [kamuflasy] kamuflase, penyamaran; *v* menyamar

camp *n* perkemahan, kamp; *v* berkemah

campus *n* lokasi universitas, kampus

can *n* kaleng

can *aux, v* **could/was able, been able** dapat, bisa

Canada *n* Kanada; **Canadian** *n* [Kanédian] orang Kanada; *adj* berasal dari Kanada

canal *n* terusan

canary *n* [kanéri] burung kenari

cancel *v* membatalkan, mencoret, menghapus; **cancellation** *n* pembatalan

cancer *n* kanker

candidate *n* calon, kandidat

candle *n* lilin

candy *n* permen, kembang gula

cane *sugar* ~ tebu

cane *n* tongkat

canine *n* anjing

cannibal *n* kanibal, pemakan sejenis

cannon *n* meriam, kanon

canoe *n* [kanu] kano

cantaloupe *n* [kantalop] melon, blewah

canteen *n* kantin

canvas *n* kanvas; kain terpal

canyon *n* ngarai

cap *n* topi pet; tutup; ~ *off* mengakhiri

capability *n* kesanggupan, kemampuan; **capable** *adj* bisa, mampu, dapat

capacity *n* daya tampung, kapasitas

cape *n* tanjung

capital *n* modal; huruf besar; ~ *(city)* ibukota; ~ *punishment* hukuman mati; **capitalist** *n* kapitalis; **capitalism** *n* kapitalisme

capitol *n* ibukota

capsule *n* kapsul

captain *n* kapten, nahkoda; kapitan

caption *n* [kapsyen] tulisan di bawah gambar

captivity *n* penawanan, tahanan; **capture** *n* penangkapan; *v* menangkap

car *n* mobil; gerbong; ~ *park* tempat parkir; ~ *wash* cuci mobil; *dining* ~ (gerbong) restorasi

caramel *n* gula bakar, permen rasa karamel

carat *n* karat

caravan *n* kafilah; karavan

carbohydrate n [karbo-
haidrét] karbohidrat

carbon n karbon, zat arang;
~ dioxide karbon dioksida;
carbonated ~ drink
minuman bersoda

carcass n bangkai (binatang)

card n kartu; kardus; credit
~ kartu kredit; playing ~s
kartu remi; to play ~s main
kartu

cardboard n karton, kertas
tebal

care n pemeliharaan, pe-
rawatan; ~ of (c/-) dengan
alamat (d/a); v peduli,
memedulikan; ~ for suka
pada; child ~ penitipan
anak-anak; to take ~
berhati-hati, jaga diri; to
take ~ of memelihara,
mengurus

career n karir; ~ woman
wanita karir

carefree adj tanpa beban,
riang; **careful** adj hati-hati;
careless adj teledor, lalai
← **care**

carer n perawat, penjaga
anak ← **care**

caretaker n penjaga ←
care

cargo n muatan kapal; ~
boat kapal barang

Caribbean the ~ (Sea)
Laut Karibia

carnation n anyelir

carnival n pesta, pasar
malam, karnafal

carnivorous adj yang
makan daging

carol n lagu Natal

carp n ikan gurame;
Japanese ~ ikan koi

carpenter n tukang kayu

carpet n permadani, karpet

carport n garasi, atap untuk
perlindungan mobil

carriage n [karij] kereta;
gerbong ← **carry**

carrier n [karier] pembawa
(penyakit dsb); ~ bag
plastik, keresek ← **carry**

carrot n wortel; insentif

carry v mengangkut, mem-
bawa; ~ on meneruskan;
~ out menjalankan,
melakukan, melaksanakan

cart n kereta, pedati, gerobak;
horse and ~ kereta kuda

cartographer n orang yang
membuat peta

cartoon n (film) kartun;
komik

cartridge *n* [kartrij] pelor, peluru; isi pulpen

carve *v* mengukir

case *n* peti, koper; kasus, perkara, hal, perihal; in ~ jika, kalau

cash *n* uang kontan, uang tunai; ~ *crop* hasil pertanian yang akan dijual

cashew *n* kacang mede

cashier *n* [kasyir] kasir, kassa ← **cash**

casino *n* tempat berjudi, kasino

casserole *n* [kaserol] masakan yang berkuah

cassette *n* kaset; ~ *player* radio kaset, tape

cast *n* lemparan; tuangan; pemain-pemain sandiwara; *v* **cast cast** melempar, melontar; menuangkan; memilih untuk peran; ~ *iron* besi tuang

caste *n* [kast] kasta

castle *n* [kasel] puri, benteng, istana

castor ~ *oil* minyak jarak, kastroli

casual *adj* santai

casualty *n* korban kecelakaan; ~ *(ward)* Unit

Gawat Darurat (UGD)

cat *n* kucing; ~ *nap* tidur sebentar

catalog *n* katalog, daftar; *v* mendokumentasi

catastrophe *n* [katastrofi] bencana, malapetaka

catch *n* angkapan, hasil; jepitan, gesper; *v* **caught caught** [kort] menangkap; terkena, terjangkit (penyakit); ~ *(a) cold* masuk angin; ~ *up* mengejar; mengobrol setelah lama tidak bertemu; **catchphrase** *n* semboyan

category *n* kategori, golongan

cater *v* melayani; menyediakan makanan; **caterer** *n* perusahaan jasa boga; **catering** *n* jasa boga

caterpillar *n* ulat

cathedral *n* [kathidral] katedral

Catholic *n* orang Katolik; *adj* Catholic; *Roman* ~ Katolik

cattle *n* sapi, ternak

Caucasian *n* [kokésyan] orang kulit putih

caught *v, pf* ← **catch**

cauliflower *n* [koliflauer] kembang kol

cause *n* [coz] sebab; *v* menyebabkan, mengakibatkan

caution *n* sikap hati-hati, kewaspadaan; *v* mengingatkan

cave *n* gua

caviar *n* telur terubuk (ikan)

cavity *n* rongga, lubang (gigi)

cc *cubic centimeter* cc (sentimeter kubik)

CD *abbrev compact disk* CD

cease *v* [siis] berhenti; menghentikan; ~ *fire* gencatan senjata

cedar *n* sejenis pohon

ceiling *n* [siling] langit-langit, plafon

celebrate *v* [sélébrét] merayakan; **celebrated** *adj* ternama, masyhur, termasyhur; **celebration** *n* perayaan

celebrity *n* selebriti

celery *n* seledri

cell *n* sel; bilik penjara; ~ *phone* telepon seluler (ponsel), telepon genggam

cellar *n* besmen, ruang bawah tanah

cement *n* semen, beton; perekat; *v* menyemen; merekat

cemetery *n* kuburan, tempat pemakaman umum (TPU)

censor *n* sensor; *v* menyensor

census *n* sensus

center *n* pusat; ~ *of attention* pusat perhatian; *shopping* ~ pusat perbelanjaan, mal; **central** *adj* pusat, tengah, pokok; ~ *Jakarta* Jakarta Pusat (Jakpus); ~ *Java* Jawa Tengah (Jateng)

centimeter *n* senti, sentimeter

centipede *n* [sentipid] kaki seribu, lipan

century *n* abad

cereal *n* [sirial] sereal

ceremony *n* upacara

certain *adj* [serten] tentu, pasti, yakin; **certainly** *adj* tentu saja

certificate *n* sertifikat, ijazah, surat; **certified** *adj* berijazah

cervical *adj* berhubungan dengan leher (rahim); **cervix** *n* leher rahim

cf *compare* dibandingkan

chain *n* rantai; kalung; serangkaian; ~*smoke* merokok terus-menerus; *in* ~*s* dibelenggu; *v* merantai

chair *n* kursi; ketua; **chairman** *n, m* **chairperson** *n* ketua

chalk *n* kapur

challenge *n* tantangan; *v* menantang; **challenging** *adj* menantang

chamber *n* [cémber] kamar; ~ *of commerce* kamar dagang

chameleon *n* [kamilion] bunglon

champagne *n* [syampéin] sampanye

champion *n* juara

chance *n* kesempatan, peluang; *by* ~ secara kebetulan; *to take a* ~ mengambil risiko

chancellor *n* kanselir; *vice-~* pembantu rektor

change *n* perubahan; uang kembali; *v* menukar, mengubah; ~ *your clothes* ganti pakaian; ~ *your mind* berubah pikiran

channel *n* saluran, selat; *v* menyalurkan

chant *n* lagu yang dinyanyikan atau diucapkan; *v* bernyanyi; menyanyikan (berulang-ulang)

chaos *n* [kéos] kekacauan

chap *n, sl, m* orang, lelaki

chapel *n* [capel] kapel, gereja kecil

chapter *n* bab, pasal

character *n* [karaktér] sifat, peran; huruf; **characteristic** *n* ciri; *adj* khas

charade *n* [syerad] adegan, sandiwara

charcoal *n* arang

charge *n* muatan; ongkos, harga; serangan, serbuan; tuduhan; *in* ~ berkuasa, berwenang; *free of* ~, *no* ~ gratis, cuma-cuma; *v* menyerang; meminta bayaran, menagih; (me)ngecas

charity *n* amal

charm *n* pesona; sihir; gantungan gelang; *v* memesonakan, menarik hati; menyihir; **charming** *adj* jelita, juwita, memesonakan

chart *n* grafik; peta; *v* memetakan

charter *n* piagam; *v* mencarter

chase *n* pengejaran; *v* mengejar

chastity *n* [castiti] kesucian

chat *n* percakapan; *v* meng-

obrol; **chatter** *n* celotehan,
obrolan; *v* berceloteh,
mengobrol; **chatting** *n*
kegiatan berkomunikasi
lewat internet

chauffeur *n* [syofer] supir,
sopir

cheap *adj* murah; **cheapen**
v menurunkan harga,
merendahkan

cheat *n* penipu; *v* menipu,
curang; **cheating** *n* curang,
kecurangan

check *n* motif kotak-kotak

check, cheque *n* cek

check *n* pemeriksaan, uji,
cek; *v* memeriksa, menguji,
mengecek; ~ *in* melapor (di
hotel), cek in; ~ *out* membayar lalu meninggalkan
hotel

checkmate *ejac* skakmat

checkout *n* kasir, kassa
(terutama di swalayan)

cheek *n* pipi; keberanian,
kelancangan; **cheeky** *adj*
berani, nakal

cheer *n* kegembiraan;
sorak; *v* memberi semangat,
bersorak; mendukung;
cheerful *adj* gembira,
senang hati; **cheerleader** *n*

pemandu sorak

cheese *n* keju

chef *n* [syéf] juru masak

chemical *n* [kémikel] bahan
kimia; *adj* kimiawi; **chemist** *n* ahli kimia; apoteker;
chemistry *n* ilmu kimia

cheque → **check**

cherry *n* buah ceri

chess *n* catur; **chessboard**
n papan catur

chest *n* dada; peti, kopor

chew *v* mengunyah; ~*ing
gum* permen karet

chic *adj* [syik] anggun,
bergaya, modis

chicken *n* (rasa) ayam; ~ *pox*
cacar air

chief *n* **chiefs** kepala
(suku), pemimpin; *adj*
utama, pokok; **chiefly** *adv*
terutama, pertama-tama

child *n* [caild] **children**
[cildren] anak, putra; **child-
hood** *n* masa kanak-kanak,
masa kecil; **childish** *adj*
kekanak-kanakan

Chile *n* [Cili] Cile

chili → **chilli**

chill *n* udara dingin

chilli *n* cabe; ~ *sauce* (saus)
sambal

chilly *adj* sejuk, dingin ←
chill

chimney *n* **chimneys**
cerobong asap

chimpanzee *n* simpanse

chin *n* dagu

China *n* [Caina] (negeri)
Cina; **china** *n, adj* porselen;
Chinatown *n* Pecinan;
Chinese *n* orang Cina,
orang Tionghoa; *adj* Cina,
Tionghoa

chip *n* keping; keripik; *hot*
~s kentang goreng; *v* pecah

chipmunk *n* tupai atau bajing
tanah dengan gigi besar

chiropractor *n* [kairoprak-
tor] ahli pengobat tulang
punggung

chisel *n* [cizel] pahat; *v*
memahat

chives *n, pl* lokio

chlorine *n* klorin

chloroform *n* kloroform,
obat bius

chock ~-*a-block*, ~-*full*
penuh sesak

chocolate *n, adj* coklat

choice *n* pilihan, terpilih
← **choose**

choir *n* [kuaier] koor

choke *v* mencekik

cholera *n* kolera

cholesterol *n* kolesterol;
high ~ kolesterol tinggi

choose *v* **chose chosen**
memilih

chop *n* potong; steik yang
bertulang; *v* memotong,
mencincang; **chopper** *n*
parang; helikopter

chopsticks *n, pl* sumpit

chore *n* tugas (rumah)

choreographer *n* pencipta
tarian, koreografer

chose, chosen *v, pf* ←
choose

Christ *n* [Kraist] (Yesus)
Kristus; **christen** *v* [krisen]
mempermandikan, mem-
baptis; memberi nama;
christening *n* permandian; **Christian** *n* orang
Kristen atau Katolik; *adj*
Kristiani, Nasrani, Masehi;
Christmas *n* (hari) Natal;
~ *card* kartu Natal

chronic *adj* kronis, menahun

chronological *adj* menurut
tanggal

chubby *adj* gemuk,
berlebihan berat badan

chuck *v, sl* membuang

chunky *adj* berisi, berat

church *n* gereja; **churchyard** *n* kuburan dekat gereja

CIA *abbrev* Central Intelligence Agency Badan Intelijen Pusat (Amerika Serikat)

cicada *n* sejenis jangkrik

cider *n* sari buah (terutama apel)

cigar *n* [sigar] cerutu; **cigarette** *n* [sigarét] rokok

cinema *n* [sinema] (gedung) bioskop

cinnamon *n* kayu manis

circle *n* [serkel] lingkaran, bulatan; kawasan, lingkungan; *v* melingkari; mengedari

circular *n* [serkyuler] surat edaran; *adj* bulat, bundar; **circulate** *v* beredar; mengedarkan; **circulation** *n* peredaran, sirkulasi

circumcise *v* menyunat; ~*d* disunat; **circumcision** *n* [sirkumsisyen] sunatan

circumstances *n, pl* keadaan

circus *n* sirkus

citizen *n* [sitizen] warganegara; **citizenship** *n* kewarganegaraan

city *n* [siti] kota; ~ *hall* balaikota

civil *adj* sipil; sopan; **civilian** *n* orang sipil; **civilization** *n* [sivilaizésyen] peradaban; **civilized** *adj* beradab

Ck *creek* K. (kali)

claim *n* tuntutan; tagihan; pengakuan; *v* menuntut; menagih; mengaku; meminta

clam *n* kerang

clamber *v* memanjat, naik

clamor *n* keriuhan, keramaian, kegaduhan

clan *n* suku bangsa, kaum, marga

clap *n* tepuk; *v* bertepuk tangan; **clapper** *n* anak lonceng

clarify *v* [klarifai] menjelaskan, menerangkan; **clarification** *n* [klarifikésyen] penjelasan, penerangan ← **clear**

clarinet *n* klarinet

clash *n* bentrokan; *v* bentrok

clasp *n* jepitan, gesper; pelukan; *v* menjepit, memegang

class *n* kelas; pelajaran; golongan; *first* ~ terbaik; *science* ~ kelas IPA; **classify** *v* menggolongkan; **classroom** *n* ruang kelas

class *n* mutu, kualitas (tinggi); **classic** *adj* klasik; **classical** ~ *music* musik klasik

clause *n* ayat, klausa; syarat; anak kalimat

claw *n* cakar, jepit

clay *n* tanah liat

clean *adj* bersih; *v* membersihkan; **cleaning** *n* pembersihan; **cleanser** *n* pembersih

clear *adj* terang, jernih, jelas; nyaring, nyata; *to keep* ~ menghindari, mengelakkan; *v* membereskan; **clearance** *n* izin; ~ *sale* cuci gudang

clench *v* menggenggam; ~*ed fist* kepalan tangan

clerk *n* [klark] juru tulis

clever *adj* [klever] pandai, cerdas, pintar

cliché *n* klise

client *n* [klaient] nasabah, pelanggan, tamu, klien

cliff *n* tebing; ~*hanger* sangat menegangkan

climate *n* [klaimet] iklim

climax *n* [klaimaks] puncak, klimaks, orgasme

climb *n* [klaim] perjalanan naik; *v* memanjat; menaiki

cling *v* **clung clung** melekat; ~ *wrap* plastik pembungkus makanan

clinic *n* klinik, pusat kesehatan masyarakat (puskesmas)

clip *n* jepitan; *v* menjepit, menggunting, memotong; **clippers** *n* gunting; **clipping** *newspaper* ~ guntingan koran, kliping

clitoris *n* kelentit, klitoris

clock *n* jam; *alarm* ~ weker; *three o'*~ jam tiga; *v* mencatat waktu

clog *n* kelom, bakiak

close *v* [kloz] menutup; ~*d* tutup

close *adj* [klos] dekat, akrab; ~ *up* dari dekat; gambar yang diperbesar

closet *n* [klozet] lemari baju

closure *n* [klosyer] penutupan ← **close**

clot *n* gumpal; *v* bergumpal

cloth *n* kain, bahan; *table*~ taplak meja; **clothes** *n, pl* pakaian, baju

cloud *n* awan; *v* memperkeruh; **cloudy** *adj* berawan

clove *n* cengkeh; ~ *cigarette* (rokok) kretek

clown n badut, pelawak; v melucu

club n perhimpunan, klub, kelab; ~ *sandwich* roti dengan isi daging dan selada; *night*~ kelab malam, diskotek; **clubbing** n pergi ke diskotek

clue n tanda, petunjuk

clumsy adj canggung, kikuk

clung v, pf → **cling**

cluster n gugus, tandan; v berkerumun

clutch n genggam; kopling; v menggenggam

cm *centimeter* cm (sentimeter)

coach n pelatih; bis pariwisata; kereta kencana; v melatih

coal n batu bara; ~ *mine* tambang batu bara

coalition n koalisi

coarse adj [kors] kasar

coast n pantai, pesisir; **coastal** adj berkaitan dengan pantai

coast v meluncur, jalan bebas

coaster n alas gelas

coastline n garis pantai ← **coast**

coat n mantel, jas; lapisan; kulit atau bulu binatang; ~ *of paint* lapisan cat; v melapisi

coax v membujuk

cobble ~*stone arch* batu trotoar; **cobbler** n tukang reparasi sepatu

cobra n kobra, ular sendok

cobweb n sarang laba-laba

cocaine n [kokéin] kokain

cock n ayam jantan; ~ *fighting* sabung ayam; **cocky** adj arogan

cockatoo n [kokatu] burung kakatua

cockpit n kokpit

cockroach n kecoa

cocktail n sejenis minuman keras, koktil

cocoa n [koko] (biji) coklat

coconut n (buah) kelapa; ~ *palm* pohon kelapa, pohon nyiur

cocoon n [kekun] kepompong

code n sandi, kode; undang-undang, peraturan

coffee n kopi; *white* ~, *milk* ~ kopi susu

coffin n peti mati

cog n roda gigi

coherent *adj* jelas; masuk akal

coil *n* gulungan, gulung; *v* bergelung

coin *n* uang logam, koin

coincidence *n* [koinsidens] kebetulan

coke → **cocaine**

cold *n* masuk angin, pilek; rasa dingin; *adj* dingin

collaborate *v* bekerja sama; **collaborator** *n* orang yang bekerja sama

collapse *n* keruntuhan, kerobohan; *v* runtuh, ambruk, roboh

collar *n* kerah, leher baju; **collarbone** *n* tulang selangka

colleague *n* [kolig] rekan, kolega, teman kantor

collect *v* mengumpulkan, memungut; **collection** *n* kumpulan, koleksi; **collector** *n* kolektor

college *n* [kolej] sekolah, kolese; perguruan tinggi, universitas; ~ *student* mahasiswa; *to go to* ~ (sudah) kuliah

collide *v* bertabrakan, menabrak; **collision** *n*

[kolisyen] tabrakan

colloquial *adj* percakapan, sehari-hari

colon *n* titik dua

colonel *n* [kernel] kolonel; *lieutenant*-~ letkol (letnan kolonel)

colonial *adj* kolonial, penjajah; ~ *house* rumah Belanda; **colonization** *n* penjajahan; **colonize** *v* menjajah, menduduki; **colony** *n* jajahan

color *n* [kaler] warna; *v* mewarnai; ~*blind* buta warna; **colorful** *adj* berwarna-warni

colt *n* kuda jantan yang muda

column *n* tiang; barisan; kolom; **columnist** *n* pengasuh rubrik

coma *n* koma, mati suri

comb *n* [koom] sisir; *v* menyisir

combat *n* peperangan, pertempuran; *v* memerangi

combination *n* gabungan, kombinasi; ~ *lock* kunci kombinasi; **combine** *v* menggabungkan, memadukan

come *v* [kam] **came come** datang, tiba, sampai; ~

406

forward tampil, maju; ~ *from* berasal dari, datang dari; ~ *in* masuk; ~ *out* keluar; ~ *through* lewat, menempuh; **comeback** *n* kembali

comedian *n* [komidien] pelawak, komik; **comedy** *n* lawak, komedi

comet *n* bintang berekor

comfort *n* [kamfert] kenyaman; hikmah, hiburan; *v* menghibur; **comfortable** *adj*, **comfy** *sl* nyaman

comic *n* pelawak, komik; *adj* lucu ← **comedy**

coming *n* [kaming] kedatangan; *adj* mendatang ← **come**

comma *n* koma

command *n* perintah; komando; *v* memimpin

commemorate *v* memperingati, merayakan; **commemoration** *n* peringatan, perayaan

commence *v* mulai, memulai

comment *n* komentar; *no* ~ tidak ada keterangan; *v* berkomentar, memberi komentar; mengomentari;

commentator *n* komentator

commerce *n* perdagangan, perniagaan; *chamber of* ~ kamar dagang (kadin); **commercial** *n, adj* dagang, perniagaan; komersial

commission *n* pesan; komisi; **commissioner** *n* komisaris

commit *v* berjanji; melakukan; **commitment** *n* janji, tanggung jawab, ikatan

committee *n* [komiti] panitia, komite

commodity *basic* ~ bahan pokok

common *adj* biasa, umum; bersama; rendah; *to have something in* ~ memiliki persamaan

commune *n* komunitas yang hidup bersama

communicate *v* berkomunikasi; memberitahu, menghubungi; **communication** *n* komunikasi, perhubungan

communism *n* komunisme; **communist** *n* orang komunis; *adj* komunis; *Indonesian* ~ *Party* Partai Komunis Indonesia (PKI)

community *n* masyarakat, umat, komunitas ← **commune**

commuter *n* pelaju

compact *adj* kompak; padat

companion *n* kawan, teman; *longtime* ~ pasangan hidup; **company** *n* [kampeni] kawan-kawan; perusahaan, maskapai (penerbangan)

comparative *adj* perbandingan, komparatif; **compare** *v* membandingkan; **comparison** *n* perbandingan

compass *n* [kampas] pedoman, kompas; jangka; ~ *point* mata angin

compassionate *adj* mengasihani, berbelas kasih

compensate *v* mengganti (rugi); **compensation** *n* ganti rugi, kompensasi

compete *v* [kompit] bersaing, bertanding

competence *n* kemampuan, kompetensi; **competent** *adj* mampu, kompeten

competition *n* persaingan; pertandingan; **competitive** *adj* (suka) bersaing; **competitor** *n* pesaing, saingan

← **compete**

compile *v* menyusun; **compilation** *n* antologi, koleksi, susunan, kompilasi

complain *v* mengadu, mengeluh; **complaint** *n* pengaduan, keluhan

complete *adj* lengkap, komplit; *v* menyelesaikan; **completely** *adj, neg* sama sekali

complex *n* kompleks; *adj* rumit, ruwet; **complexion** *n* [kompléksyen] kulit wajah

complicate *v* mempersulit; ~*d* rumit, kompleks; **complication** *n* kesulitan; komplikasi (penyakit)

compliment *n* pujian; *v* memuji; **complimentary** *adj* cuma-cuma, gratis; memuji

comply *v* [komplai] mengikuti, memenuhi

component *n* unsur, komponen, suku cadang

compose *v* menyusun, membentuk, mengarang; **composer** *n* komponis; **composition** *n* karangan; susunan

compose ~*d* tenang, tidak mudah tergoncang

compost *n* kompos

compound *n* kompleks (perumahan); gabungan; senyawa

comprehend *v* mengerti, memahami; **comprehension** *n* pengertian, pemahaman

compress *n* kompres; *v* memampatkan, memadatkan; ~ed padat

comprise *v* mencakup; ~d of terdiri dari, terdiri atas

compromise *n* [kompromaiz] kompromi; *v* mencari jalan tengah, berkompromi

compulsion *n* paksaan; **compulsory** *adj* paksa, wajib

computer *n* komputer

comrade *n* [komrad] kawan, teman; kamerad

concave *adj* cekung

conceal *v* menyembunyikan; ~ed tersembunyi

concede *v* [konsid] mengaku, menerima

conceited *adj* sombong, angkuh

conceive *v* [konsiv] menjadi hamil; mengerti, membayangkan

concentrate *v* memusatkan (perhatian), konsen; **concentration** *n* pemusatan, konsentrasi

concern *n* perkara, hal; perhatian; perusahaan; ~ed prihatin; tersangkut

concert *n* konser

concession *n* izin, kelonggaran; konsesi ← **concede**

concise *adj* pendek, ringkas, singkat

conclude *v* menyimpulkan; memutuskan; **conclusion** *n* kesimpulan; akhir; *in ~* sebagai kata akhir

concrete *n* [konkrit] semen, beton; *adj* nyata

concussion *n* gegar otak

condemn *v* [kondém] menghukum; menghakimi, mengutuk

condensation *n* pengembunan, kondensasi

condition *n* keadaan, kondisi; syarat; **conditional** *adj* dengan syarat; ~ *tense* bentuk pengandaian

condolences *our ~* kami ikut berduka cita, kami ucapkan belasungkawa condom *n* kondom

conduct *n* kelakuan, cara;
conductor *n* dirigen
(musik); kondektur (angkutan umum); penghantar

cone *n* kerucut; marka
jalan

confectionery *n* permen,
gula-gula

confederation *n* persekutuan

confess *v* mengaku; **confession** *n* pengakuan

confetti *n* guntingan kertas
yang dilempar saat berpesta,
hujan kertas

confidence *n* kepercayaan;
in ~ rahasia; *self-*~ percaya
diri (PD); **confident** *adj*
berani, percaya diri; **confi-
dential** *adj* [konfidénsyel]
rahasia

confine *v* membatasi,
mengurung; memingit

confirm *v* menegaskan,
memastikan; **confirmation**
n kepastian, penegasan,
konfirmasi

confiscate *v* menyita

conflict *n* perselisihan,
pertikaian, percekcokan,
konflik; perang; *v* bertentangan

conform *v* menurut, sesuai
dengan

confound *v* mengherankan,
membingungkan

confront *v* **confronting** *adj*
menghadapi; menentang,
melawan; **confrontation** *n*
konfrontasi

confuse *v* membingungkan;
~*d* bingung

congested *adj* macet,
sesak; **congestion** *n* kese-
sakan, kemacetan

conglomeration *n* konglo-
merasi

congratulate *v* mengu-
capkan selamat; **congra-
tulations** *n, pl* ucapan
selamat; *ejac* selamat

congregate *v* berkumpul;
congregation *n* jemaah
(gereja)

congress *n* kongres,
muktamar; **Congress** *n*
Perwakilan Rakyat Amerika
(Senat dan Dewan Perwa-
kilan Rakyat)

conical *adj* kerucut,
mengerucut ← **cone**

conjunction *n* kata sam-
bung, kata penghubung; *in*
~ *with* bersama

conjure v [konjer] menyulap, menyikir

connect v menyambung, menghubungkan; **connection** n hubungan, sambungan; koneksi

conquer v [konker] mengalahkan, menaklukkan, merebut; **conquest** n penaklukan

conscience n [konsyens] hati nurani; **conscientious** adj rajin

conscious adj [konsyus] sadar; **consciousness** n kesadaran

consecutive adj berturut-turut

consensus n mufakat; **consent** v menyetujui; adj izin

consequence n akibat, dampak; **consequent** adj yang berikut; **consequently** adv oleh karena itu, maka

conservation n perlindungan, pemeliharaan; **conservative** adj kolot, konservatif

consider v menganggap, mengindahkan; mempertimbangkan; **considerable** adj cukup banyak; **consideration** n pertimbangan; **considering** conj mengingat

consist v terdiri atas, terdiri dari

consistent adj konsekuen, tetap; **consistently** adv terus-menerus

console n meja atau papan (untuk peralatan) konsol; v menghibur

consonant n huruf mati, konsonan

conspiracy n [konspirasi] komplotan, persekongkolan; **conspire** v bersekongkol, berkomplot

constable n [kanstabel] polisi

constant adj tetap, selalu; **constantly** adv selalu, terus-menerus

constellation n gugus bintang, konstelasi

constipated adj sembelit

constitute v merupakan; terdiri dari; **constitution** n undang-undang dasar (UUD), konstitusi

construct v membangun, membuat, membentuk;

411

construction *n* bangunan, pembangunan (gedung), konstruksi; ~ *site* proyek

consul konsul, wakil; **consulate** konsulat; ~*-General* konjen (konsulat-jenderal)

consult *v* menanyakan, mencari pendapat, berkonsultasi; **consultation** *n* perundingan, konsultasi

consume *v* memakan, menghabiskan; memakai; **consumer** *n* pengguna, pemakai, konsumen; **consumption** *n* pemakaian

contact *n* hubungan, kontak; ~ *lenses* lensa kontak; *v* menghubungi

contagious *adj* menular, menjangkit

contain *v* berisi, memuat, mengandung; **container** *n* tempat; ~ *ship* kapal barang

contaminate *v* mencemari; **contamination** *n* kontaminasi

contemplate *v* merenungkan

contemporary *n* teman seangkatan; *adv* modern, kini, kontemporer

contempt *n* penghinaan

contend *v* berpendapat

content *n* [kentént] kepuasan; ~*(ed)* puas, senang

content *n* [kontént] isi, bahan; **contents** *n, pl* isi, muatan; *table of* ~ daftar isi

contentious *adj* kontroversial, dapat diperdebatkan ← **contend**

contest *n* pertandingan, lomba; *v* bertanding; memperjuangkan; **contestant** *n* peserta

context *n* hubungan, kaitan; konteks

continent *n* benua; **continental** *adj* berhubungan dengan benua

continual *adj* selalu, terus-menerus; **continuation** *n* terusan, lanjutan, sambungan; **continue** *v* terus; melanjutkan, meneruskan; *to be* ~*d* bersambung; **continuous** *adj* terus-menerus

contour *n* garis bentuk; ~ *map* peta kontur

contraceptive *n, adj* kontrasepsi; ~ *pill* pil KB

contract *n* kontrak, surat perjanjian; *v* mengecil; memborong; mengontrak; **contraction** *n* kontraksi;

contractor *n* kontraktor, pemborong; **contractual** *adj* menurut kontrak

contradict *v* membantah, menyanggah; **contradiction** *n* pertentangan, kontradiksi

contrary *on the ~* sebaliknya

contrast *n* perbedaan, kontras; *v* berbeda; membandingkan; *~ing* berbeda, berlawanan

contribute *v* menyumbang, memberikan; **contribution** *n* sumbangan, kontribusi

control *n* kendali, kontrol; *in ~ of* mengendalikan; *v* mengendalikan

controversial *adj* kontroversial; **controversy** *n* isu, kontroversi

convene *v* [konvin] bersidang

convenience *n* kesempatan; kemudahan; **convenient** *adj* enak; dekat

convention *n* seminar, rapat, konvensi; kebiasaan; **conventional** *adj* biasa ← **convene**

conversation *n* percakapan, pembicaraan; **converse** *v* berbincang, bercakap-cakap; **conversely** *adj* sebaliknya

conversion *n* perubahan; **convert** *n* orang yang telah masuk agama lain; *Isl* mualaf; *v* masuk agama baru; mengubah

convex *adj* cembung

convey *v* [konvé] membawa, mengangkut; menyampaikan

convict *n* narapidana; *v* menghukum

conviction *n* keyakinan, kepercayaan

convince *v* meyakinkan; *~d* yakin

convoy *n* iring-iringan, konvoi

cook *n* juru masak, koki; *v* memasak; *~book* buku resep; *~ing* masakan; **cookery** *n* cara memasak; **cookie** *n* kue kering yang keras

cool *adj* sejuk, dingin; *v* menyejukkan

coolie *n* kuli

co-operate, cooperate *v* bekerja sama; **co-operation** *n* kerja sama; **co-operative** *n* (toko) koperasi

cop *n, sl* polisi

cope *v* menghadapi, hidup dengan (kesulitan)

copper *n* tembaga; *adj* warna tembaga

copy *n* salinan, kopi; *v* menyalin, meniru; memfotokopi; **copyright** *n* hak cipta

coral *n* karang

cord *n* tali

cordial *n* sirop

core *n* inti, hati

coriander *n* ketumbar

cork *n* gabus; sumbat; **corkscrew** *n* kotrek

corn *n* jagung; katimumul

corned ~ *beef* kornet

corner *n* sudut, penjuru; *v* memojokkan

coronation *n* upacara penobatan

coroner *n* petugas pemeriksa mayat

corporal *n* kopral

corporate *adj* berkaitan dengan perusahaan; **corporation** *n* perusahaan, perkumpulan, persekutuan, grup

corpse *n* [korps] mayat (manusia)

correct *adj* benar, betul; *v* membetulkan, memperbaiki; **correction** *n* pembetulan, perbaikan

correspond *v* suratmenyurat; sesuai dengan; **correspondence** *n* suratmenyurat; **correspondent** *n* orang yang menulis surat atau artikel; wartawan

corridor *n* lorong

corrosive *adj* keras; merusak

corrupt *adj* korup, dapat disuap; *v* menyuap; merusak; **corruption** *n* korupsi, suap

cosmetic *adj* berkaitan dengan kecantikan; ~ *surgery* bedah plastik; **cosmetics** *n, pl* alat-alat kecantikan (seperti lipstik, perona pipi dsb)

cosmopolitan *adj* internasional, kosmopolitan

cost *n* **cost cost** harga (barang), ongkos (perjalanan), biaya (jasa); *v* berharga; **costly** *adj* mahal

costume *n* pakaian, busana, kostum

cosy, cozy *adj* enak, mungil

cottage *n* pondok, bungalo; ~ *cheese* keju putih untuk mengisi makanan

cotton *n, adj* kapas, katun;

~ *field* kebun kapas; ~ *wool* kapas

cough *n, v* [kof] batuk

could *v* [kud] bisa, dapat, mampu; *pf* → **can**

council *n* dewan; pemerintah setempat (seperti kecamatan); **councillor** *n* anggota dewan

counsel *n* pengacara; nasihat; *v* menasihati, memberi nasihat; **counsellor** *n* konselor

count *n* penghitungan; *v* berhitung; menghitung; **countdown** *n* penghitungan dari nomor besar sampai zero

count *n, m* gelar bangsawan

counter *n* loket; *v* melawan, menangkis

counterfeit *adj* [kaunterfét] palsu

country *n* [kantri] negeri, negara; tanah air; *in the* ~ di pedesaan, di pedalaman; **countryside** *n* pedesaan, pedalaman

county *n* kabupaten, wilayah tingkat bawah

coup *n* [ku] kudeta

couple *n* [kapel] pasang, pasangan

coupon *n* kupon

courage *n* [karej] keberanian; **courageous** *adj* [karéjus] berani

courier *n* kurir; ~ *service* jasa pengiriman barang

course *n* [kors] kursus; jalan, arah; *golf* ~ padang golf; *of* ~ tentu saja, memang, pasti

court *n* [kort] pengadilan

court *n* [kort] jalan buntu; taman; lapangan main

court *n* [kort] *at* ~ di istana

courtesy *n* [kertesi] kesopanan, sopan-santun

courtship *n* [kortsyip] masa pacaran

cousin *n* [kazen] (saudara) sepupu; *first* ~ saudara sepupu

cove *n* teluk kecil

cover *n* [kaver] tutup, penutup; sampul (buku); sarung (bantal); perlindungan; *v* menutup; meliputi

cow *n* sapi, lembu; ~'s *milk* susu sapi; *dairy* ~ sapi susu

coward *n* pengecut, penakut; **cowardly** *adj* penakut, pengecut

coyote *n* [koyoti] sejenis anjing liar

crab *n* kepiting, rajingan

crack *n* retak; bunyi; *sl* kokain; ~*ed* retak; gila; *v* retak, pecah dengan bunyi gemeretak; ~ *up* menjadi gila, **cracker** *n* petasan, biskuit kering

cradle *n* [krédel] buaian, ayunan

craft *n* kerajinan tangan; ketrampilan; **craftsman** *n* perajin, tukang

crafty *adj* licik

cram *n* keadaan penuh sesak, macet; *v* memasukkan dengan paksa; belajar mati-matian sebelum ujian

cramp *n* kejang

crash *n* tabrakan, ambruknya; *plane* ~ kecelakaan pesawat, pesawat jatuj; *v* bertabrakan, menubruk; jatuh (pesawat terbang)

crate *n* peti kayu

crater *n* kawah

crave *v* mengidamkan, merindukan; **craving** *n* idaman

crawl *v* merangkak, merayap

crayon *n* krayon, kapur tulis lilin

craze *n* tren, kegemaran; **crazy** *adj* gila

cream *n* krim, kepala susu; *adj* (warna) krem

crease *n* lipatan, wiron; *v* membuat lipatan

create *v* [kriét] menciptakan, membuat; **creation** *n* ciptaan, kreasi; Kejadian; **creature** *n* makhluk

credit *n* penghargaan; kredit; ~ *card* kartu kredit

creek *n* kali, sungai kecil

creep *n, sl* orang yang menjijikkan atau mengerikan; *v* merangkak, merayap, menjalar; **creepy** *adj* angker, mengerikan

cremate *v* membakar mayat, memperabukan; **cremation** *n* kremasi, pembakaran mayat

crescent *n* jalan yang melingkar; ~ *moon* bulan sabit; *the Red* ~ Sabit Merah

crest *n* jambul

crew *n* awak kapal; regu, kru

cricket *n* jangkrik, belalang; semacam olahraga seperti kasti

crime *n* kejahatan; **criminal** *n* penjahat; *adj* jahat

crimson *adj* merah tua

cripple *n* orang pincang; *v* melumpuhkan, membuat pincang

crisis *n* [kraisis] krisis

crisp *n* (kripik) kentang; *adj* garing; segar

criteria *n, pl* syarat; patokan, norma

critic *n* pemerhati; **critical** *adj* kritis, genting; **criticism** *n* kritik; **criticize** *v* mengritik

croak *n* suara kodok; *v* menguak

crochet *n* [krosyé] rajutan; *v* merajut

crockery *n* tembikar

crocodile *n* buaya

crony *n* kawan seper-kongkolan, konco

crooked *adj* bengkok

crop *n* panen; *v* memotong

croquet *n* [kroké] semacam permainan seperti mini-golf

cross *n* silang; salib; per-simpangan, persilangan; *v* melintasi, menyeberangi; ~-*eyed* juling; **crossing** *n* penyeberangan; **crossroads** *n* simpang, perempatan;

crossword *n* teka-teki silang (TTS)

crouch *v* berjongkok

crow *n* [kro] burung gagak; *v* berkokok

crowbar *n* [krobar] linggis

crowd *n* orang banyak, gerombolan orang, kerumun-an orang; *v* berkerumunan, mengerumuni; ~*ed* penuh sesak, ramai

crown *n* mahkota; ubun-ubun

crucial *adj* [krusyel] utama, pokok; penting

crude *adj* kasar, mentah; primitif; ~ *oil* minyak mentah

cruel *adj* bengis, kejam; **cruelty** *n* kebengisan, kekejaman

cruise *n* [kruz] pelayaran pesiar; ~ *ship* kapal pesiar; *v* menjelajah

crumb *n* [kram] remah; **crumble** *v* merepih, ambruk, merapuh

crumpet *n* sejenis roti panggang

crumple *v* rebah; menggum-palkan

crunch *v* mengerkah, men-

imbulkan bunyi berderak;
crunchy *adj* garing
crusade *n* perjuangan;
perang salib; **crusader**
n orang yang memper-
juangkan sesuatu
crush *n*, *sl* cinta monyet; *v*
menghancurkan; menekan
crust *n* kerak, kulit
crutch *n*; **crutches** *pl* kruk
cry *n* [krai] teriak, pekik;
tangis; *v* berteriak, memekik; menangis
crystal *n*, *adj* hablur, kristal
Cuba *n* Kuba; **Cuban** *adj*
berasal dari Kuba
cube *n* kubus; **cubic** ~
meter (cm³) meter kubik
cubicle *n* bilik
cucumber *n* [kyukamber]
timun, mentimun
cuddle *n* [kadel] pelukan;
v memeluk, mengemong;
cuddly *adj* enak diemong
atau dipeluk
cue *n* petunjuk, isyarat; kiu
(bilyar)
cuff *n* ujung tangan, manset
cuisine *n* [kuisin] santapan,
masakan
culprit *n* pelaku, yang
bersalah

cult *n* kultus; *personality* ~
kultus individu
cultivate *v* memelihara,
menanam; ~*d* sopan,
beradab, berpendidikan;
cultivation *n* pemeliharaan,
penanaman
cultural *adj* **culture** *n* kebudayaan, budaya; ~ *shock*
gegar budaya
cunning *n*, *adj* cerdik, licik
cup *n* cangkir, cawan; piala;
cupboard *n* [kaberd]
lemari; **cupcake** *n* kue
kecil
cure *n* obat, pengobatan; *v*
mengobati (sampai sembuh)
curfew *n* jam malam
curiosity *n* penasaran, kein-
gintahuan; keajaiban; **curious** *adj* penasaran, ingin
tahu; aneh
curl *n*, *v* keriting; **curly** *adj*
ikal, keriting
currant *n* kismis (kecil,
berwarna hitam)
currency *n* mata uang;
foreign ~ mata uang asing
current *n* arus; *adj* kini;
berlaku; ~ *affairs* berita kini
curriculum *n* kurikulum
curry *n* kari, gulai

curse *n* kutukan; umpatan, makian; *v* mengutuk; mengumpat, memaki

curtain *n* [kerten] horden, gorden, tirai

curve *n* lengkung; *v* melengkung

cushion *n* [kusyen] bantal; *v* melindungi dengan bantalan

custard *n* sejenis puding

custody *n* tahanan, kurungan

custom *n* adat, kebiasaan; langganan; **customer** *n* langganan, nasabah (bank)

customs *n* bea cukai, pabean; ~ *officer* petugas bea cukai

cut *n* **cut cut** potongan; *final* ~ versi terakhir; *short* ~ jalan pintas; *v* memotong, menggunting; ~ *down* menebang; mengurangi; ~ *off* memutuskan

cute *adj* lucu; mungil, manis

CV *abbrev curriculum vitae* CV, riwayat kerja

cyberspace *n* dunia maya

cycle *n* [saikel] daur, siklus; *v* bersepeda, naik sepeda; **cyclist** *n* pengendara sepeda; pembalap sepeda

cyclone *n* [saiklon] angin topan, siklon

cylinder *n* silinder

cynical *adj* suka mengejek

cypress *n* [saipres] pohon eru

Czech *adj* Ceko; *the* ~ *Republic* Republik Ceko

D

dabble *v* mencoba-coba

Dad *n, sl* Pak; *my* ~ ayahku; **Daddy** *n, sl, child* Papa

dagger *n* keris

daily *n* harian; ~ *newspaper* koran harian; *adv* tiap hari, setiap hari, sehari-hari

dairy *n* perusahaan susu; *adj* susu

daisy *n* bunga aster

dam *n* bendungan; *v* membendung

damage *n* [damej] kerusakan; rugi, kerugian; *v* merugikan, merusak

dame *n, f* gelar bangsawan

dammit *ejac* persetan! ← **damn it**

damn

damn v mengutuk; adj terkutuk; ejac perselan; ~ it persetan

damp n kelembaban, iklim lembab; adj lembab

dance n tari, tari-tarian; dansa; v menari; berdansa; **dancer** n penari; **dancing** n tari-tarian, seni tari

dandruff n ketombe; anti-~ shampoo sampo anti ketombe

danger n [dénjer] bahaya; **dangerous** adj berbahaya

Danish adj berasal dari Denmark

dare n tantangan; v menantang; adj berani; **daring** n keberanian; adj berani

dark n gelap, kegelapan; adj gelap; ~ glasses kacamata hitam; ~ green hijau tua; **darkness** n kegelapan

darling n sayang, buah hati; adj tersayang

darn v menambal, menjerumat; ejac sialan; ~ed sialan; ~ing needle jarum tisik

dash n garis datar; v berlari

dashboard n dasbor, panel peralatan

data n data; **database** n bank data

date n korma; ~ palm pohon korma

date n tanggal; kencan; best before ~, use-by ~ tanggal kedaluwarsa; out of ~ kolot, kuno; up to ~ modern, mutakhir; v mengencani, memacari; ~ from sejak; ~d tertanggal; ketinggalan jaman, kuno

daughter n, f [doter] anak perempuan, putri; god-~ putri baptis; grand~ cucu; ~-in-law menantu

dawn n dini hari, fajar; permulaan; v fajar menyingsing

day n hari; siang; all ~ sepanjang hari; one ~ sekali waktu; the good old ~s tempo dulu; the other ~ baru-baru ini; twice a ~ sehari dua kali; during the ~ siang hari; **daybreak** n dini hari, fajar; **daydream** n lamunan, khayalan; **daylight** n siang; sinar matahari; ~ saving kebijakan memajukan jam selama musim panas; **day-**

time *n, adj* siang hari

daze *n* keadaan pusing

dazzle *v* menyilaukan, memesonakan

dead *v, pf* [déd] → **die**; *adj* mati; sunyi senyap; ~ **end** jalan buntu; ~ **heat** seri (dalam perlombaan);
deadline *n* batas waktu;
deadlock *n* jalan buntu;
deadly *adj* mematikan; sungguh-sungguh

deaf *adj* [déf] tuli; ~**mute** bisu tuli

deal *n* persetujuan; *a great ~, a good ~* sebagian besar; cukup banyak; *it's a ~* setuju; *v* **dealt dealt** [délt] membagi (kartu); ~ *in* jual-beli; ~ *with* memperlakukan, menghadapi; **dealer** *n* pedagang; **dealings** *n, pl* urusan, transaksi

dear *n* yang baik, yang terhormat (in letters); *my ~* sayangku; *adj* mahal

death *n* [déth] kematian; ~ *penalty* hukuman mati

debate *n* perdebatan; *v* berdebat; memperdebatkan; **debating** *n* kegiatan berdebat

debt *n* [dét] hutang; ~ *collector* petugas penagih hutang; *in ~* berhutang

debut *n* [débyu] penampilan pertama

decadent *adj* merosot

decaffeinated ~ *coffee (decaf)* kopi tanpa kafein

decapitate *v* memenggal kepala

decathlon *n* dasalomba

decay *n* kerusakan, kebusukan; *tooth* ~ karis; *v* melapuk, membusuk

deceased *n the* ~ orang yang meninggal; *adj* telah meninggal, mangkat, wafat

deceit *n* [disit] tipu daya; **deceitful** *adj* penuh tipu daya, bersifat menipu; **deceive** *v* menipu; ~*d* tertipu

December *n* bulan Desember

decency *n* kesopanan; **decent** *adj* sopan, patut, layak

decentralization *v* desentralisasi

deception penipuan ← **deceit**

decide *v* memutuskan, menentukan, menetapkan

deciduous *adj* [desidyues] berganti daun

decimal *n* persepuluhan, desimal; ~ *point* koma (desimal)

decision *n* [desisyen] keputusan; **decisive** *adj* [desisif] menentukan ← **decide**

deck *n* geladak, dek; ~ *chair* kursi pantai, kursi malas

declaration *n* pernyataan, pengumuman, maklumat, deklarasi; **declare** *v* menyatakan, mengumumkan

decline *n* kemunduran, kemerosotan; *v* mundur, menjadi kurang; menolak

decode *v* membaca atau memecahkan sandi

decompose *v* membusuk; ~*d* busuk

decorate *v* menghiasi; **decoration** *n* hiasan, perhiasan; tanda kehormatan

decrease *n* pengurangan, penurunan; *v* berkurang; mengurangi, menurunkan

dedicate *v* mempersembahkan, mengabdikan; **dedication** *n* pengabdian, persembahan

deduct *v* memotong, mengurangi; **deduction** *n* potongan, pengurangan

deduction *n* kesimpulan ← **deduce**

deep *adj* dalam; *a* ~ *sleep* tidur pulas, ~ *freeze* lemari es; ~*rooted* berurat-berakar; **deepen** *v* mendalam; memperdalam; **deeply** *adv* dalam

deer *n* rusa, menjangan

default *v* gagal; lalai membayar; *by* ~ dengan tak hadir; secara otomatis

defeat *n* kekalahan; *v* mengalahkan, menggagalkan

defecate *v* buang air besar, berak

defect *n* [difékt] cacat, cela, kerusakan

defect *v* [defékt] durhaka, menyeberang ke pihak lain

defective *adj* rusak, cacat ← **defect**

defend *v* membela, mempertahankan; **defendant** *n* tergugat; **defender** *n* pembela; bek; **defense** *n* pertahanan, pembelaan, perlawanan; **defensive** *adj* bersikap bertahan, defensif

defiant *adj* bersifat menentang, bersifat melawan

deficit *n* kekurangan (uang), defisit

define *v* menentukan, menetapkan, mengartikan; **definite** *adj* tertentu, pasti; **definitely** *adv* tentu; **definition** *n* definisi

deflate *v* kempes; mengempeskan

deflect *v* menangkis, membelokkan; **deflection** *n* pembelokan

deforestation *n* deforestasi, penebangan hutan

deformed *adj* cacat

degradation *n* penurunan pangkat; pelecehan

degree *n* (suhu) derajat; gelar sarjana; *Bachelor's* ~ S1; *Master's* ~ S2

dehydrated *adj* [dihaidréted] dehidrasi, kurang minum

dejected *adj* murung, tanpa semangat

delay *n* keterlambatan, penundaan; *v* menunda, memperlambat

delegate *n* wakil, utusan; *v* menyerahkan; mengutus;

delegation *n* delegasi, perwakilan

delete *v* menghapus, mencoret

deliberate *v* menimbang-nimbang; berembuk; *adj* (dengan) sengaja; **deliberation** *n* pertimbangan, perundingan

delicate *adj* halus; sering sakit; **delicatessen** *n* toko makanan kering (seperti daging, keju)

delicious *adj* [delisyus] enak, sedap, lezat

delight *n* [delait] kesenangan, kegembiraan; **delightful** *adj* menyenangkan, membahagiakan

delinquent *adj* nakal

delirious *adj* mengigau, berdemam tinggi

deliver *v* mengirim, menghantarkan, memberi; membidani; melahirkan; **delivery** *n* penyerahan, pengiriman; ~ *boy* kurir

demand *n* tuntutan; persediaan; *v* menuntut, minta

democracy *n* demokrasi, kerakyatan; **democrat** *n*

demolish

ENGLISH–INDONESIAN

demokrat; **democratic** *adj*
demokratis

demolish *v* membongkar,
merobohkan

demonstrate *v* berunjuk
rasa; menunjukkan, mem-
perlihatkan, membuktikan;
demonstration *n* pertunjukan; demonstrasi, demo,
unjuk rasa

dengue [déngi] ~ *fever*
demam berdarah

denim *n* (bahan) jins

denomination *n* satuan;
pecahan, lembaran (uang)

dense *adj* padat, rapat,
lebat; *sl* bodoh; **density** *n*
kepadatan

dent *n* peot, peyok; *v* mele-
kukkan

dental *adj* berhubungan
dengan gigi; **dentist** *n*
dokter gigi

deny *v* [denai] menyangkal,
memungkiri, menolak

depart *v* berangkat, pergi;
departure *n* keberangkatan

department *n* departemen;
bagian; ~ *store* toko serba
ada (toserba)

depend *v* bergantung, tergantung; **dependent** *adj*

tergantung pada; tang-
gungan

deport *v* mendeportasi,
membuang

deposit *n* deposito, simpanan; endapan; *v* menaruh,
menyimpan

depot *n* [dépo] depot, depo,
gudang

depreciate *v* [deprisyét]
turun nilai; **depreciation** *n*
penurunan nilai, depresiasi

depress *v* menekan, menyusahkan hati; ~*ed* tanpa
semangat, murung; ~*ing*
menyedihkan; **depression**
n bagian yang rendah;
depresi, jaman meleset;
kehilangan gairah hidup

deprive *v* [depraiv] mengambil, merampas

Dept *Department* Dep
(Departemen)

deputy *n* wakil; ~ *head*
wakil kepala (waka)

derail *v* anjlok, keluar dari
rel; **derailment** *n* kejadian
anjlok

derivation *n* asal; **derive** *v*
berasal

derrick *n* kerekan, derek,
menara pengeboran minyak

424

descend v turun; ~ed from keturunan; ~ing order dari atas ke bawah; **descendant** n keturunan, anak cucu; **descent** n jalan turun; keturunan

describe v melukiskan, menggambarkan; **description** n penggambaran, deskripsi

desert n [désert] gurun, padang pasir; ~ island pulau tak terhuni

desert v [desert] meninggalkan, membelot; desersi; **deserted** adj sunyi (senyap)

deserve v berhak mendapat, patut (menerima); **deserving** adj patut terima

design n rancangan, contoh, gambar, desain; v merancang, mendesain

designer n perancang, desainer; fashion ~ perancang busana; adj bermerek ← **design**

desirable adj yang diinginkan; **desire** n keinginan, nafsu, hasrat; v ingin, menginginkan, mendambakan

desk n meja (tulis); bangku (di sekolah)

despair n keputusasaan; v putus asa; **desperate** adj sudah putus asa

despite prep meskipun, kendati

dessert n [desert] pencuci mulut, puding

destination n tujuan, jurusan

destined adj [déstind] ditakdirkan; **destiny** n nasib, takdir

destroy v menghancurkan, memusnahkan, membinasakan; **destroyer** n (kapal) perusak; **destruction** n kerusakan, kehancuran, pemusnahan, pembinasaan; **destructive** adj merusak, membinasakan

detail n rinci, perincian, seluk-beluk; in ~ secara terinci; v merincikan; ~ed terinci

detain v menahan

detect v menemukan, mendapatkan, mendeteksi; **detective** n reserse, detektif

detention n penahanan, penawanan; in ~ disetrap ← **detain**

deter v [detér] menghalangi

detergent n sabun, obat, deterjen

deteriorate v [detiriorét] memburuk, merosot

determination n tekad bulat; **determine** v menetapkan, menentukan, memutuskan; ~d bertekad, bersikeras

detest v membenci

detract ~ *hom* mengurangi, menurunkan nilai, mengecilkan nilai

devastate v menghancurkan; **devastating** adj menghancurkan; **devastation** n penghancuran

develop v mengembangkan, membangun, membina; mencuci (film); **developer** n pengembang, pemborong; **development** n pembangunan, perkembangan; pengembangan, pembinaan

deviate v [diviét] menyimpang, melenceng

device n alat

devil n setan, iblis

devise v memikirkan, merencanakan

devolution n devolusi; ~ to the provinces otonomi daerah (otda)

devote v mengabdikan, menyediakan; **devoted** adj tekun; **devotion** n ketaatan, kebaktian; rasa sayang

devour v melahap

devout adj soleh, beriman ← **devote**

dew n embun

diabetes n [daiabitis] penyakit gula, kencing manis; **diabetic** n [daiabétik] penderita kencing manis

diagnose v mendiagnosa, menentukan; **diagnosis** n diagnosa

diagonal n garis sudut-menyudut, diagonal; adj sudut-menyudut, diagonal

diagram n denah, bagan

dial n [daial] piringan, muka jam; v memencet (nomor telepon)

dialect n dialek

dialogue adj percakapan, dialog

diameter n garis tengah, diameter

diamond n berlian, intan

diaper n popok; disposable ~ pamper

diarrhoea, diarrhea n [daiaria] mencret, sakit perut, diare

426

diary *n* [daiari] buku harian;
to keep a ~ menulis buku
harian

dice *n, pl* dadu → **die**

dictate *v* mendikte; **dictation** *n* dikte, imla

dictator *n* diktator

dictionary *n* kamus

did *v, pf* → **do**

die *v* [dai] **died dead** mati,
meninggal, wafat; gugur,
wafar (dalam perang); ~
out menjadi punah; padam

diesel *n* [disel] minyak
solar; mesin disel

diet *n* [daiet] diet; makanan;
on a ~ (mengikuti) diet; *v*
mengikuti diet, membatasi
makan

differ *v* berbeda; **difference**
n beda, perbedaan; **different** *adj* beda, lain,
berbeda

difficult *adj* susah, sulit,
sukar; **difficulty** *n* kesulitan,
kesusahan

dig *v* **dug dug** menggali;
diggings *n, pl* penggalian

digest *v* mencerna

digit *n* [dijit] angka; jari;
digital *adj* digital

dignified *adj* [dignifaid]

bermartabat, mulia; **dignity**
n martabat

dike *n* pematang, bendung,
tanggul

dilapidated *adj* [dilapidéted]
telantar, bobrok, buruk

dilate *v* membesar

dilemma *n* pilihan sulit,
dilema

diligent *adj* rajin, telaten

dilute *v* mengencerkan; *adj*
encer

dim *v* meredup; meredupkan;
adj redup, suram

dime *n* sepuluh sen (Amerika)

dimension *n* matra, dimensi;
dimensional *three-*~ tiga
dimensi

dimple *n* lesung pipi

dine *v* bersantap (malam);
diner *n* rumah makan kecil

dining *n* santapan; ~ *car*
restorasi, gerbong makan; ~
room ruang makan ← **dine**

dinner *n* makan malam;
makan siang; ~ *party* acara
makan malam

dinosaur *n* [dainosor]
dinosaurus

dip *n* bagian yang turun; *v*
mencelupkan

diploma *n* ijazah, diploma

diplomat *n* pegawai kedutaan, diplomat; **diplomatic**
adj diplomatik, berkaitan
dengan kedutaan

dipper *n* gayung ← **dip**

direct *adj* langsung; serta
merta; terus terang; ~
current arus searah; *v* memimpin, mengarahkan,
memerintahkan, menun-
jukkan; menyutradarai;
direction *n* arah, petunjuk;
directly *adv* secara langsung, serta merta, segera;
director *n* direktur, pemimpin; sutradara

directory *n* buku alamat,
buku daftar

dirt *n* kotoran, debu; tanah;
~*cheap* murah sekali; ~
poor miskin sekali; ~ *road*
jalan tanah; **dirty** *adj* kotor,
dekil; ~ *word* kata jorok

disable *v* [disébel] mematikan; ~*d* cacat; orang cacat

disadvantage *n* rugi,
kerugian

disagree *v* tidak setuju;
disagreeable *adj* tidak enak,
marah-marah; **disagree-
ment** *n* percekcokan, perbedaan pendapat

disappear *v* hilang, lenyap

disappoint *v* mengecewa-
kan; **disappointment** *n*
kekecewaan, rasa kecewa

disapproval *n* sikap tidak
setuju atau suka; **disapprove**
v tidak menyetujui, tidak
suka, menolak

disarmament *n* perlucutan
senjata

disaster *n* musibah, malapetaka, bencana; **disas-
trous** *adj* malang, celaka

disbelief *n* rasa tidak percaya

disc, disk *n* cakram; *compact* ~ *(CD)* CD; *floppy* ~
disket

discharge *n* pemecatan,
pemberhentian; cairan yang
keluar, keputihan; *v* memecat, melepaskan

disciple *n* [disaipel] murid

discipline *n* disiplin, tata
tertib, ketertiban

discomfort *n* rasa tidak
nyaman, kesusahan

disconnect *v* mencabut,
memutuskan; ~*ed*
terputus(-putus)

discontent *n* rasa kurang
senang, rasa tidak puas

discontinue v memberhentikan

discord n perselisihan, bunyi sumbang

discount n potongan (harga), diskon, korting; v memotong harga, mendiskon

discourage v [diskarej] mengecilkan hati, tidak menganjurkan

discover v menemukan, mendapat; **discovery** n penemuan

discredit v tidak percaya; mencoreng nama

discreet adj sopan, bijaksana, berhati-hati

discrepancy n [diskrépansi] selisih, perbedaan

discretion at your ~ tergantung anda ← **discreet**

discriminate v membedakan, mendiskriminasikan; **discrimination** n pembedaan, diskriminasi; racial ~ diskriminasi berdasarkan ras

discus n (lempar) cakram; ~ throw lempar cakram

discuss v [diskas] berembuk membicarakan; **dis-**

cussion n pembicaraan, diskusi

disease n penyakit

disembark v mendarat, turun dari kapal

disgrace n aib, malu; in ~ kena aib; v mencoreng muka, memalukan; **disgraceful** adj memalukan

disguise n [disgaiz] samaran; in ~ menyamar; v menyamar

disgust n rasa muak; v menjijikkan, memuakkan

dish n piring, pinggan; sajian, hidangan; ~cloth lap piring

dishonest adj [disonest] tidak jujur, suka bohong

dishwasher n mesin pencuci piring ← **dish**

disillusion v mengecewakan

disinfect v membasmi kuman; **disinfection** n pembasmian kuman

disinterested adj tidak memihak, obyektif, netral

disjointed adj terpotong-potong, terputus-putus

disk → **disc**; **diskette** n disket

dislike n ketidaksukaan; v tidak suka

dislocate v keluar dari tempatnya, tergelincir

dismantle v membongkar

dismay n kecemasan; v mencemaskan

dismiss v menolak; membubarkan, memecat; **dismissal** n pembubaran, pemecatan

dismount v turun (dari kuda)

disobedience n ketidakpatuhan; **disobedient** adj tidak patuh, nakal; **disobey** v melawan, tidak mematuhi

disorder n kekacauan; penyakit

disparity n selisih

dispatch n pengiriman; v mengirimkan

dispensation n kelonggaran, dispensasi

dispenser n alat atau mesin dengan persediaan; water ~ tempat akua

dispersal n berhamburnya; **disperse** v berhamburan; menghambur

displace v menggantikan; ~d person pengungsi

display n pameran, per-

tunjukan; v memperlihatkan, mempertunjukkan, memamerkan

disposal n persediaan; pembuangan; **dispose** ~ of membuang; menjual

disposition n kepribadian, kecenderungan

dispossess v menyita, mencabut hak milik

disproportionate adj [disproporsiyonet] tidak sebanding

disprove v [dispruv] membantah, menyangkal; membuktikan salah

dispute n perselisihan, percekcokan; v membantah; mempermasalahkan

disqualified adj, v dinyatakan tidak berhak atau keluar, dibatalkan

disregard v tidak mengindahkan, mengabaikan

disreputable adj bernama buruk

disrespectful adj tidak hormat

dissatisfaction n ketidakpuasan, kekecewaan

dissect v [daisékt] membedah, membelah

dissimilar adj tidak sama, berbeda

dissolve v larut; melarutkan

distance n jarak, kejauhan; in the ~ dari kejauhan; **distant** adj jauh

distaste n rasa tidak suka; **distasteful** adj memuakkan

distinct adj jelas, kentara; **distinction** n perbedaan; nilai unggul; **distinctly** adv secara jelas

distinguish v membedakan; ~ed terhormat, ternama

distorted adj berubah; diubah

distract v mengalihkan perhatian; menyesatkan; ~ed tersesat, bingung; **distraction** n selingan; gangguan, kesesatan

distress n kesulitan, kesusahan; ~ed menderita

distribute v menyebarluaskan, membagikan, menyalurkan, mendistribusikan; **distribution** n penyebarluasan; pembagian; penyaluran, pendistribusian; **distributor** n penyalur, pengecer

district n, adj distrik, daerah; ~ court pengadilan

wilayah, pengadilan negeri

disturb v mengganggu; **disturbance** n kekacauan, kegaduhan, gangguan

ditch n selokan, parit

ditto adj sama

dive v menyelam, terjun; **diver** n penyelam; sky~ penerjun payung; **diving** n selam; loncat indah; ~ board papan loncat

diverse adj berbagai (macam), aneka, pelbagai; **diversion** n sesuatu yang mengalihkan perhatian; hiburan; **diversity** n keanekaragaman; **divert** v menangkis, mengalihkan perhatian; menghibur

divide n jurang, kesenjangan; v membagi; **divisive** adj bersifat memecah-belahkan

divine adj ilahi; hebat

division n pembagian; bagian; divisi

divorce n perceraian; v bercerai; ~d cerai; **divorcée** n, f janda

DIY abbrev do it yourself barang yang dirakit atau dikerjakan sendiri

dizzy *adj* pusing (kepala), pening, bingung

do *v* [du] **did done** berbuat, bikin; membuat, melakukan, mengerjakan; ~ *up* memperbaiki, mempercantik; ~ *without* jalan tanpa; *how do you* ~ apa kabar; ~ *your best* kerjakan sebaik-baiknya

dock *n* galangan, dok; **dockyard** *n* galangan

doctor *n* dokter; doktor (S3)

document *n* surat, dokumen; *v* mendokumentasi; **documentary** *n* film dokumenter; **documentation** *n* catatan, dokumentasi

dodge *v* mengelakkan, menghindar

dog *n* anjing

dog *v* membuntuti, selalu menjadi masalah

dogma *n* dogma, kepercayaan agama

doing *n* [duing] perbuatan; *v what are you* ~? sedang apa? → **do**

dole *n* tunjangan pengangguran

doll *n* boneka; ~'*s house* rumah boneka; **dolly** *n*,

child boneka

dollar *n* dolar; *US* ~ dolar AS

dolphin *n* [dolfin] lumba-lumba

domain *n* daerah, wilayah

dome *n* kubah

domestic *adj* dalam negeri, domestik; ~ *servant* pembantu (rumah tangga, PRT)

dominant *adj* berkuasa, berpengaruh, dominan; **dominate** *v* menguasai, mendominasi; **domination** *n* penguasaan, dominasi

domino *n* gaplek, domino; ~ *effect* efek domino

donate *v* menyumbangkan; **donation** *n* sumbangan

done *v, pf* [dan] → **do**

donkey *n* keledai

donor *n* pemberi, donor; *blood* ~ donor darah ← **donate**

don't *v* jangan ← **do**

donut *n* donat

doom *n* malapetaka, ajal

door *n* pintu; ~*bell* bel (pintu); ~*man* petugas pembuka pintu; ~*mat* keset; ~*step* ambang pintu; ~*way* pintu

dope *n, sl* obat-obatan, obat bius, ganja

dorm, dormitory *n* asrama

dosage *n* takaran, dosis; **dose** *n* dosis

dot *n* titik, noktah, percik; *on the* ~ tepat, pas pada waktunya; *polka* ~ bercorak bulatan besar; **dotty** *adj* pikun

double *adj* [dabel] ganda; kembaran; *v* melipatgandakan; ~ *bed* tempat tidur untuk dua orang; *on the* ~ segera

doubt *n* [daut] ragu, keraguan; *v* menyangsikan, meragukan; **doubtful** *adj* sangsi, ragu-ragu

dough *n* [do] adonan; **doughnut** → **donut**

dove *n* [dav] burung merpati

down *n* bulu halus (burung); *adv* di bawah, ke bawah; ~*hearted* *adj* kecil hati; ~ *and out* melarat, sengsara; ~*to-earth* sederhana, bersahaja; **downfall** *n* jatuhnya; **downstairs** *adv* di lantai bawah; **downtown** (di) pusat kota; **downward,**

downwards *adv* ke bawah

dowry *n* [dauri] mas kawin, mahar

doze *n* tidur sebentar, tidur ayam

dozen *n* [dazen] lusin; ~*s* berpuluh-puluh, puluhan

Dr *Doctor* dr (dokter)

draft *n* rancangan; *bank* ~ wesel; *v* merancang

drag *n* gaya tolak; *v* menyeret, menarik

dragon *n* naga

dragonfly *n* capung

drain *n* saluran, parit, got; kali; aliran; *v* menguras, mengalirkan, mengeringkan; ~*ed* capek, lemas; **drainage** *n* pengaliran, drainase; **drainer** *n* rak piring

drama *n* seni peran, drama, sandiwara; **dramatic** *adj* mengesankan, dramatis

drank *v, pf* → **drink**

drastic *adj* drastis, radikal

draught *n* [draft] angin (di dalam bangunan); sejenis bir; **draughty** *adj* berangin

draw *v* **drew drawn** menggambar; menarik; **drawback** *n* kekurangan,

433

sisi buruk; **drawer** n laci;
chest of ~s (lemari) laci;
drawing n lukisan, gambar

dreadful *adj* menakutkan,
dahsyat

dream n mimpi, impian; v
mimpi; bermimpi, mengimpikan; **dreamer** n pemimpi;
orang yang melamun

dregs n, pl sisa (minyak,
kopi)

drench v membasahi; ~ed
basah kuyup

dress n rok; pakaian, baju,
kostum; v berpakaian, mengenakan pakaian; menghiasi;
~ *rehearsal* gladi bersih; ~
up berdandan, berpakaian
formal; **dressing** n perban;
saus (untuk salada); **dressy**
adj bergaya formal

drew *v, pf* → **draw**

drift n arus, aliran, arah; v
terbawa arus, terhanyut;
driftwood n kayu yang
terbawa arus

drill n bor; latihan; v
mengebor; melatih

drink n **drank drunk** minuman; v minum, meminum;
drinker n peminum; *heavy*
~ peminum berat

drip n tetes, tetesan; v
menetes; ~-*dry* tidak perlu
disetrika

drive n semangat, dorongan; v **drove driven** [driven]
membawa (mobil), menge-
mudikan, menyupir; **driver**
n supir, sopir, pengemudi,
pengendara (mobil); kusir,
sais (kendaraan berkuda);
engine ~, *train* ~ masinis;
driveway n jalanan masuk
halaman untuk mobil;
driving *adj* mendorong;
~ *lesson* les mengemudi

drizzle n, v hujan rintik-rintik

droop v merana, lemas

drop n titik, tetes; *cough* ~
permen obat batuk; v jatuh,
turun, terjun; menjatuhkan,
menurunkan; ~ *by*, ~ *in*
mampir

drought n [draut] masa
kering tanpa hujan

drove *v, pf* → **drive**

drover n gembala

drown v tenggelam;
menenggelamkan

drowsy *adj* mengantuk

drug n obat (bius), obat-
obatan; v membius; ~*store*
toko kecil; apotik

drum *n* gendang, tambur; *v* mengetuk; **drummer** *n* penabuh

drunk *n* mabuk; *v, pf* → **drink**

dry *adj* kering, haus; membosankan; *v* menjemur, mengeringkan; *~-cleaning* binatu, waserai; *~ season* musim kemarau; **dryer** *n* alat atau mesin pengering; *clothes ~* mesin pengering baju; *hair ~* pengering rambut

dual *adj* dwi, (rangkap) dua

dubbing *n* sulih suara

dubious *adj* ragu-ragu, meragukan

duck *n* itik, bebek; *v* berjongkok menghindari; **duckling** *n* anak itik

due *adj* jatuh tempo; perlu, wajib

dug *v, pf* → **dig**; **dugout** *n* bungker

dull *adj* bodoh, dungu

dumb *adj* bisu; bodoh; **dumbfound** *~ed* tercengang

dummy *n* manekin, orang-orangan; *n, adj* tiruan

dump *n* (*rubbish*) *~* tempat pembuangan sampah,

tempat pembuangan akhir (TPA); *~ truck* truk sampah; *v* membuang

dumpling *n* pangsit

dunce *n* orang bodoh

dune *n* bukit pasir

dung *n* tahi, pupuk

duplicate *n* rangkap kedua, salinan, kopi, duplikat; *v* membuat kopi atau rangkap

durable *adj* awet

duration *n* lamanya

during *conj, prep* selama, sementara

dusk *n* senja

dust *n* abu, debu; *v* membersihkan, menghilangkan debu; **dustbin** *n* tempat sampah; **duster** *n* lap debu, penyapu; **dusty** *adj* berdebu

Dutch *n* bahasa Belanda; *adj* berasal dari Belanda

dutiful *adj* patuh, menurut; **duty** *n* kewajiban; pekerjaan, tugas; bea; *~ free* bebas bea cukai

dwarf *n* katai, cebol

dwelling *n* tempat tinggal

dye *n* zat pewarna; *v* mencelupkan, mengecat (rambut)

dyke *n, sl* lesbi, orang lesbian

435

dynamic *adj* dinamis, hidup
dynamite *n* dinamit, bahan
peledak
dynasty *n* keluarga, dinasti

E

each *adj* masing-masing;
tiap-tiap, saban; ~ *other*
saling, satu sama lain
eager *adj* ingin sekali, pengen
eagle *n* burung rajawali
ear *n* telinga, kuping; **ear-
drum** *n* gendang telinga
early *adj* [érli] pagi-pagi, dini
earn *v* [érn] mendapat gaji,
memperoleh
earnest *adj* [érnest]
sungguh-sungguh
earnings *n, pl* pendapatan,
gaji, upah ← **earn**
earplug *n* penyumbat telinga
earring *n* anting ← **ear**
earth *n* [érth] bumi, dunia;
tanah, debu; *on* ~ di dunia;
earthquake *n* gempa bumi
ease *n* kemudahan, kese-
nangan; *v* mempermudah,
meringankan

easel *n* kuda-kuda
east *adj* timur; *the Middle*
~ Timur Tengah (Timteng);
~ *Timor* Timor Loro Sae
Easter *n* Paskah
eastern *adj* (daerah) timur
←**east**
easy *adj* mudah, gampang;
~*going* bersikap santai ←
ease
eat *v* **ate eaten** makan
eaves *n, pl* ujung bawah atap;
eavesdrop *v* menguping
ebb *v* surut; ~ *tide* air surut
ebony *n* kayu eboni
eccentric *adj* [éksentrik]
aneh, antik
echo *n* [éko] gema, gaung,
kumandang; *v* bergema,
bergaung, berkumandang
eclipse *n* gerhana; *lunar* ~
gerhana bulan; *solar* ~
gerhana matahari
ecological *adj* berkaitan
dengan ekologi; **ecology** *n*
ekologi
economic *adj* berkaitan
dengan ekonomi; **econo-
mical** *adj* hemat, ekono-
mis; **economics** *n* ilmu
ekonomi; **economist**
n ekonom; **economy** *n*

ekonomi, dunia usaha; kehematan

ecstasy *n* kegembiraan, kebahagiaan; ekstasi; **ecstatic** *adj* sangat gembira atau bahagia

eczema *n* eksema

ed. *editor* red. (redaksi); *edition* edisi, cetakan

edge *n* [éj] pinggir, sisi, tepi; mata (pisau); *on* ~ tegang

edible *adj* dapat dimakan

edit *v* menyunting, mengedit; **edition** *n* terbitan, keluaran, edisi, cetakan; **editor** *n* redaktur, penyunting, editor; ~*in-chief* pemimpin redaksi; **editorial** *n* tajuk rencana

educate *v* mendidik; **education** *n* pendidikan; **educational** *adj* mendidik

eel *n* [iel] belut

eerie *adj* ngeri

effect *n* pengaruh, efek; akibat, hasil; **effective** *adj* berhasil, efektif

efficiency *n* daya guna, efisiensi; **efficient** *adj* berdaya guna, tepat guna, efisien

effort *n* usaha, upaya

eg *exempli gratia = for*

example mis., (seperti) misalnya

egg *n* telur; ~ *cup* tempat telur rebus; **eggplant** *n* terong; **eggshell** *n* kulit telur

Egypt *n* [Ijipt] Mesir; **Egyptian** *adj* berasal dari Mesir

eight *adj, n* [éit] delapan; **eighteen** *adj, n* delapan belas; **eighteenth** *adj* kedelapan belas; **eighth** *adj* kedelapan; **eighty** *adj, n* delapan puluh

either *adj* [ither, aither] salah satu; ~ … *or* … … atau…; *I don't like* ~ duaduanya saya tidak suka

eject *v* mengeluarkan, mengusir

elaborate *v* menguraikan, menjelaskan secara panjang lebar; *adj* rumit, panjang lebar, teliti

elastic *n* karet; *adj* karet, kenyal, elastis

elated *adj* bahagia; **elation** *n* kegembiraan

elbow *n* siku; *v* menyikut

elder *n* yang lebih tua; sesepuh; *adj* kakak;

437

~ *brother* kakak (laki-laki);
elderly *adj* sepuh, sudah
tua; **eldest** *n* anak sulung;
adj anak paling tua, sulung
elect *v* memilih; **election** *n*
pemilihan; *general* ~ pemilihan umum (pemilu);
elective *n* mata pelajaran
pilihan
electric *adj* listrik; *the* ~
chair kursi listrik; **electri-
cian** *n* tukang listrik; **electricity** *n* listrik
electronic *adj* elektronik;
electronics *n, pl* barang
elektronik, elektronika
elegant *adj* anggun, elok
element *n* unsur, bagian,
bahan, elemen; **elementary**
adj dasar; ~ *school* sekolah
dasar (SD)
elephant *n* [élefant] gajah
elevate *v* menaikkan,
mengangkat; **elevation** *n*
ketinggian; **elevator** *n* lift
eleven *adj, n* sebelas;
eleventh *adj* kesebelas
elf *n* **elves** peri
elicit *v* memperoleh (arti),
mengeluarkan
eligibility *n* memenuhi
syarat; kepantasan; **eligible**

adj memenuhi syarat, dapat
dipilih
eliminate *v* menyisihkan,
menyingkirkan; **elimination**
n penyisihan, eliminasi;
~ *round* babak penyisihan
elite *the* ~ para elit, kaum
atas; *adj* elit
elope *v* kawin lari
eloquent *adj* fasih, pandai
bicara
else *adv* lain; *or* ~ jika tidak;
someone ~ orang lain;
what ~ apa lagi; **elsewhere**
adv di lain tempat
emancipate *v* memerdekakan, membebaskan;
emancipation *n* kemerdekaan, pembebasan
embankment *n* tepi
embarrass *v* memalukan,
mempermalukan; **embar-
rassment** *n* keadaan yang
membuat malu, rasa malu
embassy *n* kedutaan
embellish *v* menghiasi,
membesar-besarkan, mem-
bumbui
embers *n, pl* bara
embezzle *v* menggelapkan;
embezzlement *n* korupsi,
penggelapan uang

emblem n lambang, tanda
embrace n pelukan; v
memeluk
embroider v menyulam,
membordir; **embroidery** n
sulaman, bordiran
embryo n [émbrio] janin
emerald n zamrud; adj
hijau
emerge v [emérj] timbul,
muncul; **emergence** n
timbulnya, munculnya
emergency n [emérjénsi]
keadaaan darurat; ~ brake
rem bahaya; ~ exit pintu
darurat
emigrant n emigran; **emi-grate** v pindah, beremigrasi;
emigration n emigrasi
eminent adj [éminent]
ternama, terpandang,
unggul
emission n pancaran,
buangan, emisi; **emit** v
memancarkan, mengeluarkan
emotion n perasaan, emosi;
emotional adj emosi
emperor n kaisar ← empire
emphasis n [émfasis]
tekanan; **emphasize** v me-nekankan, menitikberatkan
empire n kekaisaran, kera-

jaan; the British ~ Kerajaan
Inggris
employ v mempekerjakan;
menggunakan, memakai;
employee n pegawai,
buruh, pekerja, karyawan,
karyawati; **employer** n
majikan; **employment** n
pekerjaan
empower v memperdaya-kan; **empowerment** n
pemberdayaan
empress n, f kaisar wanita
← empire
empty adj kosong, hampa;
v mengosongkan
enable v memungkinkan
enact v menjadikan
enamel n glasir, cat halus;
email
enchant v memesonakan,
memikat, menyihir;
enchantment n sihir
enclave n daerah kantung
enclose v memagari;
melampirkan, menyertakan;
enclosure n kandang
encounter n pertemuan; v
bertemu, berjumpa
encourage v [énkarej]
mendorong, mendukung,
memberi semangat; **en-**

439

couraging *adj* menggembirakan; **encouragement** *n* dorongan, desakan

encyclopedia *n* ensiklopedi

end *n* akhir, ujung; *The ~* tamat; *in the ~* akhirnya; *v* berakhir; menyudahi; mengakhiri

endanger *v* [endênjer] membahayakan, mengancam; *~ed species* binatang yang terancam punah

endearing *adj* manis, lucu

endeavor *n* [éndévor] usaha

endless *adj* tanpa ujung, tiada hentinya, tidak ada akhirnya, tak terhingga, tidak berkeputusan ← **end**

endorse *v* menyokong, mendukung; **endorsement** *n* dukungan

endurance *n* daya tahan; **endure** *v* bertahan; menahan, menderita, menempuh

enemy *n* musuh, seteru; *arch ~* musuh bebuyutan

energetic *adj* [énerjétik] energik, bersemangat; **energy** *n* tenaga, usaha; *geothermal ~* tenaga panas bumi; *hydro-electric ~* tenaga air

enforce *v* menjalankan, melaksanakan; menegakkan

engage *v* memasang; *~d* bertunangan; **engagement** *n* janji; pertunangan

engine *n* [énjin] mesin; *~ driver* masinis; *train ~* lokomotif, lok, **engineer** *n* insinyur; masinis; *v* merekayasa; **engineering** *n* ilmu teknik; *civil ~* teknik mesin; *electrical ~* teknik elektro

England *n* [Ingland] Inggris; **English** *n* bahasa Inggris; *adj* berasal dari Inggris

engrave *v* mengukir pada batu atau logam; membuat etsa; **engraver** *n* pembuat etsa; **engraving** *n* etsa

enhance *v* meningkatkan; **enhancement** *n* peningkatan, perbaikan

enigma *n* teka-teki

enjoy *v* menikmati; *~ yourself* bersenang-senang; **enjoyable** *adj* menyenangkan; **enjoyment** *n* kenikmatan, kesenangan

enlarge *v* membesarkan, memperbesar, memperluas;

440

enlargement *n* pembe-saran

enormous *adj* sangat besar

enough *adj* [enaf] cukup, sudah

enrich *v* memperkaya;
enrichment *n* pengayaan

enroll *v* mendaftarkan;
enrolled *adj* terdaftar;
enrollment *n* pendaftaran

ensure *v* memastikan, menjamin

enter *v* masuk; memasuki, memasukkan

enterprise *n* perusahaan, usaha; **enterprising** *adj* yang mengambil inisiatif, yang berusaha

entertain *v* menghibur;
entertainer *n* artis, penghibur; **entertainment** *n* hiburan

enthusiasm *n* semangat, gairah, antusiasme, gelora; kegemaran, hobi; **enthusiastic** *adj* antusias, bersemangat

entire *adj* seluruh, seantero;
entirely *adv* benar-benar

entitled *adj* berhak

entrance *n* pintu masuk ← **enter**

entrepreneur *n* [ontreprenur] pengusaha, wiraswasta

entrust *v* memercayakan kepada

entry *n* jalan masuk, pintu masuk; pembukuan; masuk-an, kata kepala ← **enter**

envelope *n* amplop

envious *adj* iri ← **envy**

environment *n* lingkungan;
environmental *adj* berkaitan dengan lingkungan;
~*ly friendly* ramah lingkungan; **environmentalist** *n* aktivis lingkungan

envy *n* (rasa) iri

epic *n* cerita panjang, epik;
adj hebat, patut dikenang

epicenter *n* titik pusat gempa bumi, episentrum

epidemic *n* wabah

epilepsy *n* penyakit ayan, epilepsi, sawan

episode *n* bagian (waktu), episode

equal *n* [ikuel] bandingan;
v menyamai, menyamakan;
adj sama, setara; **equality** *n* kesamaan; **equation** *n* persamaan

equator *n* katulistiwa

equestrian *n* atlet penunggang kuda; *adj* berkaitan dengan penunggangan kuda

equine *adj* berkaitan dengan kuda

equinox *n* saat malam dan siang sama panjangnya

equip *v* melengkapi; **equipment** *n* perlengkapan; *play* ~ tempat bermain anak-anak, ayunan

equivalent *n* yang sama atau setara; *adj* sama harga atau nilainya

eradicate *v* membasmi

erase *v* menghapus; **eraser** *n* penghapus; *board* ~ penghapus papan

erect *v* mendirikan, membangun; *adj* tegak, tegang; **erection** *n* pembangunan; ereksi

erosion *n* kikisan, erosi

erotic *adj* erotis, merangsang

errand *n* urusan, pesan

erratic *adj* tidak menentu, tidak teratur

error *n* salah, kesalahan ← **err**

erupt *v* meletus; **eruption** *n* letusan, erupsi

escalate *v* naik, tambah; meningkatkan; **escalator** *n* tangga berjalan, eskalator

escape *n* pelarian; *v* melarikan diri, kabur, menghindari

escort *n* pendamping, rombongan; *v* mendampingi, mengiringi

ESP *abbrev extra-sensory perception* indera keenam

especially *adv* khususnya, terutama ← **special**

espionage *n* [éspionaj] pengintaian, spionase

essay *n* karangan

essence *n* inti, sari, esensi; **essential** *adj* mutlak; ~ *oil* minyak esensial

establish *v* mendirikan, mengadakan; menentukan, menetapkan; **establishment** *n* pendirian, penentuan, penetapan; pembangunan

estate *n* tanah milik; kebun, perkebunan

estimate *n* taksiran, anggaran, perkiraan; pendapat; *v* menaksir, memperkirakan

estuary *n* muara, kuala

ETA *abbrev estimated time of arrival* perkiraan waktu kedatangan

etc *et cetera* dll (dan lain-lain), dsb (dan sebagainya)

eternal *adj* abadi, kekal; **eternity** *n* keabadian, kekekalan

ethical *adj* etis; ~ *Policy* Politik Etis; **ethics** *n*, *pl* etika

ethnic *adj* etnis, kesukuan; tradisional; ~ *group* suku (bangsa), kelompok etnis

etiquette *n* tata cara, sopan santun, etiket

EU *abbrev European Union* UE (Uni Eropa)

Europe *n* [Yurop] Eropa; **European** *n* orang Eropa; *adj* berasal dari Eropa; ~ *Union* Uni Eropa

euthanasia *n* [yutanésia] mencabut jiwa karena belas kasihan, eutanasia, mati tenang

evacuate *v* mengungsi; mengungsikan; **evacuation** *n* pengungsian, evakuasi

evade *v* mengelakkan

evaluate *v* menilai; **evaluation** *n* evaluasi, penilaian

evangelical *adj* yang menyebarkan agama Kristen

evaporate *v* menguap; **evaporation** *n* penguapan

evasion *n* [ivéisyon] *tax* ~ tidak membayar pajak;

evasive *adj* mengelak ← **evade**

eve *n* [iv] malam (sebelumnya); *Christmas* ~ malam Natal; *New Year's* ~ Malam Tahun Baru; *on the* ~ *of* malam sebelum; **Eve** *n* Hawa; *Isl* Siti Hawa

even *adj* rata; genap; pun; *prep* bahkan; ~ *if* kalaupun; ~ *though* meskipun; *to get* ~ membalas dendam

evening *n* sore, petang; malam; *good* ~ selamat malam; *this* ~ nanti malam; *yesterday* ~ tadi malam, kemarin malam

event *n* peristiwa, kejadian, acara; ~ *organizer* penyelenggara (acara); **eventually** *adv* akhirnya

ever *adj* [éver] pernah; ~ *since* (mulai) sejak; *have you* ~? pernahkah?; **everlasting** *adj* kekal, abadi

every *adj* [évri] setiap, tiap; ~ *day* setiap hari, saban hari; ~ *other day* selang hari; **everybody, everyone** *adj* semua orang, setiap orang; **everyday** *adj* sehari-hari; **everything** *n* semua; **everywhere** *adj* di mana-mana

evict *v* mengusir, menggusurkan; **eviction** *n* pengusiran, penggusuran

evidence *n* bukti; *to give ~* menjadi saksi; **evident** *adj* jelas, nyata, terang

evil *n* [ivel] kejahatan; *adj* jahat

evolution *n* evolusi

exact *adj* tepat, persis; betul; **exactly** *adv* persis

exaggerate *v* [egzajerét] membesar-besarkan; **exaggeration** *n* pernyataan yang berlebihan

exam, examination *n* ujian; **examine** *v* menguji, memeriksa

example *n* contoh, teladan; *for ~* (seperti) misalnya, seumpamanya

exasperate *v* menjengkelkan, membuat kesal

excavation *n* penggalian

exceed *v* melebihi, melampaui; **exceedingly** *adv* teramat, sangat

excellency *Your ~* Yang Mulia; **excellent** *adj* bagus sekali, hebat

except *prep* kecuali; *v* mengecualikan; **exception** *n* kekecualian, pengecualian; **exceptional** *adj* luar biasa, istimewa

excess *n* kelebihan; **excessive** *adj* berlebihan, melampaui batas

exchange *n* pertukaran, penukaran; kurs; *foreign ~* mata uang asing, devisa; *v* menukar

excite *v* merangsang, membangkitkan; **excitement** *n* kegembiraan

exclaim *v* berseru; **exclamation** *n* seruan; *~ mark* tanda seru

exclude *v* mengecualikan; **excluding** *v* tidak termasuk; **exclusion** *n* pengecualian; **exclusive** *adj* eksklusif, elit

excrete *v* mengeluarkan cairan; buang air

excursion *n* kunjungan

excuse *n* [ékskyus] alasan, dalih; *v* [ékskyuz] memaafkan; *~ me* permisi

execute *v* melakukan, melaksanakan; menjalankan keputusan; melakukan hukuman mati; **execution**

n pelaksanaan (hukuman mati); **executioner** *n* algojo; **executive** *n* pemimpin (harian), eksekutif; *adj* eksekutif

exempt *adj* bebas dari; *v* membebaskan

exercise *n* olahraga; latihan, pelajaran; *v* berlatih; melakukan; ~ *bike* sepeda stasioner; ~ *book* buku tulis

exhale *v* mengeluarkan napas

exhaust *n* [ekshost] asap kendaraan; *v* menyelesaikan sampai tuntas; menguras tenaga; **exhaustion** *n* kecapekan yang luar biasa

exhibit *n* [éksibit] barang yang dipamerkan; *v* mempertunjukkan, memperlihatkan; **exhibition** *n* pameran

exhilaration *n* rasa gembira

exile *n* buangan; pembuangan; *v* membuang

exist *v* ada; **existence** *n* keberadaan

exit *n* pintu atau jalan keluar; kepergian

exodus *n* kepergian, eksodus

exotic *adj* eksotik, dari negeri asing

expand *v* memperluas, mengembangkan; memuai; **expansion** *n* perluasan, pengembangan

expat, expatriate *n* orang asing, orang yang tinggal di luar negeri, ekspatriat

expect *v* berharap; mengharapkan, menantikan; **expectancy** *life* ~ harapan hidup; **expectation** *n* harapan

expedition *n* perjalanan, ekspedisi

expel *v* membuang; mengeluarkan

expend *v* mengeluarkan, membelanjakan, memakai; **expense** *n* belanja, biaya, ongkos; **expensive** *adj* mahal

experience *n* pengalaman; *v* mengalami

experiment *n* percobaan, uji coba; *v* mengadakan percobaan, menguji coba

expert *n* ahli, pakar; *adj* ahli

expire *v* kedaluwarsa, jatuh tempo; mati; **expiry** ~ *date* tanggal kedaluwarsa

explain *v* menjelaskan, me-

nerangkan, menyatakan;
explanation n penjelasan

expletive n [éksplitif] kata
umpatan

explicit adj tegas, jelas, eks-
plisit; ~ language kata-kata
jorok

explode v meletus, meledak

exploit v memanfaatkan,
mengeksploitasi; **exploita-
tion** n eksploitasi

exploration n penjelajahan,
eksplorasi; **explore** v menjelajah; mengadakan pene-
litian; **explorer** n pen-
jelajah

explosion n letusan, ledakan;
explosive adj dapat meledak; **explosives** n, pl
bahan peledak ← **explode**

export n, adj ekspor; v
mengekspor; **exporter** n
pengekspor, eksportir

expose v menyingkapkan,
mempertunjukkan, mema-
merkan, membuka

express n yang cepat, kilat,
ekspres; adj cepat, kilat; v
mengucapkan, mengung-
kapkan, menyatakan, meng-
utarakan; **expression** n
ucapan, peribahasa; raut

muka; **expressive** adj
ekspresif, menyatakan
perasaan

expulsion n pengeluaran
← expel

extend v merentangkan,
membentangkan; memper-
luas; memperpanjang;
extension n perpanjangan;
extensive adj luas, panjang lebar; **extent** n luas
cakupan, derajat, tingkat;
to what ~ sejauh mana

exterior n luar, luarnya

exterminate v membasmi,
memusnahkan

external adj (di) luar

extinct adj punah;
extinction n pemadaman;
kepunahan

extinguish v [ékstinguisy]
memadamkan

extra adj ekstra; ~-curri-
cular ekskul

extract n sari, ekstrak,
petikan; v mencabut (gigi);
mengambil; **extraction** n
pencabutan; asal

extraordinary adj [ékstro-
dinari] luar biasa, istimewa

extravagant adj boros,
berfoya-foya

extreme *adj* terlampau, ekstrem; **extremely** *adv* sangat, teramat

exuberant *adj* riang gembira, bersemangat

eye *n* [ai] mata; *black* ~ lebam biru di mata; *v* melirik; **eyeball** *n* bola mata; **eyebrow** *n* alis; **eyelash** *n* bulu mata; **eyelid** *n* kelopak mata; **eyesight** *n* penglihatan; **eyewitness** *n* saksi mata

F

fable *n* dongeng, cerita rakyat; **fabulous** *adj* hebat

fabric *n* kain, bahan

fabulous *adj* hebat, menakjubkan

face *n* muka, paras, wajah; ~ *value* harga nominal; *v* menghadapi; **facial** *n* perawatan wajah; ~ *expression* raut wajah

facility *n* sarana, fasilitas; kemudahan

facsimile *n* salinan, kopi; ~ *machine* mesin faks → **fax**

fact *n* kenyataan, fakta; *in* ~ sebenarnya

factor *n* unsur, faktor, elemen

factory *n* pabrik

faculty *n* daya, kemampuan; fakultas

fade *v* luntur, pudar; mengecil (suara)

faeces → **feces**

fail *v* gagal; tidak jadi; jatuh; tidak lulus; *without* ~ pasti; **failure** *n* kegagalan, gagalnya

faint *n* pingsan; *v* (jatuh) pingsan; *adj* lemah, kecil

fair *n* pameran, pekan raya, pasar malam; *adj* adil, berimbang; **fairly** *adv* cukup, agak; dengan adil

fairy *n* peri; ~ *floss* kembang gula; ~ *godmother* ibu peri; ~ *tale* dongeng, cerita rakyat

faith *n* iman, kepercayaan; *in good* ~ dengan itikad baik; **faithful** *adj* beriman, setia; **faithfully** *yours* ~ hormat kami

fake *n* tipuan; *adj* palsu; ~ *ID* identitas palsu

447

falcon *n* burung elang

fall *n* kejatuhan, keruntuhan, keguguran; musim gugur, musim rontok; *v* **fell, fallen** jatuh, runtuh, gugur; ~ *apart* pecah; ~ *ill* jatuh sakit

fallen *v, pf* → **fall**

falls *n, pl* air terjun

false *adj* palsu; **falsify** *v* memalsukan

fame *n* ketenaran, nama harum

familiar *adj* dikenal; akrab; **family** *n* keluarga; rumah tangga

famine *n* [famin] kelaparan

famous *adj* terkenal, ternama ← **fame**

fan *n* kipas; penggemar, fans; *electric* ~ kipas angin; *v* mengipasi, mengembusi

fanatic *adj* fanatic

fancy *v* menginginkan; *adj* rumit, megah

fang *n* taring

fantastic *adj* ajaib, fantastis, tidak masuk akal; **fantasy** *n* fantasi, khayalan

FAQ *abbrev* frequently-asked questions pertanyaan biasa

far *adj* jauh; *as* ~ *as* sejauh, sepanjang; *so* ~ sejauh ini, selama ini

fare *n* ongkos perjalanan

farewell *n* perpisahan; *ejac* selamat tinggal, selamat jalan

farm *n* pertanian, peternakan; **farmer** *n* petani; **farming** *n* pertanian

fart *n, coll* bunyi kentut; *v* kentut, membuang angin

farther, further *adj, adv* lebih jauh; **farthermost, farthest** *adj, adv* terjauh, paling jauh

fascinate *v* memesonakan, menarik hati; **fascination** *n* pesona

fascism *n* [fasyisem] fasisme, sayap kanan; **fascist** *adj* fasis, sayap kanan

fashion *n* mode; cara; *v* membentuk; **fashionable** *adj* bergaya, gaya

fast *n* puasa; *v* berpuasa; ~*ing month* bulan puasa

fast *adj* cepat, laju; kokoh; ~*track*, ~ *lane* jalur cepat; ~ *train* kereta api cepat

fasten *v* [fasen] mengikatkan, menambatkan

fat *n* lemak; *adj* gemuk, tambun

448

fatal *adj* mematikan

fate *n* nasib

father *n* ayah, bapak; *adopted* ~ ayah angkat; *founding* ~s bapak-bapak bangsa; **father-in-law** *n* mertua (lelaki)

fatigue [fatig] *n* kelelahan, kecapekan; kerusakan; *v* capek

fatty *adj* lemak ← **fat**

faucet *n* keran

fault *n* kesalahan, salah; cacat; pemukulan awal yang meleset (tenis); *to find* ~ mencari kesalahan; **faulty** *adj* cacat, rusak, kurang sempurna

favor *n* pertolongan; karunia, anugerah; ampun; *in our* ~ menguntungkan kita; *in* ~ *of* mendukung; *v* lebih suka; **favorable** *adj* baik, menguntungkan

favorite *n* kesukaan, anak emas; *adj* kesukaan, yang paling disukai, favorit

fax *n* ~ *(machine)* mesin faks; *v* (me)ngefaks, mengirim lewat faks ← **facsimile**

FBI *abbrev Federal Bureau of Investigation* Biro

Nasional Penyelidikan (Amerika Serikat)

fear *n* ketakutan, rasa takut; *v* takut akan; ~*ed* menakutkan; **fearless** *adj* tidak takut, berani

feast *n* pesta, perjamuan, perayaan; *v* ~ *on* melahap, makan

feather *n* bulu

feature *n* ciri (khas); ~*s* wajah, paras; *v* mempertunjukkan; memperlihatkan

February *n* bulan Februari

feces *n, pl* [fisiz] tinja

fed *v, pf* → **feed**

federal *adj* federal, berserikat; **federation** *n* federasi, perserikatan

fee *n* upah, gaji, biaya

feed *n* pakan, makanan hewan; *v* **fed fed** memberi makan; ~ *on* makan (dari); ~ *up* bosan, jenuh; **feedback** *n* tanggapan

feel *n* rasa; *v* **felt felt** berasa, merasa; meraba; **feeler** *n* sungut; peraba; **feeling** *n* perasaan

feet *n, pl* → **foot**

feline *n* (binatang dari keluarga) kucing

449

fell *v* menebang, memotong (pohon); *v* → **fall; felling** *n* penebangan

fellow *n* lelaki; ~ *worker* teman sekerja; *adj* sesama; ~ *man* sesama manusia

felt *n* bulu kempa; *v, pf* → **feel**

female *n, adj* perempuan, wanita; betina (binatang)

feminine *adj* feminin; yang berkaitan dengan kewanitaan; **feminism** *n* feminisme, gerakan menuju persamaan hak perempuan

fence *n* pagar; *v* memagari; bermain anggar; **fencer** *n* pemain anggar; **fencing** *n* anggar

fermentation *n* fermentasi, peragian

fern *n* paku

ferocious *adj* ganas, buas

ferret *n* semacam musang

ferry *n* feri; *v* membawa penumpang bolak-balik, menyeberangkan

fertile *adj* subur; **fertilizer** *n* pupuk; **fertility** *n* kesuburan

fervent *adj* bersemangat, bernafsu, bergairah

festival *n* pesta, perayaan,

hari raya, festival; **festive** *adj* perayaan, pesta; ~ *season* masa Natal; **festivity** *n* pesta, perayaan, acara

fetch *v* menjemput (orang), mengambilkan

fete *v* [féit] pekan raya, pasar malam

fetus *n* [fítus] janin

feud *n* [fyuud] permusuhan, perseteruan; *v* bertengkar, berkelahi

feudal *adj* feodal; **feudalism** *n* feodalisme

fever *n* demam; *dengue* ~ demam berdarah; **feverish** *adj* demam, panas

few *adj* (hanya) sedikit; *a* ~ beberapa

fiancé *n* [fiansé] tunangan (laki-laki); **fiancée** *n* tunangan (perempuan)

fiber *n* [faiber] serabut, serat; **fiberglass** *n, adj* kaca serat

fiction *n* fiksi

fiddle *n, arch* biola; **fiddler** *n* pemain biola

fidget *n* orang yang tidak bisa duduk diam; *v* bergerak terus karena gelisah

field *n* bidang, daerah;

padang, medan, ladang; *v*
mengambil bola (olahraga)
fierce *adj* buas, galak,
ganas
fiery *adj* berapi-api ← **fire**
fifteen *adj, n* lima belas;
fifteenth *adj* kelima belas
← **five**
fifth *adj* kelima; *one-~*
seperlima ← **five**
fiftieth *adj* kelima puluh;
fifty *adj, n* lima puluh
fig *n* buah ara
fight *n* [fait] pertengkaran;
perkelahian; pertempuran;
perjuangan; *v* **fought fought**
bertengkar; berkelahi; bertempur, berperang, berjuang;
fighter *n* pejuang; pesawat
tempur
figure *n* rupa, bentuk; bagan,
gambar; angka; harga;
~-skating main sepatu es; *v*
menghitung, berpikir
file *n* berkas, arsip, dokumentasi; *single ~* antri satu
per satu; *v* menyimpan;
mengikir
fill *n* jatah; *v* mengisi,
menempati, memenuhi
fillet *n* filet, potongan daging
tanpa tulang

film *n* film
film *n* selaput
filter *n* saringan, filter; *v*
menyaring, menyeleksi; *~
paper* kertas saring
filth *n* kotoran, sampah;
filthy *adj* kotor sekali
filtration *n* penyaringan
fin *n* sirip; *shark ~ soup*
sup sirip ikan hiu
final *n* (pertandingan) final;
adj final, penghabisan, terakhir; **finally** *adv* akhirnya
finance *n* keuangan; *v* membiayai, mendanai; **financial**
adj keuangan
find *n* [faind] (hasil)
temuan; *v* **found found**
menemukan; menyimpulkan
fine *n* denda, tilang; *v* mendenda, menilang
fine *adj* bagus, baik; halus
finger *n* jari; *~ food* makanan kecil; *index ~* telunjuk;
~nail kuku jari; *little ~*
kelingking; *middle ~* jari
tengah; *ring ~* jari manis;
fingerprint *n* sidik jari
finish *n* (garis) akhir; penghabisan, penyelesaian;
v berhenti; mengakhiri,
menghentikan; menyele-

451

saikan; menghabiskan; ~
off menghabiskan; ~ *up*
menyelesaikan

Finland *n* Finlandia

fire *n* api; kebakaran; ~
brigade, ~ *department*
pasukan pemadam kebakar-
an; ~ *engine* mobil
pemadam kebakaran; ~
escape tangga darurat; ~
extinguisher alat pemadam
kebakaran; *on* ~ sedang
terbakar; *v* melepaskan
tembakan, menembak; ~ *up*
memberi semangat; *to
catch* ~ terbakar; *to set* ~
to membakar; **firearm** *n*
senjata api; **firefighter** *n*
anggota pasukan pemadam
kebakaran; **fireplace** *n* perapian; **fireproof** *adj* tahan
api; **fireworks** *n, pl* kembang api, petasan, mercon

firm *adj* tetap, pasti, tegas

first *adj* pertama; ~*-born*
anak sulung, anak pertama;
~ *cousin* (saudara) sepupu;
~ *name* nama depan;
~*-rate* terbaik, nomor satu;
~ *prize* hadiah utama; *at* ~
pada awalnya, semula;
firstly *adv* pertama-tama

fish *n* ikan; *v* memancing;
fisherman *n* nelayan; **fisheries** *n* perikanan; **fishing**
n memancing; ~ *rod* joran;
fishy *adj* mencurigakan

fist *n* tinju, kepalan tangan

fit *adj* pas, tepat, layak,
patut; fit, sehat; *v* menyesuaikan, **fitness** *n* kebugaran, kesehatan; ~ *center*
pusat kebugaran, tempat
fitnes

five *adj* lima; ~*-star hotel*
hotel bintang lima

fix *n* masalah; *v* memperbaiki;
menetapkan, memasang;
fixed *adj* tetap; ~ *price*
harga pas

fizz *n* busa

flab *n* lemak; **flabby** *adj*
gemuk, tidak berotot

flag *n* bendera

flake *n* serpih, lapis, keping;
v hancur

flame *n* (kobaran) api; **flam-
mable** *adj* dapat terbakar

flank *n* sisi

flannel *n* kain panas, fla-
nel; handuk kecil untuk
menyabuni

flap *n* tutup, penutup; *v*
mengepak

flare *n* nyala api; *v* bernyala, menyala

flash *n* kilau; blits; *a ~ of lightning* halilintar, kilat; *in a ~* dalam sekajap mata; *v* berkilat-kilat; **flashlight** *n* (lampu) senter

flask *n* botol minuman

flat *n* apartemen; *adj* rata, datar; *~ tire* ban kempes; **flatten** *v* meratakan

flatter *v* membujuk, merayu, menyanjung

flautist *n* pemain suling, pesuling ← **flute**

flavor *n* rasa; *v* membumbui

flaw *n* **flawed** *adj* cacat, cela; **flawless** *adj* sempurna, tanpa cacat

flea *n* kutu (binatang); *~ market* pasar loak

fled *v, pf* → **flee**

flee *v* **fled fled** melarikan diri, kabur, minggat

fleet *n* armada (angkatan laut)

flesh *n* daging

flexible *adj* lentur; fleksibel

flick *n* sentilan; *v* menyentil; **flicker** *v* berkedip-kedip

flight *n* [flait] penerbangan; terbangnya; *~ of stairs* tangga

flinch *v* bereaksi terhadap sesuatu yang mengagetkan

fling *v* **flung flung** melemparkan

flip *n* salto; *v* membalik, memutar-balikkan

flippant *adj* enteng, sembrono

flirt *n* orang genit; *v* bermain mata

float *n* pelampung; semacam minuman es; *v* mengapung, terapung

flock *v* datang berbondong-bondong, berkumpul, berhimpun

flood *n* banjir, air bah; *v* banjir; membanjiri; **flooded** *adj* banjir; **floodlight** *n* lampu sorot

floor *n* lantai, tingkat; *~ cleaner* obat pel, obat pembersih lantai; *~ plan* denah

flop *v* gagal; jatuh, tidak berdiri; **floppy** *adj* tidak tegak, lembut

floral *adj* berkaitan dengan bunga; **florist** *n* (pemilik) toko bunga

floss *(dental)* ~ benang pembersih gigi

flour *n* tepung (terigu); *corn~* tepung maizena

453

flourish n [flarisy] gerakan yang lincah; v mekar, tumbuh subur

flow n aliran; v mengalir

flower n bunga, kembang; ~-seller penjual bunga

flown v, pf → **fly**

flu n flu, selesma; bird ~ flu burung ← **influenza**

fluent adj lancar, fasih

fluff n bulu (kain), debu; isi yang tidak berarti; **fluffy** adj berbulu

fluid n cairan; adj cair, tidak tentu

flung v, pf → **fling**

flush v memerah (muka); ~ the toilet menyiram WC

flute n suling

flutter v berkibar-kibar; mengepakkan

fly n lalat; **flyswat, flyswatter** n pemukul lalat

fly v **flew flown** [flon] terbang; berkibar-kibar; mengibarkan; frequent ~er orang yang sering naik pesawat; ~ a kite main layang-layang

flyer, flier n selebaran, brosur

foam n buih, busa; v berbuih, berbusa

focus n titik perhatian, pusat perhatian, fokus; v memfokuskan, memusatkan perhatian; **focused** adj terarah

foetid → **fetid**

foetus → **fetus**

fog n kabut; ~ up berembun; **foggy** adj berkabut

foil n kertas perak; v menggagalkan

fold n lipatan; v melipat

folk n orang; ~ tale cerita rakyat; my ~s keluarga saya

follow v mengikuti, menuruti; **follower** n pengikut, anggota; **following** yang berikut

fond adj suka, gemar

font n jenis huruf (cetakan)

food n makanan, pangan, pakan (hewan); World ~ Organization Organisasi Pangan Sedunia

fool n orang bodoh; **foolish** adj bodoh

foot n **feet** kaki; athlete's ~ jamur (di kaki); **football** n sepak bola; **footballer** n pemain sepak bola; **footpath** n jalan setapak, trotoar; **footprint** n tapak kaki; **footwear** n sepatu

for *prep* bagi, untuk; selama; ~ *hours* berjam-jam; ~ *my mother* untuk ibuku; *Kelvin was sick ~ two days* Kelvin sakit selama dua hari; ~ *all I know* sepengetahuan saya; *conj* karena

forbid *v* **forbade forbidden** melarang; **forbidden** *adj* terlarang, dilarang

force *n* kekuatan, tenaga, daya; *armed ~s* angkatan bersenjata; *by ~* dengan paksa; *v* memaksa

forecast *n* ramalan; *weather ~* ramalan cuaca; *v* meramalkan; **forecaster** *n* peramal, analis

forefinger *n* jari telunjuk

forehead *n* dahi, kening

foreign *adj* [foren] asing, luar negeri; ~ *exchange*, ~ *currency* mata uang asing, devisa; **foreigner** *n* orang asing

foresee *v* **foresaw foreseen** meramal, memprediksi

forest *n* hutan; **forestry** *n* perhutanan

forever, forevermore *adv* untuk selamanya

forgave *v, pf* → **forgive**

forge *v* memalsukan; **forgery** *n* pemalsuan, tiruan

forget *v* **forgot forgotten** lupa, melupakan, terlupa; **forgetful** *adj* pelupa

forgive *v* **forgave forgiven** memaafkan, mengampuni

forgot, forgotten *v, pf* → **forget**

fork *n* garpu; belokan, pertigaan

forlorn *adj* memelas

form *n* bentuk, rupa; formulir, blangko; *v* merupakan, membentuk

formal *adj* formal, resmi; **formality** *n* formalitas

format *n* bentuk, format; **formation** *n* pembentukan, formasi ← **form**

former *adj* dahulu, bekas, mantan (orang), lama; **formerly** *adj* dahulu, sebelumnya

formula *n* rumus, formula; *milk ~* susu bubuk, susu formula

fort *n* benteng ← **fortress**

forth *adj* ke depan; *and so ~* dan seterusnya (dst)

fortieth *adj* (ulang tahun

455

yang) keempat puluh ←
forty

fortnight *n* dua minggu;
fortnightly *adj, adv* tiap
dua minggu

fortress *n* benteng

fortunate *adj* beruntung;
fortunately *adv* secara
beruntung; **fortune** *n* rezeki; harta karun; *to seek
your* ~ merantau; ~*teller*
peramal, dukun

forty *adj, n* empat puluh ←
four

forward *adj, adv* ke depan,
maju; *v* mengirimkan

fossil *n* fosil; **fossilized**
adj telah menjadi fosil;
tidak dapat berubah lagi

foster *v* memelihara; ~ *child*
anak angkat, anak pungut; ~
mother ibu angkat

foul *adj* jorok, kotor, najis,
jijik; *v* melanggar peraturan
(olahraga); mengotori

found *v* mendirikan; *v, pf* →
find; **foundation** *n* yayasan;
fondasi, alas; bedak dasar;
founder *n* pendiri

fountain *n* air mancur, pancuran air; ~ *pen* pulpen

four *adj, n* empat; **fourteen**

adj, n empat belas; **fourteenth** *adj* keempat belas;
fourth *adj* keempat

fowl *n* unggas; ayam

fox *n* rubah; *v* menipu

fraction *n* pecahan

fracture *n* keretakan, patah;
v patah, retak; mematahkan,
meretakkan

fragile *adj* mudah pecah
atau patah

fragment *n* potong, pecahan,
keping

fragrance *n* [frégrant] **fragrant** *adj* harum, wangi

frail *adj* lemah, rapuh

frame *n* rangka, kerangka;
bingkai, lis (gambar); kusen
(pintu); tubuh, badan; *v*
membingkai

France *n* Perancis

frangipani *n* bunga kamboja

frank *adj* terus terang,
ceplas-ceplos

frantic *adj* kalang kabut

fraternity *n* persatuan,
persaudaraan; *college* ~
perkumpulan mahasiswa
laki-laki

fraud *n* penipuan, penipu

fray ~*ed* compang-camping

freak *n* orang dengan cacat

yang luar biasa; *adj* luar biasa, kebetulan; **freakish, freaky** *adj* luar biasa, kebetulan

freckle *n* bintik-bintik

free *v* membebaskan, melepaskan; *adj* bebas, merdeka; cuma-cuma, gratis; ~ *trade* perdagangan bebas; **freestyle** *n* gaya bebas; **freedom** *n* kemerdekaan, kebebasan; **freeway** *n* jalan bebas hambatan

freeze *v* **froze frozen** membeku; **freezer** *n* lemari es; **freezing** *adj* membekukan, sangat dingin

freight *n* [frét] muatan, kargo; *v* mengirim; **freighter** *n* kapal barang

French *n* bahasa Perancis; *adj* berasal dari Perancis

frequency *n* gelombang, frekuensi; **frequent** *adj* berulang kali, sering; *v* sering mengunjungi

fresh *adj* segar; baru; sejuk; ~ *graduate* orang yang baru tamat; **freshwater** *adj* air tawar

friction *n* gesekan

Friday *n* hari Jumat; *Good* ~ Jumat Agung

fried *adj* goreng → **fry**

friend *n* [frénd] kawan, sahabat, teman; **friendly** *adj* ramah, bersahabat; **friendship** *n* persahabatan

fright *n* [frait] rasa takut; **frighten** *v* menakut-nakuti, menakutkan

frill *n* embel-embel; *no* ~*s* sederhana, polos

fringe *n* pinggir; poni

frisky *adj* berlompat-lompat

frizz *v* mengeriting; **frizzy** *adj* keriting, kribo

frog *n* kodok, katak; **frogkick** *n* gaya kodok

from *prep* dari

front *n* bagian muka; hadapan; *adj* muka; ~ *door* pintu depan, pintu masuk; *in* ~ *of* di depan, di muka; **frontier** *n* tapal batas, perbatasan

frost *n* embun beku; **frostbite** *n* radang dingin; **frosty** *adj* dingin, tidak ramah

froth *n* busa, buih; *v* berbusa, berbuih

frown *n* [fraun] muka cemberut; *v* mengernyit dahi

froze, frozen *v, pf* → **freeze**

frugal *adj* pelit, sederhana, bersahaja

fruit *n* buah, buah-buahan; **fruiterer** *n* penjual buah

frustrate *v* menghambat; **frustration** *n* frustasi

fry *v* menggoreng; menjadi panas; ~ *pan* penggorengan, kuali

ft *foot* kaki

fudge *n* semacam gula-gula

fuel *n* bahan bakar

fulfill *v* memenuhi

full *adj* penuh; kenyang; lengkap; ~*blood* totok; ~ *moon* bulan purnama; ~*grown* akil balig, dewasa

fumble *v* meraba-raba, salah tangkap

fumes *n, pl* asap, uap, emisi

fumigate *v* menyemprot

fun *n* keasyikan; *adj* asyik; ~ *park* taman hiburan; *to make* ~ *of* memperolok-olokkan

function *n* fungsi; *v* berfungsi, berjalan, bekerja

fund *n* dana

fundamental *n* dasar-dasar; *adj* dasar, asasi

funeral *n* (upacara) pemakaman; ~ *parlor* pelayanan pemakaman

fungus *n* **fungi** [fanggai] jamur, cendawan

funky *adj* ngetren, gaya, gaul

funnel *n* corong

funny *adj* lucu, jenaka; aneh

fur *n* bulu (binatang); **furry** *adj* berbulu

furious *adj* marah sekali, geram, naik pitam ← **fury**

furnace *n* [fernes] oven, tungku

furnish *v* melengkapi; **furniture** *n* mebel, perabot rumah

further *adj* lebih jauh, lebih lanjut; **furthermore** *adv* lagipula; **furthermost** *adj* yang paling jauh

fury *n* kemarahan, berang

fuse *n* sumbu, sekering; *v* melebur, menyatu; **fusion** *n* fusi; santapan yang memadukan dua unsur

fuss *n* repot; kekacauan; *v* cerewet; **fussy** *adj* teliti, cerewet

future *n* masa depan; *adj* yang akan datang, mendatang, bakal, calon (orang)

fuzz *n* bulu; **fuzzy** *adj* berbulu

FYI *abbrev for your information* agar diketahui

G

g *gram* g (gram)

gabble *v* bicara terlalu cepat dan kurang jelas

gadget *n* alat, perkakas

gag *n* ikat mulut; lelucon; *v* menyumbat mulut

gain *n* untung, keuntungan, laba; *v* memperoleh, mendapat, mencapai; ~ *weight* bertambah berat badan

gale *n* angin besar, badai; ~ *force wind* badai

gall *n* [gol] empedu; keberanian

gallery *n* serambi, ruang pameran, galeri

gallon *n* galon (4.54 liter)

gallop *v* mencongklang, lari congklang, berlari cepat

galore *adj* sesukanya

galvanized ~ *iron* besi berlapiskan seng

gamble *v* berjudi, bertaruh; **gambler** *n* penjudi; **gam-**

bling *n* judi, perjudian

game *n* permainan, pertandingan; satwa buruan; *adj* berani

gang *n* kawanan, gerombolan, geng; **gangster** *n* preman, penjahat, perampok, garong

gaol *n* [jéil] penjara

gap *n* lubang, celah, jurang pemisah; ~ *year* tahun sesudah tamat SMA sebelum kuliah

garage *n* [garaj] garasi; bengkel

garden *n* kebun, taman; ~ *center* pusat perbelanjaan perlengkapan kebun; ~ *party* pesta taman; **gardener** *n* tukang kebun; **gardening** *n* berkebun

gargle *v* berkumur

garlic *n* bawang putih

garment *n* garmen, pakaian; ~ *factory* pabrik garmen

garnish *n* hiasan; *v* menghiasi

gas *n* gas; bensin; ~ *chamber* kamar gas; ~ *cooker* kompor gas

gash *n, v* luka

gasoline *n* [gasolin] bensin; ~ *station* pompa bensin ← **gas**

gasp *n* embusan napas; *v* menarik nafas dengan cepat; *last* ~ mati-matian

gate *n* pintu (masuk), gerbang; **gatekeeper** *n* penjaga pintu; juru kunci; **gateway** *n* pintu masuk

gather *v* berkumpul; mengumpulkan, memetik; **gathering** *n* perkumpulan

gaudy *adj* norak, mencolok

gauge *n* [géj] ukuran, kadar; *v* mengukur, menaksir

gauze *n* kain kasa

gay *n* orang homoseksual; *adj* homoseksual; senang hati, meriah

gaze *n* pandangan; *v* menatap, memandangi

gazelle *n* semacam rusa

gazette *n* [gazét] surat berita, koran

gear *n* peralatan, perkakas, perabot; persneling, gigi; gir; *second* ~ gigi dua

gecko *n* cicak

gee *ejac, sl* wah, aduh

geese *n, pl* → **goose**

gelatine *n* semacam agar-agar

gem, gemstone *n* permata

gender *n* jenis kelamin; jender; ~ *studies* kajian jender

gene *n* gen

general *n* jenderal; *adj* umum; *Attorney-*~ Jaksa Agung; *director-*~ direktur-jenderal (dirjen); *in* ~ pada umumnya; **generally** *adv* biasanya, umumnya

generate *v* menghasilkan, membangkitkan

generation *n* angkatan, generasi; pembangkitan

generator *n* pembangkit listrik ← **generate**

generous *adj* murah hati, dermawan

genesis *n* asal; *Chr* Kejadian

genetic *adj* genetik

genial *adj* [jinial] ramah

genital *n* kemaluan; *adj* berhubungan dengan kemaluan

genius *n* [jinius] kecerdasan; jenius, orang berotak cemerlang

genocide *n* pembunuhan massal

genre *n* [jonre] gaya, aliran

gentle *adj* (lemah) lembut, halus, jinak; **gentleman** *n* **gentlemen** tuan; orang pria; orang sopan; *ladies* *and gentlemen* bapak-bapak dan ibu-ibu; **gently** *adv* perlahan-lahan, lemah lembut

genuine *adj* [jényuin] asli, sejati, tulen

geography *n* [jiografi] ilmu bumi, geografi

geologist *n* [jiolojist] geolog, ahli geologi; **geology** *n* geologi

geometry *n* ilmu ukur sudut, geometri

geothermal *adj* [jiotérmal] berhubungan dengan panas bumi; ~ *springs* air panas (gunung)

geriatric *adj* sangat tua

germ *n* kuman

German *n* bahasa Jerman; *adj* berasal dari Jerman; **Germany** *n* Jerman

gesture *n* isyarat, gerak-gerik tangan; *v* memberi isyarat

get *v* **got gotten** mendapat, menerima; mengerti; menjadi; ~ *along*, ~ *on* maju; berangkat; bergaul; ~ *away* pergi; lari, kabur; ~ *back* (mendapat) kembali; ~ *better* sembuh; menjadi lebih

baik; ~ *by* bertahan; ~ *into trouble* mendapat masalah; ~ *off* turun; ~ *up* bangun; ~ *well soon* semoga lekas sembuh

geyser *n* [giser] air mancur panas

gherkin *n* mentimun (yang diasamkan)

ghost *n* hantu

GI *abbrev government issue* tentara Amerika Serikat

giant *n, adj* [jaiant] raksasa

gibbon *n* [gibon] siamang

giddy *adj* [gidi] pusing, pening

gift [gift] kado, hadiah, pemberian; bakat; ~ *voucher* kupon belanja

gigantic *adj* [jaigantik] besar sekali, raksasa

giggle *n* [gigel] kikikan; *v* cekikik; tertawa terkikik-kikik

gills *n, pl* [gils] insang

gilt *n* [gilt] sepuh ← **gild**

gin *n* [jin] jenewer, minuman keras

ginger *n* [jinjer] jahe; *adj* merah (rambut); kuning (bulu kucing); **gingerbread** *n* roti keras rasa jahe

461

gipsy → **gypsy**
giraffe n [jiraf] jerapah
girl n [gerl] anak perempuan,
putri, gadis
give v [giv] **gave given**
memberi; ~ *away* memba-
gikan; membuka rahasia; ~
birth bersalin, melahirkan; ~
in mengalah; ~ *up* menyerah, menyerahkan; ~ *off*
mengeluarkan, menghasil-
kan; **given** *adj* tertentu
glacier n gletser
glad *adj* gembira, senang
glamorous *adj* memesona,
menarik, menawan, glamor;
glamor n kemewahan,
daya tarik, pesona
glance n pandangan sekilas;
v melirik, memandang
sekejap mata
gland n kelenjar
glare n cahaya yang menyilaukan; v membelalak,
melihat dengan sikap marah
glass n kaca; gelas; *look-
ing*-~ cermin; **glasses** n
kacamata; *dark* ~ kacamata
hitam; **glasshouse** n
rumah kaca
gleam n sinar, cahaya,
kilap

glide v meluncur; **glider** n
pesawat peluncur, pesawat
layang; *hang*-~ gantole
glimmer n cahaya redup
glimpse n pandangan
sekilas; v melihat sekilas
glitter n kegemilapan,
kemegahan; v gemilap
global *adj* seluruh dunia;
~ *warming* pemanasan
bumi; **globalization** n
globalisasi; **globe** n bola
dunia; bola lampu, bohlam
gloom n remang-remang,
kesuraman
glorious *adj* megah, mulia,
agung; **glory** n kemuliaan,
kemenangan
gloss n kilau, kilap
glossary n daftar istilah
glossy *adj* licin, mengkilap
← **gloss**
glove n [glav] sarung
tangan
glow n sinar, cahaya; v
bersinar, berseri; menyala;
~-*worm* ulat yang menge-
luarkan cahaya
glucose n glukosa
glue n [glu] lem, perekat; v
mengelem
glum *adj* murung

GMT *abbrev Greenwich Mean Time* waktu GMT

gnaw *v* [noa] menggerogoti

gnome *n* [nom] orang kerdil, katai; *garden* ~ patung kerdil sebagai hiasan taman

go *v* **went gone** [gon] pergi, berjalan; hilang; *~-between* perantara, calo; ~ *along* ikut serta; ~ *back* kembali; ~ *before* mendahului; ~ *by* berlalu; ~ *in* masuk; ~ *on* meneruskan; ~ *out* keluar; ~ *out with* berpacaran dengan; ~ *through with* menyelesaikan; ~ *under* bangkrut; *to have a* ~ berusaha; *no* ~ tidak bisa

goal *n* gawang, gol; tujuan; *v (to score a)* ~ mencetak gol; **goalkeeper** *n* penjaga gawang, kiper

goat *n* kambing

god *n* dewa; **God** *Isl, Chr* Allah, Tuhan; *Chr* Bapa; *~mother* ibu baptis, ibu permandian; ~ *bless you* Tuhan memberkati; **goddess** *n, f* dewi

going ~ *to* mau, akan; naik ← **go**

gold *n* emas; *~-leaf* emas

prada; ~ *mine* tambang emas; **golden** *adj* terbuat dari emas; ~ *anniversary* hari ulang tahun perkawinan yang kelimapuluh; **goldfish** *n* ikan emas

golf *n* golf; ~ *course* padang golf; **golfer** *n* pegolf, pemain golf

gone *v, pf* ← **go**

good *adj* baik, bagus; ~ *at* pandai; ~ *evening* selamat malam; ~ *Friday* Jum'at Agung; ~ *lord* astaga; ~ *night* selamat tidur; *for* ~ untuk selama-lamanya; *no* ~ tidak ada gunanya, tidak ada baiknya; **goodbye** *ejac* selamat tinggal, selamat jalan; **goodness** *n* kebaikan; ~ *me* ampun; **goods** *n, pl* barang-barang; ~ *train* kereta (api) barang

goose *n* **geese** [gis] angsa

gorge *n* jurang, ngarai

gorgeous *adj* [gorjes] sangat menawan atau menarik, indah

gorilla *n* gorila

gosh *ejac* wah!

gospel *n* injil, ajaran; ~ *music* musik gospel

gossip *n* gosip, isu, gunjingan, buah bibir, kabar burung; raja gosip (ragos); *v* bergosip; menggosipkan

got, gotten *v, pf* ← **get**

gout *n* asam urat

govern *v* [gavern] memerintah

governess *n, f* [gavernés] guru pribadi

government *n* [gaverment] pemerintah, pemerintahan; **governor** *n* gubernur; ~ *general* gubernur-jenderal ← **govern**

gown *n* gaun; jubah; *dressing* ~ kimono

GPA *abbrev grade point average* IP (indeks prestasi)

GPO *abbrev General Post Office* Kantor Pos Besar

grab *n* rampasan; *v* merampas, menjambret, menyerobot, menangkap

grace *n* keanggunan; rahmat, anugerah, karunia; masa tenggang; **graceful** *adj* anggun, lemah gemulai

grade *n* tingkat, pangkat, derajat; nilai (rapot); kelas; *first* ~ kelas satu; *v* memberi

angka atau nilai; memeriksa, menyortir; **gradual** *adj* lamakelamaan, berangsur-angsur

graduate *n* [gradyuet] lulusan, tamatan; sarjana; *v* [gradyuét] lulus, tamat; wisuda; **graduation** *n* tamat sekolah, acara lululusan; wisuda

graft *n* [graft] korupsi, kolusi

grain *n* butir; sereal, bijibijian; urat kayu

gram *n* gram

grammar *n* tata bahasa, gramatika; ~ *school* sekolah swasta

grand *n* besar, agung; bagus, mewah

grandchild *n* cucu; **granddaughter** *n* cucu (perempuan); **grandfather** *n* kakek; **grandma** *n, sl* nenek; nek; **grandmother** *n* nenek; **grandpa** *n, sl* kakek; kek; **grandson** *n* cucu (lelaki)

granny *n* nenek, perempuan tua ← **grandmother**

grant *n* (dana) pemberian, sumbangan, subsidi, beasiswa; *v* memberi, meng-

anugerahkan; *taken for*
~*ed* dianggap sudah begitu,
diramehkan

grape *n* buah anggur; *adj*
(rasa) anggur; **grapefruit** *n*
semacam jeruk kuning
yang besar

graphic *adj* grafik, bergambar, jelas; ~ *artist*
pelukis grafis

grasp *v* memegang,
menggenggam, menangkap,
mengerti

grass *n* rumput; **grasshopper** *n* belalang

grate *v* memarut; meng-
ganggu; **grate, grating** *n*
riol, kisi; *adj* kasar, mengganggu

grateful *n* berterima kasih

grater *n* parut ← **grate**

grave *adj* berat, genting,
gawat, serius

grave *n* kuburan, makam

gravel *n* [gravel] batu kerikil

graveyard *n* kuburan,
tempat pemakaman ←
grave

gravity *n* daya tarik bumi,
gaya berat

gravy *n* [grévi] saus atau
kuah daging

gray *adj* (warna) abu-abu,
kelabu; suram; ~ *matter*
sel-sel otak; **grayhound** *n*
anjing pacu

graze *n* goresan pada kulit;
v mendapat goresan pada
kulit

grease *n* [gris] gemuk,
minyak; *v* [griz] memberi
gemuk, meminyaki; **greasy**
adj berlemak, berminyak

great *adj* [grét] besar, agung,
mulia, raya; ~ *Britain* Inggris Raya, Britania Raya

great-grandchild *n* cicit;
great-grandfather *n* kakek
buyut; **great-grandmother**
n nenek buyut

Greece *n* Yunani

greed *n* kerakusan, keta-
makan; **greedy** *adj* rakus,
tamak, loba

Greek *n* bahasa Yunani;
orang Yunani; *adj* berasal
dari Yunani ← **Greece**

green *adj* hijau; mentah;
baru, muda; ramah ling-
kungan; ~ *light* lampu
hijau; izin; **greengrocer** *n*
tukang sayur; toko sayur;
greenhouse *n* rumah
kaca; ~ *effect* efek rumah

kaca, pemanasan bumi; ~
gas gas yang ikut mem-
perparah efek rumah kaca;
greens *n, pl* sayuran,
sayur-mayur; partai hijau,
partai peduli lingkungan

greet *v* memberi salam,
menegur, menyambut;
meet and ~ acara ramah
tamah; **greeting** *n* salam,
ucapan selamat; *season's*
~*s* Selamat (Hari Natal)

grenade *n* granat

grew *v, pf* → **grow**

grey → **gray**

grid *n* jaringan

gridiron *n* sepak bola
Amerika

grief *n* kesedihan, duka cita

grill *n* pemanggangan,
barbekiu; *v* memanggang;
griller *n* pemanggangan (di
kompor)

grim *adj* seram

grime *n* kotoran, daki;
grimy *adj* kotor

grin *n* senyum, seringai; *v*
tersenyum, menyeringai

grind *v* **ground ground**
menggerinda, menggiling,
mengasah; **grinder** *n*
gerinda

grip *n* pegangan, genggam-
an; *v* memegang, meng-
genggam; **gripping** *adj*
menegangkan, menga-
syikkan

grit *n* kerikil, pasir;
kenekatan

grizzle *v* mengadu, rewel,
cengeng

groan *n* keluh, erang; *v*
berkeluh, mengeluh,
mengerang

grocer *n* penjual bahan
makanan; **grocery** *n* toko
bahan makanan; **groceries**
n, pl bahan makanan

groom *n (bride)*~ mempelai
pria, pengantin pria, calon
suami

groom *n* pengasuh kuda;
v memelihara penampilan,
merias

groove *n* alur; gaya

grope *v* meraba-raba

gross *n* gros, 12 lusin, 144;
adj sangat gemuk; *sl* kotor;
jorok; ~ *national product
(GNP)* pendapatan (kotor)
nasional

ground *v, pf* → **grind**

ground *n* [graund] tanah,
bumi; *v* mendasarkan;

melarang (pergi); **grounds** n, pl pekarangan, taman; alasan; *on the ~ of* berdasarkan

group n kelompok, grup; v mengelompokkan

grow v [gro] **grew grown** tumbuh; bertambah; menjadi; menanam; *~ up* jadi besar, tumbuh

growl n [graul] geram; v menggeram

grown v, pf → **grow**

growth n pertumbuhan, pertambahan; benjolan ← **grow**

grudge n dendam; *to bear a ~* menaruh dendam

grumble n keluhan; bersungut-sungut, menggerutu

grumpy adj mengomel, marah-marah

grunt n dengkur; v mengeluarkan bunyi dengkur

GST abbrev Goods and Services Tax PPN (Pajak Pendapatan Nasional)

guarantee n [garanti] jaminan; v menjamin, menanggung

guard n [gard] jaga, penga-

wal; kondektur; v menjaga, pengawal; **guardian** n wali, orang tua asuh; penjaga

guava n jambu

guerilla, guerrilla n, adj gerilya, gerilyawan

guess n [gés] tebakan, terkaan, sangkaan; v menebak, menerka

guest n [gést] tamu; *~house* losmen, hotel kecil; *~ room* kamar (tidur untuk) tamu

guidance n [gaidans] pimpinan, bimbingan; **guide** n pemandu, pembimbing; v membimbing, memandu; **guidebook** n buku petunjuk, buku panduan; **guidelines** n, pl pedoman

guilt n [gilt] kesalahan, rasa bersalah; *~free* tanpa rasa bersalah; **guilty** adj bersalah

guitar n gitar; *bass ~* gitar bas; *electric ~* gitar listrik; **guitarist** n pemain gitar; gitaris

gulf n teluk besar; jurang

gull n (sea)~ burung camar

gully n jurang

gulp n teguk; v meneguk, menelan

H

gum *n* getah

gum *n* gusi

gun *n* bedil, senapan, revolver, pistol; *v* menembak

gurgle *v* berdeguk; mendeguk

gush *n* pancaran, semburan; *v* memancar, mengalir dengan deras

gusto *n* cita rasa; semangat, kesukaan

gusty *adj* berangin ← **gust**

gut *n* usus; **guts** *n, pl* nyali, keberanian

gutter *n* parit, selokan

guy *n, sl* [gai] orang, lelaki, cowok

gym *n* [jim] aula, tempat senam; pusat kebugaran;

gymnasium *n* aula, tempat senam, gimnasium; **gymnast** *n* pesenam; **gymnastics** *n* senam

gynecologist *n* [gainekolojist] ginekolog

gypsy, gipsy *n* nomaden, orang jipsi; *Sea* ~ orang Bajau

habit *n* kebiasaan; *bad* ~ kebiasaan buruk; **habitat** *n* tempat tinggal, habitat

hack *v* memotong-motong, mencincang; memasuki jaringan komputer; **hacker** *n* orang yang memasuki jaringan komputer

had *v, pf* → **have**

hadn't (**had not**) ← **have**

haemorrhage → **hemorrhage**

haemorrhoid → **hemorrhoid**

hail, hailstone *n* hujan es

hair *n* rambut, bulu; ~ *pin* tusuk konde; *body* ~ bulu; **hairbrush** *n* sikat rambut; **haircut** *n* potong rambut; **hairdresser** *n* penata rambut, potong rambut; **hairspray** *n* semprot rambut; **hairy** *adj* berbulu

half *n* [haf] **halves** *adj* setengah, separuh; ~~*hearted* setengah hati; ~ *time* istirahat (dalam pertandingan); ~ *a dozen* setengah lusin; ~ *past three* (jam) setengah empat;

halfway *adj* setengah jalan

hall *n* [hol] aula, balai, ruang; lorong, koridor; *concert* ~ gedung konser, gedung pertunjukan

hallo → **hello**

Hallowe'en malam 31 Oktober

hallucinate *v* berhalusinasi; **hallucination** *n* khayal, halusinasi

hallway *n* lorong, koridor

halo *n* [hélo] lingkaran cahaya di sekitar kepala

halt *n* [holt] pemberhentian; *v* berhenti; memberhentikan

halter *n* [holter] tali leher

halve *v* [hav] membagi dua ← **half**

ham *n* irisan daging babi

hamburger *n* burger

hammer *n* palu; *v* memalu, memukul

hammock *n* tempat tidur gantung

hamper *n* bakul, keranjang (makanan)

hamster *n* marmot

hand *n* tangan; jarum (jam); ~ *out* membagi-bagikan; ~*s off* jangan ikut campur, jangan disentuh; ~*s up*

angkat tangan; *on* ~ hadir, tersedia; *on the other* ~ di sisi lain; *v* memberi, menyampaikan; ~ *in* menyerahkan; **handbag** *n* tas tangan; **handbook** *n* buku panduan, pedoman; **handcuff** *n* borgol, belenggu; *v* memborgol; **handful** *n* segenggam

handicap *n* rintangan, cacat; ~*ped* cacat

handicraft *n* kerajinan tangan ← **hand**

handkerchief *n* sapu tangan

handle *n* pegangan; *v* menangani, memegang; **handlebar** *n* setang

handmade *adj* buatan tangan ← **hand**

handphone → **phone**

handsome *adj* [handsam] ganteng, tampan

handwriting *n* [handraiting] tulisan tangan ← **hand**

handy *adj* berguna, praktis; **handyman** *n* tukang ← **hand**

hang *v* bergantung; menggantung; ~ *out* tongkrong; ~ *up* memutuskan sambungan telepon; ~*gliding* gantolé; ~*up* masalah

hangman *n* algojo

hangout *n* tempat tong-
krongan

hangover *n* tidak enak badan
setelah banyak minum

happen *v* terjadi; **happening**
n kejadian, peristiwa

happiness *n* kebahagiaan;
happy *adj* bahagia, berbahagia, senang

harass *v* mengganggu,
mengusik; **harassment** *n*
gangguan; *sexual ~* pelecehan seksual

harbor *n* [harber] pelabuhan

hard *adj* keras; susah, sulit;
adj dengan rajin; *~ labor*
kerja paksa; *~ up* tidak
punya uang banyak; *~ of
hearing* agak tuli; **harden** *v*
mengeras

hardly *adv* nyaris tidak,
hampir tidak

hardware *n* alat-alat pertu-
kangan; barang-barang dari
logam dan besi; peranti
keras ← **hard**

hare *n* kelinci besar

harm *n* bahaya; kerugian,
kerusakan, kejahatan; *v*
merusak, mengganggu; *no
~ done* tidak apa-apa;

harmful *adj* membahayakan, merusak, merugikan;
harmless *adj* tidak jahat

harmonica *n* harmonika

harmony *n* keselarasan,
kerukunan, kecocokan

harness *n* tali pengaman, tali
keselamatan; pakaian kuda;
v memasang; memanfaatkan

harp *n* harpa

harsh *adj* kasar, keras hati;
tidak ramah

harvest *n* (hasil) panen; *v*
memanen, memotong (padi)

has → have

hash *n* pagar (#)

hasty *adj* tergesa-gesa,
tergopoh-gopoh

hatch *n* pintu kecil; *v*
mengeram, menetas

hate *n* kebencian, rasa
benci; *v* membenci; **hatred**
n [hétred] kebencian, rasa
benci

haughty *adj* [hoti] sombong,
angkuh

haul *n* hasil tangkapan;
muatan; *long-~ flight*
penerbangan jarak jauh; *v*
menarik, menghela

haunt *v* menghantui; *~ed
house* rumah hantu

470

have *v* [hav] **had had** mempunyai, memiliki; ada; mendapat; menyuruh; ~ *a shower* mandi; ~ *lunch* makan siang; ~ *on* memakai, berpakaian; ~ *to* harus, terpaksa, wajib

haven *n* pelabuhan, tempat berlindung

hawk *n* burung elang

hawker *n* penjaja, pedagang kaki lima; ~ *center* pujasera, tempat pedagang kaki lima

hay *n* rumput kering, jerami; ~ *fever* alergi rumput; ~*stack* tumpukan rumput kering

hazard *n* bahaya, risiko

haze *n* kabut, asap

hazel *adj* warna mata yang hijau kecoklatan; **hazelnut** *n* semacam buah kemiri

he *pron, m* [hi] dia, ia (subyek); **He** *pron* Dia, Tuhan

head *n* [héd] kepala; pemimpin, direktur; *v* mengepalai; menyundul (bola); ~*dress* hiasan kepala; ~ *for* menuju; ~*hunter* pengayau; ~ *office* kantor pusat; ~ *start* mulai

lebih awal; ~*s or tails* mengundi dengan keping logam; *Rp 60.000 a* ~ Rp 60 000 rupiah per orang; *section* ~ kepala bagian; *v* mengepalai, memimpin; **headache** *n* sakit kepala, pusing; **heading** *n* judul (karangan); **headlights** *n, pl* lampu depan (mobil); **headline** *n* kepala berita; **headmaster** *n, m* **headmistress** *f* kepala sekolah; **headquarters** *n* markas besar

heal *v* menyembuhkan, menyehatkan; **health** *n* [hélth] kesehatan; **healthy** *adj* sehat

heap *n* timbunan, tumpukan, susunan; *v* menimbun

hear *v* **heard heard** [hérd] mendengar; ~ *from* mendapat kabar dari; ~ *of* mendengar tentang; mengetahui; **hearing** *n* (indera) pendengaran, sidang; ~ *aid* alat bantu dengar

heart *n* [hart] jantung; hati, inti; ~ *attack* serangan jantung; ~ *disease* sakit jantung; ~*shaped* ber-

bentuk hati; ~ *of gold*
berhati baik; ~ *of stone*
tidak berhati; *by* ~ hafal;
cross my ~ bersumpah;
heartbeat *n* denyut jantung;
heartbreak *n* patah hati
heat *n* panas, kepanasan,
hangat; *v* memanaskan,
menghangatkan; **heater** *n*
alat pemanas
heaven *n* [héven] surga;
heavens *ejac* masya Allah;
for ~*'s sake* demi Allah
heavy *adj* [hévi] berat,
berbobot
Hebrew *n* [Hibru] bahasa
Ibrani; *arch* orang Ibrani
hedge *n* pagar hidup
hedgehog *n* landak
heed *n* perhatian
heel *n* tumit; hak; *high* ~*s*
sepatu hak tinggi
height *n* [hait] ketinggian;
tinggi badan; puncak
heir *n* [ér] **heiress** *f* ahli
waris
held *v*, *pf* → hold
helicopter *n* helikopter,
heli; **helipad** *n* landasan
helikopter; **heliport** *n*
lapangan helikopter
hell *n* neraka

hello, hallo *ejac* halo; apa
kabar?
helm *n* kemudi
helmet *n* helm
help *n* pertolongan, bantuan;
v menolong, membantu; *it
can't be* ~*ed* apa boleh
buat; **helpful** *adj* suka
menolong; berguna; **help-
less** *adj* tidak berdaya
hem *n* kelim; *v* mengelim
hemisphere *n* [hémisfir]
belahan (bumi)
hemorrhage *n* [hémerej]
perdarahan; *v* berdarah
hemorrhoid *n* [hémeroid]
wasir, ambeien
hen *n, f* ayam betina
hepatitis *n* [hépataitis]
hepatitis, radang hati
her *pron, f* -nya (kepunyaan); dia, ia (obyek)
herb *n* jamu, bumbu; ~*s*
ramuan bumbu
herd *n* kawanan; *v*
menggembala
here *adv* di sini; *come* ~
(ke) sini; ~ *and there* di
sana-sini; ~ *she is* ini dia;
~ *is my card* ini kartu nama
saya; *Eileen lives* ~ Eileen
tinggal di sini

hereditary *adj* turun-temurun, genetik

heritage *n* [héritej] warisan, harta pusaka

hermit *n* petapa

hernia *n* burut

hero *n* [hiro] pahlawan

heroin *n* [héroin] heroin, putau

heroine *n, f* [héroin] pahlawan (wanita)

heron *n* burung bangau

herring *n* ikan haring

hers *pron, f* miliknya; **herself** *pron* dirinya, sendiri; *by* ~ sendiri

hesitant *adj* **hesitate** *v* ragu-ragu, bimbang

heterosexual *n* hetero *sl* heteroseksual, orang yang suka lawan jenis

hey *ejac* he, oi

hibernate *v* tidur selama musim dingin

hiccup *n* cegukan, sedu; *v* cegukan, bersedu

hid, hidden *v, pf* → **hide**

hide *n* kulit (binatang)

hide *v* **hid hidden** bersembunyi, berlindung, mengumpet; menyembunyikan; ~*-and-seek* petak umpet,

sembunyi-sembunyian

hiding *n* persembunyian; *in* ~ bersembunyi; ~ *place* tempat sembunyi, tempat berlindung ← **hide**

high *adj* [hai] tinggi, mulia; ~ *chair* kursi bayi; ~*-class* kelas satu; ~ *jump* loncat tinggi; ~ *noon* tengah hari, jam 12 siang; ~*-rise* bertingkat tinggi; ~ *school* sekolah menengah (atas); ~ *tide* air pasang; *on a* ~ sedang bahagia; **highlands** *n* tanah tinggi, pegunungan; **highness** *Your* ~ Yang Mulia; **highway** *n* jalan raya, jalan besar

hijack *v* membajak; **hijacker** *n* membajak; **hijacking** *n* pembajakan

hike *n* perjalanan kaki; *v* berjalan kaki, mendaki gunung; **hiker** *n* pendaki gunung, orang yang gemar berjalan kaki; **hiking** *n* mendaki gunung; berjalan kaki

hilarious *adj* [hilérius] lucu sekali, sangat menggelikan

hill *n* bukit; **hillside** *n* lereng bukit; **hilly** *adj* berbukit-bukit

him *pron, m* dia, ia (obyek);
himself *pron* dirinya,
sendiri; *by* ~ sendiri

hind [haind] ~ *leg* kaki
belakang (binatang)

hindsight *n* [haindsait]
peninjauan kembali, melihat
ke belakang

Hindu *n* orang Hindu; *adj*
Hindu; **Hinduism** *n* agama
Hindu

hinge *n* [hinj] engsel; sendi

hint *n* tanda, isyarat, sindiran; *v* mengisyaratkan;
handy ~ tips

hip *n* pangkal paha, pinggul;
hipsters *n, pl* celana
dengan pinggang rendah

hire *n* sewa; *v* menyewa,
mempekerjakan; ~ *car* mobil
sewaan; ~ *out* menyewakan;
~ *purchase* sewa beli

his *pron, m* -nya (kepunyaan)

hiss *n* desis; *v* berdesis,
mendesis

historic *adj* bersejarah;
historical *adj* historis,
berkaitan dengan sejarah;
history *n* sejarah, hikayat;
medical ~ riwayat medis

hit *n* pukulan; *v* **hit hit**
memukul, kena, mengenai;

~ *out* menyerang; ~*-and-run*
tabrak lari

hit *n* (lagu) yang sedang naik
daun; *adj* laku, populer

hitchhike *v* menumpang
mobil orang yang lewat

HM *abbrev* Her Majesty, His
Majesty Yang Dipertuan
Agung

hoard *n* timbunan; *v* menimbun, mengumpulkan;
hoarder *n* penimbun

hoarse *adj* serak, parau

hoax *n* [hooks] tipuan,
cerita bohong; *v* menipu

hobby *n* hobi, kegemaran,
kesukaan; ~ *farm* pertanian
sebagai tempat peristirahat-
an; ~*-horse* kuda-kudaan,
kuda mainan

hockey *n* hoki; *ice* ~ hoki
es

hoe *n* [ho] pacul, cangkul

hog *n* babi; orang rakus

hoist *clothes* ~ jemuran
(baju); *v* menaikkan

hold *n* pegangan, geng-
gaman; palka; *v* **held held**
memegang, menggenggam;
bermuatan; ~ *off* menahan;
~ *fast* bersikukuh; ~ *out*
bertahan; ~ *up* tahan; me-

nodong; ~-*up* perampokan, penodongan

hole *n* lubang, liang

holiday *n* hari libur; *religious* ~ hari raya; *v* berlibur

holiness *His* ~ Yang Mulia Sri Paus ← **holy**

Holland *n*, *sl* Belanda

hollow *n* rongga, ruang; *adj* hampa, kosong

holocaust *n* [holokost] bencana (pembakaran), pemusnahan; *The* ~ pembinasaan orange Yahudi selama Perang Dunia Kedua

holy *adj* suci, kudus; *Cath* ~ *Father* Sri Paus; ~ *water* air suci

home *n* rumah; panti (jompo); *adj* di rumah, di kandang sendiri; ~ *economics* pendidikan kesejahteraan keluarga (PKK); ~ *ground* kandang sendiri, lapangan sendiri; *at* ~ di rumah; betah, mapan; **hometown** *n* kampung (halaman); **homemade** *adj* buatan sendiri; **homesick** *adj* rindu pada rumah, kampung halaman atau

negeri sendiri; **homeward** *adv* pulang, ke (arah) rumah; **homework** *n* pekerjaan rumah (PR); **homing** ~ *pigeon* merpati pos

homicide *n* [homisaid] pembunuhan

homo *n*, *sl* orang homo; **homoseksual** *adj* homoseksual, suka sesama jenis

honest *adj* [onest] jujur; **honesty** *n* kejujuran

honey *n* [hani] madu; sayang, sayangku; **honeymoon** *n* bulan madu; *v* berbulan madu

honk *n* bunyi klakson; *v* mengklakson, menyembunyikan klakson

honorable *adj* terhormat; *The* ~ Yang Terhormat; **honorary** *adj* kehormatan; **honor** *n* hormat, kehormatan; *v* menghormati; *in* ~ *of* untuk menghormati

hoof *n* **hooves** kuku (binatang)

hook *n* kait, kali; *v* mengait; ~ *up* memasang, menghubungkan; ~ *and eye* kancing cantel, kait; *off the* ~ lepas, selamat; **hooked**

adj keranjingan; ~ *nose* hidung bengkok

hooligan *n* penggemar sepak bola yang brutal

hoop *n* gelindingan, simpai; *hula* ~ hulahup

hoot *n* suara burung hantu; bunyi klakson; suara tertawa; *v* bersuara (burung hantu); tertawa; **hooter** *n* klakson

hop *n* lompat (pada satu kaki); *v* melompat-lompat, melonjak-lonjak

hope *n* harapan; *v* berharap; mengharapkan; *no* ~ tidak ada harapan; **hopeful** *adj* penuh harapan; **hopeless** *adj* putus asa

horizon *n* [horaizon] cakrawala, kaki langit, ufuk, horison; **horizontal** *adj* [horizontel] melintang, horisontal

hormone *n* hormon

horn *n* tanduk; terompet, klakson; **horned** *adj* bertanduk

hornbill *n* burung enggang

hornet *n* penyengat, langau

horrible, horrific *adj* mengerikan, dahsyat; **horrify**

v mengerikan; **horror** *n* kengerian, ketakutan, horor

horse *n* kuda; *clothes* ~ jemuran (baju); *saw-*~ kuda-kuda; **horseback** *on* ~ berkuda; **horsepower** *n* daya kuda, PK *(paardekracht)*; **horseshoe** *n* ladam, sepatu kuda

horticulture *n* perkebunan, hortikultura

hose *n* selang

hospital *n* rumah sakit; *mental* ~ rumah sakit jiwa

hospitality *n* keramahtamahan

host *n, m* [hoost] tuan rumah

hostage *n* sandera, tawanan; *to take* ~ menyandera

hostel *n* asrama

hostess *n, f* [hoostés] nyonya rumah ← **host**

hostile *adj* bermusuhan

hot *adj* panas, hangat; pedas; *sl* seksi, menggairahkan; ~ *plate* tungku; ~ *water bottle* botol karet

hotel *n* hotel; *four-star* ~ hotel bintang empat

hotline *n* sambungan langsung, nomor telepon langsung ← **hot**

hound *n* anjing pemburu

hour *n* [auer] jam; ~ *hand* jarum pendek; *half-~, half an* ~ setengah jam; *quarter of an* ~ seperempat jam; **hours** *(for)* ~ berjam-jam; *after* ~ *(ah)* setelah jam kerja

house *n* rumah; dewan; ~ *of Representatives* Dewan Perwakilan Rakyat; **houseboat** *n* rumah perahu; **household** *n* rumah tangga; **housekeeper** *n* kepala pembantu; **housemaid** *n, f* pembantu, pramuwisma; **housewarming** *n* pesta atau selamatan untuk rumah baru; **housewife** *n, f* ibu rumah tangga; **housework** *n* pekerjaan rumah; **housing** *n* perumahan

hovel *n* gubuk (derita)

how *adv* bagaimana; betapa; ~ *about* bagaimana kalau; ~ *beautiful* betapa cantiknya; ~ *do you do?* apa kabar?; ~ *much?, ~ many?* Berapa banyak?; ~ *much is it?* Berapa harganya?; **however** *adv* biarpun, akan tetapi, namun; bagaimanapun

howl *n* gonggong; teriak, tangis; *v* melolong; menangis (dengan keras)

HQ *abbrev headquarters* mabes (markas besar)

HR *abbrev human resources* SDM (sumber daya manusia)

HRH *abbrev His/Her Royal Highness* Yang Dipertuan Agung

HS *abbrev high school* SMA, sekolah menengah

hub *n* pusat (kota)

hug *n* pelukan; *v* berpelukan; memeluk; *bear-~* memeluk erat

huge *adj* besar sekali

hull *n* lambung kapal

hum *v* bersenandung; mendengung

human *n, adj* manusia, orang; ~ *rights* hak azasi manusia (HAM); **humane** *adj* manusiawi, berperikemanusiaan; **humanitarian** ~ *aid* bantuan kemanusiaan

humble *adj* rendah hati; *v* merendahkan

humid *adj* lembab; **humidity** *n* kelembaban

humiliate *v* menghina,

merendahkan; **humiliation** *n* penghinaan

hummingbird *n* semacam burung kolibri

humorous *adj* lucu, kocak, menggelikan; **humor** *n* kelucuan; sifat; *sense of ~* selera humor

hump *n* ponok (unta), bongkol

hunch *n* perasaan, firasat, dugaan

hunchback *n, adj* bungkuk

hundred *n* ratusan; *adj* seratus; *adj* keseratus

Hungarian *n* [Hanggérian] *adj* berasal dari Hongaria; **Hungary** *n* Hongaria

hunger *n* [hangger] rasa lapar; **hungry** *adj* lapar

hunt *n* perburuan, buruan; *v* berburu; memburu; **hunter** *n* pemburu; **hunting** *n* pemburuan, perburuan

hurdle *n* gawang; rintangan; *v* melompati; mengatasi; **hurdles** *n, pl* lari gawang; **hurdler** *n* pelari gawang

hurl *v* melempar, melemparkan

hurrah, hurray *ejac* hore; *hip, hip ~* hip hip hore

hurricane *n* angin topan

hurry *n* ketergopoh-gopohan; *v* bergegas; menggegaskan; *~ up* ayo cepat; *sl* cepatan; *in a ~* tergesa-gesa

hurt *n* sakit hati, luka; *v* melukai, menyakiti, mencederai, merusak

husband *n* suami

hush *v* diam; *~ up* menutupnutupi

husk *n* kulit (biji)

hut *n* pondok, gubuk

Hwy *Highway* Jl Ry (Jalan Raya)

hydraulic *adj* [haidrolik] hidrolik, hidrolis

hydroelectric *~ power station* pembangkit listrik tenaga air

hydrogen *n* [haidrojen] hidrogen, zat air

hygiene *n* [haijin] kebersihan; higiene; **hygienic** *adj* bersih; higienis

hypertension *n* hipertensi, darah tinggi

hypnotist *n* (ahli) hipnotis; **hypnotize** *v* menghipnotis

hypocrite *n* [hipokrit] orang munafik; **hypocritical** *adj* munafik

hypodermic ~ *syringe* jarum suntik

hypothesis *n* [haipothesis] hipotesa

hysterical *adj* histeris

I

I *pron* saya, aku

IBRA *abbrev Indonesian Bank Restructuring Agency* BPPN

ice *n* es; ~ *block* es batu; ~*d tea* es teh; ~*skating* bermain sepatu (luncur) es; **ice cream** *n* es krim; **iceberg** *n* gunung es; **icing** *n* lapisan gula di atas kue

icy *adj* [aisi] dingin sekali, sedingin es ← **ice**

ID *abbrev* identification identitas, jati diri

IDD *abbrev international direct dialing* SLI (sambung-an langsung internasional)

idea *n* [aidia] ide, gagasan; **ideal** *adj* [aidil] yang diinginkan atau diidamkan, ideal, yang terbaik

identical *adj* sama, serupa, identik

identification *n* pengenalan, identifikasi; **identify** *v* mengenal, mengidentifikasi; **identity** *n* identitas, jati diri; ~ *card* kartu pengenal, kartu tanda penduduk (KTP)

idiom *n* ungkapan, idiom

idiot *n* orang dungu

idol *n* idola; berhala; **idolize** *v* mendewakan, memuji

ie *id est = that is* yaitu, yakni

if *conj* kalau, jika; apabila, bila

ignite *v* menyala, membakar; menyalakan; **ignition** *n* starter, kontak; ~ *key* kunci kontak

ignorant *adj* tidak tahu; **ignore** *v* tidak menghiraukan, tidak mengindahkan

iguana *n* iguana, sejenis biawak

ill *n* penyakit; *adj* sakit; jahat, salah

illegal *adj* melanggar hukum, tidak sah, ilegal

illegitimate *adj* lahir di luar nikah; ~ *child* anak yang lahir di luar nikah, anak haram

illiterate *adj* buta huruf

illness *n* penyakit; *mental*
~ penyakit jiwa

illusion *n* ilusi, khayal;
illusionist *n* tukang sulap

illustrate *v* menggambarkan,
melukiskan; **illustration** *n*
gambar, lukisan, ilustrasi;
illustrator *n* pelukis

image *n* gambar; **imagi-
nary** *adj* khayal; **imagination** *n* daya cipta, khayal,
fantasi; **imagine** *v* membayang; membayangkan

IMF *abbrev International
Monetary Fund* Dana
Moneter Internasional

imitate *v* meniru; **imitation**
n tiruan, imitasi; ~ *leather*
kulit palsu; **imitator** *n* peniru

immediate *adj* langsung;
immediately *adv* serta
merta

immense *adj* sangat besar;
immensely *adv* sangat

immerse *v* mencelupkan,
membenamkan; **immersion**
n pencelupan

immigrant *n* pendatang,
imigran; **immigrate** *v*
datang dari daerah lain
untuk menetap; **immigra-
tion** *n* imigrasi

immoral *adj* tuna susila, cabul

immortal *adj* kekal, abadi,
baka

immune *adj* kebal, imun;
immunity *n* kekebalan;
immunization *n* imunisasi,
pengebalan

impartial *adj* tidak memihak,
adil, obyektif

impatience *n* [impésyens]
ketidaksabaran, rasa tidak
sabar; **impatient** *adj* tidak
sabar

impeach *v* menuduh, men-
dakwa, memanggil ke
pengadilan; **impeachment**
n dakwaan, tuduhan;
pemanggilan

impede *v* menghalangi,
merintangi

imperative *n* bentuk perintah; *adj* harus

imperfect *adj* kurang sempurna, tercela

imperial *adj* [impirial] kaisar;
imperialism *n* imperialisme;
imperialist *n* orang penjajah,
imperialis; *adj* imperialis,
penjajahan ← **empire**

impersonal *adj* bersikap
dingin; tidak mengenai
orang tertentu

480

impersonate *v* menyamar sebagai

impertinent *adj* kurang ajar

implement *n* perkakas, perabot, alat; *v* menerapkan, melaksanakan; **implementation** *n* penerapan, implementasi

implicate *v* melibatkan; **implication** *n* implikasi, dampak

impolite *adj* kurang sopan

import *n* barang impor, pemasukan; *v* mengimpor, mendatangkan

important *adj* penting

importer *n* pengimpor, importir

impossible *adj* mustahil, tidak mungkin

impostor *n* penipu, penyamar, gadungan

impotent *adj* tidak berkuasa; lemah syahwat, impoten

impractical *adj* tidak praktis

impress *v* memberi kesan, mengesankan; **impression** *n* kesan; cetakan; **impressive** *adj* mengesankan, hebat, dahsyat

imprison *v* [imprizon] memenjarakan; **imprisonment** *n* hukuman penjara

improper *adj* tidak layak, tidak senonoh

improve *v* [impruv] memperbaiki; meningkatkan; menjadi sembuh, membaik; **improvement** *n* perbaikan, peningkatan, kemajuan

impulse *n* kata hati, dorongan hati; **impulsive** *adj* menurut kata hati

impure *adj* kotor, cemar, najis, tidak murni, tidak suci

in *prep* di (dalam), dalam, pada; *adj, coll* laku, populer; ~ *addition* lagipula; ~ *contrast* sebaliknya, di sisi lain; ~ *Indonesian* dalam Bahasa Indonesia; ~ *Semarang* di Semarang; ~ *spite of* walaupun, meskipun; ~*depth* secara mendalam; ~*service* latihan dalam perusahaan

inability *n* ketidakmampuan

inaccuracy *n* kesalahan; **inaccurate** *adj* tidak teliti, tidak tepat

inactive *adj* tidak aktif, tidak bergerak

481

inadequate *adj* kurang, tidak cukup

inappropriate *adj* tidak pantas

inaudible *adj* tidak kedengaran, tidak terdengar

inaugural *adj* [inogyural] perdana; **inauguration** *n* pelantikan; pembukaan

incarnation *n* penjelmaan

incendiary ~ *device* bom pembakar

incense *n* dupa, kemenyan

inch *n* inci

incident *n* peristiwa, kejadian, insiden; **incidentally** *adv* ngomong-ngomong

incinerator *n* tempat pembakaran sampah

incite *v* menghasut; **incitement** *n* hasutan

inclination *n* [inklinasyen] kecenderungan, kecondongan; **incline** *v* cenderung, condong

include *v* mengandung, meliputi; **including** *conj* termasuk; **inclusive** *adj* inklusif; sampai dengan

incoherent *adj* tidak jelas

income *n* [incam] pendapatan, penghasilan, gaji;

~ *tax* pajak penghasilan; **incoming** *adj* yang masuk

incompatible *adj* tidak cocok

incompetent *adj* tidak mampu

incomplete *adj* kurang lengkap, tidak komplet

inconsiderate *adj* tidak memperhatikan (perasaan orang lain)

inconsistent *adj* tidak konsisten

inconvenient *adj* merepotkan, mengganggu

incorporated *adj* perseroan terbatas

incorrect *adj* tidak benar, salah

increase *n* pertambahan, kenaikan; *v* tambah, bertambah; menambah, menaikkan, meningkatkan

incredible *adj* luar biasa, tidak dapat dipercaya, hebat

incubation *n* penetasan, pengeraman; ~ *period* masa perkembangan (penyakit)

incur ~ *expenses* memakan biaya

incurable *adj* [inkyurabel]

tidak dapat diobati, tidak
dapat disembuhkan

indecent *adj* tak senonoh,
tidak sopan

indecision *n* kebimbangan,
kebingungan; **indecisive**
adj ragu-ragu, bimbang

indeed *adj, adv* betul,
sebetulnya; *conj* memang;
bahkan; *it is* ~ benar sekali

indefinite untuk jangka
waktu tidak terbatas

indent *v* memasukkan ke
dalam (alinea)

independence *n* kemerdekaan; kebebasan; ~
Day Hari Kemerdekaan;
independent *adj* mandiri,
merdeka, bebas, tidak
tergantung

indestructible *adj* tidak
dapat dibinasakan atau
dimusnahkan

index *n* daftar, indeks; ~
finger telunjuk

India *n* India; *the Dutch
East* ~ *Company* VOC;
Kompeni; **Indian** *n* orang
India; orang Indian; *adj*
berasal dari India

indicate *v* menunjukkan;
indication *n* tanda, petunjuk,

alamat; **indicator** *n* penun-
juk; indikator; lampu sein

Indies *the East* ~ Hindia
Belanda; *the West* ~
Hindia Barat

indigenous *adj* asli; ~
people penduduk asli

indigestion *n* salah cerna

indignant *adj* marah,
jengkel

indigo *n* nila; *adj* biru tua

indirect *adj* tidak langsung

indistinct *adj* kurang terang,
kurang jelas, samar-samar

individual *n* pribadi, orang,
oknum; *adj* perseorangan;
~*ly* masing-masing

Indochina *n* [Indocaina]
Indocina; **Indochinese** *adj*
berasal dari Indocina

Indonesia *n* Indonesia;
Indonesian *n* Bahasa Indo-
nesia; orang Indonesia; *adj*
berasal dari Indonesia; ~
Embassy Kedutaan Besar
Republik Indonesia (KBRI)

indoor *adj* **indoors** *adv* di
dalam rumah atau gedung

induction *n* pelantikan;
induksi

indulge ~ *in* menikmati

industrial *adj* berkaitan

dengan industri atau pabrik;
industry *n* industri, perin-
dustrian; kegiatan

inefficient *adj* tidak efisien,
tidak jalan dengan baik

ineligible *adj* tidak dapat
dipilih

inequality *n* ketidaksamaan,
kesenjangan

inert *adj* lembam, tidak
bergerak; ~ *gas* gas lembam, gas mulia

inevitable *adj* tidak dapat
dielakkan, mau tidak mau

inexpensive *adj* tidak mahal

infant *n, adj* bayi, balita,
anak kecil

infect *v* menulari, menjangkiti; **infection** *n* penyakit, infeksi, penularan;
infectious *adj* menular

infer *v* mengambil kesimpulan; **inference** *n* kesimpulan, dugaan

inferior *adj* [infirior] kurang
bagus atau baik, bermutu
rendah

infertile *adj* mandul, tidak
subur; **infertility** *n* keman-
dulan

infidel *n* [infidél] kafir

infiltrate *v* menyusup,

(diam-diam) memasuki

infinite *adj* [infinit] tak terhitung; **infinitive** *n* bentuk
dasar kata kerja; **infinity** *n*
jumlah tak berakhir

inflame *v* meradangkan;
memperparah; **inflammable**
adj dapat terbakar

inflate *v* membesar; **inflation** *n* inflasi; ~ *rate* laju
inflasi

inflexible *adj* kaku

inflict *v* membebankan;
memberikan, menimbulkan

influence *n* [influens] pengaruh, efek; *v* memengaruhi;
influential *adj* berpengaruh

influenza *n* flu, selesma

inform *v* memberitahu,
mengabarkan, meng-
informasikan

informal *adj* santai, tidak
resmi

informant *n* sumber,
narasumber; **informer** *n*
pelapor, pengadu; **information** *n* informasi,
keterangan, penerangan;
informed *adj* berpengetahuan luas ← **inform**

infra ~*red* infra merah;
infrastructure *n* prasarana

infringement *n* pelanggaran

infusion *blood* ~ tambah darah

ingenious *adj* [injinius] sangat pandai

ingredient *n* [ingridient] bahan (mentah)

inhabit *v* mendiami, menghuni; **inhabitant** *n* penduduk, penghuni

inhale *v* menarik nafas, mengisap; **inhaler** *n* isapan, sedotan

inherit *v* mewarisi; **inheritance** *n* warisan

initial *n* huruf pertama, paraf; *v* teken, memaraf; *adj* pertama, perdana, permulaan; **initially** *adv* awalnya; **initiate** *v* memulai, memprakarsai; **initiation** *n* (upacara) pengenalan; **initiative** *n* prakarsa, inisiatif

inject *v* menyuntik, menyuntikkan; **injection** *n* suntik, suntikan; injeksi

injure *v* merugikan, melukai; **injury** *n* luka; kerugian; hinaan

injustice *n* ketidakadilan

ink *n* tinta; **inky** *adj* berwarna gelap

inland *n* pedalaman

inlet *n* teluk kecil

inn *n* penginapan

inner *adj* (di) dalam; batin

innocence *n* keadaan tidak bersalah, keadaan tanpa dosa; **innocent** *adj* tidak bersalah, tanpa dosa

innovation *n* ciptaan baru; **innovative** *adj* mampu menciptakan yang baru

input *n* masuknya; *v* memasukkan

inquest *n* pemeriksaan, penyelidikan

inquiry, enquiry *n* pertanyaan; penyelidikan, pemeriksaan

insane *adj* gila, sakit jiwa

inscribe *v* menulis, memahat, menoreh; **inscription** *n* tulisan, suratan, prasasti

insect *n* serangga; **insecticide** *n* obat pembasmi serangga

insemination *artificial* ~ inseminasi buatan

insert *n* sisipan; *v* menyisipkan, menyelipkan, memasukkan

inside *prep, adj* (di) dalam; ~ *information* informasi

dari orang dalam; ~ out terbalik; **insider** n orang dalam

insight n [insait] wawasan, pemahaman

insignificant adj tidak berarti, sepele

insist v mengotot, bersikeras, bersikukuh; mendesak

insolent adj tidak sopan, kurang ajar

insoluble adj tidak dapat larut

insolvent adj bangkrut, palit, tidak mampu membayar

insomnia n (keadaan) sulit tidur

inspect v memeriksa; **inspection** n pemeriksaan, inspeksi; **inspector** n pemeriksa

inspiration n ilham, inspirasi; **inspire** v mengilhami, memberi inspirasi

instability n ketidakstabilan

install, instal v melantik; memasang; **installation** n pelantikan; pemasangan; **instalment, installment** n angsuran; to pay in ~s mencicil, membayar dengan mengangsur

instance for ~ misalnya, seumpamanya

instant n saat; ~ coffee kopi instan; **instantly** adv saat itu juga, serta-merta

instead conj [instéd] alih-alih, melainkan, malah; ~ of daripada, sebagai pengganti

institute n lembaga, institut; **institution** n adat (istiadat); lembaga, institusi

instruct v mengajar; memerintahkan, menginstruksikan; **instruction** n pengajaran; perintah, instruksi; **instructor** n pengajar, guru, instruktor

instrument n alat, perkakas, pesawat

insufficient adj kurang cukup

insult n cemoohan, hinaan; v menghina, mencemoohkan

insurance n asuransi, pertanggungan; ~ agent agen asuransi; ~ policy polis asuransi; **insure** v mengasuransikan; memastikan

insurgent n, adj pemberontak

insurrection n pemberontakan

intact adj utuh

intake *n* masukan, asupan

integral *adj* perlu; pokok;
integrity *n* ketulusan hati,
kejujuran

intellect *n* akal budi, intelek;
intellectual *n* cendekiawan;
adj pandai

intelligence *n* kecerdasan;
intelijen; **intelligent** *adj*
cerdas, pandai

intend *v* berniat, bermaksud

intense *adj* hebat, mendalam, kuat, intens; **intensify**
v meningkatkan; **intensive**
adj intensif

intent, intention *n* maksud,
niat, kehendak, tujuan;
intentional *adj* sengaja ←
intend

interaction *n* pergaulan,
interaksi

interchange *n* simpang,
belokan

intercom *n* radio antar
ruangan

intercontinental *adj* antar-
benua

intercourse *(sexual)* ~ persetubuhan

interest *n* kepentingan;
perhatian, minat; daya tarik;
bunga (uang); ~ *rate* suku

bunga; *of* ~ menarik perhatian; *v* menarik perhatian;
interested *adj* tertarik,
berminat; **interesting** *adj*
menarik (perhatian)

interfere *v* [interfir] campur
tangan; mencampuri, meng-
ganggu; **interference** *n*
campur tangan, gangguan

interim *n, adj* sementara

interior *n* [intirior] pedalaman, dalamnya; *adj*
(bagian) dalam

interjection *n* kata seru

intermediary *n* perantara;
intermediate *adj* sedang

intermission *n* waktu
istirahat

intern *v* menawan, meng-
internir

internal *adj* dalam (negeri);
international *adj* internasional, antar bangsa

internment *n* penawanan,
penahanan; ~ *camp* kamp
tawanan; **internship** *n* masa
magang (di rumah sakit) ←
intern

interpret *v* menafsirkan;
menerjemahkan (secara li-
san); **interpretation** *n*
penafsiran; **interpreter** *n*

penerjemah, juru bahasa;
interpreting n penerjemahan
interrogate v [intérogét]
memeriksa, menginterogasi,
menanyai; **interrogation**
n pemeriksaan, interogasi;
interrogator n pemeriksa
interrupt v menyela, men-
yeletuk, memotong pem-
bicaraan
intersection n perempatan,
simpang; persilangan
interval n antara, selang,
jeda, waktu istirahat
intervene v [intervin]
campur tangan, mengha-
langi; **intervention** n
halangan, campur tangan,
intervensi
interview n wawancara,
tanya jawab, interpiu; v
mewawancarai; **interview-
ee** n orang yang diwawan-
carai; **interviewer** n
pewawancara
intestine n [intéstin] usus,
isi perut
intimate [intimet] adj mesra,
intim, karib
intimidate v menakuti-
nakuti, mengintimidasi;
intimidation n intimidasi

into prep ke (dalam); menjadi; menuju
intolerant adj tidak tenggang rasa, tidak bertoleransi
intoxicate v memabukkan
intransitive adj tanpa
pelengkap atau obyek; ~
verb kata kerja tanpa
pelengkap
intravenous ~ drip infus
intricate adj [intriket]
berbelit-belit, ruwet
intrigue membuat penasaran,
menuntut berpikir
introduce v memperkenal-
kan; **introduction** n perkenalan; (kata) pengantar;
introductory adj awal
intrude v mengganggu;
intruder n orang yang
memasuki tempat tanpa
izin; maling; **intrusive** adj
yang mengganggu urusan
pribadi
intuition n intuisi, gerak hati
invade v menyerang, men-
yerbu; **invader** n penyerang
invalid n [invelid] orang
sakit, orang cacat; adj
[invalid] tidak berlaku,
tidak sah

invaluable *adj* tak ternilai

invasion *n* serangan, serbuan ← **invade**

invent *v* menciptakan, menemukan; membuat-buat; **invention** *n* ciptaan; **inventor** *n* pencipta

inventory *n* inventaris

inverse *n* kebalikan; *adj* terbalik; **invert** *v* mem-balikkan; *~ed commas* tanda kutip

invest *v* menanamkan (modal), menginvestasikan

investigate *v* menyelidiki; **investigation** *n* penyeli-dikan; **investigator** *n* penyelidik

investment *n* penanaman modal, investasi; **investor** *n* penanam modal ← **invest**

invisible *adj* tak terlihat, gaib

invitation *n* undangan, ajakan; **invite** *v* mengundang, mengajak; mempersilakan

invoice *n* faktur, surat tagihan

involve *v* melibatkan

inward *adj* ke dalam; batin

IOC *abbrev International Olympic Committee*

Komite Olimpiade Inter-nasional

iodine *n* [aiodin] yodium

IOU *abbrev I owe you* saya berhutang kepada anda

Iran *n* Iran; **Iranian** *adj* [Irénian] berasal dari Iran

Iraq *n* Irak; **Iraqi** *adj* berasal dari Irak

Ireland *n* Irlandia

iris *n* bunga iris; selaput pelangi, iris

Irish *adj* [Airisy] berasal dari Irlandia ← **Ireland**

iron *n* besi; setrika; *the ~ Curtain* Tirai Besi; *v* menyetrika; **ironing** *n* setrikaan; kegiatan menye-trika; *~ board* papan setrika

ironic *adj* ironis; **irony** *n* ironi

irrational *adj* tidak masuk akal

irregular *adj* tidak teratur, luar biasa

irrelevant *adj* tidak relevan

irresponsible *adj* tidak bertanggung jawab

irrigate *v* mengairi; **irriga-tion** *n* pengairan, irigasi

irritable *adj* cepat marah, marah-marah; **irritant** *n*

yang mengganggu;
irritate v mengganggu,
membuat jengkel
Is. *island* P. (pulau)
Islam n agama Islam;
Islamic adj berkaitan dengan agama Islam
island n [ailand] pulau; *the
Andaman ~s* Kepulauan
Andaman
isolate v mengasingkan,
menjauhkan; **isolation** n
pengasingan
Israel n [Isrél] Israel; **Israeli**
adj berasal dari Israel
issue n [isyu] masalah, isu;
terbitan; v menerbitkan;
mengeluarkan, memancarkan
isthmus n tanah genting
it pron dia, ia (barang); -nya;
itu; ~ *is (it's) hot* hari ini
panas
Italian adj berasal dari Italia
← **Italy**
italics n, pl [italiks] tulisan
miring
Italy n Italia
itch n, v **itchy** adj gatal
item n [aitem] barang; pasal,
ayat; nomor
itinerary n [aitinereri]
rencana perjalanan

its pron -nya (barang)
it's → **it**
itself pron sendiri
IUD abbrev intra-uterine
device IUD
ivory n [aivori] gading
ivy n tanaman menjalar,
tanaman merambat

J

jab n tusukan; pukulan
pendek
jack n dongkrak, tuas, kuda-
kuda
jackal n serigala
jacket n jaket; sampul buku
jackfruit n buah nangka
jackpot n hadiah utama
jade n batu giok
jagged adj [jaged] bergerigi
jaguar n semacam macan di
Amerika
jail, gaol n penjara
jam n selai; *~-packed*
penuh sesak; *~ session*
bermain musik bersama;
traffic ~ kemacetan lalu
lintas; *in a ~* dalam kesu-

litan; *v* macet; menyumbat, menjepit

jamboree *n* jambore

janitor *n* petugas pembersihan, penjaga

January *n* bulan Januari

Japan *n* Jepang; **Japanese** *n* bahasa Jepang; *adj* berasal dari Jepang

jar *n* kendi, stoples, botol

jargon *n* bahasa khusus, istilah di bidang tertentu

jasmine *n* [jasmin] bunga melati

jaundice *n* [jondis] kuning

Java *n* pulau Jawa; *West ~* Jawa Barat (Jabar); **Javanese** *n* bahasa Jawa; *adj* berasal dari Jawa Tengah atau Timur

javelin *n* lembing; *~ throw* lempar lembing

jaw *n* rahang

jazz *n* musik jazz; **jazzy** *adj* bergaya, menyolok

jealous *adj* [jélus] cemburu; **jealousy** *n* kecemburuan, rasa cemburu

jeep *n* mobil jip

jeer *n* ejekan, cemoohan; *v* mengolok-olok, mencemooh

jelly *n* agar-agar; **jelly-bean**

n semacam gula-gula agar; **jellyfish** *n* ubur-ubur

jerk *n* sentakan, renggutan; *sl* orang bodoh; *v* menyentak, merenggut

jersey *n* [jérsi] switer

jest *n* kelucuan, senda gurau

Jesus *n* [Jisus] Yesus; *Isl* Isa; *~ Christ* Yesus Kristus

jet *n* semburan air; pancar gas; jet; *v, sl* terbang; **jetset** *n* gaya hidup yang sering terbang ke luar negeri; *~ fighter* pesawat perang jet

jetty *n* jeti, dermaga

Jew *n* orang Yahudi

jewel *n* [jul] (batu) permata; **jeweler** *n* tukang emas; **jewelry** *n* perhiasan

Jewish *adj* Yahudi ← **Jew**

jiffy *in a* ~dalam sekejap mata

jigsaw *n* gergaji ukir; *~ puzzle* teka-teki menyusun potongan kayu

jingle *v* bergemerincing

jinx *n* nasib malang, sial

jittery *adj* gelisah, gugup

job *n* pekerjaan, tugas; *~-hunting* mencari pekerjaan; *part-time ~* pekerjaan paruh waktu; **jobless** *adj* menganggur

jockey *n* joki

jog *n, v* lari pagi, lari sore; **jogging** *n* kegiatan lari; ~ *track* jalan untuk lari

join *v* bergabung, ikut serta; menghubungkan, menggabungkan

joint *n* sendi, ruas; *adj* bersama; ~ *venture* usaha patungan

joke *n* senda gurau, lelucon, guyonan; *v* bersenda gurau, melucu, melawak; *only joking* bercanda kok; **joker** *n* pelawak; joker (kartu)

jolly *adj* riang, gembira

jolt *n* goyangan, guncangan

Jordan *n* Yordania; **Jordanian** *adj* berasal dari Yordania

jot *v* mencatat; ~*ting pad* kertas catatan

journal *n* (buku) harian, majalah; **journalism** *n* kewartawanan, jurnalisme; **journalist** *n* wartawan, jurnalis

journey *n* [jurni] perjalanan

joy *n* kebahagiaan, kegembiraan

JP *abbrev Justice of the Peace* hakim setempat

jubilant *adj* bergembira

jubilee *n* peringatan, hari ulang tahun; *silver* ~ peringatan 25 tahun

Judaism *n* [Judéizem] agama Yahudi

judge *n* hakim; *v* menghakimi, menilai; **judgment** *n* keputusan

judo *n* judo, yudo

jug *n* tempat untuk saus atau minuman; teko

juggle *v* bermain sunglap; bermain sulap; **juggler** *n* tukang sunglap; **juggling** *n* sunglapan

juice *n* air (buah), sari buah, jus; *orange* ~ air jeruk; **juicy** *adj* berair banyak

jukebox *n* kotak musik, mesin pemutar lagu

July *n* bulan Juli

jumbo *adj* (berukuran) besar

jump *n* lompatan, loncatan; *v* melompat, meloncat; melompati

jumper *n* switer, baju hangat

junction *n* simpang (jalan), perempatan; *T-*~ simpang tiga

June *n* bulan Juni

jungle *n* [janggel] hutan, rimba (raya)

junior *n* yunior; *adj* yunior, lebih muda, lebih rendah pangkatnya; ~ *high school* sekolah menengah pertama (SMP)

junk *n* barang bekas, barang loak, sampah

jury *n* juri

just *adj, adv* hanya, saja; tepat, persis; ~ *now* baru saja

just *n* adil; **justice** *n* keadilan; **justify** *v* membenarkan

juvenile *adj* kekanak-kanakan; muda

K

kangaroo *n* kanguru, kangguru

kayak *n* dayung; kayak, kano; sampan; **kayaking** *n* dayung kayak

keen *adj* antusias; tajam

keep *v* **kept kept** menyimpan, memegang, menaruh, memelihara, menjaga; ~ *a promise* menepati janji; ~ *a secret* menyimpan rahasia;

~ *on* terus melakukan; ~ *off* tidak mengganggu; ~ *out* dilarang masuk; ~ *up* melanjutkan, meneruskan; *for* ~*s* untuk selamanya; **keeper** *n* pemegang, penjaga, kurator; **keepsake** *n* kenang-kenangan, oleh-oleh

keg *n* tong

kennel *n* kandang anjing

kept *v, pf* → **keep**

kernel *n* biji, inti

kerosene *n* [kerosin] minyak tanah

kettle *n* teko; **kettledrum** *n* genderang kecil

key *n* [ki] (anak) kunci; tuts; nada; *adj* pokok; ~*chain* rantai kunci; ~ *ring* gantungan kunci; *major* ~ nada mayor; *piano* ~ tuts (piano); *v* ~ *in* memasukkan, mengetik; **keyboard** *n* kibor; papan tuts; **keyhole** *n* lubang kunci

kg *kilogram* kg (kilogram)

kick *n* tendangan; *v* menendang, menyepak; ~ *off* memulai

kid *n* anak kambing; *sl* anak; **kiddie, kiddy,**

kids adj, coll kanak-
kanak

kidnap v menculik;
kidnapper n penculik

kidney n [kidni] ginjal;
~-**bean** kacang merah

kill v membunuh; ~ed in
action gugur, tewas; ~ off
menghancurkan, mem-
binasakan; ~ time meng-
habiskan waktu; **killer** n
pembunuh; **killing** n pembunuhan

kilogram, kilo n kilo,
kilogram

kilometer, kilo n kilo,
kilometer

kind n [kaind] macam, jenis,
ragam; adj baik hati,
simpatis; ~-**hearted** baik
hati; ~ of agak

kinder, kindergarten n
taman kanak-kanak (TK)

kindly adv [kaindli]
dengan baik hati; tolong;
~ inform me tolong dibe-
ritahu ← **kind**

kindness n [kaindness]
kebaikan hati ← **kind**

king n raja; **kingdom** n
kerajaan

kiosk n kios, loket, warung

kiss n ciuman, sun, kecupan;
v mencium, (memberi) sun;
hugs and ~es peluk cium

kit n peralatan, perlengkapan

kitchen n dapur

kite n layang-layang

kitten n anak kucing; **kitty**
n, coll kucing (kecil)

kiwi n burung kiwi; **kiwi-
fruit** n (buah) kiwi

km kilometer km (kilometer)

knee n [ni] lutut, dengkul; ~
deep, ~ high selutut; **kneecap** n tempurung lutut

kneel v [nil] **knelt knelt**
berlutut

kneepad n pelindung lutut
← **knee**

knew v, pf → **know**

knife n [naif] pisau; v
menikam; at ~point
ditodong

knight n [nait] kesatria

knit v [nit] merajut; **knitting**
n rajutan; ~ needle jarum
rajut; **knitwear** n baju
rajutan, busana rajutan

knob n [nob] tombol,
pegangan

knock n [nok] pukulan,
ketok; a ~ at the door

ketukan di pintu; *v* mengetuk; memukul; ~ *down*
membongkar; memukul
sampai jatuh; **knockout**
n (pukulan) yang sangat
hebat

knot *n* [not] simpul; buku,
mata kayu; mil laut; *v*
menyimpulkan

know *v* [no] **knew known**
tahu, mengetahui; mengenal;
mengerti; ~*all* sok tahu; *in
the* ~ tahu; **knowledge** *n*
[nolej] pengetahuan; *to my*
~ setahu saya; **knowledge-
able** *adj* banyak tahu;
known *adj* dikenal

knuckle *n* [nakel] buku jari

KO *abbrev knockout*
pukulan yang sangat hebat

koala *n* koala

Koran *the* ~ al-Quran

Korea *n* [Koria] Korea
(Selatan); *North* ~ Korea
Utara; **Korean** *n* bahasa
Korea; *adj* berasal dari Korea

kph *kilometers per hour*
kilometer per jam

L

L. *abbrev Lane* Gg (Gang)

L *abbrev liter* liter

label *n* merek; nama; *v*
memberi nama, menulis
nama pada barang

laboratory, lab *n* laboratorium

labor *n* pekerjaan (kasar); ~
Day Hari Buruh; *in* ~
sedang bersalin; *v* bekerja;
~ *Party* Partai Buruh;
laborer *n* buruh, tukang,
pekerja

labour → labor

labyrinth *n* susunan yang
simpang siur, labirin

lace *n* renda

lack *n* kekurangan; *v* kurang,
tidak memiliki, tidak mempunyai

lacquer *n* [laker] lak, pernis;
v memberi pernis

lacrosse *n* [lakros] permainan yang memakai tongkat
dengan keranjangan kecil
dan bola

lad *n* anak lelaki

ladder *n* tangga, jenjang

lady *n, f* [lédi] nyonya,
wanita; gelar bangsawan;
ladies and gentlemen

bapak-bapak dan ibu-ibu;
ladybird, ladybug *n* kepik;
ladylike *adj* seperti wanita
(yang sopan)

lag *v* tertinggal, ketinggalan

lagoon *n* laguna

laid *v, pf* → lay

lain *v, pf* → lie

lake *n* danau, telaga; **lake-
side** *adj* di tepi danau

lamb *n* [lam] anak domba,
anak biri-biri

lame *adj* lumpuh, pincang;
lemah

lament *n* [lamént] ratapan;
v meratapi

laminate *v* melaminasi,
melapis dengan lembaran
plastik, laminating

lamp *n* lampu, pelita;
kerosene ~ lentera, lampu
petromaks; *~post* tiang
lampu, tiang lentera

land *n* tanah, bumi, darat;
negeri, negara; ~ *tax* pajak
tanah; *by* ~ jalan darat,
lewat darat; *v* mendarat;
landing *n* pendaratan;
tempat beristirahat di
tangga; **landlady** *n, f* induk
semang; **landlocked** *adj*
tidak berbatasan dengan

laut; **landlord** *n, m* tuan
tanah, pemilik rumah; **land-
mark** *n* patokan, petunjuk;
peristiwa penting; **land-
mine** *n* ranjau (darat);
landowner *n* tuan tanah;
landscape *n* pemandangan,
lanskap; **landslide** *n* tanah
longsor

lane *n* gang, lorong; jalur;
lajur; *slow* ~ jalur lambat;
to change ~s pindah jalur

language *n* [languej]
bahasa; *bad* ~ kata-kata
jorok, makian

lantern *n* lentera; *Chinese* ~
lampion

Lao *n* bahasa Laos; **Laotian**
adj berasal dari Laos

lap *n* haribaan, pangkuan;
lapdog *n* anjing piaraan
yang kecil; penjilat

lapse *n* jatuh; kehilangan;
selang; *v* kambuh, menjadi;
habis

laptop *n* komputer laptop

large *adj* besar, luas; ~ *size*
ukuran besar; *at* ~ bebas

lark *n* semacam burung

larva *n* **larvae** jentik-jentik

larynx *n* pangkal teng-
gorokan

laser *n* (sinar) laser

lass, lassie *n, sl* anak
perempuan

last *v* tahan, bertahan,
berlangsung; awet; *adj*
terakhir, penghabisan; ~
month bulan lalu; ~ *night*
semalam; *at* ~ akhirnya;
lasting *adj* awet, abadi

latch *n* palang pintu, kunci,
grendel

late *adj* lambat, terlambat;
mendiang; *lsl* almarhum; *f*
almarhumah; **lately** *adv*
belum lama, belakangan
ini, baru-baru ini

latent *adj* tersembunyi,
terpendam, laten

later *adj, adv* nanti; kemudian ← **late**

latest *adj, adv* terakhir,
paling akhir; ~ *news* berita
terkini; *at the* ~ paling
lambat, selambat-lambatnya

latex *n* getah

lather *n* buih, busa (sabun);
v menyabun

Latin *n* bahasa Latin,
bahasa Romawi; ~ *America*
Amerika Latin

latitude *n* lintang

latter *n, adj* yang kemudian,
yang tersebut

laugh *n, v* [laf] tertawa,
ketawa; ~ *at* menertawakan,
menertawai; **laughter** *n*
ketawa, tawa

launch *n* peluncuran; kapal
berkas; *v* meluncurkan; ~
into memulai

laundromat *n* tempat cuci
pakai mesin otomat; **laundry**
n cucian, baju kotor; binatu

lava *n* lahar, lava

lavatory *n* [lavetori] kamar
kecil, WC

lavender *adj* ungu muda;
n semacam bunga harum
berwarna ungu

lavish *adj* mewah, berlebihan

law *n* hukum, undang-
undang; peraturan;
~-*abiding* taat hukum;
against the ~ melanggar
hukum; **lawmaker** *n*
pembuat undang-undang

lawn *n* lapangan rumput;
~ *bowls* boling taman; ~
mower mesin potong
rumput; ~ *tennis* tenis

lawsuit *n* perkara, dakwaan; *to bring a* ~ *against*
menuntut ← **law**

lawyer *n* pengacara, advokat, praktisi hukum ← **law**

laxative *n* obat peluntur, pencahar

lay *v* **laid laid** meletakkan; ~ *eggs* bertelur; ~ *off* memberhentikan, mempehakakan; membiarkan

layer *n* lapis, lapisan

layout *n* tata letak; rancangan, rencana ← **lay**

laziness *n* kemalasan; **lazy** *adj* malas

lb *pound* pon (berat)

lead *n* [léd] timbal, timah hitam, plumbum

lead *v* [lid] **led led** memimpin; ~ *role* peranan utama; ~ *the way* memelopori, merintis; **leader** *n* pemimpin; **leadership** *n* kepemimpinan; **leading** *adj* penting, utama, terkemuka

leaf *n* **leaves** daun

leaflet *n* selebaran

leafy *adj* rimbun, rindang ← **leaf**

league *n* [lig] liga, persatuan, perserikatan

leak *n, v* bocor, merembes; **leaky** *adj* bocor, rembes

lean *n* kurus; sedikit

lean *v* tidak lurus, condong, bersandar; **leaning** *n* kecenderungan

leap *n* lompatan; ~ *year* tahun kabisat; *v* melompat

leapt *v, pf* [lépt] → **leap**

learn *v* belajar; mendengar berita; **learner** *n* pelajar; **learning** *n* pembelajaran

lease *n* sewa; *v* mempersewakan

leash *n* pengikat binatang; *on a* ~ dirantai

least *adj* terkecil, paling sedikit; *at* ~ setidak-tidaknya, sekurang-kurangnya; *not in the* ~ tidak sama sekali

leather *n* [léther] kulit

leave *n* cuti; *maternity* ~ cuti hamil; *paternity* ~ cuti untuk ayah baru; *on* ~ sedang cuti; *v* **left left** berangkat, pergi, bertolak; membiarkan; meninggalkan; ~ *me alone* biarkan saya sendiri; jangan ganggu saya; *to take* ~ pamit, mohon diri; (mengambil) cuti

Lebanese *adj* berasal dari Libanon; **Lebanon** *n* Libanon

lecture *n* kuliah, ceramah,

pidato; v memberi kuliah; memberi teguran; **lecturer** n dosen, lektor

led v, pf → **lead**

leech n lintah

leek n bawang perai

left adj (sebelah) kiri; ~ handed kidal

left adj, v, pf tertinggal → **leave**; **leftover** n, adj sisa

leg n kaki

legacy n [légasi] warisan, harta pusaka

legal adj sah, legal, menurut undang-undang

legend n legenda; kunci peta; **legendary** adj terkenal

leggings n, pl [légings] stoking tebal ← **leg**

legible adj [léjibel] dapat dibaca

legislate v [léjislét] membuat undang-undang; **legislation** n perundang-undangan; **legislative** adj legislatif

legitimate adj sah

legroom n ruang untuk kaki (selama duduk) ← **leg**

leisure n [lésyer] waktu luang, waktu senggang

lemon n jeruk nipis, limun;

lemonade n air jeruk nipis; Sprite

lend v meminjamkan; ~ a (helping) hand menolong; **lender** n pemberi pinjaman

length n panjang; jarak, lama; at ~ panjang lebar; at arm's ~ menjaga jarak; **lengthen** v memperpanjang; **lengthy** adj panjang lebar; panjang, lama

lens n lensa; contact ~ lensa kontak

leopard n [lépard] macan kumbang

lesbian lesbi

less adj kurang, lebih kecil; the ~er Sundas Nusa Tenggara; **lessen** v mengurangi, mengecilkan

lesson n pelajaran; les; piano ~ les piano

let v **let let** membiarkan; menyewakan (rumah); ~ alone apalagi, jangankan; ~ down mengecewakan; menurunkan; ~ fly melepaskan; ~ go melepaskan; ~ up reda, berhenti; ~ us, let's marilah; to ~ disewakan; **let-down** n kekecewaan

lethal adj [lithal] mematikan

499

let's → **let us**
letter *n* surat; huruf, aksara;
~ *box* kotak surat; bis surat;
letterhead *n* kop surat
lettuce *n* [létes] selada
leukaemia, leukemia *n*
[lukimia] kanker darah
level *adj* [lével] datar, rata;
n tingkat; permukaan; *v*
meratakan; ~*headed*
berkepala dingin; ~ *off*, ~
out mendatar; *on the* ~ jujur
lever *n* pengungkit, tuas,
tuil
levy *n* [lévi] pajak, retribusi
liaison [liéson] ~ *officer*
pegawai hubungan mas-
yarakat (humas)
liar *n* [laier] pembohong
← lie
liberal *adj* murah hati;
liberal; **liberate** *v* membebaskan; **liberation** *n* pembebasan; **liberator** *n* pihak
yang membebaskan; **liberty**
n kemerdekaan, kebebasan
librarian *n* [laibrérian]
pustakawan, kepala per-
pustakaan; **library** *n* perpustakaan
license, licence *n* [laisens]
izin, ijazah; ~ *plate* pelat

polisi; *driving* ~ surat izin
mengemudi (SIM); **license** *v*
mengizinkan, membolehkan
lick *n* jilatan; *v* menjilat;
mengalahkan dengan telak
lie *v* bohong; *v* berbohong,
membohong
lie *v* **lay lain** terletak, berada;
berbaring; ~ *down* merebah-
kan diri, berbaring, tiduran
lieutenant *n* letnan
life *n* hidup, kehidupan;
~ *insurance* asuransi jiwa;
~*size* berukuran yang
sebenarnya; *for* ~ sepanjang
hidup; *to save a* ~ menyelamatkan jiwa; **lifeboat** *n*
sekoci (penyelamat); **life-**
buoy *n* pelampung; **life-**
guard *n* penjaga pantai,
penjaga kolam renang; **life-**
jacket *n* baju pelampung;
lifelong *adj* seumur hidup,
sepanjang hidup; **lifesaver**
n penjaga pantai; **lifestyle**
n gaya hidup; **lifetime** *n*
seumur hidup ← **live**
lift *n* lift, pengangkat barang;
v mengangkat; *to get a* ~
menumpang, tebeng
light *n* [lait] cahaya, sinar;
lampu; *sl* korek api; *adj*

terang; ringan, enteng; *v* **lit**
lit menyalakan, memasang
(lampu); *~-fingered* tangan
panjang; *~-headed* pusing;
~-hearted enteng, menyenangkan; *to bring to ~*
membukakan; *to come to*
~ terbuka, terkuak; **lighten**
v meringankan, menerangkan; **lighter** *n* korek api,
geretan; **lighthouse** *n* mercu suar; **lightning** *n* kilat,
halilintar, geledek

like *adj* sama, serupa, sepa-
dan, setara; *conj* seperti,
sama dengan; *v* suka,
menyukai, gemar; **likeable**
adj ramah, menyenangkan;
likely *adj* agaknya,
kemungkinan; **likewise**
adv begitu juga, demikian
pula

lilac *adj* ungu muda; *n*
semacam tanaman yang
berbunga ungu

lily *n* [lili] teratai

lime *n* limau; kapur; *~ green*
hijau lumut

limelight *n* [laimlait] pusat
perhatian; sorotan

limit *n* batas, limit; *v* membatasi; *that's the ~* itu

keterlaluan; **limited** *adj*
terbatas

limousine *n* [limosin], **limo**
n, sl limosin, limo

limp *v* berjalan pincang; *adj*
lemah

line *n* garis, gores; tali; baris,
deret; *~ manager* atasan;
shipping ~ perusahaan perkapalan, *in ~ with* sesuai
dengan; *out of ~* menyimpang; *to stand in ~* antri; *v*
melapisi

linen *n* kain linan; *~ cupboard* lemari seprei

liner *n* kapal penumpang
yang besar

lingerie *n* [lonjeri] pakaian
dalam wanita

linguistics *n* ilmu bahasa,
ilmu linguistik

lining *n* lapisan, furing ←
line

link *n* mata rantai, hubungan

lino *coll* linolium

lion *n* [laion] singa

lip *n* bibir; **lipread** *v*
lipread lipread [lipréd]
membaca gerakan bibir;
lipstick *n* lipstik

liquid *adj* cair; *n* cairan, zat
cair

501

liquor *n* [liker] minuman keras

lisp *n* cadel, pelat; *v* berbicara cadel

list *n* daftar; *short ~* daftar pendek; *v* mendaftar, menyebutkan

listen *v* [lisen] mendengarkan, menyimak; **listener** *n* pendengar; **listening** *n* (pelajaran) menyimak

lit *v, pf* → **light**

liter *n* liter; *per ~* seliter, per liter

literacy *n* [literasi] (angka) melek huruf; **literally** *adv* secara harfiah; benar-benar; **literate** *adj* melek huruf; terpelajar; **literary** *adj* sastra; **literature** *n* kesusastraan

litre → **liter**

litter *n* usungan, tandu

litter *n* seperindukan (anak binatang)

litter *n* sampah (di jalan); *v* membuang sampah sembarangan

little *adj* kecil; sedikit; *~ finger* kelingking; *n* sedikit; *~ by ~* lambat laun, sedikit demi sedikit

live *v* [liv] hidup, tinggal, berdiam; *~ off* hidup dari; *~*

with hidup dengan; kumpul kebo dengan; **live** *adj* [laiv] langsung; hidup; *~ broadcast* siaran langsung; **livelihood** *n* rezeki, nafkah

liver *n* [liver] hati, lever

livestock *n* hewan ternak

living *n* [living] mata pencarian; *to make a ~* mencari nafkah; *~ room* kamar keluarga ← **live**

lizard *n* [lizerd] kadal, biawak, cicak

llama *n* sejenis binatang di Amerika Selatan seperti unta

LLB *abbrev Bachelor of Laws* SH (Sarjana Hukum)

load *n* muatan, beban; *v* memuat, diisi; **loading** *~ bay* tempat bongkar muat

loaf *n* **loaves** roti; sejenis sepatu santai

loan *n* pinjaman; *v* meminjamkan, meminjami → **lend**

lob *n* bola yang dipukul tinggi; *v* memukul tinggi-tinggi

lobby *n* lobi (hotel); gerakan; *v* berusaha memengaruhi, memperjuangkan

lobe *ear ~* cuping

lobster *n* udang karang, udang laut

local *adj* setempat, lokal; *n* orang setempat; **locate** *v* mencari; **location** *n* lokasi, tempat; penempatan

lock *n* kunci, gembok; pintu air; *~-up* sel tahanan; *v* mengunci; **locker** *n* loker

locket *n* liontin

locksmith *n* tukang kunci ← lock

locomotive *n* lokomotif, lok

locust *n* belalang

lodge *n* pondok, pemondokan; *v* mondok, menginap; *~ a complaint* mengajukan pengaduan; **lodger** *n* pemondok, anak kos; **lodging** *n* pemondokan; akomodasi

loft *n* loteng; **lofty** *adj* tinggi, mulia

log *n* catatan, buku harian; *v* mencatat; *~ in* memasukkan nama atau kata kunci; *~ off*, *~ out* keluar dari program

log *n* batang kayu, kayu gelondongan; *v* menebang (pohon); **logging** *n* penebangan; *illegal ~* penebangan liar

logic *n* [lojik] logika, akal; **logical** *adj* logis, masuk akal

lone *adj* tunggal, sendiri;

loneliness *n* (rasa) kesepian; **lonely** *adj* sepi, kesepian, sunyi, sendirian; **loner** *n* penyendiri

long *adj* panjang; lama; *~-haired* berambut panjang; *~-haired cat* kucing angora; *~-range* jarak jauh; *~-sighted* rabun dekat; *~house* rumah panjang; *~ jump* lompat jauh; *~-distance call* telepon interlokal; *before ~* tidak lama kemudian; *so ~* sampai jumpa; *as ~ as* selama

long *~ for* rindu akan, merindukan, mengidamkan; **longing** *n* hasrat, kerinduan

look *n* penampilan, gaya; *v* melihat; *~ after* merawat, menjaga; *~ around* melihat-lihat; *~ at* melihat; *~ back* menoleh ke belakang; *~ for* mencari; *~ forward to* menantikan; *~ on* menonton; *~ out!* awas!; **lookout** *n* tempat meninjau; pengintai; **looks** *n, pl* paras, wajah, penampilan

loop *n* lingkaran, ikal, putaran; *v* menyimpulkan; **loophole** *n* jalan keluar

loose *adj* longgar, kendur, terurai; lepas; **loosen** *v* melonggarkan, mengendurkan

loot *v* merampas, menjarah; **looter** *n* penjarah; **looting** *n* penjarahan

lord *pron* tuan; **Lord** *n, Chr* Tuhan

lorry *n* truk

lose *v* [luz] hilang, kehilangan; rugi, kalah; ~ *face* malu; ~ *your way* tersesat; **loser** *n* yang kalah; **loss** *n* rugi, kerugian, kehilangan; *at a* ~ tidak mengerti; **lost** *adj* hilang; tersesat; tewas

lot *n* undi

lotion *n* salep

lottery *n* lotere, undian ← **lot**

lotus *n* bunga seroja, bunga teratai

loud *adj* berisik, riuh, gempar, bising; **loudspeaker** *n* pengeras suara

louse *n* **lice** kutu; **lousy** *adj, sl* [lauzi] jelek

love *adj* [lav] kosong (dalam permainan tenis); *forty* ~ empat puluh kosong (40-0)

love *n* [lav] cinta, asmara; kasih (sayang); *pron* kekasih, sayang; *v* mencintai, menya-

yangi; ~ *triangle* cinta segitiga; *in* ~ kasmaran; *to fall in* ~ jatuh cinta; *to make* ~ bercinta; **lovely** *adj* manis, cantik, asri; **lover** *n* kekasih; penggemar

low *adj* rendah, hina; murah; *n* titik rendah, nadir; ~ *tide* air surut; **lower** *adj* lebih rendah; *v* menurunkan

loyal *adj* setia, setiakawan; **loyalty** *n* kesetiaan, kesetiakawanan

lubricant *n* [lubrikant] pelumas

luck *n* untung; *bad* ~ sial; *good* ~ untung; semoga; **lucky** *adj* beruntung

luggage *n* bagasi, barang-barang

lukewarm *adj* [lukworm] suam, suam kuku

lullaby *n* [lalabai] (kidung) ninabobo

lumber *n* kayu; *v* berjalan dengan berat; **lumberjack** *n* penebang kayu

luminous *adj* terang, bercahaya

lump *n* gumpal, bongkah; benjolan; *v* menaruh tanpa banyak berpikir; menyatu-

504

M

kan; *to have a* ~ *in your throat* ingin menangis;
lumpy *adj* bergumpal, tidak encer

lunar *adj* berkaitan dengan bulan; ~ *eclipse* gerhana bulan

lunatic *adj* gila; *n* orang gila

lunch *n, v* makan siang

lungs *n, pl* paru-paru

lure *n* iming-iming, bujuk-an; *v* memancing, mengiming-iming

lurk *v* bersembunyi, menunggu diam-diam

lush *adj* lebat, subur

lust *n* hawa nafsu, berahi

lusty *adj* kuat, bersemangat

luxurious *adj* [laksyurius] mewah, lux; **luxury** *n* kemewahan

lychee *n* buah leci

lymph *n* [limf] getah bening; ~ *node* kelenjar getah bening

lyric *n* lirik, kata-kata yang dinyanyikan

m *meter* m (meter)

ma'am *pron* Nyonya, Nona ← **madam**

macaroni *n* makaroni

Macau *n* Makau

Macedonia *n* [Masedonia] Makedonia

machine *n* [məsyin] mesin, alat; **machinery** *n* mesin-mesin, alat-alat

mackintosh, mac, mack *n* jas hujan

mad *adj* gila, tergila-gila; marah; *like* ~ cepat sekali; ~ *about cars* tergila-gila akan mobil

Madagascar *n* Madagaskar

madam *pron* Nyonya

madman *n* orang gila

madness *n* kegilaan, penyakit gila

maestro *n* [maistro] musisi ternama, maestro

magazine *n* majalah

maggot *n* belatung

magic *n* [majik] ilmu sihir, ilmu sulap; **magical** *adj* berkaitan dengan sihir; ajaib; **magician** *n* penyihir, penyulap

magistrate *n* [majistrét] hakim

magnet *n* magnet, maknit; **magnetic** *adj* magnetik

magnificent *adj* sangat bagus, mewah

magnify *~ing glass* kaca pembesar

magpie *n* burung murai

mahogany *n* pohon mahoni, kayu mahoni

maid *n* pembantu; gadis; *old ~* perawan tua; **maiden** *adj* perdana; *n* perawan, gadis

mail *n* pos; surat email; *v* mengepos, mengirim lewat pos; *~ order* pesanan lewat pos; **mailbox** *n* kotak surat; **mailman** *n* tukang pos

main *adj* utama; *~ road* jalan utama, jalan raya; *in the ~* umumnya; **mainland** *n* daratan; **mainly** *adv* terutama

maintain *v* memelihara, mempertahankan; **maintenance** *n* pemeliharaan

maize *n* jagung

majesty *n* keagungan; *Your ~* Baginda, Sri Paduka

major *adj* utama, terbesar;

n mayor; **majority** *n* kebanyakan, mayoritas

make *n* jenis, macam; *v* membuat, membikin, mengadakan; *~-believe* khayalan; *~ do* puas; *~ for* menuju; *~ off* lari, kabur; *~ up* merias; mengarang, berdusta; mengganti; *~ fun of* meledek; *~ up your mind* memutuskan, mengambil keputusan; **make-up** *n* rias wajah; *~ artist* perias; **makeover** *n* perubahan gaya rambut atau rias; **maker** *n* pembuat, pencipta; **makeshift** *adj* sementara

Malagasy *~ Republic* Madagaskar

Malay *adj* Melayu; *n* bahasa Melayu, bahasa Malaysia; orang Melayu; *the ~ Annals* Sejarah Melayu; **Malaysia** *n* Malaysia; *East ~* Sarawak dan Sabah; **Malaysian** *n* orang Malaysia

Maldives [Maldivs] *the ~* (Kepulauan) Maladewa

male *adj* lelaki, pria; jantan

malfunction *n* kerusakan, kegagalan, *v* gagal

mallet *n* palu dari kayu

mama, mamma *n, pron* ibu

mammal *n* mamalia, binatang menyusui

man *n* **men** orang laki-laki, pria; suami, pasangan, pacar; *arch* orang, manusia; ~*made* buatan manusia; *v* bertugas di

manage *v* mengelola, memimpin; mengurus, menangani; **management** *n* pimpinan, direksi; pengelolaan, pemerintahan, pengurusan, manajemen; **manager** *n* manajer, pemimpin, pengurus; **managing** ~ *director* direktur pelaksana

mandatory *adj* wajib, keharusan

mane *n* surai; rambut yang lebat

maneuver, manoeuvre *n* [manuver] latihan perangperangan; tipu daya; manuver

mango *n* mangga

mangosteen *n* manggis

mangrove *n* bakau

mania *n* [ménia] kegilaan, demam

manicure *n* perawatan tangan, manikur

manipulate *v* memanipulasi; memainkan, mendalangi; **manipulative** *adj* suka memanipulasi

mankind *n* [mankaind] umat manusia ← **man**

mannequin → **manikin**

manner *n* cara, jalan; macam; ~*s* sopan santun; **mannered** *adj* well-- sopan, beradat

mansion *n* [mansyen] rumah besar

manslaughter *n* [mansloter] pembunuhan yang tidak disengaja

mantelpiece *n* rak di atas perapian

manual *adj* dengan tangan, tidak otomatis; *n* pedoman, buku panduan; ~ *labor* pekerjaan kasar

manufacture *n* pembuatan; *v* membuat; **manufacturer** *n* pabrik

manure *n* pupuk (kotoran)

manuscript *n* naskah

many *adj* [méni] banyak

map *n* peta; *v* memetakan

marble *n* marmer, pualam; kelereng

March *n* bulan Maret

march *n* perjalanan (militer); mars; *v* jalan kaki

margarine *n* [marjarin] mentega

marginalized *adj* terpinggirkan

marijuana *n* [marihuana] ganja

marina *n* dermaga; **marine** *adj* berhubungan dengan laut; **maritime** *adj* berhubungan dengan laut

marinade *n* saus perendam; **marinate** *v* merendam

marital *adj* berhubungan dengan perkawinan

mark *n* tanda, alamat; cap; sasaran; bekas; nilai; *good* ~s nilai (rapot) yang baik; *v* menandai, mengecap; mencatat, memperhatikan; mengoreksi; **marker** *n* penanda; spidol besar; penilai

market *n* pasar, pasaran; **marketing** *n* pemasaran

marmalade *n* selai jeruk

marriage *n* [marij] perkawinan, pernikahan; *related by* ~ berkerabat karena perkawinan; ~ *certificate* surat kawin, akte pernikah-

an; **married** *adj* kawin, nikah; *m* beristri; *f* bersuami ← **marry**

marry *v* menikah, kawin; menikahi; ~ *off* menikahkan, mengawinkan

marsh *n* rawa

marshal *n* marsekal; *field-*~ panglima; *v* memanggil

marshmallow *n* penganan manis yang putih dan empuk

martyr *n* martir

marvel *n* keajaiban; **marvelous** *adj* ajaib, hebat, mengagumkan

mascara *n* perona mata, maskara

masculine *adj* [maskulin] laki-laki, lelaki, jantan

mash *v* menghancurkan, mengaduk sampai halus

mask *n* topeng; masker; *v* menyamarkan

masquerade *n* [maskeréd] pesta bertopeng; *v* menyamar

mass *n* massa; banyak sekali; misa; ~ *rally* demo, unjuk rasa

massacre *n* [masaker] pembunuhan atau pembantaian

besar-besaran; *v* membunuh secara besar-besaran

massage *n* pijatan; *v* memijat, mengurut

massive *adj* raksasa, besar sekali ← **mass**

mast *n* tiang (kapal)

master *n* tuan (rumah); ahli, guru; *v* menguasai; *~'s (degree)* S2, magister; **mastermind** *n* dalang, otak; **masterpiece** *n* adikarya

masturbate *v* beronani,

masturbation *n* onani, masturbasi

mat *n* tikar; matras

match *n* korek api; tara, jodoh; pertandingan; *v* menyesuaikan; menyamai, menandingi; **matchbox** *n* tempat korek api; **matchmaker** *n* mak jomblang

mate *n* kawan, sahabat; pasangan; *v* kawin (binatang)

material *n* bahan, perkakas, alat; materi; **materialism** *n* materialisme; **materialistic** *adj* materialistis

maternal *adj* keibuan; dari pihak ibu; **maternity** *adj* masa kehamilan; *~ clothes* pakaian hamil

mathematics *n, pl* **math, maths** *sl* matematika

matron *n* [métron] kepala perawat, suster

matter *n* perkara, hal, perihal; bahan; *as a ~ of fact* ngomong-ngomong; *~-of-fact* terus terang; *what's the ~?* ada apa?; *v* berarti; *it doesn't ~* tidak apa-apa; *no ~ what* bagaimanapun juga

mattress *n* kasur

mature *adj* dewasa, tua, matang; *~-age student* mahasiswa dewasa

maximal *adj* maksimal, sebanyak-banyaknya;

maximum *adj, n* maksimum, sebanyak-banyaknya

May *n* bulan Mei

may *v, aux* boleh, dapat; **maybe** [mébi] *adv* mungkin, barangkali, boleh jadi

mayor *n* [mér] walikota

maze *n* labirin, jalan yang ruwet atau simpang siur

MBA *abbrev Master of Business Administration* MBA

MD *abbrev medical doctor* dr, dokter

me *pron, obj* saya, aku

509

meadow *n* [médo] padang rumput

meal *n* makanan, santapan

mean *adj* sedang, rata-rata; kurang, hina

mean *adj* jahat, membuat sakit hati

mean *v* **meant meant** [mént] berarti, bermaksud; memaksudkan, menghendaki; **meaning** *n* arti, maksud

means *n* harta, kekayaan; alat; cara; *by all* ~ tentu, pasti

meant *v, pf* → **mean**

meantime *in the* ~ sementara itu; **meanwhile** *adv* sementara itu

measles *n, pl* [mizels] penyakit campak

measure *n* [mésyer] ukuran, takaran; besarnya; tindakan; *v* mengukur; **measurement** *n* ukuran

meat *n* daging

mechanic *n* [mekanik] montir, ahli mesin; **mechanical** *adj* teknik; ~ *engineering* teknik mesin

medal *n* medali

meddle *v* campur tangan

media *n, pl* [midia] pers; perantara, bahan; *print* ~ media cetak

mediator *n* perantara

medical *adj* kedokteran, medis; ~ *school* jurusan kedokteran; **medicine** *n* [médisin] obat; jurusan kedokteran, ilmu kedokteran

medieval, mediaeval *adj* [médiivel] dari Abad Pertengahan

meditate *v* bermeditasi, bersemadi; **meditation** *n* meditasi, semadi

Mediterranean *the* ~ *(Sea)* Laut Tengah

medium *adj* sedang; **media** *n* cenayang, dukun, perantara; bahan

medley *n* campuran (lagu)

meet *n* perlombaan atletik atau renang; *v* **met met** bertemu, berjumpa; menemui; berkumpul; **meeting** *n* rapat, pertemuan

melody *n* lagu

melon *n* semangka

melt *v* meleleh, mencair, melebur; melelehkan, meleburkan

member *n* anggota; **membership** *n* keanggotaan

membrane *n* selaput

memo *n* memorandum, surat peringatan; **memorial** *adj* peringatan; *n* tanda atau tugu peringatan; **memorize** *v* menghafalkan; **memory** *n* ingatan, memori

men *n, pl* → **man**

mend *v* memperbaiki, membetulkan; menambal; ~ *your ways* mengubah kebiasaan buruk; *on the* ~ mulai sembuh

menstrual ~ *cycle* siklus datang bulan; **menstruate** *v* **menstruation** *n* datang bulan, mens

mental *adj* jiwa; ~ *arithmetic* mencongak, berhitung di kepala; **mentality** *n* mentalitas, cara berpikir

mention *n* [ménsyen] sebutan; *v* menyebutkan; *don't* ~ *it* (terima kasih) kembali, sama-sama

menu *n* daftar makanan, menu

merchandise *n* (barang) dagangan; **merchant** *n* pedagang, saudagar

mercury *n* air raksa

mercy *n* belas kasih,

kemurahan hati

merge *v* menyatu; menggabungkan; **merger** *n* pemersatuan, penggabungan

merit *n* jasa; manfaat

mermaid *n* putri duyung

merry *adj* ria; ~-*go-round* komedi putar, korsel

mesh *n* mata jala, lubang

mess *n* kekacauan, keadaan berantakan; *in a* ~ dalam kesulitan, biro erasing; *v* mengacaukan; ~ *around* tidak memperlakukan dengan jujur; ~ *up* mengacaukan

message *n* pesan; **messenger** *n* pesuruh, kurir

messy *adj* berantakan, tidak rapi ← **mess**

met *v, pf* → **meet**

metal *n* logam

metaphor [métafor] *n* kiasan, ibarat, perumpamaan

meteor *n* [mitior] bintang jatuh

meter *n* meter

method *n* metode, cara, jalan

metre → **meter**

Mexican *adj* berasal dari Meksiko; **Mexico** *n* Meksiko

511

mezzanine *adj* [mézanin] lantai tengah

mg *milligram* mg (miligram)

mice *n, pl* ← **mouse**

microphone *n* [maikrofon] mikrofon, corong radio

microscope *n* [maikroskop] mikroskop

midday *n* tengah hari, jam 12 siang

middle *adj* tengah, menengah; *n* pertengahan, titik tengah; *~-aged* setengah baya; *~-class* kelas menengah

midget *n* katai, cebol

midnight *n* [midnait] tengah malam, jam 12 malam

mid-sized *adj* berukuran sedang

midst *n* tengah; *in the ~ of* di tengah

midway *adj* di pertengahan jalan, di tengah jalan

midwife *n* bidan

might *v, aux* [mait] mungkin, boleh jadi

might *n* [mait] kuasa, kekuasaan; **mighty** *adj* berkuasa; besar

migraine *n* [maigrén] migren, sakit kepala sebelah

migrant *n* [maigrant] pendatang; **migrate** *v* pindah, bermigrasi; **migration** *n* migrasi

mild *adj* [maild] lembut, ringan, enteng; *~ weather* cuaca yang tidak panas atau dingin

mile *n* mil

military *adj, n* militer, ketentaraan

milk *n* susu; *v* memerah susu; *~ bar* warung (susu); *~ cow* sapi perah; **milky** *the ~ Way* Bimasakti

mill *n* penggilingan, kilang; **miller** *n* penggiling

millimeter *n* mili, milimeter

million *n* juta; **millionaire** *n* jutawan, milyuner

mimic *n* pemain mimik; *v* **mimicked mimicked** meniru

minaret *n* [minarét] menara (mesjid)

mince *n* (daging) cincang; *v* mencincang, mengiris

mind *n* [maind] akal (budi), pikiran, jiwa; *to keep in ~, to bear in ~* ingat akan, mempertimbangkan; *to lose your ~* menjadi gila; *v*

512

ingat akan, memperhatikan, mengindahkan; merasa keberatan; *never ~* tidak apa-apa; *~ your own business* jangan ikut campur; *do you ~?* apa anda keberatan?

mine *pron, poss* milikku, saya punya

mine *n* ranjau; **minefield** *n* daerah ranjau

mine *n* tambang; **miner** *n* buruh tambang; **mineral** *n* [mineral] barang tambang, barang galian; *~ water* air dari sumber gunung

mini *adj, sl* kecil, mungil, mini; **miniature** *adj* kecil; *in ~* berskala kecil, berukuran kecil

minimum *adj, n* minimum, sedikit-sedikitnya, terendah

mining *n* [maining] pertambangan

minister *n* menteri; pendeta; *~ of Agriculture* Menteri Pertanian (Mentan); *Prime ~* Perdana Menteri; **ministry** *n* kementerian, departemen

minor *adj* [mainor] kecil; di bawah umur, belum dewasa;

n anak; **minority** *n* golongan kecil, minoritas

mint *n* percetakan mata uang; *v* menempa uang

mint *n* sejenis kemangi; permen penyegar mulut

minus *v* [mainus] kurang; tanpa; *six ~ one is five* enam kurang satu sama dengan lima

minute *adj* [mainyut] kecil sekali

minute *n* [minet] menit; *~s* notulen, laporan; *~ hand* jarum panjang

miracle *n* [mirakel] keajaiban, mukjizat

mirage *n* [miraj] fatamorgana

mirror *n* cermin; *v* mencerminkan

misbehave *v* berkelakuan buruk

miscalculation *n* salah hitung

miscarriage *n* [miskarej] keguguran

miscellaneous *adj* [miselénius] beraneka ragam; lain-lain

mischief *n* [mischef] kenakalan, kejahilan; **mischievous** *adj* nakal, jahil misconduct *n* kelakuan buruk

miser *n* orang kikir, orang pelit; **miserable** *adj* [mizerabel] sedih, murung

misfortune *n* kecelakaan

misgovernment *n* pemerintahan yang buruk

misinformation *n* salah informasi

mislead *v* **misled misled** menipu, menyesatkan

misprint *n* salah cetak

miss *n, pron* Nona (before a surname)

miss *v* meleset; rindu akan, merindukan; *~ing* tidak hadir; hilang, kurang; *~ person* orang hilang

missionary *n* misionaris

mist *n* kabut, halimun

mistake *n* kesalahan; *by ~* tidak sengaja; *v* **mistook mistaken** keliru, salah mengerti

mister *pron* Tuan (before a surname); **mistress** *n* kekasih, gundik

mistook *v, pf* → **mistake**

misty *adj* berkabut ← **mist**

misunderstand *v* **misunderstood misunder-**

stood salah mengerti, salah paham, salah tangkap; **misunderstanding** *n* kesalahpahaman

misuse *n* penyalahgunaan; *v* menyalahgunakan

mitten *n* sarung tangan, kaus tangan

mix *n* campuran; *v* mencampur(kan); *~ up* mencampuradukkan; membingungkan; *~ed marriage* perkawinan campuran; **mixture** *n* campuran, adonan

ml *milliliter* mili, mililiter

moan *n* erangan; keluhan; *v* mengerang, mengeluh

mob *n* orang banyak

mobile *adj* dapat bergerak, dapat dipindahkan; *~ phone* telepon genggam, ponsel

mock *adj* palsu, pura-pura, tiruan; *v* mengejek

mode *n* cara, jalan

model *adj* contoh; *n* contoh, macam, model; peragawati, peragawan; *v* memperagakan

moderate *adj* sedang, moderat; *n* orang moderat

modern *adj* modern, baru, kini; **modernize** *v* memperbarui

modification *n* perubahan, modifikasi; **modify** *v* mengubah

moist *adj* basah, lembab; **moisture** *n* embun, kelembaban; **moisturizer** *n* pelembab

molar *n* gigi geraham

mold, mould *n* cetakan; jamur; *v* membentuk, mencetak

moldy, mouldy *adj* berjamur, jamuran, apak ← **mold**

mole *n* sejenis tikus; tahi lalat

molecule *n* molekul

molt, moult *v* berganti bulu atau kulit

molten *adj* cair, leleh ← **melt**

Moluccas *the* ~ Maluku

Mom, Mum *pron* Bu, Mak

moment *n* saat; *in a* ~, *just a* ~ sebentar

mommy, mummy *pron* Ibu, Mama, Mami ← **mom**

monarch *n* [monark] raja, ratu; **monarchy** *n* kerajaan

monastery *n* [monastri] biara

Monday *n* [Mandé] hari Senin

monetary *adj* [manetéri] keuangan, moneter; ~ *crisis* krisis moneter (krismon);

money *n* uang; ~ *changer* penukar uang asing; ~ *order* poswesel; **moneybox** *n* celengan

Mongolia *n* Mongolia; **Mongolian** *adj* berasal dari Mongolia

mongrel *adj, derog* [manggrel] campuran; *n* anjing kampung

monitor *n* pengawas; layar (komputer); *v* mengawasi

monk *n* [mank] biarawan, rahib

monkey *n* [mangki] monyet

monopoly *n* monopoli

monorail *n* monorel, kereta api rel tunggal

monsoon *n* musim hujan, muson

monster *adj* raksasa; *n* makhluk besar yang mengerikan

month *n* [manth] bulan; *at the end of the* ~ akhir bulan; **monthly** *adj, adv* bulanan; *n* majalah bulanan

monument *n* monumen, tanda peringatan, tugu peringatan

515

mood *n* suasana hati

moon *n* bulan, rembulan; *new* ~ bulan muda; **moonlight** *n* [munlait] sinar bulan

moose *n* rusa besar (di Amerika Utara)

moral *n* [morel] kesusilaan, etika; moral, moril; ~ *support* dukungan moral

more *adv* lebih, lagi; ~ *and* ~ semakin; ~ *or less* kurang lebih; *one* ~ *glass* satu (gelas) lagi; *the* ~ *the merrier* makin banyak, semakin ramai; **moreover** *adv* lagipula

morgue *n* [morg] kamar mayat

morning *n* pagi (hari); ~ *paper* koran pagi; *good* ~ selamat pagi (diucapkan sampai jam 12 siang)

Morocco *n* Maroko

moron *n* orang bodoh

mortality *n* kematian; ~ *rate* tingkat kematian

mortar *n* adukan semen dan pasir; mortir

mortgage *n* [morgej] hipotek

mosaic *n* [moséik] mosaik

Moslem → **Muslim**

mosque *n* [mosk] mesjid

mosquito *n* [moskito] nyamuk; ~ *net* kelambu

moss *n* lumut; **mossy** *adj* berlumut

most *adv* paling, maha; *at (the)* ~ sebanyak-banyaknya, paling-paling; **mostly** *adv* kebanyakan

motel *n* hotel transit

moth *n* ngengat; ~ *ball* kapur barus

mother *n* [mather] ibu; induk; *pron* Ibu; ~–*in-law* (ibu) mertua; ~–*of-pearl* kulit mutiara; ~ *ship* kapal induk; ~ *tongue* bahasa ibu

motion *n* gerak; mosi, usul; ~ *sickness* mabuk (jalan); **motionless** *adj* tidak bergerak, diam

motivation *n* dorongan, dukungan, motivasi; **motive** *n* [motiv] alasan, dalil, motif

motor *n* motor, mesin; **motorboat** *n* perahu bermotor; **motorcycle** *n* **motorbike** *sl* sepeda motor; **motorcyclist** *n* pengendara motor; **motorist** *n* pengendara mobil; **motorway** *n* jalan bebas hambatan

motto *n* semboyan, slogan, moto

mould → **mold**

mount *n* (nama) gunung; ~ *Bromo* Gunung Bromo; *v* naik; menaiki, menaikkan; memasang; **mountain** *n* [maunten] gunung

mourn *v* [morn] berkabung; meratapi, menangisi; **mourner** *n* orang yang berkabung; **mourning** *n* perkabungan

mouse *n* **mice** tikus; **mousehole** *n* lubang tikus; **mousetrap** *n* perangkap tikus

mouth *n* mulut; muara; ~ *organ* harmonika; **mouthful** *n* sesuap; **mouthwash** *n* obat kumur

move *n* perpindahan, gerakan; *v* bergerak; berpindah (rumah); menggerakkan, memindahkan; **movement** *n* gerak, gerakan, pergerakan

movie *n*, *sl* [muvi] film

mow *v* [mo] memotong rumput; **mower** *n* mesin pemotong rumput

MP *abbrev Member of*

Parliament anggota DPR

mph *miles per hour* mil per jam

Mr *Mister* Tn (Tuan) (harus dipakai dengan nama keluarga, mis. *Mr Brown*)

Mrs *Mistress, Missus* Ny (Nyonya) (harus dipakai dengan nama keluarga, mis. *Mrs Thatcher*)

Ms Ny, Ibu (status perkawinan tidak disebut. Harus dipakai dengan nama keluarga, mis. *Ms Smith*)

Mt *Mount* Gg., (gunung)

much *adv*, *n* banyak; *so* ~ sekian; *as* ~ *as* sebanyak

mucus *n* lendir, ingus, dahak

mud *n* lumpur

muddle *n* kekacauan, kekusutan; *v* mengacaukan

muddy *adj* berlumpur ← **mud**

mudguard *n* [madgard] sepatbor ← **mud**

muffled *v* tidak jelas kedengaran; **muffler** *n* kenalpot; selendang

mug *n* cangkir besar; *v* menodong, merampok; **mugger** *n* penodong

muggy *adj* lembab (cuaca)

mule *n* bagal; semacam selop wanita

multi- *pref* lebih dari satu, aneka; **multi-colored** *adj* warna-warni, beraneka warna

multiple *adj* [maltipel] berlipat ganda; **multiplication** *n* perkalian; **multiply** *v* berkembang biak; mengalikan

Mum → **Mom**

mumble *v* bergumam, berkomat-kamit

mummy *n* mumi → **mommy**

mumps *n* penyakit gondok; *to have the* ~ gondokan

munch *v* mengunyah

municipality *n* [munisipaliti] kota (praja), kotamadya; **municipal** *adj* berkaitan dengan kotamadya

mural *n* lukisan pada tembok atau dinding

murder *n* pembunuhan; *v* membunuh; **murderer** *n* pembunuh

murmur *n* bisikan; *v* berbisik; membisikkan

muscle *n* [masel] urat, otot;

kekuatan

muse *v* termenung, melamun

museum *n* musium

mushroom *n* cendawan, jamur

music *n* musik, lagu; **musical** *adj* (berbakat) musik; **musician** *n* musikus, pemain musik

Muslim, Moslem *adj* Islam, Muslim; *n* orang Islam

must *n* keharusan; *v, aux* harus, wajib, terpaksa

mustache, moustache *n* [mustasy] kumis, misai

mustard *n* mostar

mutation *n* mutasi, perubahan

mute *adj* bisu

mutilate *v* memotong; **mutilation** *n* mutilasi, pemotongan

mutter *v* bergumam, berkomat-kamit

mutual *adj* [myutyual] saling, dari kedua pihak, timbal balik; ~ *friend* saling berteman

muzzle *n* moncong, mulut; *v* membredel, memberangus

my *pron, poss* saya, -ku

myself *pron* saya sendiri; sendirian

mysterious *adj* gaib, misterius; **mystery** *n* kegaiban, misteri

mystical *adj* **mysticism** *n* mistik, aliran kebatinan

myth *n* [mith] isapan jempol, dongeng, mitos

N

nail *n* paku; kuku; ~ *file* kikir kuku; ~ *polish* cat kuku, kuteks; ~ *scissors* gunting kuku; *v* memaku; **nailbrush** *n* sikat kuku

naked *adj* [néked] telanjang

name *n* nama; *v* menamai, menamakan, memberi nama; ~*dropping* menyebut orang ternama sebagai kenalan; *to call* ~*s* mengejek; **named** *adj* bernama; *in the* ~ *of* atas nama, demi; **namely** *conj* yakni, yaitu; **nameplate** *n* papan nama

nanny *n* penjaga anak, pengasuh anak

nap *n* tidur siang; *v (to take a)* ~ tidur sebentar

napkin *n* serbet; popok;

nappy *n* popok; *disposable* ~ pampers, popok plastik

narrate *v* menceritakan; **narrative** *n, adj* cerita; **narrator** *n* orang yang bercerita

narrow *adj* sempit; ~ *escape* nyaris celaka; *v* menyempitkan; ~*minded* picik, berpikiran sempit

NASA *abbrev National Aeronautics and Space Administration* Administrasi Angkasa dan Aeronautika Nasional

nasal *adj* berhubungan dengan hidung, sengau

nastiness *n* kejahatan, keburukan; **nasty** *adj* buruk, jahat

nation *n* [nésyen] negara, bangsa; **national** *n, adj* [nasyonal] nasional, kebangsaan; ~ *anthem* lagu kebangsaan; **nationality** *n* kebangsaan, kewarganegaraan

native *adj* [nétif] asli; ~

speaker penutur asli; *n* orang asli, pribumi

NATO *abbrev North Atlantic Treaty Organization* NATO, Pakta Pertahanan Atlantik Utara

natural *adj* [natyurel] alami, alamiah; **naturally** *adj* tentu, memang; **nature** *n* alam (semesta); tabiat, kepribadian, sifat

naught → **nought**

naughty *adj* [noti] nakal, jahil

nausea *n* [nozia] (rasa) mual, mabuk

navel *n* pusar

navigate *v* [navigét] melayari, mengemudikan kapal; **navigation** *n* pelayaran, navigasi; **navigator** *n* mualim, navigator; **navy** *n* [névi] angkatan laut

nb. *nota bene = note well* catatan

near *adj* dekat; **~-sighted** rabun jauh; *a ~ thing, a ~ miss* hampir saja, nyaris; **nearby** *adv* [nirbai] dekat; **nearly** *adv* hampir

neat *adj* apik, rapi, bersih; *sl* hebat, bagus

necessary *adj* [néseséri] perlu; **necessity** *n* kebutuhan, keperluan

neck *n* leher; *to break your ~* leher patah; *to stick your ~ out* mengambil risiko; **necklace** *n* kalung; **neckline** *n* garis leher; **necktie** *n* dasi

need *n* kebutuhan, keperluan; *in ~* perlu bantuan; *if ~ be* jika perlu; *no ~* tidak usah, tidak perlu; *v* membutuhkan, memerlukan

needle *n* jarum; *v, sl* mengejek, menyindir; **needlepoint, needlework** *n* semacam sulaman

negative *adj* negatif, buruk; *n* klise

neglect *n* keadaan telantar; *v* mengabaikan

negotiate *v* bermusyawarah, berunding; merundingkan; **negotiation** *n* negosiasi, perundingan; **negotiator** *n* juru runding

neigh *v* [néi] meringkik

neighbor *n* [nébor] tetangga; **neighborhood** *n* lingkungan (dekat rumah); **neighboring** *adj* bertetangga, berdekatan

neither *conj* [nither, naither] kedua-duanya (tidak); ~ ... **nor** bukan ... maupun

Nepal *n* Nepal; **Nepalese** *adj* berasal dari Nepal

nephew *n, m* [néfyu] keponakan (lelaki); *great-~* anak (lelaki) dari keponakan

nepotism *n* [népotizem] nepotisme

nerve *n* saraf; nyali, keberanian; *~-racking* menggelisahkan; **nervous** *adj* gelisah, gugup

nest *n* sarang; *v* bersarang; ~ *egg* tabungan, persediaan

net *adj* bersih, netto; *n* jala, jaring

Netherlands *the* ~ (negeri) Belanda

nettle *n* jelatang

network *n* jaringan; *v* menjalin hubungan

neutral *adj* [nutral] netral, tidak memihak

never *adv* [néver] tidak pernah; ~ *again* tidak pernah lagi; ~ *before* belum pernah; *well I* ~ astaga

nevertheless *conj* [néverthelés] walaupun demikian, namun

new *adj* baru; ~ *Year* tahun baru; ~ *Year's Eve* malam tahun baru; ~ *Zealand* Selandia Baru; *Papua* ~ *Guinea* Papua Nugini; **newborn** *adj* baru saja lahir; ~ *baby* orok; **newcomer** *n* pendatang baru; **newly** *adv* baru saja, belum lama; ~ *weds* pengantin baru; **news** *n, s* berita, warta, warta berita; kabar; **newsletter** *n* selebaran; **newspaper** *n* surat kabar, koran

next *prep* berikut, sebelah, samping; ~ *door* rumah sebelah; ~ *month* bulan depan; ~ *of kin* keluarga terdekat; ~ *time* lain kali

NGO *abbrev* *non-governmental organization* LSM (lembaga swadaya masyarakat)

NHS *abbrev* *National Health Service* Pelayanan Kesehatan Nasional

nib *n* mata pena

nibble *n* [nibel] gigit; *v* menggigit, mengunggis

nice *adj* enak, sedap; manis, cantik, apik

nick *n* torehan; *v, sl* mengutil

nickel *n* nikel
nickname *n* nama kecil, nama panggilan
nicotine *n* nikotin
niece *n, f* [nis] keponakan (perempuan); *great-~* anak perempuan dari keponakan
night *n* [nait] malam; *~ club* kelab malam, kafe; *~ owl* orang yang suka bangun waktu malam; *~ school* kursus malam; *~ and day* siang malam; *at ~* pada waktu malam, malam hari; *good ~* selamat tidur; *last ~* tadi malam, semalam;
nightie *sl* daster; **nightfall** *n* senja, magrib; **nightingale** *n* bulbul; **nightlife** *n* kehidupan malam; **nightly** *adv* tiap malam; **nightmare** *n* mimpi buruk; **nightwatchman** *n* jaga (malam)
nimble *adj* [nimbel] cekatan, tangkas, gesit
nine *n, adj* sembilan; **nineteen** *n, adj* sembilan belas; **nineteenth** *adj* kesembilan belas
ninetieth *adj* kesembilan puluh; **ninety** *adj, n* sembilan puluh ← **nine**

ninth *adj* [nainth] kesembilan ← **nine**
nip *n* gigitan kecil; *v* mencubit, menggigit
nipple *n* [nipel] puting, pentil, dot
no. *number* no. (nomor)
no tidak; bukan; *~ way, ~ chance* tidak mungkin
noble *adj* bangsawan, ningrat
nobody *n* [nobodi] bukan siapa-siapa; *pron* tidak seorang pun
nocturnal *adj* (hidup pada waktu) malam
nod *n* anggukan, tanda setuju
noise *n* bunyi, kegaduhan, keributan, suara bising; *~ pollution* polusi suara; **noisy** *adj* gaduh, ribut, berisik, bising
nomad *n* pengembara, nomaden
nominate *v* mencalonkan; **nomination** *n* pencalonan, nominasi
non- *pref* tidak, non-; *~existent* tidak ada; *~profit* nirlaba; *~stop* tanpa berhenti
nonchalant *adj* [nonsyalant] enteng, tanpa beban

522

none *n* [nan] seorang pun tidak, sesuatu pun tidak; tidak sama sekali; *there's* ~ *left* tidak ada sisanya

nonsense *n* omong kosong

noon *(at)* ~ jam duabelas siang

noose *n* jerat

nor *neither* … ~ bukan … maupun; juga tidak

normal *adj* biasa, lazim, lumrah, umum; normal; **normally** *adv* biasanya, pada umumnya

north *adj, adv* utara; *n* (sebelah) utara; ~ *Korea* Korea Utara (Korut); ~ *Pole* Kutub Utara; *to the* ~ *of* di sebelah utara; **northeast** *adj, n* timur laut; **northern** *adj* utara; *the* ~ *Hemisphere* belahan bumi utara; **northwest** *adj, n* barat laut

Norway *n* Norwegia; **Norwegian** *adj* [Norwijen] berasal dari Norwegia

nose *n* hidung; *to have a blood* ~ mimisan; *to look down your* ~ *at* memandang rendah; *to stick your* ~ *in* ikut campur; **nostril** *n* lubang hidung; **nosy** *adj*

ingin tahu

not *adv* tidak, tak; belum; bukan; ~ *ready* belum siap; ~ *yet* belum; ~ *at all* sama sekali tidak

notch *n* takik, torehan

note *n* catatan, peringatan; nada, not; nota; *v* mencatat, menulis; memperhatikan; *to take* ~ *of* memperhatikan; **notebook** *n* buku catatan, buku tulis, notes; **noted** *adj* masyhur, tersohor, kenamaan; **notepaper** *n* kertas tulis

nothing *n* [nathing] tidak sesuatu pun; ~ *like* tidak seperti; *to come to* ~ gagal

notice *n* [notis] perhatian; pemberitahuan, maklumat; *at short* ~ dengan mendadak, serta merta; *v* melihat; memperhatikan; *to take* ~ *of* mengindahkan, memerhatikan; **noticeable** *adj* [notisabel] nyata, tampak, kelihatan

notification *n* [notifikésyen] pemberitahuan, surat panggilan; **notify** *v* memberitahu; memberitahukan

notorious *adj* [notorius] mempunyai nama buruk

nougat *n* [nuga] gula-gula keras terbuat dari kacang

nought, naught *n, arch* [not] nol, kosong; tanpa hasil

noun *n* [naun] kata benda

nourish *v* [narisy] memberi gizi, memelihara; **nourishing** *adj* bergizi

novel *adj* baru; *n* buku roman, novel; **novelist** *n* pengarang novel

November *n* bulan November

now *prep* [nau] sekarang, kini; ~ *that* sejak; *just* ~ baru saja, tadi; *(every)* ~ *and then,* ~ *and again* sekali-sekali, kadang-kadang; *from* ~ *(on)* mulai sekarang; *conj* nah; **nowadays** *prep* sekarang (ini)

nowhere *adv, pron* [nowér] tidak di mana-mana; *to go* ~ tidak ke mana-mana, tidak bergerak

nuclear *adj* nuklir; ~ *energy* tenaga nuklir

nude *adj* telanjang, bugil; *in the* ~ telanjang

nudge *n* [naj] sentuhan; *v* menyentuh, menyinggung

nuisance *n* [nusens] gangguan; orang peng-

ganggu; *what a* ~ mengganggu saja, mengganggu sekali

numb *adj* [nam] mati rasa, kesemutan

number *n* nomor; bilangan, angka; banyaknya; ~ *plate* plat polisi; **numeral** *n* angka; *Roman* ~*s* angka Romawi

nun *n* biarawati, suster

nurse *n* juru rawat, perawat; *v* merawat; menyusui; **nursery** *n* kamar anak; toko tanaman; ~ *rhyme* lagu anak-anak; **nursing** *adj* menyusui; ~ *home* panti asuhan

nut *n* kacang; *sl* penggemar berat, penggila; *to go* ~*s* menjadi marah, menjadi gila; **nutmeg** *n* pala

nutrient *n* [nutrient] gizi; **nutrition** *n* [nutrisyen] ilmu gizi; **nutritious** *adj* bergizi

nutty *adj* berasa kacang; *sl* gila ← **nut**

nylon *n* [nailon] nilon; **nylons** *n, pl* stoking

NZ *abbrev* *New Zealand* Selandia Baru

O

o/s *overseas* LN (luar negeri)

oar *n* dayung

oatmeal *n* havermut

oath *n* sumpah; umpatan; *under* ~ di bawah sumpah; *to take an* ~, *to swear an* ~ bersumpah

oats *n, pl* sejenis gandum

obedient *adj* taat, patuh
← **obey**

obese *adj* [obis] gemuk sekali; **obesity** *n* keadaan sangat gemuk

obey *v* [obé] taat, patuh

obituary *n* berita duka, berita kematian, obituari

object *n* benda, obyek; *v* berkeberatan; **objection** *n* keberatan; **objective** *adj* obyektif, tidak memihak; *n* tujuan

obligation *n* [obligésyen] kewajiban; **obligated** *adj* diharuskan

oblivious *adj* [oblivius] tidak sadar, tidak meng-indahkan

oblong *adj, n* persegi panjang

oboe *n* obo

obscene *adj* [obsin] cabul, jorok

obscure *adj* tidak terkenal, terpencil; *v* mengaburkan

observant *adj* suka mem-perhatikan; taat; **observa-tion** *n* pengamatan, penin-jauan; **observe** *v* menga-mati, meninjau; meng-hormati; **observer** *n* pen-gamat, peninjau

obsession *n* obsesi

obstacle *n* [obstakel] rin-tangan, hambatan

obstinate *adj* [obstinet] keras kepala

obstruct *v* merintangi, menghalangi; **obstruction** *n* rintangan, halangan

obtain *v* memperoleh, mendapatkan, menerima

obvious *adj* [obvius] jelas, terang, nyata; **obviously** *adv* dengan jelas

occasion *n* [okésyen] kesempatan; peristiwa, acara; **occasional** *adj* **occasion-ally** *adv* kadang-kadang

occupant *n* penghuni; **occupation** *n* pekerjaan; pendudukan; **occupy** *v* [okupai] mengisi; menduduki

occur *v* terjadi; **occurrence** *n* kejadian, peristiwa

ocean *n* [osyan] samudera, lautan; *the Indian* ~ Samudera Hindia

o'clock jam, pukul; *it's six* ~ sekarang jam enam

octagon *n* segi delapan

October *n* bulan Oktober

octopus *n* ikan gurita

OD *abbrev overdose* overdosis

odd *adj* aneh, ganjil; **odds** *n, pl* kemungkinan; *~~-on* kemungkinan besar; *against the* ~ kemungkinan kecil

odor *n* bau; *body* ~ *(BO)* bau badan

of *prep* [ov] milik; dari, daripada

off *prep* jauh; *adj* mati, tidak hidup; basi (makanan); tidak jadi; *~~ duty* tidak sedang dinas; *~~-key* bersuara sumbang; *~~-limits* tidak boleh; ~ *the record* (dikatakan) secara tidak resmi; ~ *and on* sekali-sekali; *day* ~ hari libur; *the milk is* ~ susu sudah basi

offend *v* menghina, membuat tersinggung; melanggar

hukum; **offender** *n* yang bersalah, yang melakukan;

offense *n* pelanggaran hukum, kesalahan; **offensive** *adj* menghina, tidak sopan; serangan

offer *n* tawaran, penawaran; *v* menawarkan, menawari; mempersembahkan;

offering *n* persembahan, sesajen

office *n* [ofis] kantor, ruangan, tempat kerja; jabatan; ~ *hours (OH)* jam kerja; *at the* ~ di kantor; **officer** *n* pegawai, petugas; perwira; *police* ~ polisi; **official** *adj* resmi; *n* pegawai, pejabat

offspring *n* anak, keturunan ← **off**

often *adv* sering

ogre *n* [oger] raksasa; makhluk yang menakutkan

oil *n* minyak; *v* meminyaki; ~ *colors,* ~ *paint* cat minyak; ~ *palm* kelapa sawit; ~ *tanker* kapal minyak; **oilfield** *n* ladang minyak; **oilwell** *n* sumur minyak; **oily** *adj* berminyak

ointment *n* salep, balsem

OK, okay [oké] baik, oke, jadi; *v* menyetujui

old *adj* tua; sepuh, lanjut usia; *~-fashioned* kuno, kolot; **olden** *~ days* masa lalu, tempo dulu, zaman baheula

olive *n* [oliv] (buah) zaitun; *~ green* berwarna hijau pudar

Olympic *adj* Olimpiade; *~ Games* Pertandingan Olimpiade; **Olympics** the *~* (Pertandingan) Olimpiade

omelet, omelette *n* telur dadar

omen *n* tanda, pertanda, alamat

omit *v* melupakan, menghilangkan

omnibus *n* kumpulan, antologi → **bus**

on *adj* hidup; *~ and off* kadang-kadang; *prep* di (atas), pada; *~ the phone* sedang menelepon; *~ the way* sedang dalam perjalanan; *from that day ~* mulai hari itu; *adv* terus; sedang berjalan, sedang berlangsung; *~ and ~* terus-menerus

once *adv* [wans] sekali (waktu); dahulu kala; *all at ~* serentak; tiba-tiba; *at ~* pada saat itu juga, segera; *~ upon a time* sekali waktu; *just this ~* sekali ini saja ← **one**

oncoming *adj* [onkaming] yang mendekat

one *n, adj* [wan] satu, suatu; seorang; *pron* orang; *~ another* satu sama lain; *~ apple* sebuah apel; *~ day* kapan-kapan; suatu hari, sekali waktu; *~ hundred* seratus; *~ of* salah satu (dari); *~-sided* sepihak, berat sebelah; *~-way street* jalan satu arah; *as ~* serentak; *not ~* tidak satu pun; *the ~* yang satu itu; *~ by ~* satu per satu

ongoing *adj* terus-menerus ← **on**

onion *n* [anien] bawang; *spring ~* daun bawang

only *adj* tunggal; *~ child* anak tunggal; *one and ~* satu-satunya; *adv* saja, hanya; *if ~* kalau saja; *not ~ ... but also* tidak hanya ... tetapi juga

onward *adv* ke depan, seterusnya ← **on**

onyx *n* [oniks] batu akik

opal *n* opal, baiduri

opaque *adj* [opék] tidak tembus pandang, buram

open *adj* buka, terbuka; terang-terangan; ~ *house* acara menerima tamu di rumah sepanjang hari; ~*minded* berpandangan terbuka; ~ *secret* rahasia umum; *v* membuka; **opener** *n* pembuka; **opening** *adj* pembuka; *n* pembukaan; lubang, celah, lowongan

opera *n* opera

operate *v* [operét] membedah, mengoperasi; beroperasi; menjalankan (mesin), mengoperasikan; **operation** *n* pembedahan, operasi; cara menjalankan; **operator** *n* penjaga mesin, penjaga telepon

opinion *n* [opinion] pendapat; *in my* ~ menurut pendapat saya

opium *n* candu

opossum, possum *n* semacam tupai

opponent *n* lawan

opportunity *n* kesempatan, peluang; *job* ~ lowongan kerja; ~ *shop* toko loak

opposite *n, adj* [opozet] berlawanan, bertentangan, lawan (kata); **opposition** *n* perlawanan, oposisi

oppression *n* penindasan, tekanan; **oppressive** *adj* menekan; menyesakkan napas

optical *adj* optik; ~ *illusion* tipu mata; **optician** *n* ahli kaca mata

optimist *n* **optimistic** *adj* optimis

option *n* [opsyen] opsi, pilihan; **optional** *adj* bebas (memilih)

optometrist *n* dokter mata; ahli kacamata

or *conj* atau; *either* ... ~ salah satu

oral *adj* lisan, berkaitan dengan mulut

orange *adj* [orenj] oranye, jingga; *n* jeruk

orangutan *n* orang hutan

orchard *n* [orced] kebun buah

orchestra *n* [orkestra] orkes

orchid *n* [orkid] (bunga) anggrek

order *n* urutan; peraturan; perintah; pemesanan; *in ~* teratur; beres; *in ~ to* supaya; *on his ~s* atas perintahnya; *out of ~* rusak; *v* memerintahkan, menyuruh, mengatur, memesan

ordinary *adj* [ordineri] biasa, lazim

organ *n* orgel, organ

organ *n* bagian badan; **organic** *adj* organik; **organism** *n* makhluk

organization *n* organisasi, persatuan; penyusunan, pengaturan; **organize** *v* menyusun, mengatur, mengurus; **organizer** *n* pengurus

orgasm *n* [orgazem] orgasme, puncak (nafsu)

oriental *adj* timur, ketimuran

orientation *n* orientasi, pencarian jalan

origin *n* asal, asal-usul; **original** *adj* orisinil, asli, semula

ornament *n* hiasan

orphan *n* [orfan] anak yatim (piatu); **orphanage** *n* rumah yatim piatu

orthodox *adj* ortodoks, biasa

ostrich *n* burung unta

other *pron, adj* [ather] lain, berlainan; *every ~ day* selang sehari; *the ~ day* kemarin, belum lama ini; *the ~ woman* orang ketiga; **otherwise** *conj* kalau tidak, bila tidak

otter *n* berang-berang

ouch *excl* [auc] aduh, sakit

ought *aux v* [out] seharusnya, semestinya, sebaiknya

ounce *n* [auns] ons

our *pron* kita, kami; **ours** *pron* milik kita, milik kami; **ourselves** *pron* kita sendiri, kami sendiri

out *prep* (di) luar; *adj* di luar, tidak ada; tidak berlaku lagi; *~-of-date* ketinggalan zaman, kolot; *~-of-work* menganggur; **outbreak** *n* pecahnya, meletusnya (perang); terjangkitnya (penyakit); **outburst** *n* letusan, ledakan; **outcome** *n* hasil, kepu-

tusan; **outdated** *adj*
ketinggalan zaman, kuno;
outdoor *adj* **outdoors**
prep (di) luar (rumah);
outer *adj* bagian luar; **outfit** *n* busana; **outgoing** *adj*
ramah; **outlet** *n* jalan keluar, saluran pembuangan;
toko, cabang; **outline** *n*
garis besar; **outlook** *n*
wawasan; **outpost** *n* pos
yang terpencil; **output** *n*
hasil, produksi; keluaran;
outright *adj* langsung,
terus terang, tulus; **outside**
n, prep (di) luar, ke luar,
bagian luar; **outsider** *n*
orang luar; **outspoken** *adj*
blak-blakan, terang-terangan; **outstanding** *adj* luar
biasa; **outward** *adj* berpe-
nampilan; *adv* keluar
oval *adj* lonjong; *n*
(lapangan) bulat panjang
ovary *n* [overi] indung
telur
oven *n* [aven] oven, kompor, tungku
over *adj* selesai, rampung;
prep di atas; melalui;
tentang, mengenai; lebih
daripada; *all* ~ seluruh;

selesai semua; ~ *and* ~
berulang kali; ~ *there* di
sebelah sana, di seberang;
overact *v* bertindak secara
berlebihan; **overall** *adj*
secara keseluruhan; **overcast** *adj* mendung, berawan;
overcharge *v* meminta
bayaran terlalu tinggi;
overcome *adj* **overcame**
overcome kewalahan; *v*
mengalahkan, mengatasi;
overcrowded *adj* penuh
sesak; **overdose** *n* overdosis, OD; *v* OD; **overdue**
adj kedaluwarsa, terlambat;
overflow *v* banjir; ~ *into*
menggenangi, membanjiri;
overhead *adj* di atas
(kepala); *n* ongkos eks-
ploitasi; **overhear** *v*
overheard overheard
menguping; terdengar;
overload *v* kebanyakan
(muatan); **overnight** *adj,
prep* semalaman; **overpass**
n jembatan penyeberangan;
overpower *v* menguasai;
overrated *adj* tidak sebagus
rekomendasinya, dinilai terlalu tinggi; **overseas** *adv,
adj* (di) luar negeri; **over-**

shadow v membayangi; **oversight** n kelupaan; **overtake** v **overtook overtaken** menyalip; **overthrow** v **overthrew overthrown** menjatuhkan, meruntuhkan; **overweight** n kelebihan berat (badan)

owe v [o] berhutang; **owing** ~ *to* berkat, sebab, karena

owl n [aul] burung hantu

own *adj* [oun] sendiri; v memiliki, mempunyai; **owner** n pemilik; **ownership** n kepemilikan, hak milik

ox n **oxen** sapi, lembu

oxygen n [oksijen] oksigen

oxtail ~ *soup* sop buntut

← **ox**

oyster n tiram

oz *ounce* ons

ozone n, *pl* ozon; ~ *layer* lapisan ozon

P

p *page*, **pp** (*pages*) halaman

pa *per annum* per tahun, setahun

PA *abbrev personal assistant* asisten pribadi

Pa *pron, sl* Pak, Yah

pace n langkah; kecepatan

Pacific ~ *Ocean* Lautan Teduh, Samudera Pasifik

pack n bungkusan, pak; ~*ed* penuh (sesak); v membungkus, mengepak, menyusun; **package** n bungkus; bingkisan, paket; ~ *deal* paket; **packet** n paket, pak, bungkus; **packing** n pengepakan, pengemasan

pact n pakta, perjanjian

pad n bantalan; *writing* ~ bloknot

paddle n [padel] kayuh; v mengayuh

paddy n ~ (*field*) sawah

padlock n gembok; v mengunci, menggembok

page n halaman, lembar; v memanggil

pageant n [pajent] lomba; arak-arakan

pagoda n kuil

paid v, *pf* → **pay**

pain n rasa sakit, rasa nyeri; *in* ~ kesakitan; **painful** *adj* sakit, pedih

531

paint *n* cat; *oil ~* cat minyak; *wet ~* cat basah; *v* mengecat; **painter** *n* tukang cat; pelukis; **painting** *n* lukisan; seni lukis

pair *n* pasang, rangkap; pasangan; *~ of glasses* kacamata; *a ~ of shoes* (sepasang) sepatu; *~ of trousers* celana

pajamas → **pyjamas**

Pakistan *n* Pakistan; **Pakistani** *adj* berasal dari Pakistan

pal *n, sl* kawan, sobat

palace *n* [pales] istana, puri

palate *n* [palet] langit-langit

pale *adj* pucat, lemah

Palestine *n* [Palestain] Palestina; **Palestinian** *adj* [Palestinian] berasal dari Palestina

palm *n* [pam] palem; telapak tangan; *~reading* membaca garis tangan; *~ oil* minyak kelapa sawit; *~ sugar* gula aren

palsy [polzi] *cerebral ~* kelumpuhan akibat penyakit otak

pamphlet *n* brosur, selebaran, pamflet

pan *n* panci, wajan, kuali; **pancake** *n* panekuk

panel *n* panel; sehelai papan; *~ beating* ketok

panic *n* panik, ketakutan; *v* panik

panorama *n* pemandangan

pansy *n* sejenis bunga

pant *v* terengah-engah

panther *n* macan kumbang

pantry *n* [pantri] gudang (dapur), lemari untuk menyimpan makanan kering

pants *n, pl* celana; **pantsuit** *n* setelan celana dan baju atas

panty *~ liner* pembalut (tipis); **panties** *n, pl* celana dalam wanita

papa *pron* pak, ayah

papaya *n* pepaya

paper *n* kertas; koran, surat kabar; makalah; *~book* buku bersampul tipis; *~s* surat-surat, dokumen; *~ clip* jepitan kertas; **paperboy** *n* tukang koran, loper koran; **paperwork** *n* pekerjaan tulis-menulis

Papua *n* Irian (Jaya); *~ New Guinea (PNG)* Papua

Nugini; **Papuan** *n* orang Papua

parachute *n* payung, parasut; *v* terjun payung

parade *n* [paréid] pawai, arak-arakan; jalan; *v* berpawai, berbaris

paradise *n* surga

paragraph *n* paragraf, alinea

parakeet *n* burung bayan; burung parkit

parallel *adj* sejajar, paralel; *n* garis lintang

paralysis *n* [paralisis] layuh, kelumpuhan; **paralyzed** *adj* lumpuh

paranoid *adj* takut sekali (sakit jiwa)

paraphrase *v* [parafréiz] menguraikan dengan kata-kata sendiri, memfrasakan

parasite *n* [parasait] parasit, benalu

parcel *n* bingkisan, paket; parsel

pardon *n* ampun, maaf; grasi; *v* mengampuni, memaafkan; ~ *me* maaf

parent *n* [pérent] orang tua, ibu bapak, ayah bunda

park *n* taman; *car* ~ tempat parkir; *v* parkir; memarkir-

kan mobil; ~*ing lot* tempat parkir; *no* ~*ing* dilarang parkir

parliament *n* Dewan Perwakilan Rakyat (DPR), parlemen

parody *n* parodi; *v* memarodikan

parrot *n* burung nuri

parsley *n* [parsli] peterseli

parson *n* pendeta

part *n* bagian, potong; peranan; belahan; *in* ~ sebagian; *side* ~ belahan samping; *on my* ~ dari pihak saya; *to play a* ~ memainkan peranan, berperan; *to take* ~ *(in)* ikut serta, mengambil bagian; *v* membagi, memisahkan; ~ *with* melepaskan

participant *n* peserta; **participate** *v* ikut serta, mengambil bagian; **participation** *n* keikutsertaan, partisipasi

particle *n* butir; unsur; partikel; **particular** *adj* istimewa, spesial, khusus; *in* ~ khususnya, terutama; **particularly** *adv* terutama, khususnya

parting *n* perpisahan; belahan (rambut) ← **part**

partly *adv* sebagian ← **part**

partner *n* pasangan, mitra; **partnership** *n* persekutuan, kemitraan

party *n* pesta, perayaan; partai, kelompok, pihak; rombongan; *third* ~ pihak ketiga; *v* berpesta

pass *n* surat izin masuk, pas jalan; *v* lulus ujian; lewat; melalui, melewati; mengesahkan; ~*er-by* orang lewat, orang di jalan; ~ *away* meninggal dunia, berpulang; ~ *for* dipandang sebagai, mirip; ~ *out* pingsan; ~ *up* melewatkan; ~ *sentence* menjatuhkan hukuman; ~ *wind* kentut; **passage** *n* [pasej] jalan lintas, jalan tembus, lorong, terusan; bagian dari tulisan; pelayaran; **passenger** *n* [pasenjer] penumpang; **passing** *in* ~ sepintas lalu

passion *n* [pasyen] hawa nafsu, gairah; **passionate** *adj* [pasyenet] bernafsu, bergairah, bersemangat

passive *adj* pasif, terdiam

passport *n* paspor

password *n* kata sandi

past *adj* lalu, lewat, lampau, silam; ~ *tense* bentuk lampau; *n* masa lalu

paste *n* [pést] adonan, pasta; *v* tempel

pastel *n* warna pastel; kapur berwarna

pastor *n* pastor, pendeta

pastry *n* [péstri] kue

pat *n* tepukan; *v* menepuk, mengelus

patch *n* tambal, tempelan; *v* menambal; **patchwork** *n* penjahitan kain perca; campur aduk

paternal *adj* [patérnal] dari pihak bapak

path *n* jalan (tapak), lorong

pathetic *adj* [pathétik] menyedihkan, memelas

patience *n* [pésyens] kesabaran; soliter; **patient** *adj* sabar; *n* pasien

patio *n* teras, emper terbuka

patriotic *adj* cinta tanah air; **patriotism** *n* patriotisme, kecintaan kepada tanah air

patrol *n* patroli, ronda; *v* berpatroli, meronda

pattern *n* pola, corak; patron, contoh

patty *n* perkedel; ~ *cake* kue mangkuk

pause *n* [pouz] jeda, waktu istirahat; *v* berhenti sebentar; menghentikan sementara

pavement *n* trotoar

pavilion *n* [pavilion] anjungan; tenda besar; bangunan dekat taman atau lapangan

paw *n* kaki binatang

pawn *n* gadai; pion; *v* menggadaikan; **pawnshop** *n* rumah gadai, pegadaian

pay *n* pembayaran; gaji, upah; *v* **paid paid** membayar; ~ *attention* memperhatikan; ~ *back* mengganti, membayar kembali; ~ *off* melunasi; berhasil; ~ *TV* TV kabel; ~ *a visit* berkunjung; mengunjungi; **payday** *n* (hari) gajian; **payment** *n* pembayaran; **payphone** *n* telepon umum

PC *abbrev* (personal computer) komputer

PC *abbrev* *police constable* polisi

pea *n* kacang polong

peace *n* perdamaian; ~ *of mind* ketenteraman hati; **peaceful** *adj* damai,

tenteram, tenang

peach *n* buah persik

peacock *n, m* burung merak

peak *n, adj* puncak; ~ *hour* jam-jam sibuk (di jalan); ~ *season* musim ramai; *v* memuncak

peanut *n* kacang tanah; ~ *butter* selai kacang, pindakas; ~ *sauce* bumbu kacang

pear *n* [pér] buah pir

pearl *n* mutiara

peasant *n* [pézent] petani

peck *v* mematuk

peculiar *adj* [pekyulier] aneh, ganjil; ~ *to* khas

pedal *n* [pédel] injakan kaki, pedal; *v* mengayuh (sepeda)

pedestrian *n* [pedéstrien] pejalan kaki; ~ *crossing* penyeberangan jalan

pediatrician *n* [pidiatrisyen] dokter anak-anak

pedicab *n* [pedikab] becak

pedicure *n* pedikur, perawatan kaki

pedigree *n* [pédigri] trah; silsilah

pee *v, sl* kencing, pipis; *to have a* ~ kencing

535

peek *v* mengintip, menengok sejenak

peel *n* kulit (buah); *v* mengelupas; menguliti, mengupas; **peeler** *n* alat pengupas

peep *v* mengintip, mengintai; menengok; **peephole** *n* lubang pengintai

peer *v* melihat dengan susah

peg *n* pasak; sangkutan; patokan; *v* mematok, memasak; ~ *doll* boneka pasak; *(clothes)* ~ jepitan (baju)

pelican *n* [pélikan] burung pelikan, burung undan

pelvis *n* panggul, tulang pinggul

pen *n* pena, kalam; bolpoin, pulpen; ~ *name* nama samaran

penalize *v* menghukum; **penalty** *n* denda, hukuman, penalti

pencil *n* pensil; ~ *case* tempat pensil; ~ *sharpener* rautan pensil

penetrate *v* tembus; menerobos, menembus; **penetration** *n* penerobosan, penembusan, penetrasi

penguin *n* pinguin

penicillin *n* penisilin

peninsula *n* [peninsula] semenanjung

penis *n* [pinis] penis, zakar

penknife *n* [pén naif] pisau lipat ← **pen**

penny *n* pence *n, pl* sen Inggris

penpal *n* sahabat pena

pension *n* [pénsyen] pensiun; **pensioner** *n* orang pensiunan

penthouse *n* [pént haus] apartemen (mewah)

people *n, pl* [pipel] orang, bangsa, rakyat, kaum

pepper *n* merica, lada; *salt and* ~ garam merica; **peppermint** *adj* mentol; *n* permen

per *prep* setiap, tiap, per; *two dollars* ~ *person* satu orang dua dolar

percent *adj* persen; **percentage** *n* persentase

perch *n* tempat bertengger di sangkar burung; sejenis ikan; *v* bertengger

percolator *n* penyaring kopi

percussion *n* perkusi

perfect *adj* [pérfekt]

sempurna; *v* [perfékt] menyempurnakan

perforate *v* melubangi

perform *v* melakukan, menyelenggarakan, memainkan (peran); **performance** *n* pertunjukan; **performer** *n* pemain, pemeran; **performing** ~ *arts* seni peran, musik dan tari

perfume *n* wewangian, minyak wangi, parfum; wangi

perhaps *n* mungkin, barangkali

period *n* [piried] zaman, masa, kala, waktu; titik; *coll* datang bulan, haid; **periodical** *n* terbitan berkala, majalah

periscope *n* periskop

perk *n, sl* untung, sisi baik; ~ *up* menjadi bersemangat

permanent *adj* tetap, permanen; ~ *resident* penghuni tetap

permission *n* izin; **permissive** *adj* serba boleh; **permit** *n* surat izin; *v* mengizinkan, memperboleh

perpendicular *adj, n* tegak lurus

persecute *v* menyiksa, mengejar-ngejar

persevere *v* bertekun, gigih

Persian *adj* berasal dari Persia; ~ *cat* kucing angora

persist *v* tetap (melakukan), bertekun, bertahan; **persistent** *adj* gigih, tekun

person *n* **people** [pipel] orang, pribadi; *in* ~ sendiri; **personal** *adj* pribadi; perorangan; **personality** *n* kepribadian; tokoh; **personally** *adv* secara perorangan; **personnel** *n* [pérsonél] personalia, para karyawan

perspiration *n* [pérspirésyen] keringat, peluh

persuade *v* [pérsuéd] meyakinkan; **persuasive** *adj* meyakinkan

pervert *n* orang yang mengidap kelainan seksual; orang yang suka mengintip

pessimist *n* orang pesimis; **pessimistic** *adj* pesimis, bersangka buruk

pest *n* hama; gangguan; **pester** *v* mengganggu, mengusik

pesticide *n* [péstisaid]
pestisida, obat pembasmi
serangga

pestle *n* alu

pet *adj* kesayangan; *n*
hewan peliharaan; ~ *shop*
toko yang menjual hewan
peliharaan dan keperluan-
nya; *teacher's* ~ murid
kesayangan; *v* mengelus

petal *n* [pétel] daun bunga

petition *n* [petisyen] permohonan, petisi; *v* memohon

petrol *n* bensin; **petroleum**
n [petrolium] minyak bumi
olahan

petticoat *n* rok dalam

petting *n* cumbuan ← **pet**

petty *adj* kecil, remeh,
sepele; ~ *cash* uang kecil;
coll uang receh

phantom *n* [fantom] hantu,
momok

pharmacist *n* [farmasist]
apoteker; **pharmacy** *n*
apotik

phase *n* [féiz] tahap, masa;
~ *out* menghapus secara
bertahap

Ph.D. *abbrev Doctor of
Philosophy* S3

phenomenon *n* fenomena

philanthropist *n* [filan-
tropist] dermawan

Philippines [filipins] *the* ~
Filipina

philosopher *n* [filosofer]
filsuf, ahli filsafat; **philosophy** *n* (ilmu) filsafat

phlegm *n* [flém] dahak

phobia *n* penyakit ketakutan,
fobi

phone *n, sl* telepon; ~ *book*
daftar nomor telepon; ~
box telepon umum; *on the*
~ sedang telepon; *v* menelepon ← **telephone**

phonetic *adj* fonetik, sesuai
dengan abjad

photo *n, sl* foto; **photocopy**
n fotokopi; ~ *machine* mesin
fotokopi; *v* memfotokopi;
photograph *n* foto, potret,
gambar; *v* memotret; **photographer** *n* tukang foto,
tukang potret, fotografer;
photography *n* potret-
memotret, fotografi

phrase *n* [fréz] frasa, ke-
lampok kata; **phrasebook** *n*
buku ungkapan bahasa asing

physical *adj* (secara) fisik;
jasmani

physics *n, pl* ilmu fisika

physiotherapy *n* fisioterapi
pianist *n* [pienist] pemain
piano; **piano** *n* piano; ~
key tuts piano
pick *n* pilihan; beliung; *first*
~ pilihan pertama; *v* memilih; mencungkil; memetik; ~
flowers memetik bunga; ~
on mengganggu, mengusik;
~ *up* mengambil; menjem-
put; ~ *your nose* mengupil
picket ~ *fence* pagar kayu;
~ *line* barisan pemogok
pickle *n* [pikel] acar; *v*
mengasinkan
pickpocket *n* copet, pen-
copet
pickup *n* pikap
picnic *n* piknik
picture *n* gambar, lukisan; *v*
membayangkan; melukiskan;
in the ~ sudah tahu
pie *n* pai; sejenis kue
piece *n* [pis] potong, keping,
bagian; *a* ~ *of music*
sebuah lagu; *v* ~ *together*
menyusun
pier *n* [pir] jeti, dermaga,
pelabuhan
pierce *v* [pirs] menembus,
menindik, menusuk
pig *n* babi; orang yang

bengis atau jorok; ~-*headed*
keras kepala
pigeon *n* [pijen] burung
merpati, burung dara;
pigeonhole *n* kotak pribadi
piggybank *n* [pigibank]
celengan
pigment *n* pigmen, zat warna
pigsty *n* [pigstai] kandang
babi
pigtail *n* ekor kuda; kepang
dua
pile *n* timbunan; *v* menimbun
pilgrim *n* haji; peziarah; **pil-**
grimage *n* ziarah, peziarah;
to make a ~ berziarah; *to*
make the ~ naik haji
pill *n* pil, obat; *the (contra-*
ceptive) ~ pil KB; **pillbox**
n tempat obat
pillar *n* [piler] tiang, soko
guru; ~ *box* bis surat
pillow *n* [pilo] bantal; ~
case, ~ *slip* sarung bantal
pilot *adj* percontohan; *n* pilot,
penerbang, pandu; contoh
pimple *n* [pimpel] jerawat
pin *n* peniti; *v* menyematkan
pinafore *n* [pinafor] sejenis
rok anak
pincers *n, pl* sepit, capit

539

pinch *n* cubitan; sedikit; *a* ~ *of salt* sedikit garam; *v* mencubit

pine *n* ~ *(tree)* pohon pinus

pineapple *n* nanas

pingpong *n* tenis meja, pingpong

pink *adj* merah muda, merah jambu, pink

pint *n* [paint] ukuran cairan sebesar seperdelapan galon (0.568 liter)

pioneer *n* [payonir] perintis, pelopor; *v* memelopori

pipe *n* pipa; *v* menyalurkan; **pipeline** *n* saluran pipa

pirate *n* [pairat] bajak laut, pembajak; **pirated** *adj* bajakan

pit *n* lubang, terowongan dalam tambang; biji (buah); *v* mengadu

pitch *n* pola titinada; lempar-an (bisbol); usaha; *v* melemparkan; ~*dark*, ~ *black* gelap gulita; **pitcher** *n* pelempar; kendi, tempat air

pitiful *adj* [pitiful] memelas, menyedihkan; **pity** *n* belas kasihan; *v* mengasihani; *what a* ~ sayang (sekali); *to*

have ~ *on, to take* ~ *on* mengasihani

pixie *n* [piksi] peri, makhluk halus

place *n* tempat; kedudukan; ~ *card* kartu nama tempat duduk; ~ *mat* tatakan piring; *first* ~ pemenang, juara; *my* ~ rumah (saya); ~ *of worship* rumah ibadah; *in* ~ *of* sebagai pengganti; *v* menempatkan, meletakkan; *to take* ~ terjadi, berlangsung

plagiarism [pléjerizem] *n* plagiat

plague *n* [plég] penyakit sampar, wabah; *v* sangat mengganggu

plain *adj* polos; sederhana, bersahaja; nyata; *n* medan, dataran; **plainly** *adv* terus terang

plait *n* [plat] kepang; *v* mengepang

plan *n* rencana, rancangan, bagan, denah; *v* merancang, merencanakan; **planning** *n* perencanaan

plane *n, sl* pesawat terbang ← **aeroplane**

planet *n* planet; ~ *Earth* Bumi

plank *n* papan

planner *n* perencana; *daily ~* buku agenda ← **plan**

plant *n* tetumbuhan, tanaman; pabrik; *v* menanam, menanamkan; **plantation** *n* perkebunan

plaster *n* kapur, gips, plester; *~ cast* gips; *v* memasang secara sembarangan

plastic *adj, n* plastik; *~ bag* keresek, kantong plastik; *~ surgery* bedah plastik

plate *n* piring; pelat; *number ~* pelat polisi

plateau *n* [plato] dataran tinggi

platform *n* peron; panggung; *~ heels* hak tinggi yang tebal

platinum *n* [platinum] platina, emas putih

play *n* pertunjukan, sandiwara; permainan; *v* main, bermain; memainkan; *~ along* berpura-pura kerjasama; *~ around* berfoya-foya; *~ back v* memutar kembali; *~ down* mengecilkan; *~ truant* membolos dari sekolah; **playboy** *n* lelaki yang suka mempermainkan perempuan; seorang Arjuna; **player**

n pemain; **playground** *n* tempat bermain, tempat ayunan; **playpen** *n* boks (bayi); **playwright** *n* pengarang drama

plaza *n* alun-alun

plea *n* permohonan, permintaan; pembelaan, dalih

pleasant *adj* [plézant] menyenangkan, enak, nyaman, nikmat; sopan; **please** tolong; silahkan; coba; *~ help me* tolong bantu saya; *~ sit down* silahkan duduk; *~ try* cobalah; *v* menyenangkan; **pleasure** *n* [plézyur] kesukaan, kenikmatan

pledge *v* [pléj] berjanji, berikrar; menjanjikan

plenty *adj* banyak, cukup

plot *n* sebidang tanah; alur cerita; komplotan; *v* merencanakan; berkomplot, bersekongkol

plow, plough *n* [plau] bajak; *v* membajak

plug *n* sumbat; steker, stopkontak; *v* menyumbat

plum *n* buah prem

plumber *n* [plamer] tukang ledeng

plump *adj* tambun, subur

plunder *v* merampas, menjarah

plunge *n, v* terjun, cemplung

plural *adj* jamak

plus [plas] *n* nilai plus; *v* plus, ditambah

pm *post meridiem* siang, sore, malam (jam 12.00–24.00)

PM *abbrev Prime Minister* PM (Perdana Menteri)

pneumonia *n* [nyumonia] radang paru-paru

PNG *abbrev Papua New Guinea* PNG (Papua Nugini)

pocket *n* saku, kantong, kocek; ~ *money* uang saku, uang jajan; *v* mengantungi; **pocketknife** *n* [poketnaif] pisau lipat

poem *n* [poem] syair, pantun; **poet** *n* penyair; **poetry** *n* puisi

point *n* titik, noktah; tanjung; ~*blank* langsung, terus terang; *compass* ~ mata angin; ~ *of view* (sudut) pandangan, pendapat; *beside the* ~ tidak penting; *to the* ~ tepat, pendek; *v* menunjuk, menunjukkan; ~

out menunjukkan; **pointed** *adj* runcing, tajam; **pointless** *adj* tiada gunanya

poison *n* racun; bisa; *food* ~*ing* keracunan makanan; *v* meracuni; **poisonous** *adj* beracun, berbisa

poke *v* menyodok, menusuk

Poland *n* Polandia ← **Pole**

polar *adj* berhubungan dengan kutub; ~ *bear* beruang kutub; **pole** *n* kutub

pole *n* tiang

police *n* [polis] polisi; ~ *station* kantor polisi, pos polisi; **policeman** *n, m* polisi; **policewoman** *n, f* polisi wanita (polwan)

policy *n* kebijaksanaan; *insurance* ~ polis (asuransi)

polio *n* penyakit lumpuh layuh, penyakit polio

polish *n* pelitur, semir; *shoe* ~ semir sepatu; *v* menggosok, menyemir

polite *adj* sopan (santun); **politeness** *n* kesopanan, kesopan-santunan

political *adj* politik; **politician** *n* [politisyen] politikus, politisi; **politics** *n* [ilmu] politik poll *n* pemberian suara; *opinion* ~ jajak pendapat

pollute *v* mencemarkan; **polluted** *adj* tercemar; **pollution** *n* pencemaran, kecemaran, polusi; *air* ~ polusi udara

polo *n* polo

polygamy *n* poligami

pond *n* kolam

pony *n* kuda kerdil, kuda poni; **ponytail** *n* ekor kuda

poo, pooh *n, sl* tahi; *v* berak

pool *n* kolam (renang); bilyar; pul

poor *adj* miskin, papa; hina, malang

pop *n* ~ *(musik)* lagu pop, musik populer ← **popular**

pop *v* meletup; ~ *in*, ~ *over* mampir; ~ *up* muncul

Pope *the* ~ Sri Paus

poppy *n* bunga opium, bunga madat

popular *adj* populer, laku; **population** *n* (jumlah) penduduk, populasi

porcelain *adj, n* porselen, keramik

porch *n* serambi, beranda, teras

porcupine *n* [porkyupain] landak

pore *n* pori

pork *n* daging babi

pornography *n* pornografi

porpoise *n* [porpus] lumba-lumba

porridge *n* [porij] bubur

port *adj* kiri (di kapal); *n* pelabuhan; lubang, colok-an; anggur port

portable *adj* dapat dibawa ke mana-mana, jinjing

porter *n* kuli

portfolio *n* tas, map, sampul; koleksi

porthole *n* [port hol] ting-kapan kapal

portion *n* porsi, bagian

portrait *n* potret, lukisan, gambar

Portugal *n* Portugal; **Portuguese** *adj* [Portugis] ber-asal dari Portugal; *n* bahasa Portugal

pose *n* [poz] gaya, lagak; *v* bergaya

position *n* [posisyen] letak, kedudukan, pangkat, jabatan; keadaan

positive *adj, n* positif, pasti, tentu

possess v memiliki, mempunyai; **possession** n kepunyaan, (harta) milik; **possessive** adj [pozésif] ingin memiliki, posesif

possibility n kemungkinan; **possible** adj [posibel] mungkin; **possibly** adv barangkali, mungkin

possum, opossum n semacam binatang malam seperti tupai

post adj sesudah, pasca; ~-graduate pascasarjana; ~-mortem otopsi

post n pos; jabatan; tiang; layanan pos; ~ office kantor pos; v mengeposkan; menempelkan; **postage** n [postej] perangko, ongkos kirim; **postcard** n kartu pos; **poster** n plakat, gambar

postman n tukang pos ← **post**

postpone v menunda, mengundurkan

posture n [postyur] sikap badan, postur

pot n pot, periuk, tempat bunga, tempat tanaman; ~ belly gendut; ~ luck bisa baik, bisa tidak; seadanya;

~ scourer penggosok panci

potato n [potéto] kentang; ~ chips kentang goreng; ~ crisps kripik kentang

potential adj mungkin, berpeluang, calon; n kemungkinan, kekuatan, tenaga

pothole n [pot hol] lubang di jalan

potter n perajin tembikar; **pottery** n tembikar, pecah belah, keramik

poultry n [poltri] unggas

pound n pon; tempat penerimaan barang yang hilang; ~ sterling pon sterling, pon Inggris; v menumbuk; memukul-mukul

pour v mengalir; menuangkan, mencurahkan; menyiram; ~ (with rain) hujan lebat

poverty n [poverti] kemiskinan

POW abbrev prisoner-of-war tawanan perang

powder n [pauder] bubuk, serbuk, puyer; bedak; ~ed milk susu bubuk; v membedaki

power n kekuasaan, kekuatan, daya, tenaga; **powerful**

adj berkuasa, kuat

practical *n* praktis, berguna; **practically** *adv* hampir-hampir, benar-benar; **practice** *n* praktek, kebiasaan, adat; latihan; mempraktekkan, melatih

praise *n* [préiz] pujian; *v* memuji; ~ *the Lord* puji Tuhan

pram *n* kereta bayi, kereta anak-anak ← **perambulator**

prank *n* gurauan, permainan

prawn *n* udang

pray *v* berdoa, sholat, bersembahyang; **prayer** *n* [préir] doa, sembahyang; ~ *beads* *Isl* tasbih; *Cath* rosario; ~ *mat* sejadah

pre- *pref* [pri] pra-, sebelum; ~*-school* taman kanak-kanak (TK)

preacher *n* pemuka agama; *Isl* khatib, dai

precaution *n* tindakan pencegahan

precious *adj* [présyus] berharga, mahal; mulia; ~ *metal* logam mulia

precise *adj* tepat, saksama; **precision** *n* kesaksamaan, ketelitian

predator *n* [prédater] pemangsa, pemakan hewan lain

predict *v* meramalkan; **prediction** *n* ramalan

preface *n* [préfas] pendahuluan, kata pengantar, prakata

prefer *v* lebih suka, memilih; **preferably** *adv* [préferabli] lebih baik; **preference** *n* kecenderungan, pilihan

prefix *n* awalan

pregnancy *n* (masa) kehamilan; **pregnant** *adj* hamil, mengandung

prehistoric *adj* prasejarah

prejudice *n* [préjudis] prasangka; **prejudiced** *adj* berprasangka

preliminary *adj* pendahuluan, persiapan, awal

premature *adj* prematur, sebelum waktunya, pradini

premier *adj* utama, terbaik

premiere *n* [prémiér] pemutaran perdana, pertunjukan perdana

prepaid *adj* prabayar; *v, pf* → **prepay**

preparation *n* [préparésyen] persiapan; **prepare** *v* menyiapkan, mempersiap-kan; **prepared** adj siap, bersedia

prepay v membayar di muka

preposition n [préposisyen] kata depan

prerequisite n [prirekuisit] prasyarat, syarat

prescription n resep

presence n [prézens] hadirat, hadapan; kehadir-an; **present** adj [prézent] sekarang, kini; hadir; n hadiah, kado, pemberian; at ~ sekarang ini; v [prezént] menyajikan, memper-sembahkan; **presentation** n penyajian, presentasi; **presently** adv segera

preservation n [préservé-syen] perlindungan; preservasi; **preservative** n [presérvativ] pengawet; **preserve** n [presérv] cagar; selai; v mengawetkan, melindungi, memelihara

president n presiden; ketua

press n percetakan; pers; alat penekan; ~ agency kantor berita; ~ clipping guntingan koran; ~

conference jumpa pers; ~ gallery ruang wartawan; in ~ sedang dicetak; v menekan, menindih, mendesak; ~ on maju, menekan; **pressure** n [présyur] tekanan

prestigious adj bergengsi

presumably adv kiranya, agaknya; **presume** v men-ganggap; mengira

pretend v berpura-pura, berdalih

pretty adj [priti] manis, cantik, molek; adv cukup

pretzel n cemilan kering yang asin

prevent v [prevént] mencegah, menghalangi, menangkis; **prevention** n pencegahan

preview n previu

previous adj yang dahulu, yang sebelumnya

price n harga; ~ list daftar harga; **priceless** adj tidak ternilai

prick n tusukan; v menusuk; **prickly** adj tajam, berduri, menusuk

pride n kesombongan, kebanggaan, harga diri

priest *n, Cath* [prist] pastor; *Hin* pedanda

primary *adj* pertama, terpenting, dasar; ~ *school* sekolah dasar (SD); **prime** *adj* perdana, utama; ~ *minister (PM)* Perdana Menteri (PM)

primitive *adj* sederhana, primitif

prince *n, m* pangeran; **princess** *n, f* putri, permaisuri

principal *adj* utama; *n* kepala sekolah; uang pokok

principle *n* [prinsipel] asas, prinsip; *in* ~ pada prinsipnya, pada dasarnya; *on* ~ karena keyakinan

print *n* tapak (kaki); gambar, reproduksi; tulisan, ketikan; *fine* ~ tulisan kecil; *in* ~ masih dicetak; *out of* ~ sudah tidak dicetak lagi; *v* mencetak; menulis dengan huruf cetak; **printer** *n* printer, pencetak; ~*s* percetakan; **printout** *n* hasil cetak

prior *adj* [praior] terlebih dahulu; **priority** *n* prioritas

prison *n* [prizon] penjara; *in* ~ dipenjara; **prisoner** *n* orang yang dipenjara,

terpidana

private *adj* [praivet] pribadi; swasta; milik sendiri; ~ *sector* (perusahaan) swasta; *in* ~ tidak di depan umum

privilege *n* [privilej] hak istimewa

prize *n* hadiah; *v* menilai tinggi

pro *adj* pro, setuju dengan

probably *adv* kemungkinan besar, mungkin

problem *n* masalah, soal

procedure *n* prosedur, tata cara; **proceed** *v* maju, jalan; meneruskan; **process** *n* cara, proses; *v* memproses, mengolah; ~*ed meat* daging olahan; **procession** *n* arak-arakan, prosesi

proclaim *v* menyatakan, memproklamasikan, mengumumkan; **proclamation** *n* proklamasi, pengumuman

produce *n* hasil; *v* menghasilkan; **producer** *n* produsen; **product** *n* hasil, produk; **production** *n* produksi, pertunjukan

profession *n* profesi, pekerjaan; pernyataan; **professional** *adj* profesional

professor *n* guru besar

profile *n* profil

profit *n* untung, keuntungan, laba; ~ *and loss* laba rugi; *v* beruntung, memperoleh keuntungan; **profitable** *adj* menguntungkan

program, programme *n* acara, program; *v* memprogram

progress *n* kemajuan; *v* maju; *in* ~ sedang berlangsung; **progressive** *adj* berpikiran maju, progresif

prohibit *v* melarang

project *n* proyek; *v* memproyeksikan; **projector** *n* proyektor

prominent *adj* terkemuka, menonjol

promise *n* [promis] janji; *v* berjanji; menjanjikan

promote *v* memajukan, menaikkan pangkat, mempromosikan; **promotion** *n* kenaikan pangkat; promosi

prompt *adj* cepat; *n* bisikan

pronoun *n* kata ganti

pronounce *v* melafalkan; menyatakan; **pronunciation** *n* lafal

proof *n* bukti; ~*read* mengoreksi naskah

prop *n* penopang, sangga; alat-alat yang diperlukan di panggung

propeller *n* baling-baling

proper *adj* benar, betul, patut, layak; **properly** *adv* benar-benar, dengan betul

property *n* kepunyaan, (harta) milik; sifat

prophet *n* nabi, rasul; *Isl the* ~ *(Muhammad)* Nabi Mohammad (s.a.w.)

proportion *n* perbandingan, proporsi

proposal *n* usul; lamaran; **propose** *v* mengusulkan; meminang

prosecute *v* menuntut; **prosecution** *n* pihak penuntut; **prosecutor** *n* jaksa, penuntut

prosper *v* berhasil, menjadi makmur; **prosperous** *adj* makmur

prostate *n* (kelenjar) prostat

prostitute *n* [prostitut] pelacur, pekerja seks komersial (PSK), wanita tunasusila (WTS)

protect *v* melindungi;

protection *n* perlindungan; **protective** *adj* [protéktif] bersifat melindungi; pencegah

protest *n* protes, pembangkangan, unjuk rasa; *v* memprotes, melawan, membangkang, berunjuk rasa; **Protestant** *adj* Kristen; *n* orang Kristen

proud *adj* bangga; angkuh, sombong

prove *v* [pruv] membuktikan; **proven** *adj* ternyata, terbukti

proverb *n* peribahasa

provide *v* menyediakan, membekali, melengkapi; **provided, providing** ~ *(that)* asal, asalkan

province *n* propinsi; **provincial** *adj* berhubungan dengan provinsi; picik, kampungan

provoke *v* menghasut, memancing

prune *n* buah prem kering

PS *abbrev postscript* catatan tambahan pada akhir surat

PS *abbrev primary school* SD (sekolah dasar)

pseudonym *n* [siudonim] nama samaran

psychiatric [saikiatrik] ~ *hospital* rumah sakit jiwa; **psychiatrist** *n* [saikayetrist] psikiater, ahli jiwa

psychic *adj, n* [saikik] mempunyai indera keenam, cenayang

psychologist *n* psikolog, ahli ilmu jiwa; **psychology** *n* ilmu jiwa, psikologi

PTO *abbrev please turn over* di halaman berikut

Pty Ltd, Pte *Proprietary Limited* PT (Perseroan Terbatas), CV, NV

puberty *n* masa puber, pubertas; **pubic** *adj* ~ *hair* bulu yang tumbuh di sekitar kemaluan

public *n* orang banyak, umum; ~ *health* kesehatan masyarakat; ~ *relations* (PR) hubungan masyarakat (humas); ~ *servant* pegawai negeri; *in* ~ di depan umum; **publication** *n* terbitan, keluaran; pengumuman

publish *v* menerbitkan, mengeluarkan, mengumumkan; **publisher** *n* penerbit

pudding *n* puding, pencuci mulut, podeng

puddle *n* [padel] genangan

puff *n* embusan; isapan; tiupan; *v* terengah-engah; mengepul; meniup

puke *v, sl* muntah

pull *n* tarikan, daya tarik; *v* [pul] menarik; ~ *back* menarik ke samping; mundur; ~ *down* menarik ke bawah; membongkar, merobohkan; ~ *out* batal; mencabut; ~ *over* minggir, menepi; **pullover** *n* switer, baju hangat

pulp *n* bubur; daging buah; ampas; *wood* ~ bubur kayu

pulse *n* nadi

pumice *n* [pamis] batu apung

pump *n* pompa; *v* memompa

pumpkin *n* labu

punch *n* pukulan, tonjokan; *v* menghantam, meninju, menonjok

punctual *adj* tepat waktu; **punctuality** *n* sikap selalu tepat waktu

punctuation *n* [pangktyué-syen] pemberian tanda-tanda baca; ~ *mark* tanda baca

punish *v* [panisy] meng-hukum; **punishment** *n* hukuman

pupil *n* murid; anak mata, pupil

puppet *n* boneka; wayang; **puppeteer** *n* dalang

puppy *n* [papi] anak anjing

purchase *n* [perces] pem-belian, belanjaan; *v* mem-beli

pure *adj* murni, bersih

purple *adj* ungu, lembayung

purpose *n* maksud, niat, tujuan; *on* ~ dengan sengaja

purr *n* dengkur (kucing); *v* mendengkur

purse *n* dompet

purser *n* penata usaha di kapal atau pesawat terbang

pursue *v* mengejar, mengi-kuti, memburu

push *n* [pusy] dorongan; *v* mendorong; ~ *in* menye-robot, mendorong masuk; ~ *off* pergi; **pusher** *n* kereta anak; **pushy** *adj* suka memaksa kehendak, lancang

puss, pussycat *n, sl* [pus, pusikat] kucing

put *v* **put put** [put] meletak-

kan, menaruh, menyimpan;
menempatkan; ~ *down*
memadamkan; mereme-
hkan; menyuntik mati
binatang; ~ *on weight*
menjadi lebih gemuk; ~ *off*
menunda, mengundurkan;
~ *up* memasang; menginap;
~ *up with* tahan; ~~*down*
hinaan

puzzle *n* [pazel] mainan,
teka-teki; **puzzled** *adj*
[pazeld] bingung

pygmy *adj* [pigmi] kerdil

pyjamas, pajamas *n, pl*
piyama, baju tidur

pyramid *n* piramida

python *n* [paithon] ular
sanca, piton

Q

quadrilateral *adj, n* segi
empat

quadruple *v* [kuodrupel]
berlipat empat

quadruplet *n* [kuodruplet]
kembar empat

quail *n* burung puyuh

quaint *adj* kuno, aneh

quake *n* gempa; *v* gemetar

qualification *n* kualifikasi, ijazah; **qualified** *adj*
berkualifikasi, berhak,
berijazah; **qualify** *v* memenuhi syarat, lolos

quality *n* mutu, kualitas;
sifat

quantity *n* [kuontiti] banyaknya, kuantitas

quarantine *n* [kuorantin]
karantina

quarrel *n* [kuorel] pertengkaran, percekcokan; *v*
bertengkar, ribut

quart *n* [kuort] ukuran
cairan (944 ml)

quarter *n* [kuorter] perempat; kampung, daerah,
lingkungan; *three* ~*s* tiga
perempat

quartet *n* [kuortét] empat
sekawan, kwartet

quay *n* [ki] dermaga

queen *n* ratu

queer *adj* aneh; *adj, n, sl*
homoseksual

query *n* [kuiri] pertanyaan;
v menanyakan, meragukan

quest *n* pencarian; *in* ~ *of*
mencari

551

R

question n pertanyaan; masalah, soal; ~ *mark* tanda tanya; *out of the* ~ tidak mungkin; *without* ~ tentu saja, niscaya; v bertanya; menanyai, menanyakan; meragukan; mempersoalkan; **questionnaire** n [kuéstionér] angket

queue n [kyu] antre, antrean; v antri, berantri

quick adj cepat; **quicken** v menjadi lebih cepat

quid n, sl pon sterling

quiet adj [kuayet] teduh, tenang; *to be* ~ diam; *on the* ~ diam-diam; n keteduhan, ketenangan; **quieten** v menenangkan, meredakan

quilt n selimut tebal

quinine n [kuinin] kina

quit v **quit quit** putus asa, berhenti, meninggalkan

quite adv cukup sama, rada, lumayan

quiz n kuis, ulangan singkat, tanya jawab; v menanyai

quota n jatah, kuota

quotation n kutipan; penawaran; ~ *marks* tanda kutip; **quote** v mengutip, menyebut, mencatat

R. *river* S. (sungai)

rabbi n [rabai] pendeta Yahudi

rabbit n kelinci

rabies n [rébis] penyakit anjing gila, rabies

raccoon n sejenis musang, rakun

race n lomba, balap, pacuan; v berlomba, membalap; **racecourse** n pacuan kuda; **racehorse** n kuda pacu, kuda balap; **racetrack** n sirkuit; pacuan kuda

race n (suku) bangsa, ras; **racism** n [résizem] rasisme, pembedaan rasial; **racist** adj rasis; n orang yang membenci suku bangsa lain

rack n rak; *luggage* ~ tempat barang

racket, racquet n raket

radiation n radiasi, penyinaran

radical adj [radikel] radikal, ekstrem; n orang radikal

radio n [rédio] radio

radioactive adj [rédioaktif] radioaktif

radish n [radisy] lobak

radius n [rédius] jari-jari,

radius

RAF *abbrev Royal Air Force* Angkatan Udara Kerajaan (Inggris)

raffle *n* [rafel] undian; *v* mengundi

raft *n* rakit; *white water* ~*ing* arung jeram

rag *n* lap, kain jelek; *in* ~*s* compang-camping

rage *n* kemarahan, geram; *all the* ~ sangat digemari

raid *n* razia, serangan, penggerebekan; *v* merazia, menyerang, menyerbu; **raider** *n* perompak

rail *n* rel; *by* ~ dengan kereta api; **railing** *n* susuran; **railroad, railway** *n* jalan kereta api; ~ *station* stasiun kereta api

rain *n, v* hujan; *heavy* ~ hujan deras; *light* ~ gerimis; **rainbow** *n* pelangi, bianglala; **raincoat** *n* jas hujan; **rainfall** *n* curah hujan; **rainy** *adj* banyak hujan; ~ *season* musim hujan

raise *v* mengangkat, menaikkan, meninggikan; membesarkan (anak-anak); menimbulkan

raisin *n* kismis

rake *n* penggaruk; *v* menggaruk, menyapu

rally *n* reli; pertemuan; *v* berkumpul, berhimpun

ram *n* biri-biri jantan; *v* membenturkan

ramp *n* jalur mendaki, jalur yang melandai

ran *v, pf* → **run**

ranch *n* peternakan, pertanian

random *at* ~ secara sembarangan, membabi buta

rang *v, pf* → **ring**

range *n* [rénj] jajaran, barisan; kisaran, jangkauan; lapangan, tempat; *v* berkisar; **ranger** *n* penjaga hutan

rank *n* pangkat, derajat; *v* menduduki; mengatur, menyusun; menggolongkan; **ranking** *n* urutan

ransom *n* (uang) tebusan, penebusan

rap *n* musik rap; ketukan; *v* mengetuk

rape *n* perkosaan, pemerkosaan; *v* memerkosa, menggagahi

rapid *adj* [rapid] cepat, lekas; **rapids** *n, pl* jeram

rapist n pemerkosa ← **rape**

rare adj mentah; jarang; **rarely** adv jarang

rascal n bangsat

rash n gatal-gatal; nappy ~ ruam popok

raspberry n frambozen

rat n tikus (besar); ~ poison racun tikus; ~ race kehidupan kota yang amat sibuk

rate n tarif, perbandingan, angka; kecepatan; birth ~ angka kelahiran; exchange ~ kurs; at any ~ bagaimanapun; v menilai; **rated** adj dinilai, dianggap

rather adv agak, rada, cukup; melainkan; ~ than daripada

rating n penilaian

ratio n [résyio] perbandingan

ration n rangsum, jatah; v merangsum

rational adj rasional, masuk akal

rattan n rotan

rave n ~ (party) pesta dansa

raven n burung gagak

raw adj mentah; kasar; ~ materials bahan mentah; ~ silk sutera kasar

ray n sinar; ikan pari

razor n pisau cukur

Rd Road Jl (Jalan), Jl Ry (Jalan Raya)

reach n jangkauan; v sampai, tiba, mencapai; menghubungi

react v [riakt] bereaksi; menanggapi; **reaction** n tanggapan, reaksi; **reactive** adj reaktif

read v read read [réd] membaca; ~ aloud membaca dengan suara keras; ~ to membacakan; ~ the Koran mengaji; ~ someone's mind membaca pikiran orang; **reader** n pembaca; buku bacaan

reading n membaca; bacaan ← **read**

ready adj [rédi] siap, sedia; selesai, sudah; ~ to use siap pakai

real adj nyata, betul, sejati; adv sangat, benar-benar; ~-life story kisah sejati; **reality** n kenyataan, realitas; **realize** v sadar; mewujudkan, melaksanakan; **realistic** adj realistis; **really** adv sangat, benar-benar

rear adj, n (bagian)

belakang; pantat; ~ *view mirror* kaca spion; *at the ~* di belakang; *v* membesarkan
reason *n* sebab, alasan; akal (budi); *within ~* yang pantas, yang masuk akal; *without ~*, *no ~* tanpa sebab; *v* berunding; **reasonable** *adj* masuk akal
rebel *n* [rébel] pemberontak; *v* [rebél] memberontak; **rebellion** *n* pemberontakan
recall *n* [rikol] ingatan; pemanggilan kembali; *v* ingat; memanggil kembali, menarik kembali
receipt *n* [risit] kuitansi, tanda terima, struk; penerimaan; *on ~ of* setelah menerima; **receive** *v* menerima, mendapat, memperoleh; menyambut; **receiver** *n* (pesawat) penerima
recent *adj* baru; **recently** *adv* baru-baru ini
reception *n* resepsi; penyambutan; tangkapan ← **receive**
recess *n* istirahat; *in ~* sedang istirahat, tidak bersidang
recharge *v* mengecas, mengisi ulang

recipe *n* [résipi] resep
recital *n* pertunjukan, konser; **recite** *v* membaca dari luar kepala, mendeklamasikan
reckon *v* menghitung; *sl* pikir
reclaim *v* memperoleh kembali; menguruk pantai; **reclamation** *n* pengurukan pantai, reklamasi
recognition *n* pengenalan; penghargaan; **recognize** *v* mengenal, mengenali; mengakui, menghargai
recommend *v* menganjurkan; memuji; **recommendation** *n* rekomendasi, saran
record *n* [rékord] catatan; daftar; rekor; piringan hitam; dokumen; *~s* arsip; *off the ~* (pernyataan) tidak resmi; *to break a ~* memecahkan rekor; *v* [rekord] mencatat, mendaftar, merekam
recorder *n* semacam suling
recover *v* [rikaver] sembuh, pulih; menemukan kembali, menyelamatkan
recreation *n* [rékriésyen] hiburan, rekreasi

recruit *n* rekrut; *v* merekrut;
   recruitment *n* penerimaan
   pegawai
rectangle *n* [rektanggel]
   empat persegi panjang
recycle *v* [risaikel] didaur
   ulang; **recycling** *n* daur
   ulang
red *adj* merah; ~ *Cross*
   Palang Merah; ~ *tape* birokrasi; *caught ~~handed*
   tertangkap basah; **redden** *v*
   memerah
redhead *n* [rédhéd] orang
   yang berambut merah
reduce *v* mengurangi,
   memperkecil; **reduction** *n*
   potongan, pengurangan,
   penurunan, reduksi
reef *n* (batu) karang
ref. *reference* rujukan
refer *v* mengacu; menunjukkan; mengenai; **referee** *n*
   wasit; **reference** *n* surat
   keterangan, referensi;
   referral *n* (surat) rujukan
refill *n* isi ulang; pengisian
   kembali
refine *v* menghaluskan,
   menyaring; **refinery** *n*
   kilang
reflect *v* membayang; men-

cerminkan, memantulkan;
   merenung, merenungkan;
   reflection *n* bayangan;
   renungan; **reflective** *adj*
   memantulkan sinar; termenung
reforestation *n* reboisasi
reform *n* perubahan, refor-
   masi; *v* berubah; mengubah;
   menyusun kembali
refresh *v* menyegarkan;
   refresher ~ *course* kursus
   penyegaran; **refreshments**
   n, pl minuman, makanan
refrigerator *n* lemari es,
   kulkas
refuge *n* tempat suaka,
   perlindungan; **refugee** *n*
   pengungsi
refund *n* pembayaran
   kembali; *v* mengembalikan
   uang
refusal *n* penolakan; **refuse**
   v [refyuz] menolak
regard *n* hormat; *in* ~ *to*,
   with ~ *to* sehubungan
   dengan, mengenai; *v* menganggap; *my* ~s salam saya;
   regarding *conj* mengenai,
   tentang
regency *n* kabupaten;
   daerah; **regent** *n* bupati

region *n* daerah, wilayah;
  regional *adj* daerah
register *n* [réjister] daftar; *v*
  daftar; mendaftarkan; mencatat; ~ed mail pos tercatat;
  registration *n* pendaftaran,
  pencatatan; **registry** *n*
  (kantor) pendaftaran; ~
  office kantor catatan sipil
regret *n* rasa sesal; *v*
  menyesal
regular *adj* biasa; teratur;
  tetap
regulation *n* aturan,
  peraturan
rehearsal *n* [rihérsal]
  latihan
reign *n* [réin] pemerintahan,
  masa bertakhta; *v* memerintah, bertakhta
reindeer *n* [reindir] **reindeer** rusa kutub
reinforce *v* [riinfors] memperkuat, memperkokoh
reject *v* [rejékt] menolak;
  rejection *n* penolakan
rejoice *v* bergembira,
  bersyukur
relate *v* menceritakan; mengaitkan, menghubungkan;
  ~ *to* memahami, bersimpati; **related** *adj* berkaitan,

berhubungan; **relation** *n*
  saudara, keluarga; hubungan; *in ~ to* mengenai, tentang; **relationship** *n* hubungan; **relative** *adj* relatif;
  n saudara, keluarga
relax *v* bersantai-santai;
  mengendurkan; **relaxation** *n*
  relaksasi; **relaxing** *adj* santai
relay *n* (lari) estafet; *v* menyampaikan, meneruskan
release *n* pembebasan;
  rilis, keluaran; *v* melepaskan, membebaskan,
  memerdekakan
relevant *adj* bersangkut
  paut, relevan
reliable *adj* andal, tepercayar
  ← **rely**
relief *n* [rilif] bantuan, pertolongan, sumbangan; rasa
  lega; *what a ~* syukur; *Isl*
  alhamdulillah; *in ~* timbul;
relieve *v* membantu,
  menolong; ~ *yourself* buang
  air; **relieved** *adj* lega, plong
religion *n* [rilijen] agama;
  religious *adj* beragama,
  saleh, religius
reluctance *n* keengganan;
  reluctant *adj* enggan
rely *v* [relai] mengandalkan

remain *v* tinggal, tetap; ~*s* sisa; **remainder** *n* sisa

remark *n* komentar; catatan; *v* berkomentar, mengomentari; berkata; **remarkable** *adj* pantas diperhatikan, luar biasa

remedy *n* [rémédi] obat, penawar

remember *v* ingat; ~ *me to* salam saya untuk

remind *v* [remaind] mengingatkan; **reminder** *n* surat peringatan

remote *adj, n* terpencil; ~ *control* remot

removal *n* [remuvel] pemindahan; **remove** *v* memindahkan; menjauhkan

rendezvous *n* [rondévu] (tempat) pertemuan

renew *v* memperbarui, memperpanjang; **renewal** *n* pembaruan

renovate *v* merenovasi, memperbaiki; **renovation** *n* perbaikan, renovasi

rent *n* (uang) sewa; *v* menyewa; ~ *out* menyewakan; **rental** *adj* sewaan; ~ *car* mobil sewaan; *DVD* ~ rental DVD

repair *n* perbaikan, reparasi; *v* memperbaiki

repay *v* **repaid repaid** membayar kembali, mengganti

repeat *n* tayangan ulang; *v* mengulangi; **repeatedly** *adv* berulang kali

replace *v* mengganti, menggantikan; **replacement** *n* pengganti; pergantian

reply *n* [replai] jawaban, sahutan, balasan; *v* menjawab, menyahut, membalas

report *n* laporan, pemberitaan; *v* melapor; melaporkan, memberitakan; **reporter** *n* wartawan

represent *v* mewakili; menggambarkan, melambangkan; **representation** *n* perwakilan; gambaran; **representative** *n* wakil, utusan

reprint *n* cetak ulang; *v* mencetak ulang

reproduce *v* mempunyai keturunan, berkembang biak; meniru; **reproduction** *n* reproduksi, perkembangbiakan reptile *n* binatang melata

republic *n* republik; *the People's ~ of China (PRC)* Republik Rakyat Cina (RRC); **republican** *adj* berkaitan dengan republik, republikan; pro-republik; *n* pendukung republik

reputation *n* nama baik, reputasi

request *n* permohonan, permintaan; *by ~* atas permintaan; *v* memohon, minta

require *v* memerlukan; **requirement** *n* syarat; *~s* kebutuhan

rescue *n* penyelamatan; *v* menolong, menyelamatkan

research *n* penelitian, riset; *~ and development (R & D)* penelitian dan pengembangan (litbang); *v* meneliti, meriset

resemble *v* menyerupai, mirip

resent *v* benci, marah; **resentment** *n* rasa marah, dendam

reservation *n* reservasi, pesanan, buking; **reserve** *n* cadangan, persediaan; *nature ~* cagar alam; *v*

memesan, menyediakan

reservoir *n* [résérvwar] waduk

reshuffle *n* perombakan; *v* merombak

residence *n* kediaman; *permanent ~ (PR)* hak tinggal secara tetap; **resident** *n* penduduk, penghuni; *arch* residen; **residential** *adj* berkaitan dengan perumahan

resign *v* [rizain] mundur, mengundurkan diri, berhenti bekerja; **resignation** *n* [rézignésyen] pengunduran diri

resist *v* [rezist] melawan, menahan; **resistance** *n* perlawanan, pertahanan

resolution *n* keputusan, resolusi; **resolve** *v* memutuskan, bermaksud

resort *n* tempat beristirahat, resor

resource *n* sumber daya; *human ~ (HR)* personalia; *natural ~* sumber daya alam

respect *n* hormat; hal; *in that ~* mengenai, berhubungan dengan hal itu;

559

with ~ to dalam hal itu;
to pay your ~s melayat;
respectable adj baik-baik,
terhormat; **respectful** adj
(penuh) hormat; **respectfully** yours ~ hormat kami
respective adj masing-
masing
respond v membalas, men-
jawab, menanggapi; **res-
ponse** n tanggapan, jawaban, respons
responsibility n [respon-
sibiliti] tanggung jawab;
responsible adj bertanggung jawab
rest n (waktu) istirahat;
sisa; v berhenti, beristirahat,
mengaso; tinggal; ~ on
berdasarkan, bersandarkan;
restroom n toilet, WC
restaurant n restoran,
rumah makan
restore v memperbaiki,
mengembalikan, memugar
restrict v membatasi;
restriction n pembatasan
result n akibat, hasil; ~ in
mengakibatkan, menye-
babkan
resumé, resume n
[rézumé] riwayat hidup

resume v mulai lagi, meneruskan
resurrect v menghidupkan
kembali; **resurrection** n
kebangkitan
retail adj [ritél] eceran,
ritel; n perdagangan eceran;
v berharga eceran; **retailer** n
pengecer, pedagang eceran
retain v menyimpan, mena-
han, tetap
retarded adj tunagrahita,
terkebelakang
retire v pensiun; **retired** adj
pensiunan; **retirement** n
masa pensiun
retreat n [retrit] retret;
penarikan (diri); v mundur,
menarik diri
retrenched adj dipehakakan,
diberhentikan
retrieve v [retriv] mengambil, mendapat kembali
return n kembali, pe-
mulangan, perjalanan
pulang; ~ address alamat
pengirim; ~ ticket karcis
pulang pergi; ~ to sender
dikembalikan kepada
pengirim; in ~ for sebagai
pengganti; many happy ~s
selamat (ulang tahun); v

pulang, kembali; mengem-
balikan, membalas

Rev. *Reverend* pendeta

reveal *v* [revil] membuka,
menyingkapkan; menyatakan

revenge *n* (rasa) dendam,
pembalasan; *to take* ~ membalas dendam

revenue *n* [révenyu] penghasilan, pendapatan

reverence *n* hormat, takzim;
reverend *n, Chr* pendeta

reversal *n* pembalikan;
reverse *adj* terbalik; *n* sisi
balik; *v* mundur, memun-
durkan kendaraan; mem-
balikkan

review *n* [revyu] tinjauan;
resensi; majalah; *v* me-
ninjau kembali; menilai;
reviewer *n* penulis resensi

revise *v* memperbaiki,
memeriksa ulang, merevisi;
revision *n* perbaikan,
periksa ulang, revisi

revival *n* kebangkitan

revolt *n* pemberontakan; *v*
memberontak

revolution *n* revolusi;
peredaran

reward *n* [reword] hadiah,
imbalan, ganjaran; *v* meng-

ganjar; menghadiahi;
rewarding *adj* menguntungkan, berguna

rheumatism *n* [rumatizem]
encok, rematik, sengal

rhinoceros *n* [rainoseres]
rhino *sl* badak; *one-horned*
~ badak bercula satu

rhyme *n* [raim] sajak; *v*
bersajak; **rhythm** *n* [rithem]
irama, ritme

rib *n* tulang rusuk, iga;
spare ~s iga panggang

ribbon *n* pita

rice *n* padi; beras; nasi; ~
cake krupuk; lontong; ~
field sawah; ladang; *fried* ~
nasi goreng

rich *adj* kaya, subur; ~ *in
protein* kaya akan protein

rickshaw *n* becak

rid *v* membersihkan, membebaskan; *to get* ~ *of*
menyingkirkan, menghi-
langkan

ridden *v, pf* → **ride**

riddle *n* teka-teki

ride *n* perjalanan; *v* **rode**
ridden mengendarai, naik; ~
a horse menunggang kuda;
~ *a motorbike* mengenda-
rai sepeda motor; **rider** *n*

penunggang; pengendara

ridge *n* punggung gunung

ridiculous *adj* menggelikan

rifle *n* [raifel] senapan, bedil; *air* ~ senapan angin

rift *n* celah; keretakan

rig *n* perlengkapan; *oil* ~ alat pengebor minyak, rig; *v* melakukan dengan curang

right *adj* [rait] (sebelah) kanan; betul, benar; patut, layak; ~ *angle* sudut siku-siku, tegak lurus; ~ *away* segera; ~ *now* sekarang juga; *all* ~ baiklah; *n* hak; *by* ~s sebetulnya, sebenar-nya; *human* ~s hak azasi manusia (HAM); *on the* ~ di sebelah kanan

rim *n* tepi (roda, piring); *wheel* ~ velg

ring *n* cincin; lingkaran; jaringan; gelanggang; de-ring; ~ *finger* jari manis; ~ *road* jalan lingkar; *boxing* ~ ring; *v* **rang rung** berdering; *coll* telepon, menelepon; ~ *the bell* membunyikan bel, memukul lonceng

rink *ice (skating)* ~ gelang-gang es

rinse *n* bilasan; *v* membilas

riot *n* [raiot] kerusuhan; kegaduhan

RIP *abbrev rest in peace* beristirahat(lah) dengan tenang

rip *n* robekan, sobekan; *v* menyobek, merobek

ripe *adj* masak, matang

rise *n* kenaikan; *pay* ~ kenaikan gaji; *v* **rose risen** [rizen] bangkit, terbit, berdiri

risk *n* risiko; *v* mengambil risiko; **risky** *adj* berisiko

ritual *n* upacara (agama)

rival *n* saingan, lawan; *v* menyaingi

river *n* [river] sungai, kali

RM *abbrev Malaysian ringgit* ringgit

road *n* jalan (raya); ~ *accident* kecelakaan lalu lintas; ~ *map* peta per-jalanan; *to hit the* ~ jalan, berangkat; **roadwork** *n* perbaikan jalan

roar *n* aum; deru; *v* meng-aum; menderu

roast *adj* panggang; ~ *beef* sapi panggang; *n* daging panggang; *v* memanggang, membakar rob *v* merampok, merampas; **robber** *n* perampok; **robbery** *n* perampokan; *armed* ~ perampokan bersenjata

robe *n* jubah

rock *n* batu, cadas; ~ *music* musik rock; *v* mengayunkan; menggoncang

rocket *n* roket; *v* meroket

rocky *adj* berbatu-batu ← **rock**

rod *n* batang

rode *v, pf* → **ride**

rodeo *n* pertunjukan ketrampilan menangani kuda dan hewan ternak

role *n* peran, peranan

roll *n* gulung, gulungan; roti bulat; daftar; ~*ing pin* gilingan adonan;~ *call* apel; *v* berguling, berputar; menggulung, menggulingkan, menggelindingkan; ~ *over* berguling; **roller** ~ *blades*, ~ *skates* sepatu roda; *hair* ~ alat penggulung rambut

Roman *adj* Romawi; *n* orang Romawi

romance *n* cerita cinta

romantic *adj* romantik ← **romance**

roof *n* atap

room *n* ruang, ruangan; kamar; *v* kos

rooster *n* ayam jago

root *n* akar; *to take* ~ berakar; *v* berakar

rope *n* tali

rosary *n, Isl* tasbih; *Cath* rosario

rose *n* bunga mawar, bunga ros; *v, pf* → **rise**

rot *v* membusuk

rotate *v* berputar, berkisar; **rotation** *n* perputaran, perkisaran

rotten *adj* busuk ← **rot**

rouge *n* [ruj] perona pipi

rough *adj* [raf] kasar; mentah; ~ *draft* naskah pertama; **roughly** *adv* kurang lebih, kira-kira; secara kasar

round *adj* bulat, bundar; di sekitar; ~ *table* meja bundar; ~ *trip* perjalanan pulang pergi; ~ *the world* keliling dunia; *all year* ~ sepanjang tahun; *n* giliran, putaran, ronde; *v* mengelilingi; **roundabout** *n* bundaran; komidi putar

route *n* [rut] trayek, jalur, rute

routine *adj* biasa, sehari-hari, rutin; *n* kebiasaan sehari-hari

row *n* [rau] pertengkaran; keributan

row *n* [ro] baris, jajar, deretan

row *v* [ro] berkayuh; mendayung, mengayuh

rowdy *adj* [raudi] berisik ← **row**

royal *adj* kerajaan; *n* anggota kerajaan; **royalty** *n* keluarga kerajaan

RSA *abbrev Republic of South Africa* Afsel (Republik Afrika Selatan)

RSVP *abbrev répondez s'il vous plaît* tolong dikonfirmasi

Rt Hon. *Right Honorable* yang terhormat

rub *v* menggosok, menggosok-gosok; ~ *out* menghapus; **rubber** *n* karet; penghapus

rubbish *n* sampah; omong kosong

ruby *n* batu mirah

rucksack *n* ransel

rude *adj* kasar, tidak sopan

rug *n* permadani

ruin *n* reruntuhan, puing-

puing; *v* meruntuhkan, merobohkan, merusak

rule *n* aturan, peraturan; pemerintahan; ~ *out* mengesampingkan; *as a* ~ biasanya; *v* memerintah; ~ *a line* membuat garis, menggaris; **ruler** *n* kepala pemerintah; penggaris

rum *n* room

rumor *n* kabar angin, kabar burung, desas-desus

run *n* perjalanan, latihan berlari, perlombaan; ~-*down* lesu; tidak terpelihara; *fun* ~ lomba lari untuk amal; *on the* ~ sedang melarikan diri; *in the long* ~ lambat laun, lama-lama, dalam jangka panjang; *v* **ran run** lari; berlangsung; mengalir; memimpin; menjalankan; ~ *away* kabur, melarikan diri; ~ *over* melindas; **runaway** *n* pelarian

rung *v, pf* → **ring**

runner *n* pelari; pesuruh, pengantar; ~-*up* juara kedua ← **run**

runway *n* landasan terbang

rural *adj* pedesaan, pedalaman

rush *n* ketergesa-gesaan;
~ *hour* jam padat; *v* terburu-
buru; menyerbu

Russia *n* Rusia; **Russian**
adj berasal dari Rusia; *n*
bahasa Rusia; orang Rusia

rust *n* karat; *v* berkarat;
rusty *adj* berkarat, karatan

ruthless *adj* [ruthles] keji,
kejam, tanpa belas kasihan

rye *n* [rai] gandum hitam

S

sabotage *n* [sabotaj]
sabotase; *v* menyabotase

sachet *n* [sasyé] sase, saset,
kemasan (kecil) (berisi
saus, sampo dll)

sack *n* karung, goni

sacred *adj* [sékred] suci,
kudus

sacrifice *n* [sakrifais]
korban, pengorbanan; *Isl*
kurban, qurban; *v* berkur-
ban; mengorbankan

sad *adj* susah, sedih

saddle *n* pelana, sadel,
tempat duduk

sadness *n* kesedihan ← **sad**

safari *n* wisata melihat atau
memburu binatang liar
(terutama di Afrika)

safe *adj* selamat; aman,
dapat dipercaya; ~*keeping*
penyimpanan yang aman; ~
bet pasti, tentu; *n* brankas;
~*deposit box* kotak tempat
menyimpan barang ber-
harga di bank; **safely** *adv*
dengan selamat; **safety** *n*
keselamatan; keamanan; ~
net jaringan keselamatan;
jaringan pengaman; ~ *pin*
peniti cantel; ~ *vest* baju
pelampung

saffron *n* kunyit, kuning

sag *v* turun, mengendur,
terkulai

saga *n* [saga] hikayat,
zcerita yang panjang

said *v, pf* [séd] → **say**

sail *n* layar; *v* berlayar; **sailing** *n* berlayar; **sailor** *n*
pelaut, anak buah kapal
(ABK)

saint (St) *n, Chr, m* santo; *f*
santa; orang suci, orang
kudus

sake *for God's* ~ demi
Allah

salad *n* selada; ~ *dressing*
bumbu selada

salary *n* [salari] gaji

sale *n* obral; *for* ~ dijual; *on*
~ diobral, didiskon; **sales** *n*
penjualan; **salesperson** *n*
agen; pelayan toko

saliva *n* [selaiva] air liur

salmon *n* [samen] ikan
salmon

salt *n* garam; ~ *cellar,* ~
shaker tempat garam; **salty**
adj asin

salute *n* pemberian hormat;
v memberi hormat

same *adj* sama; serupa; *all
the* ~, *just the* ~ walaupun
begitu; *adv* sama, seperti
itu

sample *n* [sampel] contoh;
v coba

sanction *n* [sangsyen]
persetujuan; sanksi; *v* menyetujui; memberi sanksi

sand *n* pasir; ~ *dune* bukit
pasir

sandal *n* [sandel] sepatu
sandal

sander *n* mesin penggosok

sandpaper *n* kertas gosok,
ampelas; *v* mengampelas
← **sand**

sandwich *n* [sandwij] roti
lapis

sandy *adj* mengandung
pasir ← **sand**

sane *adj* waras, berakal sehat

sang *v, pf* → **sing**

sanitary *adj* bersih, saniter;
~ *pad* pembalut (wanita)

sank *v, pf* → **sink**

Santa *n* ~ *(Claus)* Sinterklas,
Santa

sap *n* getah

sapphire *n* [safair] batu
nilam, batu safir

sarcasm *n* [sarkazem]
sarkasme, sindiran tajam;
sarcastic *adj* sarkastis,
menyindir

sardine *n* [sardin] ikan
sarden

sarong *n* sarung

Satan *n* [séten] setan, iblis

satchel *n* tas sekolah, tas
buku

satellite *n* [satelait] satelit;
bulan; ~ *dish* parabola

satisfaction *n* kepuasan;
satisfactory *adj* memuaskan, cukup; **satisfy** *v*
[satisfai] memuaskan; me-
menuhi; **satisfied** *adj* puas

Saturday *adj, n* [saterdé]

hari Sabtu
sauce n kuah, saus; *tomato*
~ saus tomat
saucer n piring cawan; *fly-ing* ~ piring terbang
Saudi Arabia n Arab Saudi;
Saudi, Saudi Arabian adj
bcrasal dari Arab Saudi
savage adj [savej] buas,
liar, ganas
savanna, savannah n
sabana, padang rumput
save n penyelamatan,
tangkapan; *prep* kecuali; v
menyelamatkan; ~ *money*
menghemat uang; mena-bung uang; ~ *up* mena-bung; **savings** n, pl (uang)
tabungan, simpanan
saw n gergaji; v mengger-gaji; v, pf → **see**; **sawdust**
n serbuk kayu
sax, saxophone n saksofon
say v **said said** [séd] kata,
berkata; mengatakan; **say-ing** n pepatah, peribahasa
scale n skala, ukuran; sisik,
kulit; *large*-~ secara besar-besaran; **scales** n, pl
timbangan, neraca
scalp n kulit kepala
scalpel n pisau bedah

scan n peninjauan; v menin-jau; pindai, memindai
scandal n skandal, keonaran
scanner n pemindai, scanner
← **scan**
scapegoat n kambing hitam
scar n bekas (luka); v mem-bekas, menggoresi;
scarred adj terluka
scarce adj [skérs] jarang;
kurang; **scarcely** adv ham-pir tidak, nyaris
scare n [skér] peristiwa
yang menakutkan; v
menakut-nakuti, menakutkan;
~ *away* mengusir; **scare-crow** n orang-orangan
untuk mengusir burung di
ladang; **scared** adj takut
scarf n syal
scarlet adj merah tua
scary adj [skéri] mena-kutkan ← **scare**
scatter v menaburkan,
menyebarkan
scavenger n pemulung
scene n [sin] pemandang-an; adegan; ~ *of the crime*
tempat kejadian perkara
(TKP); *to make a* ~ mem-buat heboh; **scenery** n
pemandangan alam

scent *n* [sént] (minyak) wangi, harum, bau

sceptic, sceptical → **skeptic, skeptical**

schedule *n* [skédyul] jadwal, program, daftar acara; *behind* ~ terlambat; *v* merencanakan, mengatur

scheme *n* [skim] rencana; bagan, skema, rancangan; *v* merekayasa

scholar *n* [skolar] pelajar; orang terpelajar; **scholarship** *n* beasiswa; **school** *n* sekolah; ~ *year* tahun ajaran; *elementary* ~, *primary* ~ sekolah dasar; *junior high* ~ sekolah menengah pertama (SMP); *medical* ~ fakultas kedokteran; *night* ~ kursus malam; *secondary* ~ sekolah menengah

science *n* ilmu (pengetahuan alam, IPA); sains; **scientist** *n* ilmuwan

scissors *n, pl* [sizers] *pair of* ~ gunting

scold *v* menegur, menghardik

scoop *n* sendok, ciduk, gayung; *v* menyendok, menciduk, menyekop

scooter *n* otopet, skuter

scope *n* ruang lingkup, jangkauan; bidang

scorch *v* membakar (tidak sengaja)

score *n* skor, angka, nilai; *v* mencetak gol, angka atau poin; memperoleh nilai; **scoreboard** *n* papan angka

scorn *v* mencemoohkan, mencaci-maki

scorpion *n* kalajengking

scotch *n* wiski Skotlandia; **Scotland** *n* Skotlandia; **Scottish** *adj* berasal dari Skotlandia

scout *n* pandu, pramuka; pengintai; *girl* ~ pandu puteri

scramble *n* perebutan; *v* berebut; mengocok; ~*d eggs* telur kocok goreng

scrap *adj* bekas; ~ *metal* besi tua; ~ *paper* kertas bekas; *n* sisa, carik; *sl* perkelahian; **scrapbook** *n* buku tempel, album

scrape *v* bergeseran; menggores, menggesekkan

scratch *n* goresan; *v* menggores, menggaruk, mencoret

scrawl *n* tulisan cakar ayam

scream *n* jeritan; *v* berteriak, menjerit

screech *n* ciutan; jeritan; *v* menciut-ciut; menjerit

screen *n* tabir; layar putih; *v* menyaring; memutarkan (film); **screening** *n* pemutaran film

screw *n* sekrup; *v* menyekrup; *vulg* bersetubuh; **screwdriver** *n* obeng

scribble *v* mencoret-coret

script *n* tulisan; naskah; *Latin* ~ huruf Romawi

scroll *v* menggulung, naik

scrub *n* semak, belukar

scrub *n* mandi, pencucian; sabun cair yang mengandung butir; *v* menggosok

scuba ~ *diving* selam dengan tangki udara

sculptor *n* perupa, pematung, pemahat patung

SEA *abbrev South East Asia* Asia Tenggara

sea *n* laut; ~ *cow* duyung; ~ *cucumber* teripang; ~ *level* permukaan laut; ~ *urchin* bulu babi; *the Java* ~ Laut Jawa; **seafood** *n* makanan laut; **seagull** *n*

burung camar; **seahorse** *n* kuda laut

seal *n* anjing laut

seal *n* meterai, cap; *v* menutup; ~*ed road* jalan beraspal

sealion *n* [silayon] singa laut ← **sea**

seam *n* kelim, pelipit

seaplane *n* pesawat terbang air ← **sea**

search *n* [sérc] pencarian, penggeledahan; ~ *party* rombongan pencari; ~ *warrant* surat kuasa untuk menggeledah; ~ *and rescue (SAR)* regu penyelamat; *v* mencari, memeriksa, menggeledah

seashell *n* kerang (laut) ← **sea**

seashore *n* pantai laut ← **sea**

seasick *adj* **seasickness** *n* mabuk laut ← **sea**

seaside *n* tepi laut ← **sea**

season *v* [sizen] membumbui

season *n* [sizen] musim; ~ *ticket* karcis terusan; *the dry* ~ musim kemarau

seasoning *n* bumbu ← **season**

seat *n* tempat duduk, bangku, kursi; **seated** *adj* sedang duduk

seaweed *n* ganggang laut, rumput laut

second *n* [sékond] detik

second *adj* [sékond] kedua; ~ *gear* gigi dua; ~*hand* bekas; ~*rate* bermutu rendah; *every* ~ *day* selang sehari, dua hari sekali; **secondary** *adj* sekunder; ~ *school* sekolah menengah

secrecy *n* [sikresi] kerahasiaan; **secret** *adj, n* rahasia

secretary *n* sekretaris, panitera; ~ *of State* Menteri Luar Negeri (AS)

secretly *adv* [sikretli] diam-diam, mencuri-curi ← **secret**

sect *n* sekte, aliran; **sectarian** ~ *violence* kekerasan berbau SARA

section *n* seksi, bagian, belahan; **sector** *n* sektor, bidang

secular *adj* [sékuler] sekuler

security *n* keamanan; ~ *police* polisi rahasia; *UN* ~ *Council* Dewan Keamanan PBB

sedimentary ~ *rock* batu endapan

seduce *v* menggoda, merayu

see *v* **saw seen** melihat; berkunjung, ~ *Paris* berkunjung Paris; *I* ~ saya mengerti; ~ *someone off,* ~ *someone out* mengantarkan; ~ *to* mengurus

seed *n* biji, benih

seek *v* **sought sought** [sot] mencari

seem *v* nampak; ternyata, kelihatannya; rupanya, rasanya

seen *v, pf* → **see**

segment *n* bagian, golongan, pangsa, segmen

segregation *n* pemisahan

seismic *adj* [saizmik] yang berkaitan dengan gempa bumi; **seismograph** *n* [saizmograf] seismograf

seize *v* [siz] menangkap; menyita; **seizure** *n* penyitaan

seldom *adv* jarang

select *v* [selékt] memilih, menyaring; **selection** *n* pilihan, pemilihan, seleksi

self *pron* sendiri, pribadi; ~*centred* egois; ~*confi-*

dence percaya diri (PD);
~*control* pengawasan diri
sendiri; ~*conscious* sadar
akan dirinya, canggung;
~*defense* bela diri;
~*educated* otodidak;
~*employed* swausaha,
wiraswasta; ~*government*
otonomi, swapraja; **selfish**
adj egois, suka mementingkan diri sendiri

sell *v* **sold sold** menjual,
berjualan; ~ *off* menjual
habis, mengobral; ~ *out*
habis terjual; **seller** *n* penjual

semi- *pref* tengah, separuh;
~*colon* titik koma

Semitic [Semitik] *anti-*~
anti Yahudi

send *v* **sent sent** mengirim, mengirimkan, men-
girimi; ~ *for* memanggil,
minta datang; ~ *off* mengantarkan; ~ *on* meneruskan;
~ *away for,* ~ *out for* memesan; **sender** *n* pengirim

senile *adj* pikun

senior *adj* [sinior] lebih tua,
tertua, senior; *n* orang yang
lebih tua; ~ *high school*
sekolah menengah atas
(SMA)

sensation *n* kegemparan,
sensasi; **sensational** *adj*
menggemparkan, sensasional

sense *n* indera; perasaan;
arti, pengertian; *common* ~
akal sehat; *the five* ~*s* pan-
caindera; *to make* ~ masuk
akal; **sensible** *adj* waras,
berpikiran sehat, berakal
sehat; **sensitive** *adj* peka,
sensitif

sent *v, pf* → **send**

sentence *n* kalimat; keputusan, hukuman; *death* ~
hukuman mati; *v* meng-
hukum

sentimental *adj* sentimentil

sentry *n* [séntri] penjaga;
~ *box* gardu jaga, rumah
(jaga) monyet

separate *adj* [séperet]
terpisah; *v* [séperét]
berpisah; pisah ranjang;
memisahkan; **separation** *n*
pemisahan

September *n* bulan
September

sequel *n* [sikuel] lanjutan,
sambungan

sequence *n* [sikuens]
urutan, rangkaian

sergeant *n* [sarjent] sersan

serial *n* [siriel] seri; film seri; cerita bersambung (cerber); ~ *killer* pembunuh berantai; ~ *number* nomor seri, nomor urutan; **series** *n* seri, rangkaian

serious *adj* sungguh-sungguh, serius

sermon *n* khotbah, ceramah

servant *n* pembantu, pelayan, pramuwisma; babu; **serve** *v* melayani, mengabdi; menghidangkan; **service** *n* pelayanan; pemeliharaan; kebaktian; masa bakti, jasa; ~ *station* pompa bensin; *v* memperbaiki (mobil)

serviette *n* [sérviét] serbet

sesame *n* [sésami] wijen

session *n* [sésyen] sidang; *in* ~ bersidang

set *adj* sudah ditentukan; siap; *n* sepasang, seperangkat, perlengkapan; pesawat (radio/televisi); kelompok; *v* **set set** menaruh; memasang, menyetel; menetapkan; terbenam (matahari); ~ *(down)* meletakkan; ~ *aside* menyisihkan; ~ *off*, ~ *out*

berangkat; ~*-up* susunan; **setting** *n* penyetelan; lingkungan, latar belakang

settle *v* [sétel] berdiam; menempati; menyelesaikan, menenangkan; mengatur, mengurus; **settlement** *n* perkampungan; penyelesaian; **settler** *n* pendatang, pemukim awal

seven *adj, n* [séven] tujuh; **seventeen** *adj, n* tujuh belas; **seventh** *adj* ketujuh; **seventy** *adj, n* tujuh puluh

several *adj* [séveral] beberapa

sew *v* [so] menjahit; ~*ing machine* mesin jahit

sewn *v, pf* [son] → **sew**

sex *n* jenis kelamin; (hubungan) seks, persetubuhan, sanggama; ~ *education* pendidikan seks; *to have* ~ bersetubuh, bersanggama; **sexual** *adj* seksual; ~ *harassment* pelecehan seksual; **sexy** *adj* seksi

shabby *adj* lusuh, jelek

shack *n* gubuk, pondok

shade *n* naungan, tempat teduh; krei; warna

572

shadow *n* [syado] bayangan; *v* membayangi; membuntuti

shaft *n* lubang, terowongan; batang

shaggy *adj* tidak rata, kasar (rambut, bulu)

shake *n* minuman bercampur (coklat, dsb) ← **milkshake**; goncangan, gelengan (kepala); jabat tangan; *v* **shook shaken** mengguncang, mengocok; ~ *hands* berjabatan tangan; **shaky** *adj* goyang, goyah, kurang kuat

shall *v, aux* akan; ~ *not* (*shan't*) takkan, tidak akan

shallow *adj* dangkal

shame *n* malu; *what a ~* sayang sekali

shampoo *n* [syampu] sampo; *v* berkeramas

shan't *v* takkan, tidak akan ← **shall**

shanty *n* gubuk, pondok

shape *n* bentuk; *v* membentuk

share *n* bagian, andil, saham; *v* berbagi; membagi; **shareholder** *n* pemegang saham

shark *n* ikan hiu

sharp *adj* tajam, runcing; cerdik; *ten o'clock ~ jam* sepuluh tepat; **sharpen** *v* meruncingkan, mengasah, meraut; **sharpener** *n* raut pensil

shave *v* bercukur; mencukur; mengiris; **shaving** ~ *cream* sabun cukur; **shaver** *n* alat cukur (listrik)

shawl *n* syal, selendang

she *pron, f* [syi] dia

shear *n* [syir] mencukur (domba), memotong; **shearer** *n* pencukur domba

sheath *n* [syith] sarung; pelapah; *penis* ~ koteka

shed *n* gudang

shed *v* rontok; ~ *leaves* merontokkan daun; ~ *tears* mencucurkan air mata

sheep *n* **sheep** domba, biri-biri; *a flock of ~* sekawanan domba; **sheepdog** *n* anjing gembala

sheer *adj* tipis; curam; belaka

sheet *n* helai, lembar; seprai; *a ~ of paper* sehelai kertas

shelf *n* papan, rak

shell *n* bom kecil, peledak; ~ *shock* trauma (karena

573

perang); **shelling, shellfire**
n penembakan atau
peledakan (dalam perang)
shell *n* kulit, kerang; *coconut* ~ tempurung kelapa;
v mengupas; **shellfish** *n*
kerang-kerangan
shelter *n* tempat berlindung, tempat teduh; *bus* ~
halte bis; *v* berlindung,
bernaung; melindungi
shepherd *n* [shéperd] gembala; *German* ~ anjing
herder
sheriff *n* [syérif] kepala
polisi daerah (AS)
shield *n* [syild] perisai,
tameng; *v* melindungi
shift *n* perubahan, pergeseran; jam kerja; *v* berpindah tempat, beralih; men-
gubah, menggeser
shine *n* cahaya, sinar; *v*
shone shone [syon] bercahaya, bersinar; meman-
carkan; ~ *shoes*
menggosok sepatu
shiny *adj* berkilap, mengkilap
← **shine**
ship *n* kapal, perahu; *v*
mengirim (lewat kapal);
shipping *n* perkapalan,

pengiriman dengan kapal;
shipwreck *n* [syiprék]
peristiwa kapal karam;
shipyard *n* galangan kapal
shirt *n* baju, kemeja; *polo* ~
kaus berkerah
shiver *v* menggigil, gemetar
shock *n* guncangan; kejutan; *electric* ~ kena setrum;
shocking *adj* mengejutkan
shoe *n* [syu] sepatu; ~ *polish*
semir sepatu; *running* ~*s,*
sports ~ sepatu olahraga;
shoelace *n* tali sepatu
shone *v, pf* → **shine**
shook *v, pf* → **shake**
shoot *n* tunas
shoot *v* **shot shot** menembak; merekam; ~ *a goal*
mencetak gol; **shooting** *n*
penembakan; menembak
(olahraga); syuting, pengambilan gambar
shop *n* toko; ~ *assistant*
pramuniaga, pelayan toko;
v berbelanja; ~ *around*
melihat-lihat; **shopkeeper**
n pemilik toko; **shoplift** *v*
mengutil atau mencuri dari
toko; **shopper** *n* orang
yang berbelanja, pembeli;
shopping *n* hasil belanja,

belanjaan; ~ *center*, ~ *mall* (pusat) pertokoan, mal

shore *n* pantai, tepi

shorn *v*, *pf* → **shear**

short *adj* pendek, ringkas, singkat; kurang; kekurangan; ~*-changed* dapat uang kembali yang kurang; ~*-sighted* rabun jauh; ~*-tempered* cepat marah; ~*-term* jangka pendek; ~ *circuit* kortsleting; ~ *story* cerita pendek (cerpen); *for* ~ singkatannya, nama pendeknya; *in* ~ singkatnya, pendek kata; *to cut* ~ memperpendek, memotong; *n* film pendek; **shortage** *n* [shortej] kekurangan; **shorten** *v* memendekkan, memperpendek; **shortly** *adv* tidak lama lagi; secara ketus; **shorts** *n*, *pl* celana pendek, kolor

shot *n* tembakan; suntikan; ~ *glass* seloki; ~ *put* tolak peluru; *v*, *pf* → **shoot**

should *v*, *aux* [syud] seharusnya, sebaiknya, semestinya

shoulder *n* [syolder] bahu, pundak; *hard* ~ bahu jalan; *v* memikul, menanggung

shout *n* [syaut] teriakan; *v* berteriak

shove *n* [shav] dorongan; *v* mendorong dengan kasar; ~ *off derog* pergi

shovel *n* [shavel] sekop; *v* menyekop

show *n* [sho] pertunjukan, tontonan; acara di televisi; pameran; ~ *business*, *showbiz* dunia hiburan; ~*-off* orang yang berlagak; *no* ~ tidak jadi, tidak datang; *v* memperlihatkan, mempertunjukkan; menunjukkan, menampakkan; membuktikan; ~ *off* beraksi; berlagak, sok; memamerkan; **showdown** *n* [shodaun] bentrokan

shower *n* [syauer] pancuran (mandi); hujan sebentar; ~ *cap* tutup kepala; *v* mandi (di pancuran); menghujani, menabur

shown *v*, *pf* → **show**

showroom *n* ruang pameran, ruang pajangan ← **show**

shrank *v*, *pf* → **shrink**

shred *n* carik, sobekan; *v* mencarik, memarut

shriek *n* [syrik] jeritan, pekikan; *v* menjerit

shrimp *n* udang

shrine *n* kuil, tempat keramat

shrink *v* **shrank shrunk** susut; menyusutkan

shrub *n* tanaman kecil

shrug *n* angkat bahu; *v* mengangkat bahu

shrunk *v, pf* → **shrink**; **shrunken** *adj* berkerut, menyusut

shudder *n* gigil, getar; *v* menggigil, gemetaran

shuffle *v* mengocok; menyeret kaki; ~ *cards* mengocok kartu

shut *v* **shut shut** tutup; menutup; ~ *down* mematikan; ~ *up* tutup mulut, diam; **shutter** *n* daun penutup jendela

shuttle *adj* [syatel] ulang-alik; ~ *bus* bis ulang-alik; *n* kendaraan ulang-alik; *space* ~ pesawat ulang-alik

shuttlecock *n* kok

shy *adj* [syai] malu, pemalu

sibling *n* saudara (kandung)

sick *adj* sakit; ~ *bay* kamar

untuk orang sakit; ~ *leave* cuti sakit; ~ *of* bosan, jenuh, jemu

sickle *n* [sikel] sabit; *hammer and* ~ palu arit

sickly *adj* sering sakit, sakit-sakitan ← **sick**

sickness *n* sakit, penyakit ← **sick**

side *n* sisi, segi; samping; ~ *effect* efek samping; ~ *by* ~ bersebelahan; *both* ~s kedua belah pihak; *to take* ~s berpihak, memihak; **sideburns** *n* brewokan, cambang; **sidecar** *n* sespan; **sidetrack** *v* melenceng; menggelincirkan; **sidewalk** *n* trotoar; **sideways** *adv* miring, ke samping

sieve *n* [siv] ayakan, saringan

sift *v* mengayak; menyaring

sigh *n* [sai] keluh, nafas panjang; *a* ~ *of relief* menarik nafas lega; *v* menarik nafas panjang; mendesah

sight *n* [sait] pemandangan; penglihatan; *in* ~ kelihatan; *long*-~*ed* rabun dekat; **sightseeing** *n* wisata, tamasya

sign *n* [sain] tanda, pertanda, isyarat; rambu; plang; ~ *language* bahasa isyarat; *v* menandatangani; teken, memberi paraf; ~ *up* mendaftar; **signal** *n* [signal] tanda, isyarat; *v* memberi tanda; mengisyaratkan; **signature** *n* [signatyur] tanda tangan

significant *adj* berarti, penting

signpost *n* [sainpost] rambu

silence *n* keheningan; *v* mendiamkan; **silent** *adj* diam; ~ *letter* huruf yang tidak diucapkan

silk *adj, n* sutera

silly *adj* bodoh, tolol; lucu

silver *adj, n* perak; ~ *anniversary* ulang tahun perkawinan perak

similar *adj* [similer] serupa, mirip

simple *adj* [simpel] sederhana, bersahaja; **simply** *adv* dengan sederhana; hanya; benar-benar, sungguh-sungguh

simulation *n* simulasi

simultaneous *adj* [simulténius] serentak, serempak

sin *n* dosa; *v* berdosa

since *conj* sejak, sedari, sebab, karena

sincere *adj* [sinsir] tulus (hati), ikhlas; bersungguh-sungguh; **sincerely** *yours* ~ salam hormat

sing *v* **sang sung** bernyanyi, menyanyi; menyanyikan; **singer** *n* penyanyi

Singapore *n* Singapura; **Singaporean** *adj* [Singaporian] berasal dari Singapura; *n* orang Singapura

singer *n* penyanyi

single *adj* [singgel] tunggal, sendiri; lajang, *m* bujangan; lagu; ~*-handed* sendirian; ~ *bed* tempat tidur untuk satu orang; *every* ~ *time* setiap kali; *women's* ~*s* pertandingan tunggal putri; *v* ~ *out* memilih (satu)

singlet *n* singlet

singular *adj, n* [singguler] tunggal

sink *n* tempat cuci (piring); *v* **sank sunk** tenggelam, mengendap; menenggelamkan; ~ *in* meresap, masuk ke dalam hati

sinus *adj* berkaitan dengan lubang antara hidung dan mulut

sip *n* isapan; *v* mengisap, meminum sedikit

sir *pron* tuan

siren *n* sirene

sister *n* saudara perempuan, adik atau kakak perempuan; kepala perawat, suster; ~*in-law* kakak/adik ipar (perempuan)

sit *v* **sat sat** duduk; ~ *down* (pergi) duduk

site *n* lokasi, situs; *archeological* ~ situs purbakala; *web*~ situs (di) internet

sitting *adj* ~ *room* kamar duduk; *n* sidang ← **sit**

situated *adj* [sityuéted] terletak; **situation** *n* keadaan, situasi

six *adj*, *n* enam; **sixteen** *adj*, *n* enam belas; **sixth** *adj* keenam; ~ *sense* indera keenam; **sixty** *adj*, *n* enam puluh

size *n* ukuran, nomor; besarnya

skate *n* sepatu luncur, sepatu es; *ice*-~ sepatu es; *v* bermain sepatu luncur

atau sepatu roda; **skating** *n* bermain sepatu luncur

skeleton *n* [skéleton] kerangka

skeptical, sceptical *adj* ragu-ragu, kurang percaya, skeptis

sketch *n* sketsa; gambar; *v* membuat sketsa; menggambar

skewer *n* [skyuer] tusuk daging, tusuk sate

ski *n* (sepatu) ski; *v* main ski; **skiing** *n* main ski

skid *n* bekas gelincir; *v* gelincir, tergelincir, selip

skill *n* keterampilan, keahlian; **skillful, skilful** *adj* terampil

skim *v* membaca secara pintas; ~ *milk* susu tanpa kepala susu

skin *n* kulit; ~ *cancer* kanker kulit; *v* menguliti

skinny *adj* [skini] kurus, ceking

skip *v* melompat-lompat; melewati; meloncati; ~*ping rope* tali lompat

skirt *n* rok

skull *n* tengkorak, batok kepala

skunk *n* sigung

sky *n* langit, angkasa, udara; ~*high* setinggi langit, selangit; **skydiving** *n* terjun payung; **skyscraper** *n* pencakar langit

slab *n* papan, potong

slack *adj* kendur, lesu; tidak rajin; **slacken** *v* mengendur, berkurang

slacks *n, pl* celana panjang (perempuan)

slam *n* gerdam; *Grand* ~ empat kejuaraan tenis yang besar; *v* membanting, menggerdam, menutup dengan keras

slang *n* bahasa percakapan, bahasa gaul

slant *n* kemiringan, sudut, pandangan

slap *n* tampar, tamparan; *v* menampar

slate *n* batu tulis

slaughter *n* [sloter] pembantaian; penyembelihan; *v* membantai; memotong, menyembelih

slave *n* budak; **slavery** *n* perbudakan

sleazy *adj* jorok, tidak

senonoh, tidak sopan (pakaian)

sled, sledge *n* kereta luncur

sleep *v* **slept slept** tidur; ~ *in* bangun siang; ~ *together*, ~ *with* tidur bersama; bersetubuh; ~ *well* selamat tidur; **sleepwalk** *v* mimpi jalan; **sleepy** *adj* mengantuk

sleet *n* hujan bercampur es dan salju

sleeve *n* lengan baju; sisipan kertas di CD; **sleeveless** *adj* tanpa lengan

slender *adj* ramping, langsing

slept *v, pf* → **sleep**

slice *n* irisan, sayatan; *a* ~ *of cake* sepotong kue; *v* mengiris, menyayat

slide *n* perosotan; *v* **slid slid** meluncur; tergelincir; ~ *down* merosot

slight *adj* [slait] sedikit; mungil; **slightly** *adv* sedikit

slim *adj* ramping, langsing, lampai; *v* ~ *down* menjadi (lebih) langsing

slime *n* kotoran, lumpur, lumut; **slimy** *adj* berlumpur, kotor

sling *n* ambin; **slingshot** *n* ketapel

slip *n* kesalahan; longsor; rok dalam; *v* tergelincir; terlupa; ~ *up* keliru, berbuat salah

slipper *n* selop; sandal

slippery *adj* licin ← **slip**

slit *n* celah, belah; *v* membelah

slob *n* orang yang sembrono

slogan *n* semboyan, slogan

slope *n* lereng; *v* melandai; **sloping** *adj* miring

sloppy *adj* tidak rapi; cengeng

slot *n* celah, lubang (kunci); tempat

slow *adj* perlahan-lahan, pelan-pelan; lambat, lamban; lama; ~ *down* mengurangi kecepatan; memperlambat; **slowly** *adv* pelan-pelan

slug *n* semacam siput; **sluggish** *adj* malas

slum *n* daerah kumuh

slump *n* kemerosotan; *v* merosot; terjatuh

sly *adj* cerdik

smack *n* tampar, tamparan, tempeleng; *sl* heroin; *v* menampar, menempeleng

small *adj* kecil; ~ *change* uang kecil, uang receh; ~ *fry* ikan teri; ~ *talk* basa-basi, obrolan ringan; *too* ~ kekecilan; ~ *is beautiful* kecil itu indah

smart *adj* cerdas, pintar; cantik, tampan; cepat; *quick* ~ sekarang juga; *v* pedih, sakit

smash *n* tabrakan, kecelakaan (mobil); smes; ~ *hit* laku keras; *v* memecahkan, menghancurkan

smell *n* bau; *delicious* ~ harum; *sense of* ~ indera penciuman; *v* bau; ~ *sweet* wangi; mencium; **smelly** *adj* berbau (tidak sedap)

smile *n* senyum, senyuman; *v* tersenyum

smith *n* pandai besi

smog *n* asbut (asap kabut)

smoke *n* asap; *sl* rokok; *v* berasap; merokok; **smoker** *n* perokok; **smoking** *no* ~ dilarang merokok; **smoky** *adj* berasap

smooth *adj* licin; lancar

smuggle *v* [smagel] menyelundupkan; **smuggling** *n* penyelundupan

snack *n* makanan kecil, camilan; ~ *bar* warung, tempat menjual makanan kecil

snail *n* keong, siput

snake *n* ular

snap *n* bunyi yang keras; *v* mematahkan; ~ *at* membentak; ~ *up* cepat membeli; **snapshot** *n* potret, foto

snatch *v* menjambret, merampas

sneak *n* orang yang melaporkan kawan; *v* menyelinap; ~ *off* pergi secara diam-diam, kabur; ~ *out* diam-diam keluar; **sneakers** *n* sepatu kets, sepatu olahraga; **sneaky** *adj* tidak terus terang

sneer *n* mimik wajah yang menyeringai; *v* menyeringai

sneeze *n*, *v* bersin

sniff *n* hirupan; *v* mencium, mencium-cium; *~er dog* anjing pencium

sniffle *n* [snifel] pilek; *v* tersedu-sedu

sniper *n* penembak jitu

snob *n* orang sombong

snooze *n*, *sl* tidur sebentar

snore *v* mendengkur; *sl* mengorok

snout *n* moncong

snow *n* salju; *v* hujan salju; ~ *line* garis salju; **snowball** *n* bola salju; **snowman** *n* boneka salju; **snowy** *adj* bersalju

snug *adj* hangat, nyaman; pas

so *adv* begitu; sangat; demikian; ~~~ biasa saja; *I think* ~ saya kira begitu; *conj* jadi, maka, oleh sebab itu; ~ *that* supaya; sehingga; ~ *what* terus; *~-and-~* (si) anu

soak *v* merendam; **soaked, soaking** ~ *wet* basah kuyup

soap *n* sabun; ~ *opera* opera sabun; ~ *powder* sabun cuci baju

sob *n* sedu; *v* tersedu-sedu

soccer *n* sepak bola; ~ *field* lapangan sepak bola

social *adj* [sosyal] sosial, kemasyarakatan; ramah; ~ *studies,* ~ *sciences* ilmu pengetahuan sosial (IPS); ~ *worker* pekerja sosial; **socialism** *n* [sosyalizem] sosialisme; **socialist** *n* sosialis; **society** *n* [sosayeti]

581

masyarakat; perkumpulan, perhimpunan; **sociologist** n sosiolog; **sociology** n sosiologi, ilmu masyarakat

sock n kaus kaki

socket n lubang, stop-kontak

soda ~ water air soda

sofa n dipan, sofa, kursi empuk

soft adj lunak, lembek, lem-but; ~ toy boneka; **soft-ball** n sofbal; **softener** n [sofener] pelembut

soil n tanah; v mengotori

solar adj [soler] berhu-bungan dengan matahari; ~ eclipse gerhana matahari

sold v, pf → **sell**

soldier n [soljer] tentara, laskar, serdadu

sole adj satu-satunya, tung-gal; ~ parent orang tua tunggal; n telapak kaki, alas sepatu

solemn n [solem] khidmat, serius

solicitor n [solisiter] pengacara, ahli hukum

solld adj padat; kuat, kokoh; n zat padat

solitary adj sendiri; sepi

solo adj, adv sendiri, solo; **soloist** n solois, penyanyi atau pemain tunggal

solution n cara pemecahan, cara penyelesaian, solusi;

solve v memecahkan; menyelesaikan

some adj [sam] beberapa; kurang lebih; salah satu; sedikit; **somebody** pron seseorang, ada orang; **somehow** adv bagaimana-pun juga; **someone** pron [samwan] seseorang, ada orang

somersault n [samersolt] jungkir balik

something pron [samthing] sesuatu ← **some**

sometimes adv [samtaimz] kadang-kadang ← **some**

somewhat adv [samwot] agak, sedikit ← **some**

somewhere adv [samwér] entah di mana ← **some**

son n [san] anak (lelaki), putera; ~~in-law menantu

song n nyanyian, lagu; **songwriter** n pencipta lagu

soon adv segera, lekas; the ~er, the better makin cepat makin baik

582

sophisticated *adj* [sofisti-kéted] canggih, pintar, berpengalaman

sore *adj* sakit, pedih; *a ~ throat* sakit tenggorokan; *sl* marah

sorry *adj* menyesal; maaf

sort *n* macam, jenis; *v* menyortir, memilih, memilah-milah

SOS *abbrev save our souls* tolong, selamatkan jiwa kami

sought *v, pf →* **seek**

soul *n* sukma, nyawa, jiwa, semangat; *~ (music)* musik khas orang hitam

sound *adj* sehat, kuat; *n* bunyi, suara; *v* berbunyi, kedengaran; **soundtrack** *n* musik dari film

soup *n* [sup] sop, sup

sour *adj* [saur] asam, kecut; *sweet and ~* asam manis

source *n* [sors] sumber, mata air; narasumber

south *adj, n* [sauth] selatan; *~ Africa* Afrika Selatan (Afsel); *~ Pole* Kutub Selatan; **southeast** *adj, n* [sauth ist] tenggara; **southern** *adj* [sathern] sebelah selatan

souvenir *n* [suvenir] oleh-oleh, kenang-kenangan, cenderamata

sow *v* [so] menaburkan

soy *~ milk* susu kedelai; **soya** *~ bean* kacang kedelai

space *n* ruang, tempat; spasi, jarak; angkasa; **spacious** *adj* [spésyus] luas, lapang

spade *n* sekop

spaghetti *n* spageti

Spain *n* Spanyol

span *n* jangka; masa; rentang; *v* merentang

Spanish *adj* [Spanisy] berasal dari Spanyol; *n* bahasa Spanyol ← **Spain**

spare *adj* cadangan; *~ part* suku cadang, onderdil

spark *n* (percikan) api; **sparkle** *n* kilau; *v* berkilau-kilauan, bergemerlapan

sparrow *n* [sparo] burung gereja

speak *v* **spoke spoken** berbicara, berkata; *~ about, ~ on* membicarakan; *~ up* berbicara dengan keras; *~ well of* memuji; **speaker** *n* pembicara; Ketua Dewan; **speaking** *n* berpidato

spear *n* tombak, lembing

special *adj* [spésyal] istimewa, khusus, spesial; **specialist** *n* spesialis, ahli

species *n* [spisyis] jenis, macam

specific *adj* khusus, tertentu, spesifik; **specification** *n* spesifikasi

specimen *n* [spésimen] contoh

specs *n, coll* **spectacles** *n, pl, arch* kacamata; **spectacular** *adj* hebat, spektakuler; **spectator** *n* penonton

sped *v, pf* → **speed**

speech *n* pidato; cara bicara ← **speak**

speed *n* laju, kecepatan; *v* **sped sped** ~ *up* mempercepat; **speedboat** *n* perahu motor cepat; **speedy** *adj* lekas, cepat

spell *n* pesona; masa; *v* mengeja, **spelling** *n* ejaan

spend *v* **spent spent** membelanjakan, memakai

sperm *n* sperma, air mani

sphere *n* [sfir] bulatan, bola; bidang

spice *n* bumbu, rempah-

rempah; **spicy** *adj* pedas

spider *n* laba-laba

spill *v* tumpah; menumpahkan

spin *v* **spun spun** berputar-putar; memintal

spinach *n* [spinec] bayam

spine *n* tulang punggung

spiral *adj* [spairal] spiral; *v* bergerak naik/turun

spirit *n* [spirit] semangat; roh, hantu; **spirits** *n* minuman keras; **spirited** *adj* bersemangat; **spiritual** *adj* batin, rohani; keagamaan; *n* lagu rohani

spit *n* air ludah; *v* **spat spat** meludah

spite *n* dendam, dengki; *in* ~ *of* kendati, walaupun

splash *n* bunyi ceburan atau cemplungan; *v* bepercikan; memercikkan

splendid *adj* bagus sekali

splinter *n* serpih; *v* memecah, menyerpih

split *adj* retak, sobek; *n* belahan, retakan; *v* **split split** retak, membelah; membagi

spoil *v* memanjakan; merusak; **spoilt** *adj* manja

spoke, spoken v, pf → **speak; spokesperson** n juru bicara

sponge n [spanj] spons, bunga karang

sponsor n sponsor; v mendukung, mensponsori

spontaneous adj [sponténius] spontan

spooky adj angker, ngeri

spoon n sendok

sport n olahraga; **sporting** adj sportif; **sportsperson** n olahragawan; **sporty** adj suka berolahraga

spot n titik, noda; sl jerawat; v melihat; **spotlight** n lampu sorot; **spotty** adj berjerawat, jerawatan

spouse n pasangan; suami, isteri

spout n bibir, corot; v memancar

sprain n, v salah urat, keseleo

sprang v, pf → **spring**

spray n percikan, semprotan; v menyemprot, memerciki

spread n [spréd] penyebaran; sajian; mentega, selai; v **spread spread** mengolesi; menyiarkan, menyebarkan, membentangkan

spring n musim semi, musim bunga; sumber (air); per, pegas; v **sprang sprung** melompat, meloncat

sprinkle v [sprinkel] menaburkan, membubuhi; **sprinkler** n alat penyiram

sprint n lari cepat (jarak pendek); v berlari dengan cepat

sprout n tunas; v bertunas, tumbuh

sprung v, pf → **spring**

spun v, pf → **spin**

spurt v berlari atau bekerja dengan cepat; menyembur; menyemburkan

spy n mata-mata, spion; v memata-matai; **spyglass** n teropong, keker

Sq square alun-alun

squad n [skuod] regu, pasukan

square adj [skuér] persegi; 55 ~ meters 55 meter persegi; n persegi empat; alun-alun, medan; hasil perkalian

squash n [skuosy] semacam labu; v memasukkan dengan paksa

squat *v* [skuot] jongkok, berjongkok

squeak *n* [skuik] ciutan; cicit; *v* menciut-ciut; mencicit; **squeaky** *adj* menciut-ciut

squeeze *v* memeras; memeluk; *a tight* ~ sempit

squint *n* mata juling; *v* melihat dengan susah

squirrel *n* bajing

Sri Lanka *n* Sri Lanka; **Sri Lankan** *adj* berasal dari Sri Lanka

St *Saint* Santo, Santa

St *street* Jl (jalan)

stab *n* tikam, tikaman; *v* menikam

stable *adj* [stébel] mantap, stabil; kandang kuda, istal

stadium *n* stadion, gelang-gang, arena

staff *n* staf, para karyawan, para pegawai; para guru atau pengajar; tongkat

stag *n* rusa jantan

stage *n* panggung, pentas; tahap; *v* mengadakan, menyelenggarakan

stagnant *adj* tidak bergerak atau berkembang

stain *n* noda; *v* menodai,

mencemarkan; **stainless** ~ *steel* baja anti karat

stair *n* anak tangga; **stairs** *pl* tangga; **staircase, stairway** *n* tangga

stake *n* pancang; taruhan; bagian

stale *adj* keras (roti); basi, pengap, apak

stalk *n* [stok] tangkai; **stalker** *n* orang yang mengikuti atau mengejar

stall *n* [stol] warung, kedai, kios; kandang; *v* mogok, tidak langsung hidup

stamina *n* daya tahan

stammer *n* kegagapan; *v* menggagap

stamp *n* perangko; meterai, segel, tera, cap; *v* membubuhi prangko, memberi meterai, mengecap

stand *n* tribune; pendirian, sikap; kios; *v* **stood stood** berdiri; tahan; ~ *down* mundur, mengundurkan diri; ~ *for* berarti, melambangkan

standard *adj* baku, standar, tolok; *n* patokan, ukuran, norma, standar

stank *v, pf* → **stink**

staple *v* [stépel] menjepret (kertas); **stapler** *n* jepretan

staple *adj* [stépel] pokok; *n* makanan atau bahan pokok

star *n* bintang; *shooting ~* bintang berekor

starboard *adj, n* [starbed] sebelah kanan kapal

starch *n* kanji; sari pati

stare *v* memelototkan mata; memandang, menatap

starfish *n* bintang laut ← **star**

start *n* awal, permulaan; *v* mulai, berangkat; memulai; menghidupkan mesin

startle *v* [startel] mengejutkan, mengagetkan

starve *v* (mati) kelaparan

state *adj* kenegaraan; *~ Department* Departemen Luar Negeri (Amerika Serikat); *n* negara (bagian); keadaan, suasana; *v* menyatakan, menyebutkan, memaparkan; **stateless** *adj* tanpa kewarganegaraan; **statement** *n* pernyataan, pengumuman

station *n* stasiun, pos; pangkalan; *~ master* kepala stasiun

stationary *adj* tetap, tidak bergerak

stationery *n* alat tulis

statistics *n, pl* statistik, angka

statue *n* [statyu] patung

status *n* keadaan, kedudukan, status; pangkat, derajat

stay *n* (masa) tinggal; *v* tinggal, menginap; bertahan

STD *abbrev sexually transmitted disease* PMS (penyakit menular seksual)

steady *adj* [stédi] tetap, terus-menerus, teguh, mantap

steak *n* [sték] stek, bistek

steal *v* **stole stolen** mencuri; *~ into* menyelinap

steam *n* uap; *v* beruap; mengukus; **steamboat** *n* kapal api; jenis masakan yang direbus di tempat; **steamroller** *n* penggiling jalan

steel *n* baja; **steelworks** *n* pabrik baja

steep *adj* curam, terjal; *sl* mahal

steer *v* mengemudikan

stem *n* batang

stencil *n* stensil

stenographer *n*
[sténografer] juru steno
step *n* langkah, jejak; anak
tangga; tahap; *in* ~ sejalan;
out of ~ tidak sejalan, salah
langkah; *v* melangkah; ~
down meletakkan jabatan,
mengundurkan diri; ~ *on*
menginjak; **stepfather** *n*
bapak tiri, ayah tiri; **stepmother** *n* ibu tiri

stereo *n* [stério] peralatan
pemutaran musik

sterile *adj* [stérail] steril,
sucihama; mandul; **sterilize**
v menyucihamakan, men-
sterilkan

stern *adj* keras, tidak
senyum; *n* buritan (kapal)

stew *n* rebusan; *v* merebus

stick *n* tongkat, batang;
walking ~ tongkat; *v* **stuck**
stuck bertekun, bertahan;
melekatkan; **sticker** *n*
stiker, tempelan; **sticky** *adj*
lengket, lekat

stiff *adj* keras, kaku; pegal

still *adj* tenang, teduh, sepi;
adv masih; *conj* bahkan,
tetapi

stimulate *v* mendorong,
merangsang

sting *n* sengat; *v* **stung**
stung menyengat

stink *n* bau (busuk); *v* **stank**
stunk berbau (busuk)

stir *n* [ster] keributan, kekacauan; *v* bergerak; mengaduk; mengacaukan

stitch *n* jahitan; *v* menjahit

stock *n* persediaan; hewan
ternak; **stockbroker** *n*
pedagang saham

stocking *n* stoking

stockpile *v* menimbun ←
stock

stocky *adj* berbadan pendek
gemuk

stole, stolen *v, pf* → **steal**

stomach *n* [stamek] perut,
lambung

stone *n* batu; biji (buah)

stood *v, pf* → **stand**

stool *n* bangku, dingklik

stoop *v* membungkuk,
merendahkan diri

stop *n* perhentian, akhir;
v berhenti, menahan;
stopper *n* penyumbat,
tutup

storage *n* penyimpanan;
gudang; **store** *n* toko;
persediaan, perbekalan,
gudang; *v* menyimpan

storey → **story**

stork *n* (burung) bangau;

storm *n* angin badai;
stormy *adj* (berangin) ribut

story, storey *n* lantai,
tingkat

story *n* cerita, riwayat,
kisah, dongeng

stove *n* kompor; *gas ~*
kompor gas

straight *adj* [strét] lurus,
terus; *sl* heteroseksual; *adv*
langsung; jujur, terus
terang; **straighten** *v* meluruskan; **straightforward**
adj terus terang

strain *n* ketegangan; *v*
bersusah payah; mengejan;
menyaring; memaksakan;
strainer *n* saringan

strait *n* selat

stranded *adj* terdampar

strange *adj* [strénj] aneh,
ganjil, asing; **stranger** *n*
orang asing, orang luar

strangle *v* [stranggel]
mencekik

strap *n* tali; cambuk; **strap-
less** *adj* tanpa tali baju

strategic *adj* [stratijik]
strategis; **strategy** *n*
[strateji] strategi, siasat

straw *n* sedotan; jerami,
merang

strawberry *n* stroberi, arbei

stray *adj* yang tersesat;
tidak bertuan (binatang)

streak *n* garis, coret, coreng

stream *n* sungai, kali; aliran;
v mengalir; **streamer** *n*
pita hiasan; **streamlined**
adj ramping, efisien

street *n* jalan; **streetcar** *n*
trem

strength *n* kekuatan, tenaga,
kekuasaan; **strengthen** *v*
memperkuat, memperkokoh
← **strong**

stress *n* tekanan; ketegangan, stres; *v* menekan,
mementingkan, menitik-
beratkan; **stressful** *adj*
menegangkan

stretch *n* bagian, ruas
(jalan); jangkauan; *v* menegangkan; merentangkan

stretcher *n* usungan

strict *adj* keras; streng
(guru); **strictly** *adv* dengan
ketat; hanya

strike *n* pukulan; pemo-
gokan, mogok kerja;
serangan; *v* **struck struck**
memukul; menyerang;

589

mogok; **striker** *n* pemogok; pemain depan, ujung tombak (sepak bola)

string *n* tali; senar (raket, alat musik); untaian

strip *n* garis, jalur; *v* menghilangkan, membersihkan; membuka baju; menari telanjang; **stripper** *n* penari telanjang

stripe *n* garis, belang

stroke *n* pukulan; gaya (renang); serangan otak

stroll *v* berjalan kaki

strong *adj* kuat, kokoh; keras (minuman)

struck *v. pf* → **strike**

structure *n* bangunan, susunan, struktur; *v* menyusun

struggle *n* [stragel] perjuangan; *v* berjuang

strung *v, pf* → **string**

stubborn *adj* keras kepala

stuck *adj* terjebak, terjepit; *v, pf* → **stick**

student *n* pelajar, murid, mahasiswa; **studies** *n, pl* pelajaran, penelitian

studio *n* studio; sanggar

study *n* [stadi] pelajaran, studi; penelitian, riset;

ruang belajar; *v* belajar, mempelajari, mengkaji

stuff *n* bahan; barang-barang; *v* mengisi; **stuffing** *n* isi, pengisi; busa

stumble *v* [stambel] tersandung

stun *v* membuat tertegun atau pingsan; mengagetkan; **stunning** *adj* memesonakan, cantik sekali

stung *v, pf* → **sting**

stunk *v, pf* → **stink**

stunt *n* perbuatan yang luar biasa; pertunjukan, akrobatik

stunt *v* menghalangi, memperlambat; **stunted** *adj* kerdil, terhalang

stuntman *n* pemeran pengganti ← **stunt**

stupid *adj* bodoh, dungu

sturdy *adj* kokoh

style *n* [stail] gaya, cara; **stylish** *adj* bergaya

sub- *pref* (di) bawah

subconscious *adj, n* bawah sadar

subcontinent *the (Indian)* ~ Asia Selatan

subcontractor *n* pemborong bawahan

subject *n* soal, topik, subyek; mata pelajaran; *v* menaklukkan, menundukkan; **subjective** *adj* subyektif, berat sebelah

submarine *adj* [sabmarin] di bawah (permukaan) laut; *n* kapal selam

submission *n* penyerahan, pengajuan; ketundukan; **submit** *v* menyerahkan, menyampaikan

subordinate *adj, n* [sabordinet] bawahan

subscribe *v* berlangganan; menganut; **subscriber** *n* pelanggan; **subscription** *n* langganan

subsequent *adj* berikut; **subsequently** *adv* kemudian, setelah itu

subsidize *v* mensubsidi, memberi subsidi; **subsidy** *n* tunjangan, subsidi

subsistence ~ *agriculture* pertanian untuk bertahan hidup

substance *n* zat; bahan; isi pokok; hakikat

substitute *adj, n* ganti, pengganti; wakil; *v* mengganti; **substitution** *n*

penggantian

subtitles *n, pl* teks

subtract *v* **subtraction** *n* mengurangi

suburb *n* [sabérb] daerah perumahan, daerah perkotaan; **suburban** *adj* [sebérben] di daerah perumahan atau perkotaan; **suburbia** *n* daerah perumahan

subway *n* kereta api bawah tanah; terowongan penyeberangan

succeed *v* [saksid] berhasil, menjadi sukses; mengganti; **success** *n* keberhasilan, sukses; **successful** *adj* berhasil, sukses

such *adj* seperti itu, sedemikian; sungguh; *adv* demikian, begini, begitu; *pron* demikian, begitu

suck *v* mengisap, mengemut

sudden *adj* tiba-tiba, mendadak; **suddenly** *adv* tiba-tiba, secara mendadak

suds *n, pl* busa

sue *v* menggugat, menuntut

suede *n* [suéd] kulit halus

suffer *v* menderita; **suffering** *n* penderitaan

sufficient *adj* [safisyent]
cukup

suffix *n* akhiran

suffocate *v* mati lemas;
mencekik

sugar *n* [syuger] gula

suggest *v* [sejést] menyarankan, mengusulkan,
menganjurkan; **suggestion**
n saran, usul, anjuran; **sug-
gestive** *adj* sugesti

suicide *n* [suisaid] bunuh
diri

suit *n* [sut] setelan (pakaian);
rupa (kartu); *v* cocok; ber-
padanan; **suitable** *adj*
patut, layak, cocok; **suitcase** *n* koper

suite *n* [swit] setelan;
sederetan (kamar); rangkaian (musik)

sulfur, sulphur *n* belerang

sultan *n* [saltan] sultan

Sumatra *n* (pulau)
Sumatera; **Sumatran** *adj*
berasal dari Sumatera

summarize *v* meringkas;
summary *n* ringkasan,
ikhtisar

summer *n* musim panas

summon *v* memanggil;
summons *n* (surat)

panggilan

sun *n* matahari; **sunbathe**
v [sanbéth] berjemur; **sun-
burn** *n*, *v* terbakar sinar
matahari; **sunny** *adj* cerah;
riang

sundae *n* [sandé] es krim
dengan sirop

Sundanese *adj* [Sundaniz]
berasal dari daerah Jawa
Barat atau Banten; *n* bahasa
Sunda; orang Sunda

Sunday *n* hari Minggu ← **sun**

sundown *n* matahari terbenam, matahari tenggelam,
magrib ← **sun**

sung *v*, *pf* → **sing**

sunglasses *n*, *pl* kacamata
hitam ← **sun**

sunk *adj* tenggelam; *v*, *pf*
→ **sink**; **sunken** *adj*
cekung; tenggelam

sunlight *n* [sanlait] cahaya
matahari ← **sun**

sunrise *n* matahari terbit
← **sun**

sunset *n* matahari ter-
benam, matahari tenggelam,
magrib; ~ *prayer* (sholat)
magrib ← **sun**

sunshine *n* sinar matahari,
cahaya matahari ← **sun**

suntan *n* kulit berwarna coklat karena kena sinar matahari ← **sun**

super *adj* luar biasa, hebat

superb *adj* bagus sekali, istimewa

superintendent *n* pengawas, pemimpin, kepala instansi

superior *adj* [supirior] ulung, unggul, tinggi; sombong; *n* atasan

supermarket *n* (toko) swalayan

superstitious *adj* [superstisyes] sering percaya takhayul

supervise *v* mengawasi; **supervision** *n* [supervisyen] pengawasan; **supervisor** *n* [supervaizer] pengawas

supper *n* makan malam

supplement *n* [saplement] tambahan, pelengkap, suplemen; **supplementary** *adj* tambahan, pelengkap

supplier *n* [saplayer] pemasok; **supply** *n* pasokan, persediaan, suplai; *v* memasok, menyediakan

support *n* dukungan, bantuan; *v* mendukung, membantu; **supporter** *n*

pendukung

suppose *v* mengandaikan, menganggap, mengira

supreme *adj* unggul, teratas

sure *adj* [syur] tentu, pasti; yakin; **surely** *adv* tentu, tentu saja, pasti

surf *n* buih ombak; *v* berselancar; **surfer** *n* peselancar; **surfing** *n* (main) selancar, berselancar

surface *n* [sérfes] muka, permukaan

surfboard *n* papan selancar ← **surf**

surgeon *n* [serjen] ahli bedah; *plastic* ~ ahli bedah plastik; **surgery** *n* pembedahan, operasi; tempat praktek dokter

surname *n* nama keluarga, nama marga

surprise *n* kejutan; *v* membuat kejutan, mengejutkan

surrender *n* penyerahan; *v* menyerahkan

surround *v* mengelilingi, mengepung

survey *n* angket; penelitian; peninjauan; *v* meneliti, meninjau survival *n* kelangsungan hidup; **survive** *v* bertahan (hidup), tetap hidup, selamat; **survivor** *n* orang yang selamat

suspect *n* [saspekt] tersangka; *v* [saspékt] menyangka

suspend *v* menggantung; menangguhkan, menunda; **suspension** *n* penskorsan; suspensi

suspicious *adj* curiga, mencurigakan

SUV *abbrev sports utility vehicle* mobil jip

swallow *v* [swolo] menelan

swam *v, pf* → **swim**

swamp [swomp] paya, rawa

swap, swop *n* pertukaran; *v* bertukar; menukar

swarm *n* [sworm] sekawanan; *v* berkerumun

swat *v* [swot] memukul (serangga)

sway *n* goyangan; *v* bergoyang; menggoncangkan

swear *v* [suér] **swore sworn** bersumpah; mengumpat

sweat *n* [swét] keringat, peluh; *v* berkeringat; **sweatband** *n* gelang pen-

yerap keringat; **sweatshirt** *n* semacam baju hangat; **sweatshop** *n* pabrik dengan upah rendah; **sweaty** *adj* berkeringat, keringatan

Sweden *n* Swedia; **Swedish** *adj* berasal dari Swedia

sweep *v* **swept swept** menyapu

sweep, sweepstakes *n* taruhan, undian

sweet *adj* manis; *n* permen; ~ *and sour* asam manis; **sweetheart** *n* kekasih

swell *adj, sl* hebat; *n* gelombang; *v* membesar

swept *v, pf* → **sweep**

swift *adj* cepat, lancar

swim *v* **swam swum** berenang, mandi; **swimming** *n* renang; ~ *pool* kolam renang; *synchronized* ~ renang indah; **swimsuit, swimwear** *n* baju renang

swine *n* babi

swing *n* **swung swung** ayunan; pergeseran; *v* bergoyang, berayun

swipe *v* menggesek; memukul; mencuri

Swiss *adj* berasal dari Swis ← **Switzerland**

switch *n* sakelar, penghubung; pertukaran; ~ *off*
  mematikan; ~ *on* meng-
  hidupkan, memasang
Switzerland *n* (negeri) Swis
swollen *adj* bengkak,
  kembung ← **swell**
swop → **swap**
sword *n* [sord] pedang
swore, sworn *v, pf* → **swear**
swum *v, pf* → **swim**
swung *v, pf* → **swing**
syllable *n* [silabel] suku kata
syllabus *n* [silabus]
  rencana pelajaran, daftar
  pelajaran
symbol *n* lambang, simbol
symmetry *n* [simetri] simetri
sympathy *n* [simpathi]
  simpati
symphony *n* simfoni
symptom *n* gejala
synagogue *n* sinagoga
syndrome *n* sindroma;
  Down's ~ sindroma Down
synonym *n* padanan,
  sinonim
synthetic *adj* sintetis
Syria *n* Suriah; **Syrian** *adj*
  berasal dari Suriah
syringe *n* [sirinj] alat suntik,
  suntikan

syrup *n* sirop
system *n* sistem, susunan,
  jaringan

T

T ~-*bone steak* sejenis
  steik; ~-*shirt* kaus (oblong)
tab *n* label
tabby *n* kucing belang
table *n* [tébel] meja; daftar; ~ *tennis* tenis meja,
  pingpong; **tablecloth** *n*
  taplak meja; **tablespoon** *n*
  sendok besar
tablet *n* pil, tablet
tabloid *n* koran, tabloid
taboo *adj* tabu; *n* pantangan
tactful *adj* bijaksana,
  diplomatis
tactic *n* taktik, siasat, kiat;
  tactical *adj* taktis
tadpole *n* kecebong
tag *n* label, merek, nama,
  kartu; *v* memberi tanda
tail *n* ekor, buntut; bagian
  belakang; *v* membuntuti,
  mengikuti secara diam-
  diam

tailor *n* tukang jahit, modist

Taiwan *n* Taiwan; **Taiwanese** *adj* berasal dari Taiwan

take *v* **took taken** mengambil, membawa (pergi); mengganggap; menangkap, menerima; makan (waktu), memerlukan; ~ *after* mirip; ~ *for* mengira, menyangka; ~ *it* tahan; ~ *off* lepas landas; membuka; ~ *on* menerima, menanggung; ~ *over* mengambil alih; ~ *to* suka; **takeaway** *adj, n* dibungkus, bawa pulang; **taking** ~*s* pendapatan (selama masa tertentu)

talc *n* bedak; **talcum** ~ *powder* bedak

tale *n* cerita, dongeng

talent *n* [talent] bakat; **talented** *adj* berbakat

talk *n* [tok] percakapan, pembicaraan, ceramah; ~*s* perundingan; *v* berbicara, berunding, bertutur; **talkative** *adj* [tokatif] cerewet, banyak omong; **talkback** ~ *radio* acara kontak pendengar; **talkshow** *n* acara diskusi

tall *adj* [tol] tinggi, jangkung

tambourine *n* [tamburin] rebana

tame *adj* jinak; *v* menjinakkan

Tamil *adj* berasal dari kebudayaan Tamil atau Keling; *n* bahasa Tamil

tamper *v* merusakkan, mengubah

tan *adj* coklat muda; *n* kulit berwarna coklat

tandem *in* ~ bersama, berdua

tangerine *n* [tanjerin] jeruk garut, jeruk keprok

tangle *n* [tanggel] kekusutan, kekacauan

tango *n* [tanggo] (dansa) tango; *v* berdansa tango

tank *n* tangki; panser; **tanker** *n* kapal tangki

tap *n* keran; ketukan; *v* mengetuk; menyadap

tape *n* pita; plester; kaset; ~ *recorder,* ~ *deck* mesin pemutar kaset, tep; *sticky* ~ isolasi, selotip; *v* membalut; merekam; **tapeworm** *n* cacing pita

taper *v* meruncing

tapir *n* babi alu

tar *n* ter; aspal

tarantula *n* sejenis laba-laba besar

target *n* sasaran, tujuan, target; *v* mengincar

tariff *n* tarif, ongkos

taro *n* talas

tarpaulin *n* terpal

tart *n* kue kecil yang bulat

task *n* tugas, pekerjaan

taste *n* [tést] (cita) rasa; nuansa; selera; *v* mengecap, merasai; **tasteful** *adj* berselera (baik); **tasteless** *adj* tidak berselera, norak; **tasty** *adj* enak, sedap

tattoo *n* tato, rajah; *v* merajah, menato

taught *v, pf* → **teach**

tax *n* pajak, bea; *v* mengenakan pajak atau bea; **taxation** *n* pajak, perpajakan

taxi, taxicab *n* taksi; *metered* ~ taksi argo

taxpayer *n* pembayar pajak ← **tax**

TB *abbrev* *tuberculosis* TBC, radang paru-paru

tea *n* [ti] teh; ~ *bag* celup teh, kantong teh; ~ *plantation* kebun teh; *afternoon* ~ makan sore

teach *v* **taught taught** [tot]

mengajar; **teacher** *n* guru, pengajar; **teaching** *n* pengajaran; ~ *and learning* hal belajar-mengajar; **teachings** *n, pl* ajaran

teacup *n* cangkir teh, cawan teh ← **tea**

teak *n* (kayu) jati

team *n* regu, tim; ~ *spirit* semangat tim; **teammate** *n* kawan (seregu); **teamwork** *n* kerjasama sekelompok

tear *n* [tér] sobekan, robekan; *v* **tore torn** menyobek, merobek, mengoyak

tear *n* [tir] air mata

tearooms *n, pl* restoran kecil tempat minum teh ← **tea**

tease *v* mengganggu, meledek, mengusik

teaspoon *n* sendok teh ← **tea**

technical *adj* [téknikel] teknis; **technician** *n* teknisi

technique *n* [téknik] cara, teknik

technology *n* teknologi; *science and* ~ ilmu pengetahuan dan teknologi (iptek)

teen *n* remaja, anak baru gede (ABG); **teenage** *adj* remaja, umur belasan tahun; **teenager** n (anak) remaja; **teens** n, pl umur belasan tahun

teeth n, pl ← **tooth**

tel. *telephone* tlp (telepon)

telecast n [télekast] tayangan (langsung); v menayangkan, menyiarkan

telecommunications n, pl telekomunikasi

telegram n, arch telegram, surat kawat; **telegraph** n, arch telegraf

telephone n (pesawat) telepon, telefon; v menelepon

telescope n teropong (bintang), teleskop

television (TV) n televisi (teve, tivi)

tell v **told told** bercerita; menceritakan, memberitahukan; menyuruh, memerintahkan; ~ *on* melaporkan, mengadukan; ~ *off* menegur

teller n kasir

temper n sifat, watak

temperate ~ *zone* daerah beriklim sedang

temperature n suhu

temple n pelipis

temple n candi, kuil; *Hind* pura, kuil

temporary adj untuk sementara

tempt v menggoda

ten adj n sepuluh

tend v cenderung; merawat, memelihara; **tendency** n kecenderungan

tender adj (berhati) lembut; lunak, halus; kurang matang (daging); **tenderness** n kelembutan (hati)

tendon n urat

tennis n tenis

tenpin ~ *bowling* boling

tense n masa; *past* ~ bentuk lampau; *present* ~ (kata kerja) masa kini

tense adj tegang; **tension** n ketegangan, tegangan

tent n kemah, tenda

tenth adj kesepuluh ← **ten**

term n istilah; jangka waktu, triwulan, caturwulan (cawu); ~ *deposit* deposito berjangka; **terms** n, pl syarat-syarat; hubungan; *on good* ~ berhubungan baik

terminal adj penghabisan, terakhir; n terminal, pangkalan; mengakhiri

termite n rayap, anai-anai

terrace n teras

terrible *adj* [téribel] mengerikan, menakutkan, buruk sekali

terrific *adj* [terifik] hebat; **terrify** *v* menakutkan, membuat ngeri

territory *n* daerah, wilayah

terror *n* rasa takut, teror; **terrorism** *n* [térorizem] terorisme; **terrorist** *n* teroris; **terrorize** *v* meneror

tertiary *adj* [térsyeri] ketiga; ~ *education* pendidikan di perguruan tinggi

test *n* ujian, pemeriksaan, tes; percobaan, uji coba; *v* memeriksa, menguji; mengujicoba

testicle *n* [téstikel] buah pelir

testimony *n* kesaksian

testing *n* pengujian, percobaan

text *n* naskah, teks; *v* mengirim pesan singkat; **textbook** *n* buku pelajaran

textiles *n, pl* tekstil, barang tenunan

Thai *adj* berasal dari Thailand; *n* bahasa Thai; **Thailand** *n* Thailand

than *conj* daripada, dari; *bigger* ~ lebih besar daripada

thank *v* mengucapkan terima kasih; ~ *God Isl* alhamdulillah; *Chr* puji Tuhan; **thanks** *coll* terima kasih, makasih; ~ *to* berkat; ~ *very much* terima kasih banyak

that *conj* bahwa; yang; supaya; ~*'s all* sekian; ~*'s* ~ *habis perkara*; ~ *way* begitu; ke arah sana; *pron* **those** itu

thatch *n* jerami, rumbia

thaw *n* cair; *v* mencair, menjadi cair

the *art* itu, -nya

theater *n* (gedung) teater

theft *n* pencurian ← **thief**

their *pron, poss, pl* [thér] **theirs** mereka (punya), milik mereka; **them** *pron, obj, pl* mereka; **themselves** *pron, pl* mereka sendiri

theme *n* tema, pokok

then *adv* pada waktu itu; *conj* sesudah itu, kemudian, lalu; maka; *n* waktu itu

theory *n* teori

therapy *n* terapi

there *adv* [thér] (di) situ; (di) sana; *ejac* nah; *n* sana; itu; ~ *is,* ~ *are* ada; **there-**

fore *conj* maka, oleh sebab itu

thermometer *n* termometer

thermos *n* [thérmes] termos

thesaurus *n* [tesorus] sejenis kamus

these *pron, pl* ini ← **this**

thesis *n* **theses** [thisis] skripsi, disertasi, tesis; dalil

they *pron, pl* [thé] mereka

thick *adj* gemuk; tebal; kental; *coll* bodoh; **thickness** *n* ketebalan, kekentalan

thief *n* [thif] **thieves** pencuri, maling

thigh *n* [thai] paha

thimble *n* [thimbel] bidal, sarung jari

thin *adj* kurus; tipis; encer

thing *n* barang, benda, alat; *just the* ~ inilah dia

think *v* **thought thought** [thot] pikir, berpikir; berpendapat; ~ *about* memikirkan; ~ *over* menimbang, mempertimbangkan; **thinker** *n* pemikir

thinner *adj* lebih kurus, lebih tipis ← **thin**

third *adj, n* ketiga; pertiga; ~ *party* pihak ketiga; ~

world dunia ketiga; *two-*~*s* dua pertiga

thirsty *adj* haus

thirteen *adj, n* tiga belas; **thirteenth** *adj* ketiga belas

thirty *adj, n* tiga puluh

this *pron* **these** ini; ~ *evening* nanti malam; malam ini; ~ *morning* tadi pagi; pagi ini

thong *n* celana dalam berbentuk tali; **thongs** *n, pl* sandal jepit

thorn *n* duri

those *pron, pl* itu ← **this**

though *adv* [tho] bagaimanapun; *conj* sungguhpun, meskipun, biarpun; *even* ~ walaupun

thought *n* [thot] pikiran, ide; *v, pf* → **think**; **thoughtful** *adj* penuh perhatian

thousand *adj, n* ribu; *one* ~, *a* ~ seribu; *the* ~ *Islands* Pulau Seribu

thrash *v* menggelepar-gelepar; mencambuk

thread *n* [thréd] benang; urutan; *v* ~ *a needle* memasang benang

threat *n* [thrét] ancaman; **threaten** *v* mengancam

three *adj, n* tiga

threw *v, pf* → **throw**

thrifty *adj* hemat, irit

thrill *n* getaran (jiwa); sensasi; *v* menggetarkan; **thriller** *n* film atau buku yang menyeramkan; **thrilling** *adj* menggetarkan

throat *n* tenggorokan, kerongkongan; *ear, nose and ~ specialist* dokter THT (telinga, hidung dan tenggorokan)

throb *n* debar, denyut; denyutan; *v* berdebar, berdenyut-denyut

throne *n* takhta, singgasana

through *adj* [thru] selesai; *adv* terus; *prep* melalui, melewati, oleh, karena, terus; *to go ~ a lot* mengalami banyak kesulitan, banyak menderita; **throughout** *prep* di mana-mana; sepanjang

throw *v* **threw thrown** *n* lemparan; *v* membuang, melemparkan; *~ out, ~ away* membuang (sampah); *~ up* muntah

thrust *n* daya dorong; serangan; tusukan; *v* men-

dorongkan; menyerang; menusuk

thud *n* gedebuk; *v* bergedebuk

thumb *n* [tham] jempol, ibu jari; *v* membaca sepintas lalu (buku); **thumbnail** *n* kuku jempol

thump *n* gebukan; bunyi gedebuk; *v* menggebuk; berdebar (hati, jantung)

thunder *n* gemuruh, geluduk; **thunderbolt, thunderclap** *n* petir; **thunderstorm** *n* gemuruh dan petir

Thursday *adj, n* (hari) Kamis

thus *conj, arch* maka; *~ far* selama ini; sampai sekarang, hingga kini

thyroid *~ gland* kelenjar gondok

tiara *n* mahkota kecil, tiara

tick *n* tanda √; detik; kutu (binatang); *v* berdetik; *~ off* mencoret satu per satu

ticket *n* karcis, tiket

tickle *v* [tikel] menggelitik; **ticklish** *adj* geli

tidal *adj* berhubungan dengan air pasang dan surut; *~ wave* gelombang pasang; **tide high ~, ~'s in**

601

air pasang; *low ~, ~'s out*
air surut

tidy *adj* apik, rapi; *n* tempat
menyimpan barang; *v* merapikan; *~ up* merapikan,
memberes-beres

tie *n* tali, ikat; dasi; pertalian;
seri; *v ~ in* bersambung,
menyambung

tiger *n* harimau, macan

tight *adj* [tait] erat, tegang,
ketat; *coll* sukar, sulit;
~ squeeze keadaan terjepit;
~-fisted pelit; **tighten** *v*
mengeratkan, mengetatkan;
tights *n* stoking tebal

tile *n* ubin, tegel, keramik;
genteng

till *conj, coll* sampai, sehingga

till *n* laci uang till; *v* bercocok tanam

timber *n* kayu (bahan
bangunan)

time *n* waktu, masa; kali;
~ bomb bom waktu; *~ limit*
batas waktu; *~ off* waktu
cuti, istirahat; *~ out* istirahat (olahraga); *~ zone* zona
waktu, wilayah waktu; *in ~*
sebelum waktunya; *on ~*
tepat waktu; *that ~* waktu
itu; *~ after ~* berkali-kali; *a*

good ~ pengalaman yang
menyenangkan; *all the ~*
selalu, senantiasa; sejak
semula; *all this ~* selama
ini; *at a ~* sekaligus; *to
have ~* sempat, ada waktu;
to pass ~ iseng, mengisi
waktu; *to take ~* memakan
waktu; *v* mencatat waktu;
timekeeper *n* pencatat
waktu; **times** kali; **timer** *n*
jam (pasir), pencatat waktu;
timetable *n* jadwal

timid *adj* [timid] malu-malu,
takut-takut

tin *n* timah; kaleng; *~
opener* pembuka kaleng; *v*
mengalengkan; **tinfoil** *n*
kertas perak

tint *n* warna; *v* memberi warna

tiny *adj* [taini] kecil sekali,
mungil

tip *n* ujung; uang rokok, tip;
saran, tips; tempat pem-
buangan akhir (TPA); *v*
memberi tip; menumpahkan

tiptoe *v* jalan berjinjit

tire, tyre *n* ban

tire *v* menjadi lelah; melelahkan; **tired** *adj* lelah,
capek, letih

tissue *n* tisu; jaringan

title *n* [taitel] gelar; judul;
titleholder *n* pemegang
gelar, juara bertahan

T-junction *n* pertigaan,
simpang tiga

to *prep* [tu] ke, kepada;
untuk; lawan; *five (minutes)*
~ *three* jam tiga kurang
lima (menit)

toad *n* katak, kodok;
toadstool *n* cendawan,
jamur payung

toast *n* sulangan; *v* bersulang

toast *n* roti panggang; *v*
memanggang; **toaster** *n*
alat pemanggang roti

tobacco *n* tembakau

toboggan *n* kereta peluncur;
v main kereta peluncur

today *adv, n* [tudé] hari ini;
(masa) kini

toddler *n* (anak) batita
(bawah tiga tahun)

toe *n* [to] jari kaki; ujung
(kaus kaki); **toenail** *n* kuku
(jari) kaki

together *adv* [tugéther]
bersama, bersama-sama

toil *n* kerja keras; *v* bekerja
keras, membanting tulang

toilet *n* kamar kecil, WC;

kloset; **toiletries** *n, pl*
perlengkapan mandi, alat-
alat kecantikan

token *n* tanda (penghargaan),
tanda masuk

tolerant *adj* tenggang rasa,
toleran, sabar

toll *n* tol, bea; jumlah
korban; ~ *road* jalan tol;
road ~ jumlah korban
kecelakaan; **tollgate** *n*
pintu tol, gerbang tol

tomato *n* **tomatoes** tomat

tomb *n* [tum] kuburan,
makam

tomorrow *adv, n* [tumoro]
besok, esok (hari); masa
depan; *the day after* ~ lusa

ton *n, arch* [tan] ton; **tonne**
n [ton] ton (1,000 kg)

tone *n* bunyi, nada; warna,
rona; *v* ~ *down* mengurangi
(sifat)

tongs *n, pl* jepitan

tongue *n* [tang] lidah;
bahasa; *to hold your* ~
tutup mulut, diam

tonight *adv, n* [tunait]
malam ini, nanti malam

tonsils *n, pl* amandel

too *adv* terlalu, terlampau;
sekali; juga; ~ *late* terlambat;

~ *much* keterlaluan, kebanyakan

took *v, pf* → **take**

tool *n* alat, perkakas; **tools**
n, pl peralatan; **toolbox** *n*
tempat peralatan

tooth *n* **teeth** gigi; **toothache** *n* [tuthék] sakit gigi;
toothbrush *n* sikat gigi;
toothpaste *n* pasta gigi;
toothpick *n* tusuk gigi

top *adj* atas; teratas, terbaik,
tertinggi; ~ *secret* sangat
rahasia; ~ *speed* kecepatan tertinggi; *n* puncak,
(bagian) atas, ujung; tutup;
gasing; *v* melebihi

topic *n* topik, isu; **topical**
adj hangat

topless *adj* dengan dada
terbuka ← **top**

topping *n* saus, lapisan atas
← **top**

topsoil *n* lapisan atas
tanah

torch *n* obor, suluh; senter;
v membakar

tore *v, pf* → **tear**

torment *v* menyiksa, meny-
engsarakan

torn *v, pf* → **tear**

torpedo *n* [torpido]

torpedo; *v* menorpedo,
menenggelamkan

torrent *n* aliran air yang
deras, semburan

tortoise *n* [tortes] kura-
kura

torture *n* siksaan; *v*
menyiksa

toss *n* lemparan; *v* melemparkan, melontarkan,
melambungkan; mengundi

total *adj* sama sekali,
seluruh; *n* jumlah, total

touch *n* [tac] sentuhan,
nuansa; *in* ~ berhubungan;
tahu; *a* ~ *of* sedikit; *to lose*
~ kehilangan hubungan; *v*
menyentuh, menyinggung,
mengenai; ~ *up* memper-
baiki; ~*and-go* hampir-
hampir; **touching** *adj* bersentuhan; mengharukan

tough *adj* [taf] kasar; liat,
alot, awet; ~ *guy* orang
kuat; ~ *luck* sayang sekali

tour *n* tamasya, tur, perjalanan, pelayaran; *v* mengikuti
tur, menjelajahi; **tourism** *n*
wisata, pariwisata, turisme;
tourist *n* wisatawan, turis;
domestic ~ wisnu (wisa-
tawan nusantara); *foreign* ~

wisman (wisatawan mancanegara)

tournament n kejuaraan, pertandingan, turnamen

tow v [to] menarik, menderek; ~*truck* mobil derek

toward [tuwod] **towards** *prep* ke (arah); kepada, akan, untuk, terhadap; menjelang, menuju

towel n [taul] handuk

tower n [tauer] menara

town n kota; *to go into* ~ pergi ke kota; ~ *planning* planologi; **township** n kota

toxic *adj* beracun

toy n mainan

trace n bekas, jejak; v merunut, mengikuti jejak, memetakan

track n jejak, tapak jalan; ~ *event* olahraga lari; ~ *and field* olahraga lari, lompat dan lempar; v mengikuti jejak

tractor n traktor

trade n niaga, perniagaan, perdagangan; ~ *union* serikat kerja, serikat buruh; v berdagang, berbisnis; bertukar; tukar-menukar; ~ *in* tukar tambah; **trademark**

n merek dagang; **trader** n pedagang; **tradesman** n tukang

tradition n [tradisyen] adat (istiadat), tradisi; **traditional** *adj* menurut adat, tradisional

traffic n lalu lintas; peredaran, perdagangan; v mengedarkan; **trafficking** n pengedaran

tragedy n [trajedi] cerita sedih; kecelakaan; **tragic** *adj* tragis, menyedihkan

trail n tapak jalan, bekas, jejak; ~ *bike* (sepeda) motor gunung; v mengikuti jejak; **trailer** n kendaraan gandengan

train n kereta api

train v melatih; **trainee** *adj* calon; n orang yang ikut latihan, orang yang magang; **trainer** n pelatih; **training** n latihan, pelatihan, pendidikan

tram n trem

tramp n gelandangan, orang gila

trample v [trampel] menginjak-injak

trance n kerasukan, keadaan tidak sadar diri

tranquilizer *n* obat penenang

trans- *pref* lintas, melalui

transaction *n* transaksi

transfer *n* pemindahan, mutasi; *v* memindahkan

transform *v* berubah bentuk; **transformation** *n* perubahan bentuk, transformasi

transfusion *n* transfusi; *blood* ~ transfusi darah

transit *in* ~ dalam perjalanan

transition *n* peralihan, transisi

transitive *adj* transitif, mempunyai obyek

translate *v* menerjemahkan; **translation** *n* terjemahan, penerjemahan; **translator** *n* penerjemah

transmigration *n* transmigrasi

transmit *v* mengirimkan, menyiarkan, memancarkan; **transmitter** *n* pemancar

transparent *adj* bening, tembus cahaya

transplant *n* cangkok, pencangkokan; *v* mencangkokkan

transport *n* angkutan, pengangkutan, transportasi; *v* mengangkut, membawa; **transportation** *n* transportasi

transvestite *n* bencong, banci

trap *n* perangkap, jerat, jebakan; *v* memerangkap, menjerat, menjebak; **trapdoor** *n* pintu di lantai atau plafon

trash *n* sampah

trauma *n* [troma] pengalaman buruk, trauma

travel *v* jalan, berjalan; bepergian; **travels** *n, pl* perjalanan-perjalanan; **traveler** *n* orang yang sedang dalam perjalanan, musafir

tray *n* dulang; baki

tread *n* [tréd] alas sepatu, telapak (ban); *v* **trod trodden** menginjak, memijak; **treadmill** *n* mesin latihan jalan atau lari

treasure *n* [trésyur] barang berharga tinggi

treasurer *n* [trésyurer] bendahara; Menteri Keuangan; **treasury** *n* Departemen Keuangan

treat *n* [trit] sesuatu yang menyenangkan; *v* mengobati;

tropic

memperlakukan; **treatment** n pengobatan, perawatan; perlakuan

treaty n [triti] pakta, per-janjian

tree n pohon

trek n perjalanan (yang jauh dan melelahkan); v berjalan jauh

tremble n gemetar, getaran; v bergetar, gemetar

tremendous adj [treméndus] hebat, dahsyat

tremor n gemetaran; gempa bumi

trend n mode, gaya, tren; kecenderungan; **trendy** adj gaya, bergaya, modis

trespass v memasuki tem-pat tanpa izin; no ~ing dilarang masuk

trial n [trail] sidang peng-adilan, proses; percobaan; on ~ sedang diadili; ~ and error mencoba-coba; v menguji

triangle n [trayanggel] segi tiga; kerincing

tribal adj suku (bangsa), kesukuan; **tribe** n suku (bangsa)

tribute n penghargaan; upeti

trick n tipu daya; permainan; v menipu; **tricky** adj sulit, rumit

tricycle n [traisikel] sepeda roda tiga

trigger n [triger] pelatuk, picu, pemicu; v memicu, menyebabkan

trillion adj, n trilyun (1 000 000 000 000)

trim adj langsing, rapi; n potong sedikit; garis hiasan; v menggunting; menghiasi

trip n perjalanan; v tersandung; menjebloskan

triple adj [tripel] lipat tiga; n rangkap tiga; v berkem-bang tiga kali lipat; **triplet** n kembar tiga

tripod n [traipod] (tumpuan) kaki tiga, tripod

triumph n [trayemf] keme-nangan, keberhasilan; v menang, berhasil

trod, trodden v, pf → **tread**

trolley n kereta dorong, troli

troop n pasukan; v jalan ramai-ramai; **trooper** n polisi

trophy n [trofi] piala

tropic the ~s daerah kha-tulistiwa, daerah tropis; **tropical** adj tropis

607

trot n lari derap, lari kecil; v berderap, menderap

trouble n [trabel] kesusahan, kesulitan; gangguan; kerusakan; repot; v menyusahkan; **troublemaker** n pengacau

trousers n, pl [trauzerz] celana panjang

trout n semacam ikan air tawar

truce n gencatan senjata

truck n truk

true adj [tru] benar, betul, sungguh; setia; **truly** adv sesungguhnya, sungguh-sungguh

trumpet n trompet

trunk n belalai; batang (tubuh); arch koper

trust n kepercayaan; in ~ sebagai titipan; v percaya akan, mempercayai; **trustee** n wakil, wali; **trustworthy** adj andal, tepercaya; **trusty** adj setia

truth n [truth] kebenaran; in ~ sebenarnya; some ~ ada benarnya; to tell the ~ mengatakan dengan jujur; **truthful** adj jujur

try n usaha, percobaan; v

mencoba, berusaha; **tryout** n seleksi, percobaan

T-shirt n kaus (oblong)

← **T**

tub n bak mandi

tube n tabung; pipa, pembuluh; the ~ sl kereta api bawah tanah di London

tuber n akar umbi, ubi

tuberculosis n radang paru-paru, tebese, TBC

tuck n lipatan; v ~ in memasukkan baju ke dalam celana

Tuesday adj, n [Tyusdé] (hari) Selasa

tug n sentakan, tarikan; v menarik, menyentak; **tugboat** n kapal penarik

tuition n [tuwisyen] pengajaran; uang belajar

tulip n bunga tulip, tulpen

tumble n, v [tambel] jatuh terguling-guling

tumor n benjolan, tumbuhan, tumor

tuna n ikan tongkol

tune n bunyi, lagu; melodi; v menyetel; menala; ~ in ikut mendengar; ~ out berhenti mendengar; ~ up menyetel (mesin), memperbaiki

tunnel *n* terowongan; *v*
menggali terowongan atau
lubang

turbulence *n* pergolakan;
cuaca buruk; **turbulent** *adj*
bergolak

Turk *n* orang Turki; **Turkey** *n*
Turki

turkey *n* kalkun

Turkish *adj* berasal dari
Turki ← **Turk**

turn *n* putaran; giliran;
belok; *v* berputar, membelok,
menoleh; memutar, mem-
balikkan; ~ *away* menolak;
~ *down* menolak; menge-
cilkan; ~ *into* berubah
menjadi; ~ *off* mematikan;
~ *on* menghidupkan; ~ *up*
muncul; menemukan

turnip *n* lobak cina

turnoff *n* pintu keluar (jalan
tol) ← **turn**

turnout *n* jumlah hadirin ←
turn

turnover *n* penjualan,
omzet; pergantian ← **turn**

turpentine *n* [térpentain]
terpentin; **turps** *n, coll*
turpentin

turquoise *adj* [térkoiz] biru
toska; *n* (batu) pirus

turtle *n* kura-kura, penyu

tusk *n* gading

tutor *n* guru pribadi; wali
kelas; *v* memberi les privat
kepada; **tutorial** *n* kelas
diskusi

TV *abbrev television* teve,
tivi, TV (televisi)

tweezers *n, pl* pinset,
penyepit

twelfth *adj* kedua belas;
twelve *adj, n* dua belas

twenty *adj, n* dua puluh

twice *adv* dua kali

twilight *adj, n* [twailait]
senjakala

twin *n* kembar; ~ *sister*
saudara kembar

twinkle *n* kelip; *v* berkedip-
kedip, berbinar-binar

twist *n* tikungan; pelintir;
putaran; *v* memutar, me-
mintal, menganyam

two *adj, n* [tu] dua; ~-*edged*
bermata dua; ~-*legged*
berkaki dua; ~-*way* dua
arah

tycoon *n* [taikun] hartawan,
taipan

type *n* macam, jenis, bentuk;
tipe; golongan; huruf cetak;
v mengetik; *to touch-*~

mengetik tanpa melihat;
typewriter *n, arch* mesin tik
typhoid *n* [taifoid] ~ *(fever)*
tifus, tipus
typhoon *n* [taifun] (angin)
topan
typing *n* bahan untuk diketik;
typist *n* juru ketik
tyrant *n* orang yang kejam
tyre → **tire**

U

UAE *abbrev United Arab
Emirates* UEA (Uni Emirat
Arab)
UFO *abbrev unidentified
flying object* piring terbang
ugly *adj* buruk (rupa), jelek
UHF *abbrev ultra-high
frequency* UHF
UK *abbrev United Kingdom*
Kerajaan Inggris
Ukraine *n* [Yukrén] *(the)* ~
Ukraina
ukulele *n* [yukulélé] gitar
kecil, ukulele
ulcer *n* bisul, borok; *mouth*
~ sariawan

ultimate *adj* [altimet] terakhir, penghabisan, mutakhir; paling (mewah); pokok
ultra- *pref* [altra] teramat
sangat; **ultraviolet** *adj*
[altravayolet] ~ *rays* sinar
UV
um *interj* anu, er
umbrella *n* payung
umpire *n* wasit
UN *abbrev United Nations*
PBB (Persatuan Bangsa-
Bangsa)
un- *pref* tidak, tak
unable *adj* [anébel] tidak
mampu, tidak dapat, tidak
bisa ← **able**
unacceptable *adj* [anak-
séptabel] tidak dapat
diterima ← **accept**
unanimous *adj* [yunani-
mus] **unanimously** *adv*
dengan suara bulat, secara
aklamasi
unarmed *adj* [anarmd]
tidak bersenjata ← **arm**
unattached *adj* [anatacd]
sendiri, belum kawin; tidak
terikat ← **attach**
unattended *adj* [anaténded]
tanpa pengawasan ←
attend

unauthorized *adj* [anotho-raizd] tanpa wewenang, tidak sah ← **authorize**

unavoidable *adj* [anavoida-bel] tidak dapat dihindar-kan, tidak dapat dielakkan ← **avoid**

unaware *adj* [anawér] tidak sadar, tidak menyadari ← **aware**

unbalanced *adj* tidak waras

unbearable *adj* [anbérabel] tak tertahankan ← **bear**

unbelievable *adj* [anbeliv-abel] tidak dapat dipercaya, bukan main; **unbelieving** *adj* tidak percaya ← **believe**

unbiased *adj* [anbayesd] tidak memihak, berimbang ← **biased**

unbleached *adj* [anblicd] tidak diputihkan ← **bleach**

unbolt *v* membuka (kunci selot) ← **bolt**

unborn *adj* belum lahir; ~ *baby,* ~ *child* janin ← **born**

unbreakable *adj* [anbréka-bel] tahan banting, anti pecah ← **break**

unchain *v* melepaskan ← **chain**

uncivilized *adj* [ansivil-aizd] biadab ← **civilized**

uncle *n* [angkel] paman, om; ~ *Sam* Paman Sam

unclean *adj* tidak bersih, kotor ← **clean**

unclear *adj* kurang jelas ← **clear**

uncomfortable *adj* [ankamftabel] tidak enak, kurang nyaman ← **comfortable**

unconscious *adj* [an-konsyus] pingsan, tidak sadar; **unconsciously** *adv* tanpa disadari ← **conscious**

unconstitutional *adj* [ankonstityusyenel] tidak berdasarkan undang-undang dasar, inkonstitusional ← **constitutional**

uncontrollable *adj* [ankon-trolabel] tidak terkendali ← **control**

uncover *adj* [ankaver] membuka ← **cover**

undated *adj* tak bertanggal ← **date**

under *conj* menurut; *prep* (di) bawah; **underage** *adj* di bawah umur; **underclothes** *n, pl* pakaian dalam; **undercover** *adj* rahasia, menyamar; **underdog** *n* pihak yang lemah; **underestimate** *v* meremehkan; **underfed** *adj* kurang mendapat makanan; **undergo** *v* **underwent undergone** menempuh, mengalami; **undergraduate** *adj, n* sarjana muda; **underground** *adj* (di) bawah tanah; *n the* ~ kereta api bawah tanah (di London); **underline** *v* menggarisbawahi; **underneath** *adv, prep* (di) bawah; **underpaid** *adj* dibayar tidak selayaknya; **underpass** *n* terowongan (di bawah jalan); **underscore** *n* tanda _; **undersigned** *the* ~ yang tertanda tangan (ytt)

understand *v* **understood understood** mengerti, paham; memahami; **understanding** *adj* pengertian; *n* pengertian, pemahaman

undertake *v* **undertook undertaken** menjalankan, melakukan

undertaker *n* pengurus jenazah

undertook *v, pf* → **undertake**

underwater *adj* [anderwoter] (di) dalam air ← **under**

underway *adv* sedang berlangsung ← **under**

underwear *n* pakaian dalam ← **under**

underworld *n* [anderwerld] dunia penjahat, dunia bawah tanah ← **under**

undies *n, pl, coll* celana dalam ← **underwear**

undo *v* [andu] **undid undone** membuka ← **do**

undoubtedly [andautedli] tentu saja, tidak diragukan lagi ← **doubt**

undress *v* membuka pakaian, melepas pakaian ← **dress**

uneasy *adj* [anizi] gelisah

uneducated *adj* [anédyukéted] tidak berpendidikan ← **educate**

unemployed *adj, n* [anemploid] pengangguran; **unemployment** *n* pengangguran ← **employ**

unequal *adj* [anikwel] tidak sama, tidak sederajat, tidak seimbang; **unequaled** *adj* tidak ada bandingnya, tiada tara ← **equal**

uneven *adj* [aniven] tidak rata, bergelombang; tidak konsisten, tidak seimbang ← **even**

unexpected *adj* [anékspékted] tidak terduga; **unexpectedly** *adv* tiba-tiba ← **expect**

unfair *adj* tidak adil, tidak jujur

unfaithful *adj* tidak setia, durhaka; menyeleweng ← **faithful**

unfit *adj* tidak sehat; tidak patut ← **fit**

unforgettable *adj* [anforgétabel] tak terlupakan ← **forget**

unforgivable *adj* [anforgivabel] tidak dapat dimaafkan ← **forgive**

unfortunate *adj* [anfortyunet] malang, sial; **unfortunately** *adv* sayang ← **fortunate**

ungrateful *adj* [angrétful] tidak tahu berterima kasih ← **grateful**

unhappiness *n* [anhapines] kesedihan, rasa tidak bahagia; **unhappy** *adj* tidak bahagia, sedih; malang ← **happy**

unhealthy *adj* [anhélthi] tidak sehat ← **healthy**

UNICEF *abbrev United Nations International Children's Fund* Organisasi Persatuan Bangsa-Bangsa untuk Anak-anak, Organisasi Anak Sedunia

unidentified *adj* [anaidéntifaid] ~ *flying object (UFO)* piring terbang ← **identify**

uniform *adj, n* [yuniform] (pakaian) seragam; *school* ~ seragam (sekolah)

unify *v* [yunifai] menyatukan, mempersatukan

uninhabited *adj* tidak dihuni ← **inhabit**

uninvited *adj* [aninvaited] tak diundang ← **invite**

union *n* [yunien] persatuan, serikat, uni

unique *adj* tunggal, unik, tiada duanya

unison [yunison] *in* ~ serentak, bersama

unit *n* [yunit] unit, satuan

unite *v* [yunait] bersatu, menyatu; menyatukan, mempersatukan; **united** *adj* bersatu, serikat; *(the)* ~ *Arab*

Emirates (UAE) Uni Emirat Arab; *the ~ States of America (USA)* Amerika Serikat (AS)

universal *adj* [yunivérsel] umum, universal; **universe** *n* alam semesta

university *n* [yunivérsiti] universitas

unkind *adj* [ankaind] kejam, bengis ← **kind**

unknown *adj* tidak ketahuan, tidak dikenal ← **knowing**

unless *conj* (kecuali) kalau

unlike *adj* tidak seperti, tidak sama ← **like**

unlikely *adj* kemungkinan kecil; tidak dapat dipercaya ← **likely**

unload *v* membongkar (muatan), mencurahkan ← **load**

unlock *v* membuka (kunci, gembok) ← **lock**

unlucky *adj* celaka, sial, malang ← **lucky**

unmarried *adj* [anmarid] belum kawin, tidak kawin, lajang ← **married**

unnatural *adj* [an-natyurel] tidak wajar ← **natural**

unnecessary *adj* [an-néseseri] tidak perlu, tidak usah ← **necessary**

unpack *v* membongkar ← **pack**

unpaid *adj* tidak dibayar, belum dibayar ← **pay, paid**

unpleasant *adj* [anplézent] kurang menyenangkan, tidak enak ← **pleasant**

unpredictable *adj* [anprediktabel] tidak dapat diramalkan ← **predict**

unprepared *adj* [anprepérd] tidak siap, belum siap; tidak disiapkan, belum disiapkan ← **prepared**

unprofessional *adj* [anprofesyenel] tidak profesional ← **professional**

unprotected *~ sex* hubungan seks tanpa alat kontrasepsi ← **protect**

unqualified *adj* [ankuolifaid] tidak berijazah, tidak memiliki kualifikasi ← **qualified**

unreal *adj* tidak nyata; **unrealistic** *adj* tidak realistis ← **real**

unreasonable *adj* [anriznabel] tidak masuk akal ← **reasonable**

unreliable *adj* [anrelayabel] tidak dapat dipercayai, tidak dapat diandalkan ← **reliable**

unripe *adj* mentah, kurang matang ← **ripe**

unsafe *adj* tidak aman, berbahaya ← **safe**

unsatisfactory *adj* [ansatisfaktori] tidak memuaskan ← **satisfactory**

unscrew *v* membuka sekrup, melepaskan sekrup ← **screw**

unseen *adj* tidak terlihat, tidak kelihatan ← **seen**

unskilled *adj* [anskild] tidak terampil, tidak mahir; ~ *labor* tenaga buruh ← **skilled**

unsolved *adj* [ansolvd] belum terbongkar ← **solve**

unstable *adj* [anstébel] goyah, tidak stabil; mudah tergoncang ← **stable**

unsteady *adj* [anstédi] tidak tegak, goyah ← **steady**

unsuccessful *adj* [ansaksésful] tidak berhasil,

tidak lulus, gagal ← **successful**

unsuitable *adj* [ansutabel] tidak cocok ← **suitable**

unsure *adj* [ansyur] tidak yakin, tidak pasti ← **sure**

unsweetened *adj* [answitend] tanpa gula, tanpa pemanis ← **sweeten**

unthinkable *adj* [anthinkabel] tak terpikirkan, tak terbayangkan ← **think**

untidy *adj* [antaidi] tidak rapi, tidak teratur, jorok ← **tidy**

untie *v* [antai] membuka (tali), menguraikan ← **tie**

until *conj* sampai; *prep* hingga, sampai (dengan)

untrained *adj* tidak terlatih, tanpa pendidikan ← **train**

untrue *adj* [antru] tidak benar; **untruthful** *adj* tidak benar, bohong ← **true, truth**

unusual *adj* [anyusyuel] tidak biasa, tidak lazim ← **usual**

unwanted *adj* [anwonted] tidak diinginkan ← **wanted**

unwelcome *adj* [anwélkem] tidak dikehendaki, tidak disambut ← **welcome**

unwell *adj* tidak enak badan ← **well**

unwilling

ENGLISH–INDONESIAN

unwilling *adj* tidak mau, segan, malas ← **willing**

unwind *v* [anwaind] **unwound unwound** beristirahat; melepaskan ← **wind**

unwise *adj* tidak bijaksana, bodoh ← **wise**

unwound *v, pf* → **unwind**

unwrap *v* [anrap] membuka (bungkus)

unwritten *adj* [anriten] tak tertulis ← **written**

unzip *v* membuka ritsleting ← **zip**

up *adj* habis; bangun; naik; *what's ~?* apa kabar? ada apa?; *adv* ke atas; naik; *~ and down* naik turun; mondar-mandir; *prep* (di) atas; ke atas; *~ against* menghadapi; *~ front* di muka; *~ to* sampai; sedang; *what are you ~ to?* sedang apa?; *~-to-date* modern, terbaru, mutakhir; **upbringing** *n* asuhan, didikan; **upcoming** *adj* [apkaming] yang mendatang; **update** *n* laporan terbaru; *v* memperbarui; **upfront** *adj* [apfrant] terus

terang, jujur; **upgrade** *n* penataran; *v* menaikkan kelas; **uphill** *adj* sulit, berat; *adv* ke atas (bukit), menanjak

upholstery *n* kain pelapis atau bantal di kursi, sofa dll

upkeep *n* perawatan, pemeliharaan ← **up**

upon *prep* [apon] (di) atas → **on**

upper *adj* (tingkat) atas; tinggi; *~ case* huruf besar ← **up**

upright *adj* [aprait] tegak (lurus); jujur ← **up**

uprising *n* pemberontakan ← **up**

uproar *n* kegaduhan, keributan ← **up**

upset *adj* tersinggung; tidak tenang; terbalik; terganggu; *v* membuat tersinggung, mengganggu, merusak

upside *~ down* terbalik ← **up**

upstairs *adj* di (lantai) atas; *adv* ke (lantai) atas; *n* lantai atas ← **up**

upward *adj* [apwerd] naik; *adv* (menuju) ke atas ← **up**

616

uranium *n* [yurénium] uranium

urban *adj* [érben] perkotaan

urge *n* [érj] dorongan; *v* mendorong, mendesak; **urgent** *adj* mendesak, penting, genting

urinate *v* [yurinét] kencing, buang air kecil; **urine** *n* air kencing, air seni

US *abbrev* *United States* AS (Amerika Serikat)

us *pron, obj* kita (termasuk lawan bicara); kami

use *n* [yus] pemakaian, penggunaan; *what's the ~?* apa gunanya? *it's (of) no ~* tidak ada gunanya, percuma, sia-sia; *v* [yuz] memakai, menggunakan; *~ up* menghabiskan; **used** *adj* bekas (pakai); *~ to* terbiasa; dulu; **useful** *adj* [yusfel] berguna, bermanfaat; **useless** *adj* tidak berguna, sia-sia; tidak dapat dipakai; **user** *n* [yuzer] pemakai

USG *abbrev* *ultrasonogram* USG

usual *adj* [yusyual] biasa, lazim, lumrah; *as ~* seperti biasa; *the ~* yang biasa;

usually *adv* biasanya ←
use

utensil *n* [yuténsil] alat (masak)

uterus *n* [yuterus] rahim, kandungan, peranakan

utilities *n, pl* keperluan (air, listrik, gas); **utilize** *v* mempergunakan

utmost *adj* yang sepenuhnya; *n* sepenuhnya

utter *v* mengucapkan, memanjatkan (doa)

utter *adj* **utterly** *adv* sama sekali

UV *abbrev* *ultra violet* ultra-violet

V

vacancy *n* lowongan; ada kamar; **vacant** *adj* kosong

vacation *n* [vakésyen] liburan

vaccinate *v* [vaksinét] memvaksinasi, menyuntik; **vaccination** *n* vaksinasi, pencacaran

vacuum [vakyum] *v* menyedot debu

vagina *n* [vejaina] vagina, liang peranakan

vague *adj* [vég] tidak jelas, samar-samar

vain *adj* bangga pada penampilan sendiri

Valentine [Valentain] ~'s *Day* Hari Kasih Sayang, Hari Valentin (tanggal 14 Februari)

valet *n, m* [valé] pelayan pria; ~ *parking* pelayanan parkir

valiant *adj* [valient] berani

valid *adj* [valid] berlaku, sah; **validate** *v* mengesahkan, memvalidasi

valley *n* [vali] lembah

valuable *adj* [valyuabel] berharga; mahal; *n, pl* barang-barang berharga; **value** *n* nilai; *good* ~ harga baik; *pl* norma, nilai; *v* menghargai, menilai

valve *n* [valv] klep, katup, pentil

vampire *n* [vampair] vampir, drakula, pengisap darah

van *n* mobil bagasi; gerbong

vandal *n* perusak, orang iseng yang merusak sarana umum; **vandalism** *n* [vandelizem] kerusakan akibat orang iseng; **vandalize** *v* merusak sarana umum

vanilla *n* panili, vanili

vanish *v* [vanisy] hilang, menghilang, lenyap

vanity *n* [vaniti] kebanggaan pada penampilan sendiri ← **vain**

vapor *n* uap

variable *adj* [vériabel] berubah-ubah, tidak tetap; *n* variabel; **variation** *n* perubahan, variasi ← **vary**

varied *adj* [vérid] berbagai, berbeda-beda; **variety** *n* [varayeti] macam; keanekaragaman; **various** *adj* [vérius] berjenis-jenis, bermacam-macam ← **vary**

varnish *n* pernis

vary *v* [véri] berubah-ubah, berbeda-beda; mengubah

vase *n* vas, jambangan

vast *adj* luas, besar sekali; **vastly** *adv* sangat, amat

VAT *abbrev value added tax* PPN (pajak pertambahan nilai)

vat *n* tong

Vatican *the* ~ kediaman Sri Paus di Roma, Vatikan

vault *n* kuda-kuda loncat;

pole ~ loncat galah; *v* meloncat (dengan galah)

veal *n* daging anak sapi

vegan *n* orang yang tidak makan atau memakai produk dari hewan

vegetable *adj* [véjtebel] nabati; *n* sayur, *pl* sayur-sayuran, sayur-mayur; **vegetarian** *n* [véjétérien] orang yang hanya makan sayur, orang vegetarian; **vegetation** *n* [véjetésyen] tetumbuhan, tumbuh-tumbuhan

vehicle *n* [viekel] kendaraan, wahana

veil *n* [vél] kerudung, kudungan; jilbab; tudung; selubung; *v* menyelubungi

vein *n* [vén] urat, pembuluh balik, vena

velvet *adj, n* beludru, beledu

vendor *n* penjaja, penjual; *street* ~ pedagang kaki lima

veneer *n* lapisan (tipis)

venereal [veniriel] ~ *disease (VD)* penyakit menular seksual (PMS)

venom *n* [vénem] bisa;

venomous *adj* [vénemus] berbisa

vent *n* lubang angin; **ventilation** *n* ventilasi, peredaran udara, sirkulasi udara

ventriloquist *n* [véntriloquist] ahli bicara perut

venture *n* usaha; *v* mengambil risiko, memberanikan diri

venue *n* [vényu] tempat acara berlangsung

veranda(h) *n* beranda

verb *n* kata kerja

verdict *n* putusan

verification *n* verifikasi, pembuktian; **verify** *v* [vérifai] membuktikan, membenarkan

vermicelli *n* [vérmicéli] ~ *noodles* bihun, soun

verse *n* [vérs] ayat; sajak, syair; pantun; bagian (dari sajak)

version *n* [vérsyen] versi

versus (vs) *conj* lawan, melawan

vertical *adj* tegak lurus, vertikal

very *adv* [véri] amat, sangat, sekali; benar, betul

vessel *n* perahu, kapal; bejana

vest *n* rompi; singlet

vet *n, coll* dokter hewan (drh) ← **veterinarian**

vet *n, coll* veteran; **veteran** *adj* [vétran] kawakan; *n* veteran

veterinarian *n* [véterinérian] dokter hewan; **veterinary** ~ *surgeon* dokter hewan

veto *n* (hak) veto; *v* memveto

VHF *abbrev very high frequency* VHF

via *prep* [vaya] lewat, via; melalui

vibrate *v* bergetar; **vibration** *n* getaran, vibrasi

vicar *n, Chr* [viker] pendeta

vice *n* sifat buruk atau jahat; ~ *squad* polisi kesusilaan

vice- *pref* wakil, muda; ~*president* wakil presiden

vice ~ *versa* sebaliknya

vicious *adj* [visyes] kejam, jahat; ~ *circle* lingkaran setan

victim *n* korban

victor *n* pemenang; **victorious** *adj* jaya, yang menang; **victory** *n* kemenangan

video [vidio] alat perekam kaset video; **videotape** *n* kaset video; *v* merekam

pada kaset video

Vietnam *n* Vietnam; **Vietnamese** *adj* berasal dari Vietnam, *n* orange Vietnam

view *n* [vyu] pemandangan; pandangan, pendapat; *on* ~ dipertontonkan; *scenic* ~ pemandangan yang asri; *v* melihat, meninjau; **viewer** *n* pemirsa; **viewfinder** *n* lubang kecil untuk mengukur ruang di kamera

vigorous *adj* kuat, bersemangat

vile *adj* jorok, menjijikkan; buruk; keji, hina

villa *n* vila

village *n* [vilej] desa, kampung, dusun; **villager** *n* orang desa

vine *n* tanaman anggur; tanaman merambat

vinegar *n* [vineger] cuka

vineyard *n* [vinyerd] kebun anggur

vinyl *n* [vainel] plastik tebal

violence *n* [vayolens] kekerasan; **violent** *adj* kasar; suka memukul; keras, hebat

violet *adj* [vayolet] ungu muda; *n* sejenis bunga berwarna ungu

violin *n* [vayolin] biola

VIP *abbrev* *very important person* orang yang sangat penting

virgin *n* [vérjin] perawan, gadis; ~ *Mary* Perawan Suci; **virginity** *n* [vérjiniti] kegadisan, keperawanan

virtual *adj* [vértyuel] nyaris; maya; **virtually** *adv* nyaris

virus *n* [vairus] virus

visa *n* [viza] visa

vision *n* [visyen] penglihatan; visi

visit *n* [vizit] kunjungan; *v* berkunjung; mengunjungi; **visitor** *n* tamu, pengunjung; ~*s book* buku tamu

visual *adj* [visyuel] berkaitan dengan mata atau peng-lihatan; ~ *arts* seni rupa

vital *adj* penting sekali; **vitally** *adv* sangat, amat

vitamin *n* vitamin

vivid *adj* [vivid] hidup, jelas, terang

VJ *abbrev* *video jockey* VJ

vocabulary *n* **vocab** *coll* [vokabuleri] kosa kata

vocal *adj* bersuara; ber-kaitan dengan suara; *n* pembawaan lagu; **vocalist**

n penyanyi, vokalis

voice *n* [vois] suara; *to lose your* ~ kehabisan suara; *v* menyuarakan, mengatakan

void *adj* tidak berlaku lagi; *n* kekosongan, kehampaan

volcanic *adj* [volkanik] berkaitan dengan gunung api; **volcano** *n* [volkéno] gunung api, gunung berapi

volleyball *n* bola voli

volt *n* volt; **voltage** *n* [voltej] tegangan listrik, voltase

volume *n* [volyum] isi, muatan, volume; jilid

voluntary *adj* [volentri] sukarela; **volunteer** *adj* sukarelawan; *v* menawarkan (jasa); menjadi sukarelawan

vomit *n* muntah; *v* muntah

voodoo *n* guna-guna

vote *n* (pemungutan) suara; hak memilih; *v* memberikan suara; memutuskan; memilih; **voter** *n* pemilih; **voting** *n* pemungutan suara

voucher *n* [vaucer] vocer, bon

vow *n* janji; *marriage* ~*s* janji kawin; *Isl* ijab kabul; *v* bersumpah

vowel *n* [vaul] huruf hidup,
vokal

voyage *n* [voyej] pelayaran,
perjalanan lewat laut

vulgar *adj* [valger] kasar;
tidak sopan, jorok

vulnerable *adj* [valnerabel]
mudah diserang, rentan

vulture *n* [vultyur] burung
nasar

W

wacky *adj, coll* nyentrik

wad *n* [wod] gumpal; *a ~
of gum* permen karet

waddle *n* [wodel] *v* berjalan
terseok-seok

wade *v* berjalan dalam air;
mengarungi

wafer *n* biskuit tipis

waffle *n* [wofel] wafel; *v*
cerocos, berbicara tanpa
tujuan

wag *v* mengibas, mengibas-
ibas; mengibaskan

wage *n* upah

wagon *n* [wagon] gerbong,
kereta

wail *n* ratapan; *v* meratap

waist *n* pinggang; **waistcoat**
n rompi; **waistline** *n*
ukuran pinggang

wait *n* masa menunggu;
penantian; *v* menunggu,
menanti; *~ for* menunggui,
menantikan; *~ on* melayani;
~ and see lihat dulu; **waiter** *n, m* pelayan; **waitress**
f pelayan

wake *n* air alur kapal; selamatan sesudah upacara
pemakaman; *v* **woke
woken** membangunkan;
~ up bangun; membangun-
kan; **waken** *v* bangun;
membangkitkan

walk *n* [wok] jalan-jalan,
jarak yang dijalani; *v* jalan
(kaki), berjalan (kaki); *~
away, ~ out* meninggalkan
tempat; **walkie-talkie** *n*
woki-toki, HT; **walking** *adj*
berjalan; **walkout** *n* aksi
mogok

wall [wol] *n* tembok,
dinding

wallet *n* [wolet] dompet

wallpaper *n* [wolpéper]
kertas dinding; *v* melapisi
dinding dengan kertas

walnut *n* [wolnat] sejenis kenari

walrus *n* [wolras] singa laut

waltz *n* [woltz] vals; *v* berdansa vals

wand *n* [wond] tongkat sihir

wander *n* jalan-jalan; *v* mengembara, berkelana, berputar-putar; ~ *off* pergi ke tempat lain

want *n* [wont] keinginan; *v* ingin, menginginkan, menghendaki; membutuhkan, memerlukan; *for* ~ *of* karena tidak ada; **wanted** *adj* dicari

war *n* [wor] perang; ~ *crimes* kejahatan perang; ~*torn* hancur akibat perang

ward *n* [word] bangsal, ruang; wilayah

warden *n* [worden] pengawas, penjaga; sipir, juru kunci

wardrobe *n* [wordrob] lemari baju, lemari pakaian; koleksi busana

warehouse *n* [wérhaus] gudang

warfare *n* [worfér] peperangan, pertempuran, perjuangan

warm *adj* [worm] hangat, panas; *v* memanaskan, menghangatkan; ~ *to* menjadi tertarik atau bersemangat; ~ *up* menjadi panas; menghangatkan (makanan); memanaskan (badan); **warmth** *n* panas, kehangatan

warn *v* [worn] memperingatkan; **warning** *n* peringatan

warp *n* [worp] *v* membengkokkan, melengkungkan

warranty *n* [woranti] jaminan, garansi

warrior *n* [worier] pejuang, prajurit, kesatria

warship *n* [worsyip] kapal perang

wart *n* [wort] kutil

wartime *n* [wortaim] masa perang

was *v, pf* [woz] → **be**

wash *n* [wosy] cucian; mandi; *to have a* ~ mandi; *v* mencuci, membasuh; memandikan (orang); ~ *your hands* mencuci tangan; ~ *up* terhanyut; ~ *your hair* keramas, mencuci rambut; **washbasin** *n* tempat cuci muka, wastafel; **washcloth** *n* lap; **washing** *n* cucian;

washroom n kamar kecil, WC

wasp n [wosp] tawon

waste n [wést] sampah; pemborosan; v memboros-kan; membuang, **wasteful** adj boros; **wastepaper** ~ basket tempat sampah

watch n [woc] jam tangan; jaga; by my ~ menurut jam saya

watch v [woc] menonton; menjaga; ~ out hati-hati, waspada; ~ over menjaga, melindungi; **watchdog** n (anjing) penjaga

water n [woter] air; v ber-liur; menyirami, mengairi; ~ polo polo air; ~ pump pompa air; ~resistant tahan air; ~ supply pengadaan air, persediaan air; **watercolors** n, pl cat air; **waterfall** n air terjun; **waterfront** n tepi laut, tepi sungai, tepi danau; **watering** ~ can cerek; **watermelon** n semangka; **waterproof** adj kedap air; **waters** n, pl perairan; **waterski** n [woterski] ski air; v bermain ski air; **watertight** adj kedap air,

rapat; **watery** adj berair

wave n ombak, gelombang; v berkibar; melambaikan; ~ at melambaikan tangan; **wavelength** n panjang gelombang; **wavy** adj ber-gelombang, berombak

wax n lilin; malam (untuk batik)

way n jalan; arah; cara; on the ~ di perjalanan, sedang dalam perjalanan; to give ~ memberi jalan; to get your (own) ~, to have your (own) ~ menang sendiri

we pron, pl kami; kita

weak adj [wik] lemah; **weakness** n kelemahan

wealth adj [wélth] kekaya-an; **wealthy** adj kaya

weapon n [wépen] senjata

wear n [wér] **wore worn** pakaian; perlengkapan; v memakai; ~ away menjadi aus, tersusut; ~ out menjadi usang; menjadi capek

weasel n [wizel] semacam musang

weather n [wéther] cuaca; ~ forecast prakiraan cuaca

weave v [wiv] **wove woven** bertenun; menenun; **weaver**

n penenun, tukang tenun

web *n* jaringan; rumah laba-laba

wed *v* nikah, kawin; **wedding** *n* (acara) perkawinan, pernikahan

wedge *n* ganjalan; *v* mengganjal

Wednesday *adj, n* [Wénsdé] (hari) Rabu

weed *n* tanaman liar; gulma

week *n* minggu; **weekday** *n* hari kerja; **weekend** *n* akhir minggu, akhir pekan; **weekly** *adj, adv* tiap minggu; mingguan; *n* (majalah) mingguan

weep *v* **wept wept** menangis

weigh *v* [wé] menimbang; **weight** *n* berat, bobot; **weightlifter** *n* atlet angkat besi; **weightlifting** *n* angkat besi

weird *adj* [wird] aneh, ganjil

welcome *n* [wélkem] sambutan; *v* (mengucapkan) selamat datang

weld *v* mengelas

welfare *n* [wélfér] kesejahteraan

well *adv* baik; sehat; *as ~*

(begitu) juga, demikian juga; *~behaved* berkelakuan baik; *~loved* tercinta; *~meaning* bermaksud baik, berniat baik; *~off* kaya, berada; *~read* berpengetahuan luas

well *n* (sumber) mata air, sumur

Welsh *adj* berasal dari Wales

went *v, pf* → **go**

wept *v, pf* → **weep**

west *adj, n* barat; **western** *adj* barat; **westerner** *n* orang Barat

wet *adj* basah, berair; *v* **wet wet** membasahi

whack *n* [wak] pukulan hebat

whale *n* [wél] ikan paus

wharf *n* [worf] **wharves** dermaga

what *adj* [wot] apa; alangkah; *interrog* [wot] apa; *~'s your name?* siapa namanya?; **whatever** *adj* apa saja, apa pun; **whatsoever** *adj* apa saja, apa pun

wheat *n* [wit] gandum

wheel *n* [wil] roda; **wheelbarrow** *n* [wilbaro] kereta dorong, gerobak; **wheelchair** *n* kursi roda

when *conj* [wén] ketika;
  bila, kalau; *interrog* kapan;
  whenever *adv, conj*
  [wénéver] kapan saja
where *adv, conj, pron* [wér]
  di mana; *interrog* di mana
whereas *conj* [wéraz]
  sedangkan, padahal
wherever *adv, conj* [wéréver]
  di mana saja, di mana pun
whether *conj* [wéther] apakah
which *conj, pron* [wic]
  mana; **whichever** *pron*
  [wicéver] mana saja
while, whilst *conj* [wail]
  selama; saat, ketika; sedangkan; *n* waktu
whip *n* [wip] cambuk, cemeti;
  v mencambuk, mencemeti
whir *n* [wér] deru, desing; *v*
  menderu, mendesing
whirl *v* [wérl] berputar, berpusar; **whirlpool** *n* pusaran
  air; **whirlwind** *adj* sangat
  cepat, kilat; *n* angin puyuh,
  angin beliung
whisker *n* [wisker] kumis;
  whiskers *n, pl* cambang,
  berewok
whiskey, whisky *n* wiski
whisper *v* [wisper] ber-
  bisik; membisikkan

whistle *n* [wisel] peluit; *v*
  bersiul
white *adj* [wait] (berkulit)
  putih; ~ *lie* dusta; ~*collar*
  worker orang kantoran;
  egg ~ putih telur; *n* (orang
  kulit) putih; **whiten** *v*
  memutihkan; **whitewash** *n*
  kapur; *v* mengapur
WHO *abbrev* *World Health*
  Organization Organisasi
  Kesehatan Dunia
who *conj* [hu] yang; *inter-*
  rog, pron siapa; **whoever**
  pron [huéver] barang siapa
whole *adj* [hol] seantero,
  seluruh, semua; lengkap,
  utuh; *n* semua, keseluruhan;
  wholemeal *adj* tepung
  terigu yang masih mengandung biji-biji; **wholesale**
  adj grosir, rabat
whom *pron, obj* [hum] siapa
whoops *ejac* [wups] aduh
whore *n, derog* [hor] pelacur
whose *conj* yang; *pron,*
  poss [huz] milik siapa
why *conj, interrog* [wai]
  mengapa; *ejac* nah
wicked *adj* [wiked] jahat
wicker ~ *chair* kursi
  (anyaman) rotan

wide *adj* lebar, longgar, luas; *adv* jauh, lebar; ~ *awake* sudah bangun (dan tidak mengantuk lagi); **widespread** *adj* [waid-spréd] tersebar luas

widow *n, f* [wido] janda (mati); **widower** *n, m* duda (mati)

width *n* lebar(nya) ← **wide**

wife *n* **wives** isteri

wig *n* rambut palsu, wig

wild *adj* [waild] liar, ganas, buas; gila; **wilderness** *n* [wildernes] hutan (belantara), gurun; **wildfire** *n* [waildfair] kebakaran hutan; **wildflower** *n* bunga liar; **wildlife** *n* [waildlaif] margasatwa, fauna

will *n* kehendak, kemauan; wasiat; *political* ~ kemauan politik; *v* **would** [wud] akan, mau, hendak; ~ *not (won't)* tidak akan, takkan; **willing** *adj* rela, bersedia, sudi; *God* ~ insya Allah; **willpower** *n* kehendak

win *v* **won won** [wan] menang; memenangkan; memperoleh, mendapat

wind *n* (mata) angin

wind *n* [waind] belok, belokan, belitan; *v* **wound wound** memutar, menggulung; membelit, membalutkan; ~ *a clock* memutar jam; **winding** *adj* berliku-liku, berputar-putar

windbreak *n* [windbrék] penahan angin; **windmill** *n* kincir angin ← **wind**

window *n* [windo] jendela; ~*shopping* cuci mata

windscreen, **windshield** *n* [windsyild] kaca depan mobil ← **wind**

windy *adj* banyak angin, berangin ← **wind**

wine *n* (minuman) anggur; **winery** *n* [waineri] kilang anggur, tempat pembuatan anggur

wing *n* sayap; sisi (panggung); *left*-~ bersayap kiri

wink *n* kedip, kedipan; *forty* ~*s* tidur siang, tidur sebentar; *v* kedip, berkedip; mengedipkan mata

winner *n* pemenang; **winnings** *n* hasil kemenangan ← **win**

winter *adj, n* musim dingin; *in* ~ pada musim dingin;

627

the ~ Olympics Olimpiade
Musim Dingin

wipe *v* menyapu, menyeka,
menghapus; *~ out* menyapu
bersih; menghapuskan

wire *n* [wair] kawat; *~ netting*
kawat kasa

wisdom *n* kearifan, kebijaksanaan; *~ teeth* gigi
geraham bungsu; **wise** *adj*
arif, bijaksana

wish *n* keinginan; *best ~es*
salam; *v* ingin; menginginkan; mengharapkan

wit *n* kejenakaan; orang
jenaka; **wits** *n, pl* akal
(budi); *at your ~' end*
kehilangan akal

witch *n, f* penyihir, tukang
sihir; **witchcraft** *n* ilmu sihir

with *prep* dengan, bersama,
serta; pakai; **withdraw**
v **withdrew withdrawn**
mundur, mengundurkan
diri; menarik, mencabut;
withdrawal *n* pengunduran;
penarikan (uang); **with-
drawn** *adj* pendiam, suka
menyendiri

within *adv, prep* (di) dalam;
~ a week dalam waktu
seminggu ← **with**

without *prep* tanpa, dengan
tidak ← **with**

witness *n* saksi; *v* menyaksikan

witty *adj* jenaka, lucu,
bersifat menyindir ← **wit**

wivee *n, pl* → **wife**

wizard *n, m* [wizerd] penyihir, tukang sihir

wobble *v* [wobel] goyang,
goyah; **wobbly** *adj* goyang

woke, woken *v, pf* → **wake**

wolf *n* [wulf] serigala; *~
whistle* suitan; *to cry ~*
pura-pura memberitakan
bahaya

woman *n* [wumen] **women**
[wimen] perempuan, wanita;
~ doctor dokter wanita;
women's rights hak-hak
perempuan

womb *n* [wum] kandungan,
rahim, peranakan

won *v, pf* → **win**

wonder *n* [wander] keajaiban; *no ~* tidak mengherankan, pantas; *v* berpikir,
berpikir-pikir; **wonderful**
adj ajaib, mengherankan

won't *v, aux* takkan → **will**

wood *n* kayu; hutan; *~
carving* ukiran kayu; *touch ~*

semoga terkabul; **wooden**
adj terbuat dari kayu;
woodpecker *n* burung
pelatuk; **woods** *n, pl* hutan;
woodwork *n* prakarya,
pelajaran memotong dan
mengolah kayu
wool *n* wol, bulu domba;
woolen *adj* terbuat dari
wol; **woolly** *adj* terbuat
dari wol, berbulu
word *n* [wérd] kata; ~ *search*
teka-teki mencari kata; ~
for ~ kata demi kata; ~ *of*
mouth secara lisan; *lost for*
~*s* kehilangan kata; *in a* ~
secara singkat; *in other* ~*s*
dengan kata lain; *not a* ~
tidak sepatah kata pun; *to*
eat your ~*s* menarik kembali apa yang diucapkan; *to*
give your ~ berjanji; *what's*
the Indonesian ~? Apa
Bahasa Indonesianya?
wore *v, pf* → **wear**
work *n* [wérk] pekerjaan,
karya, kerja; kantor, tempat
kerja; *at* ~ sedang bekerja;
di kantor; *hard* ~ kerja
keras; *out of* ~ tidak bekerja,
menganggur; *v* bekerja,
berjalan, jalan; ~ *at*, ~ *on*

mengerjakan; ~ *off* mengurangi; ~ *out* menyusun,
memecahkan; berolahraga;
workbook *n* buku tulis;
worker *n* pekerja, buruh;
workforce *n* tenaga kerja;
working *adj* ~ *class* kaum
buruh, rakyat jelata; ~
holiday bekerja sambil berlibur; **workman** *n* pekerja,
tukang; **workmanship** *n*
hasil kerja; **workout** *n*
latihan; **works** *n, pl* pabrik;
mesin; **worksheet** *n* kertas
tugas belajar; **workshop** *n*
bengkel; **workstation** *n*
meja kerja
world *n* [wérld] dunia,
alam; planet; ~*class*
berkelas dunia; ~*famous*
terkenal di seluruh dunia; ~
record rekor dunia; ~ *War*
II (WWII) Perang Dunia
Kedua; *to go around the* ~
mengelilingi dunia; *it's a*
small ~ dunia ini kecil;
worldwide *adj* yang
meliputi seluruh dunia
worm *n* [wérm] cacing, ulat
worn *v, pf* → **wear**
worry *n* [wari] kekhawatiran,
beban pikiran, urusan,

kesusahan; *v* khawatir, merasa cemas; ~ *about* mencemaskan; *don't* ~ jangan khawatir; *no worries* tidak masalah

worse *adj, adv* [wérs] lebih buruk, lebih jelek ← **bad**

worship *n* ibadah, pujaan, pemujaan; *v* memuja, menyembah

worst *adj, adv* [wérst] paling buruk, paling jelek, terburuk ← **bad**

worth *adj* bernilai, bermanfaat, berharga; *n* [wérth] nilai, harga, guna; *it was* ~ *it* ada manfaatnya, ada hikmahnya; **worthwhile** *adj* berguna, bermanfaat

would *v, aux, pf* [wud] akan → **will**; **wouldn't** *v aux, neg* [wudent] tidak akan, takkan

wound *n* [wund] luka; *v* melukai; **wounded** *adj* terluka; *n* korban (luka)

wound *v, pf* [waund] → **wind**

wove, woven *v, pf* → **weave**

wow *ejac* [wau] wah

wrap *n* [rap] semacam roti isi yang digulung; *v* membungkus; ~*ping paper* kertas bungkus, kertas kado;

wrapper *n* bungkus, pembungkus

wreath *n* [rith] karangan (bunga)

wreck *n* [rék] rongsokan kapal karam; ~*ed* karam, tenggelam; *a nervous* ~ gila ketakutan; *v* merusak, menghancurkan

wrench *n* [rénc] *(monkey)* ~ kunci Inggris; renggutan; *v* merenggut; keseleo, terkilir

wrestle *n* [résel] pergumulan, pergulatan; *v* bergumul, bergulat; **wrestler** *n* [résler] pegulat; **wrestling** *n* [résling] gulat

wriggle *n, v* [rigel] geliat-geliut

wring *v* **wrung wrought** *v* memeras

wrinkle *n* [ringkel] (garis) keriput, kerut

wrist *n* [rist] pergelangan tangan; **wristwatch** *n* jam tangan

write *v* **wrote written** [rait] menulis, mengarang; ~ *down* mencatat, menuliskan; ~ *to* menyurati; ~ *a letter* menulis surat; ~ *an essay* membuat karangan; **writer** *n*

penulis, pengarang; **writing** *n* tulisan, karangan; ~ *desk* meja tulis; ~ *materials* alat tulis; ~ *paper* kertas tulis, kertas surat; *in* ~ secara tertulis; **written** *adj* tertulis
wrong *adj* [rong] salah, keliru; *n* kesalahan; *what's* ~? ada apa?
wrote *v, pf* → **write**
wrought *v, pf* → **wring**; ~ *iron* besi tempa
wrung *v, pf* → **wring**

X

X-ray *n* [éksré] rontgen, sinar X; *v* merontgen, menyinar
xylophone *n* [zailofon] xilofon

Y

yacht *n* [yot] kapal layar, kapal pesiar; **yachting** *n* berlayar
Yank, Yankee *n, coll* orang Amerika (Serikat)

yard *n* pekarangan, halaman; ukuran panjang sebesar 0.9144 m; *back* ~ halaman belakang; *railway* ~s langsiran
yarn *n* benang (rajutan)
yawn *v* menguap
yeah *sl* [yéa] ya, iya ← **yes**
year *n* [yir] tahun; *financial* ~ tahun buku; *last* ~ tahun lalu; *next* ~ tahun depan; *for* ~s bertahun-tahun; *Chinese New* ~ (Tahun Baru) Imlek; **yearbook** *n* buku tahunan; **yearly** *adj* tahunan
yearn *v* [yérn] sangat ingin; rindu
yeast *n* ragi
yell *n* pekik, pekikan; *v* memekik
yellow *adj* [yélo] kuning; *sl* takut
yes ya
yesterday *adv, n* kemarin; *the day before* ~ kemarin dulu
yet *adv* masih (belum); *as* ~ sampai sekarang, sehingga kini; *conj* namun
yield *n* [yild] hasil, produksi; *v* mengalah; menghasilkan

yoga n yoga

yogurt, yoghurt n yogurt

yolk n [yok] kuning telur

you pron [yu] kamu, engkau; form Anda; pl kalian; ~ all kalian, anda sekalian; **you'd** anda akan ← **you would**; **you'll** anda akan ← **you will**

young adj [yang] muda; ~ girl anak gadis; ~ man pemuda; ~ people remaja, kaum pemuda; anak baru gede (ABG); coll ~ woman pemudi; n anak (binatang)

your pron -mu, kamu punya, milik anda, kepunyaan anda; **you're** kamu adalah ← **you are**; **yours** pron, poss milikmu, milik anda; ~ truly, ~ sincerely, ~ faithfully hormat kami; **yourself** pron **yourselves** engkau sendiri, kamu sendiri, Anda sendiri ← **you**

youth n [yuth] masa muda; kaum muda; ~ hostel losmen; in my ~ waktu masih muda

you've [yuv] kamu sudah ← **you have**

yowl v [yaul] memeong, meraung

yum ejac sedap, enak; **yummy** adj enak, sedap; ejac enak, nyam-nyam

Z

zebra n kuda zebra, kuda belang

zero adj, n [ziro] nol, kosong

zigzag adj, v berkelok-kelok, berliku-liku

zinc n seng

zip ~ code kode pos; **zipper, zip** n ritsleting, kancing tarik; ~ up menutup ritsleting

zone n zona, daerah; war ~ daerah perang

zoo n, coll kebun binatang (bonbin); **zoologist** n [zuolojist] zoolog, ahli ilmu hewan

zoom v meningkat, meluncur; ~ in memfokuskan lebih dekat pada